NEWS WRITING AND REPORTING FOR TODAY'S MEDIA

NEWS WRITING AND REPORTING FOR TODAY'S MEDIA

SIXTH EDITION

Bruce D. Itule
Arizona State University

Douglas A. Anderson
The Pennsylvania State University

Boston Burr Ridge, IL Dubuque, IA Madison, WI New York San Francisco St. Louis
Bangkok Bogotá Caracas Kuala Lumpur Lisbon London Madrid Mexico City
Milan Montreal New Delhi Santiago Seoul Singapore Sydney Taipei Toronto

McGraw-Hill Higher Education

A Division of The ***McGraw-Hill*** *Companies*

NEWS WRITING AND REPORTING FOR TODAY'S MEDIA

Published by McGraw-Hill, a business unit of The McGraw-Hill Companies, Inc., 1221 Avenue of the Americas, New York, NY, 10020.

This book is printed on acid-free paper.

3 4 5 6 7 8 9 0 DOC/DOC 0 9 8 7 6 5 4 3

ISBN 0-07-249212-0

Editorial director: *Phillip A. Butcher*
Sponsoring editor: *Valerie Raymond*
Editorial assistant: *Jennifer Van Hove*
Project manager: *Jean R. Starr*
Production supervisor: *Carol Bielski*
Senior designer: *Jenny El-Shamy*
Producer, Media technology: *Jessica Bodie*
Supplement producer: *Matthew Perry*
Photo research coordinator: *Jeremy Cheshareck*
Photo researcher: *Jennifer Blankenship*
Cover design: *Jenny El-Shamy*
Top cover photo: *J. B. Russell / Corbis Sygma*
Bottom cover photo: *Olivier Prevosto / Corbis Tempsport*
Typeface: *10/12 Palatino*
Compositor: *Shepherd Incorporated*
Printer: *R. R. Donnelley & Sons Company*

Library of Congress Control Number: 2002107168

www.mhhe.com

ABOUT THE AUTHORS

Photo by Frank Hoy

Bruce D. Itule is an editor and writer in Phoenix. Before that he was director of student media and a clinical professor of journalism in the Walter Cronkite School of Journalism and Telecommunication at Arizona State University. He also has been a visiting professor of journalism at Penn State University. Mr. Itule has taught reporting and depth reporting to two generations of students. He also has been night city editor of the *Chicago Tribune.* He has been a reporter or copy editor at the *Arizona Daily Star* in Tucson, *The Phoenix* (Ariz.) *Gazette,* the *Boulder* (Colo.) *Daily Camera, The Denver Post* and the *Minneapolis Star.* He earned his bachelor's degree in journalism at the University of Arizona and a master's degree in journalism at the University of Colorado. He is the coauthor of *Contemporary News Reporting, News Writing and Reporting for Today's Media, Writing the News* and *Visual Editing.* He is a frequent contributor to regional and national magazines, and also has written articles for numerous professional journals. He has been honored by The Freedom Forum as a journalism teacher of the year.

Photo by Dave Shelly

Douglas A. Anderson is professor of journalism and dean of the College of Communications at Pennsylvania State University. He is author or coauthor of *A "Washington Merry-Go-Round" of Libel Actions, Contemporary Sports Reporting, Electronic Age News Editing, Contemporary News Reporting, News Writing and Reporting for Today's Media* and *Writing the News.* He also has written articles that have appeared in such academic and professional publications as *Journalism Quarterly, Newspaper Research Journal, American Journalism, APME News, Journalism and Mass Communication Educator* and *Grassroots Editor.* His teaching specialties are reporting, communication law and editing, and he was formerly the managing editor of the *Hastings* (Neb.) *Daily Tribune.* Professor Anderson was a graduate fellow at Southern Illinois University, where he received his Ph.D. A former president of the Nebraska Associated Press Managing Editors Association, the Southwest Education Council for Journalism and Mass Communication, and the Association of Schools of Journalism and Mass Communication, he has been honored by The Freedom Forum as a journalism administrator of the year.

Five editions of *News Writing and Reporting for Today's Media* have taught students what it is like to be a news reporter and writer. Our goal has always been to make the drama of news reporting come alive, to kindle excitement while painting a realistic picture. New technologies and current events now mandate more emphasis on the impact of online reporting and the importance of media ethics and fairness. In response, we have included many new features in this sixth edition.

New to the Sixth Edition

This sixth edition continues to emphasize real reporters and stories, which serve as instructional models. We have, however, updated the first-person accounts and examples of stories throughout.

We have also revised, expanded and reorganized many sections; and we have updated the Workbook and Instructor's Manual.

In addition to these changes, the sixth edition has these new features:

- *Enhanced chapter on Qualities of Good Writing.* Pulitzer-Prize winning journalist Michael Gartner emphasizes the importance of rhythm and cadence.
- *New section on the circle style of writing.* This popular writing form, particularly for feature stories, is called "writing in a circle" or "coming full circle." It is discussed in Chapter 5, Organizing a News Story.
- *New section on the handling of information and quotes from Internet and e-mail sources.* Guidelines are included in Chapter 7, Quotations and Attribution.
- *Expanded Features chapter.* Veteran *National Geographic* magazine staffers Carol Lutyk and John G. Mitchell offer helpful tips for writing feature stories.
- *Updated chapter on Speeches and Press Conferences.* The chapter now features U.S. President George W. Bush and his choice for director of the Federal Bureau of Investigation.
- *More detailed chapter on Broadcast Writing.* Fresh advice on and examples of news stories for radio are provided.
- *Enlarged chapter on Multicultural Reporting.* The Pulitzer-Prize winning series published in *The New York Times*—"How Race Is Lived in America"—is examined, largely through the eyes of one of the catalysts of the project.
- *Beefed up chapter on Business and Other Specialties.* Longtime environment writer John G. Mitchell of *National Geographic* magazine talks about the "two types of writing about the environment."
- *New sections in the Law chapter.* Material on campus rights and restrictions is included along with a discussion of individuals suing the media who increasingly are focusing their efforts on the news *gathering* tactics of journalists.
- *Expanded concluding chapter on media ethics and fairness.* A new section features practical advice from Bob Haiman's Best Practices for Newspaper Journalists.
- *Updated and expanded Where to Turn Online sections.* New material throughout the text provides help with online services.
- *New examples throughout reflect recent major stories.*

Key Retained Features

Proud as we are of the new features of the sixth edition, we have not compromised features of the text that have appealed to students and instructors for five editions.

- *First-person accounts from reporters and editors.* We enhance the practical aspects of the text with actual reporting situations. We show how concepts and principles work in real situations, and we explore the problems, philosophical questions and issues that journalists face on the job.
- *Numerous current examples of stories from a wide range of print and online newspapers.* We use examples of stories from large metros, medium-circulation dailies, small-circulation dailies and student newspapers from geographically diverse markets of all sizes.
- *Detailed, comprehensive discussions of the rudiments of news writing and reporting.* We provide chapters on leads, story organization, developing a news story from day to day, interviewing, quotes and attribution, qualities of good writing and gathering information.
- *Checklists throughout the text provide practical guidance at a glance.* Material in the checklists is useful on the job.
- *Comprehensive discussions of special kinds of reporting.* After we set forth the rudiments of writing, reporting and gathering information, we provide chapters on writing obituaries and news releases as well as covering speeches and press conferences, weather and disasters, multicultural developments and issues, police and fire departments, local government, courts, sports and business news.
- *Thorough instruction in areas that often receive only cursory treatment in other texts.* We discuss the use of survey methods to gather information for news stories, electronic retrieval strategies and legal and ethical issues.

Organization of the Text

One thing we learned as textbook authors is that virtually every school has a unique approach to teaching news writing and reporting. Because the approaches are so diverse, we wrote a textbook that is flexible enough to meet the needs of most institutions and instructors.

News Writing and Reporting for Today's Media can be used in one-semester courses in news writing, in second-semester courses in reporting or in two-semester courses in news writing and reporting. Each chapter is self-contained, and the chapters can be used in any combination.

Part One: The Fourth Estate

Part One, The Fourth Estate introduces the contemporary news media and examines how news is viewed by reporters and editors.

1. A new breed of reporter is emerging: a journalist adept at ferreting out valuable information from electronic sources. Chapter 1 explores how reporters cover the news and examines the primary jobs at newspapers.
2. Chapter 2 describes the evolution of news treatment. It outlines the traditional criteria of newsworthiness, examines the factors that affect news treatment and presents guidelines for pitching news stories to editors.

Part Two: The Rudiments

Part Two, The Rudiments, is the heart of the text. It provides instruction on the qualities of good writing, writing summary and special leads, organizing stories, developing stories, quoting and attributing, and features.

3. Chapter 3 features advice on writing from Pulitzer-Prize winning Michael Gartner and from Roy Peter Clark of the Poynter Institute for Media Studies in St. Petersburg, Fla. Then, examples are used to illustrate each of Robert Gunning's "Ten Principles of Clear Writing."
4. In Chapter 4, students are shown how to write summary leads. In the first section of this chapter, the underlying principles—including the primary elements *who, what, why, when, where* and *how*—are explained. In the second section, specific guidelines for lead paragraphs are given.
5. Chapter 5 discusses alternatives to the summary lead, explaining and providing examples of narrative, contrast, staccato, direct address, question, quote and "none of the above" leads. It also gives specifics on writing these leads, emphasizing the need for strong, vivid verbs.
6. The sixth chapter shows students how to organize news stories. It describes the steps involved in writing inverted-pyramid stories and also takes a look at the hourglass style and circle style of writing.
7. Chapter 7 discusses the development of a news story from day to day or week to week. It explains how editors and reporters determine which stories should or should not be developed beyond a single item, and it describes the phases of a developing story. As an example, the chapter uses a massive manhunt for an escaped convict, which dragged on for 55 days and brought hundreds of police and reporters into Arizona's mountain forests.
8. Students learn from Chapter 8 that strong, vivid quotations can make an ordinary news story special. This chapter describes types of quotations—direct, partial and indirect—and discusses when and how to quote. It also takes up attribution and punctuation of quotations.
9. Chapter 9 begins by distinguishing between hard news and soft news and describing types of features: personality profiles, human interest stories, trend stories, in-depth stories and backgrounders. It points out that the main function of features is to humanize, add color, educate, entertain, illuminate and analyze. It then provides advice on writing features: finding a theme, developing the story, using effective transitions and so forth.

Part Three: Gathering Information

Part Three, Gathering Information, gives students instruction in the basics of the reporting process. The chapters in this section explain how to interview, how to make maximum use of electronic databases and how to use surveys to gather information.

10. Chapter 10 underscores the importance of interviewing; it covers doing the related research, setting up interviews and conducting them. It shows students how to structure the interview, ask the right questions at the right times, establish rapport, take notes and so on.
11. Reporters increasingly are mining online databases, searching the Internet, building computer spreadsheets and using e-mail for collaboration and interviews. Chapter 11, written by Steve Doig of Arizona State University and Nora Paul of the University of Minnesota, shows students how they can strengthen their stories by making use of the latest tools. The chapter discusses how to conduct online research and provides tips on applying a healthy skepticism to the information gathered.
12. Chapter 12 explores the important concept of "precision journalism," examining the growth of survey research

as a way of gathering information for news stories. This chapter addresses basic considerations involved in conducting surveys: formulating and testing questions, developing samples, collecting and analyzing data and writing the story. Chapter 12 also presents rules for reporting polls.

Part Four: Basic Assignments

Part Four, Basic Assignments, takes up fundamental stories that reporters often encounter: obituaries, rewriting of news releases, weather, disasters, speeches and press conferences. It also examines the fundamentals of broadcast writing.

13. Chapter 13 stresses that obituaries are among the best-read items in newspapers and that reporters should strive not only to provide the basic facts but also to humanize obits with anecdotes and quotations. This chapter outlines the information typically given in obituaries and examines policies of various newspapers regarding names, nicknames, courtesy titles, ages, addresses and causes of death.
14. Chapter 14 discusses news releases and gives tips on evaluating them—deciding if they are of interest to the audience—and on rewriting them.
15. In Chapter 15, the student is shown how to prepare for speeches and press conferences, how to cover them and how to organize the information into a coherent story.
16. Chapter 16 provides guidelines for writing about weather and disasters. It describes types of weather stories: forecasts, travel conditions and closings, record-breaking weather, unusual weather and seasonal and year-end coverage. It also takes a look at AP style for weather stories. The chapter illustrates disaster coverage by examining reporting of the crash of an airliner in Texas.
17. Chapter 17 stresses that, although broadcast writing differs in several respects from print writing, the same principles of clarity and conciseness apply to both. This chapter looks at the basics of broadcast style and broadcast writing and illustrates how to write for radio and television. It also features advice from working professionals.

Part Five: Beats

Part Five, Beats, takes a look at the writing and reporting techniques that are necessary for covering typical beats: multicultural affairs, city government, police and fire departments, courts and sports.

18. Chapter 18 stresses how important it is for students to be sensitive to cultures, ethnic groups, religions and lifestyles different from their own. Reporters and editors provide plenty of useful advice on how journalists can improve coverage of minority affairs.
19. In Chapter 19, coverage of city government is explored. This chapter describes forms of municipal governments (mayor-council, council-manager and commission) and provides advice on covering city council meetings and the city budget process.
20. Chapter 20 presents strategies for effective coverage of police and fire departments. It emphasizes the importance of understanding how these organizations are structured, developing sources within them and reading and using departmental records. Advice on writing stories about arrests, accidents and rapes is given. A reporter's day on the police and fire beat—a day that includes coverage of a major fire—is described. Chapter 20 ends with suggestions for beat reporters.

21. Our next beat is the courts. In Chapter 21, students are introduced to the federal and state judicial systems and to the importance of mastering judicial structures, learning terminology and writing stories in understandable language. The basic criminal process and the basic civil process are described, and a criminal case is traced, step by step, from arrest to verdict. Advice is given on reporting both criminal and civil cases.
22. The final beat in Part Five is sports. Chapter 22 explores the evolution of sports writing and contemporary trends in sports coverage and writing styles. It gives practical advice on reporting sports—working with statistics and writing games up for critical readers—but it emphasizes that sports writing extends beyond merely reporting games to coverage of contract negotiations, courtroom battles and boardroom decisions.

Part Six: Advanced Assignments

Part Six, Advanced Assignments, looks at in-depth and investigative reporting, business news and other specialized reporting.

23. Chapter 23 explains that in-depth and investigative articles provide comprehensive accounts that go well beyond a basic news story. Students are shown, first, how to investigate these stories—how to "smell" a story, research it, conduct interviews and if necessary go undercover. Then they are shown how to write the story—how to find the best lead, how to use anecdotes and observations and how to tie the story together with a logical thread.
24. Chapter 24 explores business news and other special reporting areas. Students are given instruction on writing news and feature stories in business, technology and the environment, three areas that are representative of specialty reporting.

Part Seven: Beyond the Writing

Part Seven, Beyond the Writing, examines legal and ethical ramifications of reporting.

25. Chapter 25 introduces students to several legal issues that are of particular concern to reporters. After a discussion of the First Amendment and the press, it considers libel, protection of sources and the question of fair trial versus free press. Landmark cases are discussed, and practical guidelines are provided.
26. Our final chapter—Chapter 26—focuses on journalistic ethics and fairness; it stresses that, increasingly, society is calling for accountability in journalism. This chapter notes that, as technology has advanced at warp speed, journalists have found themselves on the hot seat of public opinion and that the movement to extricate them from the swamp of public opinion has taken on a sense of urgency. The chapter emphasizes that the country's newspaper editors have placed credibility and fairness at the top of their agendas. The chapter includes a discussion of authoritarian and libertarian press systems and the "social responsibility" theory, and then takes up public criticism of the press and the response of the press to that criticism. It examines codes of ethics and some of the most important ethical issues facing journalists today: fairness and objectivity, misrepresentation by reporters, privacy versus the public's right to know, conflicts of interest and journalistic arrogance.

Appendixes

We provide three important features as appendixes. Appendix A provides the Gannett Newspaper Division's Principles of Ethical Conduct for Newsrooms. Appendix B gives many of the style rules of The Associated

Press. And the Glossary (Appendix C) defines key terms used in the text.

Supplements

We have written an accompanying Workbook with exercises based on real news events. In addition to providing writing exercises, each chapter of the Workbook contains review questions for the corresponding chapter in the text. For instructors whose students are using the Workbook, we have also written an Instructor's Manual. Interlink, Internet and Web Online Resources for Mass Communication Students, by Joseph Bridges, Ph.D., Malone College, is a resource guide available at the McGraw-Hill Mass Communication home page: *www.mhhe.com/media.*

Acknowledgments

Some of the journalists interviewed for this book have moved to other jobs. References to them, however, remain within the context of their jobs at the time their articles were published or at the time they were interviewed.

Many people contributed to the research and preparation of our text through their insights, advice and willingness to provide examples. They include the entire staff of the *Chicago Tribune,* and in particular, environment reporter Casey Bukro; Dick Ciccone, who as managing editor allowed us to use whatever stories and resources we needed; and Mitch Dydo, a consummate copy editor.

Others who were particularly helpful include Jerry Schwartz, national writer and editor, The Associated Press; reporter David Cannella of *The Arizona Republic; Birmingham* (Ala.) *News* Managing Editor Thomas Bailey; Jake Batsell and Duff Wilson, reporters at *The Seattle Times; Beaumont* (Texas) *Enterprise* Managing Editor William Mock; Mary Beth Sammons, Chicago business writer; *Chicago Sun-Times* feature writer Mary Gillespie; Dan Gillmor, technology reporter at the *San Jose* (Calif.) *Mercury News;* Kenneth Bowling, news editor, *Dallas Morning News;* Robert H. Giles, curator, Nieman Foundation, Harvard University; *Evansville* (Ind.) *Press* Editor Tom Tuley; *Fairbanks* (Alaska) *Daily News-Miner* Managing Editor Kent Sturgis; Fort Lauderdale (Fla.) *Sun-Sentinel* investigative reporter Fred Schulte and projects editor Maren Bingham; Felix Gutierrez, senior vice president, The Freedom Forum; Ron Jenkins, editor of *The Gleaner,* Henderson, Ky.; Tim Wiederaenders, editor of the *Kingman* (Ariz.) *Daily Miner;* Mary Lou Fulton, managing editor, America Online; *Mesa* (Ariz.) *Tribune* reporter Mike Padgett; Charles Kelly, president, Kerker Marketing Communications, Minneapolis; Professor Todd F. Simon of Kansas State University; *Omaha* (Neb.) *World-Herald* reporters Lee Barfknecht and Terry Henion; University of Nebraska-Lincoln Professor Will Norton; Caesar Andrews, editor, Gannett News Service; Marie Dillon of the *Chicago Tribune;* Cynthia Scanlon, reference librarian at the Phoenix Public Library; and Roy Peter Clark, Poynter Institute for Media Studies, St. Petersburg, Fla.

In addition, we would like to thank Jerry Ceppos, vice president for news, Knight Ridder; Dawn Garcia, deputy director, John S. Knight Fellowships for Professional Journalists, Stanford University; Professor Emeritus Harry W. Stonecipher, Southern Illinois University-Carbondale; Professor James Simon, Fairfield University; City of Tempe, Ariz., Management Services Director Jerry Geiger; *Tempe* (Ariz.) *Daily News Tribune* Managing Editor Lawn Griffiths, and reporters Adrianne Flynn and Gail Maiorana; Tempe Public Library reference librarian Sherry Warren; *Topeka* (Kan.) *Capital-Journal* reporter Roger Aeschliman; syndicated technology writer Kim Komando; Doug Smith, a sportswriter, and Jack Williams, weather page editor for *USA Today;* Dorothy Gilliam, columnist, *The Washington Post;* and *National Geographic* magazine senior editorial staff members Carol B. Lutyk and John G. Mitchell.

We owe special thanks to several people who were particularly helpful with the broadcasting material: Wendy Black, KOY Radio, Phoenix; Dan Fellner, WTVN-TV, Columbus,

Ohio; Professor Dave Ogden, University of Nebraska at Omaha; Professor Joe Russomanno of Arizona State University; and Ben Silver, Arizona State University professor emeritus and a former CBS newsman.

Significant contributors to this edition were Steve Doig of Arizona State University and Nora Paul of the University of Minnesota, who wrote Chapter 11.

In addition, several faculty and staff members at Arizona State University contributed examples, advice and encouragement: Professors Roy Halverson, Frank Hoy, Richard Lentz, Richard McCafferty, W. Parkman Rankin, Dennis Russell, Frank Sackton, Sharon Bramlett-Solomon, Edward Sylvester and Kyu Ho Youm; reference librarian Harvey Sager; staff members Lisa Coleman, Mary Jo Ficklin, Fran McClung, Karen Shannon and Janet Soper.

In addition, several colleagues at Penn State University contributed: Angie Brown, Clay Calvert, John Curley, Gene Foreman, Patricia Kidder, Robert Richards and John Yingling.

We would like to thank the reviewers who read the fifth edition and offered thoughtful suggestions on how to improve the book in this sixth edition: Roberta Kelley, Washington State University; David Ogden, Wayne State College; Henry Wefing, Westfield State College; William Dickinson, Louisiana State University; Terry Dalton, Western Maryland College; Mark Witherspoon, Iowa State University; Connie Stevens Henson, Radford University; Kenton Bird, University of Idaho; Jae-Won Lee, Cleveland State University.

We would also like to acknowledge those professors who reviewed all or parts of the previous editions: Fred Bales, The University of New Mexico; Jerry E. Brown, University of Montana; Jerry Chaney, Ball State University; Anne Collins, Hudson Valley Community College; J. Laurence Day, University of West Florida; Tom Dickson, Southwest Missouri State University; Carolyn Stewart Dyer, The University of Iowa; Wallace B. Eberhard, University of Georgia; Thomas Fensch, University of Texas at Austin; Gilbert Fowler, Arkansas State University; Bruce Garrison, University of Miami; Randy Hayman, Marist College; John R. Hetherington, California State University, Chico; Bruce E. Johansen, University of Nebraska at Omaha; Mike Kautsch, University of Kansas; Cecil Leder, Mott Community College; Thomas B. Littlewood, University of Illinois; Sue A. Lussa, San Diego State University; Gary Morgan, Oxnard College; Donald Morrisseau, Florida Junior College; June Lytel-Murphy, Villanova University; Marlan Nelson, Oklahoma State University; Eric M. Odendahl, San Diego State University; Edith Pendleton, Edison Community College; Jay Perkins, Louisiana State University; Jane W. Peterson, Iowa State University; Kim Peterson, Bethel College; William C. Porter, Brigham Young University; Richard P. Preiss, Suffolk University; Donald Reed, Oklahoma State University; Humphrey A. Regis, Hampton University; Schyler Rehart, California State University, Fresno; Marshel D. Rossow, Mankato State University; Don Seaver, University of North Carolina at Chapel Hill; Susanne Shaw, University of Kansas; Jeff South, Virginia Commonwealth; Jean Stapleton, East Los Angeles College; Renee Studebaker, University of Texas at Austin; Skip Surguine, Indiana Wesleyan University; and Michael Turney, Northern Kentucky University.

We would also like to thank Valerie Raymond, our sponsoring editor for this edition; Sally Constable, our marketing manager; Jean Starr, our project manager; Jenny El-Shamy, our designer; and Jennifer Van Hove, our editorial coordinator.

Special appreciation goes to our friends and families for their patience, understanding and willingness to handle extra responsibilities while we wrote this book: Claudia, Laura and Mary Anderson and Carol Carney. This book is dedicated to them; to our mothers, Tamaam Itule and Wilma Anderson; and to a special uncle and aunt, Carol and Lois Shuck.

Bruce D. Itule

Douglas A. Anderson

BRIEF CONTENTS

CONTENTS

TODAY'S MEDIA

Sept. 11, 2001. No one will forget the day terrorists attacked America.

At 8:50 a.m., Eastern time, *The New York Times* sent its first news alert and story over computer screens worldwide:

> A plane crashed into Manhattan's World Trade Center this morning, causing heavy damage and fires to several floors.

The initial report came five minutes after a hijacked airliner loaded with passengers and jet

(©AFP / Corbis)

fuel crashed into the building. It was the beginning of much more from *The Times* throughout the morning.

9:04 a.m. Eastern time:

> A second plane crashed into the World Trade Center towers, according to The Associated Press.

9:45 a.m. Eastern time:

> An airplane has reportedly crashed near the Pentagon just outside Washington, D.C. Fire can be seen coming from the building.
>
> There are reports of a large fire in the mall, and the west wing of the White House is being evacuated.
>
> The Federal Aviation Administration has shut down all airports in the country.

One of the worst days in American history had started. Soon, another jetliner would crash near Pittsburgh. Both 110-story towers of the World Trade Center would collapse, raining dust and debris over lower Manhattan and killing thousands.

President Bush, who was in Florida at the time of the attacks, later called them "a national tragedy" and said the United States "will hunt down and punish those responsible."

Within days, America would be at war against worldwide terrorism.

The enormity of the story was incomprehensible, but journalists throughout the United States and the world went to work immediately. One reporter on the job in New York was Jerry Schwartz of The Associated Press.

Schwartz had arrived at AP headquarters in Rockefeller Center at 8:30—as usual, the first national writer to arrive for the day. He looked up from his desk to a nearby television in time to see images of the burning trade center. Moments later, executive editor Jonathan Wolman charged through the office, grabbed Schwartz by the arm and ran with him into the New York City bureau. Schwartz found himself at a computer terminal, writing the biggest story of his life.

"I've been in this business for more than a quarter century," Schwartz said, "and these were the most chaotic moments I have ever experienced." Phones rang incessantly, reporters and editors shouted out developments and questions—"The tower collapsed? The whole tower?"—and Schwartz struggled to keep up with it all, and to write a coherent story.

He wrote the breaking story for a couple of hours before he was detached to do a minute-by-minute chronology of an unbelievable day. Then, along with colleague David Crary, he wrote the story that would top many of the daily newspapers in the United States and abroad the day after the attack. It began:

> NEW YORK—In the most devastating terrorist onslaught ever waged against the United States, knife-wielding hijackers crashed two airliners into the World Trade Center Tuesday, toppling its 110-story towers. The deadly calamity was witnessed on televisions across the world as another plane slammed into the Pentagon, and a fourth crashed outside Pittsburgh.
>
> "Today, our nation saw evil," President Bush said in an address to the nation Tuesday night. He said thousands of lives were "suddenly ended by evil, despicable acts of terror."

Said Adm. Robert J. Natter, commander of the U.S. Atlantic Fleet: "We have been attacked like we haven't since Pearl Harbor."

Establishing the U.S. death toll could take weeks. The four airliners alone had 266 people aboard and there were no known survivors. At the Pentagon, about 100 people were believed dead.

In addition, a firefighters union official said he feared at least 200 firefighters had died in rescue efforts at the trade center—where 50,000 people worked—and dozens of police officers were believed missing.

"The number of casualties will be more than most of us can bear," a visibly distraught Mayor Rudolph Giuliani said.

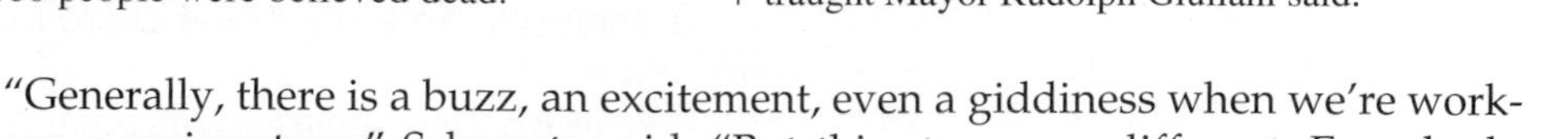

"Generally, there is a buzz, an excitement, even a giddiness when we're working on a major story," Schwartz said. "But this story was different. Everybody knew how important it was, how big it was, but nobody took any pleasure in it.

"When Rockefeller Center officials announced that the building was being evacuated as a precaution against attack, nobody moved a muscle. Nobody even looked up. There was a grim determination. We knew we were writing history, but it wasn't the kind of history anybody wanted to write.

"We were all so close to the story, just a couple of miles away. There was no escaping the sorrow and the tragedy. We are journalists, we're supposed to keep a distance from what we report. But we could not be immune to the horror of it, the heartbreak ot it."

The story developed quickly over minutes, days, weeks, months. Each day, newspapers reported the last 24 hours of developments. Each moment, online editions and broadcast outlets were able to report even more. Less than a month later, news organizations worldwide began reporting that the United States and Britain launched waves of heavy air and missile attacks against southern Afghanistan in the hunt for the al Qaeda terrorist network controlled by Osama bin Laden and the Taliban government that protected it.

Other news occurred during those hours and days in September and October. Anxious consumers in various parts of the country lined up for an hour or more in mid-September to fuel up on gasoline amid fears that supplies would be disrupted after the terrorist attacks. Officials in New York, Florida and Nevada reported incidents or information involving anthrax exposure, and anxiety about bioterrorism spread nationwide.

In Washington, D.C., the U.S. Postal Service announced that the cost of mailing a letter would go up again, this time to 37 cents. There were local traffic accidents to report, tornadoes caused damage in the Midwest, companies laid off more employees as the U.S. economy slipped deeper into recession.

Students and others were glued to televisions, radios and the Internet to find out the latest developments on the attacks and their aftermath. They were also wondering where to eat lunch or about the score of Saturday's game. University dailies were covering campus events. Television stations were reporting the weather and other local stories. The Major League Baseball playoffs and World Series were about to start.

There was so much information to report, to process. It was available, it was instantaneous, and people worldwide wanted it. And thousands of people were working throughout the world and at any one moment to gather the information and disseminate it.

Not too long ago, in the past century, a majority of students coming out of journalism schools used their talents primarily at newspapers. Now, many graduates still look for newspaper internships and jobs, but others seek and find work at a variety of media outlets such as magazines, television, online services, radio, public relations and advertising.

This book is aimed primarily at students who want to be news reporters and writers in the print media, but the skills they learn and use are required in any media-related job. Writing needs to be clear, concise and accurate. Reporting needs to be aggressive and precise, and it must be based on careful research and interviewing. It makes no difference if it is a memo to an advertising client or an understandable story for tens of thousands of people.

Regardless of the medium for which they work, journalists must be able to gather information, find the most important elements, put the story together and communicate it effectively within the parameters of the medium.

How people receive the information and the form in which it is sent is changing dramatically, but it still comes from a reporter/writer in the field, on the phone or on a computer. He or she is pounding out sentences, paragraphs and stories that summarize every type of event or life imaginable. And he or she is working under a tight deadline, realizing that every second and word count, and that accuracy is essential.

The newspaper business in the United States began modestly nearly three centuries ago as an offshoot of the community print shop. Today, it is one of the nation's giant industries that depends heavily on technology. We already have virtual newspapers. Who knows what will come next?

Wherever the newspaper industry is headed, it still will need reporters working with telephones, notepads and computers. They can gather incredible amounts of information from credible and not-so-credible sources on the Internet. They can interview via e-mail. Online databases offer them government, corporate and organizational data.

The **Internet** is a sprawling, ill-defined, unimaginably large network-of-networks of computers that can communicate. It is not a place, nor is it a database. It is where organizations or people can communicate worldwide. On it can be found conspiracy theories, Supreme Court decisions, daily White House briefings and even pornography. It is an invaluable tool for a journalist because it means instant information about anything.

All it takes to get on the Internet is a computer with a modem or hard-wired or wireless "Ethernet" connection. Commercial online companies such as America Online, as well as local firms and telephone companies, offer Internet access at costs that have been dropping steadily.

How Reporters Cover the News

When aspiring journalists talk about where they would like to work, they usually mention huge metropolitan newspapers that would make them a foreign or Washington correspondent. Or they talk about television networks or large radio stations with news departments. They want to work for the places that pay the best wages and have scores of "specialists" traveling around the world. They want to have fun, interview the president, cover a Super Bowl, golf full time and write about it, or spend time with Academy Award winners.

The truth is that most reporters never will work in New York, Chicago, Los Angeles or Washington, D.C. The majority will work for the hundreds of other metro dailies, community newspapers and small broadcast outlets throughout the United States, covering everything from a pie-eating contest, to a traffic accident, to a new business opening, to a double homicide.

Some reporters like community journalism and will spend their careers at small dailies or weeklies. Others will use their first job to gain experience and clippings so that they then can move first to a medium-sized newspaper or station and then to a major American city.

Reporting takes three forms:

- General assignment
- Beats
- Specialties

Each of these areas has distinct characteristics, but their borders are fuzzy. Daily news and feature stories do not fall neatly into a single category. They tend to spill over into all three. That means good reporters must be prepared to operate in any of these areas.

General Assignment Reporting

General assignment reporters cover breaking news or feature stories as they come up. Assignments for general assignment reporters usually come directly from an editor or from assistants who have read something in the mail, on the wires or in another publication or who have heard about a story from a public relations person, another editor or reporter, or someone who telephones the newsroom.

General assignment reporters—they are called GAs for short—mainly cover **spot news,** which is news occurring now. They are important to any newsroom operation because they are there when a story breaks. For example, there may be a report on the radio that protesters are marching on a suburban town hall to demonstrate against an increase in water rates. A GA is sent to the scene immediately. Later in the day, the same GA may cover a parade downtown, then a community meeting in which political candidates are questioned.

The most successful GAs are excellent and quick writers who know their communities well. The stories they write range from crime to crops, from weather to widgets. They must know what is going on and who the main players are around town.

Working a Beat

Beat reporters cover breaking news and features in specific geographic and subject areas every day, such as police and fire departments; county and federal courts; and city, county and state governments. They generally come up with their own story ideas, based on knowledge of their beats and constant contact with sources. They may also be given assignments by their editors. Beat reporters usually write at least one story a day.

Specialty Reporting

Specialty reporters cover breaking news and features in even more specialized areas than beat reporters, such as transportation, energy, medicine, the environment, technology, education, culture, law and aviation. Like beat reporters, they are responsible for finding and writing the stories that originate in their areas.

Their story ideas come from contacting sources and from public relations people, the wires and other editors, reporters and publications. While general assignment and beat reporters are concerned with spot news, specialty reporters are often interested in long-range stories, the roots of problems and the reasons behind the news. This means that they often operate under the most flexible deadlines, spend a lot of time researching and must learn computer-assisted reporting methods.

For instance, if there is serious contamination in the largest lake in town, the environmental reporter will first write a spot news story reporting it. Then the reporter may go on to study the problem in depth over a period of time to find out what caused the contamination, how it will affect the community in years to come, what can be done about it and what lessons it has taught city officials.

Specialty reporters have to talk to experts in a specialized field and then write stories in language readers will understand. Thus they must be experts as well as skilled news writers.

They must also be excellent reporters who can cross over into many areas. In the story on the contamination of the lake, the environmental reporter would have to talk to people at City Hall to find out why it happened, sources in the medical field to check on its health effects, police and fire officials who are keeping people away from the lake and researchers who are studying long-term effects of water pollution.

The Newspaper Newsroom

People in the Newsroom

Most newspaper newsrooms are structured the same way. At the top is the **editor,** whose role changes depending on the size of the paper. At a community newspaper the editor also may be a publisher, a business manager, a reporter, a photographer and an advertising salesperson. At a metro the editor may have nothing to do with the day-to-day editorial process; the *managing editor* is in charge. There may also be an **executive editor** above the managing editor, but his or her responsibilities extend beyond the newsroom.

At the other end of the ladder are the beginning reporters, who are trying to make their mark on the profession and hoping to get their names on front-page stories—that is, to get a **byline.** The number of newsroom personnel between the beginning reporter and the top editor is determined by the circulation of the newspaper and its budget.

Managing Editor

At most newspapers the **managing editor** runs the newsroom. It is his or her job to make sure that the newspaper is out on time each day and that costs are kept within a budget. The managing editor is usually responsible for hiring and firing newsroom personnel and serves as a spokesperson for the paper. At smaller newspapers the managing editor is also involved in selecting stories, photos and graphics; making assignments; laying out pages; and editing copy and writing headlines.

In a typical newsroom the managing editor has a number of subeditors, each responsible for one facet of putting out the paper.

News Editor and Copy Desk

The **news editor** is in charge of the **copy desk,** where **copy editors** work. Their job is to edit copy and write headlines for the wire and locally written stories that go on the news pages each day. At larger papers there is a national copy desk that handles stories from other cities, a foreign copy desk that edits copy from other countries and a local copy desk that handles stories by "cityside" reporters. Larger newspapers also employ **designers** who are responsible for **pagination,** the electronic layout process. Individual departments, such as sports and lifestyle, may also have their own copy desks. Some newspapers have a "universal copy desk," which edits stories from every department.

Most daily newspapers are members of The Associated Press (AP) and supplemental news services, which give them a steady flow of stories from cities and battlefields throughout the United States and world. Once the news editor decides which "wire stories" and cityside stories go into the paper, they are sent to an editor or designer, who positions them on a page and assigns the size and style of the headline. Then each story is sent to the **slot editor** on the copy desk. The slot editor distributes the story to a copy editor who edits it and writes the headline. The copy desk is the last desk to handle the story before it appears in print.

City or Metropolitan Editor

The **city editor** runs the city (or metropolitan) desk and is in charge of the cityside general assignment, beat and specialty reporters. Assistant city editors may help hand out assignments and review stories. Reporters come to the city desk for ideas, with ideas, for counseling and with stories ready for editing.

It is the city editor's job to make sure that the news in the city (or metropolitan area) is covered and as many local stories as possible get into each edition. There is only so much space between the first and last pages of a newspaper, and ads fill up much of that space. What is left is called the **editorial news hole.** The city editor and the other subeditors at the paper are hoping to fill as much of the editorial news hole as possible with stories or photographs from their staffs; thus much of their time is spent trying to sell their material to the managing and news editors.

The number of reporters reporting to the city editor is determined by the size of the newspaper. Major metropolitan newspapers have hundreds of reporters; community newspapers may have only a few.

State Editor

The **state editor**—alternatively called the **area** or **suburban editor**—supervises reporters who cover communities and areas outside the city in which the newspaper is published. At a big newspaper, reporters may staff bureaus in communities throughout the state. They write news and feature stories about events and people in those communities, then call them in or send them by computer to the state editor, who edits the stories and finds space for them in the newspaper.

Even small newspapers have state or area desks, but instead of covering the entire state, they often cover only other communities in the county or in the circulation area of the paper. Coverage of neighboring communities or other cities in the state is important to newspapers because they always are trying to increase their circulation and advertising base.

National and Foreign Editors

Metropolitan newspapers usually have **national** and **foreign editors** who work much like the state editor, but they supervise reporters in bureaus throughout the country or the world. Some newspapers may have reporters in Washington and New York. Others may have fully staffed bureaus in Washington, New York and other major American cities. They may also have reporters in London, Rome, Moscow, Beijing and other major foreign cities. Community newspapers generally do not have national and foreign correspondents; they depend on the wire services to supply them with national and foreign news and features.

Photo Editor

The **photo editor** supervises a newspaper's photographers. At many papers the photo editor sits at or near the city desk, assigning photographers to accompany reporters on news and feature assignments. Some papers have one photographer who handles everything, including pictures for advertisements. Others have several who divide assignments; a few have dozens who are specialized in the types of events they cover.

Graphics Editor

The **graphics editor** serves as the liaison between reporters, editors, photographers, artists and designers to coordinate the production of maps, charts, diagrams, illustrations and other informational graphics that accompany stories. At papers where there is no graphics editor, the photo editor or news editor is usually responsible for the graphics. An artist or staff of artists works for the graphics editor.

Sports Editor

The **sports editor** is in charge of sportswriters and the desk people who process their copy. The writers cover sports events and features in a community's high schools and colleges. They also cover professional sports in their area. The desk people on the sports staff edit stories and lay out the daily sports pages. The sports editor often writes a column.

Lifestyle Editor

The **lifestyle editor,** who might also be called a **features editor,** heads what is usually a paper's main feature section. The section may include articles by lifestyle writers, a food editor, an entertainment writer, a drama critic, a television writer and other reviewers and critics. It may include engagement and wedding announcements. The lifestyle editor, like the sports editor, is also responsible for editing and laying out pages each day.

Financial Editor

The **financial editor** is in charge of the business news that goes into the newspaper. Most papers have a business page or business section each day, and many have a staff of financial reporters who cover area businesses. Financial news has grown in popularity in recent years, and many papers are expanding their staffs to cover it. Newspapers have always printed closing stock averages and press releases on business openings, expansions and closings, but now they are assigning their own reporters to cover financial news as aggressively as any other news.

The News Meeting

At least once each day, the foreign, national, state, city, news, photo and graphics editors meet with the managing editor in what may be called a **news meeting, doping session, news conference, editors' meeting** or **editorial conference.** In this meeting they discuss the top foreign, national, state and local stories and photographs. They decide which stories will make it into the paper and which of those stories will be on the front page. A breaking news story could change their plans, but after about 20 minutes of give and take, these editors have determined what their readers will get that day. The sports, lifestyle and financial editors also meet with the managing editor each day, and they will be called into the meeting if they have stories that are being considered for the news section.

A.M. and P.M. Coverage

Morning newspapers are called **A.M.s.** They report news that breaks on the **A.M. cycle,** generally from noon to midnight, as well as other non-breaking stories. Their news meetings are held in the late afternoon because deadlines are in the evening and the papers are printed and delivered during the night, while most people are sleeping. Beat reporters for an A.M. generally work during the day, but many staff members work during the evening.

Evening newspapers are called **P.M.s,** and the **P.M. cycle** runs from about midnight to noon. Editors at P.M.s hold their news meetings in the morning because their deadlines are usually before noon. P.M.s try to get the latest news to their readers, but they realize that by the time the paper is printed and distributed in the afternoon, most of their readers will have had a chance to hear the news on radio, watch it on television or read it online. Therefore, they try to offer their readers a bigger and more comprehensive news report and more local feature stories than other media can. Larger evening papers also have more than one edition each day, which helps them deliver the latest news possible.

Evening newspapers are fighting an uphill battle, however. Some newspapers in small, one-paper cities are P.M.s, but many have shut down or switched to A.M. (People still like to look at their morning newspaper before work each day, while they are drinking coffee, to find out what happened since they went to bed the night before.) There are many complicated reasons for the decline of evening newspapers, but it can be attributed partly to changing lifestyles. In most households today there are two wage earners, and they are bombarded by the Internet, e-mail, radio and television throughout the day. When they get home, they often want to use their leisure time in some other way than reading an evening newspaper.

CHAPTER TWO

INGREDIENTS OF NEWS

Two people are injured in a car wreck. Now that's news. Or is it? Some places, yes. Other places, no.

The definition of *news* is elusive. It can be:

- "Man bites dog."
- Something you haven't heard before.
- Happy or sad. Disturbing or entertaining.
- What editors and reporters say it is.

Whatever it is, *news* is an extremely complex term, and it is different things to different people. It is information, and today's media are in the information business.

(*Erlend Aas / Scanpix*)

What's news today might not be news tomorrow. What's news in one geographic area is not necessarily news in another. News of unemployment in the steel industry will be on the front page in Pittsburgh but might not even make the paper in Great Bend, Kan. Conversely, a 15-cent increase in wheat prices will get front-page treatment in Great Bend but might not rate a mention in Pittsburgh.

In a small town served by a community newspaper, a car accident with two injuries may be the biggest news of the day. At a large metropolitan newspaper, such an occurrence may not be reported unless the accident involves well-known people. In the big cities, it would take a major accident with fatalities to make the news.

One important thing about news is that it is always changing. In a speech to the Organization of News Ombudsmen in 1998, Sandra Mims Rowe, editor of *The Oregonian* in Portland, said: "Part of what is going on is that other media (besides newspapers) are recasting the definitions of news. The newest news dispenser, the runaway Internet, makes a journalist out of anybody who has a modem. It values speed and sensationalism above accuracy. New media will not adopt the highest standards."

Later in her speech, Rowe added: "The high road is there if newspapers will take it. If newspaper journalism and journalists long for greater respect, then newspaper editors must supply the discipline to play down—not play up—the trivial, the perverse, the bizarre."

What Is News Treatment?

People have always been hungry for news. Colonial Americans hurried to meet arriving ships, to pick up letters and newspapers from Europe. The first attempt to publish a colonial newspaper was on Sept. 25, 1690, when Benjamin Harris of Boston issued *Publick Occurrences Both Foreign and Domestick.* His unauthorized paper was shut down by Massachusetts Bay officials after the first issue—and the next newspaper in the colonies was not printed until 1704—but *Publick Occurrences* began a wave of American newspapers that over the last three centuries has brought readers news of diverse happenings.

In *Publick Occurrences* Harris said that he would furnish his readers "with an account of such considerable things as have arrived unto our notice."

Hard News and Soft News

In today's media-conscious world, news comes from many print, electronic and broadcast fronts. Sometimes news is bad; sometimes it is good. It can be hard; it can be soft.

Hard news events, such as killings, city council meetings and speeches by leading government officials, are timely and are reported almost automatically by the media.

Soft news events, such as a lunch to honor a retiring school custodian or a car wash by fourth-graders to raise money for a classmate with cancer, are not usually considered immediately important or timely to a wide audience. These events still contain elements of news, however, and the media often report them. (A more complete discussion of hard and soft news appears in Chapter 9.)

Most media strive to present a mix of hard and soft stories. People today lead busy lives, and they are bombarded with print and electronic information

24 hours a day. They want to know what is happening in Russia and China, on Capitol Hill, in their state legislature and down the street. They also want to know what movies are the most popular, what celebrity marriage is on the rocks, the best way to keep roses healthy and what to do this weekend.

The Need for Flexibility

Reporters and their editors are always debating the word *news*. They know that if an airplane crashes near downtown and people are killed, the story will be the top news of the day. But the rest of the news isn't so easy to peg, and it's changing as rapidly as you're reading this sentence.

Sue Clark-Johnson, chairman, CEO and publisher of the Gannett-owned *Arizona Republic* in Phoenix, told a group of high school journalism students in 2001 that those thinking of a career in journalism are entering at an exciting time, when "things continue to change at lightning speed."

She said: "Our challenge as newspaper professionals is to adapt to the needs of today's technologically savvy, time-starved readers. We can't sit back and wait for people to come to us. We need to aggressively pursue new readers and make the paper more relevant, exciting and packed full of information for many different segments of our population."

Clark-Johnson said her newspaper will rely on **convergence** to reach new audiences in the future. "Convergence is a collaboration that leverages the strengths of newspapers, TV and the Internet to gather and distribute information in new ways to new audiences," she added. "Convergence has literally changed the way we do business at *The Republic*. The ultimate goal is to benefit our readers and viewers.

"Newspapers can provide depth and breadth to stories because we have more resources and space to devote to issues. TV can help put a face on these issues and add a human side. And online gives us the ability to report on the news instantly and lets you pick what you want to read about and when you want to read about it."

In her speech, Clark-Johnson also talked about what she called "community connectedness," which she said means not only defining what a community is, but also helping build it. "It means making sure the newspaper thoroughly and accurately reflects the communities we serve. It's getting more names and faces in the paper. Making sure our stories, our reporters and our columnists represent the full diversity of our community. And I'm not just talking about ethnic diversity."

Civic Journalism

Journalists often define news by connecting with residents in their communities. They refer to these connections and the resulting stories as **civic journalism.**

The Pew Center for Civic Journalism (*www.pewcenter.org*) says that at its heart civic journalism "is a belief that journalism has an obligation to public life—an obligation that goes beyond just telling the news or unloading lots of facts. The way we do our journalism affects the way public life goes. Journalism can help empower a community or it can help disable it."

Each year, the Pew Center honors excellence in civic journalism through the James K. Batten Award, named for the late chairman and chief executive of

Knight-Ridder Inc. In 1989, Batten said in a speech at the University of California—Riverside, "I think we need to cultivate a journalistic ethic that celebrates the magic of writers and editors and photographers and artists who are blessed with the gift of connecting—not just wafting self-indulgent messages out of the newsroom's door." His speech outlines much of the philosophy of what has come to be known as civic journalism.

In 2001, for example, the Batten Award went to *The Herald Dispatch* in Huntington, W.Va., and West Virginia Public Broadcasting for their coverage of the state's future without coal. In announcing the award, the Pew Center said the coverage "built multiple entry points and had a strong online component that fostered wide community development. It also demonstrated the potential of moving beyond simple publication towards application of the journalism."

The Gatekeeping Process

Selection of news for print or broadcast is subjective. It is based on a journalist's feelings, thoughts and experiences. Communication researchers refer to people who make news decisions as **gatekeepers.** These editors, news directors and reporters can open the gate to let news flow; they can close the gate to keep news from oozing out. Sources can also be considered gatekeepers. If they refuse to supply information, possibly there will be no story.

One person seldom has complete control over all the gates in the process of disseminating news. For example, the managing editor of a newspaper reads a story in a national news magazine about contemplated congressional action to cut benefits to military veterans. While mulling the possibility of developing a local angle, the managing editor notices that The Associated Press has just moved a similar national story. Seeing the AP story reinforces the editor's belief that it should be further developed by a reporter.

The managing editor then talks to the city editor about assigning the story to a reporter. The managing editor suggests that the reporter interview some local veterans for their reactions to the contemplated cutbacks. The city editor, however, has just seen a local television interview and says the interview was not enlightening. The city editor suggests that, rather than putting together a quick local story based on off-the-cuff emotional reactions, a reporter first conduct some interviews with state congressional representatives and review the specific proposals. Then, the reporter could get reactions from local residents. The story would have to be held a day or so, but the managing editor agrees that a stronger article would be worth the delay. The city editor assigns the story to a reporter who has been out of college for only two years and has had no contact with the military.

The gatekeeping process continues: The reporter must decide whom to interview and what to ask, which answers to include in the story, which element to play up in the lead and which sources are the most knowledgeable and quotable.

The reporter writes the story and turns it in to an assistant city editor for review. The assistant city editor thinks that more emphasis should be placed on comments made by a veteran's widow who was interviewed. The reporter obliges.

The news editor determines that the story should run 20 inches and be given a four-column headline. It is to be a front-page story.

A copy editor reads the story and removes some of the material the assistant city editor asked the reporter to add. The reporter rants and raves about the cut.

An assistant managing editor is called in to resolve the dispute. A compromise is reached; the widow's comments are left in the story, but because the article must still be cut, a comment from an American Legion member who says that a local congressman is antimilitary is deleted. The assistant managing editor says that the publisher is a good friend of the congressman, but that this is not a factor in the decision to delete the remark.

Thirty minutes before deadline, a reporter calls the city desk to say that the superintendent of schools has just been fired by the board of education. This story will run 20 inches. The news editor decides to take the story on veterans off the front page and move it to an inside news section. The managing editor intervenes, saying that it should remain on the front page, where readership is highest. The managing editor then orders an international story to be shifted from the front page to an inside page.

This scenario could be extended, but the point is clear: There is no scientific formula for deciding what is news and where it should be placed in a newspaper. At several junctures in the process of gathering and writing news, decisions to include or exclude information are made. Reporters and editors, consciously or unconsciously, often rely on time-honored news elements to help them make these decisions.

What Makes News?

Criteria for Newsworthiness

For decades, textbooks on reporting have discussed the classic elements of news. Criteria most often considered as determining newsworthiness include these:

- *Timeliness.* Is it a recent development, or is it old news?
- *Proximity.* Is the story relevant to local readers?
- *Conflict.* Is the issue developing, has it been resolved or does anybody care?
- *Eminence and Prominence.* Are noteworthy people involved? If so, that makes the story more important.
- *Consequence and Impact.* What effect will the story have on readers?
- *Human Interest.* Even though it might not be an earth-shattering event, does it contain unique, interesting elements?

Some examples will illustrate these classic criteria.

Timeliness

Freshness strengthens a news story. For example, when a storm hits, readers immediately need to know its effects. The first two paragraphs from an article in *The Evansville* (Ind.) *Press* illustrate the timely nature of such a story:

> Tri-State roads called "hazardous at best" by the National Weather Service won't improve until at least tomorrow when sunny skies, temperatures near freezing and drying winds should help road clearing work.
>
> Police throughout the Tri-State urged residents to stay home as drifting snow closed roads throughout the Evansville area. Some could remain closed for days, weather officials said.

When the Kansas Board of Education decided on math requirements for schoolchildren, *The Kansas City Star* reported the story while it was still timely. It began:

> TOPEKA—The Kansas Board of Education reached a compromise Tuesday on math requirements for kindergarten through 12th grade.
>
> After several hours of discussion, the board agreed to send a list of suggestions to the advisory committee that wrote the standards. Once the committee makes the revisions, the board will consider adopting the requirements.

Breaking news stories such as the two above command space at most newspapers. They are timely, and readers want to know what is happening now.

Of course, readers who want the most timely stories can go online or turn on their televisions. This access to instantaneous news puts increased pressure on reporters. They always have had to be accurate and quick. Now they have to be even quicker but still maintain the highest standards of accuracy.

Proximity

Events close to home are naturally of interest to the news media. Note the following lead paragraph from *The Gleaner,* Henderson, Ky.:

> The city's stormwater management consultant Monday night unveiled a proposal designed to handle Henderson's stormwater problems and estimated cost of the plan at $26 million.

Henderson's stormwater problems might not interest readers in Biloxi, Miss., or Laramie, Wyo., but they deserve front-page treatment in Henderson.

The lead on a story published in *The Colorado Springs Gazette* would not have raised an eyebrow among readers anywhere else. But it was news in Colorado Springs.

> Two people who had been expected to run for the Colorado Springs City Council District 1 seat said Tuesday they will not be candidates.

Local economic developments are naturally of significant interest to readers. One story in the *Plano* (Texas) *Star Courier* led with:

> The Plano Chamber of Commerce initiated a program Wednesday to emphasize to local consumers and merchants the importance of spending money within the city.

Conflict

Conflict—whether it involves people, governmental bodies or sports teams—is often considered newsworthy. For example, note the lead on a story published in *The Star-Herald* of Scottsbluff, Neb.:

> A request from Nebraska Western College to install a storm sewer along the north side of East 27th Street was denied by the Scottsbluff City Council Monday night based on opposition from property owners in the area.

Here is another lead from *The Gleaner* in Henderson, Ky.:

> Efforts to block the city's purchase of land that could be used to expand the city landfill appeared this weekend to be headed for defeat at Tuesday's city commission meeting.

Eminence and Prominence

Some happenings are newsworthy simply because well-known people are involved. People tell jokes in this country every day. That generally would not be considered to be worth a news story. Nearly every time President Bush joked early in his presidency, however, it made the news.

Stabbings in metropolitan areas normally do not receive front-page treatment—unless the victims are prominent. The lead paragraph from an *Evansville Press* story follows:

> A former Indiana State University Evansville basketball player was fatally stabbed and another ex-player was seriously hurt in a fight early today at the North Park Village parking lot.

Newspapers routinely publish obituaries. Only when a person of particular prominence dies, however, does the story make news in papers around the country. Here's the lead on an Associated Press story that was widely published:

> NASHVILLE, Tenn. (AP)—John Hartford, a versatile and wry performer who wrote the standard "Gentle on My Mind" and turned his back on Hollywood to return to bluegrass music, died Monday after a long battle with cancer. He was 63.

Consequence and Impact

Few developments hit a community as hard—economically and emotionally—as mass layoffs by major employers. It is not surprising, then, that media give prominent play to these occurrences. Here are the first two paragraphs of a story published in *The Gleaner*, Henderson, Ky.:

> Alcan Aluminum Corp. announced Thursday it will shut down one of three potlines at its Sebree smelter, resulting in the layoff of about 250 employees.
>
> "Alcan has no proposed date when the employees might be called back," the company said in a statement.

The impact of layoffs is not limited to the employees and their families. An economic domino effect is felt throughout the area. Readers are always interested in stories that have considerable impact on their communities.

Projects that would involve millions of dollars naturally have a major impact on an area. Recognizing this, *The Evansville Press* led a story with:

> A group of western Kentucky businessmen quietly is planning to build a Tri-State airport that would replace commercial airports in Evansville and Owensboro.

An action taken by the County Commission in Birmingham, Ala., would eventually have an impact on residents there, as emphasized in the first two paragraphs of a story in *The Birmingham News:*

> In two to three weeks, Jefferson County's Family Court complex should be a safer place.
>
> The County Commission Tuesday gave tentative approval to stationing security guards at the entrance of the Family Court building while it is open and at the entrance to the county's detention center around-the-clock.

Human Interest

It may be a cliché that there are a lot of interesting people in the world, but it is a fact that newspaper readers like to hear about them. Human interest stories often appeal to the emotions of readers, pulling them into the lives of others or into subjects of broad concern. Bob Dvorchak wrote a story for The Associated Press that undoubtedly captured the interest of his readers in the first two paragraphs. The story was about an aide to a Pennsylvania state senator:

> On weekdays, Dennis Sciabica toils in politics as an aide to a state senator. In his free time, he's a professional cowboy, wrestling steers and riding snorting bulls.
>
> "Both are high risk businesses," Sciabica says. "I've had people tell me that I sling the bull during the week and ride it on weekends."

When the 2000 U.S. Census figures were released, Jeff McDonald of *The San Diego Union-Tribune* wrote a story about the only place in San Diego County where a majority of the residents are under 18. His story began:

> They wait months, years even, to move into the 1970s tract homes rising from the hills and mesas between Interstate 15 and Admiral Baker Golf Course.
>
> Theirs is an enclave of three-, four- and five-bedroom homes with milk- and chocolate-colored garage doors fronting well-tended streets that end in quiet cul-de-sacs standing guard over Mission Valley.

In this corner of Tierrasanta, where a generation ago the Navy built thousands of homes for its sailors, and private developers rounded out the neighborhood with cookie-cutter precision, children outnumber adults.

Other Factors Affecting News Treatment

In addition to the classic criteria of newsworthiness, other factors influence whether a story should be done. These include:

- *Instincts of Editors and Reporters.* They know news when they see it.
- *Audience.* Would inner-city residents of Los Angeles, for example, be interested in the death of a former governor of North Carolina?
- *"News Holes."* Depending on available space, some stories could make the paper one day, but be left out on another.
- *Availability of News.* Depending on what is happening locally and in the world, there are simply more stories to choose from on some days. On slow news days, editors and reporters will scratch for stories of borderline value. On heavy news days, some good stories don't merit dissemination.
- *Philosophy of the Medium.* The business-oriented *Wall Street Journal,* for example, selects stories on the basis of criteria different from those of a metropolitan arts and entertainment publication.
- *Pressure from the Publisher.* Most publishers try not to interfere openly with the news process, but most editors and reporters are aware of the political and social leanings of owners.
- *Influence of Advertisers.* Usually it is a subtle consideration, but some editors might think twice, for example, about giving prominent space to the formation of a "committee for decency in movies" if local theaters are major advertisers.
- *News Mix.* News media often strive to balance hard news with soft news and to provide local, national and international stories.
- *Competition among Media.* To some extent, community and metropolitan newspapers supplement each other, as do the print and electronic media. Each medium has its strengths and weaknesses in coverage of news. But most media try to keep one step ahead of the competition, and this sometimes affects handling of news.
- *Changing Demographics.* Demographics—the distribution, density, size and composition of the American population—are changing, and the nation's media need to adjust their news coverage accordingly.

An elaboration of these factors follows.

Instincts of Editors and Reporters

William Mock, managing editor of *The Beaumont* (Texas) *Enterprise* (circulation: 62,000 weekdays), said that "gut instincts and common sense" often take over when making news decisions: "We have to second-guess what our readers really want to know."

If, for example, local teachers are threatening to strike and the wire services move a story about a school strike 2,000 miles away, the assumption is that local readers will be interested. If local teachers were not poised for a walkout, the instinct of the editor would probably be that local readers are not interested in the far-from-home strike story.

Experienced editors and reporters develop a sense of what readers want. Readership surveys and demographic breakdowns, of course, provide editors and reporters with background information that can help hone their instincts.

The Audience

"To determine news value, editors and reporters should put themselves in the reader's easy chair," Mock said. "You have to keep in mind that the reader probably is going to listen to the radio driving to and from work and very likely will watch some television news." According to Mock, when readers pick up the newspaper in the morning, they already have an idea of what is going on in the world. When they are getting ready for work or school, *The Enterprise* must compete for their attention. It must compete not only with the radio, television and electronic news providers but with scrambled eggs, bacon, toast, spilled orange juice and kids jockeying for position in the bathroom. The readers may know what they saw on television the night before and what they heard on the radio that morning, but they may be confused about the details. *The Enterprise* has to tell readers what is behind the news—put it into perspective for them.

Mock makes it a point to know his readers. Beaumont, a city of 125,000, has "a fairly good mix of socioeconomic demographics," he said. The area is heavily dependent on the petrochemical industry. "Developments that in any way touch this industry, nationally or internationally, ripple down to many of our readers," Mock added. "Our unemployment rates often run above the average. When a company closes in Beaumont, that is a big story. It means more people will be out there competing for scarce jobs. The closing of a company might not be a big deal in areas with relatively low unemployment rates, but it means a lot to our readers and to our economy."

The News Hole

The size of the **news hole**—the number of column inches available for news—varies at most publications from day to day. On days when the pages are *wide open* (when there are comparatively few advertisements and many column inches are available for news) stories of borderline importance might be published. When pages are *tight* (if comparatively little space is available for news), stories that would be published on a day when even average space is available simply cannot be worked into the news hole.

The Gleaner in Henderson, Ky., is an 11,000-circulation publication. On most days, the paper runs 20 to 24 pages (with the equivalent of 10 to 12 full pages available for news); on Sundays, it averages 42. In a year, *The Gleaner* devotes about 48 percent of its total space to news.

At some daily papers, when the news side is given the **dummy**—a page-by-page mark-up that has ads with specific sizes keyed in—editors are locked into the assigned space. At *The Gleaner,* however, the editor, Ron Jenkins, has authority to get additional space when it is necessary.

"On a lot of days, it seems that we have 10 gallons of water to put in a 5-gallon bucket," Jenkins said. "When the news hole is really tight, the emphasis in our paper is on local news. We do a lot of cutting on national and international stories on those days. If we have five significant wire stories, but room to run only three of them, we'll slice all five at the bottom just to get them in the paper. On tight news days, we run a lot of national and international news briefs [capsulized accounts of longer news stories]."

Availability of News

Some days are slower than others in terms of available news stories. News stories that would not merit publication on relatively brisk news days might make their way into print in a Saturday paper. Saturdays are often slow news days because government offices and other news-making institutions are closed. Newspapers stockpile non-timely features and trend stories for use on these days.

Major-market electronic media and large-circulation newspapers naturally have more resources for gathering news than smaller operations do. A large-circulation newspaper, for example, has scores of reporters and editors for gathering and processing news. It also subscribes to a wide variety of news services in addition to The Associated Press. For a fee, newspapers can subscribe to any number of supplemental news services, such as Knight-Ridder, Gannett and The New York Times News Service. Because of budget restrictions, smaller newspapers may not subscribe to several supplemental services. Instead, they rely primarily on a major wire service and a skeleton news staff. Thus, available resources limit how news media gather and handle the news.

Philosophy of the Medium

Some newspapers, such as *The New York Times,* consider themselves papers of record. It is not unusual for *The Times* to devote a full page to the text of a public official's speech or to verbatim excerpts from a significant Supreme Court decision. Most newspapers do not have the space to provide such detail. Instead, most American dailies would publish a story highlighting the speech or the court case.

Radio, television stations and online publications emphasize breaking news and stories where sound and video are logical supplements. These media are technologically well suited to keep pace with breaking news stories; newspapers are not. Radio and online reporters can literally update stories by the minute. Television does not update stories as often as other electronic sources, but if a story merits it, television news is in a position to provide live coverage or interrupt regular programming.

Pressure from the Publisher

Warren Breed, in an early research study of socialization in the newsroom, found that newspaper publishers have much to say in both long-term and immediate news policy decisions. His study, which was published in an article in *Social Forces* in 1955, concluded that many publishers hesitate to issue direct commands to slant a news story. It is logical, however, to assume that some subtle influence is always present, and low-key inferences or suggestions by publishers are philosophically and ethically more acceptable than open commands.

Managing editors of daily newspapers in Kansas and Nebraska perceive little direct pressure from their publishers when making news and editorial decisions, according to a mail questionnaire survey in the two states. The study, which was reported in the *Nebraska Newspaper* magazine, noted, however, that editors often respond to subtle suggestions from their publishers. The study showed a tendency on the part of managing editors to consider the same persons (on the basis of occupation) influential in the community as they believe their publishers consider influential.

The study also showed that editors of daily newspapers in Kansas and Nebraska enjoy some management autonomy—far greater freedom than that of "middle management" employees in other businesses. Still, there is a limit to an editor's management freedom when the most difficult decisions must be made: it often extends, in those cases, only to the publisher's door.

Publishers seldom pressure reporters directly about how to handle a news story. If they are pressured, however, reporters must react on a case-by-case basis. Naturally, their response depends on several factors. For example, does the publisher have a reputation for applying pressure to reporters? If so, how have other reporters dealt with it? What is the working relationship of the publisher, editors and reporters at the newspaper? Is the publisher one who might admire reporters who stand by their opinions in the teeth of pressure? Or is the publisher one who would just as soon fire reporters as look at them?

Possibly the best way for reporters to deal with pressure from publishers, or advertisers, is to seek advice from experienced editors who have probably encountered similar situations.

Influence of Advertisers

The potential always exists for advertisers to influence the dissemination of news. Theoretically, however, the news side of any medium is independent of the advertising arm; and virtually all of the time, it works out that way.

Editors and reporters instinctively bristle at the thought of an advertiser's attempt to blackmail the newspaper into running—or not running—a story. News organizations that would give in to blackmail are few and far between—particularly if a significant story hangs in the balance. Suppression of major news events because of pressure from advertisers is unlikely. For example, it is difficult to imagine a newspaper, television station or radio station spiking a story about an investigation into alleged bid rigging by a local contractor simply because the contractor is a big advertiser.

The potential for spiking a story about a minor news event, however, is probably greater. An editor, for example, might exercise "news judgment" (by rationalizing that "no one really cares") not to publish a story if the same contractor was convicted of first-offense drunken driving. Also, few news media delve deeply into consumer news reporting about local products and services. Some larger newspapers and television stations do, but they are in the minority. Reporters are generally more aggressive in tackling government issues than business issues.

Even though "the wall" between editorial and advertising remains, there is a growing alliance between the two areas as newspapers strive to become information companies and increase profits. For example, at the *Los Angeles Times,* the former publisher, who had worked for the Federal Reserve System and General Mills, appointed "general managers" from the business side to serve as "partners" with editorial department section editors.

In a three-part examination of what happened at the *Times* under publisher Mark Willes, the paper's media critic, David Shaw, reported: "Many in the

newspaper industry question whether Willes can devise new strategies that have eluded people who have spent their lives running big newspaper companies. More important, reporters and editors at the *Times* and elsewhere wonder if, in his gut, he realizes that newspapers are a public trust, not just another moneymaking enterprise."

Newspaper editors and reporters, for the most part, make every effort to avoid any appearance of catering to advertisers. This noble stand, of course, is economically less risky at large-circulation newspapers (where a single advertising account would not make a crucial profit-loss difference) than at smaller dailies and weeklies, where one large account could contribute a disproportionate share of overall revenue.

The News Mix

Most daily media strive for a **news mix**—a combination of hard news stories and lighter feature pieces. Also, these media present a combination of local, regional, national and international news.

Ron Jenkins, editor of *The Gleaner,* said that his newspaper uses a "smorgasbord approach" to the presentation of news. "We've had readership surveys show that the appetite among readers is spread fairly evenly among local, national and international news," he said.

The Gleaner emphasizes local news, but Jenkins reported that the newspaper hopes to add a half page of national news each day. "We hope the advertising growth will allow us to do that," he said.

Competition among Media

Competition has an effect on news coverage by various outlets. In Henderson, Ky. (population: 27,000), for example, Jenkins has to look over his shoulder at the media of metropolitan Evansville, Ind., a city of 137,000 just 6 miles away.

"We must provide our readers with the news that they won't get in the Evansville newspaper," Jenkins said. "Our policy is to keep the design of our newspaper simple, clean and inviting. But, when you open up the package, there has to be some substance in it."

For example, *The Gleaner* publishes major stories at the end of every month about the number of building permits that were issued locally. "Following the trend in building permits is a way of monitoring our local economy," Jenkins said. "Sometimes the stories are played on Page 1—if there is a significant upward or downward movement—but usually we play the story on the business page." The Evansville media would be unlikely to carry the story at all.

Clearly, editors and reporters at local media react to one another in making their news judgments. It is common for reporters and editors to monitor not only other newspapers but electronic news media as well. Some events, such as a press conference at which the mayor announces his or her intention to seek reelection, would naturally be covered by the print and electronic media.

Occasionally, however, a newspaper will cover an event that it normally would not simply because a television station is giving the event substantial attention. For example, a television station might do updates on its 6 p.m. and 10 p.m. newscasts about a 14-year-old who is attempting to break the world's record for sit-ups. Because television is giving so much attention to the event, a newspaper might also carry a picture and short story. Editors would not want readers to believe that the newspaper was missing a "big" story. Editors and reporters at the newspaper might have felt that the teenager doing sit-ups wasn't really newsworthy, but because television gave it so much coverage, the newspaper had to provide some.

Changing Demographics

Many newspapers across the United States are expanding and enhancing their coverage of the many cultures that make up the population. That's because the demographics in this country are changing rapidly.

In 2001, for example, *San Diego Union-Tribune* staff writer Leonel Sanchez reported that 2000 Census numbers showed that Mexicans and Mexican-Americans make up 84 percent of San Diego County's more than 750,000 Latinos and 22 percent of the county's 2.8 million population.

Sanchez also reported:

- Latinos, who can be of any race but are linked by their Spanish culture, make up nearly 27 percent of the country's population.
- The numbers of Cubans, Puerto Ricans and Central and South Americans all grew during the 1990s.
- Peruvians formed their own chamber of commerce and set up polling places to participate in Peru's presidential elections from abroad.
- Other associations formed by Hispanic groups continue to thrive.

Clearly, news coverage must be responsive to these significant changes, many more of which are being reported in the wake of the 2000 U.S. Census. It is increasingly imperative for journalists to be sensitive to and knowledgeable about racial and social diversity. In fact, the United States is fast becoming a country where virtually any group can call itself a "minority." The media must alter their traditional patterns of coverage if they are to paint consistently accurate portraits of various ethnic groups and to examine, on a day-to-day basis, the impact of cultural trends and changing demographics on society. (See Chapter 18 for a more complete discussion of multicultural reporting.)

Pitching News Stories to Editors

Competition for space in a newspaper is fierce. Reporters must compete aggressively for valuable inches. Those who develop the knack of ferreting out stories and effectively presenting their ideas often win the favor of their supervisors. A reporter who has good news judgment will capture the attention of an editor. These reporters are acknowledged and appreciated because good story ideas take some of the pressure off busy editors who are always seeking them.

Following are some ingredients in the successful pitching of stories.

Specificity

When approaching an editor with a story idea, don't just name the subject. Do not, for example, tell an editor that you would like to do a story on a star volleyball player who is ready to return to the team after sitting out from competition for a season. That general idea, in itself, has some merit. But it will probably generate the most common comeback of editors: "That's interesting, but what's the angle?"

Always go to your editor with a proposed angle. In the case of the story about the volleyball player, for instance, the reporter might emphasize that the player had to sit out her junior year because of pregnancy and that the article would explore her feelings about making it back into the sport and the hard work she went through to get into physical and mental condition to play. But this does not mean that, on the basis of further interviews and research, the angle could not change. Reporters should guard against having such a firm fix on one angle that they would not react to new material. Reporters should not be bound to a preconception.

If you have done a good job preparing your story pitch, you have virtually written your lead. Obviously, the key to submitting a solid story proposal is to conduct sufficient preliminary research. It does not take much effort to make an extra telephone call to a source, to consult the clip file or to check the Internet. Taking these steps before you pitch the story enables you to be more precise.

Succinctness

Editors are busy. They have other reporters and stories competing for their attention. Do not waste the editor's time with a long-winded story proposal.

For example, assume that you want to do a story about pick-up basketball games that take place in your school's gymnasium during noon hours on weekdays. It would be unwise to saunter up to an editor and say: "You know, there are about 50 students, dropouts, faculty members and alumni who gather at the gymnasium on weekday noons to play basketball. I stopped by there the other day, and it looked as though they were having a lot of fun. I think it is interesting that a lot of people from various stations in life skip lunch to play basketball. You know, I even saw a couple of our varsity players over there the other day. I think this is more than a sports story. I think it's a good story about people who enjoy playing games to break up the tension of the day. What do you think? Shall I give it a try?"

In all likelihood, the editor would shut you off before you reached the fourth sentence. Remember: You are trying to sell the merits of your proposal. You will not do that by boring the editor to the point of frustration.

Get to the point: "Each weekday noon, about 50 students, dropouts, faculty members and alumni play basketball in the school's gymnasium. This is an unusual group. You can find 45-year-old nationally known physicists and department administrators out there trading elbows, glares and high fives with students half their age. These people form a subculture of sorts on the campus. I want to interview several of them to find out what brings them together."

Enthusiasm

If you are not enthusiastic about your story idea, chances are your editor will not be. Editors want meat and bone on story ideas—not generalities. If you excite your editor about the story, you probably will be given the time and support to explore it fully. If the editor is not interested in the idea—if you cannot sell the story—chances are you will be discouraged from writing it. Editors often make decisions to go with stories on the basis of the effectiveness of a reporter's pitch. If you are blasé about the story, you can't expect your editor to get excited about it.

An editor will know if you are just throwing out ideas without adequate thought. Go to the editor with a game plan. Explain not only the specific angles you intend to pursue but also how long you think it will take to write the story and how long you think the story will run.

Monitoring the Media

Editors sometimes complain that reporters are interested in reading only the stories they write themselves. Don't fall into this trap. Read the newspaper from cover to cover; listen to newscasts on television and radio. National stories might trigger local possibilities. For example, assume that there is a serial rapist on the rampage in California. What are the tendencies of this rapist and others like him? Are there certain high-risk situations that women should avoid? Local law enforcement officials and psychologists could help you develop an angle. Stories like this are both current and timely. They are timely because a series of rapes is taking place now in another state—and that, in itself, is newsworthy. They are current in the sense that this is a topic which has been and remains on the minds of many. So many of these stories have been written that the subject has acquired a news value independent of whether such a serial rape might have occurred the previous night. In addition, the topic has impact and involves conflict.

Don't forget that old local stories can trigger new ones, called **follows.** Such stories are often appropriate and newsworthy. For example, assume that you read an article about a radiation leak in the life sciences building on your campus. The building was evacuated. Check to see if classes were held in the building the next day; check to see if additional precautions will be taken to prevent future leaks; check to see if the leak posed a danger to nearby buildings. Don't hesitate to pitch the follow to your editor.

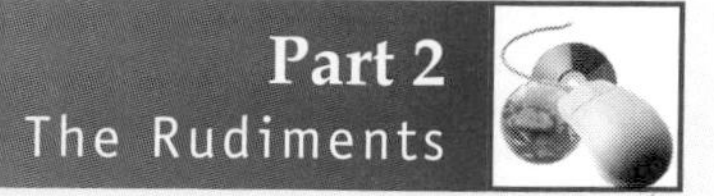

QUALITIES OF GOOD WRITING

Michael Gartner, Pulitzer Prize-winning journalist, said he writes leads—over and over—in his mind while he is driving to work in the morning or home in the evening.

"I compose as I drive, and then I say the leads out loud, listening for rhythm and cadence, hunting for the lyric—much the way, I suspect, a songwriter taps out different notes on his piano in search of just the right tune."

Gartner has served at various times during his career as president of NBC News, page one editor of *The Wall Street Journal*, editor and president of *The Des Moines Register*, editor of *The Courier-Journal* in Louisville and general

(*Photo Courtesy of Iowa Cubs*)

news executive for Gannett Corporation and *USA Today*. In 1997, he won the Pulitzer Prize for the editorials he wrote for *The Tribune* of Ames, Iowa, where he was then the editor and co-owner.

He said in his keynote address for Penn State's Foster Conference of Distinguished Writers that good writers develop their own *voice.*

"You just can't do that if you don't listen to yourself," he said. "And the best way to listen to yourself is to read to yourself—out loud. Listen for the cadence—or the discordance. Listen for the beat—and the offbeat. Listen for the rhyme and the reason. Sometimes, you'll hear the jarring word, the awkward phrase—the word that looked fine but sounded junky, the phrase that typed nice but sounded clunky."

Anna Quindlen, Pulitzer Prize-winning journalist and novelist, said in a Foster Conference talk that "writing is a constant process of rejection; sometimes you have to produce a lot of bad paragraphs to get a good sentence."

She noted, however, that she loves "having written." She said: "Writing is immortality. Writing is a guaranteed afterlife."

Gartner agreed that writing is not always fun.

"Sometimes it's painful," he said. "Sometimes, it's frustrating. Sometimes, it's embarrassing. The fun of writing? That, sometimes, is like the fun of a headache. Or the fun of cavities. Or the fun of divorce."

He emphasized, though, how important it is "to love the meanings and sounds of words . . . the rhythms of phrases, the cadence of sentences."

Indeed, he said: "You have to love, even, the look of paragraphs as they sit atop one another."

Gartner said the best newspaper advice he ever received came when he was 21 years old. He was just out of college, working as a copy editor at *The Wall Street Journal* in New York.

"I was working nights, and late one evening I looked up and this big, gentle man was standing there watching me," Gartner said. "When he saw me pause, he introduced himself as Barney Kilgore. Barney Kilgore was the man who invented the modern-day *Wall Street Journal*. He was a genius. He had been a reporter and editor, but by this time he was president of the company, though—like all good managers—he spent a lot of time walking around the place.

" 'What are you doing?' he asked me. I explained that I was trying to rewrite a story I'd been given, because it was murky. 'Good,' he said, and then he added: 'Remember, the easiest thing for the reader to do is to quit reading.'

"Oh, what wonderful advice to a newspaperman. I pasted it on my typewriter, and I've kept it written on my computers and notebooks—and etched in my brain—ever since."

Clearly, newspaper editors are placing more emphasis on good writing today than ever before. Seminars, workshops and conventions often feature sessions on how reporters can improve their writing—how, as Gartner noted, they can "cut the complex to the simple . . . [and] turn the simple into the eloquent."

Some newspapers designate editors to serve as in-house writing coaches; other newspapers import writing coaches to work with reporters who need to polish their skills.

This chapter, then, will present guidelines for good writing by two acknowledged experts.

Roy Peter Clark: Fourteen Traits of Good Writers

Roy Peter Clark, who may be the best known writing coach in the United States, described one of his first days in the newsroom of the *St. Petersburg* (Fla.) *Times.*

It was more than two decades ago; Clark had left a comfortable niche as a university professor to become a writing coach. Most of the reporters in the newsroom were not particularly impressed with his Ph.D. in English literature. He knew little of the day-to-day practicalities of journalism.

Writing in the *Washington Journalism Review,* Clark recalled the need he felt "to interview every reporter on the staff to learn much more than I could hope to teach." He told of an early experience:

> One day, I found myself sitting beside Howell Raines, then political editor in St. Petersburg, now [with] *The New York Times.* Howell had written a series of political profiles that became legendary in the newsroom. They were powerful and influential character studies so well written that other reporters could quote passages verbatim.
>
> The week I interviewed Howell, *two* of his books had been published, a terrific novel called "Whiskey Man," and an oral history of the civil rights movement, "My Soul Is Rested." I felt humbled at the prospect of coaching him. What could I tell him, "Use more active verbs in your next novel, Howell"?
>
> I decided to become student instead of teacher, and asked Howell a dozen questions about political reporting. I recorded his responses. Howell described how to write about politicians as human characters and not just authority figures. He got down to nitty-gritty matters of interviewing and lead writing.

Clark used portions of the interview in his in-house newsletter; it was well received. It occurred to him that advice from respected writers could be both instructional and inspirational to reporters.

Clark served as writing coach at the *St. Petersburg Times* for two years, worked as a reporter and then joined the staff of the Modern Media Institute, which in 1983 became the Poynter Institute for Media Studies. Nelson Poynter, publisher of the *St. Petersburg Times* and *Evening Independent,* willed the controlling stock of the Times Publishing Co. to the institute. Clark, who continues to function as a writing coach, serves as senior scholar at the institute, which serves students of all ages and professionals from all over the nation.

In his article in the *Washington Journalism Review* (now *American Journalism Review*), Clark told how he had interviewed dozens of reporters during writing seminars at the institute and during his years as editor or co-editor of "Best Newspaper Writing," which is published each year by the institute. The book features award-winning stories in the American Society of Newspaper Editors' annual writing contest.

Clark began to see similar qualities in the outstanding reporters he interviewed. In turn, he developed a list of 14 qualities often shared by good writers.

Here is Clark's discussion of the common traits, adapted from the article in *Washington Journalism Review.*

Trait 1

Good writers see the world as their journalism laboratory, a storehouse of story ideas. If they can get out of the office, they can find a story. In fact, they can't walk down the street or drive to the mall or watch television without finding something to write about.

Trait 2

Good writers prefer to discover and develop their own story ideas. They have an eye for the offbeat and may find conventional assignments tedious. They appreciate collaboration with good editors but spend more time avoiding bad editors and what they perceive to be useless assignments.

Trait 3

Good writers are voracious collectors of information. This usually means that they take notes like crazy. They are more concerned with the quality of information than with flourishes of style. They more often describe themselves as reporters than as writers.

Trait 4

Good writers spend too much time and creative energy working on their leads. They know that the lead is the most important part of their work, the passage that invites the reader into the story and signals the news. They are inclined to describe how they rewrote a lead a dozen times until they "got it right."

Trait 5

Good writers talk about "immersing themselves" in the story. They live it, breathe it and dream it. They plan and rehearse the story all day long, writing it in their heads, considering their options, talking it over with editors, always looking for new directions and fresh information.

Trait 6

Most good writers are bleeders rather than speeders. When they write, in the words of the great *New York Times* sportswriter Red Smith, they "open a vein." This is because their standards are so high that their early drafts seem painful and inadequate. But when deadline comes or a big story breaks, adrenaline kicks them into a different warp factor. They can speed when they have to.

Trait 7

Good writers understand that an important part of writing is the mechanical drudgery of organizing the material, what the AP's Saul Pett describes as "donkey work." They may respond to this by developing careful filing systems. They also develop idiosyncrasies that help them build momentum during the writing process: pilgrimages to the bathroom, taking walks, daydreaming, junk food orgies or self-flagellation.

Trait 8

Good writers rewrite. They love computer terminals, which permit maximum playfulness during revision. They move paragraphs around, invert word order for emphasis, find stronger verbs and occasionally purge the entire story to make a fresh start. Alas, they are rarely satisfied with their final stories and, burdened with imperfection, can hardly bring themselves to read their own work in the newspaper. Writing is an expression of ego, making the writer vulnerable and, at times, insufferable.

Trait 9

In judging their work, good writers tend to trust their ears and their feelings more than their eyes. Some stare at the screen with their lips moving, praying that the inner music will reach their fingers. Editors "look for holes in the story." Writers want to "make it sing."

Trait 10

Good writers love to tell stories. They are constantly searching for the human side of the news, for voices that enliven the writing. Their language reflects their interest in storytelling. Rather than talk about the five W's, they are more inclined to discuss anecdotes, scenes, chronology and narrative. During interviews, they tend to answer even the most theoretical questions with war stories, jokes and parables.

Trait 11

Good writers write primarily to please themselves and to meet their own exacting standards, but they also understand that writing is a transaction between writer and reader. Unlike many journalists, these writers have confidence that sophisticated work will not be lost on their readers. They treasure the reader and want to reward and protect and inform the reader and take responsibility for what the reader learns from a story.

Trait 12

Good writers take chances in their writing. They love the surprising and the unconventional approach to a story. They prefer failing in print on occasion because those failures are a test of their inventiveness. They love editors who tolerate experimentation but who will save them from falling on their faces. Their secret wish is to produce the best, most original piece in the newspaper every day.

Trait 13

Good writers are lifelong readers, mostly of novels, and they like movies. They collect story ideas and forms from other genres. They love words, names and lists.

Trait 14

Good writers write too long, and they know it. Unlike other journalists, who stop caring for the reader after the lead is complete, these writers use transitions and endings to keep their readers going. Their endings are so good that it is almost impossible to cut stories from the bottom. They want their stories to be "seamless" or "connected by a single thread" or "to flow." They want readers to read every word.

Robert Gunning: Ten Principles of Clear Writing

Robert Gunning's book "The Techniques of Clear Writing" is one of several that should be read by anyone who is interested in writing. The others are "The Elements of Style," by William Strunk Jr. and E. B. White; "On Writing Well," by William Zinsser; and "The Art of Readable Writing" and "A New Way to Better English," both by Rudolf Flesch. There are, of course, still others, but these form a solid nucleus. In this section, we'll concentrate on Gunning's guidelines for writers, relating them to the advice offered by Zinsser, Flesch and Strunk and White.

Gunning, a former consultant to more than 100 daily newspapers, including *The Wall Street Journal,* and to United Press International, developed what he called the *ten principles of clear writing.* The principles, which are examined in his book, are:

1. Keep sentences short, on the average.
2. Prefer the simple to the complex.
3. Prefer the familiar word.
4. Avoid unnecessary words.
5. Put action into your verbs.
6. Write the way you talk.
7. Use terms your reader can picture.
8. Tie in with your reader's experience.
9. Make full use of variety.
10. Write to express, not to impress.

These principles are straightforward. Examples and quotations from Gunning and the other writing experts, however, will bring them into even sharper focus.

1: Keep Sentences Short, on the Average

Gunning wrote: "I know of no author addressing a general audience today who averages much more than 20 words per sentence and still succeeds in getting published." The key to that statement is the word *averages.* Gunning noted that "sentences must vary in length if the reader is to be saved from boredom." Indeed, don't hammer at the reader with a continuous flow of short staccato sentences. Changing the length of sentences creates variety and enhances readability.

Note the first five paragraphs of this article by Michael Allen, which was published in *The Arizona Republic* (the number of words in each sentence or transition phrase is in parentheses):

> ARMERO, Colombia—Five helicopters darted about like dragonflies over what had once been one of the most prosperous agricultural towns in Colombia. (20)
>
> Viewed from several thousand feet in the air, it looked as if an immense cement mixer had spilled its load in the heart of the valley's rich, green field. (29)
>
> Up close, it was a scene of unrelieved horror. (9)
>
> Very little stuck out of the soupy, gray mud: the tops of a few trees, a church steeple, glimpses of a neighborhood near the old cemetery. (26)
>
> And bodies. (2) Scores of blackened, putrefying corpses baking in the intense morning sun, a groping arm here, a blank, unseeing face there. (20)

Allen's sentences and transition phrases averaged 18 words. The sentences or transition phrases ranged, however, from 2 words to 29. The change of pace from long sentences to short ones helped to keep the story flowing.

2: Prefer the Simple to the Complex

Gunning wrote that the emphasis in his second principle is on the word *prefer.* "The principle does not outlaw the use of complex form," he wrote. "You need both simple and complex forms for clear expression. At times the complex form is best. But if in your preferences, you use as good judgment as Mark Twain and other successful writers, you will give the simple forms more than an even break." Zinsser wrote: "Clutter is the disease of American writing. We are a society strangling in unnecessary words, circular constructions, pompous frills and meaningless jargon. . . . The secret of good writing is to strip every sentence to its cleanest components."

Variety is achieved by blending some complex sentences with a staple of simple sentences. A **simple sentence** has only one **independent clause:** The council passed the resolution. A **complex sentence** has only one independent clause and at least one **dependent clause:** This is the council member who cast the deciding vote. (*This is the council member* is an independent clause because it is a complete sentence when left standing alone. *Who cast the deciding vote* is a dependent, or subordinate, clause; it is an adjective clause, modifying *member,* a noun.)

Greta Tilley, a reporter for the *Greensboro* (N.C.) *News & Record* and a journalism graduate of the University of South Carolina, won an American Society of Newspaper Editors Distinguished Writing Award for a six-part series on life at the Dorothea Dix Hospital, a state mental institution in Raleigh. Tilley's writing was precise and vivid. Simple sentences were the staple of her writing. Through clear, well-paced writing, Tilley introduced readers to shock treatments:

> RALEIGH—The clock above Anthony's head says 11 past eight.
>
> It's morning. Anthony hasn't eaten or drunk since midnight.
>
> He's strapped to a blue-sheeted hospital bed on wheels. Close by are two psychiatrists, two nurse anesthetists, one psychiatric nurse and two technicians.
>
> "One-ten over 64," the psychiatric nurse says through the hiss of the blood pressure machine. She puts her fingers against Anthony's pulse.

"Sixty. After his treatment the last time he had a bit of a temp, so we need to watch that."

Anthony wears a medium Afro, a full mustache and a blue hospital gown. His tall, strong frame fills the skinny bed.

His bare feet, propped on a pillow, stick out from the end of the sheet covering his body. His eyes are half closed. A stethoscope rests on his stomach.

The technicians have just rolled him from the admissions ward, where he has lived for four months, to a small, clean room in the medical/surgery unit.

Thirty minutes before, he got an injection of atropine to dry his saliva.

In 17 minutes, 140 volts of electrical current will be shot into his brain.

This is Anthony's seventh treatment. He will have one more to go.

When the mental health center in his county sent him to Dorothea Dix Hospital, he couldn't talk, wouldn't eat and didn't respond. His chart described him as catatonic. Drugs didn't help.

Anthony's depression could be coming from a chemical abnormality or stress, or both.

The psychiatrist assigned to his case, Dr. Joe Mazzaglia, asked him to try electroshock therapy. He explained that an electrically induced grand mal seizure would release chemical substances in the brain that could jolt life back into his system.

Anthony gave a reluctant yes.

The writing in the remainder of the lengthy story was equally descriptive and powerful. The story illustrated that a careful blend of simple and complex sentences—with the emphasis on the former—is a solid formula for good writing.

3: Prefer the Familiar Word

Gunning wrote: "Big words help you organize your thought. But in putting your message across you must relate your thoughts to the other fellow's experience. The short, easy words that are familiar to everyone do this job best." The authors of "The Elements of Style" wrote: "Avoid the elaborate, the pretentious, the coy and the cute. Do not be tempted by a twenty-dollar word when there is a ten-center handy, ready and able."

David Finkel of the *St. Petersburg* (Fla.) *Times,* in a story about a teen-ager who was entering a drug rehabilitation program, crafted a gripping lead paragraph that consisted entirely of one- or two-syllable words:

> Sitting tensely in a chair, he is a young man not to be messed with, a coil of barbed wire. His mouth is in a sneer. His eyes could burn holes. His name is Paul Kulek, and he's doing his best to look as if he's in control.

A newspaper carried this wire-service lead paragraph on a national weather story published in mid-November:

> Tempestuous weather spanned the nation Tuesday as record snow and freezing temperatures swept out of the Rockies into the Plains.

Tempestuous? The Random House College Dictionary defines the adjective form as "being characterized by or subject to tempests." The dictionary defines *tempest* as "an extensive current of wind rushing with great velocity and violence, esp. one attended with rain, hail, or snow; a violent storm." *Spanned?* The dictionary defines a *span* as "the full extent, stretch, or reach of anything."

The weather map, published on the same page as the story, clearly showed that at least one-third of the country had clear skies, although temperatures were cold. Obviously, "an extensive current of wind . . . attended with rain, hail, or snow" was not blowing across "the full extent" of the United States. The weather, indeed, was tempestuous in the Rockies and Plains, but the story would have been more accurate—and understandable—had it read:

> Winter-like weather spanned the nation Tuesday as record snow and freezing temperatures swept out of the Rockies into the Plains.

4: Avoid Unnecessary Words

"The greater part of all business and journalistic writing is watered down with words that do not count," Gunning wrote. According to Gunning, such words tire readers and dull their attention.

Note this sentence:

> One of the primary aims of the extremely new master's degree program, which will offer an innovative curriculum not now available to the area's population, will be to draw them back into postgraduate education to improve their communication skills.

That sentence can be cut from 40 words to 24 without changing its meaning:

> A primary aim of the new master's degree program, which will offer a curriculum currently unavailable to area residents, is to improve communication skills.

Arizona Republic reporter Dave Cannella wasted few words in his account of an assisted suicide. In the lead paragraphs of his story, note how Cannella made each word, each sentence, count:

> SOUTHFIELD, Mich.—After two canceled appointments with death, Nicholas Loving died smiling Friday.
>
> The 27-year-old Phoenix man, wasted by Lou Gehrig's disease, is the 23rd, and youngest, person assisted in suicide by Dr. Jack Kevorkian. It was the second suicide this week at which Kevorkian was present.
>
> Death came, finally, for Nick at 9:45 a.m. in an unremarkable home in this suburb 20 miles north of Detroit, said his mother, who was at his side when he died.

5: Put Action into Your Verbs

"Strong-flavored, active verbs give writing bounce and hold a reader's attention," Gunning wrote. Use of the **active voice** (subject acting upon object) rather than **passive voice** (subject acted upon) is considered more direct and vigorous. The passive voice: *The avalanche was caused by an explosion.* The active voice: *An explosion triggered the avalanche.*

Note the strength of the verbs in this paragraph by Terry Henion, a sportswriter at the *Omaha* (Neb.) *World-Herald:*

Under a slate-gray sky, the 28-degree temperature and a 23-mph north wind combined to plummet the wind chill to minus 5 degrees. The Husker defense chilled the Cyclones, too, holding Iowa State to 137 total yards. Nebraska's offense churned out 573 total yards, including 538 on the ground.

Mark Fineman of the *Los Angeles Times* selected a particularly strong, precise verb in this paragraph:

The rebellion plunged the nation into one of the worst political crises in its history and raised the prospect of a military showdown between Marcos and two of his closest aides, but Manila was calm this morning.

Partly because of the verb chosen by John Archibald of *The Birmingham* (Ala.) *News,* readers could visualize this scene:

Birmingham-Jefferson County Transit Authority Board Chairman Bernard Kincaid hobbled into the refurbished board room on crutches Wednesday, the swelling in his left foot visible beneath a thick white athletic sock.

6: Write the Way You Talk

Reporters should work to avoid formal, stilted language, especially in leads. Readers will appreciate it. When the Arizona Department of Public Safety raided a home brewery, Emil Venere, a reporter for the *The East Valley Tribune* in suburban Phoenix, could have written:

Arizona Department of Public Safety officials, for the first time since 1923—four years after prohibition began—on Monday closed down a moonshine still near Gila Bend that was capable of producing 500 gallons of the tequila-like liquid a week.

Instead, Venere wrote:

In a throwback to the days of bootleggers and speakeasies, Arizona officials raided a pig farm near Gila Bend Monday and dismantled what they claim is the biggest moonshine still ever found in the state.

Be specific. Capsulize the thrust of the story in the lead paragraph. But don't bog readers down with alphabet-soup acronyms and bulging details.

James H. Kennedy of *The Birmingham News* was conversational in this lead paragraph:

Buddy Wesley grimaced as he looked at the mess the tornado had made of his cherished antebellum home.

Arnold Hamilton of *The Dallas Morning News* also was conversational—yet brutally vivid—as he described the scene shortly after the bombing of the Alfred P. Murrah Federal Building in Oklahoma City:

> The destruction was incredible. Black smoke streamed across the skyline. Nine floors worth of brick, glass and other materials rained onto Northwest Fifth Street, killing several people outside the building and injuring scores of others. Cars burned on the street.
>
> Assistant Fire Chief Jon Hansen described the first 30 minutes after the bombing as "pure mayhem." Streets were choked with walking wounded, some bloodied and their clothes in tatters, as emergency crews and passers-by swelled the downtown area.

7: Use Terms Your Reader Can Picture

Gunning warned reporters to avoid "foggy" writing. A sports reporter who has played basketball and covered it for years will know, for instance, what a "box and chaser" defense is. But the reporter should not assume that all readers will. If such a term is to be used, it should be explained so that readers can understand it: "Metropolitan State will play a box and chaser defense against City College. In this defense, four team members will play a zone—they will cover a specific area of the floor, rather than guarding a particular player—while the fifth member will guard, or chase, City College's star everywhere."

Craig Medred of the *Anchorage* (Alaska) *Daily News* won a Distinguished Writing Award from the American Society of Newspaper Editors for his coverage of the Iditarod dogsled race from Anchorage to Nome. Medred's writing was marvelously descriptive. Readers could picture scenes he painted. One of his award-winning articles began with these paragraphs:

> HAPPY RIVER GORGE—Coming down into this cleft through the Alaska Range, the Iditarod Trail is an angry serpent.
>
> It snakes through deep snow across a steep hillside covered with birch. The trail zigzags all the way. Gravity wants the sleds to slip off the edge and tumble.

Note the first two paragraphs of this story by Medred:

> McGRATH—For two days now, battered and jerry-rigged dogsleds have come trickling one by one into this community of 500 on the Kuskokwim River.
>
> The sleds are pulled by teams of dogs fit and ready to run, but they are ridden by tired and bloodied mushers—men and women who have known the horrors of the snowless Farewell Burn.

Blaine Harden of *The Washington Post* won an ASNE Distinguished Writing Award for his articles on Africa. Few of Harden's readers had ever been in Nigeria, but the following paragraph would have enabled them to conjure up images:

> Nigeria is hot, crowded and noisy. Totems of its culture are hard work and armed robbery, doctorates and tribal hatred, family loyalty and fast cars. Its people heap scorn upon themselves as corrupt, inefficient and self-destructive.

In another ASNE award-winning story, Rick Bragg of *The New York Times* quickly escorted his readers to an Alabama prison with these words:

> Grant Cooper knows he lives in prison, but there are days when he cannot remember why. His crimes flit in and out of his memory like flies through a hole in a screen door, so that sometimes his mind and conscience are blank and clean.

Later, in the same story, Bragg wrote:

> All Jessie Hatcher's life, the devil in him would come swimming out every time a drink of whiskey trickled in.

In a riveting story about life in the bowels of the criminal court system in the nation's capital, *Washington Post* staff writer Henry Allen grabbed readers by their nostrils with this descriptive lead paragraph:

> The Superior Court cafeteria, where a lot of criminal law gets practiced in the District of Columbia, has a warm, used smell like a pay phone that somebody just hung up, somebody with a cough—a smell like a wet bathing suit you left in your car, a compost smell, a smell like the inside of an old Halloween pumpkin with sanitary overtones provided by the wall-mounted deodorizers pumping out a smell like a space station where they replaced the air with something that's supposed to be just as good as air, except it isn't.

8: Tie In with Your Reader's Experience

"A statement cut off from context is a 'figure' that simply floats about," Gunning wrote. "There must be another point of reference, a 'ground' to give it stability and meaning. And you can't count on the reader's going farther than the end of his nose to construct that ground."

What does it mean to the reader if the city budget is increased by $25 million? Not much. Most readers cannot fathom $25 million. But they can understand the tax consequences that a $25 million increase will have on them as homeowners. Break the $25 million down. Tell the reader how much taxes will increase on a house valued at $100,000, on a house valued at $125,000 and so forth.

After a preliminary census, officials of one Arizona city thought they had been shortchanged. The lead paragraph in *The East Valley Tribune* read:

> Tempe stands to lose up to $3 million if a preliminary census count of 130,000 holds up, according to city officials.

Most readers cannot relate to the impact of $3 million on an entire city, and so the reporter, Dave Downey, ued the next paragraph to help put the figure into perspective. And, to borrow Gunning's phrase, Downey saw to it that readers didn't have to go farther than the ends of their noses to comprehend the impact:

> City Manager Jim Alexander said the city could lose about $200 annually for each person not counted in the special mid-decade census being conducted in Maricopa County this fall.

When a volcano erupted in Colombia, it was difficult for most readers who had not experienced such an occurrence to imagine the devastation. Michael Allen, in the *Arizona Republic* article excerpted earlier, painted a word picture most readers could understand:

> Viewed from several thousand feet in the air, it looked as if an immense cement mixer had spilled its load in the heart of the valley's rich, green field.

Most readers never will experience serving on a grand jury or testifying before one. *Washington Post* national correspondent David Maraniss won an ASNE award for deadline writing for his account of proceedings involving the wife of the president of the United States. His words made readers feel as if they were standing outside the U.S. District Court building in Washington, D.C., helping them to relate to the scene:

> Human beings arrive in the world alone and depart alone—and appear before a grand jury alone. Even the first lady of the United States.
>
> Hillary Rodham Clinton, the best-known woman in America, never seemed more of a solitary figure than at that moment yesterday when she disappeared inside the federal courthouse on Constitution Avenue to answer questions for more than four hours from an independent counsel and 23 grand jurors investigating the swirl of events that have come to be known as Whitewater.

9: Make Full Use of Variety

The authors of "The Elements of Style" wrote: "Every writer, by the way he uses the language, reveals something of his spirit, his habits, his capacities, his bias. This is inevitable as well as enjoyable. All writing is communication; creative writing is communication through revelation—it is the Self escaping into the open. No writer long remains incognito."

Indeed, all of us put our personal brand on our writing. We work toward and nurture a style we find comfortable. Gunning wrote that style must be developed—that one "cannot be satisfied with imitation and do any job of writing well." He continued: "You must be able to size up each new situation, see how it is different, and fit the different words to it that do the job best. To do this, you need a wide knowledge of the flexibility and variety of the language."

Zinsser noted that it is important for writers to believe in their own identities and opinions. "Proceed with confidence, generating it, if necessary, by pure will power," he wrote. "Writing is an act of ego and you might as well admit it. Use its energy to keep yourself going."

Readers could feel Tim Povtak's energy flowing through his article on the sprinter Houston McTear. Writing as if he were sitting in a living room telling his best friend about McTear, Povtak began his story in *The Orlando Sentinel* as follows:

> It took only nine seconds for Houston McTear to make history in 1975. It took nearly 10 years for him to cope with what he had done. His sudden rise to fame was so pure and innocent. The following fall, though, was so adulterated and complex.
>
> He was once the "world's fastest human." He later would become the world's most misguided athlete.
>
> McTear is alive and well today, quietly plotting his grand comeback that very few really believe is possible anymore. Too many years have passed, too many other "I'm back" claims have disintegrated, for people to take him seriously.
>
> Ten years ago, on May 9, 1975, in Winter Park, Fla., McTear ran 100 yards in 9.0 seconds during an afternoon preliminary heat in the Class AA Florida boys track meet. It stunned the track and field establishment. He tied the world record.
>
> He had an incredible gift—the ability to run faster than anyone else—yet the care-and-maintenance instruction packet got lost in the mail. The blessing became a curse.
>
> Track and field experts across the country lost interest in McTear long ago. They grew weary of his unkept promises. They don't know, or even care to know, about him now.
>
> Yet things are different now, McTear says. Things have changed, he says. This one's for real, he says. "I used to be the 'world's fastest human.' " McTear says. "I can do it again. I can prove that America didn't waste time on Houston McTear."

The article went on to detail McTear's overnight burst into the national spotlight a decade earlier, to quote his high school track coach, to describe his record-setting performance, to quote one of the timers at that meet, to tell of McTear's lax training habits in his early career and to describe a drug habit that had plagued the sprinter. It was a difficult story to write; it told of developments that spanned a decade. But Povtak's style, his personal stamp on the facts, made the story flow.

10: Write to Express, Not to Impress

Gunning said it succinctly: "The chance of striking awe by means of big words is about run out in the United States." The late sports broadcaster Howard Cosell might have said:

> With his not-so-gallant gladiators finding themselves in the unenviable, precarious position of losing by six touchdowns, the sideline mentor, with unwavering resoluteness, dispatched his less-talented players into the fray.

But it would be better to write:

> With his team losing by six touchdowns, the coach decided to let his substitutes play.

Indeed, note the simplicity—the clarity—of the words of *Newsday* reporter Craig Gordon as he described the scene in the sky off Long Island when TWA Flight 800 exploded and plummeted:

As a languid summer day gave way to night, witnesses turned their eyes upward—from fishing boats, surfboards bobbing in the waves, even other planes in the sky—to watch a disaster play out before them.

At first, there was a slow-motion quality to the descent of TWA Flight 800, a number of witnesses said—just a spot of brightness out over an ocean horizon, a light that some said looked like a flare from a distant boat.

In a horrible instant, though, that curious flicker exploded into a mass of flame that lit up the sky and sent a streamer of fire toward the ocean below.

Where to Turn Online

The Poynter Institute for Media Studies—a pioneer in promoting, emphasizing and teaching good writing—remains a premier destination and source for journalists who want to hone their skills.

Each year since 1979, Poynter, in tandem with the American Society of Newspaper Editors, has published a splendid book that features reprints of and commentary on the year's best news writing.

Reporters also can turn to Poynter's superb online site (*www.poynter.org*) for writing tips as well as information on a variety of journalistic topics. The site contains research/resource files (such as computer-assisted reporting, copy editing, diversity, media ethics, new media, visual journalism, and writing and editing); "hot research," which steers people to Web resources on contemporary news topics; journalism Web sites (such as libraries, newspapers, television stations, organizations and schools); and bibliographies (for topics such as interviewing, investigative reporting, media leadership and management, public journalism, news libraries and world press).

CHAPTER FOUR

SUMMARY LEADS

The news in April 1995 from Oklahoma City was terrifying:

OKLAHOMA CITY—A thundering, half-ton car bomb blew away nearly half of a nine-story federal building Wednesday in downtown Oklahoma City, killing at least 31 people, including 12 children, leaving 200 people missing and stabbing an icy fear of terror into the American heartland. (*The Arizona Republic*)

OKLAHOMA CITY—Somber rescue workers picked through bloody rubble Wednesday night, searching for hundreds of victims of a car bomb that tore apart a federal office building and shattered America's sense of security. (*The Kansas City Star*)

(J.Pat Carter / Getty Images)

The news stories on Page 1 of the nation's newspapers the day after the bombing of the Alfred P. Murrah Federal Building reflected a sense of devastation. Ultimately the death toll would climb to 168.

Newspapers reporting this deadly act of terrorism tried to do one thing in their main stories: summarize the catastrophe for their readers.

The bombing was the beginning. This story continued for years, and each time a new development occurred, there were more Page 1 stories summarizing the news. They included the arrest of suspect Timothy McVeigh, his 1997 trial and conviction and his ultimate execution by lethal injection in 2001.

Along with his final days came a flurry of stories:

Six days before Timothy McVeigh's scheduled execution, the FBI turned over thousands of documents from the Oklahoma City bombing investigation to Mr. McVeigh's defense team. An attorney said the material may form the basis for a stay of execution request. (*The New York Times*)

WASHINGTON—Just six days before Timothy McVeigh's scheduled execution, the FBI turned over thousands of documents from the Oklahoma City bombing investigation to McVeigh's defense team Thursday. An attorney said the material may form the basis for a stay of execution request. (The Associated Press)

Attorney General John D. Ashcroft today ordered the execution of Timothy J. McVeigh delayed from May 16 until June 11. (*The New York Times*)

TERRE HAUTE, Ind.—Timothy McVeigh will seek a delay of his June 11 execution for the Oklahoma City bombing and ask for a hearing to investigate federal investigators' "fraud upon the court," his lawyers said Thursday. (The Associated Press)

DENVER—The judge in the Oklahoma City bombing case refused Wednesday to delay the execution of Timonthy McVeigh, saying newly released documents do not change the fact that he is guilty. (The Associated Press)

DENVER—A federal judge on Wednesday rejected a stay of execution for convicted Oklahoma City bomber Timothy McVeigh, who sought the delay after FBI officials admitted they failed to hand over 4,000 pages of evidence.

McVeigh is scheduled to be executed on Monday. (Reuters)

DENVER—His hopes dashed for the second day in a row, Oklahoma City bomber Timothy McVeigh abandoned all appeals Thursday and prepared to be executed Monday for the worst terrorist attack ever on U.S. soil. (The Associated Press)

Timothy McVeigh was executed by lethal injection on Monday for setting off a truck bomb in front of a federal building in Oklahoma City in 1995 that killed 168 people in the worst act of terrorism on U.S. soil. (Reuters)

TERRE HAUTE, Ind.—The government Timothy McVeigh so despised executed him by chemical injection Monday, taking his life in exchange for the 168 lives lost when he blew up the Oklahoma City federal building six years ago. He died silently, with his eyes open, and with no trace of remorse. (The Associated Press)

Witnesses say convicted Oklahoma City bomber Timothy McVeigh died swiftly and silently this morning, the first federal inmate to be put to death since 1963. President Bush said the 168 victims of the bombing "have been given not vengeance, but justice," but said McVeigh's death "cannot recover the loss" of the families. (CNN)

Reporters are the eyes and ears of their audiences. When reporters cover a breaking news event, their first stories summarize what happened, to whom, where, when, why and how. More in-depth stories may be written later about people and things touched by the event, but initially, reporters are there to gather the essential facts and write their stories as quickly and as near their deadlines as possible.

Such hard news stories usually begin with a **summary lead,** a terse opening paragraph that provides the gist of the story and invites readers inside. The summary lead should be brief, generally no more than 35 words. It is usually a single sentence, but it can be broken into more than one sentence.

Summary leads are used on news stories because they give the major points immediately. That way, people do not have to guess or wait to find out the news. Most people do not have time to read a newspaper from start to end. Because they spend so little time with the news and often do not read entire articles, they demand the most important points at the start of the story.

Concepts: Principles of Summary Leads

The Inverted Pyramid

A summary lead generally tops a traditional form of writing called an **inverted pyramid,** in which the news is stacked in paragraphs in order of descending importance. The lead summarizes the principal items of a news event. The second paragraph and each succeeding paragraph contain secondary or supporting details in order of decreasing significance. All the paragraphs in the story contain newsworthy information, but each paragraph is less vital than the one before it. Inverted-pyramid form puts the climax of a story at the beginning, in the lead, and so it is different from a form often used for novels, short stories and drama—and for some news features—in which an author begins with background and works to a climax.

Examples of inverted-pyramid form can be found before the mid-19th century, but most journalism historians say that the concept was developed during the American Civil War. Newspaper correspondents in the field sent their dispatches by telegraph. Because they were afraid that the system would malfunction or the enemy would cut the wires, the correspondents

squeezed the most important information into the first few sentences. Wire services, which used telegraphers to transmit stories until computers were introduced in the early 1970s, have continued to use the inverted pyramid as their staple form of news reporting. That enables the wire services to move stories quickly in small chunks and their customers to use the stories in whatever lengths they need.

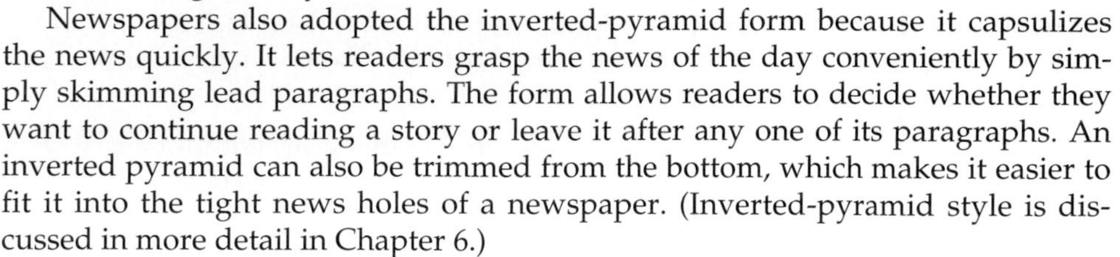

Newspapers also adopted the inverted-pyramid form because it capsulizes the news quickly. It lets readers grasp the news of the day conveniently by simply skimming lead paragraphs. The form allows readers to decide whether they want to continue reading a story or leave it after any one of its paragraphs. An inverted pyramid can also be trimmed from the bottom, which makes it easier to fit it into the tight news holes of a newspaper. (Inverted-pyramid style is discussed in more detail in Chapter 6.)

The Five W's and H

A summary lead tells an audience the most important of the six primary elements of an event, the **five W's and H.** They are:

- *Who* the event happened to, or who acted on whom
- *What* happened or will happen
- *Where* the action occurred
- *When* it happened
- *Why* the action took place; the reason behind it
- *How* it happened

Reporters look for these six elements whenever they cover a news event. It makes no difference how big or small the story is. Reporters gather the facts to answer *who, what, where, when, why* and *how;* they rate the importance of each fact; then they are ready to write a lead and news story.

The most important of the six elements go into a summary lead. The less important elements go into the second and succeeding paragraphs. In most cases it would take too many words to try to put all six elements into one lead paragraph.

Identifying the W's and H

For example, this is what could occur after a press conference at City Hall. The name and the situation are not real, but they are typical. In the press conference, the mayor—we will call her Kathy Riedy—announces that there will be no increase in property taxes this year, even though the city will lose more than $3 million in community development grants from the federal government. She says:

> There will be no increase in property taxes this year. We are not going to ask our residents to pay for the cuts they are suffering because of slashes in the federal budget. We had planned to spend $3 million in community development block grants to rebuild sidewalks that are crumbling in the downtown area, but those funds have been cut. These sidewalks were built during the Depression, and we need to replace them. We will go ahead with the sidewalk project this year, but increased property taxes will not fund it. If we cannot find alternative federal funds, we will attempt to raise the city sales tax, at least for a year, to pay for this vital project.

While taking notes, a reporter for the local newspaper decides that *what* the mayor has said about the sidewalk project is the most important point of the press conference; therefore, this will become the top of the inverted pyramid. Riedy has covered several topics during the press conference, but she concentrated on the tax issue. Although the mayor says that property taxes will not be increased, she also says that sales taxes may be. In a nice political way, Riedy says that the city will not take any money out of one pocket; it will try to take it out of another pocket.

While taking notes, the reporter highlights the five W's and H. That will make it easier to find them while the story is being written. The reporter notes:

> *Who.* Mayor Kathy Riedy.
> *What.* Downtown sidewalks will be rebuilt this year, without an increase in property taxes and even though federal funds are being cut.
> *Where.* City Hall press conference.
> *When.* Monday.
> *Why.* Cuts in federal budget will cost the city $3 million in community block grants.
> *How.* Look for alternative federal funds or increase sales tax.

Rating the W's and H

After the five W's and H are identified, they must be rated according to their importance. This is not always easy for beginning reporters, but here are three principles that will help:

- *Conduct Research.* If possible, do not cover a news event without researching the subject and the people involved. That will make it easier to spot the freshest news, the key issues, the elements that have been reported before and the embellishments.
- *Try to Identify the Five W's and H during the Reporting Process.* A news story is based on the six primary elements; look and listen for them. While taking notes, highlight them with an asterisk. Underline or put a double asterisk on those that are most important.
- *Talk to Editors.* They will often say what direction they want a story to take.

The Thought Process Behind the Lead

Reporters all say the same thing about news writing: while they are interviewing a source, covering a speech or working at the scene of a traffic accident, they are thinking about their leads and stories. This thought process begins even before they start taking notes and continues until their stories are completed. They often have their leads in mind before they actually write their stories.

Several factors can influence how a reporter thinks about a story:

- *What Has Been Reported in the Past.* Reporters are always looking for something new. In our example, if Mayor Riedy has given six speeches this week in which she has said exactly the same things about the sidewalk project, the reporter will probably quit thinking about that as the best lead.
- *How the Reporter Feels about the Subject.* Reporters bring their own prejudices and emotions to every story they cover. Reporters concerned

about the city's sidewalks will probably concentrate on what the mayor says about them.

- *How the Audience Feels about the Subject.* If the sidewalk project has been an ongoing and controversial issue in the city, reporters should know this. They will want to keep their readers, viewers or listeners informed on the latest developments.
- *Instructions from an Editor.* If the boss says, "Get a lead on the sidewalks," the reporter will probably concentrate on this issue.

As the mayor talks, the reporter begins thinking about a lead, perhaps in this way:

> "The mayor says no increase in property taxes this year. Sounds like rhetoric. What does she mean? She's going ahead with the sidewalk project. How is she going to pay for it? Bingo! No new property taxes, but she's willing to raise the sales tax. This means that ultimately the taxpayers are going to pay for it. Get as much as possible on that."

In the newsroom, composing the story at a computer terminal, the reporter has to decide how many of the W's and H can be put into the lead while still keeping it brief and easy to understand. *Who* is important because whenever the mayor speaks, everyone in the city can be affected. *When* she spoke, *what* she said and the reason behind what she said (*why*) are also critical in summarizing the story. *Where* she said it and her solution to the problem are also important, but the reporter decides that these elements are not vital to the summary and can appear in the second paragraph.

The first lead the reporter writes emphasizes *what* and *why:*

> The city will not increase property taxes this year but still will rebuild downtown sidewalks, even if it loses $3 million in federal community development funds, Mayor Kathy Riedy said Monday.

The second paragraph provides *how* and *where:*

> However, the mayor said that the city sales tax may need to be increased to pay for the project. "If we cannot find alternative federal funds, we will attempt to raise the city sales tax, at least for a year," Riedy said in a City Hall press conference.

Like any journalist, the reporter looks over the initial lead. It is not wrong, but it should have emphasized two key elements: the property tax and the sales tax. By moving up *how* and then putting the sidewalk project in the second paragraph, the reporter can make the lead stronger. The rewritten lead also begins with *who,* rather than ending with it, to emphasize who is saying "no new taxes here, but new taxes there."

The new lead:

> Mayor Kathy Riedy said Monday that the city will not increase property taxes this year to pay for federal funding cuts, but it may have to increase sales taxes.

Second paragraph:

> "We had planned to spend $3 million in community development block grants to rebuild sidewalks that are crumbling in the downtown area," Riedy said in a City Hall press conference. "We will go ahead with the sidewalk project this year, but increased property taxes will not fund it."

The reporter can write still other summary leads on the story that emphasize other W's or H. The lead can emphasize *how:*

> The city sales tax may be increased this year if the city cannot find alternative funding sources for a project to rebuild sidewalks, Mayor Kathy Riedy said Monday.

Why can be emphasized:

> A $3 million cut in federal community block grants will not stop the city from rebuilding downtown sidewalks this year, Mayor Kathy Riedy said Monday.

What and *where* can be emphasized:

> Downtown sidewalks will be rebuilt this year without an increase in property taxes, Mayor Kathy Riedy said Monday during a City Hall press conference.

Multiple-Element Summary Leads

The lead on Riedy that combined the property and sales taxes is an example of a **multiple-element lead** or **double-barreled lead.** Such a lead gives equal rating to two or more of the primary elements in a story and informs the audience immediately that more than one major event is occurring.

Here is another example of a news story topped by a multiple-element summary lead:

> TERRE HAUTE, Ind.—Oklahoma City bomber Timothy McVeigh met with one of his lawyers Thursday about his chances of avoiding execution, even as prison officials moved full speed ahead to carry out the death sentence in five days. (Reuters)

This 35-word lead summarized the news event. It answered the W's:

Who. Timothy McVeigh, lawyer, prison officials.
What. Met about avoiding execution, moved full speed ahead.
Where. Terre Haute, Ind.
When. Thursday.
Why. Not much time is left. Everything must be done quickly.

The lead informed readers that up until the last moment, McVeigh and his lawyers, as well as prison officials would be working feverishly. Each one of the primary elements could have opened the story, but each one was equally important, warranting a multiple-element lead.

Here is another multiple-element lead from The Associated Press. It used only 29 words to report three important elements: There's a new margarine, it will be out next year and it could open new interest in certain foods.

> WASHINGTON—A margarine specially made to reduce cholesterol is headed for American grocery stores next year—and experts say it could open new interest in foods with added healing properties.

Summary Leads on Features

Summary leads can also be used on *feature* stories. A **feature**—an umbrella term for a variety of stories written on soft news events—is usually not structured as an inverted pyramid, and writers will often top it with a special lead (special leads are discussed in Chapter 5). However, that does not preclude a summary lead on a feature.

Feature writers design their leads to invite readers into their stories, not to report breaking news. If they are writing about a person or an occurrence connected with a news event, the breaking news has probably been reported earlier or elsewhere. Thus the most important of the five W's and H do not have to appear in a feature lead. They can be reported somewhere else in the story.

A feature lead can be a narrative, a contrast or a question. It may talk directly to the reader or be written in the first person. Or it may summarize the thrust of the story. The point is that feature writers can use many types of leads; the summary is one of their options.

For example, here is a summary lead on a feature story about the ordeal a father went through to recover his kidnapped son:

> SCITUATE, R.I.—Thirteen-year-old Robert C. Smith, abducted from his California home 21 months ago, buried his face in his father's arms in a dramatic family reunion yesterday morning outside the State Police barracks here. (*The Boston Globe*)

Here is a summary lead on a feature about how nurses who are frustrated with life in hospitals and clinics are shifting their skills to jobs in business or law:

> Tighter regulations and skimpy medical insurance reimbursements are prompting American nurses to quit their jobs to launch or work in a range of profitable health-care-related businesses. (*Los Angeles Times*)

A Reminder: No Two Leads Are the Same

Experienced reporters covering the same news event or interviewing the same people will usually come up with the same basic leads because they are able to determine which of the W's and H are the most important. This does not mean that the wording of their leads will be the same. It means that the key elements of the story will be presented in one form or another in the opening paragraph.

For instance, here are two summary leads beginning stories about a heat wave in Colorado.

> Colorado sweltered Monday but narrowly avoided blackouts, thanks to factory backup generators and consumer cutbacks. (*Rocky Mountain News*)

> LITTLETON, Colo.—A blistering heat wave sent Coloradans to malls, theaters and water parks Monday as utility companies threatened to turn off power to some customers to cope with the surging demand for electricity. (The Associated Press)

Both leads emphasized the *what* of this story—the furnace was on in Colorado. They also focused on the intense need for electricity. The one from the *Rocky Mountain News* used only 15 words to explain how people avoided blackouts. The Associated Press lead was longer—32 words—but it more colorfully illustrated what people did to stay cool and avoid power cutoffs.

Writing a Summary Lead

How Many Words?

A summary lead, which is generally written as a single sentence, should contain no more than 35 words. Of course, there will be times when more words or sentences are needed to summarize a story; but the longer the lead, the greater the risk that it will be difficult to read or understand. The general rule to follow when writing a summary lead is: *Use a single sentence of no more than 35 words to summarize an event.*

Usually, a lead can be shortened by cutting out unnecessary adjectives. For example, here is a 44-word lead:

> Two women were injured and part of Michigan Avenue was closed for nearly seven hours Saturday when a three-alarm fire at a high-rise construction site set off a series of explosions that sent metal and other debris flying across the Magnificent Mile. (*Chicago Tribune*)

This multiple-element lead was long because it tried to summarize too much information in a single sentence. It reported that two people were injured and that explosions sent metal and other debris across Michigan Avenue, which is one of Chicago's busiest streets and is called the Magnificent Mile. Even with multiple elements, however, leads can normally be written in 35 words or fewer. Here is the lead again, with nine words that could have been trimmed indicated by brackets:

Two women were injured and part of Michigan Avenue was closed [for nearly seven hours] Saturday when a [three-alarm] fire at a high-rise construction site set off a series of explosions that sent [metal and other] debris flying across the Magnificent Mile.

Leads with more than 35 words can often be tightened into sentences that are easier to read. The following 38-word lead has been rewritten in 25 words. The shorter version would have given readers a tighter and smoother summary. Original lead:

A man suspected of shooting a Dallas police officer who responded to a burglary in a North Dallas neighborhood Friday night was charged with attempted capital murder Saturday, but officials have been unable to identify him. (*Dallas Times Herald*)

Rewritten lead:

An unidentified suspect accused of shooting a police officer who responded to a North Dallas burglary was charged with attempted capital murder Saturday, police said.

Avoiding Clutter Leads

It's tough to cram the five W's and H into a 35-word sentence. Why try? Doing so usually makes for an awkward and difficult-to-understand summary lead, which means lost readers and howling editors. The general guideline to follow is: *Put the most important primary elements in the lead. Do not clutter it with all of them. Save the remaining elements for the second, third, fourth and, if needed, later paragraphs.*

Following this guideline will help avoid a **clutter lead** such as this 43-word multiple-element lead, which ran in the *Star Tribune* in Minneapolis:

From one end of the Twin Cities to the other, residents and crews dug out, wiped off and fixed up Monday in the aftermath of yet another violent spring storm that raised roofs, toppled trees and shredded power lines from Shakopee to Woodbury.

The writer simply tried to cram too much into this lead. Here is another example of a lead cluttered with too much information. It contains 45 words:

An attorney for Corey Maeweather has asked Northampton County Court to overturn the first-degree murder conviction and life sentence the Brooklyn, N.Y., man received for his role in the torture-murder of a 13-year-old Long Island runaway in Easton two years ago. (*The Morning Call,* Allentown, Pa.)

In each of these leads, some of the information could have been moved into the second or third paragraphs. Keep summary leads simple, direct and colorful, and you will stand a better chance of keeping your readers.

Avoiding Buried Leads

If the most important element of a news story is not in the summary lead, the writer has probably **buried** it in another paragraph, which means that readers have to hunt for the news. This is not good. A summary lead should provide the key point immediately; it should not keep readers guessing.

A beginning reporter handed this story to the city editor:

> Police Chief John Jones discussed the city's crime problem with interested townspeople at a meeting Monday night.
>
> Jones agreed to meet with residents who have grown increasingly concerned about the safety of their neighborhoods.
>
> The chief said that there were more serious crimes reported here in the last 12 months than during any other year in the city's history.

The editor scolded the reporter for "burying" the lead in the third paragraph. The most important element of this story was obviously the police chief's revelation that crime in the city was at its highest level ever, not the fact that he had discussed the problem. Citizens knew the topic of the meeting before it was held.

The lead should have read:

> Police Chief John Jones said Monday night that there were more serious crimes reported here last year than during any other 12 months in the city's history.

Here is another example of a lead that failed to summarize the news. It appeared in a university daily:

> Faculty members and school administrators will have a chance to reflect on academic issues in an informal manner this weekend.

Reflect on academic issues and *in an informal manner* mean nothing to readers. The second paragraph reported the news. It said that the Academic Senate would hold a retreat at a downtown hotel to discuss its structure, purpose and future. *That* should have been in the lead.

In the next lead the news is buried in the second paragraph. The writer seemed compelled to be cute in the first.

> The mantra of the midsummer meltdown has become a command: Slow down.
>
> Texas officials are urging people to check up on the sick and the elderly, while deputies travel remote neighborhoods with water and fans in an effort to prevent more heat-related deaths. (The Associated Press)

Determining the Focal Point

A reporter focuses a summary lead by choosing which of the W's and H to emphasize. If a well-known person or someone who has been in the news—as in the two examples below—is involved in the story, *who* becomes the focal point of the lead. In this case, the story would probably start with a name.

Federal Highway Administration Chief Rodney Slater said in Oakland yesterday that proposed cuts in federal transit financing would have "a significant impact on mass transit in the Bay Area." (*San Francisco Chronicle*)

Denver District Attorney Bill Ritter said Monday he will seek the death penalty for Nathan Thill, the skinhead accused of gunning down a West African immigrant. (*Rocky Mountain News*)

The above leads name people who are well-known nationally or in their communities. If a person who is not well-known does or says something newsworthy, the *what* element usually is the focal point of the lead, as in the next two examples.

FLINT—The UAW's top negotiator in the Flint labor dispute said the strikes against General Motors Corp. could last into September. (*Detroit Free Press*)

A man charged with shooting a police officer and kidnapping two women and a child has been ordered held at the City-County Jail on a cash-only bail of $200,000. (*Albuquerque,* N.M., *Journal*)

If *where, when, why* and *how* are the most important elements, one of them should be the focal point of the summary lead. In the following lead, *where* is the focal point:

HARRISBURG—Ten state and federal investigators fanned out yesterday across south-central Pennsylvania searching poultry farms for signs that an outbreak of potentially devastating avian influenza in Maryland had come from or spread to this state. (*The Philadelphia Inquirer*)

In this lead, *when* is the focal point:

From December to February, the Earth's frigid underbelly, Antarctica, makes itself habitable. (*The Dallas Morning News*)

In this lead, *why* is the focal point:

MANSFIELD—After less than two years on the job, Mansfield Area Chamber of Commerce President Letatia Teykl is leaving to pursue a higher-paying position. "It's a career move," Teykl, 36, said Wednesday. (*Star-Telegram,* Fort Worth, Texas)

In this lead, *how* is the focal point:

> Arson was blamed for a fire at the Flatbush Ave. station of the Long Island Rail Road yesterday that spread heavy smoke into nearby subway lines, delaying hundreds of thousands of commuters and straphangers. (*New York Daily News*)

Generally, the reporters covering a news event decide which of the elements are most important. Sometimes most of the elements can be put into the lead; at other times only one or two may be appropriate.

Positioning the Time Element

The **time element,** the *when* of a story, is an important part of most summary leads because it conveys immediacy to the reader. It needs to be placed so that it does not disturb the flow of the sentence.

Option 1: Time Element after the Verb

Usually, the best position for the time element is immediately after the verb:

> An 8-year-old west Phoenix girl was killed Monday morning when a car jumped a curb and ran her down as she stopped to pick up a schoolbook from the sidewalk. (*The Arizona Republic*)

> More than 400 people met Sunday to kick off a volunteer campaign in support of a $195.5 million bond election for the Dallas Independent School District, although officials said certain sections of town may not support the package. (*The Dallas Morning News*)

Option 2: Time Element after the Object

The time element may follow the object of the verb:

> Firefighters in Oregon battled a forest fire Monday that threatened 150 homes, and in California crews tried to contain a forest and brush fire that forced the evacuation of three communities. (The Associated Press)

Option 3: Time Element after an Adverb or Prepositional Phrase

The time element may follow an adverb or prepositional phrase:

> Interest rates on short-term Treasury securities rose slightly Monday to the highest level in three weeks. (The Associated Press)

CAPE CANAVERAL, Fla.—The Columbia space shuttle broke through the clouds and roared into orbit Thursday on a marathon 13-day mission that is expected to lead to even longer stays in space. (The Associated Press)

Option 4: Time Element in a "Comfortable" Spot

Sometimes, the time element cannot follow the verb directly because it reads awkwardly in that position. Therefore, it must be moved to a "comfortable" spot in the sentence:

The Colorado Springs City Council on Tuesday approved the route of an electrical transmission line near the city's eastern edge, despite objections by landowners who wanted the project relocated. (*The Colorado Springs Gazette Telegraph*)

In this lead the time element was placed between the subject and the verb, a position most grammarians would say not to use. It would be awkward, however, to say that the council "approved Tuesday." And the time element would not fit comfortably anywhere else in the sentence. Therefore, in this case, the subject and verb were split to make the sentence read more smoothly.

Option 5: Time Element at the End

Sometimes the time element is put at the end of the sentence:

KINGMAN—A chair lift-type "aerial gondola" to convey people across the Colorado River between Bullhead City and Laughlin officially received the support of the Mohave County Supervisors Monday. (*Mohave Valley News,* Bullhead City, Ariz.)

Writing in the Active Voice

Whenever possible, write summary leads (or any other leads or paragraphs) in the active voice rather than the passive voice. In the active voice the subject acts upon an object; in the passive voice the subject is acted upon.

Editors consider the active voice more direct and vigorous than the passive voice. Here are two examples:

Rescuers dragged a 61-year-old man to safety yesterday as fire nearly destroyed a house on the southwest side and killed 12 dogs and a cat. (*Arizona Daily Star,* Tucson)

NAPLES, Fla. (AP)—Three major fires and dozens of smaller ones, many of them set by arsonists, rampaged across Florida today after killing a rookie firefighter and devouring about 50,000 acres of woodland dried by cold weather.

The passive voice should be used only when the person or thing receiving the action is more important than the person or thing doing the acting, as in these examples:

Five Northwestern students were arrested Thursday at Scott Hall as more than 70 people protested recruiting on campus by the CIA. (*The Daily Northwestern,* Northwestern University)

Williston teachers were told at an informal forum Wednesday that they can pass or fail the four District 1 House candidates in the Nov. 6 general election. (*Williston,* N.D., *Daily Herald*)

In many cases, a lead written in the passive voice should be rewritten in the active voice. For example, here was the first lead written on a robbery story:

A downtown jewelry store was robbed on Saturday of $50,000 to $100,000 by a "well-dressed" gunman, police said.

It was rewritten as follows:

A "well-dressed" gunman stole $50,000 to $100,000 from a downtown jewelry store Saturday, police said.

Writing in the active voice does not mean that stories should be written in the present tense. Because news stories generally describe events that have already occurred, the sentences should be written in the past tense. Voice and tense are two different things and should not be confused.

Providing Attributions

Attribution tells an audience who gave information to a reporter. It adds authenticity and authority to a story. An audience looks at or hears what the sources say and then evaluates the worth of their statements. (Attribution is discussed more fully in Chapter 8.) There are three guidelines to follow in deciding whether to use attribution in summary leads.

Attributing Facts

Attribution is not needed when a fact—something that has actually happened or is obviously true—is reported:

An argument that began at a gourmet restaurant in Kansas City's State Line Road antique district Saturday night ended in the shooting deaths of an owner, a cook and an employee as well as the wounding of a passerby. (*Kansas City Star*)

Attributing Opinions

Attribution is needed when a reporter is repeating the voiced opinion of a source, as happens in most stories, and it usually identifies the source by name or title:

> STORRS, Conn.—The swashbuckling escapades of movie hero Indiana Jones do a good job of promoting the profession of archaeology but distort its true purpose, a state archaeologist said. (United Press International)

Vague Attributions

Vague attributions can be used if a source is speaking on behalf of a governmental or private agency:

> WASHINGTON—Seldane, a prescription drug used by millions for hay fever and allergy problems, may be fatal for patients with liver problems or if taken with some antibiotics, the Food and Drug Administration warned Tuesday. (Reuters)

Revising the Lead: Summarizing the Story and Enticing Readers

Summary leads should do two things:

1. *Summarize the Story.*
2. *Invite Readers Inside.*

Putting the most important of the W's and H into the opening paragraph will summarize the story. Using the strongest possible words will entice readers.

The trick to writing a summary lead that summarizes and entices, rather than one that simply wraps up the story, is to continue working on the lead until the best possible combination of words is used. This means:

- *Do Not Go with the First Lead.* After writing an acceptable lead, rewrite it to improve it. Keep saying, "I can make this lead better."
- *Avoid Superfluous Words.*
- *Avoid Gobbledygook.*
- *Write Clearly and Concisely.*
- *Use Vivid Verbs.*
- *Use Colorful Words.*

For example, this lead was written for a story about the traits women seek in their mates:

> Women are likely to be disappointed in their choice of a permanent mate, a study shows.

The lead did summarize the story, but it was dull. It did not sing. Readers could have taken a look at it and said, "So what?" The writer needed to work on the lead more, to use a better combination of words to better summarize the story.

Here was the rewritten version:

> Women want permanent mates who are sensitive, self-assured and warm, but they usually come up cold, a sociologist's report shows.

The rewritten lead used five more words than the original lead, but it was still concise. It did a better job of telling the story. It used more colorful words, so that readers could "see" the story better. It also identified the source more clearly. *A study* means nothing to readers unless they know who conducted it. *A sociologist's report* gave the lead authority; it told readers that an expert in the field was the source.

Writers can often improve a lead if they read it out loud after writing it. This lead was written on a story about a new freeway in town:

> Proposition 300 is a "dream list" of poorly researched proposals for a freeway system that would not benefit taxpayers who are paying for it but do not use it, a resident said Tuesday.

There are so many short words in this lead that readers would have tripped over them. They would have had to read the sentence two or three times to figure out what it was saying. And who is this resident making such a profound statement?

Here is the rewrite:

> Proposition 300 is a "dream list" of poorly researched proposals for a freeway system that would not benefit the residents who pay for it, an opponent of the measure said Tuesday.

CHAPTER FIVE

SPECIAL LEADS

TERRE HAUTE, Ind.—News trailers that carried word of Timothy McVeigh's death to the world began packing up Tuesday, dimming the spotlight on the Corn Belt city now known as the home of the federal death row.

Satellite trucks began to roll away from the grassy field in front of the federal prison after nearly round-the-clock coverage of McVeigh's final days.

Local officials who spent months preparing for the execution seemed relieved to put it behind them. (The Associated Press)

TERRE HAUTE, Ind.—No terror-twisted chaos. No bloody pandemonium. Not even any blood.

Ending the life of the man who took so many lives went exactly like clockwork. (*The New York Times*)

(*Reuters / Jeff Mitchell / Getty Images*)

Two stories, one from The Associated Press and the other from *The New York Times*, began poignantly the day after Timothy McVeigh was executed for the bombing of the Alfred P. Murrah Federal Building in Oklahoma City. One began with a colorful description of how quickly Terre Haute returned to normal. The other began with short phrases that also precisely and colorfully captured a mood.

The beginnings of both stories went beyond the summary lead.

Chapter 4 focused on the summary lead, which gives readers the gist of an entire story quickly, generally in a single paragraph. This chapter will discuss alternatives to the summary lead. On some news stories and on most features, the best lead may not be a one-paragraph summary. Instead, the beginning might be written as a block of paragraphs that invite readers into a story. It may tease them, put them in the middle of the action, talk directly to them, ask them a question or set them up for a climax.

Whenever they are about to write, journalists ask themselves, "What is the best lead for this story?" There is no easy answer. The most appropriate lead on a breaking news story, such as a fire, might be a summary that reports what happened, when and to whom. Today's media go far beyond such stories, however. They use personality profiles describing interesting people in or out of the news and "how to" stories such as simple home repairs. There are interpretative and analytical pieces that detail weaknesses in government. There are special-interest stories, entertainment pieces and fashion reviews. There also are stories that capture the mood in a city or prison during and after an execution.

Types of Special Leads

Leads that are not summaries usually fall into one of the following categories:

- Narrative
- Contrast
- Staccato
- Direct address
- Question
- Quote
- "None of the above"

Narrative Leads

Elements of the Narrative Lead

A **narrative lead**—also called an **anecdotal lead**—is the most popular lead on features and non-breaking news stories and is also popular in non-journalistic non-fiction and fiction. The narrative lead uses an anecdote or colorful scene to draw people into the story by putting them in the middle of the action.

The opening paragraphs of the Associated Press story that begins with "News trailers" is an excellent example. Readers were placed on the street, watching the trucks pull out of Terre Haute.

Lead block. Although a narrative lead can be written as a single paragraph, it is usually written as a **lead block:** two or more paragraphs building up to a paragraph that tells readers the major point of the story. Like any journalistic writing, the lead block is constructed with terse sentences.

Because a narrative lead often involves a person, it is acceptable to use that person's name in the opening paragraph. This is usually not done in a summary lead unless the person is well-known, but using a name right away in a narrative allows an audience to identify more quickly with a major player in the story.

Here is a two-paragraph narrative lead block from *The Daily Northwestern*, the campus paper at Northwestern University. The story was about an annual contest sponsored by a sorority. In the first paragraph, the writer introduced a young man, allowing readers to feel some emotional attachment to him and, it was hoped, to the story. The opening paragraph also began in the middle of the action:

> Peter Spears swiveled his hips to the tune of "Neutron Dance," turned his back to the audience and ripped off his jacket, revealing a shirt opened to the waist.

The second paragraph continued the narrative. It painted a picture, drawing readers deeper into the story:

> Spears strutted to the beat and slowly tossed off his shirt and pants. Still wearing a black bow tie and black bikini swimsuit, he dove into the Patten Gymnasium pool.

By now, the writing should have caught the readers' interest. Vivid words—"swiveled," "ripped," "revealing," "strutted," "tossed off," "black bikini"—were used to paint a colorful picture. By the end of the second paragraph, readers should have felt as if they were in the action, emotionally tied somehow to Peter Spears.

A summary lead could have been written on the story, saying:

> A freshman Sigma Nu member won the Mr. Anchor Splash title Sunday in the fourth annual contest sponsored by Delta Gamma sorority.

But the narrative worked better. The contest was not a hard news event. Readers might not have been interested in how sorority and fraternity members spent this Sunday. The narrative was used to entice them.

Nut graph. After two or three paragraphs of narrative, it is time to use a **"so what" paragraph,** telling readers precisely what the story is about. (Narrative is used to entice readers; it should not dominate the story.) The common name for the explanatory paragraph that follows the introductory narrative is **nut graph.** This paragraph explains the significance of a story or gives its **news peg,** which links the story to previously reported news. The nut graph should be placed fairly high in the story—the third, fourth or fifth paragraph. A nut graph would also be used high in stories that begin with other special leads.

Here is a nut graph for the example above; it was the third paragraph of the story:

> Spears, a CAS (College of Arts and Sciences) freshman and Sigma Nu member, won the Mr. Anchor Splash title Sunday in the fourth annual competition sponsored by Delta Gamma sorority.

In the next narrative lead block, notice how colorful writing creates a vision for readers. The narrative draws readers into the story. The news, which does not mean much to most people in a large metropolitan area such as Phoenix, is not reported until the third paragraph, the nut graph.

> TEMPE—Louella Harris doesn't relish the idea of leaving the downtown Tempe street corner where she has been peddling hot dogs for the past five years.
>
> Harris, whose Sweet Lou's cart has been a fixture at Fifth and Mill outside the post office, has lost her space to a rival area hot dog vendor looking for a second location.
>
> The longtime vendor missed a July 2 filing deadline to comply with Tempe's new sidewalk vending lease rates and regulations. (*The Arizona Republic*)

Writing a Narrative Lead

Using observation. The key to an effective narrative lead is to write it around observation—what you as a reporter see, hear, smell, taste or touch while working on a story. When interviewing people it is critical to make notes on:

- How they move
- What they are doing during the interview
- What they are wearing and the color of their clothes
- How loudly or softly they speak
- How long it takes them to answer a question
- Smells and sights around them
- Anything that makes them unusual

These observations are extremely important in stories; they are vital to a narrative lead. In the first example, the writer would not have been able to write her narrative on the Mr. Anchor Splash contest if she had not observed the action herself.

In the second example, the writer's choice of colorful language and his observations draw readers into and through the story. The news itself won't do it. The story is a feature, a slice-of-life piece about a hot dog vendor. It is not compelling, breaking news. Readers probably would not be interested in someone who missed a filing deadline. What draws their interest is the longtime hot dog vendor, just a common person like most others, who won't be in her usual downtown spot.

Keeping the story going. Additional observations and narrative should be used later and throughout the story, not only about the person in the lead but about other characters. This should keep readers so emotionally attached to the main players that they want to read the entire story, no matter how long.

Contrast Leads

Elements of the Contrast Lead

A **contrast lead** compares or contrasts one person or thing with another, or several people or things with each other. A lead from *The Daily Oklahoman* that was used the day after the 1995 bombing of the Murrah Federal Building in Oklahoma City is a strong example. The first two paragraphs explain how things were:

> Oklahoma City will never be the same.
>
> This is a place, after all, where terrorists don't venture. The heartland, people kept saying. Car bombs don't kill children here.

The third paragraph begins with a sentence that turns readers. Now they know how things really are:

> Wednesday changed everything.

These "old and new," "short and tall" or "yesterday and today" leads tell an audience the way something was and now is. They can be used on any type of news or feature story. Here is an example from the *Williston* (N.D.) *Daily Herald:*

> When Buster Jones took over the little bar on Main Street in Williston, his hair was the color sometimes referred to as "fire in the woodshed."

The opening paragraph told readers that this story would be about Buster Jones, who opened a bar on Main Street when he was a young man. The second paragraph brought them up to date:

> Now there's "snow on the rooftop," and next January Buster will celebrate his 40th year in business at the same little bar. He took a little time Wednesday to reflect on some of the changes in Buster's Old Inn since he went into business for himself.

Most contrast leads are written in two- or three-paragraph blocks. The first sentences set the stage, explaining a past event or perception. Then readers are quickly brought up to date. There is no reason to keep bouncing readers back and forth before giving them the news peg. It may even be possible to write the contrast lead as a single paragraph, as in this example from *The Arizona Republic:*

> Jose Ornelas already has spent 59 days in federal custody for the unruly party he threw for himself last New Year's Eve during a flight from El Paso to Phoenix. On Monday he got the final bill for grabbing the flight attendant as he demanded more liquor.

Writing a Contrast Lead

Using observation. As in a narrative lead, observation can make a contrast lead crackle. It can help persuade an audience to stay with a story until the end.

Here is a contrast lead from Georgia's *Savannah Morning News* that used a strong, gripping observation in the second paragraph:

> Last month, Chris Turner talked about living with AIDS. The 18-year-old hemophiliac called it a long, hard life.
>
> Before dawn on Monday, that life ended at St. Joseph's Hospital where he had been living for two days on morphine and pure oxygen—his only support—next to his family and friends.

Using "turn words." Strong **turn words,** or phrases or sentences, should be used to introduce the second half of the contrast. The most common turn words are *but, now, today* and *yesterday*. However, there is plenty of opportunity to be creative. For instance, in the above lead on the 18-year-old who died of AIDS, a prepositional phrase (*Before dawn on Monday*) made the turn for readers.

There is no need to be cute on the turn words or phrases. It is better simply to avoid the standard words, to avoid being trite. Here is an example from *The News-Sun* in Waukegan, Ill.:

> Anton Kolb, the 51-year-old Libertyville chauffeur who is the state's newest Lotto millionaire, hasn't had a vacation in 12 years.
>
> He may take a few days off now.

Using a contrast lead for a hard news story. A contrast lead is not reserved for features only. Because it often reports breaking news, it is an effective alternative to a summary lead on a hard news story. As in the above examples, contrasts can be used on news stories about the sentencing of a man who grabbed a flight attendant or a teen-ager who died of AIDS. Here is another example of a hard news story topped by a contrast lead.

> Twenty years ago, Ryan Winn and Christopher Colombi might have exchanged punches, and the loser would have gone home with a shiner and a bruised ego.
>
> But in a world where teen-agers and handguns mix with tragic results, Winn is dead and a Maricopa County Superior Court judge ruled Monday that there is probable cause to try Colombi for second-degree murder. (*The Arizona Republic*)

Staccato Leads

Elements of the Staccato Lead

A **staccato lead** is made up of a short burst of phrases that carry an audience into a news or feature story by dangling some of its key elements in front of them. It is meant to tease readers and to set the mood for the story, as in the lead from *The New York Times* used at the beginning of this chapter. Here is another example:

> WASHINGTON—A hit movie: "Outbreak." A best-selling book: "The Hot Zone." The cover of Time magazine: "Revenge of the Killer Microbes."

No wonder people worry about what's going on in the invisible world of viruses, bacteria and one-celled creatures with an attitude.

Scientists say the danger of infectious diseases is deadly serious—not just Hollywood hype. (Knight-Ridder Tribune Information Services)

Writing a Staccato Lead

After the short phrase or burst of phrases, a nut graph must tell the audience the news peg of the story. Readers or viewers should not have to wait to find out what the story is about.

An *Orlando Sentinel* story on color schemes for apartments began with a staccato lead:

> Off-white or beige walls. Brown or gray carpet. Beige vinyl kitchen floors.

These phrases should have brought readers into the story quickly. In the second paragraph they were told the reason for the story, which was about using something other than natural colors in decorating an apartment:

> These are the staples of apartment decor. Which is fine if you are into earth tones and neutrals. But what if you have a brighter color scheme in mind and the rules forbid any change?

The *Orlando Sentinel* also used a staccato lead in a story about a new play that would be performed on the roof of a downtown parking garage. It began:

> Sixth floor, Orlando City Parking Garage, 53 W. Central Blvd., downtown Orlando.

In the second paragraph, readers were told:

> Things are happening on the roof of the city parking garage, but not what the place's builders had in mind—there are hardly any cars in sight. In their place are a unicyclist, a roller skater, a rock band, a handful of parents and some three dozen kids, putting in one of their last rehearsals for the original young people's musical "Stack 'Em in the Streets."

Direct-Address Leads

Elements of the Direct-Address Lead

In a **direct-address lead,** a news or feature writer communicates directly with the audience by using the word *you.* This kind of lead gives writers an opportunity to reach out to their audience, to include them as individuals in a story. Instead of telling how experts say spark plugs should be changed, a writer tells an individual reader or viewer: "This is how you should change your spark plugs." The direct-address lead can be effective because it works like a recruiting poster, telling readers, "we want you" to take the time to complete this story. Usually, if direct address is used in the opening paragraph, it is used throughout the story.

In this example from the *Orange County* (Calif.) *Register,* the second paragraph of the story provides the news peg.

MIAMI—Your corner gas station—and the entire U.S. oil industry—is about to change more dramatically than ever in the 100-year history of the car, experts say.

Gas prices, which have been creeping up, are on the way to a nearly 20-cent jump, a leading oil analyst said. A sizable number of oil refineries face extinction, according to the federal government. Spot gas shortages are likely. And some motorists will start hearing their engines knock annoyingly.

In this example from the *The Courier Journal* in Louisville, Ky., the nut graph comes after two paragraphs of direct address and a question.

If you're a fairly frequent restaurant goer, you've probably sorted out sauvignon blanc from chardonnay and know when pinot noir will make a better food partner than merlot. Restaurant wine lists have become more varied with better selections, and patrons have been paying attention.

But it's summertime, and perhaps you're in the mood for a more thirst-quenching beverage to go with your meal. Or maybe you just want a change of pace. Ask for the beer list.

The beer list?

Absolutely. The explosion in imported and craft-brewed ales, lagers, porters and stouts has meant a growing interest in beer and an awareness of matching it with fine food. We're talking about a much more complicated—and culinarily exciting—activity than asking for a Bud with your bratwurst or a Tsingtao with your Szechuan shrimp.

Writing a Direct-Address Lead

Use direct-address leads sparingly. Direct address is not for every story. It is not appropriate on breaking news, where it is necessary to give a brief summary of the event without becoming personally involved with an audience.

If there is a fire and three people are killed, the lead would probably say:

Three people were killed today in a fire on West 35th Street.

It would not say:

Imagine what you would have seen if you were walking down West 35th Street today.

Be prepared to rewrite direct-address leads. Some editors dislike direct-address leads because they believe that reporters should never talk directly to readers. Editors also argue that direct-address leads are often aimed at a narrow segment of the readership or generalize in a way that would anger readers. For example:

You wouldn't think this city could come up with such a creative plan, but . . .

If a direct-address lead is best for a story, discuss it with an editor and defend it if necessary. Editors who say that they do not like direct-address leads can often be talked into running them if the writer makes a good enough case. Otherwise, be prepared to rewrite.

The next leads to be discussed—question leads, quote leads and "none of the above"—are the toughest ones to get into print. The reason: Editors want the news high in the story. They do not want their writers to flimflam the audience.

Question Leads

Elements of the Question Lead

Question leads begin a story by asking an audience a question or a series of questions.

Some editors would say that question leads are never acceptable because they rarely work, are overused or force people to look for answers that should have been in the opening paragraph. Also, editors contend that writers sometimes rely on question leads as crutches, using them when they cannot decide what the key point is. Despite the obstacles, however, questions can be used effectively to begin news and feature stories. Just use such leads sparingly and make certain that the question is connected to and sets the tone for the story that follows.

Writing a Question Lead

Answer the question quickly. The key to writing a question lead is to answer the question as quickly as possible. Ideally, the question should be answered in the first paragraph; if not, it must be answered in the second. Do not leave an audience hanging, trying to figure out what the story is about.

For example, here is a question lead from United Press International that worked. Notice how the writer answered each of the brief staccato questions immediately, rather than asking them all before giving the answers:

> WASHINGTON—Waltzing? It's in. Bedhopping? Out. Miss Manners etiquette? In. Raunchy locker room talk? Out.
>
> Marriage? In. Non-commitment? It's sweet history.
>
> Seems all that is left to the torrid sexual revolution is the faint smoke of candlelit romance, one on one. Even rocker Linda Ronstadt has turned to vintage torch songs—what's going on?

Tease the audience. In this question lead from *The Wall Street Journal,* the writer, Christopher Conte, waited until the second paragraph to give his readers answers:

> FAIRFAX COUNTY, Va.—Every weekday morning, Gretchen Davis drives down Fairfax Farms Road on the way to work at the Ayr Hill Country Store in nearby Vienna. Sounds pastoral, doesn't it?
>
> But a short way down the road, Mrs. Davis reaches Route 50, a major arterial highway through this Washington, D.C., suburb. There, a river of cars roars through the suburban calm. "Sometimes you have to wait 20 minutes just for a gap in the traffic big enough to get out—and even then you have to take a chance," the shopkeeper says. For Mrs. Davis, stop-and-go traffic often stretches what used to be a pleasant 20-minute commute into a nerve-wracking hour.

Conte's question lead was effective because it teased readers, telling them to read the next paragraph to find the answer. The story began in the peaceful setting of the suburbs, but, with contrast, told readers almost immediately that suburbia has grown so rapidly that it is facing the same traffic nightmares as big cities. Although it could have started with a summary lead telling readers that years of explosive and unplanned growth have flooded the suburbs with too many cars, it used a question to move readers from peaceful image to stark reality.

Combine question leads with direct address. Question leads can use direct address to ask readers, individually, a question. For example, the *Courier-Journal* lead on asking for the beer list in fine restaurants asked a question after two paragraphs of direct address.

When *The Daily Northwestern* at Northwestern University ran a story on demands by women to be paid the same as men for comparable jobs, it began:

> Okay, you're the boss. Who's worth more to you—your secretaries or your truck drivers? Your librarians or your electricians? Your carpenters or your nurses?

Quote Leads

Elements of the Quote Lead

A **quote lead** allows a central character to begin a news or feature story by talking directly to the audience. The quotation may be the most powerful one in the story, or it may set the tone for what is to follow.

Writing a Quote Lead

General guidelines for quote leads. Use quote leads sparingly. Most newspaper editors ban quote leads on breaking news stories because quotations may not provide the major points of the story.

Quote leads are particularly effective in broadcasting, where a story begins with tape of a central character speaking dramatically and then switches to the reporter, who ties the quotation to the news event.

When writing a quote lead for print, put the attribution in the first paragraph so that readers do not have to wait to find out who is speaking. Do not write a long quotation in the opening paragraph and then begin the second paragraph with *Those were the words of. . . .* Also, try to incorporate some elements of news with the quotation in the first paragraph. If this is not possible, put some news in the second paragraph.

Avoid carrying a quote lead for more than a paragraph or two. There is no need to keep an audience hanging before attributing the quotation and giving the news peg. Use more quotations after the news is reported.

Here are three examples of quote leads. The first is from the *New York Daily News,* with the attribution at the beginning; the second is from the *College Heights Herald* of Western Kentucky University, with the attribution at the end; the third is from the *Mohave Valley News* in Bullhead City, Ariz., with the attribution in the middle:

> As Yogi Berra would say: "It ain't over till it's over." But yesterday it was over—at least for now.

> "Dumb jocks are not being born, they are being systematically created," Dr. Harry Edwards said at a lecture Tuesday night in Garrett Auditorium.

> "It was bedlam," George Burden said with a smile. "It really was. My teammates told me I looked a little white in the face and that I should sit down."

Don't misrepresent in a quote lead. Before writing a quote lead, make sure it is powerful enough to draw in an audience or significant enough to set the tone of the story. Also, be careful that the quotation, if used out of context, does not misrepresent the speaker's point.

For example, the mayor might say: "I'm the boss. I'm the person who ultimately has to decide if we are going to spend all that money on the downtown renewal project. Of course, the voters can change my mind." In this case, a reporter would be misrepresenting the mayor's point if a news story began:

> "I'm the boss," the mayor said today.

Beware of libel when using a quote lead. Before using a quotation, screen it carefully for libel. The fact that someone said something does not allow a writer to use it worry-free. In this story from the *Kenosha* (Wis.) *News,* a potentially damaging quotation was used in the lead:

> "I'm glad he's in custody so he can stop killing people," said Vernita Wheat's brother, Anthony, 18, when he was told Friday the man accused of killing his sister had been taken into custody.

The suspect was later found guilty, and the chances were slim that he would take action against the paper, but the writer should have been more careful. Reporters do not have license to use anything uttered by a source.

"None of the Above" Leads

When Is a Lead "None of the Above"?

Sometimes a lead is "none of the above." It simply will not fit into any one of the categories described here. It may be a combination of several categories, or it may be what some editors call a "freak lead," which defies definition. It may be lines from a published poem or song that introduce a news or feature story. It may be a poem or song that the writer makes up, as in:

> Today is Tuesday.
>
> A day to sail.
>
> Tomorrow is Wednesday.
>
> Beware of a gale.

This example points out the fundamental problems with "none of the above" leads: they may be cute; they may be difficult to understand; or they may turn readers off.

Still, if they are used sparingly and appropriately, these leads can work, as in this story from the *Milwaukee Sentinel:*

> Dear God,
>
> Things are rather confused here at the State Senate in Madison.
>
> On Monday morning, Senate President Fred Risser (D-Madison) was quoted as saying senators had abandoned their formal opening prayer at the beginning of each session.

Here is one from *The Seattle Times:*

> If money talks, technology roars. Sometimes, it even laughs.
> Speakers at the Technology Alliance luncheon yesterday at the downtown Seattle Westin Hotel showcased the growth of high-tech and its impact on the region.
> The humor was a welcome sideshow.

Combining Several Types of Leads

"None of the above" leads probably work best when they consist of a combination of several categories of leads, rather than a poem, a song or some other strange type of beginning. Here is a lead from the *New York Daily News* on a story about an 18.6-mile walk to raise money for the March of Dimes and a 36-mile bicycle tour. It is a summary; it's an anecdote; and it also has a touch of music.

> Over hills, over dales, 40,000 people hit the city trails yesterday for charity and fun.

For a story about a new reference book on fashion in China, the *San Francisco Examiner* used a lead block that combined quotations, a narrative, a direct address, a question and a strong nut graph:

> SHANGHAI—"Bikinis are out!" yells Lo Chaotian.
> "Bikinis are out!" cries Wang Jianhua, who asks that you please call her Patty.
> "Bikinis are out!" they shout in unison.
> The message is believable. But the messengers?
> Lo and Wang are colleagues at the Shanghai Translation publishing house. They do dictionaries and other reference volumes.

For his story on women's chances in politics in Arizona, Steve Yozwiak of *The Arizona Republic* used a lead block that contained staccato, question and direct address:

> McCain. Rhodes. Stump. Kyl. Kolbe.
> Do these names look familiar?
> You may be seeing them in the newspapers for two more years—or even longer.
> In the "Year of the Woman" and in an atmosphere of anti-incumbent fever, Arizona voters may buck a national trend in November and return those five men to Congress.

Creating Effective Leads

Using Strong Verbs in Leads

Reporters must write sentences that are concise, accurate and easy to understand. A strong, colorful verb in each sentence will make the writing even better. This is particularly important in special leads, which may not provide the main news of the story right away. In these cases, the words, rather than the news, draw an audience inside.

A vivid verb can animate a sentence: "The hostages snaked their way along the dusty road to freedom." Words can paint a picture. Sentences can describe a snowstorm, a riot, a trial or a parade so accurately that an audience can see the event.

Here is a narrative lead on a story that appeared in the *Des Moines Sunday Register*. By using vivid verbs, the writer effectively drew his readers into the story.

> MESQUAKIE SETTLEMENT, Iowa—It was still dark when the 7-year-old boy was awakened by rustling mice beneath the tattered sofa that served as his bed. His little sister, still groggy and struggling with the zipper on her coat, lurched past. Judging from the wind hissing through the window cracks, the outhouse seat would be cold.
>
> "Look at this place," the father muttered as the seven-member family stirred to life in the condemned two-bedroom house just before dawn.

Imagine how dull the lead would have been with colorless verbs:

> MESQUAKIE SETTLEMENT, Iowa—Mice under his bed woke up the 7-year-old boy. His tired sister went past him. There was wind coming through the window cracks, which meant that the outhouse seat would be cold.
>
> "Look at this place," their father said as the seven-member family got up in their two-bedroom house before dawn.

In a *Kenosha* (Wis.) *News* story on an authorization by the Wisconsin Public Service Commission to withdraw party-line telephone service in areas where it is seldom used, the lead was:

> Wisconsin Bell is hanging up on the party line.

When writing a lead, or any other paragraph in a story, it is important to pick the most precise verb, the one that enhances each sentence and makes the scene clearer to an audience. This does not mean that writers should try to surprise or shock their audiences with a spectacular verb in each sentence. When a 17-year-old boy is shot and killed by a shotgun blast, the lead should simply say that he was shot and killed, not, "A 17-year-old boy was blown away today."

Be accurate and colorful, not cute, sensational or shoddy.

Choosing a Lead: Which Lead, and When?

The nice thing, but sometimes the most annoying thing, about writing leads is that there is really no "best" lead or "most correct" lead for a news or feature story. Tradition and time—either the time people spend reading or viewing news or the limited time and space journalists have to present it—still dictate that summary leads are the best on hard news stories. However, there are exceptions. A look at any front page shows that newspapers routinely top some news stories with contrasts, staccatos and other special leads.

The only real rule in writing leads is that there really are no rules. Writers are not given quotas. They do not sit at their computer terminals and say to themselves, "I'm going to write a summary lead on this story" or "This story deserves a contrast lead or a narrative lead." They usually write the lead before the story, although sometimes they construct the story before writing what they think is the best lead.

✔ A Checklist to Help Writers Decide on the Lead

Several things help writers decide on the lead:

- ❑ *Their Own Creativity.* It is always nice to be different from everyone else, as long as the audience understands the final product.
- ❑ *What Their Sources Said.* Writers have to work with what their sources said or did. They cannot make up quotations or narrative to enhance their stories.
- ❑ *Their Observations.* Writers are limited by what they see, hear, smell and touch during an interview. They are not allowed to embellish or obfuscate.
- ❑ *Tradition.* Reporters usually know when to write a summary lead and when to steer away from it.
- ❑ *Their Editors.* Face it. Reporters write for editors. Some bosses like only summaries; some will also accept narrative and contrast leads but no others; and some think that quote leads are fine.
- ❑ *Space.* A reporter may come up with a terrific three-paragraph lead that takes up 2 inches. But if an editor says, "You have only 8 inches of space," that wonderful lead probably will be abandoned.

CHAPTER SIX

ORGANIZING A NEWS STORY

Jerry Schwartz, a national writer and editor for The Associated Press, knows news writing. The veteran journalist has worked for more than 20 years in the news service's New York headquarters and has written or rewritten every type of story imaginable.

The compelling news story written by Schwartz and colleague David Crary the day of the Sept. 11, 2001, terrorist attack on America was used worldwide. The beginning of their story is used in Chapter 1 of this text. Schwartz also has covered the courts, supervised

(© *AFP / Corbis*)

coverage of state and local elections, traveled with the pope and worked on the AP's special desk established to cover the Persian Gulf War.

Inverted-Pyramid Style

When reporters cover news, they are always thinking of the stories they must write. They usually write the lead first, often composing it mentally while interviewing sources or checking records. When they write the story, they must present the news in a clear style that flows from paragraph to paragraph.

Most breaking news stories are written in *inverted-pyramid style,* in which the most important of the five W's and H are in the lead (as described in Chapter 4). What comes after the lead is also important. The lead should interest readers; the body, or middle, of the story should hold them to the conclusion.

An Example of the Inverted Pyramid

One story that Jerry Schwartz worked on illustrates an **inverted pyramid,** in which the news is reported in paragraphs arranged in order of descending importance.

The lead contained the gist of the story. *Who, what, where, when, why* and *how* were in the beginning paragraphs. A direct quote was used early in the article. Along with the hard news facts, transitions and quotations were used to keep the story flowing and readers reading. The article also ended with news, albeit the least important, which was an effective way to conclude without saying "the end." And like most inverted pyramids, the story could have been trimmed from the bottom without sacrificing key elements.

"The Mir story was written several times," said Schwartz, who had the assignment to rewrite the story under tight deadline pressure and get it ready for American media. "First, there was an A.M.s (morning newspaper) laydown, which basically provided a story for newspapers that had early deadlines. It's a tricky thing, writing this kind of story. It almost certainly would be obsolete by the time anyone read it in the newspaper. So the emphasis was on the place of Mir in the Soviet/Russian space program."

The Lead

The summary lead on the Mir space station included *who* (actually, the space station), *what, when, where* and *how.*

> By VLADIMIR ISACHENKOV
> Associated Press Writer
>
> KOROLYOV, Russia (AP)—The Mir space station returned to Earth in pieces Friday, ending its 15-year, 2.2-billion-mile odyssey with a fiery plunge into the South Pacific.

The summary lead did a good job of telling readers the focus of the story. Its 26 words gave readers a lot of information, and also used colorful words such as *returned in pieces* and *fiery plunge.*

The Body of the Story

After the lead—that is, from the second or third paragraph to the final word—an inverted-pyramid story is structured to present the news in order of descending importance. It is not built chronologically, nor does it end with a surprise. The most important of the W's and H are put into the lead. The second most important are in the second paragraph, the third most important in the third paragraph and so on. Each paragraph further explains or complements the paragraphs before it.

The next few paragraphs of the Mir story introduced key sources and also continued reporting news. In an inverted pyramid, it is important to put strong quotes as early as possible in the story to tie readers to key sources.

There was no immediate indication that remains of the spacecraft had hit anything but water. "We don't have any report of any other damage at this stage," said David Templeman, executive director of Emergency Management Australia.

Russian authorities said that an intricate series of engine firings, meant to ensure that no populated areas were placed in jeopardy, had gone as planned.

"The Mir has finished its triumphant flight," a Mission Control announcer said. Mission Control said the remains of Mir had hit the water.

Burning remnants of Mir could be seen as they shot across the sky over Fiji.

"It was at very high altitude and very high speed. It was very bright, had a long tail of smoke, which remained in the atmosphere for several minutes," said a pilot, Neli Vuatalevu, who was flying 8,000 feet above Nadi.

Engines of the cargo ship Progress, attached to Mir, fired twice to slow the spacecraft and put it into an elliptical orbit. Then, shortly after midnight Eastern time, the engines blasted one last time to hurl the station into the waters between Australia and Chile.

Transitions were used throughout the story to introduce additional sources. Notice how the story moves effortlessly from place to place, source to source.

Russian space officials were exuberant over what they characterized as a flawless achievement.

"It has been an exemplary operation, and our experts have not made a mistake in any single step, not in a millimeter. The world has become convinced that Russia knows not only how to build spacecraft but how to control them and how to forecast their flight. Russia will remain a great space power," said Yuri Koptev, the head of the Russian Aerospace agency.

The death of Mir marked the end of a proud chapter in the Russian space program; it proved that long duration space flight was possible. Its passing came with much wistfulness, and some protest. About 15 demonstrators briefly rallied Thursday outside Mission Control, holding up a portrait of Yuri Gagarin, the Russian who was the first man in space.

"Don't Give Up the Russian Space Industry," the sign read. But Mir was doomed. The impoverished Russian government could not afford to keep it in orbit—and in good repair—while fulfilling its obligations to the construction of the international space station.

After two paragraphs of *background,* which explains things for readers and brings them up to date, Schwartz used transition to move readers to another scene in the story.

Inside Mission Control near Moscow, the mood was strictly professional. Controllers bottled up regrets over Mir's demise as they pored over charts and figures in preparation for crucial commands.

"All the emotions we feel, we will only be able to express them tomorrow after the sinking of the station," said Andrei Borisenko, the shift director at Mission Control. "Today we are working without emotion and doing our jobs."

On its last day, the aging space station soaked up the sun's energy to power its fickle batteries and stabilize its alignment.

Its target area was 120 miles wide by 3,600 miles long, and centered roughly at 44 degrees south latitude and 150 degrees west longitude.

In the end, the spacecraft was only a bit off—it came down about 930 miles northwest of the planned site, in an area centered at 40 degrees south latitude and 160 degrees west longitude, Russian authorities said. That's about 1,800 miles east of Wellington, New Zealand.

Space officials said in its last moments, Mir traveled at 200 to 300 yards per second. At that speed debris could smash through a block of concrete six-feet thick.

Vsevolod Latyshev, a spokesman at Mission Control, said Russia would make no effort to recover the debris. "What for?" he asked quizzically.

Space officials had voiced confidence that they could carry out a safe descent, pointing to their experience in dumping dozens of Progress ships and other spacecraft into the same area of the Pacific.

But Mir was by far the heaviest spacecraft ever dumped, and its size and shape made it difficult to exactly predict the re-entry.

The body of the story was lengthy (we even trimmed it a little for this text), but it followed a pattern typical of inverted pyramids: readers were given the news in a series of paraphrases and direct quotes from various sources, transitions, background and additional facts.

The Conclusion

Writers do not conclude news stories by saying "the end" or by inserting an editorial comment to wrap things up. They simply quit writing after they have reported all the pertinent information they can get into the allocated space. They often conclude a story with a direct quotation, letting a source talk directly to readers. The quotation should tie readers emotionally to the story, reminding them that the writing has ended but that the story and the people involved in it have not.

The final paragraphs can also report additional facts. The facts are important to the story, but they are not as important as those earlier in the story. Such was the case of the Mir story, which ended with background and additional news:

The orbiter circled the Earth 86,331 times. Named after the Russian word that means both peace and world, Mir housed 104 astronauts in its lifetime. Sixty-two of them were from other countries, including seven Americans. Thirty-eight other Americans visited Mir when space shuttles docked there.

But NASA would have nothing to say about Mir's ending, according to spokeswoman Kirsten Larson. It was tracking the space station's return to Earth.

The space travelers performed about 23,000 experiments, growing wheat, building semiconductors, studying the effects of long-term weightlessness on humans.

But in its last years, Mir became something of an orbiting lemon. In 1997, an oxygen-generating canister caught fire, a supply ship crashed into the station, its computer system broke down and its power failed.

In December, Mission Control lost contact with the station for more than 20 hours because the aging batteries suddenly lost power. Space officials have managed to retain contact with Mir during subsequent power losses, but each incident disabled the central computer for days.

"The material for this story came from all over the place—from Russia, from American sources, from people posted in the South Pacific," Schwartz said. "Though Vladimir's name was on the story—bylines go to the reporter who was working at the dateline—I was the one who put the story together. I'm afraid some people would think that this was tedious, a thankless job. But I find it thrilling. It's like putting together a massive puzzle, and all the pieces keep changing shape and size. The challenge is to assimilate the information as you receive it, and then incorporate it into the story. It was my job to will these bits and pieces into a coherent account of what happened."

Organizing an Inverted Pyramid: Guidelines to Follow

Every story is different, but there are some basic guidelines that should generally be followed in organizing an inverted pyramid.

1: Write a terse lead. Write a brief lead paragraph of no more than 35 words that gives the major news of the story. Write a second paragraph providing major points of the news event that would not fit into the opening paragraph.

2: Provide background. Use the third or another early paragraph, and more paragraphs if necessary, to provide **background**, which explains things for readers. Background can come from a source, who explains something technical, or from the reporter, to make a story clearer. Even breaking news stories need background paragraphs to explain what happened before. For example, in a story on the first day of a murder trial, the writer may use the third, fourth and fifth paragraphs to give details of the crime.

If there is more than one major element, use background paragraphs high in the story to wrap up all of the elements. Then each one can be developed later.

3: Present news in order of descending importance. Continue reporting news of the story using paragraphs in order of descending importance. Inverted pyramids are seldom constructed chronologically. When reporters want to write a chronology, they often use another writing form, the hourglass, which will be explained later in this chapter.

4: Use quotations early and throughout. A good time to introduce direct quotations is after the audience has been given the major news and background information. Separate direct quotations by using supplementary news and paraphrases. Sprinkle quotations throughout the story instead of stringing them together. Remember, quotations are useful because they let people in the news communicate directly to an audience.

5: Use transitions. A paraphrase, a background paragraph, a paragraph with additional news or even a direct quotation can be used as transition to move readers smoothly from one paragraph to another. Transition alerts an audience that a shift or change is coming up.

Transitions can be developed in several ways:

- *Numerically*—first, second, third, etc.
- *By Time*—at 3 p.m., by noon, three hours later, etc.
- *Geographically*—in Tucson, outside the home, District 3 voters, etc.
- *With Words*—also, but, once, meanwhile, therefore, in other action, however, below, above, etc.

6: Do not editorialize. Reporters are eyewitnesses to news. Their job is to tell an audience what they saw and what other people said. They should not include their personal opinions. If they think that something is rotten, they let the direct quotations from people involved in the story support, and rebut, their own opinion.

7: Avoid "the end." Continue reporting news until the end. This helps readers know that even though the writing has stopped, the story has not. An effective way to conclude a news story is with a direct quotation.

Analyzing an Inverted Pyramid

Now let's take a look at a news story written in inverted-pyramid form and see how well it follows the seven guidelines. The Associated Press story was transmitted to member newspapers throughout the United States.

MINNETONKA, Minn. (AP)—Fifteen Boy Scouts from this Minneapolis suburb got more adventure than they expected on their summer camping expedition.

Bound for Washington state's Cascade Mountains, the private helicopter they hired dropped them off 4,000 feet higher than planned, leaving them stranded amid glaciers and snowfields.

Rock slides and a sheer mountain face blocked their way.

It took a harrowing day for a few to climb to safety and bring back help.

"We were expecting high adventure," said Scoutmaster Brad Strot. "But not to the point where we had to bushwhack our way down the mountain and put our kids in that much danger."

The pilot said the original landing spot on a private mining claim in the North Cascades National Park was unsafe, so he dropped them off higher up the mountains.

"There were glaciers above us, snowfields all around, clean running water that didn't need to be filtered and wildflowers," Strot said.

But the trail that should have led them down to their planned campsite was blocked by rockslides, waterfalls and a sheer rock face.

"Our first impression was of being in paradise, only to find you couldn't get out," recalled Gary Johnson, father of 17-year-old Scout Jordan Johnson and an adult leader in the troop. "Heaven turned into hell."

After two days, the group realized its situation. Seven older Scouts and two leaders set off to get help that put their scout survival skills to the test.

"Everybody thought they were going to die," Jordan Johnson said. "Crossing that rock face, anybody could have slipped."

After a hike of more than 15 miles, the rescue team reached a camp with a bus that drove them into Stehekin, Wash. There, they called the pilot, who drove through the night to get back to his chopper.

At 5 p.m. last Wednesday, the Scouts were airlifted out, three at a time, from the mountain. They arrived home via train Monday.

Now apply the seven guidelines in analyzing the story.

1: Write a terse lead. The lead contains 18 words. It certainly is terse. But it does not do a good job of summarizing the story. That information comes in the second paragraph. Additional important information is in the third paragraph.

2: Provide background. Not much background information is needed in this story, but the information provided is early in the story. By the end of the fifth paragraph, readers know that the group was bound for the Cascade Mountains, the Scouts hired a private helicopter and it dropped them 4,000 feet higher than planned. And the pilot said the original landing spot on a private mining claim was unsafe.

3: Present news in order of descending importance. The most important news of this story is reported at the beginning. The Scouts were stranded on their camping expedition. A few of them had to climb to safety to bring back help. The important elements are presented early in the story, and the remaining paragraphs provide additional details about them. The story could be cut from the bottom and readers still would know the basic elements.

4: Use quotations early and throughout. The story's first quote is in the fourth paragraph. That's a good spot for it. Other quotes are sprinkled throughout. The quotes introduce key players in the story to readers.

5: Use transitions. They're used whenever the story shifts. For example, the fifth paragraph shifts to what the pilot said about the landing spot. *The pilot* is the transition. The transitional word *but* is used two paragraphs later to shift readers to the trail. Two paragraphs after that, *after two days* shifts readers again. The last two paragraphs of the story also are introduced with transitions.

6: Do not editorialize. There is no editorializing in this story.

7: Avoid "the end." The last paragraph simply reports more news: the Scouts arrived home on Monday. The writer did not end with anything such as, "and they will live happily ever after."

Improving an Inverted-Pyramid Story: An Example of Revision

Many of the stories that reporters cover deal with routine occurrences, such as traffic accidents, speeches by politicians and actions by governmental bodies. To keep their audiences interested in these stories, reporters must avoid bland or disorganized writing. They must write crisply and vividly.

Initial Version

Here is a story written for a university daily. It is used to illustrate the process that a reporter often goes through to come up with a story that is well written and well organized. The story is real, but some of the writing is changed to avoid using the name of the school and the sources.

A $151 million state university appropriations request may be cut because of monetary demands from other state programs, the chairman of the Senate's Education Committee said Saturday.

Sen. William Delgado, D-Mainsville, said the budget proposal, which represents a $13 million increase over last year's request, may be limited owing to demands on lawmakers to fund new programs for the chronically mentally ill.

The appropriations request, which was approved unanimously by the Board of Regents Friday, totals $151,298,342. Last year's request was $138,298,356.

"It's kind of like a kid asking for an allowance," Delgado said, adding that the Legislature will have to determine how much money is available before approving the budget requests.

"There is just so much money to go around," Delgado said. "First of all we have to take a look and see what we have extra. I feel we may not have enough."

Delgado said the governor has been pushing for programs for the mentally ill, and the Legislature may have to consider funding those programs before allocating funds to the university.

The Legislature will begin discussion on the budgets in January, when its regular session reconvenes.

In other matters, the university will lose 22 faculty positions next year because of a decline in its full-time student equivalent counts. The regents made the announcement at their meeting on campus Friday because they said FTE decreased by 499 this year.

The Legislature provides one faculty member for every 22 FTE.

Jim Horan, associate director of university budgets, said the decline in enrollments may be attributed to increasing enrollments at state community colleges.

The regents also approved new policies for the training of graduate teaching assistants at the university.

The new policies, which were prompted by complaints from students, require that foreign teaching assistants be required to pass a proficiency test of written and spoken English before teaching.

Analysis: What's Wrong with It?

The initial version of the story missed the boat for several reasons:

Lead. The lead was wrong.

Writing Style. The writing was dull and loose.

Organization. The story was not organized effectively. There are three major elements—the appropriations request, the loss of faculty and the testing of foreign teaching assistants—yet two of them are buried at the end.

First, let's consider the lead. In the initial story, readers were told that the Legislature may cut the university's budget request. This is not news. Budget requests are wish lists. It would be news if a budget were approved exactly as proposed.

The lead also reported that something *may* happen. Avoid writing *may* leads. They are hypothetical. The action that they are reporting may or may not happen. An audience wants something definite.

The lead of this story should have been that the university is going to lose faculty members next year because of declining enrollment. Twenty-two people are going to lose their jobs, or departments that were hoping for new faculty members are not going to get them.

Next, let's look at the writing. Throughout the initial version, the writing was dull and loose. It needed tightening and sharpening.

For example, in the second paragraph the writer said that the budget proposal "may be limited owing to demands on lawmakers to fund new programs for the chronically mentally ill." The writing could have been crisper:

> The budget proposal may be pared because lawmakers are being pushed to fund new programs for the chronically mentally ill.

The sixth paragraph reported that the governor has been pushing for the new programs and that the Legislature "may have to consider funding those programs before allocating funds to the university."

Why not say:

> The Legislature will yield to the governor's demands for the mentally ill before it funds the university, Delgado said.

Finally, consider the organization. The story should be topped with the 22 cuts in the faculty. The new tests for foreign teaching assistants and the threat of budget cuts should also be mentioned high in the story. Then each can be explained later.

There are several holes in the story. FTEs need to be explained better, as do the reasons for the new tests for foreign teaching assistants. Readers also need to be told in what areas the faculty positions would be lost.

The Rewrite

The rewritten story read:

> The university will lose 22 faculty positions next year because of declining enrollments.
>
> Funding for the positions is based on full-time equivalent counts, FTEs, which decreased by 499 this year. The Board of Regents announced the decrease during its meeting on campus Friday.
>
> FTEs are the total number of hours being taken by all students divided by 12, a normal full-time load.
>
> At their meeting, the regents also:
>
> - Approved new policies for the training of foreign-born graduate teaching assistants at the university.
> - Approved a $151 million budget request for next year, an increase of $13 million over last year.
>
> Jim Horan, associate director of university budgets, blamed the decline in students here on the increasing enrollments at state community colleges.

"We cannot compete with them for first- and second-year students," Horan said. "They're easier to get into, smaller and half the price."

The Legislature uses a ratio of one faculty member to every 22 FTEs when it appropriates salaries.

University officials said that they will try to avoid laying off any faculty members. Instead, the 22 positions will be made up by attrition, they added.

The issue of training foreign graduate students came up after students in the math and history departments complained that they could not understand their instructors.

The new policies require that foreign teaching assistants pass a proficiency test of written and spoken English before they can teach.

The request for an increased budget was approved unanimously by the regents. It totals $151,298,342, an amount that Sen. William Delgado, D-Mainsville, called wishful thinking, "like a kid asking for an allowance."

Delgado, chairman of the Senate's Education Committee, said that the proposal may be pared because the governor is pushing lawmakers to fund new programs for the chronically mentally ill.

"There is just so much money to go around," Delgado said. "First we all have to take a look and see what we have extra."

The Legislature will begin debate on the budget in January, when its regular session reconvenes.

Why Is the Rewrite Better?

For a number of reasons, the rewritten and reorganized version of the regents story was better than the initial version:

The Lead Was Stronger. It reported substance rather than something that may or may not be. After reading the initial lead, someone was likely to say, "So what?" After the second lead, a reader was likely to say: "Wow! Who is going to be fired?"

The Story Was Better Organized. By using **bullets**—bold dots that begin and highlight paragraphs—the writer introduced other major elements early in the story. After six paragraphs, readers knew what the article was about. In the initial version, the three major elements were stacked on top of each other, which meant that readers did not know all of them until the end. In the rewrite, the major elements were introduced right away, and the two least important ones were developed later.

The Writing Was Tighter. More vivid verbs were used.

Holes Were Filled. FTEs were defined. Readers were told where the 22 faculty positions would come from, why community colleges were taking away students and which students complained about foreign-born teaching assistants.

Hourglass Style

Most news stories are written in the traditional inverted-pyramid form, but there are alternatives. "When we are writing stories on deadline, we have to depend on strategies that have proved themselves," said Roy Peter Clark of The Poynter Institute for

Media Studies in St. Petersburg, Fla. "We have to reach into our toolbox and pull out our handy gadgets that help us organize our thinking and communicate to readers. I think that the problem with some writers is that they have a single form that they go back to over and over again, and they don't have at their fingertips a variety of forms out of which they can find just the right one to tell a particular story."

Clark is an advocate of a writing form called **hourglass style**, which is often used by reporters covering trials or police and fire news. In this form, the writer provides the major news in the first few paragraphs of the story. The paragraphs are written in order of descending importance, as in an inverted pyramid. Then the writer uses a **turn**, a transitional paragraph to introduce a chronology of the events of the story. Transitional paragraphs include: *Police gave the following account of the accident, The victim told the jury what happened* and *Johnson said that he was attacked shortly after he left work.* After the turn, the rest of the details of the story are told in chronological order.

Advantages of Hourglass Style

Clark said that hourglass style offers these advantages:

- The important news is presented high in the story.
- The writer can take advantage of narrative.
- The most important information is repeated in the narrative so that readers have a chance to absorb it.
- Unlike the top-heavy inverted pyramid, the hourglass has a balanced structure.
- It keeps readers in the story and leads up to a real conclusion.
- It discourages editors from slashing from the bottom.

"The hourglass is a natural way to tell a story," Clark said. "You blurt out the more important information right away, and then someone says, 'That was fascinating. How did it happen?' I've seen it on an interesting range of stories, including governmental meetings in which the writer tells the news at the top of the story and then recounts how the events took place in a chronological order. I think the hourglass opens up the reporter to a level of reporting that the pyramid sometimes discourages."

An Example of Hourglass Style: A Bizarre Accident

The news story from the *Philadelphia Inquirer* that follows was written by Reid Kanaley in hourglass style. It was the story of a truck slamming into an office building and killing a man working at his desk.

The first six paragraphs of the story were written in typical inverted pyramid style, with the most important points first. The turn came in the seventh paragraph: *Anderson gave the following account of the accident.* Then the narrative followed.

A Delaware County businessman died yesterday morning after a tractor-trailer careened into a busy Chester County intersection and slammed through the office where he was sitting at his desk.

The truck driver was seriously injured in the 8:09 a.m. accident at Route 202 and Brinton's Bridge Road in Birmingham Township. There were no other injuries, officials said.

Police said the brakes of the tractor-trailer, a flatbed loaded with coiled steel, apparently had failed. The truck veered across lanes of oncoming traffic, hitting a van, plowing through the office building and into a parked van before coming to a stop, according to Birmingham Police Chief Wade L. Anderson.

The businessman, James E. Dever, 50, of Stonebridge Road, Thornton, died during emergency surgery at Chester County Hospital in West Chester about 10:30 a.m., hospital spokeswoman Donna Pennington said. She described Dever's injuries as "multiple trauma."

The truck driver, Steven Rowe, 26, of Chesapeake, Ohio, was taken to Chester County Hospital with multiple injuries. He was listed in satisfactory condition last night.

Dever was a salesman for the Logan Co., a conveyor manufacturer, according to his son, Thomas Dever, of West Chester.

Anderson gave the following account of the accident:

Rowe's tractor-trailer was northbound on Route 202. At Brinton's Bridge Road, the truck, apparently unable to stop for a red light, crossed the southbound lanes and struck the front end of a van making a left turn onto the road. The driver of the van, Joseph A. Koskoszka of New Castle, Del., was not injured.

The truck continued past the cross street and up a grade into the parking lot of the Birmingham Professional Building on the northwest corner of the intersection. Dever was the only person in the two-story building at the time. He was at his desk in a first-floor corner office when Rowe's truck crashed through the office and into a parked van owned by Anderson. The impact demolished two walls of Dever's office and pinned him under the debris.

The van rolled onto its side and smashed the front window of the neighboring building, the Patterson Schwartz real estate office.

Anderson said he had just left his office in the basement of the Birmingham Professional Building and was sitting in a patrol car when Rowe's truck skidded by.

"I could see it was out of control, and the driver was making every attempt to miss anything," he said. "He did a fantastic job. He missed me; he missed the cars. He thought the lesser of the evils would be hitting the building, but, of course, it didn't work out that way."

Anderson estimated damages of $75,000. No charges have been filed, but the accident remains under investigation, Anderson said.

Besides his son Thomas, Dever is survived by his wife, Barbara; two daughters; and two other sons.

Organizing an Hourglass

The 30-word lead on Kanaley's story clearly summarized the event: A man was killed when a truck crashed into his office. In the second paragraph readers found out the time of the accident and that the truck driver was injured. Then in succeeding paragraphs (until the seventh) readers were told:

- *How* the accident occurred
- *Who* was killed
- *Who* was injured
- *Where* the dead man had worked

This story could have been concluded after the sixth paragraph; instead, a transitional paragraph was written that invited the audience to read a blow-by-blow account of the accident. Readers had the option of stopping or continuing.

The second half of an hourglass should not repeat the first half word for word. Obviously, some facts will be repeated, but the second half of the story should make the succession of events clearer. In this example, the second paragraph said that the accident occurred at Route 202 and Brinton's Bridge Road. The eighth paragraph reported that the tractor-trailer was northbound on

Route 202 and was apparently unable to stop for a red light at Brinton's Bridge Road. This paragraph repeated the location of the accident, but it provided additional details.

When to Use the Hourglass

An hourglass cannot be used in every news story. It would be impractical, for example, for a personality profile, a weather story, an obituary or an advance on a holiday celebration. But in a story that has a succession of events, such as a trial, a meeting or a police or fire story, hourglass style can be used effectively. "A story form does not have to be a straitjacket," Clark said. "It should be a liberating device. Reporters need to look for the best structure to tell the best possible story. I would call the hourglass a way of reconciling two essential values for the writer: (1) getting the news high up and not wasting the readers' time, and (2) telling a good story in a narrative style."

Circle Style

Another popular writing form, particularly for feature stories, is what writers call "writing in a circle" or "coming full circle." In this form, a writer begins with a scene built around an event or key source. Descriptive writing draws readers into the story.

For example, in a lengthy story about Phoenix being the worst city in the nation for red-light-running accidents, Arizona State University student writer Linda Bexell began with a 20-year-old woman who was putting her life back together after suffering severe head injuries in an auto accident.

> Krystal Philippi was en route to her Chandler High School prom, wearing a long, white gown and expecting the happiest night of her life.
>
> But in an instant, the senior, who carried a 4.0 GPA, was besieged by terror in a horrific traffic accident caused by a driver who ran a red light.

In her story, Bexell quoted numerous sources. She also conducted careful research to obtain numbers on accidents, deaths and injuries from the U.S. Brain Injury Association, the Insurance Institute for Highway Safety and other organizations. She talked to state legislators and other officials.

She had a big story to tell, but throughout she kept coming back to Krystal Philippi, who made the complex story human for readers. The story's end also came full circle and ended with Philippi:

> "I want to learn about me, I want to learn about what happened to me and what is going on with me," she added. "I am a fighter. I just go and I keep on going."

Advantages of Circle Style

Writing in a circle is an effective alternative to the inverted pyramid because it helps simplify a complex story for readers and makes it human. Other advantages include:

- The writer can use narrative and descriptive writing.
- Readers can attach to a key source and feel as though the story is about the source as well as a broader topic.

- The style is not top heavy like an inverted pyramid.
- The story flows better and keeps readers involved.
- The circle is more effective storytelling and can keep readers interested until the end.
- Editors cannot slash the story from the bottom.

Other Alternatives

Besides the hourglass and circle styles already discussed there are other alternatives in constructing a news story. Stories can also be written so that they combine elements of several writing forms.

Feature Leads

It is not uncommon in today's media to see news stories with feature leads. An Associated Press story on soaring rates of suicide among children began:

> ATLANTA (AP)—It's one of the first things 16-year-old Brandy Bozeman asks her fellow students troubled by thoughts of suicide: Do you have a gun?
>
> "Weapons are so readily available," explains Brandy, who helps counsel suicidal students at Campbell High School in suburban Atlanta.

Ending with a Twist

News stories can also be constructed so that, rather than ending with the least important news element, they end with an odd twist or a climax.

Here is an example of such a news story that was written after the 1995 bombing of the federal courthouse in Oklahoma City. Tim Wiederaenders of the *Kingman Daily Miner* in Arizona wrote the story. It reported news, but its paragraphs were not stacked from the most to least important.

> The FBI took a back seat to classic cars this weekend.
>
> "We threw them all out," said Dorothy Brown, desk clerk at a local motel, referring to the 27 agents who were staying there. ". . . They're no better than anyone else."
>
> Twenty-two more FBI agents wanted rooms, she said.
>
> Brown said the motel she works at, like many others in Kingman, was booked solid this weekend—since last year—as the eighth annual Route 66 Fun Run was held.
>
> The increased numbers of FBI agents were in town investigating leads in connection with the April 19 bombing of a federal building in Oklahoma City. The FBI presence in Kingman grew from less than one dozen agents to about 50 on Friday.
>
> The bureau also went from using desks at the Mohave County Sheriff's Office to setting up a headquarters at the National Guard Armory late last week. Several four-wheel-drive vehicles full of agents were seen coming in and out of the Armory over the weekend.
>
> FBI spokesman Jack Callahan declined to comment about increased bureau actions in the Kingman area.
>
> The story was similar at several other hotels and motels in Kingman, as media groups tracking the FBI's movements were also displaced by the Fun Run.

Numerous TV trucks could be seen this weekend across the street from the Armory, waiting and watching the FBI.

Fun Run organizers were expecting more than 700 participants for this year's event, which included a car rally from Seligman to Kingman on Saturday and from Kingman to Topock/Golden Shores on Sunday. Among events held was a car show at Kingman High School North on Saturday.

FBI agents were allowed back into local motels Sunday.

Such writing is not for every news story. Many stories deal with such serious subjects that they are naturally constructed in a traditional form that will not surprise or upset readers. But remember that newspapers do not publish only serious breaking news stories. They also report and write about softer news events. Those events open the door for alternative writing styles.

CHAPTER SEVEN

DEVELOPING A NEWS STORY

When Danny Ray Horning escaped from the maximum-security Central Unit of the Arizona State Prison at Florence, newspapers and broadcast outlets hardly noticed. At most the escape received a few paragraphs on an inside page or near the end of a broadcast.

Things changed rapidly, however. Fifty-five days later, when Horning was captured nearly 200 miles away from the prison, his story had been front-page news for weeks. He had become one of the biggest stories of the year as he eluded search dogs and hundreds of police in

(*Tom Tingle, The Phoenix Gazette*)

Arizona's mountain forests. How reporters covered this story illustrates how stories are developed from day to day.

Deciding Which Stories to Develop

Even in a local market on a routine day, the media must continually decide whether stories should or should not be developed beyond a single item. Some local news events—a train derailment, a major fire, a court trial, a search for a new college president, a hunt for an escaped convict—may be worth developing into several stories. Others—the naming of a bank president, a minor fire or fender bender with no injuries, the closing of a business, a vacation Bible school—are worth only one.

A Story's Impact

A story is developed from day to day when reporters and their editors feel that it is newsworthy; that is, the event itself, its aftermath or the news it generates has a continuing impact on an audience. Of course, the fact that reporters stop covering a story does not mean that the story stops developing. It simply means that there is room each day for only so many stories, and judgments about their newsworthiness or human interest determine which ones are continued and which ones are dropped.

For example, a truck carrying a load of potatoes into town skids off the highway, overturns and spills the cargo all over the road. That is certainly worth a story. If the truck driver is not injured, the mess is cleaned up quickly and the truck leaves town two hours later, the news event deserves only a single story reporting the unusual crash. But if the driver is critically hurt and then dies, or a reporter finds out that the potatoes were stolen, or several residents are arrested with shopping bags full of potatoes, the story may be developed for days.

Other Factors Influencing Coverage

Other factors besides the impact on an audience help the daily news media decide whether or not to continue developing a story. These factors include:

- *Prejudices of Reporters and Editors.* Obviously, if a reporter or a news executive has a particular interest in a story, it tends to be given more attention than other stories.
- *Size of the Market.* The daily media in large markets are more likely to have enough resources and staff members to cover a story in depth for many days. Reporters in small markets, where everyone is doing a little bit of everything and moving from story to story, usually do not have that luxury.
- *Pressure for Exclusivity.* Every news organization would like to be the only one in town with a story. An exclusive news story or feature article means more readers, listeners or viewers.
- *What the Competition Is Doing.* All the media are highly interested in what their competition is printing, covering online or putting on the air.

A newspaper or online reporter will often go after a story because of what was reported by a television or radio reporter; broadcast reporters will often chase stories being developed by print or online reporters.

- *What Other Stories Are Developing.* If another major story breaks, it will be given priority. This means that reporters may be pulled off stories that began developing earlier.

Covering Developing Stories

Phases of a Developing Story

Whenever a major news event occurs, all the daily media strive to keep their audiences as up to date as possible. A story can be developed for hours or for months, and it is usually covered in four phases:

- *Phase 1.* The story first breaks. Journalists rush to the scene to report the news as it is happening, or they work the phones to put together an initial breaking story. They work on the story full time, and their primary function is to tell their audiences *what* happened, *when, where* and to *whom.* The story may be front-page news. Reporters will usually write **mainbars**, primary stories that report the **breaking news**, and **sidebars**, supplemental stories that explain the news or report the human element.
- *Phase 2.* Journalists try to explain the *why* and *how* of the story, but they also continue to report late-breaking developments, such as cleanup operations or a final casualty count. This means that the story is likely to remain front-page news. **Second-day stories**, which report the latest news as well as summarize the earlier news, and sidebars are written to put the news into perspective for an audience.
- *Phase 3.* The story is no longer front-page news, unless something unusual happens to warrant front-page treatment, but reporters are still covering it full time or routinely. They look for something fresh, but they also analyze and continue to humanize the story. Follow-ups and features may be written for days afterward.
- *Phase 4.* Few reporters are working on the story full time any longer, but there may be a few pursuing specific angles. Reporters still make routine checks. Weeks or months later, there may be a major development as officials release their findings or investigative reporters come up with something. The story could become front-page news again.

Whenever reporters cover a developing story, their primary consideration is their deadline. They can stretch their coverage as much as possible, but the ever-present deadline must be met. When the time comes to phone in their notes or to push the button on their stories, reporters must go with what they've got. This means that no story they write can be definitive. All they can do is report the latest and most reliable information available at the time they write their stories. There will always be more information to gather and another story to write the next day, in a week, in a month or next year.

Chronology of a Major Story

An Escaped Convict: The Story Begins

Danny Ray Horning escaped from the Arizona State Prison by donning a medical worker's clothes and simply walking out. He was in prison for robbing a bank and was a suspect in the killing and dismembering of a California man.

At the time of the escape, Judi Villa was covering the police beat for *The Arizona Republic.* Like other reporters in the Phoenix area, Villa did not begin covering the story on a daily basis until about a month after Horning's escape. By then, Horning, a wilderness survivalist, had managed to hide from everyone trying to hunt him down. There had been massive searches in several counties, but they were called off as authorities ran out of leads.

Reporting the First Big Break

A big break in the story came when a county in northern Arizona announced that it was considering hiring a survivalist to help search for Horning. Villa, who had been working the story by phone as part of her daily routine, turned her full-time attention to Horning when the announcement about the survivalist was made. She interviewed the survivalist, who told her that there were only a few places where Horning could hide for a long period. He told Villa that Horning was probably living off crayfish, fish and plants in the Clear Creek area of northern Arizona, which is filled with chasms and caves.

In her story on the survivalist, Villa reported the latest news in her opening paragraphs:

> Coconino County authorities are considering using a noted wilderness survivalist to help search for escaped convict and California murder suspect Danny Ray Horning.
>
> Larry Olsen, 52, who operates an outdoor treatment program for youths and was asked to participate in the 1987 hunt for Idaho fugitive killer Claude Dallas, said he offered to help in the northern Arizona search for Horning.
>
> The number of searchers was cut in half, from 80 to 40, over the weekend, and authorities said they were running out of leads on Horning.

As is typical in developing stories, the lead block that reported the latest news was followed by background—a report of earlier news to bring readers up to date. Villa's fourth paragraph provided this background:

> Horning, 33, escaped May 12 from the maximum-security Central Unit of the Arizona State Prison at Florence by disguising himself as a medical worker. Last Wednesday, a former Corrections Department employee spotted Horning near Clint Wells, 45 miles southeast of Flagstaff, helping three youths with their truck. As authorities approached, Horning fled into the Mogollon Rim country, where he is believed to have survived for nearly a month.

After the background material is presented, a developing story should return to the latest occurrences. Villa's story did precisely that. It went on to report more information on Olsen, the survivalist, and how he thought he could help capture Horning. Additional background is usually presented near the end of the story.

Advancing the Story

The day after she wrote the story on Olsen, Villa was sent to northern Arizona to continue working on her story. Her task was straightforward: Continue advancing the story each day. Report the latest developments in news stories, and also look for feature stories that emphasize **color**—observations, narrative or anecdotes that give an audience a clearer picture of a person or event.

"I had covered the story over the phone initially, but then it was only a prison escape," Villa said. "The story was beginning to develop into something bigger, however, as Horning eluded police."

Villa started work at 8 a.m. on the day her city editor sent her and a photographer into the field on the Horning story. She would work until 11:30 p.m. that day, the first of many 12- to 16-hour days she would spend on a quickly developing story.

She said the first stop for her and the photographer was the command post that had been set up "in the middle of nowhere" by authorities. "We were 23 miles from a phone," Villa said. "We asked for a briefing. I had been talking to the command post on the phone before we went there (about 90 miles southeast of Flagstaff)."

Villa's first day in the field produced little news. Horning was still at large, and the authorities were frustrated. She knew there was no real breaking news to report, and so she wrote a piece that emphasized color. It began:

> Glendale resident Leota Jarrel has spent many of her summers as host at Double Springs campground at Mormon Lake, where escaped convict and California murder suspect Danny Ray Horning is believed to be hiding.
>
> This summer is no different.
>
> "Every day in Phoenix the same kind of people (as Horning) are running up and down the streets," Jarrel said Wednesday.

In her next paragraph Villa "backgrounded" her readers with the same information that had been presented in her earlier stories. Then her 20-inch story turned back to Jarrel. She used more background later in her story.

Keeping up with the news. Two days later, the search for Horning was called off, but Villa did not quit working on the story. She followed it by phone. Horning was spotted a week later; this produced another flurry of stories, but the search was called off again after three days.

The developing story was rekindled later in the month when Horning took hostages and shot at law enforcement officers at the Grand Canyon. This happened in a national park in the summer, a peak time for tourists. Now the story would develop from minute to minute.

"The assistant metro editor called me at home at 9 a.m. Sunday and asked me if I wanted to go to the Grand Canyon," Villa said. "I said 'sure,' and he said to be at the newsroom in an hour. He told me to plan to stay overnight. I wasn't prepared for five days. We (Villa and a photographer) left so quickly that I didn't think to bring along a portable computer. I had to phone in everything.

"As before, we started at the command post, trying to figure out who was who. There were 12 or 13 agencies involved—FBI, county sheriffs, the National Park Service, the state Department of Corrections, dog teams, the Border Patrol—

and each had its own area. You wanted to know someone from each one. Each had its own little system, and their efforts weren't all that together. Some agencies didn't know things that the other agencies knew. There were four main spokespeople."

Providing background. Villa's first story from the Grand Canyon was filled with color based on her observations and interviews. The only news she had to report was that Horning had not yet been captured. Instead of filing a one-sentence story reporting that nothing had happened, Villa spent the day meeting people and visiting with them. Her writing illustrated how a variety of color stories or sidebars can be written as a major story develops and how important it is to "background" readers continually. A reporter can never assume that readers have been following a story from the first day.

Here is much of Villa's first story; the annotations on the right show how her writing followed a pattern typical to developing stories.

Prison escapee Danny Ray Horning continued to elude more than 200 searchers in the Grand Canyon, but park business went on as usual and visitors said they were not afraid of the convict.	*The latest news in a summary lead*
"My son has a water gun, so we are safe," said Melitta Trautvietter, a visitor from Germany who was at the canyon on Sunday with her son, Nils, 13, and daughter, Dana, 10. "We were a little scared when we first came here," Nils said. "But now it's fine. We think they lost him."	*Introduction of key sources with strong quotes; color*
Today, officials planned door-to-door searches of residential areas around the canyon.	*News*
Horning, 33, was spotted Friday night at the Grand Canyon after taking two hostages from Flagstaff on Thursday afternoon. He tried to kidnap a family at Babbitt's, a general store in the Grand Canyon's South Rim Village, just before 9 p.m. Friday. The family escaped when the teenage son started screaming, frightening Horning, who fled with the couple he already held hostage. After firing three to five rounds at pursuing officers, Horning abandoned the vehicle, turned the couple loose on the West Rim between Hopi and Mohave points and fled into the woods. Backpackers reported spotting Horning hiking down the Bright Angel trail Saturday.	*Background*
Joyce Patterson of New Jersey said she heard the shots Friday night. "We kind of wrote it off as someone doing something stupid like shooting an animal,"	*Another source; more color*

said Patterson, who was visiting the park with her husband, 6-year-old son and 11-year-old daughter. She said the family avoided the park Saturday but chose to return Sunday and finish their vacation.

"We figured they would keep people away if it wasn't safe," Patterson said.

The sightings sparked a third large-scale manhunt for Horning since he escaped May 12 from the maximum-security unit at the Arizona State Prison at Florence.

Two attempted break-ins Saturday night—one at the Maswik Lodge and one at a residential mobile home—also may be tied to Horning, said Jim Tuck, public affairs officer for Grand Canyon National Park.

Background

"After those, dogs picked up some pretty strong scents," Tuck said, but officers couldn't positively link Horning to the scenes.

Three leads turned up no signs of Horning on Sunday.

A woman entering the park shortly before noon reported seeing a man matching Horning's description in a valley 35 miles south of the park.

News

Villa's story continued for several more paragraphs. She introduced another law enforcement source, who provided more information on the search.

Persisting. As the week wore on, Villa continued to interview people and to keep up with the latest information from authorities. She was also in constant contact with her newsroom.

"Mobile phones and pagers don't work at the canyon," she said. "I called in three or four times a day from the pay phones at the command post. *The Republic* has an 800 number."

Initially, Villa had been sent to the Grand Canyon for only a day, but she said: "After the first night I wanted to stay. We just knew he was there. My editors left it up to me from day to day if I should stay. They called my husband and asked him to pack some more clothes for me."

She also had the challenge of finding a bed each night in a national park with limited hotel rooms.

"We had to move every night," Villa said. "Tourists with reservations got their rooms. Then law enforcement people got rooms. What was left went to us. Journalists had to stand in line each day, waiting for rooms."

When Villa first got to the canyon, there was only one other reporter from Phoenix. Within a few days, however, newspapers and television stations from throughout the state had sent reporters and photographers. Horning had also become national news, and journalists from throughout the country began arriving at the Grand Canyon.

"By Thursday the law enforcement people started calling regular press conferences two times a day because there were so many reporters," Villa said. "Before that it was easy to get to people.

"It got really difficult to find a new lead every day. There were a couple of days where there was real newsy stuff. A couple of days I looked for features, for things that the other papers weren't getting."

Villa had three deadlines each day. "I didn't get much in the morning that I didn't have the night before," she said. "Horning was a person who moved at night when no one could see him. I usually called in my stories at about 10 p.m., before I went to bed. Then I would be back out at 6 a.m., checking for things that I could add to my story. The search teams worked 12-hour shifts starting at 6 a.m., so 6 to 10 a.m. was a good time to talk to the new teams."

Villa was called back to Phoenix five days after she arrived at the Grand Canyon. The story was dragging, and a second *Republic* reporter was at the canyon covering another story. Her editors decided that Villa would be the one to come home.

Three days later, Horning was captured about 110 miles south of the Grand Canyon. The *East Valley Tribune* in suburban Phoenix reported:

> A defiant and unremorseful Danny Ray Horning smugly cracked jokes after being captured early Sunday near Sedona, 55 days after escaping from the state prison at Florence and embarking on a kidnapping and robbery spree while eluding scores of police.

The reporter who replaced Villa at the Grand Canyon began his story with:

> In the end, it wasn't Rambo that inspired Danny Ray Horning's nearly two-month run from the law across Arizona's high country, but a film titled "Death Hunt."
>
> "I enjoy excitement," an unbowed Horning said Sunday as he was led in shackles to a Coconino County courtroom where he faced 12 felony counts, including three counts of attempted murder. Bond was set at $2 million.
>
> Grinning from ear to ear, the crafty robber whose escapades left Arizona lawmen with red faces told reporters of his survival in the outdoors and how he wanted to win a $1 million ransom and "get the hell out of this area."

Villa said she was greatly disappointed that she was not in northern Arizona when Horning was caught, but she still had a terrific experience. "It was a total adrenaline high," she said. "I talked about it for weeks when I got back. I slept four hours a night for five days and I wasn't tired."

Reporting the news and capturing the mood. As Villa covered the Horning story at the Grand Canyon, she had two major goals: report the latest news first while providing readers with necessary background, and capture the mood of what was going on at the canyon.

"We had to be careful of spoon-fed stuff," she said. "The authorities held press conferences that weren't important."

She gave the following tips for covering a developing story:

- *Look More In-Depth.* "You have to look at things that might not seem important when you first hear them. You have to think a lot to come up with every angle."
- *Make a Conscientious Effort to Work with Sources.* "Talk to as many people as you can. I made friends with the officials. I talked to them other than just for business. I made myself a fixture. I paid a lot of attention to visitors and what people at the next table were talking about."
- *Look for the Unique.* "That's how we scooped the other papers."

Carrying on the Coverage

The Horning story entered its final phases after the convict was captured and returned to prison. Stories were written for months, but only the major stories made it to the front page or the beginning of a newscast. Reporters were no longer covering the story full time, though they were on the lookout for further developments. For example, within a month of Horning's capture, journalists reported the following:

> Horning pleaded not guilty to 12 felony counts.
>
> The state had spent more than $1 million in its largest-ever manhunt.
>
> Horning had gone right through a roadblock at the Grand Canyon because police failed to recognize him.
>
> California prosecutors were planning to seek Horning's extradition from Arizona so that they could pursue a conviction and death sentence against him in the slaying and dismemberment of a 39-year-old man.
>
> The guard who let Horning out of the state prison was fired, a deputy warden was demoted and four other prison employees were disciplined for security breakdowns that led to Horning's escape.
>
> Weeks after Horning was returned to prison, Hollywood's initial interest in turning the manhunt into a television "movie of the week" was fading.

Obviously, the Horning story could continue to develop for months or years. As long as there is interest in him, as long as reporters are checking out leads, there could be further stories.

✔ A Checklist for Developing Stories

The steps that reporters followed in covering the Horning story as it unfolded are typical in any developing story:

- ❑ *Report the Latest News First.* The first stories report the breaking news. Follow-up stories should report the latest developments first.
- ❑ *Report the Original Breaking News High in Any Follow-Ups.* Even in a major occurrence such as the crash of an airliner, reporters cannot

assume that their audiences have read or heard about the event. Reporters must still provide background of the original breaking news, although it does not have to be in the lead. In the early follow-ups, the original news should be in the second, third or fourth paragraph. It can be lower in later follow-ups, but it should still be high in the story.

- ❑ *Advance Each Follow-Up.* Reporters do not cover a developing story merely to report the old news over and over. They must continually search for fresh developments. Each story they write should move into a new phase.
- ❑ *Find as Many Sources as Possible.* When a major story first breaks, there is usually pandemonium as law enforcement officials, gapers, family members and the media rush to the scene. Sources may be easy to find in the beginning, but they may not be reliable. As more and more reporters arrive, and as the officials in charge gain better control, sources will tend to dry up. It is important to get to as many sources as possible, but it also is important to toss out unreliable information.
- ❑ *Get Color.* Major developing stories affect people, which means that stories must reflect the human element. Audiences want to hear from as many of the players as possible. They want to know what trouble the police are having or how the search dogs are trained or how difficult it is to fly a helicopter over the scene. Color can be used throughout a main news story, after the major news is reported. It can also be used in a sidebar or feature, where the color itself may become the lead and the news is supplemental.
- ❑ *Handle Continuing Deadline Pressure.* Reporters covering developing stories cannot quit working once the first deadline passes. They know that there will be more news to report at their next deadline, in an hour, later in the day or tomorrow. They can report only the latest news possible at their deadlines; their stories are never definitive.
- ❑ *Cooperate with Other Reporters.* Journalists often trade information. Of course, they do not give away their leads or key information that they gathered exclusively, but they often help each other find sources or identify developments.

CHAPTER EIGHT

QUOTATIONS AND ATTRIBUTION

Quotations can be more than strings of words with punctuation marks surrounding them. They can generate emotion; they can provide vivid description, anecdotes and explanatory or exclusive material. Quotations can be the soul of a news story or feature. They can bring a dull story to life; and they can make a good story even better. Even ordinary statements, when placed in the context of a story, can send tingles down a person's back.

Writing for the *Independent Florida Alligator,* Greg Lamm, a journalism major at the University of Florida, quoted the convicted killer James Dupree Henry, who was about to be put to death:

(Photo by Steve Manuel)

"My final words are 'I am innocent,' " Henry said softly after he was strapped in the oak chair at 7:02 a.m., two minutes before he was jolted with 2,000 volts of deadly current. He was pronounced dead at 7:09 a.m.

Lamm went on to quote Florida's governor:

Gov. Bob Graham, on the other end of an open telephone line, told prison Superintendent Richard Dugger at 7:03 that no stay would be granted. Graham ended the conversation by saying, "God bless us all."

The short direct quotations selected by Lamm enhance the narration. Lamm's description of the minutes leading up to the electrocution is vivid, but the quotation—"My final words are 'I am innocent' "—makes readers realize that there is more to the death scene than a lethal electrical charge. A life is being taken, and a person is being given a last chance to reflect on his death. The human angle is further emphasized in the governor's "God bless us all."

Quotations can make a reader want to continue with a story. The challenge is learning how and when to use them.

Using Quotations

Types of Quotations

Statements can be handled as:

- Complete direct quotations
- Partial quotations
- Indirect or paraphrased quotations

Assume that during an interview, an attorney, John Jones, says:

The Supreme Court will consider some of the most significant First Amendment cases of the decade during the coming term. Journalists have grown increasingly concerned about what they perceive to be the anti-press bias of the current court. Therefore, journalists will be watching the court with particular interest this term.

Let's see how this could be handled in each of the three ways listed above.

Direct Quotations

The reporter could consider the three sentences to be so well stated, vivid and important that they are worthy of a **complete direct quotation,** which provides readers with the precise language of the attorney. Attribution would then be placed after the first sentence:

"The Supreme Court will consider some of the most significant First Amendment cases of the decade during the coming term," attorney John Jones said Monday. "Journalists have grown increasingly concerned about what they perceive to be the anti-press bias of the current court. Therefore, journalists will be watching the court with particular interest this term."

Partial Quotations

The reporter could also conclude that only portions of the three sentences are worthy of direct quotation. In that case, **partial quotations** would be used. Partial quotations alter the language—but not the meaning—of much of the statement while retaining specific parts of the original sentences. The reporter here could make good use of partial quotations by writing:

> Attorney John Jones said Monday that the Supreme Court will hear "some of the most significant First Amendment cases of the decade" when it convenes for the coming term. Jones said that journalists will be particularly interested in the court's actions because of "what they perceive to be the anti-press bias of the current court."

Reporters should make judicious use of partial quotations, striving not to overuse them in bunched parcels, which can be confusing to the reader, or to use them merely because of a failure to get a complete quotation. Under those circumstances, it is generally better to paraphrase.

Indirect and Paraphrased Quotations

Finally, the reporter could conclude that the entire three-sentence comment would be handled best as an **indirect quotation.** In that case, he or she could *paraphrase* the attorney's statement. Being careful to provide attribution, the reporter could write:

> Some of the decade's most important First Amendment cases will come before the Supreme Court this term, attorney John Jones said Monday. He said the cases will be of particular interest to journalists because many of them view the court as being biased against the media.

When and How to Quote

Whether statements should be handled as direct quotations, as partial quotations or as indirect quotations depends on a number of factors.

Whether to quote or to paraphrase is a major consideration reporters face after conducting an interview or listening to a speech. Some reporters use direct quotations sparingly because they do not want to turn their stories completely over to their sources. Others use quotations as often as possible because only then can the source speak directly to the audience.

Quotation marks around a sentence mean that the words are exactly—or nearly exactly—what the person said. Generally, most editors allow reporters to clean up grammar or to take out profanities in direct quotations. The AP Stylebook says: "Quotations normally should be corrected to avoid the errors in grammar and word usage that often occur unnoticed when someone is speaking but are embarrassing in print."

It is a good idea to sprinkle direct quotations throughout a story, letting the source talk to the readers. However, it is important to make sure that the direct quotations are accurate. When in doubt, paraphrase what the source said. Remember, when paraphrasing what someone said, make sure to use attribution. Tell the readers *who* is behind the statement.

Never make up quotations or paraphrases. This should go without saying, but some journalists have confessed to such a practice. Also, reporters sometimes resort to a "words in your mouth" technique, especially when a source has never been interviewed. Be careful here, because this is a point when it becomes too easy to make up quotations. For instance, a reporter is interviewing an inarticulate person who seems to answer every question with "yep." The reporter appreciates the terse responses and the easy note taking, but a story cannot be filled with "yeps." The reporter says to the person, "Did the pain feel like a sharp, blinding jab in your head?" The response is, "Yep, that is how it was." The reporter then paraphrases the source: *Talmond said that the pain felt like a sharp, blinding jab in the head.* Use this technique when it is needed, but use it sparingly and never fake it and pass it off as a direct quotation.

As Pulitzer Prize-winning journalist Michael Gartner has noted: "The good writer knows how to use quotes. He knows to use them as punctuation, as transition, as reinforcement. He knows never to use them redundantly, long-windedly or confusingly. The quote . . . is just newspaperdom's sound bite—a device to move the piece along, to get the reader from here to there—by adding a dollop of fact or a dash of amusement. The good writer always uses quotes, and always uses them sparingly. But it takes a good ear to get a good quote."

Guidelines for Direct Quotations

Here are some guidelines to consider when deciding whether or not to quote directly.

1: Use direct quotations for specific, vivid statements. Do not waste a direct quotation on a statement such as, "We will consider several important items at our next regularly scheduled council meeting." That statement should be paraphrased and attributed. Direct quotations should be saved for this type of statement: "Our next council meeting will be a blockbuster," Thornton said. "The zoning issue must—and will—be hammered out at that session."

Dan Prescher, writing for *The Gateway,* the campus newspaper at the University of Nebraska at Omaha, interviewed a clinical professor of pediatrics at the Creighton Medical School and a specialist in obstetrics and gynecology at the Women's Services Clinic in Omaha about their reactions to an antiabortion film. Prescher could have paraphrased a quotation from Paul Byrne, the clinical professor of pediatrics, by writing: *Byrne said that all people have a right to life.* But Prescher chose to quote directly:

> "The basic right is the right to life," said Byrne. "The mother has a right to life. The baby has a right to life. Without life there are no other rights."

This direct quotation has punch; it is strong and vivid. Prescher was correct in using Byrne's precise words.

Prescher also chose a vivid quotation from G. W. Orr, the specialist in obstetrics and gynecology. Again, Prescher could have used a paraphrase such as: *Orr said that the question of where life begins can be answered only by individuals. He said that people should have the opportunity to decide for themselves.* But the reporter chose to use the direct quotation:

"What people need is the truth. In the area of when human life begins . . . it'll be answered by individuals in view of their own moral and religious viewpoints. Hopefully [it] will not be answered by people who try to intimidate and coerce everyone to do what they believe."

In a story published in *The Birmingham* (Ala.) *News,* Tom Gordon reported charges and countercharges made by political opponents. One candidate was quoted as saying:

"While our boys were dying in the rice paddies in Vietnam, my opponent, . . . long hair and all, was in the classroom giving lectures on the immorality of America's involvement in Vietnam."

Gordon then quoted the response of the other candidate:

"My opponent's charges are trash and ridiculous."

Direct quotations are seldom stronger than this.

2: Use direct quotations for descriptive statements. John Conway focused on Sen. Jesse Helms, R-N.C., in an article the reporter wrote for the University of North Carolina's *Daily Tar Heel.* Conway chose the following direct quotation from Helms to describe the senator's feelings about his father:

"My father had a fifth-grade education. Never made over $7,500 in any year of his life. He was a soul of honor," Helms says, grinning pleasantly at the thought. "If I had my one wish, I wish I could be as decent a human being as he was."

Later in the story, Conway quoted Helms' reaction to a legislative bill that the senator voted against:

"But it [the bill] had nothing to do with voting rights," Helms counters. "That was already established. It was instead a wolf in sheep's clothing.

"It had a good title, but the guts of it were bad."

This quotation, too, enables readers to hear Helms, vividly in his own words, describe his feelings about the proposed legislation.

Scottie Vickery, in an article published in *The Birmingham News* about the suicide of a teen-ager who was awaiting a verdict in a capital murder trial, used a direct quotation to put the impact of the death into vigorous perspective:

> "This just ripped open a wound we thought was healing," Mayor Judy Dickinson said.

Later, in the same story, Vickery quoted a city official:

> Police Chief Larry Bice summed it up this way: "You've got a brilliant boy that got life without parole, and you've got another brilliant boy lying over in the morgue and one in prison for life. And then you've got Missy [a 26-year-old woman who had been shot to death], lying over there in the grave."

3: Use direct quotations for inner feelings. Michelle Perron, in an article published in *The Daily Reveille* at Louisiana State University, quoted a gay student:

> "They [his friends who found out he was gay] didn't have any cause to be afraid of me. . . . I myself was afraid to walk into a gay bar the first time I did," he said. "I had no idea what to expect. I was afraid there would be some wild orgy going on or something. But instead what I found out was that there were a lot of normal people there just like me. That's when I first realized I could still be a normal person and be gay."

Quotations packed with such feeling do not come along in every story. When they do, make the most of them.

4: Use direct quotations to capture personality. Kelly Frankeny wrote a story about Dr. "Red" Duke, a native of Texas and professor of surgery at the medical school of the University of Texas in Houston. Duke offers free medical advice in his news health reports on television. Note the third paragraph of Frankeny's story, which was published in *The Daily Texan:*

> He's Dr. "Red" Duke.
>
> A television star?
>
> "Shit no. I have a hard time with that," says the 56-year-old doctor who's taken to the airwaves to promote "wellness." "I call myself an overexposed old man."

The story went on to say that Duke wanted to pass along health information to his viewers like an "old country schoolteacher." The quotations help to paint a picture of Duke's personality. (See "Observe taste in quotations," on page 106, for a discussion on the use of profanities in direct quotations.)

5: Use direct quotations to supplement statements of fact. In a story about Monte Johnson, athletic director of the University of Kansas, Matt DeGalan wrote in the *Daily Kansan* what Johnson said about the firing of basketball coach Ted

Owens and football coach Don Fambrough: that it was difficult. But the reporter knew that such a statement should not stand by itself. DeGalan followed up with these direct quotations from Johnson:

> "In my case it was extremely painful, because I cared about those people just like I would about one of my friends," he said. "I think the only thing that probably allows you to survive something like that is that you have to believe what you are doing is right.
>
> "There's still emotion involved in it. There's still frustration involved in it and there's still mixed reaction to it, but I just have to go ahead and put my head on the pillow at night and say I made the most conscientious decision I could make with the facts I had available, and nobody will give you total credit for that."

6: Use direct quotations for dialogue. In a personality profile on the television investigative reporter John Camp, Donna Moss of Louisiana State University's *Daily Reveille* used dialogue to illustrate how Camp got into the business. Moss recounted an early career exchange between Camp and the manager of a small radio station:

> "Camp, you ever done any news?"
> "Nope," he quickly shot back.
> "You ever want to do any news?"
> "Nope."
> "Well, you're going to do the news."
> "Okay."

7: Use direct quotations to reduce attributions. Assume, for example, that Kareem Abdul-Jabbar, retired star of the Los Angeles Lakers and the leading scorer in the history of the National Basketball Association, said this after a Laker victory over the Boston Celtics in a championship series game:

> I am uncomfortable with the threatening talk by players from both teams, with the escalation of rugged play in the games and with the possibility of a brawl at any time. I think basketball is to be played as a game of beauty, not as an exhibition of brawn. But if someone brings a tire iron to the game, I am forced to respond in kind.

If Jabbar's statement is handled as a direct three-sentence quotation, it would read like this (with attribution following only the first sentence):

> "I am uncomfortable with the threatening talk by players from both teams, with the escalation of rugged play in the games and with the possibility of a brawl at any time," Kareem Abdul-Jabbar said. "I think basketball is to be played as a game of beauty, not as an exhibition of brawn. But if someone brings a tire iron to the game, I am forced to respond in kind."

If Jabbar's statement is used as an indirect quotation, attribution would have to be provided for every sentence. This could get cumbersome. It does help, however, to vary the writing by alternating the placement of the attribution. For example:

> Kareem Abdul-Jabbar said that he is not comfortable with the talk, the escalation of rugged play and the promise of a brawl. Basketball is a game of beauty, not brawn, he said. But he added that if tire iron tactics are used by the opposition, he will respond in kind.

Pitfalls to Avoid in Quoting

Reporters can easily fall into traps when quoting sources. Here are some guidelines to consider:

1: Beware of inaccuracies in quotations. Reporters should verify quotations that sound suspect. If, for example, there is a bad connection or background noise when interviewing by telephone, always verify the quotation. This will reduce the chance of error. It is easy to say: "I was distracted by the noise on the line. Could you repeat that for me, please?" Or: "Let me make sure I have that comment right. Could I read it back to you?"

Reporters should check further if a remark that the source verifies still sounds suspect. For example, the manager of a local factory said: "My company employs 250 people—more than any other firm in town." The reporter asks for verification; and the manager confirms the quotation. However, the Chamber of Commerce figures show that his firm employs 200 workers—and there are 12 companies in town that employ more.

If follow-ups reveal that the quotation is inaccurate, the reporter could call the source back to ask if there is an explanation for the discrepancy, or the quotation could be left out.

2: Beware of rambling quotations. Some sources love to hear themselves talk. If their long, drawn-out **rambling quotations** bore the reporter, chances are they will also bore the audience. Assume that a judge has said:

> Because of the sensationalism surrounding the trial, I want to make sure that the accused receives a fair hearing. Now, of course, I understand that the press will want to cover the trial extensively. And, according to *Richmond Newspapers* v. *Virginia,* the press has a right to attend public trials, absent overriding considerations. Now, good members of the press, you won't find a more fervent defender of First Amendment rights than I am, but, as a judge sworn to perform my duties fairly, let me tell you that I will do everything in my power to see to it that the accused receives a fair trial, for he, too, has basic Sixth Amendment rights that guarantee him as much.

The judge might have said all this—and the reporter might have dutifully written it down. But getting accurate direct quotations does not carry with it a license to bore readers unnecessarily. Under these circumstances, paraphrase the statement and possibly supplement it with some partial quotations.

3: Beware of incomprehensible quotations. When reporters interview lawyers, physicians, engineers or research scientists, chances are that some of the quotations gathered will not be understandable to lay readers. In these instances, reporters must work diligently to paraphrase the quotation into understandable terms, to get the source to rephrase it or to supplement it with an explanatory paragraph.

Edward Sylvester, a journalism professor at Arizona State University and the author of three books based on science research and extensive interviews with scientists, said: "Science writing may be one of the few areas of reporting in which writers frequently show long quotes and even whole stories to sources before publication. The reason is that the material is often so complex and shades of meaning can change intention so much that even a close associate might put a statement in a way the source would consider quite wrong. On the other hand, as a popular writer/reporter, you cannot quote technical material in the precise yet dense language of the science specialty. The result of these two demands—for precision yet simplicity—is often a 'negotiated settlement,' in which the writer attempts to translate a difficult quote on the spot: 'Could we say that . . . ?' Or, 'In other words, you've found that. . . .' Often as not, the answer is no, with an attempt to elucidate by the scientist and a reattempt to interpret by the reporter.

"This process is all the more important when you consider how often the words 'breakthrough,' or 'major discovery' or, most value-loaded of all, 'cure' appear in the press. It is extremely important to the public's interest and its perception of science that such words be used with the greatest care. To further complicate matters, the journalist who has just checked technical information and quotations with a source may in the future be in an adversarial relationship with the same source and be unwilling to reveal all information in hand until publication."

4: Do not reconstruct quotations. Do not add things to a quotation to make it better or to cover up your failure to get the entire quotation. Use it merely as a partial quotation or as an indirect quotation. Do not take a partial quotation (an incomplete sentence) and add your words to make it a complete sentence.

5: Avoid using fragmentary quotations. Fragmentary quotations—quotations used in extremely small parcels that are spread throughout a paragraph—serve no purpose. When set in type, they will look confusing:

> Sen. Douglas Johnson said he wanted to take care of the problem "immediately." He said it was a "pressing issue" that should not be put "on hold." According to the senator, the issue will "come before the Legislature" before the week "is half over." He said he is "anxious" to go about "settling" the matter.

The best advice on using fragmentary quotations is: Don't.

6: Avoid illogicalities in presenting quotations. Assume that a source has said: "I intend to pursue this matter with all the energy I can summon." Do not write: Johnson said that he will "pursue this matter with all the energy he can summon." Instead, write: Johnson said, "I intend to pursue this matter with all the energy I can summon." Or: "I intend to pursue this matter with all the energy I can summon," Johnson said. Remember: Quotation marks mean that you are using the precise words of the speaker. The speaker would not have referred to himself as "he" in a direct quotation.

7: Observe taste in quotations. The Associated Press Stylebook addresses the use of obscenities, profanities and vulgarities: "Do not use them in stories unless they are part of direct quotations and there is a compelling reason for them."

8: Be alert to offensive language. The AP always alerts editors to stories that contain profanities, indicating that the language might be offensive to some readers. Editors can then decide whether to leave it in or to delete it. The AP also tries to limit the offensive language to paragraphs that can be deleted easily.

The AP Stylebook further notes:

> In reporting profanity that normally would use the words *damn* or *god,* lowercase *god* and use the following forms: *damn, damn it, goddamn it.* Do not, however, change the offending words to euphemisms. Do not, for example, change *damn it* to *darn it.*
>
> If a full quote that contains profanity, obscenity or vulgarity cannot be dropped but there is no compelling reason for the offensive language, replace letters of an offensive word with a hyphen. The word *damn,* for example, would become *d*—— or ——.

The Washington Post's Deskbook on Style notes that the test of whether to use an obscenity should be " 'why use it?' rather than 'why not use it?' " *The Post*'s stylebook urges reporters to check individual cases with appropriate editors. *The Post* advocates, when a profanity must be used, the "s—— form, which serves the purpose of communicating without jarring sensibilities any more than necessary."

Policies on the use of profanity can vary among news media. Always check with a supervising editor if you are unsure of how to handle a quotation.

9: Be certain when using dialect. The use of dialect can also be a matter of taste; dialect often appears to ridicule the subject in a condescending way. The AP Stylebook points out that dialect—"the form of language peculiar to a region or a group, usually in matters of pronunciation or syntax"—should not be used "unless it is clearly pertinent to a story."

The New York Times Manual of Style and Usage advises: "Unless a reporter has a sharp ear and accurate notes he would do well to avoid trying to render dialect."

Use of Soundbites for Broadcast

For broadcast journalists, **soundbites,** or **actualities,** are the electronic equivalent of quotations. Like quotations in print, soundbites are verbatim from the source. A soundbite is a short snippet from a recorded interview (either on audio or videotape) that is placed strategically in the story. Soundbites serve the same function as quotations by using the news source's own words to add information, to add authenticity to the story or to make the story more colorful or personalized.

Soundbites, however, should be brief. Broadcast journalists keep their stories as short as possible because of the demands of radio and TV news (see Chapter 17). A radio story may be no longer than 40 seconds, while a TV story may run one minute or slightly more. Some news directors request that soundbites be no longer than 15 seconds and stories often have no more than two soundbites. That means soundbites should "season" the story, and not be used as the main entrée.

Framing the soundbite in the story is just as important as the soundbite itself. The sentence preceding the soundbite should be a **blind lead-in**. A blind lead-in does not foretell a soundbite. That is, a blind lead-in should be a smooth transition into the soundbite, but the soundbite should not be necessary to finish the idea or thought presented in the lead-in.

Notice in the following example how the soundbite (in quotation marks) finishes the sentence or idea presented in the lead-in.

. . . HEALTH SCIENTIST REID STEINHAUS SAYS TESTING CHILD DAYCARE CENTERS THIS YEAR IS IMPORTANT, BECAUSE. . . .

"CHILDREN'S LUNGS, HEARTS AND OTHER SENSITIVE TISSUES ARE STILL DEVELOPING, AND THEY'RE MORE SUSCEPTIBLE TO DAMAGE FROM RADON. SO WE WANT TO SEE WHAT TYPE OF ENVIRONMENT THEY'RE IN."

STEINHAUS SAYS A 10-THOUSAND-DOLLAR FEDERAL GRANT WILL FUND THE TESTING.

Here's how the lead-in should be rewritten to make it a blind lead-in.

. . . HEALTH SCIENTIST REID STEINHAUS SAYS RADON MAY POSE A GREATER RISK TO CHILDREN, SO DAYCARE CENTERS WILL BE TESTED.

"CHILDREN'S LUNGS, HEARTS AND OTHER SENSITIVE TISSUES . . ."

STEINHAUS SAYS A 10-THOUSAND-DOLLAR FEDERAL GRANT WILL FUND THE TESTING.

There are several reasons for using blind lead-ins (see Chapter 17), but the foremost is ease of editing. Often reporters use shorter versions of stories without soundbites. In the first example, the lead-in would have to be edited to make sense without the soundbite. Such editing is not necessary in the second example when the soundbite is removed.

Attributing Quotations

When and How to Attribute

Attribution tells readers the source of information. Not every piece of information, however, requires attribution. In the following lead paragraphs, it is assumed that a reliable source—either an individual or a government entity—provided the factual information and that the reporters knew beyond a reasonable doubt that what they were writing was true:

Evansville will earmark $750,000 or more for resurfacing and repairing city streets this year, several times the amount spent last year. (*The Evansville,* Ind., *Press*)

The drought in south central Nebraska has forced some area cattlemen to partially liquidate their herds or find alternative feed supplies. (*The Hastings,* Neb., *Tribune*)

Attribution for some factual information would be ludicrous:

Omaha Burke blasted Lincoln High 81-54 in a non-conference high school basketball game Friday night, according to the team's statistician.

Attribution is needed, however, when an opinion or some other information subject to change or controversy is cited. For example:

> The Trans Alaska Pipeline may have to be shut down temporarily so that a sagging section of pipe under the Dietrich River can be bypassed, according to the line's operators. (*Fairbanks,* Alaska, *Daily News-Miner*)

Verbs of Attribution

Because *said* is a neutral verb, it should nearly always be used in the attribution for news stories. *Added* can also be used because it, too, is an **objective verb of attribution.** Susan Sheehan, writing in *The New York Times Magazine,* noted that the syndicated columnist Jack Anderson often allowed subjective perception to dictate his choice of verbs of attribution. She wrote: "Anderson's characters rarely have something to say, state or comment upon; they whine, huff, snort, grump, mutter, bare their fangs or worse." Such a style might be appropriate for opinion columnists such as Anderson or in some feature stories, but it is not appropriate for reporters who write straight news stories.

Using *said* as the verb of attribution might seem repetitive and unimaginative, but reporters do not have to bombard readers with it after every sentence. Some newspapers continue to follow the rule that loose-hanging quotations (quotations without an attributive tag) are unacceptable. Other newspapers allow them, however, if a source is quoted in two or more consecutive paragraphs. Here, attribution at the end of the first paragraph effectively tells readers who the speaker is:

> "I think that the budget will be approved at our next meeting," council member Susan Long said.
>
> "I am sure that the special-interest groups will be out in force. We'll have to weigh both sides carefully.
>
> "I'm confident that we'll arrive at the correct decision."
>
> Long added that she thought this year's budget was the most explosive issue the council had dealt with in four years.

Here are some verbs of attribution that generally should be avoided:

asserted	demanded	opined
bellowed	emphasized	stammered
contended	harangued	stated
cried	hinted	stressed
declared	maintained	

Because verbs of attribution refer to speech and not to conduct or action, they should *not* be used in ways that suggest physical impossibilities:

> "This is the best day of my life," Jones smiled.
>
> "It will be a difficult task," Johnson grimaced.

The reporter should write:

> "This is the best day of my life," Jones said with a smile.
>
> "It will be a difficult task," Johnson said with a grimace.

Verbs of attribution can be found in most stories. A portion of an article by Emil Venere, published in the *The East Valley Tribune* in suburban Phoenix, is reprinted below. Verbs of attribution are italicized.

> Democratic gubernatorial hopeful Bill Schulz *told* a group of supporters Saturday that inferior education for poor people and prison overcrowding are tied together and must be solved by first improving inner-city school programs.
>
> Schulz, 54, also *said* the state has failed to provide care for chronically depressed people, another factor associated with the failure to rehabilitate jail inmates and help indigent children on the road to success.
>
> The as-yet-unofficial Democratic candidate for governor spoke to about 75 members of the East Valley Democratic Breakfast Club during a regular 8 a.m. meeting in Mesa. The founder and former president of WRS Investments, an apartment-management firm in Arizona, *said* he intends to formally announce his candidacy in September.
>
> Schulz has toured eight states, speaking to governors and officials about pressing economic problems, he *said*, and expects to visit two more by the end of this year.
>
> "How can one person be really equipped to deal with all of them (issues)?" he *asked.*
>
> By studying the ways in which other states have dealt with the same kinds of problems, he *answered.*
>
> "We have got nothing in this state that can't be fixed," he *said.*
>
> Calling high costs for prison operation and inmate overcrowding a horrendous problem, he *said*, "We're going to have to raise taxes just to operate our prisons."
>
> Arizona is spending roughly $140 million, including special appropriations, to run its prisons this fiscal year. Next year, including all legislative appropriations, that figure will be closer to $167 million, he *said.*
>
> "We're getting a lousy return," he *said.* At an average annual cost of $18,000 an inmate, prisoners who are not rehabilitated are a constant drag on the state's economy, while many students from indigent families are likely to become dropouts and end up in jail because of Phoenix's poor inner-city school programs.
>
> "They're going to be tax users rather than tax producers," he *said.* "The people who need the education the most are getting the worst education."

Identification in Attributions

Seldom is a person so well-known that his or her name will stand by itself in a lead. Thus, attribution usually identifies the source by title and name. For example:

> Parking fees at the Fairbanks International Airport are scheduled to become a reality by early summer, according to airport manager Doyle Ruff. (*Fairbanks,* Alaska, *Daily News-Miner*)

> Measures ordered Monday by a federal judge to prevent suicide at the El Paso County Jail were already being taken or were being planned, Sheriff Bernard Berry said Thursday. *(The Colorado Springs Gazette Telegraph)*

Sometimes, to streamline the writing, only the title of the person is used in the lead. The person's name is used in a subsequent paragraph. For example:

> A mining company in the Circle Mining District was fined and forced to shut down its operation last summer not because it violated regulations any more than other miners, but because it dared to point it out, according to its Fairbanks attorney.
>
> Lynette and Dexter Clark were forced by the Environmental Protection Agency to shut down work at their mine last August after they refused to apply for a discharge permit. The EPA and the Clarks' attorney, William Satterberg, settled the dispute in December, but Satterberg said he is dissatisfied with the outcome. (*Fairbanks,* Alaska, *Daily News-Miner*)

Titles should also be used for attribution in leads when an opinion has been expressed by more than one person. Note also that in attributing statements to more than one person, direct quotations are not used:

> Steps have been taken to improve leadership, morale and communications within the Colorado Springs Police Department in the past year, but internal problems have not disappeared, five City Council members said Monday. *(The Colorado Springs Gazette Telegraph)*

Attribution in leads can lack specificity if a spokesperson is repeating an official position:

> An explosion and fire killed two crewmen on the aircraft carrier *USS America,* the Navy said Sunday. (The Associated Press)

In paragraphs that follow the lead, first-reference attribution should contain the person's name and title or some other means of identification. For example:

> "I didn't know her well, but I thought that she was a wonderful person," said a neighbor, Helen Johnson.
>
> "She was one of the finest students I ever taught," said Gerald Sylvester, a geography professor at State University.

Reporters also need to be aware of what some editors call "hearsay attribution." This occurs when a statement is made to sound as though it came from one source, but it actually came from another. For example: *Smith said that he knocked one mugger down and then chased the other man two blocks before bringing him to the ground with a diving tackle.* Actually, the reporter was relying on a police report and had never talked to Smith. It is dangerous, as well as misleading, to write a sentence that merely implies attribution. If the statement sounds like a good angle, check with the source. In this case, the reporter should have given Smith a call, or the sentence should have read: *Police said Smith told them that he. . . .*

Placement of Attributions: Six Guidelines

Attribution usually *follows* the information because what is said is normally more important than who said it. For example:

> What appears to be an important advance in developing an X-ray laser space weapon powered by a nuclear bomb has been made by scientists at the Lawrence Livermore National Laboratory, federal scientists said Tuesday. *(The New York Times)*

Sometimes, however, the attribution can be of such significance or relevance that it *precedes* the information. For example:

> An Illinois Central Gulf Railroad official assured Henderson and area businessmen that industries served by that company will continue to have rail service. (*The Gleaner,* Henderson, Ky.)

The following guidelines should be considered when handling attribution for direct quotations.

1: If a single sentence is quoted directly, attribution usually follows the quotation. Thus:

> "The prices will continue to escalate," he said.

It is permissible, however, to introduce the sentence with its attribution:

> He said, "The prices will continue to escalate."

2: If multiple sentences are quoted directly, attribution normally follows the first sentence. The reader should not have to meander through two or more complete sentences before being told who the speaker is. Note how confusing the following is:

> "The proposal to change school district boundaries needs to be put into operation immediately. This change is necessary to distribute students evenly throughout the various schools in our system," Superintendent Henry Smith said.
>
> "School district boundary lines do not have to be changed. Many of the building principals are merely afraid that their teachers will have to work harder if enrollments at their schools increase. The whole proposal is the self-serving idea of a handful of principals," said school board member Ben Johnson.

3: When speakers change, new attribution should be placed before the first quoted sentence. Note the confusion in the following example:

> "We must raise tuition to generate funds to pay adjunct professors so we can open up new course sections," said Susanne Graham, a member of the board of regents. "It's the only way we can meet the needs of our students."
>
> "An increase in tuition is the last thing students need," said senior class President Lisa Kelly.

The change of speakers should have been noted immediately. For example:

> "We must raise tuition to generate funds to pay adjunct professors so we can open up new course sections," said Susanne Graham, a member of the board of regents. "It's the only way we can meet the needs of our students."
>
> Senior class President Lisa Kelly said, "An increase in tuition is the last thing students need."

Often, though, a transition sentence is the most effective way to let readers know when speakers change:

> "We must raise tuition to generate funds to pay adjunct professors so we can open up new course sections," said Susanne Graham, a member of the board of regents. "It's the only way we can meet the needs of our students."
>
> Senior class President Lisa Kelly saw it differently.
>
> "An increase in tuition is the last thing students need," she said.

4: Attribution can precede a multiple-sentence direct quotation (although many editors prefer that attribution always follow the first sentence). When this occurs, the attribution should be followed by a colon:

> Council member John P. Jones said: "We expect to ratify the new budget at our next meeting. We think we have worked out all the problems. It has been a difficult four weeks."

5: Attribution to the same speaker should not be used more than once in a quotation, even if the quotation continues for several paragraphs. This construction should be avoided:

> "We expect to ratify the new budget at our next meeting," council member John P. Jones said. "We think we have worked out all the problems," he noted. "It has been a difficult four weeks," he observed.

6: If a partial quotation is followed by a complete direct quotation, use attribution between them. Thus:

> No decision has been made on whether Israel will attack "with all we have," Eitan said. "We are sitting and waiting."

Anonymous Sources

Each time reporters conduct interviews, they face the risk that their sources will request anonymity. Therefore, reporters must learn how to deal with people who are willing to provide information only if their names are not used in the story. Because every story is different, there are no hard and fast rules on dealing with requests for anonymity, but there are general guidelines to follow.

Guidelines for Reporters

Be up-front with the source. Establish rules for the interview *before* it begins. Then there should be no misunderstanding about how the material can be used. Never assume that sources, particularly sources who are not accustomed to working with the media, understand the established conventions that deal with the use of material.

These conventions are:

- *On the Record.* All material can be used, complete with the name of the source and his or her identification. For example: "We expect a quick settlement of the strike," John P. Johnson, secretary of labor, said.
- *Off the Record.* The material cannot be used. Period. Reporters must decide whether the information they could potentially gain under these circumstances is worth it. Often, reporters refuse to accept information off the record, choosing instead to ferret it out from another source.
- *On Background.* The material can be used, but attribution by name cannot be provided. For example: "We expect a quick settlement of the strike," a high-ranking Labor Department official said.
- *On Deep Background.* The material can be used, but not in direct quotations. Also, the material cannot be attributed to the source. For example: *A quick settlement of the strike is expected.* Reporters can, however, seek verification from other sources for material on deep background and possibly get these other sources to agree to being quoted. If no verification can be found, the reporter must decide whether to take a chance on using the material. Editors should also be consulted in these circumstances. If the material proves false or incorrect, the reporter and the newspaper or broadcast medium are left holding the bag.

It is a good practice to tell the source immediately, "I am a reporter working for the *River City News.*" Then it is the source's responsibility to practice self-control, because he or she should realize that everything that is said will be on the record, unless other arrangements have been worked out before the interview.

Case-by-Case Decisions

Some sources know that they are talking to a reporter and still ask for anonymity after they have talked too long and too much. When this happens—and it does happen quite often—reporters must decide whether to use the name anyway or to respect the source's wishes.

In making this decision, reporters must consider the importance of the story, the value of the source and the editorial policies of their employers.

For example, suppose that a prosecuting attorney in a murder case calls to tell you that the defendant has agreed to plead guilty to a charge of killing a 22-year-old woman. The attorney gives you the information, but then says, "The judge has told us not to discuss this, so don't use my name—this is on deep background."

You could say, "Look, you've worked with reporters before; you can't establish a non-attribution ground rule after you've given me the information." Or, you could reason that you will need the attorney again as a source. It is just as easy to make a few more calls to confirm the information as it is to use the attorney's name in the story and risk getting your source into trouble or losing your source. Once the material is checked with other reliable sources, your lead can say (without attribution):

> A Brookfield man has agreed to plead guilty to a charge of killing a 22-year-old woman.

Or you can use this construction:

> A Brookfield man has agreed to plead guilty to a charge of killing a 22-year-old woman, according to sources close to the case.

Developing a strong network of reliable sources is one key to being an effective reporter; this means that you will sometimes have to acquiesce when a source requests anonymity.

Sometimes anonymous sources are government or corporate officials who do not want their names used because they believe that their bosses or the institutions for which they work should have credit for the statement. For instance, "City Hall said today" may be the mayor's top aide discussing the police department's negotiations with City Hall for additional funding. The reporters know who said it, but they use the nameless attribution because this was the condition for the interview.

Anonymous sources are also valuable because they can lead you to other sources; do not turn them off simply because they do not want their names used. Explain to them the policies of the newspaper regarding the use of anonymous sources and the importance of their being identified in the story. Often people can be persuaded to go on the record if they realize how vital the story is and that without an identified source it may never be printed. If nothing works, look for other sources, using the unnamed source for guidance.

Quill published a story by John Doe, a person who the magazine said wanted "to remain anonymous, mostly because his bosses don't approve of anonymous sources, and he'd like to preserve his job." The magazine said that Doe covered stories of "national and international importance."

Doe wrote: "In these days of the credibility gap, decent, clean-living reporters are supposed to abhor . . . nameless sources. But if they never quoted one, their copy would lose much of its value."

Doe said that reporters for large news media, in order to gain access to and publish certain information, routinely use anonymous sources. "Refusal to do so would deprive the public of much information it needs to form opinions about national and world affairs," he wrote. Doe emphasized, however, that "a

conscientious reporter has to judge the reliability of the source, the facts that the source is professing to give and especially whether or not the source has a motive to distort the facts for a cause or for personal gain."

Policies on Anonymous Sources

Naturally, policies on the use of anonymous sources will vary. The policies discussed in this section, however, are typical.

"Reporters must name the source of information in every story whenever possible," the *Denver Post*'s policy states. "Exceptions must be thoroughly discussed with editors and house counsel." The paper also tells its reporters to avoid using unnamed sources if possible and, when confronted with them, to seek alternative sources and documentation.

The *Bangor* (Maine) *Daily News* instructs its reporters: "If reporter and editor see clear need for confidentiality, the reason for anonymity should be explained in the story as fully as possible short of identification. If the reason isn't good, scrap the source and the quote." The newspaper goes on to say: "Information from an anonymous source should be used only if at least one source substantiates the information."

At the *Detroit Free Press,* reporters are not allowed to promise news sources absolute confidentiality on their own. At least one editor must know the identity of the source, and it is up to a supervising editor, in consultation with the reporter, to decide whether or not to use the unnamed source.

In 1998, when *The Washington Post* was being criticized by some for too much reliance on anonymous sources, Managing Editor Robert Kaiser said that his newspaper would continue to adhere to its policy of calling "for maximum possible identification of sources, at least two sources of confidential information and strong efforts by our reporters to get sources on the record."

He wrote in a column: "Occasionally, *The Post* will run a story that seems to be based on a single human source. In its text, you will read only that the information came, for example, from 'a source knowledgeable about the situation.' This is a frustrating attribution, to be sure. But in this media-saturated age, many knowledgeable sources learn how to protect themselves and box us into a corner where we must choose between using their information with vague attribution, or not sharing it with readers at all."

Noting that "each situation that arises has to be dealt with individually" and that it is not always possible to provide information from named sources Kaiser wrote: "We know we will be held accountable for our accuracy. We hope that readers will judge *The Post* by its reliability. Nothing is more important to us than our credibility. We realize many readers are infuriated by anonymous sourcing. Many journalists are, too. But we also think our readers should know that sometimes granting anonymity to sources is the only way to acquire publishable information on matters of interest and importance to them. So, if we have confidence in our information, we will print it."

Information and Quotes from Internet and E-Mail Sources

The AP Stylebook warns: "Be acutely aware of the potential dangers of using information from Internet and e-mail sources. All such electronic information—from computer disk data to e-mail to material posted on the Internet—falls into the 'tangible form' category that is subject to copyright protection as well as libel guidelines."

The Stylebook also notes: "When a story mentions a specific Web site or Web service, include the Internet address, the URL **(Uniform Resource Locator)**, within the text. This is essential information for the reader. Add Internet addresses (URLs) to the end of a story when they provide additional information, but aren't specifically referred to in a story."

In addition to listing various Internet, computer and telecommunications terms, the Stylebook provides some valuable guidelines for assessing Web sources:

> Do not mistake the Web for an encyclopedia, and the search engine for a table of contents. Any information you find on the Web should be assessed with the same care that you use for everything else. In particular, check these points:
>
> - Who is sponsoring the page? Is the author identifiable? (Stay away from anonymous pages.) Is there contact information in case you want to follow up? Is the domain type (*.edu* or *.gov*, for example) appropriate for the information provided? (Web sites set up by professional groups, for example, are generally more reliable than personal home pages.)
>
>   One tool is the use of *whois*, which can be found at *www.netsol.com/cgi-bin/whois/whois*. With a brief query, it allows a user to immediately see who is behind a Web site. It also provides contact information.
> - What is the source of the information? The source should be clearly stated, whether original or borrowed. Is it a primary or secondary source? If you're looking for the text of the Americans with Disabilities Act, you may find it on the Web site of an advocacy group, but you're better off checking the congressional Web site.
>
> For accuracy, corroborate with multiple sites whenever possible.
>
> - Based on what you know, how accurate does the information seem?
> - Are there any obvious signs of bias? What type of sites does this site link to?
> - Is the page current? If it hasn't been updated lately, the information may be outdated. Right-click on the page and choose "View Info"; that often includes the date the page was last modified.

The policy of *The Philadelphia Inquirer* follows:

> - Online reporting: The use of online sources of information such as the Internet and proprietary databases requires the same level of journalistic standards as other types of reporting.
> - Online interviewing: Some newsmakers and subject experts suggest conducting an online, or e-mail, interview. Such interviews generally should be avoided. As always, a face-to-face interview is ideal and a telephone interview is a second choice. Online interviews—equivalent to submitting a list of questions ahead of time—are not spontaneous and open.
> - Online quoting: Quotations based only on e-mail, newsgroup postings or other online messages should be verified in person or by telephone. Remember, it is relatively easy to use someone else's log-on to impersonate him or her.
> - Online credibility: Apply the usual reportorial skepticism to online information. Some easy-to-access databases may contain erroneous information. Seek guidance from the News Research Library.

Russell Frank, a Penn State journalism professor, published an article in *Quill* magazine under this catchy headline: "You've Got Quotes! While e-mail can be a valuable reporting tool, it often falls short of other interview techniques."

Frank concluded that gathering information and quotes by e-mail clearly has its place, but it "is not about to supplant other interviewing methods." He gave three reasons:

- [Reporters] don't get enough of a sense of the person they're dealing with when they use e-mail.
- E-mail doesn't lend itself to give-and-take, follow-up questions or serendipitous digressions.
- E-mail responses sound canned, unspontaneous.

After noting that "a quote from an e-mail is not, strictly speaking, an utterance," Frank discussed varying styles of attribution.

Some newspapers, for example, use this style:

> "I was flabbergasted when the council took its vote," Commissioner Steve Jones wrote in an e-mail from his city hall office.

Other newspapers simply use the verb of attribution *said,* just as they would when reporting a quote from a face-to-face or telephone interview:

> "I was flabbergasted when the council took its vote," Commissioner Steve Jones said.

✔ A Checklist for Styling Quotations and Attributions

Punctuation often plagues reporters who deal with quotations and attributions. Here are some guidelines.

Rule 1. *When introducing a direct quotation with attribution, place a comma after the verb and before the opening quotation marks.* Thus:

> Jones said, "We will be there tomorrow."

Rule 2. *When introducing an indirect quotation with attribution, do not place a comma after the verb.* Thus:

> Jones said that he would be there Wednesday.

Rule 3. *When ending an indirect quotation with attribution, place a comma before the attribution.* Thus:

> He will be there Wednesday, Jones said.

Rule 4. *Always place commas and periods inside closing quotation marks.* Do not, for example, write:

> "All our transcontinental flights are full", she said.

Instead, write:

"All our transcontinental flights are full," she said.

Do not write:

She said, "All our transcontinental flights are full".

Instead, write:

She said, "All our transcontinental flights are full."

Rule 5. *Always place colons and semicolons outside the closing quotation marks.* Thus:

Coach Jones said that it was his "dumbest mistake": deciding to start an untested freshman at quarterback.

And:

Coach Jones said that it was his "dumbest mistake"; he should not have started an untested freshman at quarterback.

Rule 6. *Placement of a question mark depends on whether it belongs to the quotation or to the surrounding sentence.* Because the question mark belongs to the quoted passage—and not to the surrounding sentence—the following example is incorrect:

Coach Jones asked his team, "Can we win this game"?

It should be punctuated like this:

Coach Jones asked his team, "Can we win this game?"

Because the question mark belongs to the surrounding sentence—and not to the quotation—the following example is incorrect:

Did the coach say, "We'll have to wait and see?"

It should be punctuated like this:

Did the coach say, "We'll have to wait and see"?

Because the question mark belongs to the quoted passage—and not to the surrounding sentence—the following example is incorrect:

"Will we continue to win"? asked the coach.

It should be punctuated like this:

"Will we continue to win?" asked the coach.

Because the question mark belongs to the surrounding sentence—and not to the quoted passage—the following example is incorrect:

Why does every coach say, "We're going to win this game?"

It should be punctuated like this:

Why does every coach say, "We're going to win this game"?

Remember: If the quoted passage itself asks the question, the question mark should appear *inside* the quotation marks; if the surrounding sentence asks the question, the question mark should appear *outside* the quotation marks.

Rule 7. *A quotation within a quotation should be set off in single quotation marks.* The following example is incorrect:

> "Johnson's plea to "win this game for the community" really fired us up," Smith said.

It should be punctuated like this:

> "Johnson's plea to 'win this game for the community' really fired us up," Smith said.

Or like this:

> "Johnson made a plea to 'win this game for the community,' " Smith said.

If you use a quotation within a quotation that quotes a third party, that quotation should be in double marks. For example:

> "I was shocked," the parent added, "when coach Johnson screamed, 'As my predecessor said, "Let's kill 'em." ' "

Rule 8. *Remember to insert closing quotation marks.* When facing a deadline, it is easy to forget to provide closing quotation marks. Note the following:

> "We're so enthusiastic about this project that we can't stop thinking about it, Jones said.

It should be punctuated like this:

> "We're so enthusiastic about this project that we can't stop thinking about it," Jones said.

Rule 9. *Closing quotation marks are not used at the end of a paragraph if the same speaker continues directly to the next paragraph.* The following is incorrect:

> "We're so enthusiastic about this project that we can't stop thinking about it," Jones said. "We look forward to getting council approval."
>
> "We hope that will come at the next meeting."

It should be punctuated like this:

> "We're so enthusiastic about this project that we can't stop thinking about it," Jones said. "We look forward to getting council approval.
>
> "We hope that will come at the next meeting."

Reporters often use multiple-paragraph direct quotations when the source's words are particularly moving and packed with emotion. In a gripping story about a mother who had to make the difficult decision to send her brain-damaged infant to a child center, Tom Hallman Jr. of *The Oregonian* in Portland allowed the woman to communicate directly with readers through several extensive direct quotations sprinkled throughout the story. In each instance, he was careful not to close each paragraph of a multiple-paragraph direct quotation with marks until the mother's

precise words ended. Here is an excerpt, with beginning quotation marks and concluding marks at the end of the third paragraph:

> "Don't call me courageous. And don't tell me what you'd do, because you don't know.
>
> "Every day I tell myself that he doesn't know any different. That he doesn't feel the same emotions we all do. That he's getting wonderful care. That he's happy.
>
> "I do this so I can turn around and walk away."

Rule 10. *When a quotation is interrupted by its attribution, remember to insert additional marks.* Note the following incorrect example:

> "Get in there now," the coach said, before I make you run extra laps."

It should be punctuated like this:

> "Get in there now," the coach said, "before I make you run extra laps."

Rule 11. *When reporting dialogue, start a new paragraph with each change of speakers.* For example:

> "I think it is wise to lengthen the school year," Smith said.
>
> "It would be ludicrous to do so," Johnson said.
>
> "I think the only ludicrous thing around here is you," Smith said.
>
> "Let's keep this discussion on a higher plateau," Johnson said.

Do not run the dialogue into a paragraph such as this:

> "I think it is wise to lengthen the school year," Smith said. "It would be ludicrous to do so," Johnson said. "I think the only ludicrous thing around here is you," Smith said. "Let's keep this discussion on a higher plateau," Johnson said.

CHAPTER NINE

FEATURES

Jake Batsell, a journalism student at Arizona State University, wanted to write a feature story on Charles Barkley, who at the time was a superstar for the Phoenix Suns.

Making arrangements to spend time with the Suns' forward was no easy task. Big-time athletes are tough to reach, particularly if you happen to be a student journalist. Batsell, who became a reporter at the *Chicago Tribune* and then *The Seattle Times* once he graduated, also wanted to spend time in Barkley's hometown of Leeds, Ala., where he needed to interview the basketball player's mother, grandmother, friends and former coaches.

(*Phoenix Suns*)

His persistence and hard work paid off. Batsell produced a feature that was well researched and written. It did not report news firsthand. It was a compelling personality profile, rich in observations and quotations, that entertained and educated. It was a piece that allowed the writer space to write. It allowed readers to come much closer to Barkley and find out what makes him tick.

It had heart.

Batsell's story began with narrative:

> As multicolored spotlights danced swiftly through the vast darkness and music blared at deafening decibel levels, Charles Barkley sat patiently at the end of the Phoenix Suns' bench.
>
> The elaborate pre-game introduction routine, by now a mere ritual for Barkley and his teammates, was about to reach its usual culmination—the grand entrance of Sir Charles onto the court.
>
> The crowd of 19,023—a sellout, as every Suns' game has been since Barkley arrived in Phoenix—clapped in synchronized fashion as the America West Arena public address announcer introduced the first four members of the home team's starting lineup.
>
> The announcer paused slightly.
>
> "And at forward, from Auburn, number 34 . . . Charrrrles BARK-leeeeeeeeeey!"
>
> As Barkley rose from his seat and jogged casually toward his teammates, the fans cheered wildly for professional basketball's most celebrated and candid performer.
>
> Within seconds, the lights came back on, casting a modest glimmer off Barkley's smooth, bald head. He tore off his warm-up outfit—revealing a frame that appears stockier than his listed 6-foot-6, 252-pound dimensions—and situated himself at center court in anticipation of the opening tip.
>
> With the shrill tweet of a referee's whistle, another four-quarter episode in the life of Charles Barkley began.

What Is a Feature?

Hard News and Soft News

People get up in the morning and want to know what happened since they went to bed. They read a morning newspaper, turn on the morning news or check the Internet. They switch their car or office radios to the news during the day to find out the latest happenings. When they get home, they turn on the evening news, read an evening newspaper or go online for a recap of what happened during the day.

A news story can be *hard,* chronicling as concisely as possible the *who, what, where, when, why* and *how* of an event. Or it can be *soft,* standing back to examine the people, places and things that shape the world, nation or community.

Hard news events, such as school board meetings and bond elections, affect many people, and the primary job of the media is to report them as they happen. Soft news, such as the re-emerging popularity of soft-top automobiles or how people are coping with cold weather, is also reported by the media. Feature stories are often written on these soft news events.

"News writers love the rush they get when they run out and cover a breaking news story," said Mary Gillespie, a feature writer at the *Chicago Sun-Times.* "That's their challenge. My challenge is to grab readers and not let them go until they finish the story, to take them beyond what they may have read in the newspaper the day before."

Gillespie has spent a day on a barge in Lake Michigan, interviewing the men who drop buoys into harbors in preparation for the summer boating season; she has been to the Miss America pageant to find out what the contestants do before and after the contest; and she has traveled to Luxembourg to rekindle memories of the Battle of the Bulge.

"I've also written a feature on napping," she said. "Who naps, who doesn't nap. Voluntary and involuntary nappers. Famous nappers in history.

"There are an infinite number of features out there. To me, the best place to find a feature is to look at what's happening around you. Look at the news. Talk to people in the supermarket. In other words, live.

"A feature involves readers on the level of, 'This could happen to you.' You are teaching people something about themselves. You are telling them, 'Look what this did to this guy. Here's what we can learn from this.' It's like holding up a mirror."

Carol Lutyk, a senior text editor for *National Geographic* magazine who also has worked as an editor in the National Geographic Society's book division and on its bimonthly travel magazine, said that while there is no formula to writing a good feature, the story must be "grounded in solid reporting and accuracy, with a strong sense of individual style. A good feature gives readers a distinct sense of place and atmosphere. If appropriate, it contains some humor, though that's often hard to do without being sophomoric.

"It focuses on memorable characters, but not so many that readers are overwhelmed by the number of people they've met. It includes good quotes that have a conversational quality. A *National Geographic* feature has a few authority figures (government officials, experts) so that readers get some weight behind the anecdotal narrative, but the little guys are really the most important characters you meet in our stories."

John G. Mitchell, a senior assistant editor at *National Geographic* who often writes and edits stories that deal with the environment, said a successful feature writer must have an eye for details. He added that a good feature writer must be willing to take occasional risks, "framing a scene or a situation in unusual language that surprises the reader without confusing him."

Mitchell said the writer must also have "a light touch (i.e., a sense of humor), a personal presence that does not intrude on the purpose of the story, an ability to show rather than tell and a penchant for accuracy."

Features: When Is Soft News Appropriate?

There is no firm line between a news story and a feature story, particularly today, when many news events are "featurized." For instance, Monday may have been the warmest day so far this year. A news story may begin: "Record heat toasted the city Monday, and there's no relief in sight." A featurized story may begin: "John Hilkevich did what everyone in the city wanted to do Monday. He spent the day getting a tan at the beach."

John G. Mitchell said the lines between news and feature stories are indeed blurring. "It used to be, a news story was a factoid—who, what, when and where," he said. "It was a report of an occurrence. A feature story was a piece that permitted the writer to interpret an occurrence or a trend or a personality.

Now, as we all know, even the formerly staid *New York Times* allows interpretive reporting of breaking news. I don't think there's much difference between news and features any more. And maybe that's a good thing."

Most media offer a mix: hard news stories that chronicle significant, timely events, and features that:

- Profile people who made the news
- Explain events that moved or shook the news
- Analyze what is happening in the world, nation or community
- Teach an audience how to do something
- Suggest better ways to live in a complicated world
- Examine trends in constantly changing societies
- Take people someplace or let them see something they haven't seen before
- Entertain or humor an audience

Despite today's interest in feature stories, hard news still fills most of a newspaper's front page. However, inside the newspaper and often on the lower half of the front page, the stories become softer. Even in television and radio news, after the anchors report the major news of the day, they turn to features.

Today's daily media use many factors to determine what events they will report, including timeliness, proximity, consequence, the perceived interest of the audience, competition, editorial goals and even the influence of advertisers. All these factors put pressure on reporters to give their audiences both news and features. Readers want hard news that tells them the *who, what, where, when, why* and *how* of events that are occurring constantly in their world, nation and community. They also want to be entertained, to smile or cry, to learn and to sit back and truly enjoy a story.

One newspaper that seems to have found a successful formula for mixing hard news and soft news is *The Wall Street Journal.* Every day, *The Journal* prints sober business and finance reports. It also has a "What's News" column that summarizes the top news stories. Mixed in with these are feature stories that center on the business world.

Sometimes, the distinction between hard and soft news is clear. When people are killed in a fire, there is **immediate news value**. The breaking stories will be written in typical inverted-pyramid form that puts the most important points at the beginning.

However, when the governor visits town just to eat chili at a favorite downtown restaurant, the writer may choose an alternative to the inverted pyramid. This is where the distinction between hard news and soft news becomes hazy. The story on the governor can be written as hard news, reporting that the governor is in town to eat chili. That could be big news in a small town. However, the story can also be written as a soft news feature, letting the governor and others explain what makes this chili and this restaurant so good. Either way, the story must be written as objectively as possible in easy-to-understand language.

Here is another situation in which the distinction is not clear-cut. A student reporter is assigned to write about the increasing burglary rate in the apartment buildings near the university. The student calls the police department, sets up an interview with the officer in charge of the burglary detail and finds out that the increase is alarming. The officer says that unless the department is given additional funding, it can do little to check the skyrocketing rate.

The reporter can handle this story as hard news and write it in inverted-pyramid form, or write it as a soft news feature. Here is an example of the inverted pyramid:

> Burglaries have increased in apartment buildings here by more than 200 percent in the last year, and police say that there is little they can do about it.
>
> "Without a bigger budget and more staff, we are powerless to reduce the wave of crime," Lt. Felix Ramirez of the burglary detail said. "The best we can do is hope witnesses will come forth and help us capture the criminals."
>
> Ramirez blamed much of the increase on a climbing unemployment rate. He said another major reason is that most apartments in the area are occupied by students, who are at school all day long.

Here is an example of the soft news feature:

> It was 5 p.m. Tuesday when Herbert V. Williamson walked in on three men who were burglarizing his apartment.
>
> Panicking, the three thieves ran out and took off in their car. Williamson called the police immediately and then started to cry as he stared at his possessions dumped on the floor.
>
> Fifteen minutes later, three men were arrested by police near the Saxton Street Mall after their car stalled. On the back seat were three paintings and hundreds of dollars worth of silver coins and clothing taken from Williamson's apartment.
>
> Williamson and the three suspects are only a small part in the city's skyrocketing burglary rate, which has increased more than 200 percent near the university in the last year. Police blame much of the increase on a rising unemployment rate, and they say that there is little they can do about it.

"Jell-O Journalism": When Is Soft News Inappropriate?

When a hard news story breaks—for example, a major development in a continuing story, a killing or a fire—it should be topped with a hard news lead. Soft leads and stories are more appropriate when a major news event is not being reported for the first time. Some editors decry an overemphasis on soft writing and refer to it as **Jell-O journalism**.

In a story on the prosecutions of a motorcycle gang for allegedly raping and beating two women in a national forest in southeastern Illinois, the *St. Louis Post-Dispatch* did not report until the 11th paragraph that the court costs could plunge a rural county into a financial crisis. The lead paragraph said:

> The two-lane road winds through the hills of Hardin County deep into the Shawnee National Forest in southeastern Illinois, carrying visitors far from the interstate highways and backward in time.

The next nine paragraphs built up to the paragraph that gave the news. Even the headline was written on the 11th paragraph. It said, "Cycle Gang Violence Jars Rural County's Budget."

There was no reason to take the reader through 10 paragraphs before giving the thrust of the story. A hard news story such as this deserved a summary lead. A soft lead would have been more appropriate on a feature on the psychological effects of the attack on the two women. And even in a feature story, the news peg should have been given in the third or fourth paragraph.

Types of Features

Feature is an umbrella term for a number of soft news stories that profile, humanize, add color, educate, entertain or illuminate. A feature is not meant to deliver news firsthand. It usually recaps major news that was reported in a previous news cycle. It can stand alone, or it can be a *sidebar* to the main story, the *mainbar*. A sidebar runs next to the main story or elsewhere in the same edition, providing an audience with additional information on the same topic.

Types of features include:

- Personality profiles
- Human interest stories
- Trend stories
- In-depth stories
- Backgrounders

Let's look at each of these.

Personality Profiles

A **personality profile** is written to bring an audience closer to a person in or out of the news. Interviews and observations, as well as creative writing, are used to paint a vivid picture of the person. People enjoy reading about other people, which makes a personality profile one of the most popular features in today's media.

Examples include an interview with a judge in a sensational murder trial and the story of a man in a wheelchair who has just completed a cross-country trek to raise funds for disabled children. Mary Gillespie once wrote a personality profile on her father, who was a prisoner of war during World War II. Her lead was, "I didn't expect to cry."

When the former baseball star Willie Mays appeared at a downtown Boston bookstore to autograph copies of his autobiography, "Say Hey," Alex Beam of the *Boston Globe* wrote a personality profile that was rich in observations and quotations. By the end of the story, readers knew the news of Mays' 2 1/2-week, 10-city book tour; more important, the vivid writing offered them a snapshot of a baseball legend.

Jake Batsell's story on Charles Barkley also offered readers a clear picture of a personality.

That cannot be done simply by interviewing a single person. It is a given that the reporter has to spend as much time as possible with the "star" of the story, but he or she must also interview friends and, if possible, foes. Remember, the

aim of the profile is to bring readers closer to the personality. That can be done much easier by using multiple sources.

For example, Batsell interviewed Johnnie Mickens, Barkley's grandmother, on the front porch of her Alabama home. His observations were vivid. Her quotations were revealing.

> Ask people in Leeds where Barkley's "Granny" lives, and they'll point the way. It is the corner house where two strong women raised young Charles.
>
> A front porch greets all visitors. Inside, it is a spacious but unpretentious house cluttered with family pictures, many of Charles himself. Charles, wearing his graduation gown. Charles, equipped in equestrian gear while shooting a commercial. Charles, throwing a forceful dunk down the throats of his opponents.
>
> A 4-foot-tall brick and wrought-iron fence surrounds the large house, which has grown with Barkley's basketball career. Johnnie Mickens, known as "Granny" to her family, remembers the day when that fence was made of chain links and Charles would jump over it tirelessly to make his legs stronger.
>
> "He used to just stand upside [the fence]—I guess he was about 10 or 12—and he would jump back and forth over it," said Mickens, who teamed with her daughter, Charcey Glenn, to raise Charles and his two brothers, Darryl and John.
>
> "I was kind of scared that he was going to catch himself. And I used to get at him about it, because, I mean, he'd go for 10 or 15 minutes, he'd just go over and back and forth.
>
> "I said, 'Son, don't do that. I'll never get to be a great-granny.' He wouldn't pay me no attention until he got tired. He was building his legs then, but I didn't realize that. I was just afraid that he was going to hurt himself."

Every paragraph in the story revealed something about Barkley's personality. Batsell let the basketball player tell his own story. It was rich in direct quotations. He also let others talk, from the women who raised Barkley to others who know him, including his close friend, Michael Jordan, formerly of the Chicago Bulls.

Human Interest Stories

A **human interest story** is written to show a subject's oddity or its practical, emotional or entertainment value. Examples include what Atlantic City does each year to prepare for the Miss America pageant, how to repair a washing machine and how people are surviving in the town with the nation's highest unemployment rate.

Travel writing fits into the category of *human interest,* although these pieces could also be trend or in-depth stories. "Good travel writing displays curiosity and a genuine sense of discovery," said *National Geographic* senior editor Carol Lutyk. "Truly fine travel writers are, first, writers, not travel journalists. They either share their deep knowledge of a place, or they serve as aliens so keen on exploration that they bring an almost childlike sense of wonder to their prose. Seemingly mundane events are the cornerstone of all great travel writing. It is in these simple but significant moments that mere storytelling can become something more transcendent. It can become literature."

She said vivid imagery is as important in travel writing as in any type of feature writing. "One of the classic ways to achieve vivid imagery is to show rather than tell," Lutyk added. "Don't tell the reader that the view is 'beautiful.' Show how it's beautiful by describing it, by painting a word picture. How did the bougainvillea smell? What were the sounds of Naples at night? How did it feel to savor the silence of the Sahara?

"Details like these make one rejoice in a story. A short piece without much detail seems long and boring, whereas a long piece packed with detail just flicks the pages past. It's a question of illusion. Any piece of writing, whether it's 500 words or 15,000, should contain the kind of detail that jumps out of the page and sings and glitters."

Lutyk said writers of features should feel a surge in their stomach when they confront details that might also be of interest to their readers. "Do you feel a little surge, or do you suppress a yawn?" she said. "Write about what really makes your stomach surge. What seems dead in perception seems dead on the page."

Trend Stories

A **trend story** examines people, things or organizations that are having an impact on society. Trend stories are popular because people are excited to read or hear about the latest fads. Examples include a look at summer fashions, a new religion or the language of teen-agers.

In-Depth Stories

An **in-depth story**, through extensive research and interviews, provides a detailed account well beyond a basic news story or feature. It can be a lengthy news feature that examines one topic extensively; an investigative story that reveals wrongdoing by a person, agency or institution; or a first-person article in which the writer relives a happy or painful experience.

Examples include stories on cancer and how it has affected several families, how illegal aliens get into the United States and how one rock group made it to the top while another failed.

Backgrounders

A **backgrounder**—also called an **analysis piece**—adds meaning to current issues in the news by explaining them further. These stories bring an audience up to date, explaining how this country, this organization, this person or whatever got to be where it is now.

Examples include an analysis of the state death penalty shortly after a murderer is sentenced to death or a story explaining how the university food service won its exclusive contract.

Writing and Organizing Feature Stories

Feature writers seldom use the traditional inverted-pyramid form. Instead, they may write a chronology that builds to a climax at the end, a narrative, a first-person article about one of their own experiences or a combination of these. Their stories are held together by a thread, and they often end where the lead started, with a single person or event.

Guidelines in Organizing a Feature Story

1. *Choose the Theme.* Make sure that the theme is not too broad or too narrow.
2. *Write a Lead That Invites an Audience into the Story.* A summary may not be the best lead for a feature. A two- or three-paragraph lead block that

begins with one of the special leads may be better. The nut graph should be high in the story. Do not make readers wait until the 10th or 11th paragraph before telling them what the story is about.

3. *Write Clear, Concise Sentences.* Sprinkle direct quotations, observations and additional background throughout the story. Paragraphs can be written chronologically or in order of importance. Remember to enrich your writing with details and vivid imagery. "Show me." Don't just "tell me."
4. *Provide Vital Background Information.* If appropriate, a paragraph or two of background should be placed high in the story to bring an audience up to date.
5. *Use a Thread.* Connect the beginning, body and ending of the story.
6. *Use Transition.* Connect paragraphs with transitional words, paraphrases and direct quotations.
7. *Use Dialogue When Possible.* Feature writers, like fiction writers, often use dialogue to keep a story moving. Of course, feature writers cannot make up dialogue; they listen for it during the reporting process. Good dialogue is like a good observation in a story. It gives readers strong mental images and keeps them attached to the writing.
8. *Use Voice.* Write in a style that reveals personality.
9. *End with a Quotation or Another Part of the Thread.* A feature can trail off like a news story or it can be concluded with a climax.

We'll now consider these elements of feature writing.

1: Find the Theme and Develop the Story

Before a feature is written it should have a theme or a purpose. Writers do not simply sit down and write features. They determine the purpose of a feature—to profile someone who is unique, to teach something, to reveal something, to illuminate something—and then they do their research and organize the story to help them achieve this purpose. Each section of the story—the beginning, the body and the end—should revolve around the theme.

Writers also narrow their themes as much as possible. No one writes a feature on cancer. That would take volumes. Instead, the feature would be on the latest medicine, how certain foods reduce the risk or one person's valiant fight.

Once the theme is determined, all research, interviewing and writing should support it. Of course, something may come up during the research or interviewing process that alters the focus of the story, but writers try to stick to the original theme as much as possible.

Writers determine a theme on the basis of several factors:

- *Has the Story Been Done Before?* Writers look for something fresh or unusual. Even an old topic, such as cancer, can have a new theme.
- *The Audience.* The story should be of interest to the audience. If people cannot relate to the piece, they will not read it, no matter how well-written it is.
- *Holding Power.* The story has to keep the audience interested. Emotional appeal is important here. Will the story make an audience laugh or cry?

- *Worthiness.* Writers must also ask themselves (or their editors may ask them): "Is this story worth anything? Is the theme so narrow or so broad that it has no value?"

2: Write the Lead

As discussed in Chapter 5, possibilities for feature leads are endless. Feature writers generally write narrative, contrast, staccato, direct address or "none of the above" leads. They usually avoid summary leads because it is not necessary or practical to summarize an entire feature in a single opening paragraph.

"You can't underestimate the importance of the lead," Mary Gillespie said. "If you don't get them in the lead, you won't get them. The lead has to convey urgency, something so provocative that they'll want to read the story. You're like a carny, saying, 'Hey, don't pass me by. Stop and read me.' But you're in trouble if you can't back up your lead. You have to follow the fireworks with something just as big."

A *lead block* of two or more paragraphs often begins a feature. Rather than put the news elements of the story in the lead, the feature writer uses the first two or three paragraphs to set a mood, to arouse readers, to invite them inside. Then the news peg or the significance of the story is provided in the third or fourth paragraph, the *nut graph.* Because it explains the reason the story is being written, the nut graph—also called the *"so what" graph*—is a vital paragraph in every feature.

"Many times, I'll be sitting in an interview and I'll know the lead," Gillespie said. "I'll hear the person say something or he'll do something, and I'll think, that's great. That's the lead. Your goal in the lead is to grab readers. You're trying to tell the reader, 'I'm going to tell you a story. I'm going to tell you something you don't know. Come in here, look at this, examine this person or situation.'"

3: Write the Body

Between the lead and the ending, the story must be organized so that it is easy to follow and understand. The body provides vital information while it educates, entertains and emotionally ties an audience to the subject. Then, the ending will wrap up the story and come back to the lead, often with a quotation or a surprising climax.

According to Gillespie, the story's body should not jar the reader. "The middle should flesh out the provocative statement in the lead. It should analyze and dig deeper. It should illuminate the lead."

Important components of the body of a feature story are background information, the thread of the story, transition, dialogue and voice.

4: Provide Background Information

It is essential for feature writers to provide the appropriate background information. Thus a paragraph or more of background should appear high in the story to bring the readers up to date.

The profile of Charles Barkley included a paragraph of background after the opening paragraphs of narrative:

> Leeds, Ala., is a friendly, sleepy and distinctly Southern community of 10,000 people. The town 20 miles east of Birmingham produced Charles Barkley, and despite his $10 million annual earnings, it is the town where his family still chooses to reside. It also is the place where Barkley says he wants to die.

5: Use a Thread

In a feature story, as in a news story, transitions, paraphrases and quotations are used to connect paragraphs and move from one area to another. Because a feature generally runs longer than a news story, it is also effective to weave a **thread** throughout the story, which connects the lead to the body and to the conclusion. This thread can be a single person, an event or a thing, and it usually highlights the theme of the story.

A feature on how people fight heart disease could begin with a 13-year-old child in a hospital bed, waiting for a heart transplant and facing the deadline of death. The body of the story would explore heart disease, how many people it affects and what is being done to help those who have it. Throughout the body of the story, the writer would keep coming back to the 13-year-old, the thread. The feature should also conclude with the child, waiting.

The same feature on heart disease could begin with an event, such as an auto accident in which a 20-year-old man dies. He is rushed to a hospital, where his heart is removed and transplanted into the chest of the 13-year-old child. The event becomes the thread. Throughout the story, the writer refers to the accident that brought death to one person and life to another.

In the Barkley story the thread is a single basketball game. The game is used like a scene in a piece of fiction that the writer keeps coming back to. The story branched out into several areas, over a man's lifetime and across several states, but throughout readers are brought back to the game. The article starts with Barkley being introduced, comes back several times to his performance during the game and ends in the victorious postgame locker room.

6: Use Transition

Transition holds paragraphs together and allows them to flow into each other. Transition is particularly important in a long feature examining several people or events because it is the tool writers use to move subtly from one person or area to the next. Transition keeps readers from being jarred by the writing. It guides them through the story and keeps them comfortable until the end. Like the thread, it helps connect the beginning, the middle and the end of a story.

Transition can be a word or a phrase at the beginning or the end of a sentence, or it can be a sentence or a paragraph that connects other sentences or paragraphs. With transition, the writer says, "Now, reader, the writing is going to move smoothly into another area." Words commonly used as transitions include *meanwhile, therefore, sometimes, also, and, but, meantime, nevertheless* and *however.* Phrases include *at 8 p.m., in other action, despite the promises* or *in the time that followed.* Sentences include *Police gave the following account of the accident* and *The witness described how the crime occurred.*

7: Use Dialogue

Dialogue is an important component of feature writing because it keeps readers attached to a story's key players. It helps move readers through the writing. With dialogue, the reader—like the writer—can listen in on important conversation between two or more people.

Dialogue can be sprinkled throughout a story to introduce sources or to give depth to sources who already have been introduced. The dialogue should be part of the story's flow, and it should add important information. It should not be stuck into the story merely to illustrate the reporter's skills.

Here is some dialogue near the beginning of a feature story that appeared in *Arizona Highways,* an international travel magazine. The story was about a one-room schoolhouse serving several ranch families in an isolated part of Arizona. This particular dialogue illustrated how each school day begins. It was used after the schoolteacher, Jim Hazzard, was introduced and after the story reported that the children had said the Pledge of Allegiance. Notice how the dialogue introduced sources so that attribution was not needed at the end of each quotation.

"Let's talk about anything new," the teacher tells his pupils after the pledge. "Anything new happen on the creek?"

Hands jump.

"Bobby."

"I heard a bird call last night. It was real loud."

"Keith."

"I saw six cats and five dogs."

Hazzard changes the subject. "Let's have a little humor."

"Catherine."

"What's worse than a 300-pound witch?"

No response.

"Being a broom."

The pupils snicker as Hazzard calls on Jake.

"Why did the boy ghost whistle at the girl ghost?"

No answer.

"Because she was so booo-tiful."

This dialogue fit well in the story. It put readers inside the classroom with the teacher and his pupils. Of course, the writer could have described the scene by paraphrasing what happened, but the dialogue was much more effective. It added color and depth to the story.

8: Use Voice

Another key element that holds a feature together is **voice**, the "signature" or personal style of each writer. Yes, there is a byline on the top of the story to tell readers who the writer is, but voice inside the story allows writers to put their individual stamps on their writing. It reveals a writer's personality and subtly tells readers that this story is not by any writer; it is by this writer.

"I think if given the chance, all writers have something unique in the way they tell a story," Mary Gillespie said. "They all bring their style, their ego and all of their baggage to whatever they do. That's the voice. Therein lies the creativity and the real challenge. There is a formula for writing feature stories, as there is for news stories. But good feature writers take the basic formula and expand it. They use their own voice. When I write a story, I want readers to say that this is Mary Gillespie writing about something, not just anyone who happened to be available to cover a story."

Remember, though, that voice should be used subtly; it is not meant to scream at readers. And it can also fall victim to an editor.

Gillespie's voice pops up whenever she writes. She did not simply call the state lottery director *handsome*—she called him *cinema handsome*. That's voice; that's Mary Gillespie drawing a conclusion and putting it into the story. When she wrote a Christmas feature about families who had to spend the holidays at home while loved ones were fighting wars or were stationed overseas, Gillespie revealed some of her personality when she wrote:

> The ache is familiar to those who remember the irony of war at Christmas—those who, while their hairlines may be beginning to recede as their bellies expand, have memories of holiday duty as sharp as blood on snow.

In his story on a championship boxing match in which the two fighters brutalized each other, *Chicago Tribune* sportswriter Bob Verdi used voice when he said:

> You didn't just walk away from this fight; you sat in your chair awhile.

Because voice is a subjective expression of a writer, it is often challenged by editors, who may edit it out or even insert some voice of their own. It is best used in feature stories, where writers are given more license to reveal their opinions and personality.

"Features offer potentially a far greater chance to put in voice, but you have to be careful," Gillespie said. "There's always an editor; there's always a copy desk. Every writer has a voice. You just have to find it. The only way to grab someone is if you have been grabbed."

9: Write the Ending

A feature can trail off, like a news story, or it can end with a climax. Often, a feature ends where the lead started, with a single person or event.

Gillespie said that the ending should complete the circle and come back to the lead. "I like to end with a quote," Gillespie added. "The story then says, here's this guy, here's why he's neat, here's his final statement to the reader. By using a quote at the end, you eliminate the feeling of a chopped-off story."

Jake Batsell ended his profile of Charles Barkley where he started it, with the basketball player at a game. The readers are now in the locker room with the victorious Suns. As usual, there was a media horde surrounding Barkley's locker.

> A reporter asked Barkley if he felt at all slighted by the fact that he makes less than the opponent he just outplayed—Derrick Coleman.
>
> "I make $10 million a year," Barkley responded. "If you live to be 100, you'll never make as much money as I do in a year. I'm happy with where I'm at. I'm just trying to get my little egg, or nest of 'em."
>
> Then came the one-liner:
>
> "I'm struggling to make ends meet."
>
> His response elicited chuckles from the media crowd.

The man has the demeanor of a modern-day Muhammad Ali. In a world where conformity is often the prerequisite for success, Charles Barkley has become an icon by remaining exactly who he is.

"I don't compare myself to other people," he said. "I just try to be myself."

"A good feature has an engaging lead, followed by a billboard (nut graph) that sets up the story line, which is then developed," Carol Lutyk said. "Yes, a feature has an ending. It doesn't have to be a conclusion, but it should leave the reader feeling satisfied, like the ending of a good movie."

John Mitchell agreed a feature should have a strong beginning, middle and end, and all are equally important. "The best lead in the world, or the snappiest kicker, ain't going to hold up a boring body of text," he added. "Sometimes the best lead cuts right to the chase. On a number of occasions over the years, I've opened a story with the line: *This is a story about . . .* And it works if what follows surprises the reader."

✔ A Checklist for Effective Features

Mary Gillespie gives advice to students who want to write features:

- ❏ *Know How to Write News.* Learn the ABCs of digging for facts, interviewing and writing news stories under tight deadlines before trying to write features.
- ❏ *Do Your Homework.* Go into any story situation knowing something about the lives of the people being interviewed. Know the direction that the interview and the story should take.
- ❏ *Use Observation.* Describe the house or the office, what the people are wearing, how they talk. Are they wearing wedding rings? Do they take a lot of time to answer a question? What color socks do they wear?
- ❏ *Use a Tape Recorder.* Taping is good because it provides a precise record of what is said. It also reveals how a person answers questions. For example, it might help a story to mention that a person took a deep breath before answering a question.
- ❏ *Do Not Be Afraid to Ask Questions.* Ask as many as possible. Even fully prepared reporters sometimes have to admit their ignorance. Sometimes, a reporter will have to say, "Can you explain this all to me?"
- ❏ *Maintain a Relationship with Every Source.* Additional questions may come up while the story is being written. At the end of the interview, ask the source where he or she can be reached.

- ❑ *Transcribe Handwritten Notes as Soon as Possible.* That will help organize thoughts and prepare an outline for the story. The longer a reporter waits to transcribe notes, the more difficult it is to do.
- ❑ *Write a Rough Outline First.* Then write a rough draft, revise it, write another draft, revise it and so on. Writing is all a refinement process. In the beginning, the more drafts that are written, the better.
- ❑ *Do Not Overwrite.* Remember, features are about people. Use quotations and paraphrases throughout the story to let sources communicate to the readers. The more talking they do, the better.
- ❑ *Polish the Story.* If there is time after the story is finished, take a breather before reading it again as objectively as possible. Read the story as many times as possible before turning it in, and continue refining it.
- ❑ *Take Criticism from an Editor.* It is true that writers pour their hearts and souls into the stories they write, but a story is not final until the last minute. Just figure that an editor will ask for something to be rechecked or added.

INTERVIEWING

An interview is an exchange of information between a reporter and a source. When a reporter asks the right questions with finesse, a source becomes a window to the news. On the other hand, a story can fail if the reporter asks the wrong questions or not enough questions, does not know how to ask questions or gives up too early on a hostile or close-lipped source.

Interviewing requires patience, confidence and an uncanny ability to listen, participate, observe and absorb. Reporters must be able to ask a question and then listen to the entire

(*Photo by Steve Manuel*)

response, all the time zeroing in on the key points. Reporters who are well-prepared should be able to tell when a source is telling the truth, embellishing it or lying.

There are three stages in every interview:

1. Research
2. Setting up the interview
3. Questions and answers

Each stage requires careful attention and expertise. A shoddy job on any of the stages will show up in the final product. A thorough job on each stage will result in the best, most professional story possible.

Doing the Research

The key to a successful interview is establishing rapport with the source. To do this, reporters must do their homework so that they can go into an interview knowing both the background of the source and something about the subject of the story. Sources are more likely to relax and open up when they feel that they are talking to reporters who speak with knowledge and authority. Sources often volunteer little information when they think that reporters are not asking intelligent questions or do not understand the subject.

Using the Newspaper Library

Most newspapers have their own libraries—at one time they were called **morgues**—in which paper or electronic clipping files are kept on sources and subjects. The newspaper library was labeled a *morgue* because that was where "dead stories" were kept until they were resurrected for use as background on current stories.

Today, newspapers operate modern libraries where reporters can access information electronically or on paper. Many stories are stored electronically in *archives,* and reporters or researchers can get copies free or for a fee.

Reporters can do much of their research by using resources available through the newspaper library. Stories are generally filed under subject and reporters' bylines, and a reporter can easily call up an archived story from a newspaper computer. Electronic databases also can be searched for information on writers and subjects.

One excellent Web site to use for quick access to current news and archives is *www2.assignmenteditor.com.* Through it, and for a fee, reporters can reach U.S., world and college newspapers; television networks and stations; radio stations; school and government directories; business magazines and numerous other sites.

Let's say, for example, that a reporter has been assigned to cover the trial of a suspect in a triple slaying that occurred more than a year ago. First, the reporter would search the local and out-of-town library files to read earlier stories that were written on the slaying and on the arrest of the suspect.

Next, the reporter would scour the earlier clips for background information, making sure that facts such as spellings, dates and locations are consistent in each of the stories. If there are inconsistencies, the reporter would check with the police or court officials for corrections.

The clips would also be used to identify potential sources and to formulate questions. The prosecutors and defense attorneys may need to be interviewed before the trial begins. A story could be written on the judge, on the families of the victims and suspect or on the last time there was a triple slaying in town.

Before the trial begins, the reporter should have culled from the clips the five W's and H of the case, the names of sources and any questions that need to be asked. Doing the homework takes time, but it will help ensure that the reporter will not be lost in court or baffled or spurned by a source. Sources are much more likely to answer a reporter when the questions are formulated on the basis of facts rather than guesses.

Using Other Resources

Some small newspapers do not have libraries. In these cases a reporter who is looking for earlier stories would have to:

Look through bound volumes of the paper

Hope that somewhere in the office there is a file on the earlier stories

Hope that an Internet search will turn up something

Rely on public and private officials for necessary background

University and public libraries are also excellent resources. They offer numerous online and on-paper information on sources and subjects.

There is no reason to begin working on a story without being fully prepared. If nothing has been written on the source, thoroughly research the subject of the story. Many people have never been interviewed, but there are few subjects on which nothing has been written. Any library or Internet search is certain to produce plenty of material.

If earlier stories have been written on a source, it is a good idea to talk to the reporters who wrote those stories. They can provide insight into a person's character and mannerisms. They will know if the person is easy or difficult to interview.

Some sources will be writers themselves. If they are, take a look at what they have written. A book or article does indeed reveal much about its author, and there is nothing like saying to a person, "I read your book" or "I read the article you wrote." Those few words can make a source relax.

When preparing for an interview with someone who has never been interviewed, try to talk to some of the person's friends or professional acquaintances. Any bits of information that can be gathered before the interview will make the entire process easier; therefore, do not hesitate to call one person to ask questions about another.

Setting Up the Interview: Guidelines to Follow

Once the preliminary research has been completed, it is time to set up the interview. Here are six guidelines to follow, each of which will be discussed in turn:

1. If the deadline is not tight, telephone or write to the person in advance to request the interview.
2. Identify yourself as a reporter, and name the organization for which you work.

3. Establish a time and place that are convenient for the person being interviewed.
4. Tell the person the general type of information being sought. There is no need to reveal specific questions, but at least tell the source that you are doing a story on such and such and would like to ask him or her some questions. Also, tell the person approximately how long the interview will take.
5. Dress appropriately.
6. Be on time.

1: Make an Appointment

For features, where the deadline is somewhat flexible, there is usually time to set up the interview in advance. For a breaking news story, however, reporters seldom have time to call or write in advance to arrange interviews. In this situation, time is critical, and interviews are instantaneous. If there is an explosion at a refinery outside of town, and five people are killed and nine injured, reporters will arrive on the scene almost as quickly as the fire trucks. Fire officials are interviewed. Questions are addressed to the survivors and the families of people who died. Reporters ask their questions quickly, often speaking with anyone they can get to.

In stories with less deadline pressure, setting up an interview helps curb the adversarial relationship that can exist between reporters and sources. It allows sources to prepare for the questions and to look their best. It allows reporters to be well-prepared.

Phoning or writing in advance also helps reporters get past the secretaries, public relations people and others who are on a source's payroll and who may speak for the source. To get past these people, it may be necessary to keep calling, writing or hanging around a source's office until the appointment is made. Another effective way of making the appointment is e-mail. Electronic messages often go directly to the source and bypass secretaries and public relations people. Questions also can be asked via e-mail.

Explore every ethical avenue to arrange interviews with sources who are not interested in talking or who are hidden from the press by other people.

2: Identify Yourself

Once sources are contacted, they should be told immediately that they are talking to a reporter. If the story is for a journalism class only, say so. When people know they are being interviewed for publication, it becomes their responsibility to control what they say.

3: Consider Your Source's Convenience

Because sources tend to be more talkative if they are on their own turf, let them decide the time and place of the interview. Often they will ask, "When is it convenient for you?" If they do, then think of deadlines, dinner dates and growling editors. Otherwise, ride with them. Some of the best interviews take place in the middle of the night, at a gymnasium or on horseback. The point is, a reporter is stepping into someone else's world; therefore, an interview should be convenient for the source, not for the reporter.

Always be prepared for the interview before setting it up. That will avoid embarrassment when the source says: "I'll be busy later. Let's do it now."

4: Describe the Story

When setting up the interview, tell the source, in general terms, something about the story and how his or her information will fit into it. That will help the source relax before the questioning begins.

It is also important when setting up an interview to tell the person approximately how long the interview will take. Newsmakers are usually busy people who must budget their time. If the person will give you only a few minutes, take it. That is better than nothing. The important thing is to get the interview, because once people start talking, they often keep going past the predetermined time limit.

5: Dress the Part

There is no need to wear a coat and tie or high heels when covering a roundup on horseback. And do not wear a T-shirt, shorts, deck shoes or a sundress to interview the defense attorney in a murder trial. The best thing to do is to dress at the same level as the person being interviewed.

6: Be on Time

Once you make the appointment for the interview, keep it. If the interview is scheduled for 11 a.m., be there at 10:50. The only thing worse than coming to an interview unprepared is showing up late or out of breath. Getting to an interview early will show initiative and should impress the source. One other word of advice: Do not schedule one interview immediately after another. That way, the only person looking at a watch will be the source.

Conducting the Interview: The Questions and Answers

An interview does not just happen. It can go wrong as easily as it can go right. That is why the reporter should pay particular attention to the structure of the interview, the ways in which questions are asked and the types of questions that are asked, the theme or purpose of the story, observations and note-taking. The reporter should become adept at handling hostile sources and uncommunicative sources. It is also important for reporters to understand special types of interviews, such as features.

Let's now consider these aspects of conducting an interview.

Structuring an Interview

Interviews follow one of two patterns that are determined by the subject matter and the type of person being interviewed. One pattern is structured like a funnel; the other is like an inverted funnel.

Funnel Interview

The **funnel interview** is the most common and the most relaxing for both the reporter and the source because the toughest and most threatening questions are saved for near the end. These interviews begin with background talk, such as:

- How long have you been with this company?
- Where were you born?
- How old are you?
- Where did you get your experience?

The background questions are followed by open-ended questions, which in turn are followed by closed-ended questions or adversarial questions.

Funnel interviews are most useful when:

- The source is not accustomed to being interviewed.
- The length of the interview is not important.
- Particularly touchy closed-ended questions need to be asked.

By beginning with general, easy-to-answer questions, the reporter has a good chance of establishing rapport with the source. Then, once the tough questioning begins, the source is more likely to respond candidly.

Inverted-Funnel Interview

In an **inverted-funnel interview**, the key questions are asked immediately. This style of interview is used with people, such as law enforcement officers or government officials, who are experienced in fielding closed-ended or adversarial questions.

For example, when a senator voted for a controversial bill that would cost his state millions of dollars in lost federal aid, he was ready for adversarial questioning from reporters: "How could you do it?" "Don't you realize this vote might cost you your job?"

Inverted-funnel interviews are also used in breaking news stories when there is little time to ask questions.

Asking Questions

Planning Questions

Before an interview, memorize or write down the important questions that need to be answered. Of course, the interview might take an unexpected turn and some of the questions might go unanswered, but it's still necessary to know in advance what should be covered. This is where homework is important. Questions are formulated by reading earlier clips and conducting preliminary interviews.

Additional questions will pop up during the interview. Jot them down on a note pad, and ask them at the appropriate time. Try to avoid staring at the list or reading from it. Do not check off questions one by one as they are answered. That could intimidate the source, who will begin talking to the note pad rather than to the reporter. It could prevent the eye-to-eye contact that is important in an interview.

Using Closed-Ended and Open-Ended Questions

The timing and wording of questions during an interview can affect the source's response. Some interviews require only quick questions and short, specific answers. For these, it is best to ask **closed-ended questions**, which are structured to elicit precise answers.

For instance, a reporter questioning an irascible police chief about an investigation of the kidnapping and alleged rape of teen-age girls asked such closed-ended questions as, "Do you agree with the county sheriff that the girls were raped before they were released by their kidnappers?" and "Is it true that your department did not respond to the parents' call for five hours because you believed that the girls had run away and had not been kidnapped?" By asking carefully worded questions such as these, the reporter forced the police chief to be precise.

The questions also showed the chief that the reporter had already interviewed other people and knew most of the answers. They illustrated an important lesson in interviewing: Don't be afraid to ask tough questions, but don't talk nonsense to a busy source. The police chief probably would have halted the interview immediately if he felt the reporter was grasping for information by asking silly questions.

Open-ended questions are used when a short, precise answer is not immediately necessary. Because they allow a source more time to develop an answer, open-ended questions sound less intimidating. They are a good way to break the ice and to establish rapport with a source. Examples of open-ended questions include "How would you trace your rise from a clerk to the president of the corporation?" and "In your opinion, what should the government do to reduce unemployment?" Open-ended questions give sources an opportunity to elaborate in considerably more detail than closed-ended questions do.

Two factors determine whether a reporter should use open-ended or closed-ended questions:

1. *How the Subject Seems to React to Certain Questions.* The reporter needs to gauge how the interview is going and then decide if specific, potentially threatening questions are necessary. Closed-ended questions should be reserved for the point in the interview when the source is relaxed and beginning to open up.
2. *The Length of the Interview.* If an important source who is rushed for time is being interviewed, get to the heart of the interview right away. Chances are that sources such as these have been interviewed many times before and are used to specific questions.

Using Personal Questions

For some reporters, asking personal questions is the toughest part of an interview. Even the most experienced reporters dread the times when they have to approach a grieving mother to ask how her son was killed or a government official to ask if the rumors of financial improprieties are true.

It is not easy asking such questions, but it is something that all reporters must do. It is also the most difficult hurdle they have to clear in an interview. Usually, though, if a personal question is asked at the right time and with sensitivity, a source will respond passionately and candidly.

"I have more trouble asking personal questions when they involve interviewing people whose children died than when they involve government officials or people in the news," said Maren Bingham, who was a news reporter and features editor before becoming the projects editor of *The Sun-Sentinel* in Fort Lauderdale, Fla. Bingham said that before she asks personal questions, she tries to show a source that she is a professional and will get the information correct. "I try to establish trust," she said. "I try to sit and talk to them, not take notes or turn on the tape recorder. I ask general questions to try to get to know them."

Marie Dillon, an editor at the *Chicago Tribune,* said that for a story she once wrote on teen-age suicides she had to interview the foster mother of a 13-year-old boy who shot and killed himself. Dillon said that she was nervous about asking the woman for an interview because she would have to ask many personal questions about the boy; however, once the interview began, she realized the woman wanted to talk. "She turned out to be a great interview," Dillon said. "She really opened up to me. She was by herself and really needed someone to talk to."

Bingham and Dillon said that their chief fear when asking personal questions is that sometime after the interview, sources will regret what they said and then ask that their remarks not be printed. "I find that most people do not mind answering personal questions, but they sometimes later regret it," Dillon said. She added that in cases like these, she has to weigh the worth of the source to the current story and to future stories. Bingham said: "I usually very nicely say 'too bad.' I figure that they're responsible adults, and they knew they were talking to a reporter. But I also realize that I caught them at a bad time. I try to be sympathetic."

Bingham and Dillon offered the following guidelines for asking personal questions:

- *Do Your Homework.* Know something about a source before trying to enter his or her personal life.
- *Try to Interview the Person Face to Face.* It is a lot easier for a person to respond to a personal question when looking at another person, rather than speaking to a stranger on the telephone or using e-mail.
- *Interview in a Casual Setting.* If a source is relaxed, he or she is much more likely to respond candidly to personal questions.
- *Break the Ice with General Questions.* Sometimes it is best to begin an interview without taking notes at all or without a camera or microphone. Talk about the weather or the setting for the interview. Ask questions such as age or address. Humor—making a source smile or laugh—helps, too. There is no need to open with a joke, but smiling broadly and making a comforting comment should help put the source at ease.
- *If the Interview Is Being Taped, Try Not to Turn the Recorder on Right Away.* Give the source a chance to feel comfortable first.
- *Sometimes, It Is Easier to Elicit a Personal Response by Not Asking a Question at All.* Instead of asking, "How did your son die?" it might be easier to say, "Tell me about your son." Let the source talk about anything. Let the interview ramble for a while. Then later, if the source missed anything, ask more specific personal questions.
- *Preface the Questions.* Sometimes, a source is more likely to answer a personal question if it is prefaced with something like, "I'm sorry to bother

you, but I have to ask you this question," or "I know you are busy, but I'd like to ask you this question."

- *Coax an Uncooperative Source.* Some sources, particularly public officials, think that by saying "no comment" they can keep something out of the newspaper or off the air. If necessary, tell the source, "We're going to use this story anyway, and your comments really will make it better."

Using Follow-Up Questions

Anyone who has seen a televised news conference has seen reporters ask **follow-up questions**, in which they rearticulate their questions or ask another question to elicit a new or a more specific response from a source. The governor may be asked, "How do you plan to cut taxes?" He responds, "We'll do whatever it takes to trim taxes, including an across-the-board 10 percent decrease, but I think it will be hard to get anything through the Legislature." The reporter follows up immediately with, "Do you think the Legislature is unwilling to go along with a tax cut because of the disastrous effects it would have on the state deficit?"

The above scenario illustrates three things about the reporter who asked the two questions:

1. The reporter had done the necessary homework and asked an appropriate open-ended question.
2. The reporter listened intently to the response, realizing that the governor was placing the blame on legislators, not on himself, for high taxes.
3. The reporter knew the subject well and therefore was able to interpret the response quickly and to follow it up with another appropriate question.

Of course, beginning reporters may not be interviewing the governor. They will be talking to a variety of sources, many of whom have never been interviewed. But just like the governor, these sources are not always going to answer a question fully, for various reasons:

- They may not understand it.
- They may ramble too much and forget it.
- They may not be qualified to answer it but try anyway.
- They may not want to answer.
- They may answer another question instead.

It is up to the reporter to make certain that each question is intelligent, brief and easy to understand. This usually eliminates the problem of a source's not understanding the question. However, the other problems may be more difficult to solve. In these cases, the reporter will need to ask follow-up questions.

Framing Questions to Fit the Story's Purpose

Reporters should know where they want their stories to go before they begin the interviewing process. Every story should have a theme or purpose. Once this purpose is determined, questions can be framed so that the interviews will help the reporter achieve it.

If a story's purpose is to show that a local politician is a crook, questions are designed so that the wrongdoing will be revealed by sources during the interview.

Many of the questions will probably be adversarial. The reporter does not have to go into the interview with guns blazing and ask the incriminating questions immediately, but he or she should never lose focus of the story. All the questions should lead toward one point: the admission of wrongdoing. In the first phase of the interview, the questions are open-ended and easy to answer. By the last phase, when source and reporter should be as comfortable as they can be, the questions are closed-ended and adversarial.

If the purpose of the story is to show how a successful restaurant owner got to be where she is today, the questions should serve a much different purpose. They are meant to bring out the best in the person. In such an interview, the reporter will be looking for descriptions and anecdotes. The questions will be non-adversarial and easy to answer. For example, the executive may be asked to describe her most unusual dishes or her customers' favorite dishes. She may want to talk about the challenge of juggling her career and her family life. Or she may have a funny story to tell about her opening week.

A news story is meant to inform readers as quickly as possible about some timely occurrence. The purpose of the story is to report the news. Interviewing for the story is done so readers can better understand the occurrence. For instance, sources can be used to explain how or why an event occurred. They can add color or depth to a news story.

Interviews are vital in a feature story. They bring it to life. Without them, there often is no story. Questions must be framed so that the sources help tell the story. In the profile of the successful restaurant owner, for example, if the woman is a bad interview and does not like answering questions, the story will fail. The reporter must frame questions that allow the restaurant owner to open up and talk easily about her success.

Preparation is the key to making an interview fit a story's purpose. The reporter should have a list of questions that need to be answered during the interview. They do not have to be written down and followed precisely, but they should be inserted into the interview at the best times. That could be at the beginning, in the middle or at the end.

One caution: There is no way of knowing in advance what direction the interview will take. The anticipated questions are a guide to help the reporter plan for the interview and the purpose of the story. If the interview strays from the prepared questions, that's fine. Just try to get it back on track as soon as possible.

Establishing Rapport

Reporters must establish rapport with their sources as quickly as possible. That is the key to getting their questions answered. "You're like a door-to-door salesman selling yourself," said Jerry Guibor, a copy editor for the *Fresno* (Calif.) *Bee* who has been a news and sports writer in California, Oregon and Arizona. "You have to know the subject and not get bored with it. You have to know the person you are interviewing and ask intelligent questions. You have to have a good intro to stimulate the source."

Guibor said that rapport should be established as quickly as possible during an interview because most sources will not answer questions candidly until they have "warmed up" to the reporter. "To establish rapport, you have to tell them who you are and what you are doing," he said. "And you have to thank them for their time."

Here are some additional guidelines:

- *Try to Conduct the Interview in Person.* There are times when telephone or e-mail interviews are necessary, but they make establishing rapport extremely difficult. Sources are more likely to warm up to someone they can see, particularly if they have never met the reporter before.
- *Begin with General, Easy-to-Answer Questions, If Possible.* This will help the source relax. Hold the adversarial questions until the end of the interview, when the source is more likely to feel comfortable.
- *Do Not Ask Vague Questions.* Ask clear, concise questions that a source can understand quickly. A source is more likely to open up when the reporter is not confused or vague.
- *Do Not Pull Any Punches.* Do not beat around the bush. Ask questions straight out. Do not ask a related, non-adversarial question in the hope that the source will respond in a certain way.
- *Avoid Arguing.* Reporters have the last say when they write.
- *Listen.* Let the person being interviewed feel that he or she is conversing with a friend rather than responding to a list of questions from a reporter. A reporter so wrapped up in the eloquence of his or her own questioning may ignore what the other person is saying.
- *Be Open for Any Response.* Remember that responses to questions tend to be signals for additional questions, some that a reporter might not have thought of while preparing for the interview.

Handling Hostile and Uncommunicative Sources

Not every source is cooperative, easy to talk to or ready to admit fault. Sources can be closed-lipped and say "no comment." They may talk only "off the record," which means that they do not want anything they say to be printed. They may be **hostile,** especially if they are asked to reveal something they do not care to share with the public. In these cases, it becomes the reporter's responsibility to try to make the source open up.

If someone does not want to comment to the press, that is his or her right. No reporter can force a person to talk. Sometimes the reporter must simply give up on one source and look for another. In these cases, an audience must be told, for instance, "The mayor refused to comment."

If a source will talk only "off the record," the reporter should take notes and should try to convince the person to allow the information to be used. Sources cannot order a reporter to take information off the record. If they could, reporters would be at their mercy. Reporters violate no ethical principles of journalism if they ignore such a command, unless they have agreed before the interview to accept the information off the record. (For a further discussion of off-the-record reporting, see Chapter 8.)

Here are some ways to persuade sources to open up, to persuade them to go on the record or to keep them from becoming hostile:

- *Do Not Act Like a Prosecuting Attorney.* Avoid hostile questions. Save the tough questions for the end of the interview.

- *Be Sympathetic and Understanding.* This does not mean that a reporter has to be on the side of the source while writing the story, however.
- *Reason with the Source.* Tell the source that using a name or comment will make the story better.
- *Genuinely Try to Understand the Source's Position.* For example, try to find a reasonable explanation for any charges against a source.
- *Repeat Some of the Damaging Things That Have Been Said about a Source.* Often sources will open up to respond to charges against them.
- *Keep Asking Questions.* As long as the source does not end the interview, continue asking questions.
- *Have Several Questions to Ask.* If the source does not answer the first one, ask the second. If the source does not answer the second question, ask the third, and so on.

Making and Using Observations

When reporters accurately write what a source has said, the audience can "hear." When they observe and then report the source's mannerisms and surroundings, the audience can "see." Observations add **color** to stories, which means that they give an audience a clearer picture of a person or an event.

Whenever they are working on stories, reporters should keep in mind the following:

- *What Is Unusual—or Common—about This Person or Place?* If a photograph were taken of the source, what would it show? How is the person dressed? New clothes? Ragged clothes? Latest fashion? How does the source look? Wrinkled face? Scars? Bushy eyebrows? Full beard? Heavy makeup? Gold teeth? What are the person's mannerisms? Nervous twitch? Always winking? Never smiling? How is the office decorated? Western? Paintings? Posters? What is unusual about the person's face, hair, mouth, eyes, ears, etc.?
- *Does the Source Articulate Well?* Is the source "comfortable" discussing this subject? Can any outside sounds be heard during the interview? Are there any pleasant or unpleasant smells? Is the source distracted?

Observations are vital to features, but they can also be effective in news stories. In a story on the conspiracy trial of 15 members of a motorcycle club charged with planning two bombings, Melinda Donnelly of the *Dallas Times Herald* used an observation in her lead:

> Jim "Sprocket" Lang has spent a lot of time hanging around the federal courthouse in Dallas lately, passing the time with racing forms from local newspapers while his comrades—allegedly some of the meanest men in Texas—sit silently in court.

Donnelly also used an observation later in the story to give readers a visual impression of some of the aging gang members:

> Despite heavy security that includes an airport-type X-ray machine and two metal detectors, most visitors have little to claim but huge belt buckles or rolls of hard candy bulging from the pockets of their jeans or corduroy suits.

This news story could have been written without observations, but in using them Donnelly added color to her writing, which can help keep readers' attention.

Observations were the cornerstone of a series of articles by *The Albuquerque Tribune* that examined alcoholism in the Route 66 town of Gallup, N.M. For six days the paper devoted all or much of its front page and many inside pages to the chronic problem it called New Mexico's "black eye." In one article, David Gomez, a reporter, wrote:

> It's just 20 degrees, too cold for the four drunks from Chinle, Ariz., to continue living in Chinle Hole, an old boxcar embedded in the bank of the Rio Puerco wash west of downtown Gallup. The boxcar is open on one side and offers no protection from the cold.
>
> With nowhere warmer to go, the Chinle boys—Abel Taylor, his younger brother, George, and their cousins Stanley "Danny" Draper and Kenneth Yazzie—sleep in an abandoned automobile they call "Kenny's hotel." It has been parked for months next to a tire store near the Rio West Mall.
>
> No one ever cleans the vomit, food wrappers and wine bottles. It smells of urine and garbage.

During an interview or when covering an event, reporters make notes of their observations. Then they decide during the writing which ones are pertinent to the story. For instance, in a court trial, one of the spectators may be wearing curlers in her hair and knitting during the testimony. This is an interesting observation that is worth noting; though it may not be used in the story, it could be used to enhance a stark story:

> Spectators packed the courtroom. One woman, with curlers in her hair, sat knitting while Parker admitted that he stole the words to the song.

Usually, observations are better than punctuation. There's no need to write:

> People could tell that Johnson WANTED that fish to bite!!!!

Instead use observations to let an audience decide that Johnson did indeed want that fish to bite:

> Johnson stared at the water. He was so tense that veins in his neck were bulging. While the others joked in the boat and munched on pretzels, Johnson kept his eyes on the water, waiting, one hand on his reel, the other on the handle of his rod.

Observation is something only reporters can obtain. Editors and readers may wonder, "How many gold teeth did he have?" or "What was she wearing?" If these observations are not made during the reporting phase, they may be impossible to get later. That is why it is so important to take as many notes as possible about a source's looks, mannerisms and surroundings. Observations should not get in the way of reporting the news; they are used to enhance the news, to make an audience feel that it was there during the interview or event.

It is best to make more observations than will actually be needed in the story. Often, editors will ask for more color. This is where observation is critical. Editors do not want a reporter to say that a person is tall or old or big or young. They want the reporter to say how tall, how old, how big or how young. They may not want a story to say only that a police recruit jumped over a 6-foot wall. They may want:

> The recruit ran up to the 6-foot portable orange wall that had been rolled onto the obstacle course. He jumped up and threw one leg over the top. He grunted, pushed and rolled the rest of his body over.

Sometimes, observations are the first things to be cut when space or time is restricted. There will be times when editors cut the color to make a story fit a space. In such cases, a reporter will not be able to mention the woman in curlers or describe the portable wall that the police recruit jumped over. This is the way daily journalism is. There simply will never be unlimited space to report a story.

Logistics

Taking Notes

During an interview, the reporter must understand and at the same time transcribe what the speaker is saying. To do that, it is necessary to write fast. Most reporters devise some system for shortening words. Many journalists also use tape recorders, particularly in lengthy face-to-face interviews.

Using a tape recorder. By using a tape recorder, the reporter can establish and maintain eye contact with the source and can conduct the interview as if it were a conversation. But reporters who use recorders usually take notes, too. Every experienced reporter has probably lost at least one interview because of a malfunctioning recorder; this is enough to make some reporters abandon the machines altogether. Tape recorders have two other disadvantages:

- Sometimes they intimidate and inhibit a source. Some people simply do not like talking into a machine that will record everything they say. Because people choose their words more carefully when they are being taped, the interview may lack spontaneity.
- Tape recorders can waste time because the reporter has to go back and listen again and again to the recording until useful quotations are found. This problem can be eased if the recorder is digital and/or has a meter so that the reporter can make notes of the location of pertinent comments.

The great advantage of a tape recorder is that it provides a permanent and precise record of what is said, preventing the reporter from inadvertently misquoting. It is impossible to write down everything that is said, especially in in-depth interviews, and so the recorder is useful to back up the quotations. The reporter takes notes in order to remember key points of the interview; when the interview is over, the notes can be filled in by going over the tape.

"If I think the interview is going to be controversial or a source is going to come back later and question what I wrote, then I use a tape recorder," said Maren Bingham of the Fort Lauderdale, Fla., *Sun-Sentinel.* "But I do not use it routinely."

Taking sufficient notes. Take copious notes—more than you will need to write the story. It is not unusual to write a two-page story from 15 pages of notes. It is better to have too many notes than not enough.

Still, there is no need to take notes on everything that is said. Listen carefully to the speaker, look for inconsistencies, formulate follow-up questions and write down only the pertinent information. And, most important, relax. Reporters run into trouble when they spend so much time frantically writing notes that they miss the meaning of what a source is saying. For example, a source might say, "Yes, I did break the law." But to get to that point, he says, "Well, all I can say is, what I mean is, gee, this is difficult for me, but yes, I did break the law." A reporter so busy trying to write down the entire quotation may miss the heart of it.

Writing faster. Even reporters using tape recorders take as many notes as they can. Some reporters learn shorthand or have their own list of abbreviations to make the job quicker. Another popular trick when taking notes is to leave the vowels out of most words. Of course, this technique is difficult to use in the beginning, but it gets easier with practice. The source might say: "The black smoke looked like a huge mushroom cloud. I thought the area had been bombed." A reporter could write: Th blck smke lked lk a hg mshrm cld. i thght th ara hd bn bombd.

Whatever system they use, reporters go over their notes immediately after the interview to make sure that they understand them. Many reporters will stay in a room after a press conference or will sit in their cars for a while to review their notes. That is the time to insert the vowels in words, or correct errors.

Managing a note pad. When conducting an in-person interview, put the note pad and the tape recorder, if one is being used, in an inconspicuous place. The best spot for a note pad is on a reporter's lap. That makes eye contact easier and allows the person being interviewed to talk to the reporter rather than to the note pad. Eye contact is important in an interview. Neatness in taking notes is not.

Using symbols. Get into the habit of putting some type of symbol, such as a star, next to key phrases or quotations. That is a good way to identify possible leads or areas that need additional probing. Reporters facing a tight deadline often compose their stories mentally during an interview; when it is over, they can head directly to a telephone to call in the story.

Asking for repetitions. Do not be afraid to ask the source to repeat a quotation. It is not rude or inappropriate to say: "Excuse me, but I did not get down everything you said. Can you repeat it?" It is also acceptable for a reporter to repeat a quotation to make certain that it was transcribed correctly. After all, both the source and the reporter want to make sure that a quotation is accurate.

If the person being interviewed is using confusing terms, stop the interview. A reporter can say: "I'm sorry. I do not understand that. Can you explain it better?" Doing this will make the story better and will show the person being interviewed that the reporter is conscientious.

Using the Telephone

The telephone is a valuable aid in conducting interviews. When reporters are covering breaking news near deadline, when they need to talk to a source who is out of town or when they are interviewing one of their regular sources, they almost always use the phone.

However, in many interviews, particularly when the source does not know the reporter or when there is no immediate deadline, eye contact is important. In such cases, a telephone interview is not a suitable substitute for going out into the field. Do not use the phone if:

- There is time for an eye-to-eye interview.
- The source is nervous.
- It is a breaking news story where many interviews are needed.
- Observations are important to the story.

Here are some guidelines to follow when conducting interviews over the telephone:

- *Identify Yourself Carefully and Fully.* This is especially important if you have never met the source. Remember, the person on the other end of the line cannot see you and will be hesitant to answer questions from a complete stranger.
- *Speak Slowly and Clearly.* You have to speak so that you can be understood. Over the phone, you have only your voice to persuade the source to talk to you.
- *Do Things to Put Sources at Ease.* For example, you might want to apologize for your tight deadline or for your inability to be there in person. Sometimes, it even helps to apologize for the sound of the computer keyboard as you take your notes.
- *Ask Brief Questions.* It is easy for a source to forget a detailed question or not to understand it fully when it is asked over the phone.
- *Put the Telephone in a Comfortable Spot on Your Shoulder Before the Interview Begins.* It is best to practice typing and talking at the same time before you actually interview someone for a story. That way you will not drop the phone or have to reposition it. Such fumbling may cause you to miss an important quotation, and it could make the source worry about your abilities as a reporter.
- *Type Your Notes.* You will soon discover that, with practice, you can type much faster than you can write in longhand.
- *Do Not Worry about Sloppy Typing.* Go over your notes as soon as possible after the interview to correct mistakes.

- *Ask Permission before You Tape a Telephone Interview.* Many states have laws forbidding a person to tape over the phone unless the other party gives permission. Be familiar with your state laws. Asking in advance will also let the source know that you are not trying anything underhanded and will prevent you from being in an embarrassing position if you have to admit that you are indeed taping the interview.

Using E-Mail

Electronic communication allows a reporter to talk worldwide to anyone with an e-mail address. Such instant communication is a terrific way to get comments from people quickly and accurately. And many busy people will respond to e-mail quicker than to mail or a phone call.

Be careful, though. Although e-mail provides a precise record of what the source said, it also endangers spontaneity. Candid, spontaneous quotations are usually the most colorful. E-mail also eliminates the face-to-face contact that is essential for observation and establishing rapport. A general guideline is to use e-mail—or a fax—for an interview only when deadline or access is a problem or when the source insists upon it and refuses to do the interview in person.

For example, a reporter working on a story about a student protest knows she has to get a comment from the university president. She calls his office repeatedly and leaves messages, but he does not call her back. She sends an e-mail, which the president checks throughout the day, and he responds. In her e-mail the reporter is careful to:

- Identify herself fully and let the source know the name of the publication.
- Give the source a rough idea of what the story is about.
- Keep the e-mail as brief as possible.
- Let the source know the deadline.
- Ask the source if he will answer follow-up questions either in person, over the telephone or in another e-mail.
- If possible, confirm that the e-mail actually came from the source and not from someone else who has access to his e-mail.

Responses gathered via e-mail can be used in stories in the same way that in-person or telephone responses are used. There is no need to tell readers that *the president said in an e-mail* unless newsroom policy dictates it.

After the Interview

The more a reporter and a source talk, the better the interview and the resulting story; therefore, the reporter should try to keep the interview going as long as possible. Questions should be asked until the source stops the interview. Remember that key points for the story are often made at the end of the interview when the source is fully relaxed; therefore, keep listening intently until the interview is indeed over.

At the end of the interview, thank the source and ask, "Where can I reach you by phone or e-mail if I have additional questions while I am writing the story?"

That will provide quick contact if more information is needed later and will show the source that you are trying to be accurate. It also forestalls a request from the source to see the story before it is printed.

Under no circumstances should a reporter agree to show a source the story once it is written. People almost always want to retract or edit their statements once they see them on paper. If reporters are confused by something a source said, they should phone the person to ask for clarification or additional information. There is no reason to take the story to the source.

Notes should be reviewed immediately after the interview to make certain that they are clear. Many reporters type their notes after interviews to fill in empty spots. If a tape recorder was used and it malfunctioned, call the source back immediately and set up another interview.

✔ A Checklist for Interviews

Here are 10 important steps to follow before, during and after an interview:

1. *Do Background Research.* Assemble a file of stories you have written about a source or topic as well as stories by other writers. Don't forget to check paper and electronic sources for biographical information.
2. *Schedule the Interview, If Possible.* If there is no tight deadline, set up the interview in advance. This will help soften the adversarial relationship that can exist between a reporter and a source.
3. *Write Down Questions or Topics in Advance.* You will be better prepared for the interview if you know the topics you want to cover or the specific questions you want answered. The interview may take another path; this is fine, but you should try to cover all the topics or questions.
4. *Hide the Note Pad.* Sources are often intimidated if they can see a reporter's note pad. Try to keep yours in your lap or in an inconspicuous place. If you use a tape recorder, try to put it in an inconspicuous place, too. Make certain that it is functioning properly before the interview begins, and take along extra batteries and tape.
5. *Use Shorthand or Some Other Method to Take Notes Quickly.*
6. *Ask for Explanations.* It is not rude to ask a source to explain what he or she is saying.
7. *Observe the Little Things.* Observation is important in news and feature stories because it gives an audience a clearer picture of a person or an event.
8. *Be Tough but Fair.* Always give sources an opportunity to respond to their critics. You want your sources to know that you are trying to be fair.
9. *Keep It Going.* No interview can go on forever, but the longer the better.
10. *Relax.*

CHAPTER ELEVEN

COMPUTER-ASSISTED REPORTING AND RESEARCH

For generations, reporters have done their jobs using tools no more technical than typewriters and telephones. Carrying nothing more complicated than a pad of paper and a pencil, they could go to the scene of the crime, the mayor's press conference, the big football game. They'd talk to witnesses and participants, scribble some notes and then head back to the office to pound out the story in time for deadline.

Those skills of good interviewing, accurate note-taking, organization and fast writing are still necessary for journalists of the 21st century—but the old skills no longer are

(*Michael Newman / PhotoEdit*)

sufficient. To succeed in the newsrooms of tomorrow, reporters will need to master a range of new technical skills that the seasoned reporters of today never had to learn.

Those skills include new ways of gathering information, such as building computer spreadsheets, mining online databases, searching the Internet, and using e-mail and chat programs for collaboration and interviews. Moreover, reporters in the field will be carrying much more than a ball point pen and a hip-pocket spiral-bound pad. They'll be using laptop computers, satellite telephones, wireless Internet connections, geographic positioning systems and digital cameras.

Reporters also will need to master different ways of telling a story. Their work will go beyond simple ink-on-newsprint to meeting the demands of online news media, where sound clips, video, animation and virtual reality can add new dimensions to a story. Even writing styles will change to fit the needs of news consumers increasingly accustomed to the nonlinear possibilities of hypertext.

In this chapter, two of journalism's best-known experts in computer-assisted reporting and online research explain how even beginning reporters can make good use of such tools. Steve Doig, a journalism professor at Arizona State University, spent much of his 20-year career at *The Miami Herald* using computers and the Internet to do increasingly complex investigative projects. And Nora Paul, director of the Institute for New Media Studies at the University of Minnesota, has trained thousands of journalists in the United States and around the world.

By Steve Doig and Nora Paul

Precision Journalism

Through most of the history of journalism, stories about complicated social problems such as crime or poverty or taxation or education policy mostly were written when someone in authority—a government agency, a think tank, a professor, an expert of some kind—did some sort of study. When the study was completed, a press conference would be called, reporters would be handed packets of information, the experts would answer some questions and then stories would be written quoting the experts. This kind of journalism was easy and safe; reporters merely had to tell their readers what the authorities said they had found.

Some enterprising reporters, though, chafed at the limitations of waiting for someone else to do a study. They wanted to tackle stories that the experts weren't studying and ask questions that the experts weren't asking. These reporters knew many important stories involved the performance of government officials and powerful institutions that couldn't be relied on to recognize and make public their own failings.

So these reporters learned to examine such social problems using what could best be called an anecdotal approach. They would talk to sources and search paper records to find instances of the problem they wanted to write about, such as drunk driving or crime in schools or land fraud. They would use these examples to illustrate the problem, implying that such cases were the tip of a much larger iceberg. The trouble with anecdotal evidence, though, is that it's too easy for reporters and readers to generalize—perhaps unfairly. That's how some scattered cases of welfare fraud can lead to a general belief that people who use public assistance are freeloading, or that instances of public corruption mean that no politicians can be trusted.

Finally, a new way to do these kinds of stories began to emerge. This method came to be called "Precision Journalism," from the still-influential 1973 book written by then reporter Philip Meyer. He was among the first journalists to experiment with using such social science tools as public opinion surveys and statistical analysis to examine the social problems of the 1960s, including race relations and anti-war sentiment.

"We journalists would be wrong less often if we adopted some of the research tools of the social scientists," Meyer argued in his book. "Social science . . . is doing what we journalists like to think of ourselves as best at: finding facts, inferring causes [and] pointing to ways to correct social problems."

At first, few reporters heeded Meyer's call. His methods required use of computers for gathering and analyzing data, and in those days computers filled entire rooms and needed squads of technicians to operate them. But the desktop computer revolution that began in the early 1980s suddenly made it possible for bright journalists to begin to do the kinds of work Meyer was suggesting.

At first, the "precision journalists" were scattered in a few newsrooms across the country, largely unaware of what each other was doing. However, over time Meyer's vision evolved into a full-blown journalism specialty, and schools such as Missouri, Indiana and Arizona State began offering professional seminars at which interested reporters could learn techniques from the pioneers who had first adopted Meyer's methods.

Interest exploded among journalists as a series of Pulitzer Prizes and other major journalism awards were given to reporters who had used computer-aided techniques. These high-profile projects examined such problems as racial discrimination in mortgage lending in Atlanta, a pattern of child abuse deaths across the country or how lax building practices led to the disastrous impact of Hurricane Andrew in South Florida.

Other reporters began to realize that computers made it possible for them to do stories that otherwise would have been impossible. With the help of computers, reporters could examine not just a few records but literally millions of them. For example, *The Miami Herald*'s study of hurricane damage, titled "What Went Wrong," was accomplished by analyzing more than 50,000 damage reports, 17,200 county commission campaign contributions totaling more than $10 million and seven million building inspection records.

Today, there are hundreds of reporters in the United States, and a growing number in other countries, who are doing what has come to be called "computer-assisted reporting," or simply "CAR." Some are specialists who have learned to do the kinds of social science projects envisioned by Meyer, using sophisticated computer programs such as spreadsheets and database managers and mapping software. Here are just a few of the kinds of stories being done by CAR specialists:

- *Sentencing Patterns.* Looking at how a community's criminal justice system operates
- *Election Campaign Contributions.* Who gives and who gets

- *Election Results.* Explaining why candidates won and lost
- *Tax Roll Studies.* Seeing whether property assessments are being done fairly
- *School Test Scores.* Pointing out the factors that make some public schools more effective than others
- *Residential Segregation.* How race relations are changing
- *Dangerous Roads.* Where and when do most accidents occur
- *Hazardous Wastes.* Showing how poverty-stricken neighborhoods are affected by environmental problems

However, CAR today is more than an arcane specialty used just for big projects. Instead, many reporters have learned that their desktop computer, the same one they use to write their stories, can also be used to help them do many other everyday tasks journalists need to do: calculate percentage change in municipal budgets, organize the names and phone numbers of sources, sort a list of schools by their test scores, convert kilometers into miles and much more. Smart beat reporters, for instance, have learned to carry a blank diskette with them so they can get a computer-readable version of reports or budgets or other data that in the past they might have gotten just on paper. Before long, knowing how to use a spreadsheet or database program will be considered as basic a skill for journalists as typing or using a telephone.

However, be sure to remember this about computer-assisted reporting: The most important word in the phrase is *reporting.* Computers don't replace any of a reporter's traditional skills and instincts, any more than a telephone replaces the need to ask good questions and take accurate notes in an interview. The majority of even the most computer-intensive project will be information gathered the time-honored way: talking to sources, interviewing experts, studying documents and the like.

Online Research

CAR also involves much more than data analysis and social science techniques. The development of the Internet, and particularly the invention of the World Wide Web in 1989, has led to an incredible profusion of research resources now widely used by journalists. A survey of journalists in 2000 by Professor Steve Ross of Columbia University found that 81 percent of respondents say that they are using the Internet and commercial data sources for online research *every day.*

In decades past, it might have been enough for a reporter to research a story just by reading through yellowed news clippings from the newspaper's archives. But the journalists of the 21st century will be expected to use the Internet and commercial database archives for research and reporting. There are literally hundreds of millions of pages of information on the Internet's World Wide Web alone, not to mention the vast collections of documents gathered by commercial database vendors. Effectively searching this huge and rapidly growing information space requires skills that go beyond the old days, when all a reporter had to do was send a note to the newspaper library saying, "Give me the clip files on the mayor."

Newspaper Archives and Commercial Databases

One of the first benefits reporters got from the computer age was the creation of searchable databases of news stories from their own and other papers. In the past, back in the days when the newspaper library was called "the morgue," a paper's reporters had to dig through files of old news clippings that were catalogued only under general terms such as "Crimes—Murder" or "Education—Public Schools—High Schools." Much time was spent culling through off-target clips in order to find a single fact. The new computerized story archives, on the other hand, helped journalists go quickly to the most relevant stories, thus speeding research and improving its quality.

Another important development was the growth of large text databases, compiled by companies such as Lexis/Nexis and Dialog. These commercial services let fee-paying journalists search for stories and other information across hundreds of publications and specialty databases. For instance, Lexis/Nexis now offers access not only to the stories of newspapers large and small around the world but also to such public records as court dockets, property tax information and bankruptcies. Such services can be very expensive, but many news organizations feel the expense is worth the depth of research that is possible.

Using the Internet

The Internet is an incredible source of information—good information that's readily available, good information that's hard to find and simply wrong information. Journalists who want to use the Net for research first need to understand the Internet's various functions, which can be thought of as tools. Internet tools divide into two types: Tools that help you locate and use *primary sources* (like people, unfiltered information or correspondence), and tools that help you locate and use *secondary sources* (such as reports, documents, articles, books). In the increasingly complex world of the World Wide Web, however, you'll often find that both kinds of sources are available in one place. For example, a medical Web site might have a library of secondary-source articles, as well as a primary-source directory of experts you can e-mail and a message board with postings from individuals.

Here is the Internet Toolbox and some of the information tasks that it can be used for:

Internet Tools: E-Mail

E-mail, the electronic exchange of messages between one computer user and another, is one of the most basic ways to connect to people. This is one-to-one communication: One person sends a message to another person who can then respond back. It is the electronic equivalent of the U.S. Postal Service (which e-mail fans have dubbed "snail mail" because of the comparatively slow speed).

Anyone with access to the Internet can have an e-mail address. Just how you retrieve, read, compose and send messages through the Internet depends on the type of Internet access you use. But basically, all e-mail software allows you to receive messages into an in-box, display the messages, reply to them, compose new ones and store them.

Many Web sites are now offering free e-mail accounts, which is useful to traveling journalists who might find it easier to get onto the Web than into their home e-mail accounts. Some examples of free e-mail are at Yahoo (*mail.yahoo.com*) and Hotmail (*www.hotmail.com*).

An e-mail address, like a postal address, directs the mail handlers passing e-mail messages through the network of computers to get the message to the right mail slot. The e-mail address consists of four parts. Consider Nora Paul's e-mail address: *npaul@umn.edu*:

- *npaul.* This is the user name she chose.
- @. The "at" sign is the universal separator between the user name and the rest of the address.
- *umn.* The host computer at the University of Minnesota that handles her e-mail.
- *edu.* Indicates the type of host computer (*.org* for nonprofit organization, *.gov* for government, *.edu* for educational institution, *.com* for commercial, *.net* for network, *.mil* for military).

E-mail allows you to send personal messages to individuals, providing more privacy in the correspondence. You might post a message publicly to a newsgroup, get some responses and then continue the conversation through e-mail. Many reporters request that responses to a publicly posted message be sent only to their private e-mail.

E-mail also can be an efficient way to communicate with hard-to-reach individuals. Avoid phone tag or rambling voice mail messages by sending an e-mail request for information to someone. They can then answer at length and at their convenience by posting a message back to you.

Even better, e-mail responses put the answer into text form, making it easy (with the knowledge and permission of the sender) to incorporate your source's comments into your story.

Internet Tools: Listservs

A "listserv" (named after the software that maintains the list) is a virtual community of people who are linked together not by geography but rather by some common interest. For example, more than 1,400 journalists who are interested in computer-assisted reporting are members of the active NICAR-L list, named for the National Institute of Computer-Assisted Reporting at the University of Missouri, which operates the list.

Consider how a typical NICAR-L member might use the list. He may be building a spreadsheet of crime records for a deadline story but can't figure out how to convert each crime's date into a day of the week. So he composes an e-mail message describing his problem and then sends it to the computer at Missouri. The listserv software in that computer, which keeps a list of the e-mail addresses of everyone who has "subscribed" to the list, immediately sends copies of his message to every member of NICAR-L. Thus, a **listserv** is a "one-to-many"

communication device. Often within minutes, answers to his question will be posted from spreadsheet experts around the country.

Most listservs are open to anyone who wants to subscribe, which is done by sending a simple e-mail message to the host computer. Some listservs, though, require proof that you have the necessary credentials (usually job or experience) to belong to the list. Other listservs are set up just for members of a committee to correspond, or for people from the same organization or students in a particular class.

Some listservs also are *moderated*, which means there is a list editor who must approve any messages posted to the list to ensure that the message is on a topic for that particular listserv's discussion interest. Most lists are unmoderated, so the listserv computer passes along anything sent—which can mean a lot of off-topic "noise" on the listserv.

Uses for Listservs

Tens of thousands of listservs have been created, devoted to topics that range from the specific (such as restoring British sports cars) to more general discussion of subjects such as politics. For example, among the several listservs that deal with crime, you'll find one specifically for technical discussion of the National Crime Survey and another on the more general topic of juvenile delinquency.

People who subscribe to listservs generally are knowledgeable or interested in the topic of the list because of either their profession or their life experiences. Typically, fewer than 15 percent of the subscribers to a list actively post messages; the rest are "lurkers" who are learning from the messages they read.

Posting questions to the list can tap you into experts and others with experience in the list's topic. Listservs also can be a reporter's early alert for newsworthy events and trends. For instance, any reporter with a specific beat such as health or education or environment should subscribe to at least one listserv on that topic. This is a great way to keep up with what experts and concerned individuals are talking about, and to solicit information, advice or contacts from them. You can find beat-specific listservs by searching such listserv directories as Topica (*www.topica.com*) or Tile.net (*www.tile.net*).

A particularly good resource for journalists combines both e-mail messaging and listservs. This resource is Profnet (*www.profnet.com*), which is a listserv set up for college and university public information officers. Professional journalists (sorry, not students) seeking experts in a particular topic can send a message (*profnet@profnet.com*) or call (1-800-776-3638) or fax a request (516-689-1425) to Profnet, which posts it to the Profnet listserv. The university subscribers read these messages and, if they have such an expert on campus, put the journalist in touch with the appropriate faculty member.

Another source of ideas is the hundreds of specialty Internet publications, called 'zines, that are distributed only through listserv subscriptions. Sign up to get the latest issues. You can find 'zines of interest by using a search engine such as Google (*www.google.com*).

Listservs are good for more than finding sources. Many reporters use them to keep in touch with their journalism colleagues. Along with NICAR-L, there are numerous other listservs operating for journalists. Whether you are a copy editor, a news researcher, a computer-assisted reporting specialist, a photojournalist or a broadcaster, there is a special listserv of your colleagues.

Joining Listservs

Most listservs are free, though a few request a subscription fee to join. To subscribe to a list, you typically send a one-line message in this form—SUBSCRIBE *listname yourfirstname yourlastname*—to the computer that hosts the list. For instance, if reporter Jane Smith wanted to subscribe to SPJ-L, the free list for the Society of Professional Journalists, she would send this message—SUBSCRIBE SPJ-L Jane Smith—to this address: *LISTSERV@LISTS.PSU.EDU*. When her subscription message goes through, she'll receive a return message with instructions for posting and for signing off the list.

If you sign on to a listserv and receive an instruction sheet, save it. The most common mistake made by listserv beginners is to accidentally post listserv instructions such as SUBSCRIBE or SIGNOFF to the list itself, rather than to the listserv computer.

Internet Tools: Newsgroups

Newsgroups, also known as Usenet, are another popular way to read or take part in discussions on the Internet. The main difference between listservs and Usenet newsgroups is that listserv messages come to your e-mail box, while you use news reader software to go to a newsgroup area and read the messages that are posted as though they were on a bulletin board.

Newsgroup messages are posted publicly, available for anyone to read and respond to. There are tens of thousands newsgroup areas currently active on the Internet, covering every conceivable topic—and some inconceivable ones. They range from the sublime, like *alt.arts.ballet,* to the mundane, like *rec.autos.driving,* to the ridiculous, like *talk.bizarre.*

Like listservs, newsgroups can be good sources for story ideas. You'll see that some newsgroup messages will be more like CB radio talk, mostly drivel. But others can give you a first alert about a developing new topic or area of concern to the group. Newsgroups also are useful for finding sources; the people who read newsgroup messages often are knowledgeable in their topic, and they're likely to know others who are experts or otherwise experienced.

Newsgroups are particularly good for finding people who are affected by something you may be writing about. For instance, a reporter writing about eating disorders can't readily ask doctors or pharmacists for a list of their patients, but could post a note on *alt.support.eating-disord* asking anyone willing to comment to send the reporter a message.

To use newsgroups, you need an Internet service that has newsgroup access, and your computer network needs newsgroup reader software as part of its service to make newsgroup messages available. Even with that, some Internet providers may restrict which newsgroups you can get to.

If you don't have direct access to newsgroups, you still can read newsgroup messages and post replies by using Google Groups (*groups.google.com*), a massive archive of newsgroup messages. Use the Google search facility to locate specific messages that contain the words or topic you are interested in or to find newsgroups likely to be discussing that topic.

Internet Tools: Online Forums

Many Web sites and commercial Internet access services such as America Online host forum areas where people can post and read messages. These are similar to newsgroups but are available only to members of a specific service, rather than being seen by anyone on the Internet. Forum messages can be as useful as newsgroup postings, but they can be more difficult to find. An archive service called ForumOne (*www.forumone.com*) provides a search mechanism for forum messages that is similar to what DejaNews does for newsgroup messages.

Internet Tools: Chat

Online chat areas are real-time typed "conversations" with others who have come into that same area. A so-called *chat room* can be a waste of time unless it is a particularly active area and you want to do a quick solicitation of comments for a story. However, some journalists have found that conducting an online interview in a private chat room is an efficient and effective technique. Also, major Web sites frequently host chat sessions with prominent people, some of whom might be important or interesting story sources. You can find chat rooms at ICQ—read that as "I seek you" (*www.icq.com*). And you can locate upcoming chat events at Yahoo's chat site (*chat.yahoo.com*).

Internet Tools: World Wide Web

Today's worldwide Internet was begun in the late 1960s as a U.S. military project designed to help the country's leaders communicate in the event of a nuclear war. For the first 20 or so years, the Internet was used mostly by computer engineers, research scientists and government contractors. The problem was that using the Net to send files or operate other computers required specialized knowledge and mastery of often cryptic commands.

Over time, various methods were devised to make the Internet more widely useful. For example, one of the most popular was called Gopher, named for the mascot of the University of Minnesota, which created this method of navigating the Net. So-called gopher sites created indexes of their publicly accessible files, allowing Internet visitors to "burrow" through the sites to find useful information.

But the true explosion of today's easy Internet usage began with an idea by a physicist named Tim Berners-Lee in 1989. Working at a lab in Switzerland, he was looking for a way to make it easier for his fellow scientists to share their papers and data files across the Internet. Berners-Lee proposed a "hypertext system" of marking text and other kinds of files with consistent codes so that users anywhere could access them. His project came to be called the World Wide Web.

By 1994, as more and more organizations embraced the simplicity of the idea, the **World Wide Web** (nicknamed WWW or "the Web") had begun to eclipse Gopher as the preferred method for compiling and publishing sets of documents, files, photos, sound and video clips. Today, the Web is the primary way government agencies, news organizations, associations, interest groups and individuals are packaging, displaying and disseminating information on the Internet.

As a concept, the Web took off for a variety of reasons. For one, the use of **hypertext markup language (HTML)** coding and "Web browser" software meant that Web pages could be created that incorporate text, images, sound files and video clips all together. Web pages also could be interactive. For instance, a visitor could click on a highlighted link on a Web page and get an e-mail box for sending an immediate message to the creator of the site. Also, Web pages could be designed to easily link you to other pages or sites containing information relevant to the topic you are looking for.

You must have full Internet access through an Internet service provider or a direct line into your network to be able to use the Web. You also need "browser" software, which takes the various multimedia files from a Web site and almost instantly builds the Web page that is displayed on your computer screen. Web browser software offers the user three main functions:

Location/Go To. This is the box where you can type in the address (called the URL, or "uniform resource locator") for the Web site you want to visit.

Navigation. Buttons or arrows allow you to go to the next screen or go back to the screen just displayed.

Bookmark. When a good site is found, one you'd like to use again, this important function saves the URL to simplify its retrieval later.

The World of the World Wide Web

Think of the WWW as consisting of three parts: Web sites with useful information, Web sites that help you locate those Web sites with useful information and Web sites that are full of useless junk or images.

Web Sites with Useful Information

Web sites are created by different entities. Being conscious about who or what created a particular Web site will help you determine if it will help you find the specific information you seek. Consider a few of the useful Web site sources:

Federal Government Web Sites

Most government agencies are making their public files available on the Web, including easy-to-use search templates for finding particular types of information. Such Web addresses typically will end in *.gov.* Here are a few examples of such sites:

- Get the annual reports and other information about thousands of publicly owned companies from the Securities and Exchange Commission at *www.sec.gov.*
- Search for population statistics from the U.S. Census Bureau at *www.census.gov.*

- Read the text of presidential speeches from the White House site at *www.whitehouse.gov*.
- Get the text of statutes and proposed laws from the Library of Congress at *thomas.loc.gov*.

State and Local Government Web Sites

Just like federal agencies, state and local governments also are becoming heavy users of the Web to provide information about their work, government personnel and contact information, and legislative records. Reporters use these for checking pending legislation, text of statutes, facts and statistics about the government, biographical information about officials, tips and news releases.

Some states are providing lots of information online; others are just beginning. The addresses of state and local government Web sites can be found at Yahoo (*www.yahoo.com*) or at "State and Local Government on the Net" (*www.piperinfo.com/state/index.cfm*).

Companies

Thousands of companies, from multinational giants down to small specialty shops, are using the Web to promote and even sell their products. Today, you can use the Web to browse catalogs, buy books and music, read classified ads, see promos for new movies, comparison shop for a new car, order airline tickets, get technical help for computer software, make hotel reservations or play the stock market. Often, a company's Web site can be found using this formula: *www.companyname.com*, such as *www.ford.com* or *www.nytimes.com*. You also can use a Web directory such as Yahoo.

Associations

All sorts of organizations and interest groups have created Web sites to promote their cause and spread information about their particular position on topics. Examples of some that can be useful to reporters are:

- *Greenpeace.* Information about this environmental activist group can be found at *www.greenpeace.org*.
- *Amnesty International.* Contact information, fact sheets and urgent situation reports are available at *www.amnesty.org*.
- *World Health Organization.* Health data, statistics and reports are at *www.who.org*.

Reference Works

Like a good library, the Web has thousands of pages devoted to providing ready access to reference information. Just a few examples:

- Search the Information Please almanac at *www.infoplease.com*.
- Use the Merriam-Webster dictionary and thesaurus at *www.m-w.com/dictionary.htm*.
- Find the ZIP code for a particular mailing address at *www.usps.gov/ncsc/lookups/lookup_zip+4.html*.
- Calculate the distance between two cities at *www.indo.com/distance*.

Web Sites That Help You Find Web Sites with Good Content

The second important category of Web sites includes those that can help you find useful, information-rich sites. In the early days of the Web, good Web sites were found largely by word of mouth. But over time, methods were developed to create huge indexes of Web sites, allowing users to efficiently search for what they needed.

Today, there are a wide variety of ways to locate such resources on the Internet: directories, spider/robot generated databases, metasearch engines, Web rings, "scouting" reports, advice seeking and guessing. Understanding the advantages and disadvantages of these tools, and when it is best to use the different techniques, is an important skill in Internet use.

Before deciding which Web search tool to use for a particular problem, consider these questions:

- What is the Web search system actually searching? Some search tools work by indexing large numbers of Web pages, while others are more focused. So, just because one search tool can't find what you're looking for, it doesn't mean that another one won't. No single search system, though, covers all existing Web pages.
- How has the data in the database been indexed? Some search tools index all the words in a Web page, while others simply index page titles or other page elements.
- How does the search engine retrieve the data it finds? Often, a search can return links to hundreds or even thousands of sites. Ideally, the search engine will use some sort of weighting scheme that will put the most relevant sites at the top of the list.
- What advanced techniques for searching are available? Some search engines let you use complicated search terms, such as "recipe AND cookie AND oatmeal NOT raisin" to find a recipe for oatmeal cookies that doesn't use raisins. They may also allow truncation of search terms, such as "crim*" to find sites mentioning "crime" or "criminals." And some also allow you to make a second, narrower search within the results returned by the first search.

The answers to these questions usually can be found by reading the help or information section of a particular search tool's site.

Search Tool Categories

Web search tools fall into these broad categories:

Directories

A Web directory tool is an index organized by subject. The sites that are included usually have been evaluated by staff members of the indexing service. Web directories are not comprehensive, but the sites typically are high-quality. Examples of Web directories include:

- Yahoo: *www.yahoo.com*
- Excite: *www.excite.com*
- Health Finder: *www.healthfinder.gov*

Spiders/Robots

Web spiders or search robots are indexes that are generated by software programs that systematically roam the Web and automatically index the words from any pages they find. Such indexes can be quite comprehensive, tallying millions of Web pages, but the software can make only crude evaluations of the usefulness of any given page, such as by counting how many times your search term appears on the page. Examples include:

- Google: *www.google.com*
- AltaVista: *www.altavista.com*
- HotBot: *www.hotbot.lycos.com*

"Shaft" Search Sites

These tools work like the Web spiders, but the software search goes out only to certain selected Web sites, such as those dealing with a particular regional or special interest. Examples include:

- TotalNews, which searches only news sites: *www.totalnews.com*
- Medical World Search, which indexes the content of thousands of medical sites: *www.mwsearch.com*
- Euroseek, an index of European sites by country and language: *www.euroseek.com*

Metasearch Databases

These tools send your search term to multiple other search engines and compile the various results. Examples include:

- Dogpile: *www.dogpile.com*
- Metacrawler: *www.metacrawler.com* (Metacrawler has an interesting feature called MetaSpy, which shows you the search terms other people are using.)

Scouting Reports

These are lists of targeted Web resources that have been evaluated, annotated and compiled by "scouts," who are individuals with interest and expertise. A good way to find scouting reports is to use the more general search engines. Examples include:

- The Poynter Institute for Media Studies' "Links to the News" list, showing collections of Web sites useful for information about a wide variety of breaking news events: *www.poynter.org/dj/shedden*
- George Washington University librarian Gary Price's "Virtual Acquisition Shelf" at *resourceshelf.blogspot.com*
- FindLaw, a large collection of Internet legal resources: *www.findlaw.org*
- The News Division of the Special Libraries Association: *www.ibiblio.org/slanews*

Web Rings

These are Web sites linked by common interest, providing easy browsing of related sites. Search for such rings by subject at Yahoo's Web ring directory site: *www.webring.com*.

Guessing

Often, knowing the structure of Web addresses can help you make a good guess about the location of a likely Web site. Try building a possible Web address using a company name or acronym or a subject word, and then add a domain suffix. (Remember, common suffixes include *.com* = commercial, *.gov* = government, *.org* = organization, *.edu* = education, *.mil* = military.) Try finding these sites without using a search engine:

- The White House
- Burger King
- The United Nations Educational, Scientific and Cultural Organization
- The Mayo Clinic
- The American Medical Association

Can You Trust Internet Information?

As a journalist, you learn to apply a healthy skepticism to the information you get, whether it comes to you in a press release or out of a database or as a whispered tip from a source. It's important for you to be just as cautious in evaluating the information you get from the Internet. There's a famous *New Yorker* cartoon of a hound sitting in front of a computer and telling another pet, "On the Internet, nobody knows you're a dog." So be careful to determine who is sponsoring the site you are looking at. Do some background research about the site before you use their information as background research for your story.

Consider this example of the sometimes fuzzy nature of the Internet as an information source. Using a search engine to track down the exact wording of a famous observation by media critic A. J. Liebling, we find the following variations in just the first 10 sites visited: "Freedom of the press belongs to the person who owns one," "Freedom of the press is guaranteed only to those who own one," "Freedom of the press belongs to the man who owns one" and "Freedom of the press belongs to those who own one."

✔ A Checklist to Consider When Looking at Web Sites

Reference librarians at the Wolfgram Memorial Library of Widener University in Pennsylvania have created a useful checklist of points to consider when looking at Web sites. Some of those points vary depending on whether the site is sponsored by a special-interest advocacy group, a corporation, a government agency or an individual. A listing of the Widener evaluation guidelines for various kinds of Web sites can be found at *www2.widener.edu/Wolfgram-Memorial-Library/webevaluation/webeval.htm*. The following guidelines, useful for evaluating advocacy Web pages, are an example of their advice. The more of these questions you can answer "yes," the more likely the source is of high quality.

Criterion 1: Authority

- ❑ Is it clear what organization is sponsoring the page?
- ❑ Is there a link to a page describing the goals of the organization?
- ❑ Is there a way of verifying the legitimacy of this organization? That is, is there a phone number or postal address to contact for more information? (Simply an e-mail address is not enough.)
- ❑ Is there a statement that the content of the page has the official approval of the organization?
- ❑ Is it clear whether this is a page from the national or local chapter of the organization?
- ❑ Is there a statement giving the organization's name as copyright holder?

Criterion 2: Accuracy

- ❑ Are the sources for any factual information clearly listed so that they can be verified in another source? (If not, the page may still be useful to you as an example of the ideas of the organization, but it is not useful as a source of factual information.)
- ❑ Is the information free of grammatical, spelling and typographical errors? (These kinds of errors not only indicate a lack of quality control but can actually produce inaccuracies in information.)

Criterion 3: Objectivity

- ❑ Are the organization's biases clearly stated?
- ❑ If there is any advertising on the page, is it clearly differentiated from the informational content?

Criterion 4: Currency

- ❑ Are there dates on the page to indicate when the page was written, when the page was first placed on the Web and when the page was last revised?
- ❑ Are there any other indications that the material is kept current?

Criterion 5: Coverage

- ❑ Is there an indication that the page has been completed and is not still under construction?
- ❑ Is it clear what topics the page intends to address?
- ❑ Does the page succeed in addressing these topics, or has something significant been left out?
- ❑ Is the point of view of the organization presented in a clear manner with its arguments well supported?

The real secret to evaluating information found on the World Wide Web is to remember that the Internet is just another communication medium, no more or less inherently reliable than a voice, a printed page or a television screen. And here's a corollary to that: Never attribute online information by writing "According to the Internet . . ." That would be as silly as saying "According to the telephone . . ."

CHAPTER TWELVE

SURVEYS

In a book first published in 1973, Philip Meyer alerted working reporters and editors to the feasibility and practicality of using social science methods to gather information. The methods he advocated were quantitative—the use of numbers to measure and evaluate.

The title of Meyer's book, "Precision Journalism," is appropriate. The theme that runs throughout the book is that social science research methods—methodologically sound sampling procedures and computer analysis—can be used to gather facts, leading to more precise, more accurate news stories.

(Photo by Steve Manuel)

Some newspapers in the United States were using straw polls to predict election outcomes in the mid-19th century. Early polling procedures were often unsophisticated and prone to error. As the mid-20th century approached, however, newspapers were increasingly publishing the results of polls. President Harry Truman's smile was wide, indeed, when he proved the polls wrong in the 1948 election. But that did not stop the media from reporting polls during ensuing decades.

Today, the survey process has grown sophisticated. Results of national polls conducted by Gallup, Harris and Roper often make the news. Even individual newspapers and electronic media are polling their audiences about local issues.

Robert Teeter, a political pollster and the head of Market Opinion Research, was quoted by *Editor & Publisher* magazine: "The publishing of polls is simply another method of reporting, a more sophisticated method of reporting than we have enjoyed in the past. It is a better and more accurate reflection than having some political reporter go out and talk to eight people in two bars and then write a story about the election."

Surveys by news media extend beyond trying to predict the outcome of elections. Newspapers practicing **precision journalism** today are polling local readers on everything from their willingness to pay higher taxes for improved highways to their support for law enforcement crackdowns on distributors of pornography.

Evans Witt, who reports on politics and polls for The Associated Press, wrote in the *Washington Journalism Review* (now *American Journalism Review*) that the media are no longer "tied to colorful, but often misleading, man-on-the-street interviews to gauge public reaction to a candidate or major news event."

But as Witt pointed out, there is a downside to the increased use of polls. "The bad news about poll proliferation is the great number of poorly done surveys, the masquerading of incompetent research under the magic word 'poll,' " Witt wrote. "News organizations often refuse to spend the money necessary to do reliable polls. But there will probably be a lot more lousy polls . . . before everyone learns that a bad poll is far worse than none at all."

The rule is clear: news media should not attempt to conduct precision journalism projects if they are not capable of doing so. There are a number of dangers: the sample of people to be surveyed might not be representative of the entire group, thus rendering inaccurate any projections based on the findings; the questions might be worded awkwardly, thus causing confusion for the respondents; the results might be misinterpreted; and the media might not allow sufficient turnaround time to carry out the project with the care it requires.

If the dangers can be overcome, however, surveys can produce fascinating information for stories. Journalists will probably continue to make greater use of surveys to gather information. Several journalism schools in the United States now require courses in research methods, statistics and computer science in an effort to prepare tomorrow's journalists better for the increasingly technological field they will be entering.

Conducting a Survey: Basic Considerations

Reporters are not expected to be experts on research design or on polling procedures, but a working knowledge of these techniques is helpful. This section is not intended to cover survey research exhaustively. Books such as Meyer's "Precision Journalism" can be consulted for further information. Other sources include "Handbook of Reporting Methods," by Maxwell McCombs, Donald Shaw and David Grey; "Mass Media Research," by Roger D. Wimmer and Joseph R. Dominick; "Research Methods in Mass Communications," edited by Guido H. Stempel III and Bruce Westley; "Survey Research Methods," by Earl R. Babbie; and "How to Conduct a Readership Survey," by W. Charles Redding.

The purpose of this section is to provide a look at some basic considerations that are of value to reporters. A scenario will be constructed to illustrate these basic considerations.

In this fictional example, Mike Walters covers the board of education for the *Riverdale Daily News,* an afternoon newspaper with a circulation of 15,000 published in a community of 30,000. As is often the case in communities of this size, residents have a great interest in the public schools.

A current issue has divided the townspeople. Two school board members were recently elected on the platform that modular scheduling should be eliminated in the public schools. Under modular scheduling, students attend 20 class modules of 20 minutes each day. The newly elected board members favor a return to the traditional seven-period day with each period lasting 57 minutes. During their election campaigns, these members said that modular scheduling was fine for independent, highly motivated students but that average and below-average students—the majority of those enrolled—would be served best by a traditional system.

Walters is apprehensive at the first school board meeting after the election. No one really knows what the newly elected board members might do. When it comes time for new business, one of the newcomers moves that the board mandate a return to the seven-period day. The other newcomer seconds the motion. The motion does not carry—several members object on procedural grounds—but the board does agree to hire outside consultants to measure the effectiveness of modular scheduling in Riverdale.

Walters returns to his office. He tells his editor that he would like to do some interviewing in the district to determine what community opinion is. Walters says that he intends to station himself at various school buildings around town and interview mothers and fathers as they pick up their children after classes. He will supplement these interviews with comments from teachers, principals, the school superintendent and board members.

Walters' editor, Susan Kelly, says that these spot interviews with a limited number of district people might not paint an accurate picture of community sentiment. She suggests that a survey would provide a better picture.

Kelly says that she is familiar with survey basics, but she wants Walters to talk to a professor at Riverdale College for additional guidance. After conversations with the professor, Walters realizes that he must get to work on the project immediately. He must form questions, determine the people to be interviewed, gather data, analyze the data and then write a story on the basis of the data.

Formulating the Questions

The main goal is to develop a **focal question**, one that directly addresses the primary issue to be explored. In this case, that issue is whether most residents favor modular or traditional scheduling. First, Walters writes a brief introductory statement that capsulizes the difference between modular and traditional scheduling. Now he is ready to write his focal question. Generally, it is best to structure a **closed-ended question,** one that builds an answer into the question. Walters decides on the following focal question: "The Riverdale School Board is considering changing from modular scheduling to traditional seven-period scheduling. Do you prefer modular scheduling or the traditional seven-period scheduling?"

Walters then formulates several questions, with each fitting under the broad umbrella of the focal issue. Questions are framed so that people will understand them. Leading questions should be avoided. It is imperative that questions be phrased as neutrally as possible.

Closed-ended questions are generally preferred to **open-ended questions,** such as "Which type of scheduling do you prefer in the Riverdale schools?" Because of the built-in answers, closed-ended questions are easier to code and tabulate. Open-ended questions give respondents ample opportunity to expand at length. If the respondents are not familiar with the various types of scheduling to be considered, however, they cannot answer the question precisely and their answers are thus more difficult to tabulate. Walters structures a handful of closed-ended questions to supplement the focal question. He starts with general questions, such as the number of years the respondent has lived in Riverdale, and then proceeds to specific issue-oriented questions. He reasons that this will help put the respondent at ease.

At the end of the closed-ended questions, Walters adds an open-ended query. He asks: "Do you think that the schools have generally been responsive to the individual scheduling needs of your child? Could you give me an example to support your opinion?" Open-ended questions often lead to vivid, interesting direct quotations that make excellent additions to a story that would otherwise contain only a lot of statistics based on the closed-ended questions.

Testing the Questions

Walters asks his editor and the college professor to look over his questions and to suggest improvements. After getting their reactions, he tests the questions on some non-editorial and editorial employees at his newspaper who have children in the public schools. Several of them have difficulty understanding the wording of one of the questions, and so Walters makes the language clearer. It is always wise to test the questions to reduce the possibility of misleading or unclear questions.

Walters is now satisfied that his questions are understandable and that they will indeed help to determine what Riverdale really thinks about modular scheduling. He is ready to pose his questions. Walters writes out all the questions and makes multiple copies of them. It is important to have questions written out, to produce consistency—that is, to establish a system of asking the same question in the same way when each interview takes place.

Next, Walters must decide which people he wants to interview.

Developing the Sample

Identifying Respondents

Kelly and Walters decide that they are most interested in the opinions of parents who have children in the Riverdale schools. These are the people they want to interview. Random telephone dialing would provide a cross section of the entire community rather than only households with schoolchildren. Kelly suggests that Walters talk to the school superintendent. The district should have a list of parents, their addresses and their telephone numbers.

Walters tells the superintendent that the newspaper would like to conduct a survey to determine the opinions of parents. Walters suggests that the superintendent allow the newspaper to make **random selections** from the list of households. For the selection to be random, each household must have an equal chance of being included in the survey.

The superintendent agrees that the survey has merit, but he contends that the names cannot be released. Finally, a compromise is struck: The superintendent agrees to provide a list of addresses and telephone numbers of all households in the district. He will, however, protect the confidentiality of the parents by not providing their names. That is fine with Walters because reporters can ask names and get quotations when they conduct their interviews. Walters is pleased to get the addresses and the telephone numbers. The superintendent, of course, had no obligation to supply them. Sometimes it is difficult to get names or phone numbers for surveys. Walters considers himself fortunate.

Thirty-two hundred students are enrolled in the Riverdale schools. Because many parents have more than one child in school, however, Walters finds that 1,500 households have children enrolled. Walters does not have the time to call on all the households. The professor at Riverdale College suggests that if Walters samples 350 of the 1,500 households, the survey will be within an acceptable sampling level of confidence (see "Determining the Sampling Error" on the next page).

The professor tells Walters not to expect all the households selected to produce usable responses. (Some people will not answer their doors or their telephones on the first call or the follow-up; others will refuse to participate in the survey.) The professor tells Walters to expect about a 70 percent response. Thus, by randomly selecting 500 households to survey, Walters has a good chance of getting 350 usable responses.

Selecting a Random Sample

The professor then tells Walters to divide the **population**—the number of households that have children in the Riverdale schools (1,500)—by the number of households he will survey (500). In this case, Walters will call every third household. Instead of necessarily starting with the first number on the list, however, Walters puts the numbers 1, 2 and 3 in a hat. He draws 2. Thus he circles the second household on the list and every third (the **skip interval**) thereafter.

He now has systematic random sampling; on the basis of the "luck of the draw," every household on the original list had an equal chance of being included in the survey.

Determining the Sampling Error

Because not all parents of Riverdale schoolchildren will be interviewed, Walters should not report that his findings precisely reflect the opinions of the entire population. Because he is surveying only a portion, or **sample**, of the population, Walters must report the margin of error.

The professor consults a chart and tells Walters that for a random sample of 350, the **sampling error** is 5.2 percent. (Charts that outline these figures can be found in most survey methodology books. A mathematical formula is used to compute the percentage.) In other words, the percentage of the entire population may be 5.2 percent above or below the estimate obtained from the sample of 350. For example, assume that the survey showed that 70 percent of those questioned have lived in Riverdale for more than five years. Walters would then know that the true figure probably lies somewhere between 64.8 percent and 75.2 percent.

A sampling error for any survey based on random selection should be reported. A confidence interval is calculated to state the probable error because of chance variations in the sample. The most common interval is the 95 percent **level of confidence.** This means that the chances are only 5 in 100 that the true figure is not within the range found. The sampling error at the 95 percent level of confidence becomes smaller as the sample size is increased and larger as the sample size is decreased.

For example, the professor tells Walters that if he were to randomly survey 600 parents, the sampling error would be 4 percent. That is, if he were to talk to all those 600 households, there would be only 1 chance in 20 that the true answer would vary from the results of the poll by more than 4 percentage points. Thus, nearly doubling the sample size from 350 to 600 would reduce the sampling error by only 1.2 percent (from 5.2 to 4). Therefore, the professor and Walters agree that a sample of 350 will be adequate.

Of course, determining an acceptable sampling margin of error depends on how close the researcher expects the outcome of the survey to be. In an election that promises to be extremely tight, for example, the people conducting the research would want to survey as many voters as possible to reduce the sampling margin of error. Also, it is always important to report the "don't know" responses. In close surveys, they might be the swing vote. Make sure to consider them when determining whether or not one side has a majority.

Gathering Data

After forming his questions and developing his sample, Walters must select the best way to gather the information. Kelly promises him that he can use eight reporters and editors to help conduct the survey. Basically, Walters can use one of three methods to gather the information: *face-to-face interviews, mailed questionnaires* and *telephone interviews.* All these methods are acceptable; choice of method depends on the situation.

Face-to-Face Interviews

Walters likes the idea of conducting face-to-face interviews. This way, the reporters conducting the interviews can probe extensively during the questioning process. Because Walters wants only parents to answer the questions, face-to-face interviewing will ensure that the respondent is not a teen-ager passing himself off as an adult.

On the other hand, Walters wants to complete the survey as quickly as possible so that he can publish the story before the school board meets in two weeks. Face-to-face interviewing will take considerable time, however, for his limited cast of reporters and editors. Walters thus realizes that the project probably cannot be completed before the next board meeting. Also, Kelly will probably question the overtime pay.

Mailed Questionnaires

Walters knows that a mailed questionnaire is relatively inexpensive, but he is concerned about the possible low rate of return. Generally, a researcher can expect about a 30 percent return on mailed questionnaires. Walters wants to get the survey completed as soon as possible. He does not want to have to conduct a follow-up survey if the response rate on the first mailing is low, and he needs at least 350 responses to keep his sampling error no higher than 5.2 percent. Thus he decides against mailed questionnaires.

Telephone Interviews

Walters finally decides that the best way to conduct the survey is by telephone. The telephone affords the luxury of follow-ups and clarification of answers, which mailed surveys are too cumbersome to handle, and it is faster than face-to-face interviewing. He realizes, of course, that telephones are used to sell everything from house siding to magazines. People often resent unsolicited telephone calls. Thus, his questions must be very clearly drafted, and he must pare them down so that they can be asked in a few minutes. He does not want to irritate the people being interviewed by asking long, irrelevant questions.

Kelly and Walters go over the questions with the eight reporters and editors who have been assigned to help conduct the survey. They decide to make their calls after 6 p.m., when working parents are more likely to be home.

The professor's estimate was accurate—500 calls result in 350 usable responses.

Analyzing the Data

Walters could hand-tabulate the results, but the professor offers to show him how to computerize the data. It takes Walters about three hours to enter the data into the computer. The professor programs the computer to handle the data. Once the data and the computer instructions are completed, in less than a minute the computer spits out the results. Walters is primarily interested in percentages.

Walters goes through the information, isolating percentages that he thinks will be of most interest to his readers. He turns to the printout of the survey's key question: "The Riverdale School Board is considering changing from modular scheduling to traditional seven-period scheduling. Do you prefer modular scheduling or the traditional seven-period scheduling?"

Overall, 350 persons were asked the question. The responses were as follows: modular, 210 (60 percent); traditional, 118 (34 percent); don't know, 22 (6 percent).

Next, Walters looks at the breakdown according to age. Of the 350 who responded, 70 were under age 30; 120 were between ages 30 and 39; 100 were between ages 40 and 49; 60 were age 50 or older.

The responses:

Age	Modular	Traditional	Don't Know
Under age 30	47 (67 percent)	18 (26 percent)	5 (7 percent)
Ages 30–39	73 (61 percent)	39 (33 percent)	8 (7 percent)
Ages 40–49	65 (65 percent)	29 (29 percent)	6 (6 percent)
Ages 50 and older	25 (42 percent)	32 (53 percent)	3 (5 percent)

The percentages show that more than half of all parents polled preferred modular scheduling. In fact, 60 percent of the 350 persons surveyed said that they favored it.

With the figures in mind, Walters is ready to write his lead.

Writing the Story

The Lead

Walters is careful not to overstate or understate the significance of the figures. He determines that the most **newsworthy element** of the survey is that most of the parents favor modular scheduling. Even though the survey showed that 60 percent favor this type of scheduling, he realizes that the sampling error could lower or raise the number 5.2 percentage points. Walters decides on this safe, accurate lead:

> More than half of the parents of Riverdale schoolchildren prefer modular scheduling, a *Daily News* poll shows.

Walters continues his story with specific results of the focal question:

> Sixty percent of those surveyed said that they preferred modular scheduling; 34 percent said that they preferred traditional scheduling; and 6 percent said that they did not know.

Walters' story goes on to detail other statistical findings of the survey. He also weaves some open-ended responses into his story. He is careful, when selecting open-ended responses, to include comments from respondents who favor modular scheduling and respondents who oppose it.

Explanatory Material: Essential Information

Walters also inserts the following into his story:

> The *Daily News* randomly interviewed 350 parents in the Riverdale School District. Telephone interviews were conducted Wednesday and Thursday evenings by *Daily News* reporters and editors.
>
> As with all sample surveys, the results of the *Daily News* poll can vary from the opinions of all school district parents because of chance variations in the sample.

> For a poll based on 350 interviews, the results are subject to a margin of error of 5.2 percentage points each way because of such chance variations. That is, if one could have talked to all Riverdale School District parents by telephone on Wednesday and Thursday, there is only 1 chance in 20 that the findings would vary by more than 5.2 percentage points from the results of surveys such as this one.

Walters inserted the explanatory paragraphs about the size of the sample, the survey procedures and the sampling error to keep within the guidelines suggested by the National Council on Public Polling. The Associated Press Stylebook suggests that editors and reporters consider the guidelines before using a story about a canvass of public opinion.

The guidelines, which were discussed in the *Washington Journalism Review* article by Evans Witt, include the following:

1. State who sponsored the survey.
2. Give the dates of interviewing.
3. Define the method of interviewing.
4. Describe the population interviewed.
5. State the size of the sample.
6. Describe and give the size of any subsamples used in the analysis.
7. Release the wording of all questions.
8. Release the full results of the questions on which the conclusions are based.

Witt, however, put the guidelines into perspective. He wrote: "They provide the minimum information needed for a reporter—or a reader—to evaluate a poll. They do not guarantee that a poll will be competently conducted; they provide no guarantees against massive errors that could affect results."

The New York Times Manual of Style and Usage states that occasionally not all polling details can be included in a story. The manual concludes: "If there ever is a doubt, the reporter should include as much of the information as possible. The responsible editors can then decide how much should be used."

The manual also cautions that terms such as *opinion poll, poll, survey, opinion sample* and *cross section* "should be limited to truly scientific soundings of opinion. They should not be applied to stringer roundups and man-in-the-street stories by reporters."

Reporting Surveys: Rules and Guidelines for Journalists

General Considerations

Surveys are most commonly used at newspapers during election campaigns to measure opinions about candidates and major issues. Of course, as has been discussed, they can also be used for community issues other than elections.

Newspapers of various circulations—including student publications—can enter the arena of precision journalism relatively easily. Only those outlets that have the labor power, the expertise and the available money to do the job right, however, should base stories on precision journalism methods.

Here are some suggestions to consider when writing a story based on a survey:

- Analyze the data carefully before starting to write. Ask yourself: What findings would be of most interest to my audience?
- Make sure that you are interpreting the statistics correctly. Check with a knowledgeable editor or supervisor if you have any questions or doubts.
- Lead with the survey's most significant findings.
- Make every effort to humanize the statistics. Focus on what the statistics say about people.
- Organize the story so that readers can comprehend the most significant findings. The use of bullets (•) to outline key statistics is often an effective way to keep the story flowing while presenting a lot of information.
- Make comparisons among subgroups in the sample when appropriate. (For example: male versus female, older respondents versus younger respondents, Republicans versus Democrats and so forth.)
- Work in as many direct quotations from survey subjects as you can. This will help bring the numbers to life.
- Provide relevant details about the sample and the method for gathering the information.
- Devise charts to accompany the story, if that is the most efficient and understandable way to present some statistical information.

Avoiding Distortions: James Simon's Top-10 Factors

James Simon is an experienced political reporter and pollster. He covered government and elections for 10 years with The Associated Press, and he served also as associate director of the Cactus State Poll in the Walter Cronkite School of Journalism and Mass Communication at Arizona State University. He is currently a professor at Fairfield University in Connecticut, where he does polling for academic, public and private clients.

Simon has noted: "Public opinion polls give reporters a chance to look at the views of the public toward an issue in the news. But the results of a survey depend largely on how it is conducted. Reporters often place too much emphasis on the sampling error that is inherent in a random survey. There are many other factors that can distort the results."

Simon compiled the following list of 10 factors that can distort the outcome of polls. They are factors that all journalists should keep in mind.

1. Reflection versus Prediction: Polls as "Snapshots"

A poll is a snapshot of a population at a given moment. One hour after the poll is conducted, respondents may hear a television newscast on a given subject and change their views. Because survey data can have such a short shelf life, pollsters try to release their findings within days of collection. Be wary of data that was *collected* more than a week before the release of the survey, especially if it concerns a volatile issue.

Polls reflect; they do not predict. They can be a very good reflection of how voters feel a week before an election. In many cases, they may be a poor predictor of how a volatile electorate will feel a week later on Election Day.

2. *Sponsors: Are They Credible?*

Special-interest groups routinely commission polls to help push their agendas, and the results should be judged with skepticism.

The questions that were included—and the questions that were left out—are often invisible to reporters. For example, a group advocating nuclear power may include properly worded questions about the higher cost of power from fossil fuel plants, then report greater public support for cheaper nuclear power. But the survey probably would not ask any questions about public sentiment toward problems involved in disposing of radioactive waste, questions that would show less public support for nuclear power.

The answer received is, in part, a product of the question asked. Does the poll do a good job of getting at the overall issue? Be sure the reader/viewer understands who sponsored the survey, and why.

3. *Samples: Who Was Polled?*

The headline is clear: Candidate Jones has a 10-point lead, with a week to go before Election Day. But in reading the story, you notice that the poll is based on interviews with 600 state *residents*, not registered voters. And you know that one-third of all state residents are not registered to vote. Pollsters have to be careful when choosing their sampling framework to ensure that it is the right one for a given issue. Arizona State University's Cactus State Poll, for example, almost always uses registered voters, since so many of the surveys deal with election issues. But a sample of all state residents, not just voters, would be more appropriate to measure opinions on a non-ballot issue such as the public's view of the death penalty.

When reading poll results, reporters should ask themselves: Did the pollsters go to the right people?

4. *Neutrality and Accuracy: How Were the Questions Phrased?*

Most surveys of attitudes toward abortion show general public support for a woman's right to choose. But using the phrase *innocent fetus* in such a question could produce very different results. Good surveys include the phrasing of the questions; as a reporter, you should reread the phrasing and ask yourself whether it appears neutral.

A related problem can stem from "double-barreled" questions. For example: "Do you agree or disagree with the statement, 'the United Nations is an inefficient body and the United States should leave it'?" If you agree with the first part of the sentence and not with the second, it would be impossible to give an accurate response.

As a reporter, you should examine the phrasing of survey questions very critically.

5. *Context: In What Order Were the Questions Presented?*

Appropriate phrasing of questions is not the only concern reporters should have. Pollsters usually don't release the full list of questions, which would show the *context* in which a question appeared. Again, support for abortion would be much lower if the question was preceded by a question dealing with the rights of the unborn. Polls commissioned by non-partisan groups usually are careful about context; surveys from special-interest groups deserve closer scrutiny.

Reporters should seek a copy of the survey and examine the order of questions.

6. Respondents' Answers: Giving the "Right" Answer?

When called by a pollster, most people are reluctant to express socially undesirable views. They may feel a civic duty to give a politically correct answer or to say what they think the pollster wants to hear. But when they get to the privacy of the voting booth, they can act freely without any fear of what a pollster or anyone else might think.

This tendency made it very hard to survey Arizona residents in the 1990s when the state considered a holiday to honor the late Dr. Martin Luther King Jr. When pollsters asked residents whether they supported the plan, a large majority said they did—perhaps because it was the politically correct thing to do. But in the privacy of the voting booth, a majority initially turned down the proposal.

7. Attitudes and Non-Attitudes: Measuring Intensity

A pollster asks your opinion on your university's fine arts program. You don't really have a firm opinion, but the pollster presses and you say you have a generally favorable opinion. You are not lying: you may have a generally favorable opinion toward everything at the university. But in this case, you really don't have a clear attitude on the fine arts program. The pollster, if he or she takes down your view and builds it into the findings, is measuring a "non-attitude." The results won't really provide a clear picture of how you feel.

Pollsters can counter this problem by asking an "intensity" question—"How strongly do you feel about the issue?"—and then focusing on those respondents who have strong feelings.

8. Interpretations: Evaluating Pollsters' Conclusions

In one of the Cactus State Polls in 1992, the pollsters decided to take an early look at Ross Perot, who at that point was just talking about a possible independent bid for the U.S. presidency. In an effort to gauge what impact he might have in Arizona, voters were asked whether they would consider voting for him. The result: 27 percent said they were likely to support this little-known candidate, 49 percent were opposed and 24 percent said they had no opinion. The pollsters faced a tough question: Is 27 percent support high or low as a starting point for a potential candidate? The answer was not clear, and the pollsters simply reported the numbers without offering an evaluation.

There are many ways to interpret survey results. Be skeptical about a pollster's comments that accompany survey results. As a reporter, always ask yourself: Do the comments make sense? Should I seek out other points of view?

9. Statistical Significance: Are the Results Meaningful?

Candidate Smith is leading candidate Jones by a margin of 52 percent to 48 percent. The sampling error in the poll is 3 percent. Does Smith have a clear lead?

The answer is no. The race should be reported as a tossup, a statistical dead heat or as too close to call. The sampling error must be applied to the percentage for each candidate, not to the difference between their percentages. Smith could have anywhere from 49 percent to 55 percent of the vote. Jones could have anywhere from 45 percent to 51 percent; if it is 51 percent, then Jones is actually leading Smith. A statistically significant lead exists only when a candidate is ahead both at the high end and the low end of the sampling error.

This is a common problem. When reading poll results before writing your story, factor in the sampling error yourself to see if the pollster handled it correctly.

10. Consistency: Comparing Results Across Polls

Due to the increased number of polls that are conducted and covered by the media, there are often multiple polls on the same subjects. While survey results may vary due to the many issues discussed in this section, readers or viewers will benefit from learning how one survey compares to others done on the same topic. Avoid taking the easy way out and reporting on only one survey.

A quick examination of a news organization's "morgue" or background files, combined with a search of an online database like Lexis-Nexis, may reveal comparable surveys that can help flesh out a topic. Web sites like *pollingreport.com* also can provide background information on trends in American public opinion.

Simon emphasized that "a healthy dose of skepticism is the best attitude to have in analyzing poll results. Reporters should insist that the pollster supply enough information to demonstrate the validity of the survey."

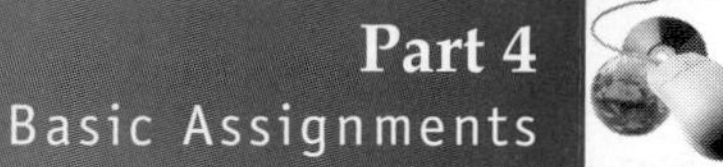

OBITUARIES

Reporters sometimes consider writing obituaries, or obits, a fate worse than death, but the fact remains that **obits**—death notices—are highly interesting to readers.

The policy of *The Berkshire* (Mass.) *Eagle* possibly best summarizes the philosophy of many newspapers: "It is our policy to run obituaries and funeral notices involving deceased persons who have any connection at all with our circulation area. If John Jones fished here in 1937 and lived happily ever after in Tacoma, we use his obit because we deem it news, it creates goodwill (or at least it avoids creating bad will) and we try to be the paper of record for our area."

(*Reuters / TimePix*)

Sometimes, death stories merit front-page treatment. Always, however, writers should craft obits to pull readers into the story and to hold them by capturing, in words, the essence of a life.

J. Y. Smith and Noel Epstein of *The Washington Post* certainly did that when one of journalism's best-known executives died:

> Katharine Graham, 84, who led The Washington Post Co. to prominence in the worlds of journalism and business and became one of the most influential and admired women of her generation, died yesterday morning at St. Alphonsus Regional Medical Center in Boise, Idaho.
>
> Mrs. Graham, former chairman and chief executive officer of The Post Co. and former publisher of *The Washington Post,* died at 11:56 a.m. of head injuries suffered when she was attending an annual conference of media business leaders. Her son, Donald, The Post Co.'s current chairman and CEO, also was attending the conference. He and many other members of the family were at the hospital in Boise when she died.

Marilyn Berger, writing in *The New York Times,* focused on Mrs. Graham's personality and her accomplishments:

> Katharine Graham, who transformed *The Washington Post* from a mediocre newspaper into an American institution, and, in the process, transformed herself from a shy widow into a publishing legend, died yesterday after suffering head injuries in a fall on a sidewalk on Saturday in Idaho. She was 84.
>
> Mrs. Graham had been attending a business conference in Sun Valley. She was flown to a hospital in Boise, where she underwent brain surgery but never recovered consciousness, her son Donald E. Graham said.

In reporting the death of Jack Lemmon, journalists across the country used a variety of approaches to summarize his life, all of which coalesced his accomplishments, his demeanor and his range as an actor.

Here's a sample:

> Jack Lemmon, a two-time Oscar winner whose 50-year career encompassed both physical comedy and intense drama, died Wednesday night at 76.
>
> One of Hollywood's most beloved figures, Lemmon died from complications related to cancer, said his publicist Warren Cowan. His wife of 39 years, Felicia, son Chris and daughter Courtney were at his bedside at University of Southern California/Norris Cancer Clinic. (*San Francisco Chronicle*)

> Jack Lemmon, who turned worry into an art form and became one of America's most beloved actors doing it, died Wednesday night in Los Angeles of complications from cancer. He was 76.
>
> Boston-bred Harvard grad Lemmon, born in an elevator in Newton-Wellesley Hospital, appeared in 90 films and won two Oscars—a supporting actor statue for his prankish laundry officer, Ensign Pulver, in "Mr. Roberts" (1955), and a best actor award for his self-loathing dress manufacturer watching his ideals crumble, in "Save the Tiger" (1973).
>
> Those Oscars span the uneasiness that Mr. Lemmon was able to steer unerringly in comic or tragic directions, pushing off in both cases from audience perceptions of him as the everyman next door, a guy who never played the boss. (*The Boston Globe*)

Jack Lemmon changed what it meant to be a movie star.

Not a stocky hero like John Wayne or a handsome charmer like Clark Gable or Cary Grant. And certainly not one of what Lemmon once called "the curly-haired pretty boys" who reigned in Hollywood when he first appeared. Lemmon was something new.

He was us.

Many watching his debut film, "It Should Happen to You," or "Mister Roberts" thought to themselves, "Hey, that guy's like me."

And he was—especially if you happened to be a neurotic little guy in a gray flannel suit that never seemed to fit quite right.

A master comedian who personified the nervous modern Everyman, Lemmon died of cancer Wednesday night. He was 76. (*USA Today*)

Jack Lemmon, the brash young American Everyman who evolved into the screen's grumpiest old Everyman during a movie career that lasted a half century, died on Wednesday at a hospital in Los Angeles. He was 76 and lived in Beverly Hills.

The cause was complications from cancer, said a spokesman, Warren Cowan.

Through most of his more than 60 movies, Mr. Lemmon was the least glamorous and most approachable of movie stars—the good-natured ordinary guy next door with a slightly skewed moral compass. He was a master of sardonic comedy and could convey urban frustrations so deftly that audiences identified with him and thus were able to laugh at themselves. (*The New York Times*)

Each of the lead blocks of the Lemmon death stories used different approaches, but they shared a common bond: in a minimum of words, they captured his persona while fusing his special qualities and achievements.

Martin Merzer of *The Miami Herald* did the same when a baseball legend died:

He possessed a sweet swing and a tortured soul. He sparkled as the centerpiece of the most famous team in sports and as the life of too many parties. He excelled at every element of his game and still left his potential unfilled.

Mickey Mantle, a former switch-hitting slugger for the New York Yankees and one of baseball's all-time greats, died in Dallas on Sunday of an aggressive form of cancer. He was 63.

Glenn Frankel of *The Washington Post*, in writing the obituary of a slain leader, dipped into his reservoir of remembrances to compose this gripping lead block:

No man—Israeli, Palestinian or American—was more essential to the Middle East peace process than Yitzhak Rabin, who was gunned down by an assassin in Tel Aviv last night.

Without his acquiescence, there would have been no secret talks between Israeli and Palestinian negotiators in Oslo. Without his support, the two sides would not have reached the 1993 agreement that granted Palestinians political autonomy, triggered Israeli military withdrawal from the Gaza Strip and Jericho and set the timetable for further withdrawal from much of the West Bank.

And without his blessing, delivered in the form of his historical handshake with Palestinian leader Yasser Arafat on the White House lawn in September of that year, the divided and wary Israeli people would never have accepted an arrangement that held great promise for peace but also contained great risks.

Selecting Obituaries to Publish

Most newspapers have an obit page. Depending on the circulation of the newspaper and the population of the area served, obituaries might fill a portion of the page or they might spill over to more than one page. Most newspapers publish obits—free—for every resident and former resident. Some larger-circulation newspapers obviously do not have sufficient space to publish an obit of everyone who dies in their area, but they do publish obits of as many people as they can. Some newspapers provide a list of the deceased with only basic facts such as age and date of death. Still other newspapers publish complete obituary information in classified advertising space purchased by funeral homes or by families.

In addition to obits published regularly on their designated page, newspapers occasionally carry front-page stories on the deaths of well-known people.

A national survey of 165 daily newspaper managing editors selected at random found that 94 percent of the country's dailies publish obits for all area residents and that nearly 9 in 10 of the dailies publish them free of charge.

The *New Haven* (Conn.) *Register* has a well-stated policy on the handling of obituaries. The *Register* "strives to run all obituaries submitted as quickly as possible after submission." If, in a space or time crunch, some obits must be held, the *Register's* policy establishes the following priority system:

1. First, obituaries of people whose deaths are significant news
2. Second, obituaries in which the funerals are on the day of publication or the next day
3. Third, obituaries in which the decedent's residence and the location of the funeral are in the New Haven area as opposed to outside the region
4. Fourth, obituaries of people who formerly lived in the area but most recently lived, and will be buried, elsewhere

The *Register* even accepts "occasional obituaries of people who never have lived in the area but have immediate family ties here or are widely known in this area." These obits, however, are kept concise, with most biographical information omitted "unless an individual is newsworthy in his or her own right."

Many newspapers are so conscious of their responsibility to publish obits that they will print an obit several days after a death if word of the death has been delayed. This often happens in the case of a person who had lived and worked in the community but had retired to another area of the country. A week after the person's death, the newspaper might receive a letter with obit information. Then, after verifying it, many papers will publish an obit beginning something like this: "John P. Jones, 75, former Riverdale electrician, died Oct. 25 at his home in Palm Springs, Calif."

Content of Obituaries

Basic Information in Obits

Obits should contain certain basic information, typically including:

- Address
- Date of death
- Cause of death

- Occupation
- Accomplishments
- Time and date of services
- Visitation information
- Place of burial
- Memorial information
- Names of survivors

In addition, some smaller-circulation newspapers carry follows to obits in which pallbearers are listed.

Many newspapers, such as *The Evansville* (Ind.) *Courier,* strive to expand obits beyond this basic information. The editor, Tom Tuley, who published a study of obit practices at various newspapers in the *Editor's Exchange,* said that he had "some uneasiness about whether we are doing as good a job with obits as we should." He cited the need to find out more about the person.

"We make an effort to call people to get additional information or anecdotes," he said. "My feeling is that there is something interesting in everyone's life. We have received good responses from our readers and the families of the deceased for our efforts."

Deadlines and limited staff, of course, keep the *Courier* from expanding all obits. But Tuley said that his newspaper tries to provide interesting details about "common people," not just celebrities and public figures.

Let's look now at the basic elements in obits.

Names

Newspapers generally use the first name, middle initial and last name of the deceased. Most do not use nicknames—particularly if a nickname sounds derogatory. If the deceased was known to most people by his or her nickname, however, some newspapers will use it. For example:

> John E. "Booster" Jones, who had not missed a Riverdale High School home basketball game since 1947, died Wednesday in Samaritan Memorial Hospital after a short illness. He was 72.

Note that the nickname is set off in quotation marks (not parentheses; in obits, the use of parentheses indicates a maiden name). Also, if the nickname would slow the cadence of the lead sentence, save it for later. For example:

> John E. Jones, who had not missed a Riverdale High School home basketball game since 1947, died Wednesday in Samaritan Memorial Hospital after a short illness. Mr. Jones, who was known to his friends as "Booster," was 72.

In the above example, a **courtesy title** (Mr.) was used on second reference. Few newspapers use courtesy titles (such as Mr., Mrs., Miss, Ms. or Dr.) on second references in news stories, but many do so in obits.

Ages

Many newspapers mandate that the age of the deceased be printed. The *News-Journal* in Daytona Beach, Fla., has a policy that states: "Always include the age of deceased and address. If necessary (but only after having exhausted all avenues) fudge a bit and say 'in his/her 70s or 80s' or whatever. There *must be* some indication of age."

The reader should never have to use arithmetic to figure out the age of the deceased (obit writers should not merely give the date and place of birth). Reporters must be careful when computing ages. Reporters and their sources often forget to take the date of birth into account. For example, a person is born Feb. 15, 1940, and dies Feb. 1, 2000. That person would be 59, not 60. A common blunder is to merely subtract 1940 from 2000 to come up with 60.

Ages can be handled in a number of ways, including these:

- John E. Jones, 72, died Wednesday in Riverdale.
- John E. Jones died Wednesday in Riverdale. He was 72.
- John E. Jones died Wednesday in Riverdale at the age of 72.
- John E. Jones died Wednesday in Riverdale at 72 years of age.

The first two examples are preferable to the last two. In the last two examples, the extra words make the language more stilted than necessary.

Addresses

Practices vary on the use of addresses. Some newspapers use full addresses (2142 S. 168th Ave., Riverdale) while others use only the town. The policy of *The Trentonian,* for example, states: "The family, usually through the funeral director, may sometimes ask that exact addresses not be used to avoid possible burglaries. We'll go along with this request, although we usually prefer using full addresses."

Causes of Death

General policies. Policies vary on stating the cause of death in obits. The national survey of managing editors cited earlier in this chapter showed that 9 percent of the papers always publish the cause of death in obituaries. Nearly 78 percent said that they sometimes do; 13 percent said that they never do.

The policy of the *New Haven Register,* for example, states: "If relatives do not want information disclosed concerning a particular disease, 'a long illness' or similar phrase may be used. If death is violent, however—for example, in an auto accident or a shooting—that fact should not be disguised. The rule of thumb is that if the funeral home does not volunteer a cause of death, ask. Too many times there have been attempts to slip obituaries through when the deaths were homicides or suspected homicides."

The policy of the *Fargo* (N.D.) *Forum* states: "Usually we do not specify the cause of death, but we ask the question in case we might miss an accident or death under suspicious circumstances. If an accident is involved, notify the city desk so that a news story can be prepared about the accident. Obituaries of accident victims should note that 'she died of injuries received in an auto accident Friday.' "

The Trentonian's policy also provides flexibility: "We do not insist on using the cause of death unless it involves accidental or other unusual circumstances. Where the deceased is young, we always ask the funeral director the cause of death. Where the deceased is prominent, regardless of age, try to determine whether it was a long or a short illness. We don't usually specify the type of illness unless the family requests it. Also, don't call it a 'lengthy' illness. It's short or long."

Most newspapers mention the cause of death if the person was well-known. Here are some examples taken from wire-service stories:

TOKYO (AP)—Emperor Hirohito, who held divine status until Japan's defeat in World War II and endured to reign for 62 years, died today of intestinal cancer. He was 87.

Crown Prince Akihito, 55, the emperor's oldest son, immediately became the 125th occupant of the Chrysanthemum Throne and received the imperial regalia.

Chief Cabinet Secretary Kenzo Obuchi said the emperor died at 6:33 a.m.

LOS ANGELES (AP)—Lucille Ball, the zany redhead who reigned for more than 20 years as the queen of television comedy, died today, a week after undergoing emergency heart surgery. She was 77.

The star of "I Love Lucy" and similar situation comedies that continue in syndication died of a ruptured aorta at Cedars-Sinai Medical Center, hospital spokesman Ronald Wise said.

BEVERLY HILLS, Calif. (UPI)—Actor Rock Hudson, the square-jawed movie hero who played the role of the suave ladies' man for three decades, died Wednesday after a yearlong battle with AIDS—the first major celebrity known to have been felled by the disease.

In Washington, the House, acting hours after Hudson's death was announced, voted 322–107 to substantially boost the amount of federal money for the battle against AIDS. The measure provides $189.7 million for AIDS work, $70 million more than President Reagan requested and 90 percent more than is being spent this year.

Policies on suicide. One of the major problems facing newspapers is how to handle obits or news stories when suicide is the cause of death. Again, policies vary. The *Bangor* (Maine) *Daily News,* for example, does not include that information in its obits. "We feel that the obit is a permanent record which families keep, and neither they nor their descendants should have to be reminded of a suicide every time they take out the family album," said Kent H. Ward, associate managing editor. "Further, we do not run suicides as news stories unless they involve prominent people or the suicide was committed in public or in some spectacular manner. In other words, if Mr. Average Joe goes down in the privacy of his basement or out behind the barn and kills himself, we do not give it a play. And his obit would probably state that he died unexpectedly."

The *Iowa City* (Iowa) *Press Citizen*'s policy states: "If someone commits suicide, it is generally handled as an obit. But calling someone's death a suicide requires confirmation from the medical examiner."

The *New Haven Register* labels deaths as suicides or apparent suicides only if "the person taking his or her life is a public figure or the suicide takes place in full view of other people. Any statement that a death is a suicide must be attributed."

The national survey of managing editors showed that 17 percent of the newspapers always use the word *suicide* in obits if it is determined to be the cause of death; 21 percent sometimes use it; and 62 percent never use it.

The most pertinent information—name, age, address, date of death and sometimes cause of death—is placed in the lead of an obit; supplementary facts fill the remaining paragraphs. Newspaper policy and the importance of the deceased are primary factors in determining the length of obits. Generally, however, the information discussed in the following sections is provided.

Background

The extent of background information will, of course, depend on the accomplishments and the community involvement of the deceased. Many obits provide the following:

- Date and place of birth
- Names of parents
- Education
- Work experience
- Honors received
- Military background

For example:

> Dr. Johnson was born Jan. 22, 1921, in Salt Lake City, Utah, the son of Joe and Carolyn Johnson. He received his medical degree from the University of Utah.
>
> He practiced medicine in Riverdale for nearly 30 years. He was honored by the Nuckolls County Medical Association in 1993 for outstanding contributions to the profession. He also served on the governor's blue-ribbon panel on hospital care.
>
> Dr. Johnson, who served in World War II, is a member of the VFW, the Knights of Columbus and the Nuckolls County Cancer Society.

Newspapers normally decide on a case-by-case basis whether potentially embarrassing or sensitive information should be used in an obituary. Common sense must be exercised. An obit writer might decide, for example, that it would serve no purpose to mention that John Smith had been convicted of income tax evasion and had served a 10-month sentence in a federal penitentiary 20 years ago. However, if John Smith had been convicted in a sensational murder trial 20 years ago and was paroled only 18 months ago, that would probably merit mention in the obit.

Many writers, out of respect for the surviving family, nevertheless try to handle these references in a matter-of-fact, unemotional way that is least offensive.

Funeral Services, Visitation and Memorials

Most newspapers list the time, day and place of the funeral, the clergyman or clergywoman and the religious affiliation. Place of burial is also mentioned. For example:

> The funeral will be at 10 a.m. Wednesday in the Butler-Blatchford Funeral Home. The Rev. Silas Smith, pastor of the First Methodist Church, will officiate. Burial will be in Evergreen Cemetery.

The Findlay (Ohio) *Courier,* like many newspapers, provides details of **visitation.** Its policy states: "In addition to the hours of visitation, we will include the hours that the decedent's family will be at the funeral home, if that information is provided. For instance: 'Visitation will be held from 2–5 and 7–9 p.m. Tuesday at the funeral home. The family will be present from 4–5 p.m.' "

Policies on mention of **memorials** differ among newspapers. The policy of the *Jamestown* (N.Y.) *Post-Journal,* for example, states: "Last paragraph notes memorials, if the family suggests same. We do not use 'In lieu of flowers.' Write instead that 'The family suggests memorials be made to the Heart Fund.' "

The Findlay Courier's policy states: "We do not say 'in lieu of flowers, memorials may be made . . .' Nor do we say that memorials 'should' be made. Simply say that 'memorials may be made to . . .' or 'the family requests that memorials be made to . . .' One other note: We do not say that memorials may be made to a specific person or family."

Survivors

The policy of the *Jamestown Post-Journal* concerning the listing of survivors is typical of many small- and medium-circulation newspapers. It states:

> (1) List names of spouse, children, grandchildren, sisters and brothers. [Many newspapers list only the number of, but not the names of, grandchildren.] Give number of, but not names of great-grandchildren. Other distant relatives, such as nieces and nephews, aunts, uncles and cousins are named if they are the only survivors in the *Post-Journal* circulation area [many newspapers never list the names of distant relatives].
>
> (2) If the deceased lived with a distant relative, but is survived by someone in his immediate family, we will include that relative by noting, "Smith lived with his nephew, John Jones."
>
> Editors will consider other special circumstances as they arise. Example: if the deceased has a lot of immediate-family survivors, but a cousin was the only one who took care of him, we will list, at the discretion of the city, regional or news editors, the cousin if the family asks us to do so. We will note, for example, that the deceased was cared for by his cousin, John Jones.

An example of a paragraph listing survivors follows:

> Survivors include his wife, the former Irene McDonald; two daughters, Susan Johnson, Evansville, Ind., and Patricia Kelly, Los Angeles; three sons, Richard, Fargo, N.D., Allan, Omaha, Neb., and William, Laramie, Wyo.; a sister, Lois Folz, Cooper City, Fla.; a brother, Sterling, Great Bend, Kan.; eight grandchildren; and three great-grandchildren.

A delicate situation can arise if the decedent was divorced or estranged from a spouse. The *New Haven Register* provides this advice: "Do not become embroiled in a family dispute over inclusion of the surviving individual in the obit. Tell the parties to work it out and have the funeral home supply the correct information. If, however, the relationship to the survivor is itself newsworthy, do not omit the survivor's name merely because other survivors do not like him or her."

The *Register* also takes into consideration surviving fiancés and companions: "If the decedent was engaged to be married, the fiancé or fiancée may be listed as a survivor if the decedent's family requests it. If the decedent had a live-in

companion and those arranging the funeral insist the name be included, put the name at the end of the list of survivors: . . . and Mary Jones, with whom Mr. Smith resided."

Obit writers should never be surprised at requests from funeral home directors or from relatives of the deceased. With this in mind, the *Register* policy states: "Never list pets as survivors."

Newspaper policies on the range of information that might be included in an obit naturally vary. It is important, therefore, that reporters who are to write obits carefully review the policy of the newspaper. If there is no written policy, study obits from past issues. If in doubt, always consult an editor.

Sources of Information

Funeral Homes

Most information for obituaries is provided to the media by funeral homes (also called *mortuaries*). However, the policy of the *New Haven Register* emphasizes the need for gathering information beyond that provided by mortuaries: "In most situations the *Register* depends on funeral homes to submit obituaries. This does not mean, however, that the newspaper's position should be supine. If a prominent person or a person violently injured is known to be near death, the newspapers should check with the hospital, the public relations officer of the person's employer or a similar authority in order not to miss the news story. Information concerning funeral services may be put off until subsequent editions."

Where to Turn Online

Background information also may be found on the Internet and online commercial services such as Lexis/Nexis. For example, many people have personal home pages, which may be found by using search engines such as AltaVista *(www.altavista.com)* or HotBot *(www.hotbot.lycos.com)*. A "people finder" database such as AnyWho *(www.anywho.com)* can help reporters quickly find the names and telephone numbers of neighbors who might have known the subject.

More information might be found in the searchable electronic clip files of many newspapers; reporters will want to check the electronic archives for their newspapers as well as the online publications listings found in the trade journal *Editor & Publisher (www.mediainfo.com)*.

Families

After gathering additional information from clippings and possibly from interviews with law enforcement officials, hospital officials, employers, fellow workers and friends, calls to family members may be in order. This, of course, should be handled delicately.

Tom Tuley of *The Evansville Courier* offers this advice to reporters who are making calls to grieving family members: "The whole problem—if you can call it a problem—can be solved by the approach of the writer. The family is under great strain. But it seems to me that about 99 percent of the people we call appreciate the fact that we want to make every effort to be accurate and to include additional information. I don't think reporters should hesitate to make a call because they fear the family member will be uncomfortable." The key, of course, to a successful interview is to establish rapport with the family member and to carry on the conversation with dignity.

Ensuring Accuracy in Obits

Confirming Information

Accuracy is immensely important in any news story, but inaccurate information in an obit can cause severe pain to surviving family members. Thus, it is particularly important to confirm all information gathered for obits. Because most of the facts contained in obits come from telephone calls from the mortuary, reporters should be diligent in checking names, cities and addresses in available directories. It is also wise to compute the age of the person from his or her date of birth to verify the age supplied by the mortuary. And when taking calls from the mortuary, always ask the caller to repeat any words or spellings that sound unusual.

According to the managing editor, Monroe Dodd, the *Kansas City Times* verified all information supplied by funeral homes by calling family members. Additional information was sought from or verified by police, coroners and other law enforcement officials. Occasionally, reporters at the *Times* would speak to business associates or close friends of the deceased if the family was vague or uncertain on some pertinent matters.

Avoiding Hoaxes

The *New Haven Register's* policy warns reporters to confirm deaths: "An obit called in by a funeral director with whom the reporter is not familiar should be confirmed by calling back. Get the number from the phone book or long-distance information; don't trust the number the caller may just have given you. If the obit is submitted by someone other than a funeral director, call the funeral home to confirm it. If the funeral home cannot be reached, the death should be confirmed with a reliable—that word should be emphasized—second source."

Some newspapers, such as *The Trentonian* in Trenton, N.J., verify calls from mortuaries by asking for the funeral director's obit code. "If he doesn't have one," the newspaper policy states, "verify that he's a funeral director by calling back the number listed in the telephone book, no matter where in the world it is. This will hopefully eliminate the dreaded hoax, the bane of all obit writers."

Obituary Styles

Routine obits at the *Chicago Tribune* and at scores of other newspapers normally follow two styles. The styles adhered to by the *Tribune* city desk are as follows: If the obit is written on the day of the death—a **same-day obit**—the fact that the person died is the lead. If the obit is written one or more days after the death—a **second-day obit**—the time of the services is the lead.

Terminology

Editors often single out words, phrases and usages that should be considered when writing obits. A sample follows.

- *Terminology for Death.* "People die—period! They don't die suddenly any more than they die slowly, although they may have died quickly after being struck in the heart with an MX missile."—Policy of *The Trentonian.*

  "Nobody dies suddenly. We all die at the same speed. Some causes of death are quicker than others, but the speed of death itself is constant. A person dies of an ailment, not from it. A person is dead on arrival at a hospital, not 'to' it. You arrive at a place, not 'to' it. Also, people are 'taken' to hospitals. If we say they are 'transported,' it sounds like they are freight."—Policy of *The Findlay Courier.*
- *Place of Birth.* "Funeral directors are fond of saying that John Jones was a 'former native' of some place. Native means the place of birth, and so a person cannot be a former native."—Policy of the *Jamestown Post-Journal.*
- *Titles for Ministers, Pastors and Priests.* Always check the AP Stylebook for proper terminology for religions and church officials.

Writing Effective Obituaries

Capturing the Flavor of a Life

Obits often fall into the standard, concise forms outlined above, but most newspapers strive to go beyond the mechanical restrictions. The policy of the *New Haven Register* makes this clear: "The obituary writer's job is not simply to report the fact of death, but also, so far as available information permits, to capture the flavor of the decedent's life. This means that, although obituary writing can be reduced to a formula, the formula never should become a straitjacket that prevents writing a better news story."

An obituary written by Belinda Brockman of *The Miami Herald,* for example, captured the qualities of an Orange Bowl official. The first three paragraphs show that obituaries can be fast-paced and descriptive:

> Hal Fleming, the Orange Bowl's "Mr. Indispensable," whose nuts-and-bolts knowledge transformed Miami's New Year's celebration from a rolling rumble of floats into true majesty, died Tuesday of lymph gland cancer. He was 65.
>
> In his 39 years with the festival, Mr. Fleming "literally developed into the closest thing that I've ever seen to an indispensable man," said Dan McNamara, executive director of the Orange Bowl Committee. "He was fantastic. My main man. We put out a lot of fires together."
>
> Those fires were all part of turning others' creative dreams into the glitter and gold that parades down Biscayne Boulevard each New Year's Eve, or marches across the playing field each New Year's night, or races through the waterways and streets of Miami each Orange Bowl season.

Writing Interesting Leads

Leads should normally contain the full name and the age of the person who has died, but other information can be added so that obits will not all read the same way. The policy of the *News-Journal,* Daytona Beach, states: "Put any interesting fact of the deceased's life in the lead, even if it is only how many years he/she lived here. Since the number of years a person had lived here is overused, dig for something else. This means the funeral home must be questioned every time it gives an obit. Occasionally, you may have to ask the director to contact the family to get something more."

John Archibald, a reporter for *The Birmingham* (Ala.) *News,* certainly recognized the potential to structure a special obituary about a retired U.S. Steel worker. After all, how many decedents are survived by 26 children? Archibald's story had an air of informality, but it was effective. The lead block of paragraphs pulled the reader inside:

> It's probably appropriate that Elisha Anderson didn't come into the world alone. He had a companion, a twin.
>
> With that kind of start, it isn't surprising that he liked children. But he never had twins of his own. He did have a few children, though.
>
> He had 26 singles.
>
> Anderson fathered his last child 20 years ago. He was 62 when Scotty Hill of Bessemer was born.
>
> By the time Hill arrived, his older siblings were in their 40s. They were starting on grandchildren.
>
> "He was getting up there by the time I was born," Hill said. "But he was a tough old guy. He was a good guy."
>
> Anderson died March 9 after a recent stroke and other medical problems, Hill said. But he was happy with his life and his passel of children. . . .
>
> With 25 brothers and sisters running around from Florida to Brooklyn, it's hard to keep up with all of them, Hill said.
>
> "Is it 26?" He wasn't sure of the number. A quick rundown of names confirmed it.
>
> There's Sara and Delorise and Cathy and Betty and Marval and Otha and Pamela and Carolyn and Teresa and Sandra and Gwendolyn and Albertina and Brenda and Gail and Joy and Justina and Jimmy and Elisha Jr. and Michael and Scotty and Thomas and Melvin and James and Marcus and Dennis and Geffery.
>
> Wow.

Archibald went on to provide anecdotes about family reunions and to report direct quotations from neighbors. After noting that only two of the 26 children would not be in Birmingham for the funeral, Archibald provided some background on Anderson, gave details of funeral services and listed full names of all surviving children.

The obituary closed with this quotation:

> "He was a nice, nice man," said Bernice Jackson, wife of Anderson's son Melvin Jackson. "He had a heap of children."

CHAPTER FOURTEEN

NEWS RELEASES

Each day, newspapers and broadcast outlets receive anywhere from dozens to hundreds of **news releases**—also called **handouts** or **press releases.** To get their message across, **public relations (PR) people** telephone or visit newspapers and broadcast outlets to describe the "news," or they send releases by mail, fax or e-mail. Many releases are posted on the Internet.

(*Photo by James Poulin*)

Some news releases are worth printing or broadcasting; many are not. It is up to the journalist to:

- Decide which releases have any local news value
- Present those with value in such a way that readers, viewers or listeners are given the most important news

Nearly every corporation, business, university, organization or political party—large or small—has one or more people whose job it is to gain the attention of the media. Many of these public relations people are former print or broadcast journalists or were journalism majors who planned careers in public relations. They know that much, most or all of the support their organizations will receive is linked directly to the publicity they receive from the media, and they know how to get this publicity.

Some firms and groups really do have news to release, and they help the media greatly by acting as news sources. Others are merely hoping to get their names in the newspaper or on the air without paying for an advertisement.

Examples of news releases include these:

A news release from the manufacturer of science and nature toys announcing a new line of products

A release from Buckingham Palace announcing the dates for this year's Swan Upping, the annual census of the swan population on certain stretches of the River Thames

A press release from the White House announcing that the president has signed a proclamation celebrating Black Music Month

A news release from Columbia University sent to local media that lists graduates from their areas

A media release from a museum announcing a new interactive exhibit that allows visitors to explore Native American cultures by using multiple senses

A release from a company that has brought together pop groups for a new album that will raise money for AIDS prevention and relief worldwide

A news release announcing that a golf course management school is sponsoring a summer tournament to benefit the Multiple Sclerosis Association

Evaluating News Releases

All these news releases were sent to newspapers and broadcast outlets for the same reason: the people who wrote them were hoping to gain publicity for their organizations and to reach as many people as possible. It is up to the journalist reviewing such releases to decide whether they have any interest for readers, listeners or viewers, and whether they have any news value or whether the organization is only seeking a free advertisement.

Factors to Consider

There are several factors that determine whether a release should be used or ignored:

- *Does It Have News Value?* Is it of interest to local readers, viewers or listeners? Does it contain timely information? If so, the release should be edited or rewritten to conform to print or broadcast style and to eliminate overuse of the name of a person or a company. Superfluous, overwritten and untimely information should be eliminated.
- *Is It Trying to Gain Free Publicity for a Person, Company or Group?* If so, toss the release into the wastebasket or tell the PR person to check with the advertising department. Remember, though, that with careful rewriting to eliminate many of the adjectives and overuse of the name of a person or company, there could be some news value in the handout.
- *Is It Worth Following Up, Perhaps as a Photograph or a Story at a Later Time?* Many releases simply announce a coming event. Even if they are not used, they may provide a good tip for later coverage.
- *Can It Be Trusted?* Always be leery of news releases, because they may have been written by a person with little or no journalism training or by someone who does not have the same standards as a professional journalist. Remember, the purpose of a release is to get information into print or on the air. It is up to the journalist handling the release to check the information to make certain that it is accurate and meets the medium's needs and style. The release should also be checked for any missing information that, had it been included, would have changed the thrust of the release.

Which Releases Will Be Used?

Every person looking at a news release has different ideas about what is newsworthy and what is not. That is why some releases are used and others are thrown away.

Some media outlets—particularly the large ones—simply frown on using news releases. They may use a release as an idea for a future story or photograph, but they seldom run the release the way it is sent in. Many editors believe that all public relations people are really selling ads and that they should pay for advertising space rather than be given news space.

There is only so much news space—the *editorial news hole*—each day, and even though a news release may be of some value, there is never enough space to run all the news releases that are received. At metropolitan newspapers and broadcast outlets, the news space is taken up by staff-produced stories; there is no room for handouts. In smaller markets, however, editors may depend heavily on news releases to help fill their news space.

There are no strict rules to follow in deciding which news releases make it into print or onto a broadcast and which ones do not. Much depends on the journalists who are looking at them. Usually, editors run releases that they believe their readers will find interesting or that they find interesting themselves. For example, an editor who likes to play golf may give the handout about the summer golf tournament to a reporter to rewrite into a story; another editor may toss it into the wastebasket.

Most news releases sent to newspapers and broadcast outlets probably have some news value, especially if the person writing them has dealt with the media in the past. PR people with journalism training usually have a solid understanding of news stories and features; this means that they can produce usable copy. They know what editors and reporters like and dislike.

It is up to the journalist at the receiving end to pick the most timely and important handouts that have the most interest to a local audience. Then, on the basis of amount of time and space available, these top handouts can be converted into news stories or used as foundations for future stories.

E-Mailed Releases

Releases have traditionally been mailed or faxed to the media, but today many are sent via e-mail. There are even companies that provide online services to companies that want to write and/or distribute news releases throughout the media.

Two Web sites that offer press release writing and/or distribution are *www.pressrelease.net* and *www.eReleases.com.*

In a section of its site titled "How to Write a Press Release," eReleases.com says, "While no one can guarantee your release will be published or used for an article, there are things you can do to improve your chances." It urges writers to be:

- *Concise.* Editors receive hundreds of releases a week (perhaps more) and appreciate releases that are brief and to the point.
- *Well-written.* A good way to ensure your release a place in the wastebasket is poor copy: bad spelling, poor grammar, and illogical or unsubstantiated claims.
- *Factual.* Stick to logical and substantiated claims, avoiding statements of belief: we're the best, the cheapest, etc.
- *Honest.* Avoid the padded quotes by company officers; even if they are experts, they come across as biased.
- *Timely.* If your release isn't topical, consider incorporating it with a recent news event—but don't stretch it.

Using News Releases

Boiling Down a Handout

Here is a release from the Ford Motor Co. about a $5 million donation to the Muhammad Ali Center in Louisville, Ky. Assume that a newspaper city editor in another community in the state has asked for a three-paragraph story on it.

Usually, when releases are sent, they include a headline and the words **for immediate release,** which tell the media that this information can be used now. Most are "immediate," but some request a future release date. The release also will provide a contact person, Web site address or telephone number for reporters who might want to ask additional questions.

FORD MOTOR COMPANY FUND GIVES GRANT TO NEW MUHAMMAD ALI CENTER

LOUISVILLE, KY, June 26, 2001—Ford Motor Company Fund today announced a $5 million donation to the Muhammad Ali Center, which will be built in downtown Louisville. Legendary athlete Muhammad Ali and his wife Lonnie received the grant on behalf of the Center—the largest private sector donation the Ali Center has received—at a Ford "Living Legends Tour" event held on the banks of the Ohio River.

Sandy Ulsh, vice president and executive director of the Ford Motor Company Fund said, "Ford is committed to building relationships in the communities where it does business, and contributing to the Muhammad Ali Center will allow us to continue our support in Louisville—as well as support people around the world."

The Muhammad Ali Center, a new not-for-profit organization, is scheduled to open in 2003 and will be located along the riverfront. The Center will offer educational programming focusing on conflict resolution, diversity and multicultural training, and personal inspiration. These programs will be available on-site and via the Internet through distance learning technology. The Muhammad Ali Institute for Peacemaking and Conflict Resolution—a partnership with the University of Louisville—will also be part of the Center.

"People everywhere are really the same. They need encouragement to achieve their dreams and the opportunity to celebrate their diversity rather than dwell on their differences," said Muhammad Ali. "With the support of the Ford Motor Company and the Ford Motor Company Fund, the Ali Center will be able to create facilities and programs that will promote respect, hope and understanding among people throughout the world."

Janet Mullins Grissom, vice president of Washington Affairs at Ford said, "This Center will stand for what Muhammad Ali has stood for all of his life—peace and the nonviolent resolution of conflict. With the partnering of Ford and the Muhammad Ali Center, truly the greatest is yet to come."

Ford Motor Company's "Living Legends Tour" showcases two of automotive history's greatest nameplates, the all-new 2002 Thunderbird and the special-edition 2001 Mustang Bullitt GT in a nostalgia-oriented tour of North America.

Ford Motor Company Fund, a not-for-profit corporation made possible by Ford Motor Company profits, supports initiatives and organizations that enhance and improve opportunities for those who live in the communities where the company does business. The Fund provides grants to not-for-profit organizations whose missions closely align with its priorities in five key areas—education, environment, health and welfare, civic affairs and public policy, and arts and humanities.

Find the Lead

The first thing to do is to find the lead, the most important point of the story. In only three paragraphs, it is impossible to be as wordy or as filled with public relations as the person who wrote this press release. Look for *who, what, where, why, when* and *how,* and then build a story around the most important of them. Not every press release contains all five of the W's or the H, but a news story can be constructed around the ones that are included. Reporters also can contact the company sending the release for additional information.

Who: Ford Motor Company Fund, Muhammad Ali and his wife, Lonnie.

What: Donation of $5 million to the Muhammad Ali Center.

Where: Along the riverfront in Louisville, Ky.

Why: To help the center offer education programming that focuses on conflict resolution, diversity, multicultural training and personal inspiration.

When: June 26, 2001, during a Ford "Living Legends Tour."

How: Ali and his wife accepted the grant. The Ford Motor Company Fund provides grants to not-for-profit organizations.

Once the five W's and H have been identified, the next step is to put them into a news story, in this case three paragraphs. Although much of this release is public relations, it does contain some news, certainly enough for three paragraphs. In the limited amount of space, only the essential ingredients can be included.

Muhammad Ali and his wife Lonnie accepted a $5 million grant Tuesday from Ford Motor Company Fund to help build their Muhammad Ali Center in downtown Louisville.

It is the largest private sector donation for the center, which is scheduled to open in 2003 along the riverfront. The center will offer educational programming focusing on conflict resolution, diversity, multicultural training and personal inspiration.

"People everywhere are really the same," Ali said. "They need encouragement to achieve their dreams and the opportunity to celebrate their diversity rather than dwell on their differences."

With more space, more specifics could have been included, such as a quote from a Ford official and a mention that the University of Louisville also would be a partner in the center. Some reporters also might want to include a sentence or two about the "Living Legends Tour."

Eliminate Fluff

Not all press releases are easy to boil down to three paragraphs. For example, the handout mentioned earlier in this chapter from the museum, which announces a new interactive exhibit, is three pages long. It clearly seeks publicity for the museum, but it also reports news about a multisensory gallery designed to demonstrate that art is not just a visual experience. The trick is to cut the **fluff** and concentrate on the news.

Some releases are already boiled down when they are sent in because the people writing them know that a release has a better chance of being used if it reads like a news or feature story. For example, here is a news release from Ithaca Industries Inc. of Wilkesboro, N.C. It is one of the most common types of releases sent to the media: it announces a corporate promotion and was written by a public relations firm.

News Release
For Release: Immediately
Contact: Mr. Jim Waller, Ithaca Industries Inc.
(919) 667-5231

WILKESBORO, N.C.—Nicholas Wehrmann, president and chief operating officer of Ithaca Industries Inc., has been elected to the additional offices of Chairman of the Board of Directors and Chief Executive Officer, replacing Gregory B. Abbott, who resigned to pursue other business interests.

Ithaca is a leading manufacturer of hosiery, underwear and sportswear.

This release gives only the basic facts. If journalists want more, they will have to call Jim Waller. Here is a rewrite of the handout, cutting the bulky 40-word lead to a more readable 24 words:

Nicholas Wehrmann, president and chief operating officer of Ithaca Industries Inc., has been elected chairman of the board of directors and chief executive officer.

The remaining facts can be given in the second paragraph:

Wehrmann replaces Gregory B. Abbott, who resigned to pursue other business interests. Ithaca manufactures hosiery, underwear and sportswear.

Avoiding Free Ads

The following news release—on an airbag repair company hoping to sell franchises—is a good example of a release that would probably not show up in print or on the air. It is nothing more than a **free ad** masked as a news release.

For Immediate Release
High Tech Automotive Franchise Looking for Expansion

Dateline: May 7, 2001
Contact Name: Elaine Credelle
Contact Phone: 1-800-224-7224
Web Address: *www.airbagservice.com*

Because of the recent roller coaster ride in the stock market many people are searching for other ways of investing their money, including starting their own business.

Franchise operations are a great investment for many people. Purchasing a franchise allows them to use the company name, logo, and business system to generate sales and profits. It can provide them with the thrill of going out on their own but with the comfort of a proven well-researched business plan at their disposal as well as ongoing support.

Individuals will often look for a business that is profitable yet offers something that is not being done by everyone else. Automotive airbags for the passenger and driver's side are in all new vehicles sold today. There has been much advancement in the systems since their inception. They provide a sense of comfort for consumers and have saved many lives. They also have greatly complicated collision repairs. The founder of Airbag Service (TM) Douglas Hansen realized that this situation would create the atmosphere for a necessary support system to the collision industry. Before Mr. Hansen left his position as Senior Project Engineer for Rocket Research Company he was involved in development work on all aspects of the airbag systems. In 1992 when he started Airbag Service (TM) he knew he had a business idea with tremendous growth potential.

Airbag Service (TM) whose corporate office is located in Seattle, Washington is an exciting automotive business with a twist. Their technicians armed with mobile service vans, lap top computers, cell phones, and much coveted and necessary tools, go to the automotive collision shops and expertly perform complicated and technological advanced procedures on automotive airbag systems. Assigned territories are set so that franchise owners have exclusive rights for that area. That means when they are not actually working on vehicles they are building sales relationships and educating shop owners on the importance of correct airbag replacement. Airbag Service (TM) firmly believes that only certified technicians using OEM parts should do airbag repairs. Technicians carry cell phones in case they need to contact the tech support line for additional repair information. Airbag Service (TM) also has their own licensed software Autopilot (TM) that helps maintain the consistency of the repair work they perform.

Airbag Service (TM) currently has 40 franchises and wants to expand to several major marketplaces. More information about Airbag Service (TM) can be found on their Web site at *www.airbagservice.com*.

This item has the same elements that would appear in any typical news release: the firm's name is mentioned more than once, its Web address is given, the name of the owner is listed and there is plenty of editorializing. There is only one thing missing: news value.

Remember: The fact that a release is sent to the media does not mean that it has news value. Many releases are merely seeking free publicity for a person, business or organization.

Determining Local News Value

What lands in the trash in one newsroom may be a candidate for a story in another simply because of **local news value**. The news release from Columbia University announcing that a student from a small city has been graduated is probably of no value to any news operation in the country, except in the small city. There, it may be worth a one-paragraph filler, a photograph or a story and picture. While one editor is cursing the university for wasting his or her time by submitting the release, another editor may be thanking the school for valuable information.

Example: A State Lottery

Here is a release from the Colorado Lottery announcing the winners of $89,000 in a lottery game. Because it deals only with Coloradans, it has strong local news value to media in the state.

"We send these news releases out several times a week," said Marlene Desmond, communications director of the Colorado Lottery.

As you read the release, try to pick out the fluff that could be cut easily.

> News Release
> For Immediate Release
> For More Information Contact: Marlene Desmond
> (303) 832-6242
>
> PUEBLO—Luck struck Colorado Lottery players twice today as a Salida man and a Golden woman became the first and second instant winners of $89,000 in the lottery's "Surprise Package '89" game.
>
> Mike McQuitty, 32, Salida, an equipment operator for the Rio Grande Railroad, said that he bought his lucky "Surprise Package '89" ticket this morning at the Stop and Save, 310 W. Rainbow Blvd., Salida. He said that his good fortune was enough to make him take the day off from work.
>
> "I scratched the ticket in our morning meeting, and when I saw what I had won, I told the rest of the guys that 'I'm taking the day off,' " McQuitty said.
>
> McQuitty said that his co-workers had no objections, and he immediately claimed the winning ticket at lottery headquarters in Pueblo.
>
> His plans for his winnings include paying some bills and taking care of his wife and three daughters.
>
> About 30 minutes after McQuitty claimed his prize, Schellia Wright, 40, a cosmetologist from Golden, claimed her $89,000 winning ticket at the lottery's Denver office.
>
> Wright bought her lucky ticket last night at 7-Eleven, 980 E. 88th, Thornton.
>
> She said that she plans on taking some time off with her husband and four children.
>
> The "Surprise Package '89" game features the top instant prize of $89,000 and the weekly Grand Prize drawing for $1 million.

What is news and what is fluff in this handout? A reporter assigned to write a three-paragraph story based on the release will need to know. Certainly, there is much publicity in the release for the Colorado Lottery: the game's name is in three paragraphs, and the tickets are usually called "lucky." However, there is also news value in the release, especially to the media serving the towns of Salida, Golden and Thornton.

To write the three paragraphs, the reporter must first determine the five W's and H:

Who: Mike McQuitty of Salida and Schellia Wright of Golden.

What: They became the first and second instant winners of the $89,000 "Surprise Package '89" game.

Where: In Salida and Thornton.

Why: Not applicable.

When: This morning and last night.

How: They each bought instant tickets at convenience stores, scratched them and realized that they had won.

Here is how the three paragraphs could have been written:

> A 32-year-old Salida man and a 40-year-old Golden woman have become the first two $89,000 instant winners in the Colorado Lottery's "Surprise Package '89" game.
>
> Mike McQuitty, an equipment operator for the Rio Grande Railroad, and Schellia Wright, a cosmetologist, bought their tickets in convenience stores. They claimed their prizes within 30 minutes of each other.
>
> McQuitty said that he plans to use his winnings to pay bills and to take care of his wife and three daughters. Wright said that she will take time off with her husband and four children.

The *Denver Post* was one of the Colorado newspapers that carried a story based on the news release. The reporter who wrote the story also interviewed a state lottery official, who provided additional information. Here are the first three paragraphs of the *Post* story, which you can compare with the release:

> The Colorado Lottery's new game—Surprise Package '89—has its first $89,000 winners.
>
> Mike McQuitty, an employee of the Rio Grande Railroad in Salida, bought two lottery tickets with the change from buying gasoline on his way to work Tuesday. He scratched off the winner while sitting in a meeting, and took the rest of the day off to drive to the lottery's headquarters in Pueblo to cash in the ticket, said Tom Kitts of the lottery.
>
> Schellia Wright, mother of four and a Golden cosmetologist, bought her winning ticket Monday night and took it into the lottery office in Denver to cash it in. She missed being the first Surprise Package '89 big winner by about 30 minutes, Kitts said.

CHAPTER FIFTEEN

SPEECHES AND PRESS CONFERENCES

Thank you all for coming. General, thank you for being here. It is my honor to nominate Robert S. Mueller of California to become the director of the Federal Bureau of Investigation. I want to welcome his wife, Anne, here, and I want to welcome you all to the Rose Garden.

When confirmed, Mr. Mueller will be only the sixth person to hold this position. He assumes great responsibilities. He was chosen with great care and he has my full confidence. Bob Mueller earned my trust and that of the attorney general when he

(*Kevin Lamarque / Reuters / TimePix*)

served as acting deputy attorney general earlier this year. He also has earned the confidence of other presidents before me.

He is the current U.S. attorney for the Northern District of California. He was appointed to that position by President Clinton. He served in my father's administration, as well. Before that, he was U.S. attorney for Massachusetts, making him one of the very few ever to serve as chief federal prosecutor in two jurisdictions.

Our next FBI director has given nearly all his career to public service, going back to his days in the Marine Corps. He served with distinction and was decorated during the Vietnam War. As a lawyer, prosecutor and government official, he has shown high ideals, a clear sense of purpose and a tested devotion to his country.

And so started a speech by President George W. Bush in the Rose Garden outside the White House. He wanted to introduce the person he was nominating for director of the FBI. Reporters were there to cover what he said.

Speeches

The Reporter and the Speech

Government officials, candidates, executives and other people give speeches to get a message across to an audience. When reporters cover a speech, they have no control over what the speaker says. They are there to be the eyes and ears of people who cannot attend. If they cannot get to the speaker before or after the speech, they merely digest what was said, mix it up and feed back the newsworthy material to their readers.

Because no interviewing is involved and reporters cannot challenge the speaker, many of the story leads are likely to be on the same point.

Speeches are usually not organized like news stories. The speaker often builds up to a major point; it is not put at the beginning. Reporters recognize this difference. As they are listening to a speech, they are editing it, anticipating its main points and cutting out all the unnecessary information.

Reporters realize that a 30-minute speech would take up considerable space in the daily news hole if it were printed in its entirety. Metropolitan newspapers occasionally print complete speeches by the president or by other important officials, but usually they rely on their reporters to pick apart speeches and to report only the *new,* the *important* or the *unusual.*

Clever speakers are aware of the reporter's function; this means that they will make every attempt to say something new, important or unusual.

Covering a Speech

Before the Speech: Preparation

It is important for reporters to do their homework *before* covering a speech. Only under the most unusual circumstances, such as an extremely tight deadline, would they cover a speech without first researching the subject and the speaker. Even if the assignment is made only a short time before the speech, it is easy to go online or to the newspaper clipping file to find out what has been written previously on the speaker or the topic of the speech.

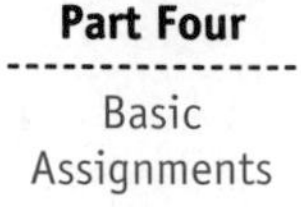

How to prepare: Tips for reporters. Here are some tips on how to prepare for covering a speech:

- *Do Your Homework.* Check news clippings and written and electronic sources. Interview friends of the speaker as well as fellow reporters for background information. Go into research asking, "Who is this person?" Come out with the answer.
- *Prepare Questions.* Know in advance the questions that the speaker needs to answer during the speech. If they are not answered, interview the speaker in person immediately after the speech or over the phone as soon as possible.
- *Catch the Speaker Early.* Every reporter covering a speech will hear the same thing; if possible, break away from the pack beforehand to obtain exclusive information. Interview the speaker over the telephone or make arrangements to see him or her just before the speech. If that is not possible, find out where the speaker will enter the room and wait there. It is sometimes possible to get in a few questions while the speaker is being introduced and before he or she walks to the podium.

Using advance texts. Advance texts of the speech are useful because they provide most of what the speaker will say; they also make the research phase easier.

Copies are usually available from the speaker or his or her agents before the speech. A well-known person who speaks will often have plenty of copies to hand out. A lesser-known person will probably not; reporters may have to ask to look at the speech or make copies of it.

A warning, though: Never write a story solely on the basis of an advance text. Speakers often wander from their prepared texts, adding some things and omitting others. Occasionally, they abandon the text altogether and speak off the cuff. Reporters who do not attend the speech and write stories from an advance text may end up looking foolish.

Use the advance text as a guide for doing the research and covering the speech. Follow the text during the speech, making changes in quotations and adding and deleting necessary phrases and sentences.

Using a tape recorder. A tape recorder will ensure that any quotations used in a news story will be precise. Just make certain that the recorder is working properly. Keep extra batteries and tapes on hand.

Also, take notes. A tape recorder is a useful backup tool for making sure that quotations are exact. Most reporters do not rely on the recorder exclusively, however, because it takes too much time to play back the tape, take notes and then write the story. (Chapter 10 lists additional guidelines on using tape recorders.)

During the Speech: Steps to Follow

Once the speech begins, there are certain steps reporters must follow.

Take copious notes. Even reporters who use tape recorders take as many notes as possible. It is impossible to transcribe the entire speech, but reporters usually take a lot more notes than they would ever need to write a story. Nearly every reporter uses shorthand or devises a personal system of speed writing.

The key here is to listen carefully for information and for quotations that can be used in the story and to write them in a notebook as quickly as possible. A tape recorder can be used as a backup for incomplete quotations.

If the speaker says something that is hard to understand, put some type of symbol in the notebook next to the confusing statement. After the speech, try to have it clarified.

When writing a direct quotation, put quotation marks around it in the notebook so that it will not be confused with a paraphrase.

Experienced reporters try to stay calm when taking notes. They know that they will often be scribbling one quotation when the speaker starts to say something else of importance. They merely quit writing the first sentence and begin the second. People are always going to speak faster than reporters can write. All a reporter can do is write down the key points and the direct quotations.

Make observations. Note the speaker's clothing and mannerisms. If the speaker smokes or laughs continually or shouts at someone in the audience, make a note of this. These observations can add color to the story.

Estimate the number of people in the room. Count small crowds. For larger crowds, count the number of chairs in each row and multiply by the number of rows. Or ask a security officer for an estimate, or ask a custodian how many chairs were set up.

Listen for news. Remember that an audience does not care about old news. There has to be a reason for each story.

If the speaker says something that could make a lead or needs further development, put a star next to it in the notebook so that it can be found easily.

Listen for summaries. A speaker will usually summarize the speech, either at the beginning or at the end. Often, that summary will make the lead for a news story. Of course, reporters might disagree on what is the best lead, but they still need to know what the speaker considered the main point.

In most cases, the speaker clearly tells the audience, "I am here to talk about . . ." or "In summary, let me say . . ." Other times, summaries are masked. Listen for changes in the speaker's voice or for points repeated several times. Also, listen for topic sentences, numbered points and transitional words. These will signal major points, which could be potential leads. Good speakers are clear about the points they want to make because they want the audience to understand what they are saying.

Ask questions afterwards. When the speech has ended, it is time to ask the questions that should have been covered but were not. Try to get the speaker alone after the other reporters have left. Follow-up phone calls to the speaker may be helpful, too.

If there is time for questioning after the speech, ask for clarification of confusing points. Never be afraid to ask a speaker to repeat a quotation, explain an unclear statement or expand on any topics of the speech. Speakers will usually answer questions when they have finished talking. They know that reporters can get mixed up, and they do not want to be misquoted.

After the Speech: Writing the Story

Questions to answer. Before writing the story, the reporter must answer several questions:

- *What Is the Key Point?* What is the speaker emphasizing? The answer to this question becomes the lead of the story.
- *What Are the Other Major Points?* All of them should be rated.
- *Which Quotations Are the Best?* The reporter must look for quotations that best illustrate the speaker's points and also make the story readable.
- *Is Any of This News?* Reporters who have done their homework will know if the speaker has given the same speech before.
- *When Is the Deadline?* If there is time, the reporter can ask more questions. Or, if the speaker has made charges, the reporter can obtain an opinion from the other side. In most speech stories, reporters simply write a brief account of what the speaker said. If there is time to interview the other side, the reporter must start the research again to find the best possible rebuttal.

Organizing the information. Most speech stories follow the same pattern. They are written as inverted-pyramid news stories. They begin with a terse (no more than 35 words) summary lead that emphasizes the key points of the speech. If the speaker is well-known, a name is used in the lead. Otherwise, a title is put in the lead to give it authority, and the speaker's name is used in the second paragraph.

After the lead, paragraphs are written in order of descending importance, but each one should contain vital information. Here is how a typical story would be organized after the lead:

- *Second Paragraph.* Back up the lead with a strong quotation or paraphrase. Name the speaker if the name was not used in the lead. Give the speaker additional authority. Tell where the speech occurred and who sponsored it. Give the speaker's age if it is appropriate for the story.
- *Third Paragraph.* Continue developing the points made in the lead, or write a transitional paragraph moving into another key point. A transitional paragraph can also introduce a set of bullets highlighting all the speaker's important points. Provide more background on the speaker. Introduce observations. Tell how many people attended the speech.
- *Fourth Paragraph or the One after the Bullets.* Continue developing the lead, or begin developing the bulleted items one by one. If possible, use a strong quotation to illustrate one of the key points.
- *Balance of the Story.* Follow up with quotations and paraphrases. Continue to sprinkle in observations.
- *Final Paragraph.* Try to end with a direct quotation, the speaker in direct communication with the reader. That will help avoid an abrupt ending and will make the reader feel that the dialogue continues even though the story has ended. Do not use an attribution such as "he concluded" in the last paragraph. Make sure that all the key points are fully developed.

The Results

President Bush certainly made news when he announced whom he wanted for FBI director. Like most speeches, his began with small talk and introductions, but he got to his point quickly. His introductory comments begin this chapter. Here is the rest of his speech:

> As director, Mr. Mueller will succeed a good and honest man, Director Louis Freeh, who has my respect and the gratitude of our nation. I also want to thank Acting Director Pickard, who has served well during this transition.
>
> The FBI has a great tradition that Mr. Mueller must now affirm, and some important challenges he must confront. Like the Department of Justice, the FBI must remain independent of politics and uncompromising in its mission.
>
> Bob Mueller's term in office will last longer than my own. And the next 10 years will bring more forms of crime, new threats of terror, from beyond our borders and within them. The tools of law enforcement will change, as well. The FBI must be ready to protect Americans from new types of criminals who will use modern technology to defraud and disrupt our society.
>
> The bureau must secure its rightful place as the premier counterespionage and counterterrorist organization in the United States. It must continue to serve as a resource and training center for law enforcement. And it must do all this with a firm commitment to safeguarding the constitutional rights of our citizens.
>
> Bob Mueller's experience and character convinced me that he's ready to shoulder these responsibilities. Agents of the bureau prize three virtues above all: fidelity, bravery and integrity. This new director is a man who exemplifies them all. Congratulations.

At this point, Mueller said a few words.

> Thank you very much, Mr. President. Thank you, sir.
>
> I am deeply honored by the trust that President Bush has shown in nominating me to head the Federal Bureau of Investigation. The FBI is the foremost law enforcement agency in the world. I look forward to the confirmation process. And, if confirmed, I look forward to working with the thousands of dedicated men and women who are agents and employees of the FBI, to enforce our nation's laws fairly and with respect to the rights of all Americans.
>
> Again, thank you, Mr. President, for the confidence you've shown in me. Thank you, sir.

The speech ended with the president saying, "Congratulations" again; Mueller saying, "Thank you very much, sir" again; and Bush telling the crowd, "Thank you all for coming."

No one doubted the newsworthiness or the significance of the president's speech. He announced a major nomination, and reporters got the announcement on the air and online within minutes.

Here is an example of how one newspaper, *The New York Times,* handled the story. This article was written by David Johnston. The summary lead contains more than 35 words, but it flows and moves readers easily into the story. Also note that *The Times* has its own style—it doesn't follow Associated Press style—on use of "Mr." and periods in F.B.I.

WASHINGTON, July 5—President Bush today nominated a seasoned criminal prosecutor, Robert S. Mueller III, to be the director of the Federal Bureau of Investigation, an agency buffeted in recent months by accusations that it has been undisciplined, mistake-prone and poorly managed.

Speaking at a Rose Garden ceremony, Mr. Bush said of Mr. Mueller, "He assumes great responsibilities, he was chosen with great care, and he has my confidence."

"The F.B.I. has a great tradition that Mr. Mueller must now affirm, and some important challenges he must confront," Mr. Bush said. "Like the Department of Justice, the F.B.I. must remain independent of politics and uncompromising in its mission."

Mr. Mueller, the United States attorney in San Francisco, said in brief remarks that he would "enforce our nation's laws fairly and with respect to the rights of all Americans."

Mr. Mueller (pronounced MULL-er) has maintained a relatively low profile, and he is regarded within federal law enforcement circles as a low-key, decisive and fair-minded prosecutor with broad experience in criminal matters.

The opening paragraphs of Johnston's article were typical of a speech story. They reported the news. The summary lead also let readers know that the reporter was knowledgeable about recent accusations against the FBI, even though those charges were not mentioned by the president or nominee.

Throughout his story, the reporter used quotes and paraphrases. It is important to sprinkle paraphrases throughout a speech story. Otherwise, it would merely be a reprint of the speech.

The body of a speech story should be a series of quotations and paraphrases, as well as important background information. Its length is determined by the amount of newsworthy information and available space.

In his story, Johnston reported much background information about the nominee as well as some of the troubles that had plagued the FBI in recent years.

Late in his story, Johnston shifted gears to get reactions to the nomination from Democratic and Republican U.S. senators. It ended with a direct quote:

> Not all Republicans expressed unqualified support. Senator Charles E. Grassley of Iowa, who has been among the Senate's chief critics of the bureau in recent years, said, "I want to make sure he's equipped to take on the serious problems facing new leadership at the F.B.I."

Press Conferences

Candidates, officials and other people hold press conferences for one or all of the following reasons:

- They feel an obligation to make information public.
- They want to get a message across to as many people as possible.
- They would like to be seen in newspapers and on newscasts.

A press conference is a **gang interview**, which means that every reporter present is going to get the same information. Also, people who hold press conferences usually know in advance what they want to say. They will get their message across and will not say much more, especially if they are experienced at fielding adversarial questions from reporters.

"Most press conferences are simply canned information," said Kenneth Reich, a political writer for the *Los Angeles Times*. "An experienced person holding a press conference is able to control it more than the reporters can. The person pretty much knows what he is going to say, and he does not go beyond that. Inexperienced people, or people who lose their temper, are the people who hold interesting press conferences."

The Press Conference as a Media Event

Press conferences often make good television or online video, which means that even on the local level they have become **media events** where both the interviewee and the reporters are in the limelight. Reich said that, in many cases, press conferences are highly stylistic shows. "Every remark is going to be 30 seconds long" to get on television, he said.

The granddaddy of press conferences is the one held by the president of the United States. It has become a major media event that features the nation's top reporters challenging the president. It is a big show for both sides; millions of people watch every move and listen to every statement.

The presidential news conference began during Theodore Roosevelt's administration. Reporters simply gathered around the president's desk for a chat. When Herbert Hoover walked into his first meeting with the 30-member Washington press corps in his office on March 5, 1929, he reportedly said, "It seems that the whole press of the United States has given me the honor of a call this morning."

By Harry Truman's presidency, the press conference drew big crowds; 322 reporters attended his last one on Dec. 31, 1952.

Television and radio coverage of presidential press conferences began during Dwight Eisenhower's first term. In the early days of his presidency, portions of film and sound track were released for broadcast hours after the conference, a practice that gave Eisenhower's staff time to delete questions and answers they felt were potentially sensitive or embarrassing. After several months, however, the entire transcript was being released for broadcast and newsreels. Eisenhower also started the practice of having reporters identify themselves and their connections before asking questions.

Today, the presidential press conference lasts about 30 minutes and draws about 300 reporters. The president is well-coached and rehearsed on the questions most likely to come from the handful of reporters who are actually allowed to ask questions.

Covering a Press Conference

Before the Conference: Preliminaries

Before a press conference begins, reporters should research the subject and the speaker thoroughly. Because they may have a chance to speak only once, reporters want to make sure that their questions are on target. Being prepared helps them find the key information in all the rhetoric.

To prepare for a press conference, reporters:

- *Read Press Releases Announcing the Conference.* Some type of press release is usually issued by an agency, organization or news bureau before a person speaks. It should give the time, date and place of the conference; provide some background information on the speaker; and tell reporters whom they can call for more information.

- *Read as Many Clippings as Possible about the Person Holding the Conference and about Its Subject.* Research should be conducted electronically, in the newspaper library or in public or university libraries. Much background information can be found on speakers through electronic sources. Hundreds of newspapers and the news wires are accessible electronically, and various online publications and databases may have information that is not available in printed form.

  Obviously, much information is available on the American president. An Internet search on President Bush offers, among other things, his speeches and administration documents online, the White House home page and White House press releases.
- *Read Articles or Books That the Interviewee Has Written.* Writings reveal much about their authors. People also warm up much more quickly to a reporter who tells them that he or she has read their work.
- *Talk to Editors.* They will often give reporters specific questions that they want answered.
- *Talk to Other Reporters.* This is particularly important for reporters who have never before covered the person holding the press conference. Reporters who have covered the person before can offer helpful advice about mannerisms or types of questions that the person will or will not answer.

The Advance Story

A release often is used to write an **advance,** a brief story announcing a coming event. For example, before President Bush holds a press conference, the following advance could be written:

> President Bush will hold a press conference Monday in which he plans to discuss his economic policies.
>
> The press conference will begin at 2 p.m. Eastern time in the White House East Room.

During the Conference: The Questions and Answers

All reporters are at a press conference for the same reason: they want to ask questions that will elicit newsworthy responses. Those who have done their homework best, and those who are actually able to ask questions, will be the most successful.

Television reporters have an advantage over print reporters during a press conference because the speaker usually wants to be seen as well as heard. Hence, television reporters are more likely to control the questioning, which is usually limited in time.

Print reporters must make themselves visible and audible. First, they should arrive at the location of the press conference early enough to get a front-row seat. That will help the speaker spot them. Print reporters must also sometimes be the most vocal in the group to make certain that the speaker calls on them. This is particularly important at a large press conference where there are many reporters and the interviewee cannot answer every question. At a local press conference attended by only several reporters, an official, candidate or newsmaker will usually try to answer all of the questions.

Because of time or space limitations, reporters often attend press conferences only to obtain answers to specific questions. Their job is to challenge the speaker to provide something more than rhetoric. They all know that they cannot report everything that is said. Still, they should listen to the other questions and the answers just in case something unexpected pops up.

Even during a White House press conference, reporters want the answers to specific questions. For example, three days before President Bush nominated Robert S. Mueller to become director of the FBI, reporters asked presidential spokesman Ari Fleischer during a routine press conference about potential candidates.

> **Question:** Ari, speaking of nominations, how come there's been such a delay in finding somebody to run the FBI?
>
> **Answer:** I just don't agree with that characterization of a delay. The FBI is a position unlike almost any other position that a president will make an appointment to. It is a fixed 10-year term. It has a jurisdiction and an impact on people's lives that is very direct, very pronounced. And it's the type of decision that a president should weigh carefully and thoroughly before naming someone. And that's the approach that the president has taken.
>
> **Question:** Is there a problem, though? Is it detrimental for the FBI to be sort of leaderless and without a permanent chief for any long period of time?
>
> **Answer:** The FBI will be under an interim director, and the president has faith that the people heading the FBI will do an excellent job. But, again, this is a serious appointment to a 10-year post. It is not a post that serves at the pleasure of the president. And, therefore, it's a post that deserves more time, more consideration, and that's what the president is giving to it.

Fleischer didn't begin the press conference by answering questions about the FBI. Instead, he began by saying:

> Good day. I have personnel announcements . . . and then I want to discuss something that is of note in the United States Senate.
>
> The president intends to nominate Wanda Nesbitt to be ambassador to the Republic of Madagascar. The president intends to nominate Mattie Sharpless to be ambassador to the Central African Republic. The president intends to nominate George McDade Staples to be ambassador to the Republic of Equatorial Guinea.
>
> I also want to note that the president is very pleased to see that a reorganization agreement has been reached in the United States Senate, which the president hopes will now allow senators and the leadership from both parties to address what is a growing confirmation gap in the United States Senate involving presidential appointments.
>
> The numbers are very simple and clear. As of June 30, President Bush has nominated more people for confirmation to the United States Senate than any of his three predecessors, despite the late confirmation, or the late inauguration of the president as a result of the transition. By late inauguration, I mean the amount of time that was available to the president during the transition.
>
> As of June 30, the president has nominated 315 people to Senate-confirmable posts. That compares with Bill Clinton, who, as of June 30, nominated 249 people; George Bush, former president, 220 people; and Ronald Reagan, 301 people. President George W. Bush has nominated more than any of these three people. Yet, the record in the Senate shows there is a growing confirmation gap.

For President George W. Bush, the Senate has confirmed only 132 of the president's nominees. Bill Clinton, at the same time, had 188 confirmed; George Bush had 147 confirmed; and Ronald Reagan had 225 confirmed.

Fleischer went on with his statement for several more minutes before he asked for questions. Now it was time for reporters to ask about what they were interested in. Some of the questions and answers follow:

Question: What is the problem in both parties, Ari?

Answer: There is a just a lag. It does not seem to be a high enough priority of the United States Senate for attention to be focused on it. We have entered an era where senators, individual senators are putting holds on individual people for a wide variety of reasons that seem to be much greater than previously done. And the numbers speak for themselves.

Question: But you think it goes beyond attributing it to just the changeover in the Senate?

Answer: Actually, because the lag began even before the changeover. I mean, there has been a lag in the last month, even more pronounced. For example, as of May 31, the Senate confirmed 129 people; as of June 30, 132. So only three people were confirmed in one month's time.

Question: Ari, which is the bigger problem, the politics on Capitol Hill or the paperwork and all the background checks these folks have to undergo?

Answer: Well, again, President George W. Bush is way ahead of the pace of previous presidents in terms of making nominations to the Senate, even with a shortened transition. I'll say the numbers again. As of June 30, the president has nominated 315 people for confirmable Senate positions. Bill Clinton, with a full transition as of June 30, only nominated 249; George Bush nominated 220; Ronald Reagan nominated 301. So President George W. Bush is way ahead of the pace of nominations. So, clearly, the problem is not on this end of Pennsylvania Avenue, in terms of filling out the paperwork and getting the nominations to the Senate.

Question: Ari, on offshore oil leases, has the president communicated at all with his brother, and is he at all concerned about his brother's political fortune, since his brother opposed this move?

Answer: I have not talked to the president about if he talked to his brother in regard to anything. There will be an announcement made later today, and I'm not going to get into the specifics of it, by the Department of Interior. I will simply say that the president has heard the voices of many people in Florida; he is concerned about the environment; he's concerned about people in Florida and their reaction to development of resources off of their shore and there will be an announcement made later today by the secretary of interior.

Question: Is this part of his energy plan and, if so, how does it fit in, per se?

Answer: This was always part of an announcement that was made by the Department of Interior, after they reviewed the sale, as is routine with all sales.

Question: Is there going to be a surprise turnabout in his views?

Answer: I think what you will hear will be a reflection of what the president said during the course of the campaign, which is he would work with the governors of all the states in the region and would have a program that is balanced, that allows our beaches to be protected, as well as development of energy in a way that is environmentally sensitive.

Question: May I ask you another question? Did the president say the *Wall Street Journal* poll was BS?

Answer: (Laughter.) He didn't say it to me, so I haven't heard that.

Question: You didn't check it out with him?

Answer: I didn't check that out.

Question: Can you tell us what his views are now on all these stories that his polls have fallen?

Answer: He shrugs his shoulders. He thinks it's a non-issue, a non-story.

Question: He doesn't follow polls, at all?

Answer: The president is cognizant of them, but the president thinks the test of a leader is what you do in office. And the president is also comforted to know that he has the solid support of the American people.

Let me reflect on that. I take a look at the polls, so let me give you little reflections on that. According to the latest Gallup Poll, the president's job approval rating is 55 to 33. That's according to Gallup, and there's some other polls—

Question: It's what?

Answer: It's 55 to 33, most recent Gallup. There are some other polls that show his job approval in the low 50s; there are some other polls show his job approval in the high 50s. Gallup is right smack in the middle. Let me give you some numbers to compare it to. In October of 1996, on his way to a landslide re-election, then-President Clinton's job approval according to Gallup was 54 to 36—

Question: Why do you always have to bring in the Clinton administration? I mean, why don't you just stick with your own—

Answer: According to the same Gallup polls of President Reagan, in October of 1984, Ronald Reagan's job approval was 58-33—

Question: What did President Truman do? (Laughter.)

Answer: —and I can get that, too. (Laughter.)

Question: There's a new budgetary environment, in part because of the tax cut and the weakening economy and the declining tax receipts as a result. And the surplus that we heard so much about during the campaign is rapidly dwindling, at least in the near years. Should Americans be concerned about that? What happened?

Answer: Well, I think people should be concerned about lack of growth in the economy. Growth is the key to revenues. And any time the economy softens it will have an impact on growth. And to review the numbers, industrial production, which is a key measure of the strength of the economy, peaked in September of 2000 and has gone down since then. Growth of the economy, as measured by the Gross Domestic Product, hit 5.4 percent in the spring of 2000. But in the summer of 2000, the slowdown began.

The solution to low growth is to cut taxes. Taxes have now been cut in an overwhelmingly bipartisan fashion. And to listen to the private sector economists tell the story, you hear that they believe that as a result of the tax cut and the fact that it's only now starting to go into law, it will give a boost to the economy, estimated anywhere from 1 percentage point to .7 percentage points. In other words, it will help grow the economy and, therefore, bring in additional revenue at a time of a weakness in the economy.

Question: In the out-years, maybe. In the near-term, revenue has declined because of the tax cut, as well. And that will force changes in the budget—

Answer: (Laughter.) Wait a minute. Wait. You just said that revenue has declined as a result of the tax cut. The tax cut hasn't gone into effect yet.

Question: As they prepare the budget for the next year and the following year, they're going to have to take into account—

Answer: The decline in revenues already exists, and it exists as a result of the slowdown in the strength of the economy, going back to last summer and last fall. That's beyond dispute. The tax cut, for the first manifestation of it, went into effect yesterday, on Sunday, as people will in their next paychecks receive bigger salaries as a result of changes in withholdings. After the $300 and $600 checks are delivered to people, that, too, will have an impact on revenue.

Question: Ari, on the death penalty, two questions. The district attorney in Houston will decide within the month whether to seek the death penalty against Andrea Yates. She's the mother who drowned her five kids. Has the president expressed an opinion on whether this woman should be put to death for that crime?

Answer: I have not heard him do so and he doesn't engage in that type of speculation. That's not the job of the president.

Question: Second question. Last week, Sara Lee plead guilty to crimes in connection with a 1998 outbreak of listeriosis, which caused the death of 16 people, eight miscarriages and 40 to 80 seriously injured people. The company pleaded guilty to the crime. Has the president expressed a view on the death penalty for corporate criminals? That is, revoking the charter of a corporation that has been convicted of a crime that has resulted in death?

Answer: No. As I indicated in your preface question, the president does not weigh in, those are matters at Justice and they should not be dictated by decisions made at the White House.

Question: Wait a second. Ari, wait a second. He's in favor of the death penalty for individuals, generally. Is he in favor of the death penalty for corporations convicted of crimes that result in death?

Answer: These are questions that are handled by officials of Justice, not by people in the White House.

Question: How can you say—

Answer: You only get three, not four.

Question: I have 18 questions, also, but I'll whittle it down to one. (Laughter.) There were four demonstrations in Arizona over the weekend, by Republicans opposed to John McCain because of his stance on issues. What is the White House's position on these disgruntled Republicans and this ongoing effort to recall Mr. McCain?

Answer: The President is working very closely with Senator McCain on a host of issues, and he looks forward to continuing his works with Senator

McCain. There are many areas where the two of them have forged a lot of consensus, and see room for a lot of good things to be done for the American people. And that's the President's ongoing approach.

Question: Ari, the president of Mexico has just gotten married this morning. Taking aside that he's a very close friend of the president of the United States, I wonder if the president has already called Fox to congratulate him?

Answer: He has not called him. And as you know, after phone calls are made, if there is one, we'll let you know.

Question: Is he sending a gift?

Answer: Is he what?

Question: Ari, on oil leasing, I was unsure from your last response whether or not you were confirming or not whether President Bush has actually conferred with his brother prior to today's announcement on—

Answer: No, I indicated I hadn't talked to the President about if he talked to his brother.

Question: Can you let me know if he does?

Answer: Yes.

A reporter in the room then said, "Thank you," and Fleischer ended the press conference by saying, "Thank you, everybody."

After the Conference: Guidelines for Reporters

Once a press conference is over, reporters whose deadlines are near must complete their stories quickly. They need to know their leads and how they will organize their stories even before the gang interview has ended.

Reporters who phone in their news stories normally do not have a computer terminal in front of them on which to compose a story, erase mistakes and rewrite if necessary. They must dictate a story that makes sense the first time. It also helps to have a good rewrite person on the other end of the phone to polish the rough edges, shuffle paragraphs if necessary and look up additional information.

The closer the deadline, the more quickly a reporter must pick out the news and compose the story. Most reporters, even those not under a tight deadline, begin to construct their stories during the press conference, while they are asking questions, listening and taking notes. They continually ask themselves:

- Which questions are best?
- Is the speaker answering candidly?
- What is new, and what has been said before?
- Is the speaker skirting any issues?
- What is the best lead?
- How should the story be organized?

The story's lead and organization are determined by several factors:

- *What Is the Most Newsworthy Response during the Press Conference?* Are the responses good enough and complete enough to be developed into a lead paragraph?

- *What Are the Other Key Points of the Conference?* Would any of them make better leads? The major points covered during the conference should be rated for importance.

Reporters covering presidential spokesman Ari Fleischer's White House press conference could choose one of several leads. Among other things, Fleischer named three presidential nominees, said the president had not yet decided on an FBI director and told reporters President Bush is concerned about the environment and the impact of offshore oil leases.

Here are examples of three leads that could have been written after the press conference.

President Bush has nominated ambassadors to Madagascar, the Central African Republic and the Republic of Equatorial Guinea, the White House announced today.

The Senate is lagging behind on confirming presidential appointments and has approved only three of President Bush's 315 nominees in one month's time, the White House said today.

A presidential spokesman said today that even if national polls show President Bush's approval rate falling, Bush believes he has the solid support of the American people.

Whatever lead is used, it would be important to use quotations in the second and third paragraphs and also name the spokesperson holding the White House press conference. Transitions would be used throughout the story to move readers from one topic to another.

CHAPTER SIXTEEN

WEATHER AND DISASTERS

Fifteen days of 110-degree heat. Disastrous flooding. Paralyzing snowstorm. Tornado. Hurricane. Airliner crash.

The media seldom ignore major weather stories or disasters. They are covered aggressively because they have a direct impact on people.

(*Richard Carson / Reuters / TimePix*)

Covering and Forecasting Weather

USA Today—Gannett's national newspaper—is among the pacesetters in weather coverage. Its weather package is highly praised and widely imitated; its coverage is colorful and comprehensive.

Jack Williams, who was editor of the *USA Today* weather page when the newspaper began publication and has been weather editor of *USA Today.com* since the service began, noted, however, that "at most newspapers, writing weather stories is looked upon as some terrible chore." Williams said that this is merely a matter of attitude. "Newspapers seem to draw people who were afraid to take calculus in college," he added. "But writing about the weather involves more than science. There's also the human side."

Williams functions as a translator when he talks to a meteorologist. According to The Random House College Dictionary, a **meteorologist** is versed in "the science dealing with the atmosphere and its phenomena, including weather and climate."

"I can use their jargon," Williams said. "But I always translate it for my readers. There are some weather concepts that are very difficult to understand. You can put them in ordinary terms that will not tell the whole story, but the story will be correct as far as it goes. Still, I worry a lot that we will oversimplify to the point that we will make the 10th-grader who has been paying attention in his earth science class cringe."

The reporter of weather stories must convey technical information in accurate, understandable terms to lay readers. Williams has the credentials for it. He attended the U.S. Naval Academy for two years, and obtained a strong engineering background, before transferring to Jacksonville University in Florida, where he was graduated with a major in history and a minor in philosophy.

Working closely with meteorologists, Williams puts together his own weather stories each day. "We also make an effort to try to get hold of people other than law enforcement officials and weather forecasters to quote in stories," he said. "We want to show how people are affected by the weather. I also try to show readers that weather, in a sense, is connected—that the storm on the East Coast is tied to the clear weather on the West Coast somehow. A lot of stories treat weather as if it popped up out of nowhere. As a national newspaper, we want to get a national perspective."

Readers often turn to the Internet or printed newspapers when they want details of weather from across the country. While most television stations focus on weather forecasting, most newspapers place primary emphasis on weather coverage. Forecasts published online and in most newspapers are based on information provided by wire services, the National Weather Service or a private **weather forecasting service** such as AccuWeather or Weather Services Corp.

Naturally, most newspapers cannot devote as much time or money to weather coverage as *USA Today* does. Nor can most newspapers match the sparkle or the sophistication of electronic media when it comes to weather forecasting. But most editors realize the importance of solid weather coverage.

Local readers, like others around the country, want to know how the weather will affect them. It is not enough merely to give high and low temperatures and precipitation totals. Readers also want to know, for example:

- If it is safe to travel
- If schools will be open
- If mail will be delivered

- If planes are on time at the airport
- If fog will make it difficult to see
- If it will be bitterly cold

Readers want to know these things—and more—because their lives are affected each day by the weather. People depend on the media for this kind of information.

Example: A Snowstorm in Fairbanks

When a storm hits, weather coverage is particularly important at the *Daily News-Miner* in Fairbanks, Alaska. Several reporters and editors play a role in gathering information when a weather story dominates the front page. This was the case when a snowstorm paralyzed Fairbanks just before Christmas. The headline in Monday's editions told the story: 17.2 inches—but don't stop counting!

The story was not routine; it went beyond providing statistical information. It contained facts, figures and direct quotations from a variety of sources.

The storm was so severe that it caused a serious circulation problem. Some of the newspapers were not delivered until the following day. *News-Miner* policy states that if it is 50 degrees below zero, the carriers have the option of delivering the newspaper the next day.

The snowstorm was a major story that required extensive interviews and the gathering of factual information. It was the type of story encountered regularly at newspapers all across the United States. The straightforward opening paragraphs of the front-page story in the *Daily News-Miner* made it clear that the weather was wreaking havoc with travel and would probably continue to do so:

> The largest snowstorm in years is continuing to dump near-record amounts in much of interior Alaska, causing slick roads and lots of accidents.
>
> Travel warnings are in effect, and the National Weather Service is predicting even more snow before the storm tapers off by noon Tuesday.
>
> "It ain't over yet," said weather service forecaster Paul Flatt this morning. "It's real tough to call, but we should pick up another six to 10 inches through Tuesday. This much snow is unusual in Fairbanks. It happens, but not very often."
>
> Weather officials at the airport tallied 17.2 inches of snowfall by 9 a.m. this morning—2.9 inches on Saturday, 11.5 inches Sunday and 2.8 inches by 9 a.m. today.
>
> "And it is still falling like mad," said National Weather Service meteorological technician Wayne Nelson this morning.

The opening paragraphs certainly provided readers with the most pertinent information: The storm was a major one; it would continue to dump snow on Fairbanks; the snow was approaching record amounts.

Had there been deaths as a result of the storm, major power outages or monetary estimates of damages, this information would probably have been included in the summary lead. However, in the relatively early stages of the storm, this information was not yet known.

After the opening paragraphs, the writing focused on facts and quotations from sources in Fairbanks and in outlying areas. The story continued with information crucial and interesting to readers:

> Fairbanks International Airport remained open this morning, but traffic was slow due to snow clearing operations on the runways, said Nelson, who also does pilot briefing.
>
> "Operation is close to normal for the major airlines," Nelson said. "But for the little guys it's different. These bush pilots can't take off in this kind of stuff."

> Alaska State Troopers are urging people to stay home to avoid the nasty driving conditions.
>
> Over the weekend, both troopers and Fairbanks city police kept busy with a string of accidents and stalled vehicles.

After the story provided readers with information that most directly touched their daily lives, it went on to discuss the origins of the storm and to provide a summary of conditions in other towns.

The story concluded with quotations from local residents, a police officer, a state trooper and managers of local towing services, who reported doing record business.

The storm continued on Monday, and so reporters and editors at the *Daily News-Miner* stayed busy gathering additional information for Tuesday's newspaper. By Tuesday, the storm was having a greater impact on readers' daily lives and on the government's coffers. This was apparent in the opening paragraphs of Tuesday's story:

> A near-record snowfall buried Fairbanks Monday, littering streets with stalled vehicles and taking an extra $10,000 bite out of the Department of Transportation's snow-clearing budget.
>
> As Fairbanksans shoveled out from under 26 inches of snow this morning, forecasters warned that two to four more inches were on the way today. Another snowstorm is expected to pass through on Thursday, but forecasters don't know how much snow it will leave behind.
>
> "This is probably about a 10-year snow," said Bob Fischer, supervising forecaster for the National Weather Service. "Storms of this magnitude are relatively rare."
>
> Heavy snow and impassable streets prevented delivery of the U.S. mail and the Fairbanks *Daily News-Miner* in some rural areas. It closed some area roads, and Eilson Air Force Base was closed to all but essential personnel today.
>
> School buses ran as scheduled, but some cut their routes short, and others stuck to main roadways, requiring children to walk there or find their own transportation.

The first five paragraphs focused on the most relevant information to readers. The story also provided these facts to aid readers:

Buses were running 15 to 30 minutes late.

Taxis were running about 30 minutes late.

Two highways were closed.

And in an additional paragraph, the newspaper advised motorists, snowmachiners and skiers "to watch for moose which are drifting from deep snow to roads, trails and railroad tracks."

Types of Weather Stories

Several reporters and editors are often mobilized in newsrooms to help cover major storms, but on a day-to-day basis, one reporter generally assumes responsibility for routine weather coverage. It is common for new staff members to be assigned the task. Examples of various types of weather stories and advice on how to write them follow.

Forecasts

The wire services routinely move **state weather forecasts.** Often, reporters will use information in wire stories to help them localize forecasts. Generally, a call to the nearest National Weather Service station will provide sufficient information for a local angle. If a region has been hit by a storm, is in the middle of a drought or is trying to dry out after several days of rain, **local weather forecasts** are particularly pertinent to readers.

Readers should be informed as completely as possible about potential weather problems, but if there is uncertainty, it is best to seek information from several sources before rushing to print with leads that overdramatize the weather. Conversely, if hazardous weather is clearly moving into an area, that should be emphasized in a story's lead.

Readers want to know what might be in store for them today and tomorrow, but *long-term forecasts* are also important. The National Weather Service and weather forecasting services provide long-range forecasts, but reporters can go beyond these by seeking details from local or regional authorities.

Clearly, the rules for putting together stories about the weather are the same as those for writing other news: select an appropriate lead; structure a concise, easy-to-understand first sentence; get quotations from authorities near the beginning of the story; and be sure to tell readers what they want to know—that is, how the weather will affect them.

Travel Conditions and Closings

Another basic weather story deals with travel conditions. Because many readers are constantly on the roads, they need to know how safe the roads are. Quite often, if travel conditions are poor, schools and other institutions are closed. Therefore, it is common for newspapers to publish stories that provide information on road conditions and details on closings of local institutions.

Information for these stories usually comes from the National Weather Service or other forecasting services, from state transportation officials, from local law enforcement personnel and, in the case of school closings, from institution officials.

Record-Breaking Weather

Newspapers routinely carry stories about record-breaking weather such as rainfall (or the lack of it) and low and high temperatures. These stories are relatively easy to write; forecasting services provide most of the information.

The importance of a weather forecasting service as a primary source cannot be stressed enough. The National Weather Service, AccuWeather and other private companies are wells of information, and reporters should routinely tap into them.

Unusual Weather

Many weather stories that the media disseminate each year are routine: forecasts, monthly rainfall totals, year-end summaries. It is a sure bet that reporters will be writing stories such as these. Occasionally, though, freak, unexpected weather can catch reporters—and everyone else—off guard. Tornadoes, hurricanes, cyclones and natural disasters such as earthquakes can wreak havoc.

When these events occur, reporters and editors must be ready to spring into action. Special problems develop when the weather goes berserk, when a tornado rips through town or when floodwaters inundate a community. While reporters and photographers are trying to work their way into restricted areas, editors and circulation employees face the problem of getting the newspaper to the readers. Reporters and editors should have emergency plans that can be implemented when freak weather strikes. In most cases, they need two plans, one for covering the freak weather and another for maintaining the production of the newspaper.

Covering unusual weather, such as tornadoes, requires many of the same reporting procedures that are followed when writing about disasters, which are discussed more extensively later in this chapter.

Seasonal and Year-End Stories

Newspapers regularly publish seasonal stories on the first day of winter, Groundhog Day, the first day of spring and so forth. Most are reported, with new approaches, each year. Newspapers also publish **year-end weather summaries**. Jan. 1 is traditionally a slow day for news. It is common for reporters to dig through the weather reports for the preceding 365 days and to base stories on the statistics. The statistical information, of course, is complemented with direct quotations from weather officials.

News reporters are sometimes assigned to write these year-end weather stories. The assignment should not be considered unimportant busy work. Good reporters will go beyond the statistics and emphasize the human ramifications of the year's weather.

Weather Terminology: AP Style

USA Today's Jack Williams noted that a basic knowledge of weather and an understanding of the language used to describe it are of great help in writing accurate, meaningful weather stories.

The Associated Press Stylebook has a comprehensive section on weather terms—ranging from *blizzard* to *flash flood* to *hurricane watch* to *travelers' advisory* to *wind chill index*. Check the stylebook if you have any questions on proper weather terms or their meanings.

✔ A Checklist for Weather Stories

Comprehensive, complete weather stories are not developed simply by incorporating a few comments from local weather-service officials into a wire-service account. Reporters must diligently ferret out information from available sources. Here are some suggestions to consider when writing stories about storms:

- ❑ *Keep in Constant Touch with the National Weather Service Bureau Nearest You or a Private Service.* Don't wait until a major storm hits to develop sources. If possible, visit the bureau nearest you. Get to know the forecasters. Then, when a major storm hits and you want information, you will not be just another voice on the telephone. Other media representatives will be in touch with the services on days of major storms; if you have taken the time to develop sources on less hectic days, it will pay dividends for you.

- *Keep in Constant Touch with the State Patrol.* The state patrol can provide you with information on accidents, road conditions and the like. As with a weather forecasting service, if you have maintained ties with the state patrol throughout the year, it will be easier to get information on days of inclement weather. It is only natural for sources to be more accommodating to those journalists who check in regularly. One way to cultivate sources such as the state patrol, the National Guard, the Army Reserve and the Coast Guard is to do an occasional feature story on their training or on new equipment or facilities they might have. Such stories will be of interest to your readers and will also help officials at the agencies remember you when you call on deadline and need some information from them.
- *Keep in Touch with the State Department of Transportation or Comparable Agency for Your Area.* Officials there can keep you posted on road closings, on bridges that are out or on areas of the state where travel is not advised.
- *Keep in Touch with Local Law Enforcement Agencies, Such as the Police and Sheriff Departments.*
- *Keep in Touch with Local Agencies Responsible for Snow Removal, Storm Cleanup and the Like.* They can provide you with information on timetables for cleanups, how many workers are on the job, whether they are working shifts around the clock and estimated costs.
- *Interview Local Residents Who Have Been Caught out in the Weather.* Do not limit weather stories to quotations from authorities; provide details and quotations from residents, too. Readers will appreciate and relate to the *human angle.*
- *Keep in Touch with Officials at Local Institutions, Agencies and Entities That Are Affected by the Weather.*

Institutions that can be affected by weather include, but are not limited to, the following:

Schools (Will classes be held? Are buses running?)

Utility companies (What effects did the storm have on use of electricity and gas?)

Telephone companies (Did the storm down lines? Did use of telephones go up during the hours of the storm?)

Civil defense departments (Are shelters being provided for the homeless or for stranded motorists?)

National Guard, Coast Guard or Army Reserve units (Have these units been mobilized to aid residents or to help clear debris or snow? If so, how many people are involved? How long will the mobilization last?)

Post office (Is the mail being delivered? If so, are deliveries running late?)

Hospitals (Have any people been hospitalized as a result of storm-related incidents? What is their condition?)

Bus companies (Are they running on schedule?)

Airport (Are planes arriving and departing? If so, are they on schedule?)

Train depots (Are trains arriving and departing? Are they on schedule?)

Taxi companies (Are they running?)

In addition to consulting with the sources listed above, reporters might want to check weather records kept by the newspaper or by local observers. And faculty members at local colleges or universities might provide additional scientific information or background on the storm.

Where to Turn Online

There are scores of weather pages available on the Internet that can help in weather research. Jack Williams of *USA Today* offers an "Ask Jack" page on *USAToday.com* in which he welcomes questions, comments and complaints from readers. Clay Thompson also answers questions and writes a daily "Outside" column on the weather page of *Arizonarepublic.com* and *The Arizona Republic*, another Gannett newspaper. *USAToday.com* and many other newspaper Web sites offer, among other things, maps, forecasts and reports. *CNN.com* offers the same type of information based on Zip codes or cities worldwide.

An excellent site that acts as a portal to newspapers, broadcast networks, graphics services, wire services and so much more worldwide is *www2.Assignmenteditor.com*. Through it, you can quickly find weather and disaster information.

The National Weather Service can be found at *www.NWS.NOOA.gov*. It offers weather and flood warnings as well as forecasts and advisories for the United States. Private services such as AccuWeather (*AccuWeather.com*) and Weather Services Corp. (*WX.com*) are also excellent resources for U.S. and international forecasts and information.

Up-to-date weather news can be found on the Weather Channel page (*Weather.com*).

These are only a sampling of what's available online if you're looking for weather information. Along with them there are local sites serving many metropolitan areas. For example, if there is a major rainstorm, a local site could provide street closings.

Covering Disasters

It was about 6 p.m. on a Friday. People were beginning their weekends. A jetliner was headed for a landing in Dallas during a severe thunderstorm.

Elements of Disaster Coverage

The First Bulletins

At about 6:15 p.m., United Press International moved a **bulletin**, which the wire services use to alert journalists that a major story is beginning to develop. A bulletin, which does not often exceed one paragraph, is sent over the wires to newspapers and broadcast outlets.

> GRAPEVINE, Texas (UPI)—An explosion was reported Friday at Dallas-Fort Worth International Airport, and there were unconfirmed reports that a Delta jetliner had crashed on landing in a severe thunderstorm.

At about the same time, The Associated Press moved a bulletin over its broadcast wire:

> (GRAPEVINE, TEXAS)—AUTHORITIES SAY A DELTA PASSENGER PLANE CAPABLE OF CARRYING MORE THAN 200 PEOPLE HAS CRASHED NORTH OF DALLAS-FORT WORTH INTERNATIONAL AIRPORT.

Editors and news directors throughout the country saw these bulletins and immediately sprang into action. As in any disaster, print and broadcast journalists relied heavily on the wire services to supply them with news until they could get their own reporters and photographers to the scene. Of course, not every newspaper and broadcast outlet would send reporters to Texas to cover this story. Only those throughout Texas, as well as the television networks and the major metropolitan newspapers, would. Many newsrooms would use wire copy exclusively. Broadcast outlets, particularly radio, would use the early stories for hourly news reports or breaks into current programming. Newspapers would use the stories that move closest to their final deadlines.

Making Every Minute Count

Several minutes after the bulletins moved, The Associated Press moved a 1st Lead-Writethru, the designation wire services use to tell newsrooms that this is the first complete story and that it replaces all earlier stories. In a developing news story such as a plane crash, where cable news networks likely will be providing live coverage as soon as they can get to the scene, wire services will move new leads, inserts to earlier stories and **writethrus** as often as they can. Within several hours of the Dallas crash, the AP would move 15 writethrus on the newspaper wire; UPI moved seven.

The 1st Writethru from the AP confirmed everyone's fears:

> GRAPEVINE, Texas (AP)—A Delta Air Lines jumbo jet crashed and exploded Friday during a heavy thunderstorm on its final approach to Dallas-Fort Worth International Airport, authorities said.

Local radio and television stations reported an unknown number of casualties.

Dense smoke streamed from the L-1011's charred hulk, and debris was scattered over several hundred yards just north of the airport.

One witness said that the plane bounced about five times and sent up smoke and flames. A pilot who witnessed the accident said that nothing was left of the plane.

The airplane crashed near oil storage tanks in a freight area. Ambulances raced to the scene, and firefighters spread foam. A car on Texas 114 was demolished.

This first story from AP was sketchy. Mention of casualties was put in the second paragraph because no one knew yet how many people were killed or injured, and AP was still relying on radio and television stations for its information. The AP still did not know how the plane crashed, where it was from, where it was going or why it crashed. Those important elements, and much more, would have to be reported in later stories.

The wire services also continued to move new stories over their broadcast wires. As it moved its 1st Lead-Writethru on the newspaper wire, the AP sent a similar story over the broadcast wire:

(GRAPEVINE, TEXAS)—LOCAL RADIO AND TELEVISION STATIONS IN THE DALLAS-FORT WORTH AREA ARE REPORTING MASS CASUALTIES FROM THE CRASH OF A DELTA AIR LINES PASSENGER PLANE. THE PLANE, CAPABLE OF CARRYING MORE THAN 200 PEOPLE, CRASHED NORTH OF THE DALLAS-FORT WORTH INTERNATIONAL AIRPORT.

WITNESSES AT THE SCENE SAY DENSE SMOKE WAS SEEN STREAMING FROM THE AIRCRAFT FOLLOWING A TREMENDOUS EXPLOSION. A PILOT WHO SAW THE ACCIDENT SAYS THERE'S NOTHING LEFT OF THE PLANE.

THERE'S STILL NO WORD ON THE FLIGHT NUMBER. EMERGENCY CREWS ARE RUSHING TO THE SCENE.

The 2nd Lead-Writethrus from AP and UPI were still unable to report the number of casualties on the airplane, but they did provide some new information. The lead paragraph of the AP's second story, for instance, was the same as in the first story, but the second paragraph was changed to update readers on casualties.

In its 2nd Lead-Writethru, UPI reported that more than 100 people were aboard the plane. It still had not confirmed the exact number, nor did it know how many people had died; but it was the first wire service to report the number of people aboard, the number of survivors, the flight number and where it originated. Here is UPI's story:

GRAPEVINE, Texas (UPI)—A Delta L-1011 with more than 100 people aboard hit two cars, crashed and exploded in a severe thunderstorm Friday at Dallas-Fort Worth International Airport, and witnesses said that there were "massive injuries."

There were at least 11 survivors, officials said, but no word on how many might have died in the fiery crash.

"Ambulances are everywhere," a witness said. "They have massive injuries."

Another witness said that the jumbo jet appeared to "nosedive" as it neared landing.

Authorities said it was believed that 147 passengers and an unknown number of crew members were on board the craft, Flight 191, originating in Fort Lauderdale, Fla.

Parkland Hospital officials in Dallas said that they received six of the injured and were alerted to "any number of people."

A witness said that about five seconds after the crash a large explosion sent flames 200 to 300 feet into the air.

"There's metal strewn all over the place," said W.J. Blankenship, a battalion chief of the Irving Fire Department.

He said that the airplane or a section of the craft apparently hit a car on Texas 114 adjacent to the airport, killing the driver.

Using Instinct

The early accounts by the wire services are typical in major breaking news stories. Coverage is based on instinct, a reporter's **nose for news,** rather than a long, carefully thought out process in which sources are cultivated. The early stories report the news as quickly as possible, and they are based on information gathered from whatever sources the reporters can get to initially. Final numbers and explanations often come hours or days later.

When reporters are able to develop a story carefully, they cultivate sources, gaining trust and ferreting out information over a period of time. In many ways a single story becomes their beat. But when they cover a fast-breaking story such as the crash of Flight 191, they must use their natural intuition and common sense to gather as much information and to make their news decisions as quickly as they can. They must react instantaneously, knowing where to go for information and knowing which witnesses, opinions, facts and figures to believe. Their intuition is based on past reporting experience.

Including the Essentials

Reporters who gather information about disasters, such as an airplane crash, strive to include essential ingredients in their stories. Each breaking story and follow-up that they write should include:

- Death count
- Number of injuries
- Condition updates from hospitals
- Update on rescue attempts
- Date of the disaster
- Time of the disaster
- Background particular to the disaster; in this case, the flight number, where the flight originated and its destination
- Factors that led to the disaster, such as the violent weather
- Latest findings in the investigation
- Quotations from survivors
- Quotations from witnesses
- Historical significance

Coordinating Coverage

Besides sending reporters and photographers to the scene of a developing story, newspaper editors and broadcast news directors coordinate coverage inside the newsroom, which becomes even more hectic than normal when a major story breaks. Here are the various responsibilities that a newsroom must handle as quickly as possible.

Checking clips. Whenever coverage of a major story begins, someone has to check the electronic or paper files of stories written in the past about similar incidents. The clips should provide information such as the number of plane crashes this year, the worst aviation disasters, the number of crashes at Dallas-Fort Worth or any problems that Delta has been experiencing.

There's one important thing to remember about clips: the fact that something has been in print does not mean that it is correct. Do not repeat an error. If there is doubt about something that has been reported earlier, check it out.

Checking hospitals. In any disaster, the busiest spots will probably be the local hospitals, where casualties are taken and where temporary morgues are often set up. Each of the hospitals should be called regularly to find out how many people were taken there and what their condition was. Usually a reporter will ask to speak to the nursing supervisor in the emergency room, but in major stories such as a plane crash, reporters are generally transferred to a single hospital spokesperson responsible for disseminating information to the media.

Checking the coroner's office. A check of the coroner's office is always important when dealing with stories in which people have been killed. The coroner, or medical examiner, can provide information on the number and the causes of deaths.

Interviewing witnesses. Interviewing witnesses over the phone is difficult, but reporters still try. The final story will rely on reporters at the scene for interviews with witnesses, but journalists working the phones can make early contacts.

Interviewing officials. Officials of companies, government agencies and other organizations must be interviewed as appropriate. In the air crash story, it was of course necessary to cover Delta Air Lines. The company would need to make some type of official statement.

Checking organizations. Because the plane had crashed in a severe thunderstorm, it was important to check with the National Weather Service or a private weather forecasting service. Someone would have to check on how violent weather affects airplane travel. For example, can lightning strike and destroy an airplane? Can a gust of wind blow it down?

Checking the wire services. No matter how well a story is staffed, the AP and supplemental wires should be checked continually to gather additional information.

Getting the Latest Lead

The media from Dallas and Fort Worth were on the air crash story instantly. By 6:30 p.m., WFAA-TV, the ABC affiliate in Dallas, began live coverage from the airport. It continued through the evening, feeding videotape via satellite to ABC News headquarters in New York. That enabled the network to break into regular programming with bulletins. Later in the evening, ABC's "Nightline" aired a full report of the crash, including live interviews with WFAA reporters on the scene.

Five hours after the crash, there was still much news to report. The crash had already been reported; but newspaper and broadcast reporters from Texas and throughout the country still had to develop the story for Saturday editions and news shows. After initial reports of the disaster, reporters turned their attention to the cleanup operation, the names of the victims and how the disaster occurred.

By the time the AP moved its 15th Lead-Writethru to member newspapers, at 10:49 p.m. Texas time, the scope of the disaster was known. The story began:

> GRAPEVINE, Texas (AP)—A Delta Air Lines jumbo jet carrying 160 people crashed and exploded Friday during a final approach to Dallas-Fort Worth International Airport, killing about 130 people, officials said.

A few minutes earlier, the AP had moved the following over its broadcast wire:

> (GRAPEVINE, TEXAS)—OFFICIALS NOW SAY ABOUT 130 PEOPLE HAVE DIED FOLLOWING THE CRASH OF A DELTA AIR LINES JUMBO JET THAT CRASHED ON APPROACH AT THE DALLAS-FORT WORTH INTERNATIONAL AIRPORT. THERE WERE 160 PEOPLE ON BOARD FLIGHT 191, AND AT LEAST 34 PEOPLE WERE INJURED.

The AP's leads reported *when* and *where* the crash occurred, but they did not mention the thunderstorm. Instead, they added the *latest* key element of the story—the number of casualties. By now, reporters knew how many people were aboard. They did not have to estimate "more than 100" as UPI did in one of its earlier leads. But they still were scrambling to get the exact number of deaths. Nearly six hours after the crash, AP could only report "about 130."

UPI also moved updated stories throughout the night, but at a slower pace than AP. In its 7th Lead-Writethru, which it moved at 11:50 p.m. Texas time, UPI reported:

> GRAPEVINE, Texas (UPI)—A Delta jumbo jet carrying 161 people nosedived while trying to land during a vicious storm at Dallas-Fort Worth International Airport Friday, killing at least 122 in a fiery explosion that scattered wreckage over a half mile.

UPI's writing continued to be more colorful than the AP's, with such vivid words as "nosedived," "vicious storm" and "fiery explosion." The AP's 15th Lead-Writethru was a terse 29 words, though. UPI used 38 words in its seventh lead.

There were other differences in the leads. While the AP reported that the plane was carrying 160 people and about 130 were killed, UPI said that there were 161 aboard and at least 122 of those had died.

Two Problems for Reporters

Problem 1: A Pitfall of Instantaneous Coverage

The wire-service leads point out a common problem in covering developing disaster stories. When scores of reporters are thrust into the middle of a major story, there is intense pressure to deliver the news faster than the competition. Because reporters are forced to go with what they've got, they are often unable to double-check each bit of information they gather.

Problem 2: Interviewing Victims' Families

One of the toughest things that a reporter has to do while covering a disaster is to interview the families of victims. At no other time does the public's right to know seem to come into such direct conflict with people's right to privacy.

Still, reporters know that by interviewing a grieving parent, spouse or child, they can add an important human element to stories that might otherwise be dominated by statistics. Professionals realize that if they handle the interviews with a great deal of sensitivity, they can offer survivors an opportunity to grieve openly and to eulogize a loved one.

Research by one reporter supports the theory that most people don't mind being interviewed during a time of grief, if they are treated with sensitivity. To fulfill the research project requirements for a master's degree in mass communication, Karen McCowan, a reporter for *The Arizona Republic* in Phoenix, sent questionnaires to 22 grieving relatives quoted in *The Republic* after the crash of a Northwest Airlines jet at Detroit Metropolitan Airport. She also sent surveys to 26 journalists who interviewed the grieving families. People who refused to be interviewed after the crash were not surveyed.

Eleven of the grieving relatives and 15 reporters answered in-depth questions concerning their feelings about the interviews. In a *Republic* article about her research, McCowan wrote that perhaps "many of the sources who refused to participate in the survey see it, like their interviews, as an invasion of privacy."

Two of the grieving relatives who responded to the survey had strong objections to being interviewed: one of them said that "privacy was more important than a story to help sell newspapers"; the other criticized the reporters' timing, saying that the first two days after the crash were "brutal." A third relative reported mixed feelings about the interviews. Eight relatives, however, said that they had not minded being interviewed. Most of these said that they wanted the public to know about their loved ones' lives, accomplishments and unexpected deaths. They also said that they saw interviews as a way to ensure accuracy in stories or to vent their emotions.

The reporters who responded to McCowan's questionnaire said that in most cases people do not mind interviews during a time of grief. "Usually, I've found that I feel much worse about asking questions than they do about answering questions," one reporter said.

All the reporters who responded said that the television interviews were most intrusive, if only because of all the equipment required. Some reporters also said that the television interviews were more exploitative emotionally because everything that the family said or did was recorded.

Three of the relatives said, however, that they found print interviews more intrusive than television interviews because of their greater length.

"Like most reporters, I dreaded having to telephone or, even worse, knock on the door of someone who had just lost a family member in a tragedy," McCowan said. "That's why I chose to do my research project on this topic.

"But my findings and personal experience have taught me that many, many people want to talk at a time like this. I think some find a great deal of comfort in the fact that they are not alone in seeing this person's death as significant."

CHAPTER SEVENTEEN

BROADCAST WRITING

Although many of the reporting concepts are the same, writing styles for print and for broadcast differ. Reporters constantly are challenged to communicate the best way they can within the parameters of their medium.

Walter Cronkite, one of the world's most revered broadcast journalists, is proud of his print heritage. When he stepped down as anchor and managing editor of the "CBS Evening News" in 1981, he was quoted by The Associated Press as saying that he worried "about the truncated nature of much of broadcast journalism." As a result, he reasoned, "a whole class of people, many of whom are capable of doing

(*Greg Pease / Getty Images*)

only the first paragraph of a story," have emerged. But, Cronkite commented, "If you don't know what belongs in the 34th paragraph of a story, how can you know what belongs in the lead?"

Cronkite told Clifford Terry, who wrote an article for the *Chicago Tribune Magazine,* that, as a broadcast journalist, he always tried to avoid superficiality by adhering to "the principles that had long been laid down in print."

Cronkite became synonymous with media coverage of America's manned space program. Viewers turned to Cronkite when Alan Shepard became the first American in space in 1961, when John Glenn became the first American to orbit the Earth in 1962 and when Neil Armstrong stepped onto the lunar surface in 1969.

Then, 36 years after Glenn's famous flight, Cronkite returned to the Kennedy Space Center in Florida to co-anchor CNN coverage of the 77-year-old astronaut-turned-senator's return to space—an event that, as Reuters reported, reunited "two old lions . . . for a last hurrah in the final frontier."

Clearly, television is first and foremost a visual medium and radio is a medium of sound. Pictures and sound can convey a tremendous amount of information—often with more impact than hundreds of words. The time constraints of broadcasting, while sometimes contributing to a superficiality, also emphasize the need for broadcast writing to be concise, clear and to the point.

Broadcast Style: Guidelines for Writers

Without a doubt, electronic journalism is easy for listeners or viewers to absorb; a person has to work much harder when reading than when listening or viewing. It is important, though, for reporters in the electronic media to write clearly and simply. The fact-filled lead including *who, what, why, where, when* and *how* can be a tongue twister and could cause the best newscaster to run out of breath. Besides, these leads normally contain too much information for the listener to digest.

Writing style for radio, as it developed through the years, became increasingly *conversational*. The rule is: Write as if you were talking to a friend. This evolution from crisp newspaper style to conversational radio style was natural. In broadcast news, the journalist should write for the *ear,* not the eye. Unlike print media, where readers have the opportunity to reread unclear passages, the broadcast news consumer has only one chance to hear and comprehend the message. Consequently, the broadcast news writer must take care to capitalize on this style opportunity to communicate with the listener or viewer.

Television writing style also evolved gradually. While it too is conversational, it developed to serve a medium different from radio. In writing for television, visuals are as important as the words. Each should be tailored to support the other. Thus, writing is often geared to available video. For example, consider a story on an environmentally unsafe chemical waste facility. The story might begin with a very wide, or "long," shot of a storage yard, with the narrative, "Officials say a three-acre chemical storage facility is an environmental time-bomb," followed by closer shots of rusting barrels, and the narrative, "Leaky and unsealed containers of chemicals like dioxin pose the biggest threat."

Broadcast journalists are not as tied to stylistic detail as their print counterparts, but hundreds of stylistic and specific writing practices are widely observed. The wire services have established rules for broadcast style, and many broadcast news departments have adopted additional rules of uniformity unique to their operations. Broadcast journalists should be familiar with these guidelines.

Professor Donald E. Brown, who taught at the University of Illinois and Arizona State University, has synthesized suggestions on stylistic practices that are followed in the broadcast industry. Practices can vary among broadcasting stations, but Brown, in his Radio and Television News Style Sheet, provides guidelines on preparation of copy, use of numerals, time references, use of quotations, use of abbreviations and punctuation. Most of the guidelines listed below are drawn from Brown's style sheet.

Rules of Style

Numbers

Of all the categories customarily covered in style sheets, numerals are perhaps of greatest importance to the beginning writer of broadcast news. Two premises should be established: First, some stories, such as those on the national budget, may have many large figures, and they are of such significance that they deserve intelligent coverage. (With such stories, reporters must decide which figures are of paramount importance, and they must weed out those that are not essential.) Second, a story that presents numerical information should be written in such a way that the announcer can read it easily and the listener can readily comprehend and remember it.

To facilitate the process, Brown gives the following suggestions:

- *Whenever Reasonable, Simplify Complicated Numbers.* It is often convenient and honest to use terms such as *approximately, more than, about* and *almost.*
- *Vary Wording to Help Both the Announcer and the Listener.* To avoid repetition and to make trends or changes clearer, use phrases such as *dropped sharply, tumbled 40 percent, more than doubled, cut in half* and *slightly more than 15 percent.*
- *Spell Out Numbers under 12.* Use numerals from 12 to 999. Keep in mind however, that such rules differ from newsroom to newsroom. Some news directors prefer that reporters spell out all numbers (twenty-five, two-thousand-two-hundred-fifty-three). That minimizes mistakes in copying numerals (such as a misplaced comma or extra numeral) and leaves no doubt about what the number is.
- *Use a Hyphenated Combination of Numerals and Words to Express Thousands;* for example, 35-thousand farmers. For millions, billions and trillions, hyphens are not needed to separate the numerals and the words, but the writer should precede the word by its first letter to help guard against typographical errors. For example: 21 (m) million families.
- *Translate Many Figures, Especially Large Ones, into Round Numbers Whenever Feasible:* $2,001,897.46, in most cases, should be written as "slightly more than two (m) million dollars."

- *Spell Out Symbols for Dollars and Cents:* 29-dollars and 60-cents.
- *Write Fractions as Words, and Hyphenate Them:* two-thirds.
- *Write Out and Hyphenate Decimals:* 5.3 percent should be "five-point-three percent." Instead of 12.3 percent, write "twelve-point-three percent."
- *Remember That, in Most Stories, Ages Are Not Essential.* In deaths, accidents or special situations where the age is needed, do not use this common newspaper style, because it is not conversational: "Marvin Smith, 6, was honored." For broadcasting, write "Six-year-old Marvin Smith was honored."
- *For Certain Types of Numerical Information, Such as Automobile Licenses and Telephone Numbers, Use a Hyphen to Break the Sequence into Its Component Parts in the Way They Would Ordinarily Be Read Aloud:* "Illinois license number J-U-M-8-3-2."

Time References

Because the **element of immediacy** is one of the biggest assets of the broadcast news media, every effort should be made to give up-to-the-minute reports and to write copy in a way that makes it sound fresh and timely. With this in mind, present tense should be used whenever possible. For example, if there is a long-running strike by truckers, it is preferable to write in the present tense: "Striking truckers are still deciding when they will return to the highways." Broadcast writers are urged to avoid the present-perfect tense, in part because it means writing in a passive rather than an active voice. For example, avoid this kind of sentence: "Striking truckers have not decided when they will return to the highways." A note of caution: While present tense is preferred in broadcast writing, it should not be forced. A writer should not take an event that occurred in the past and report it as if it is still happening. For example, do not write: "A car rolls off a bridge, and plunges into the river below." For an accident that happened hours ago, this technique might be labeled "false present tense." Instead, flesh out of a story an element that is current: "Police are still investigating an accident in which a car rolled off a bridge and into a river."

Some of Brown's suggestions on time references are:

- *As Much as Possible, Avoid Emphasizing Old Time Elements.* Be wary of emphasizing such words as *last night* in lead sentences. Look for a new development and a fresh approach when possible.
- *Avoid Undue Repetition of "Today."* In some instances, the day should be broken into its component parts: "late this morning," "this afternoon" and so forth.
- *When Appropriate, Try to Pinpoint Times in Terms That Listeners Can Relate To.* It would generally be more effective, for example, to report that one lane of the freeway will be closed "during rush hour" than to report the precise time, such as from 5 p.m. until 6 p.m.
- *In Capitalizing on Immediacy, Be Alert to Occasional Uses of Interest-Catching Time References.* These include "at broadcast time this noon," "within the past half-hour" and so forth. There is, however, no defense for referring to a "late bulletin" when the bulletin was transmitted an hour ago.

Quotations

Newspaper reporters commonly make extensive use of direct quotations. So do broadcast reporters, only they capture their quotations on audio or videotape during an interview. Those recorded sections of the interview are called **soundbites** or **actualities,** and serve the same basic function as quotations in print stories. Soundbites allow a source to provide more information while adding color and authenticity to the story. Lengthy newspaper-style quotations in the reporter's narrative should be avoided. When a reporter reads a quotation, listeners cannot see the quotation marks in the reporter's script and may become confused about who is responsible for the quotation—the newscaster or the news source. Often the reporter should paraphrase the quote and make it shorter. There are situations, however, when the reporter may want to quote a powerful word or phrase used by the news source. When this happens, attribution can be handled in a number of ways. For example, the reporter could say, "The governor calls the plan, quote, 'an abomination,' unquote, and says it should be shelved." Reporters also can introduce direct quotations with such phrases as "in what he called," "which she described as" or "in these words."

Names and Titles

Most broadcasters agree that writers should never start a lead sentence for radio or television with an unfamiliar name. Without a "warmup" for the ear, it is too easy for the listener to miss the name entirely or to misunderstand it. The newspaper style "John Jones, a well-known Hill City banker, was named chairman" would become in broadcast style "A well-known Hill City banker—John Jones—today was named chairman."

Brown gives the following suggestions:

- *Titles Should Precede Names, Preparing the Listener or Viewer for the Name to Come;* for example, Massachusetts Senator Edward Kennedy.
- *If an Official Is Well-Known within a Given Listening Area (Such as the Governor of the State in Which the Station is Located), Omit the First Name;* for example, Governor Smith. Likewise, you can omit the first name of the president of the United States.
- *If the Title Is Needed to Put the Story in Perspective But It Is So Long That the Newscaster Would Have Difficulty Running It Together with the Name, Use Two Sentences;* for example, "That's according to Jerry Smith. Smith is vice president for academic affairs at the university." This structure is suggested because it's easier not only for the newscaster to say but also for the listeners to hear and process.
- *Shorten Long Titles, or Break Them Up.* Placing part of the title in front of the name and the other part after the name can be effective; for example, "Senator John Jones, the chairman of the Armed Services Committee, said that a meeting will be held soon."

Abbreviations

One functional principle on use of abbreviations in broadcast writing is simply: Eliminate almost all abbreviations. Even with common abbreviations such as states—Pa., for instance—there is a possibility of the announcer's making an

error. And it is more than possible—in fact quite probable—that the announcer will have to hesitate while trying to make mentally sure that each abbreviation is accurately identified.

Common sense should be exercised in handling names of governmental agencies or other phrases that are sometimes conveniently identified by a series of letters. The letters Y-M-C-A and F-B-I are as easily recognized by the average listener as Young Men's Christian Association and Federal Bureau of Investigation. Broadcasters place hyphens between letters to indicate pauses. A good rule is: Use only commonly known abbreviations, and write the way you want the names to be read aloud.

Punctuation

Correct punctuation for other forms of writing is also correct for broadcast news. Punctuation marks are highly valuable to the silent reader; and they are even more valuable to the person at the microphone who is striving for instantaneous interpretation, for inflections, for phrasing, for emphasis and for other qualities that will make the reading more intelligible and more interesting to the listeners.

Two somewhat unconventional punctuation practices are popular among broadcasters. First, many announcers feel that the dash is useful in setting off certain types of explanatory or identifying material. For example, "The new chairman of the budget committee—Senator Sam Smith—will make his recommendations to the entire Legislature." The second device is the use of dots as a guide for a long, dramatic pause. Often, such dots are used where a comma would naturally be placed. For instance, "He gingerly touched the flywheel of the new machine, adjusted his safety mask and reached for the switch . . . and a deafening explosion rocked the laboratory." Three dots are sufficient. Some writers will use a series of five or more dots. This, however, takes more time, is more difficult to read and serves no functional purpose.

Always remember to end a sentence with a period.

Naturally, style elements can vary slightly based on the preferences of the anchor who reads the copy on the air. As is the case at newspapers, the nuances of style often differ from newsroom to newsroom. Broadcast journalists who are well grounded in basic style, however, can readily make appropriate adjustments.

✔ A Checklist for Broadcast Writers

In addition to stylistic considerations, broadcast journalists should always write to inform—not to impress. Professor Brown cites several taboos in broadcast writing: dialects, slang, technical terms, uncommon scientific terms and professional jargon. The last two should be translated. Also, the terms *former* and *latter* should not be used in broadcast writing. The listener cannot go back to find out what they refer to.

Brown lists three points for sentence structure in broadcast copy:

- ❑ *Avoid Long Separations of Subjects and Predicates.* Do not write, "John Jones, a resident of the Fourth Ward who was elected mayor of Riverdale by the largest margin in the city's history, will present his acceptance speech today." Instead, write, "Riverdale's new mayor, John Jones, will present his acceptance speech today. A resident of the Fourth Ward, Jones was elected by the largest margin in the city's history."
- ❑ *Break Up Lengthy Sequences of Modifiers.* Do not write, "John Jones caught a well-thrown, expertly timed, 45-yard pass from Henry Smith in Friday night's football game." If you want to emphasize what John Jones did, write: "John Jones caught a 45-yard pass from Henry Smith in Friday night's football game. The pass was well-thrown and expertly timed." If you want to emphasize the action to make a punchier lead, write: "It was well-thrown and expertly timed . . . that 45-yard pass John Jones caught from Henry Smith in Friday night's football game."
- ❑ *Avoid the Common Newspaper Structure in Which the Attribution Is Tacked On after a Quotation.* This is referred to as *dangling attribution.* Do not write, "I am going to win the election," John Jones said. Broadcasters do not use dangling attribution for two reasons: (1) people don't talk that way, and (2) the listener may think that the words are those of the broadcaster. The attribution should be handled like this for broadcast: John Jones said he will win the election, or, in these exact words, John Jones said, "I am going to win the election."

Professor Ben Silver of Arizona State University, a former CBS newsman, offers these additional tips:

- ❑ *Write Conversationally.* How do you write conversationally? Talk out loud to your typewriter or computer as you write. Talk to an audience of one or two persons when you write. Your audience may number in the thousands or even the millions, but there are rarely more than one or two people listening or watching in any one place. You are talking to one or two people driving to work. You are talking to one or two people sitting in front of the television set in the family room. The true test of broadcast writing is to read it aloud. If it sounds right, it is probably well written.
- ❑ *Broadcast Copy Should Be Written in the Active Voice.* In the active voice, the subject acts upon the object. Avoid the passive voice, in which the subject is acted upon. Passive voice: *The airliner was hit by the private plane.* Active voice: *The private plane crashed into the airliner.* Active voice is clearer, packs more punch and uses fewer words.

Writing for Radio

Professor Dave Ogden of the University of Nebraska at Omaha, longtime radio journalist, provides advice in this section for effective writing for radio.

Conciseness is key to good broadcast journalism. For many radio stations, newscasts are little more than "headline" news. The nature of the medium limits the amount of news and the length of each story. If a newspaper wants to add more news or advertising, editors can add more pages. But a radio station cannot add hours to its day, so news directors pack as much information as they can in the little time provided for news. Even at news-talk stations in large markets, stories are boiled down to their bare essence. The same story that occupies 10 to 15 column inches in a newspaper may be no longer than 30 or 35 seconds during a radio newscast. Thus, radio news writers strive for brevity and for getting to the heart of the story immediately. The soundbite, or segment of taped interview embedded in the story, should add essential information that doesn't repeat what the reporter says before or after it.

The Radio News Story, or "Wrap"

The structure of radio news stories with soundbites or actualities is called a **wrap.** That's when the reporter wraps words or sentences around one or more major soundbites. This form is also called a **donut,** since the news story surrounds the "hole" where the soundbite is placed. The sentence before the soundbite is called a **lead-in.** The lead-in helps to put the soundbite in perspective, but it should not telegraph that a soundbite follows. Such a lead-in is called a "blind" lead-in. (See Chapter 8.). The following is an example of a wrap using a blind lead-in. The report about the dissolution of a major employer in Northeast Nebraska aired on KFAB, Omaha.

NORTHEAST NEBRASKA LOSES MORE THAN ONE-THOUSAND JOBS WITH THE CLOSING OF THE BEEF AMERICA PLANT IN NORFOLK.

BEEF AMERICA VICE-PRESIDENT DEAN MILLER SAYS A TWO-WEEK STRIKE BY THE WORKERS CRIPPLED PLANT OPERATIONS AND COST THE COMPANY HUNDREDS OF THOUSANDS OF DOLLARS.

MILLER SAYS THE COMPANY CONSIDERED GETTING REPLACEMENT WORKERS.

[WE REVIEWED THE POSSIBILITY OF REOPENING AND AS A RESULT OF THE STRIKE MANY EMPLOYEES HAVE LEFT THE AREA AND SOUGHT EMPLOYMENT ELSEWHERE. THEREFORE, REOPENING IS NOT A VIABLE OPTION.]

MILLER SAYS THE STRIKE WAS OVER WAGES AND BENEFITS.

HE SAYS HIS COMPANY MADE CONCESSIONS IN THOSE AREAS, BUT NEGOTIATIONS WITH THE UNITED FOOD AND COMMERCIAL WORKERS UNION NEVER GOT OFF THE GROUND.

UNION OFFICIALS COULD NOT BE REACHED FOR COMMENT.

Notice that the lead-in to the soundbite in brackets does not signal that a soundbite follows. If the soundbite were removed, the story still would flow smoothly. One way to determine if your lead-in is a blind lead-in is to remove the soundbite and see if the story sounds natural. Lead-ins such as "Miller had this to say about reopening the plant" or "Here's what Miller says about the possibility of reopening the plant" are not blind and would have to be rewritten if the soundbite were removed.

There are several advantages to using blind lead-ins. First, editing such stories to shorter versions is easier. Second, many stations post the text of their stories on their Web sites, and that job becomes easier when simply removing the soundbite creates a Web-ready story. Third, if the tape or the file on the computer jams or doesn't "fire," the glitch is not as obvious with a blind lead-in.

Also notice in the example above that the soundbite does not repeat or resemble the lead-in. Such repetition is called *parroting* and should be avoided. Restating information wastes precious air time, adds nothing new to the story and reflects lazy writing.

In scripting for radio, soundbites are usually abbreviated to the last few words. The time of the soundbite also is included in the script, as is the identity or coding of a soundbite, whether it be the number or name of the computer file containing the soundbite or the number of the tape onto which the soundbite was dubbed. The following script example illustrates this format. This story, also aired on KFAB, focuses on reasons behind the escape of five felons from the Douglas County Corrections Center in Omaha.

DOUGLAS COUNTY OFFICIALS SAY SECURITY LAPSES PROBABLY CONTRIBUTED TO THE ESCAPE OF FIVE INMATES FROM THE COUNTY JAIL.

SHERIFF TIM DUNNING SAYS OFFICIALS KNEW SURVEILLANCE EQUIPMENT WAS NEEDED IN THE EXERCISE AREA. THAT'S WHERE THE INMATES MADE THEIR ESCAPE.

FOLDER/TAPE# :08

OC: . . . MORE EVIDENT QUICKLY.

DUNNING SAYS POLICE CAPTURED ONE OF THE ESCAPEES—TIMOTHY CLAUSEN. CLAUSEN WAS CONVICTED LAST DECEMBER OF MURDER.

DUNNING BELIEVES THE OTHER FOUR ARE STILL IN THE AREA AND ARE ARMED.

The complete soundbite by Dunning is, "Guards had requested motion detectors for that area. That type of an item might have made the escape more evident quickly." The last few words of the soundbite, or OC for **outcue,** tell the newscaster when to open the microphone and continue the story. The line above the outcue locates the soundbite in the system, be it computer or analog tape, and gives the length of the soundbite (eight seconds).

As in the first example, this latest story uses a blind lead-in and avoids parroting. As a follow-up to a previous story on the escape itself, this story took a fresher angle—why the inmates escaped.

Similarities and Differences Between Writing for TV and Writing for Radio

As in radio news, brevity is the byword in TV journalism. TV news stories also depend on soundbites gathered during an interview and the use of blind lead-ins. Unlike radio, TV news stories depend primarily on video.

Television journalists look for stories with strong visual appeal. TV journalists are striving to show, as much as tell, their audience the news. TV journalists must fashion their scripts based on the video they've shot in covering the story. These journalists let the video tell the story and provide only that information which the video does not. The reporter also uses various visual techniques to save time. For example, the reporter may not have to verbally identify a news source before a soundbite, when the name can be displayed on the screen as viewers see the source talking.

The following section details the process a reporter follows in putting together a television story and in writing a **split script,** in which the video descriptions are on the left and the audio, or reporter's narrative, is on the right.

Writing for Television

Dan Fellner, an honors broadcast-journalism graduate of Arizona State University, served an internship at KPNX-TV (an NBC affiliate in Phoenix) before he received his degree. While on assignment at the county courthouse one day, Fellner looked in on the marriage license bureau. He found that it was issuing licenses at a record-breaking rate. Fellner wrote his assignment editor a note, suggesting a story on the local marriage boom. The editor liked the idea and instructed him to put the story together. A summary of statistics would be understandable in a newspaper but would be hard to comprehend on television. Fellner had to explore ways to match the most relevant statistics with pictures—to make his story conform to the unique medium of television.

Getting Video and Conducting Interviews

The assignment editor suggested that Fellner look in the station's film-tape library to see if there was some stock video of a wedding ceremony that could be used to illustrate the story. Fellner and a photographer then went out to shoot videotape of the rest of the story. The camera crew taped some couples waiting in line for licenses and then shot videotape of the swearing-in process that they had to go through to get a license. Interviews were conducted with some couples and three of the bureau's workers.

"I feel it is important to interview as many people as possible," Fellner said. "That way you hopefully have a greater selection of interesting soundbites to choose from when putting together the story. In this case, none of the married couples I interviewed was that interesting, so I ultimately did not include any of them in the finished product."

Fellner and the photographer then went to a bridal shop for video of practically everything in stock—from flowers to wedding gowns.

He and the photographer looked over the videotape to make sure that it was technically acceptable: it was. Fellner then reviewed the interviews and selected portions. He avoided detailed statements that exceeded 20 seconds because audiences do not sit still for a longer soundbite, unless it is particularly captivating or vivid. Instead, Fellner selected brief statements from two employees at the license bureau and one from the owner of the bridal shop.

Writing was easy.

"I just had to make sure we had the pictures to go with my words," Fellner said. "After having a producer approve the script, I went into an audio booth and cut the audiotrack for the story."

Harmonizing Words and Pictures

The next day, the photographer edited the piece on videotape. Fellner, like many reporters, prefers to be present when his work is edited. The editing process took about an hour; then the story was ready to be aired. The words supplemented the pictures.

The total time, including the anchor lead-in, was about 1 minute, 45 seconds. It went as follows:

Video	Audio
Anchorperson on set.	ANCHOR LEAD-IN: IF YOU THINK MARRIAGE IS A DYING INSTITUTION, YOU'RE WRONG . . . AT LEAST NOT HERE IN THE VALLEY. IN FACT, AS DAN FELLNER REPORTS, MORE VALLEY COUPLES HAVE TIED THE KNOT THIS YEAR THAN EVER BEFORE.
Couples getting their marriage licenses at the license bureau.	REPORTER: OFFICIALS AT THE COUNTY'S MARRIAGE LICENSE BUREAU SAY THEY'VE BEEN BUSY THIS YEAR. BY THE TIME THE YEAR ENDS, MORE THAN 15,000 COUPLES WILL HAVE COME INTO THEIR OFFICE TO GET A MARRIAGE LICENSE. THAT'S SUBSTANTIALLY MORE THAN ANY OTHER YEAR IN HISTORY. THIS HAS OCCURRED DESPITE A SLUGGISH ECONOMY AND A DIVORCE RATE HIGH ENOUGH TO SCARE ANY COUPLE AWAY FROM TAKING THE PLUNGE.
Sound on videotape. Bureau worker with her name superimposed on the screen.	THERE ARE ALL AGES OF PEOPLE COMING IN, AND I REALLY DON'T KNOW WHY THEY WOULD BE DOING IT NOW MORE THAN EVER. EVERY AGE HAS BEEN IN HERE SO IT MUST BE THROUGHOUT SOCIETY . . . PEOPLE ARE GETTING MARRIED.
Another interview with a bureau worker.	I THINK PEOPLE ARE TIRED OF SHORT-LIVED ROMANCES. I THINK THEY WANT SOMETHING MORE PERMANENT.

Shots of a bridal shop. Name and address supered on the screen.	VALLEY BUSINESSES, WHICH SELL ANYTHING YOU'D EVER WANT FOR A WEDDING CEREMONY, ARE BENEFITING GREATLY FROM ALL THIS. SOME SAY THIS YEAR HAS BEEN THEIR MOST PROFITABLE EVER, AND THE OUTLOOK FOR NEXT YEAR, THEY SAY, IS EVEN BETTER.
Sound on videotape. Store owner.	WE WERE REALLY SURPRISED TO FIND THAT THE MONTH OF JANUARY—WHICH IS WHAT WE'RE FIGURING RIGHT NOW—IS 50 PERCENT OVER JANUARY OF LAST YEAR, AND WE'RE ANTICIPATING WE'LL HAVE THE BIGGEST YEAR WE'VE EVER HAD IN BUSINESS.
Wedding ceremony.	(WEDDING MUSIC FROM CEREMONY UP FULL FOR SEVEN SECONDS—THEN UNDER NARRATION.) BUT WEDDING-TYPE BUSINESSES AREN'T THE ONLY ONES TO BENEFIT FROM THE MARRIAGE BOOM. IF CURRENT STATISTICS HOLD TRUE, IN A COUPLE OF YEARS THERE ARE GOING TO BE AN AWFUL LOT OF BUSY DIVORCE LAWYERS. DAN FELLNER, TV-12, ACTION NEWS.

Fellner's story is clearly written and well-organized. The pictures and the words are coordinated. Television reporters must generally work hard to do that. But only by doing so are they able to use the medium to communicate effectively with viewers.

The Art of Storytelling

A popular concept today in broadcast news writing and reporting is "storytelling." Broadcast journalism is about people and how events affect them. Each story requires a beginning, a middle and an end. That is, each story needs a logical flow. A common technique in storytelling is presenting a problem and either showing how it is being resolved or providing an explanation as to why there is no resolution.

Broadcast writing is unique because, unlike print journalism where words are the exclusive method of communication (aside, of course, from a photograph or graphic that may accompany a story), words work in conjunction with other elements—natural sound, sound bites and, in television, video. Thus, "writing" a broadcast story may be viewed more as an exercise in producing it. It means not only writing the words but also blending them within the structure of the entire story and the other elements.

"In broadcasting, the written word must work *with* these elements in the story rather than confusing or muddling the storytelling effort," Arizona State University Professor Joe Russomanno said. "Especially in television where visuals are so important, words may be seen as only guides that help in the telling of the story. The words ought to facilitate that process. This, of course, is not meant to minimize the importance of the words and how the story is crafted. In fact, careful, skillful writing that capitalizes on the unique nature of broadcasting is critical."

✔ A Checklist for Effective Broadcast Journalism

Arizona State Professor Silver; veteran Phoenix, Ariz., radio reporter Wendy Black; and Professor Ogden of the University of Nebraska at Omaha offer the following suggestions to students who aspire to work in broadcast journalism.

- ❑ **Understand Technology.** Broadcast journalists need to understand the production techniques, capabilities and limitations of equipment used in broadcast news. In radio, reporters are expected to record and edit audiotape. Reporters in small-market television news are expected to know how to use a minicam and video editing equipment.
- ❑ **Learn to Perform.** Broadcast journalists should learn not only how to report and write but how to perform. After all, stories that are written are aired on news shows. Because of the emphasis on live coverage in broadcast reporting, reporters should learn to speak extemporaneously.
- ❑ **Keep Soundbites Short and Frame Them Appropriately.** Soundbites should be no longer than 15 seconds. Use blind lead-ins that introduce the soundbite, but do not make it obvious that a soundbite follows. Avoid parroting, or using the same words in your lead-in that follow in the soundbite.
- ❑ **Emphasize the Last Sentence of a Story.** Remember that the last sentence of a broadcast news item is the second most important part of the story. Only the lead is more important. The final sentence is the *wind-up line,* the "punch line." Winding up with the least important fact in a broadcast story would sound like a balloon with the air running slowly out of it. The reporter should use a summary line, a future angle or another important fact or merely repeat the main point to end the story. For example, in a story about a man pleading guilty to two counts of threatening to kill or harm the president of the United States, the newspaper version might end with the maximum penalties that could be imposed. That would be a logical wind-down to the story. The broadcast version, however, could end with another important, related fact, such as, "The arrest came just 10 days after another man, John

Jones, was charged in connection with an attempted stabbing of the president as he was leaving a hotel in Washington, D.C."

- **Approach Television as a Unique Medium.** Television journalists should recognize that television is a unique medium—a visual medium that can show action. Therefore, the kind and quality of visual material available for a given story frequently determine the length and position the news producer will allot to it. In fact, stories that might not otherwise be considered newsworthy may become so if they present good visual possibilities. It is not unusual for a producer to ask a reporter, "What kind of videotape do we have on the story?" One of the challenges facing the news reporter is to get motion pictures that illustrate the story.

To meet that challenge, television journalists should do two essential things:

1. *Learn to Think Visually.* To a certain extent, this is the job of the camera crew. But it is also the reporter's responsibility. News coverage is a team effort. If there is a communication breakdown and the reporter does not let the camera crew know what will be said in the script, the reporter often winds up with a well-written story but without the necessary footage to tell it visually.
2. *When Putting Stories Together for Television, Make Sure That the Words Match the Motion Pictures.* If they do not, the words will compete with the pictures and nothing will get through to the listeners. The picture is saying one thing, and the words are saying something else. Although the words should match the picture, words should not tell viewers what they can see for themselves. Let the picture tell part of the story, and use the words as a supplement—to explain or reinforce the picture or to tell the audience what the picture does not show. Words compete with the picture when there is too much narration. Use a pause now and then to allow the natural sound and picture to tell the story without narration. Natural sound adds realism to both radio and television stories.

- **Approach Radio as a Unique Medium.** Radio journalists need to recognize that radio is a unique medium—a medium that can make a strong appeal to the imagination. Learn to think aurally. It is very important in writing good radio copy to use sound when possible to give the listeners the proper "feel" to put the event together in their minds.

  Imagine, for example, a day in which the stock market has gone wild. The Dow Jones industrials have set yet another all-time high with nearly unbelievable volume. If you have access to the floor of the New York Stock Exchange, you could start your story with copy giving all the necessary information on the session, and then you could interview one of the traders. That is all pretty pat and probably pretty boring to your listeners. Instead, you could start off with the sound of cheering at the closing bell and then present a brief montage of traders and stockholders saying what a great day it had been. Listening to the sounds would set up a picture in the minds of listeners. Then you could hit the audience with the details.

It's particularly important for radio journalists to make effective use of actualities. Remember that actualities do not have to be limited to the body of a story. A radio story can be written dramatically by beginning with an actuality or sound before starting the copy.

MULTICULTURAL REPORTING

One year after a team of reporters and editors started work on a massive series of articles on race relations, *The New York Times* provided its readers with gripping, telling and often tense accounts of complex human relationships in the workplace, churches, military, schools and politics.

That series, "How Race Is Lived in America," won a Pulitzer Prize and later was packaged as a book of the same name.

Writing in the book's introduction, Executive Editor Joseph Lelyveld said: "At a minimum, *Times* editors had had this itch, this wish to do something ambitious on the theme of

(*Photo by Steve Manuel*)

race in America, for five years before we finally hit on a way into the story that promised to be something other than the usual mosaic of dreary census, school and income statistics, studded with pious quotations from the civil rights era of blessed memory or from academics and clergymen speaking earnestly."

Lelyveld wrote that the reporters and editors at *The Times* sought to learn the answers to questions they had about race relations. They decided to "simply find real stories of real people—maybe no more than two or three in each narrative—whose lives and circumstances spanned this great and enduring fault line in American life."

Each of the stories in the series unfolds over time, as Lelyveld wrote, "in all their complexity, the patterns emerging only gradually to the beholding of a patient onlooker who has won their confidence and therefore the opportunity to serve as a sympathetic witness."

Accompanied by an interactive online version that also included a database of *Times* articles on race of the past century, the series burrowed deeply into the recesses of relations across the broad spectrum of American life.

Published during June and July 2000, the series was, according to Lelyveld, "the largest commitment of time and talent *The New York Times* had ever made to a single series of articles—larger than even the Pentagon Papers."

Its 15 installments included stories on:

- Relations in a multiracial church in Decatur, Ga., whose membership during the previous three decades had seen a dramatic ethnic blending;
- Relations between a white author and black director of an HBO hit;
- Relations between black and white Internet entrepreneurs whose company prospered;
- Relations among blacks, whites, Latinos and American Indians in a raw North Carolina slaughterhouse;
- Relations among three teen-agers—an Irish-Catholic girl, an African-American Muslim girl and a girl who is half Jewish and half Puerto Rican—as they moved from middle school to high school;
- Relations between a white quarterback and players and fans at a historically black university; and
- Relations in the newsroom of the *Akron* (Ohio) *Beacon Journal* after publication of its 1994 Pulitzer Prize-winning 30-part series on race.

Each story in *The Times*'s landmark series—powerfully written, emotionally charged, and laden with telling direct quotations, subtleties and astute observations—indeed captured the issues and nuances of race in society.

Deputy Managing Editor Gerald M. Boyd and Assistant Managing Editor Soma Golden Behr were the catalysts of the project. Boyd and Behr previously had worked together on a series in 1993: 10 installments that examined the plight of inner-city youngsters. After that series was published, they knew they wanted to tackle another major project.

"Gradually, we seized upon the issue of race as something that was journalistically worthy and we spent a lot of time over the next few years figuring out what we wanted to do," Boyd, now the newspaper's managing editor, said.

Many of the nation's newspapers published lengthy stories on racial issues shortly after the verdict was handed down in the O. J. Simpson trial in 1995. (See Chapter 21.)

Boyd said his newspaper decided, however, not to explore race in depth at that time "because we wanted to do something original and different from what was typically being done."

After the Simpson trial, he said "it was clear to us that blacks and whites saw the verdict in starkly different terms." Yet, he said, life continued in the workplace: Teachers kept teaching; journalists kept putting out newspapers.

On the surface, workplace relationships did not seem to change, even though polls showed blacks and whites largely saw the issue differently.

"We thought that was fascinating," Boyd said.

Above all else, Boyd said it was clear that race in America "is a struggle" and *The Times* decided ultimately to write stories about "people who are forced to deal with each other across racial lines."

Early planning sessions focused on reporting strategies.

"We had a theme—but we didn't have stories," Boyd said. "We didn't (initially) have a sense of how many stories or how many people. We identified some areas that we needed to look into—such as the military, education, business, media, Hollywood—those kinds of things."

After an all-day meeting at Behr's home that included editors and reporters, Boyd said "about 10 or 15 reporters were sent out to see what they could come up with." As they reported back, "an outline of the series began to emerge."

Boyd likened reporting for the series to "peeling layers from an onion."

"We wanted to get a real sense of what people were going through, and that meant spending a lot of time with those people—going back and going back," he said. "We also knew the stories, by their very nature, would have to be long. We knew it would take a lot of time."

Response to the series was extraordinary: hundreds of thousands of Web site hits; an outpouring of letters to the editor; scores of invitations from communities and universities asking staff members to discuss their stories; and meaningful internal conversations among the newspaper's reporters and editors.

"It was incredible," Boyd said. "There certainly was interest in the journalism we did, but there also was interest in the lessons we had learned about the state of race in this country and the useful things we could tell people about the issue.

"Race is not something we talk about easily. But we were forced to confront that early on in the process. We had to be able to talk about our feelings in an honest way if we were going to go out and report on the topic and then edit the stories. A lot of what we had to do internally was to get comfortable—and that took some time. Once we got there, then it became much easier for us as a group of 20 to 25 reporters and editors to talk about race and share our true feelings. I think that spilled over within the newsroom and *The Times* at large. I can't tell you how meaningful and significant that was."

The series certainly met the goals of those who conceptualized it: "We wanted to focus on average, ordinary people who deal with race day in and day out and what that does to them," Boyd said.

If newspapers are going to more effectively report on the issues and dynamics of a society that increasingly is multicultural, diversity in the newsroom is paramount: diversity of thought, race and gender.

"You have to let people be themselves," Boyd said. "You have to make sure that people in a newsroom appreciate differences in class; just because somebody is of a different skin color doesn't necessarily mean that person reflects as much diversity as you might think if, for example, he has gone to the same schools (or had experiences similar to others). The most important thing is to create a climate in which you say—and you believe—that it is OK to ask when you don't understand something. That doesn't make you a racist or a militant. When we talk about race or operating across racial lines in newsrooms . . . we must be able to talk about it in ways that are open and honest.

"The failure to do that means we pay a price, as journalists and as a society. And it is a huge price. It means we have given race so much power it becomes impossible to get beyond it."

Boyd said he still believes what he had said before: "Race is not a minority issue. It's the most important domestic issue this country faces."

Executive Editor Lelyveld said the newspaper decided to let the stories unfold naturally.

"In the jargon of the newsroom, we made this revolutionary and humbling promise to ourselves by stipulating from the start that there would be no 'nut grafs' in the series," he wrote.

According to Lelyveld, the instincts of the newspaper's editors and reporters told them to "trust our readers to find their own way."

Significantly, no single event triggered the massive journalistic effort by *The Times*—and that historically has not been the case in coverage of race relations in America.

Indeed, when Los Angeles erupted in April 1992 after a jury found four police officers not guilty in the beating of a black motorist, Rodney King, renewed attention was focused on the media's ability—or inability—to cover American cultures and neighborhoods adequately on a day-to-day, non-crisis basis.

A *New York Times*/CBS News Poll conducted after the riots found that most Americans thought it was time for a new emphasis on the problems of minorities and cities. Most respondents saw the unrest more "as a symptom of festering social needs than as a simple issue of law and order." *The Times* noted that the poll "reflected a nation still struggling with the causes of urban turmoil and the most effective response to it." More than half of the respondents said that a major roadblock to solving inner-city problems was "a lack of knowledge and understanding."

Other surveys have illustrated vividly that perceptions often break along racial lines. At one point in the O. J. Simpson murder trial, a *Los Angeles Times* poll showed that 70 percent of blacks were "very" or "somewhat" sympathetic toward Simpson, compared with 38 percent of whites.

Sam Fulwood III wrote in the *Times:* "Such findings come as no surprise to many blacks and to numerous social critics, political scientists and other experts who study black American attitudes. They say a similar gulf splits blacks and whites as they interpret other facets of society. Such polarized views of reality inhibit the nation from effectively dealing with health care, crime, drugs, welfare, gang violence, out-of-wedlock births and a host of social problems."

Factors in Multicultural Coverage

Our Changing Population: Demographics

Very simply, the **demographics** of the United States—the density, distribution and composition of its population—are changing. Journalists must become increasingly cognizant of changing demographics that have created a **culturally inclusive** society.

The Role of the Media: Recommendations of the Kerner Commission

Thomas Winship, president of the Center for Foreign Journalists in Reston, Va., and former editor of the *Boston Globe,* noted in his column in *Editor & Publisher* magazine that journalists face major challenges. He wrote that "the charge to both press and politicians is to remain focused as never before on urban blight and racism in America." Winship made a plea for the media not to "duck, dance or disappear until the [political] leadership gives the same attention to the domestic urban war as we gave to the overseas Cold War."

During the past quarter-century, Winship wrote, "many metropolitan newspapers have spent untold millions on special suburban sections, with questionable bottom-line results. Yet newspapers never made a comparable commitment to the mounting rot of the inner city." He provided some suggestions for ways the media could keep "the spotlight on our city crisis over the long haul." His tips included beefing up "on-the-street coverage of the underclass in homes and barrooms, catching the everyday flavor of ghetto living." He also challenged the press to apply "investigative zeal to public housing scandals, redlining, landlord ripoffs, job training, school performance and corporate minority hiring."

Another *Editor & Publisher* article cited the concerns of Rick Rodriguez, assistant managing editor of the *Sacramento Bee,* who said that newspapers have made "no commitment to continuing coverage" of racial problems.

Rodriguez's assertion was not new. After urban rioting in the middle 1960s, President Lyndon Johnson formed the National Advisory Commission on Civil Disorders, commonly referred to as the ***Kerner Commission.*** The commission's report, issued in 1968, was far-ranging.

The commission noted, in examining the effect of the mass media on riots, "Our analysis had to consider also the overall treatment by the media of the Negro ghettos, community relations, racial attitudes, urban and rural poverty—day by day and month by month, year in and year out."

The commission concluded that the media, in covering Watts in 1967, did not "live up to their own professed standards" because the "totality of . . . coverage was not as representative as it should have been to be accurate." The commission found that "many of the inaccuracies of fact, tone and mood were due to the failure of reporters and editors to ask tough enough questions about official reports, and to apply the most rigorous standards possible in evaluating and presenting the news."

The commission noted particularly the role the media would play in an increasingly diverse America:

> The news media have failed to analyze and report adequately on racial problems in the United States. . . . By and large, news organizations have failed to communicate to both their black and white audiences a sense of the problems America faces and the sources of potential solutions. The media report and write from the standpoint of a white man's world. The ills of the ghetto, the difficulties of life there, the Negro's burning sense of grievance, are seldom conveyed. Slights and indignities are part of the Negro's daily life, and many of them come from what he now calls "the white press"—a press that repeatedly, if unconsciously, reflects the biases, the paternalism, the indifference of white America. This may be understandable, but it is not excusable in an institution that has the mission to inform and educate the whole of our society.

The commission painted a particularly bleak picture of the media's inability, at that time, to be responsible and sensitive to the diversity of their audience:

> Equally important, most newspaper articles and most television programming ignore the fact that an appreciable part of their audience is black. The world that television and newspapers offer to their black audience is almost totally white, in both appearance and attitude. Far too often, the press acts and talks about Negroes as if Negroes do not read the newspapers or watch television, give birth, marry, die, and go to PTA meetings. Some newspapers are beginning to make efforts to fill this void, but they have still a long way to go.

The commission also emphasized that inadequate coverage of the races and cultures making up the United States was not simply a matter of "white bias." The report stated that "many editors and news directors, plagued by shortages of staff and lack of reliable contacts and sources of information in the city, have failed to recognize the significance of the urban story and to develop resources to cover it adequately." The commission said that adequate coverage of different cultures and races "requires reporters permanently assigned to this beat." Although more than 30 years have elapsed, that recommendation has not been followed universally or aggressively. Some newspapers, however, are beginning to report on cultural issues with enhanced sensitivity and greater depth; and several have created "diversity beats" in response to changing demographics.

Critics are quick to point out that it has taken too long for the media to act on the major recommendation of the Kerner Commission: to diversify staffs. The report said, for example, that "the journalistic profession has been shockingly backward in seeking out, hiring, training and promoting" minorities. The report emphasized that diversifying newsrooms was essential "if the media are to report with understanding, wisdom and sympathy on the problems of the cities and the problems of the black man."

The commission was emphatic: the media needed to hire more minorities and they needed to report with greater depth and understanding on minority affairs. The report focused specifically on the plight of blacks. But the findings obviously apply to coverage of all minorities in the United States, including those with disabilities.

As Marie Hardin and Ann Preston wrote in an article in *Journalism & Mass Communication Educator:* "People with disabilities are a significant minority group that fits any definition of diversity or multiculturalism, especially in light of their status as a group (such as racial minorities or gays and lesbians) that resides outside the dominant mainstream culture." The authors noted also that, "in many ways, journalists have not afforded people with disabilities nearly the same amount of attention that they have for other minorities."

This chapter is not intended to tell you "everything you need to know" about multicultural coverage. Rather, its purposes are to provide an overview of the current status of multicultural reporting as seen by several scholars and journalists, and to offer a framework of suggestions on how reporters can be more cognizant of and responsive to the changing demographics of the United States.

Trends in Multicultural Coverage

Status and Goals of Cultural Reporting and Cultural Sensitivity: An Overview

In this section, we give a view of today's multicultural coverage, through the eyes of journalists and scholars. This is a general discussion; mass media seminars, classes in a variety of disciplines and discussions with people from all cultural and ethnic backgrounds will help put the broad issues presented here in perspective.

Sharon Bramlett-Solomon

Sharon Bramlett-Solomon, who is a journalism professor at Arizona State University, wrote in *Journalism Educator:* "If future journalists are to understand better their culturally diverse society, and if they are to meet the challenge of improved coverage of minority Americans, training in **cultural sensitivity** is imperative."

Bramlett-Solomon wrote that in her classes "students are encouraged to see, hear, smell, taste and feel life as it is experienced by people from backgrounds sometimes very different from their own." Bramlett-Solomon teaches her reporting students about other cultures by giving them assignments that require them to write about worlds far removed from their own experience. For example, one student wrote about elderly people in nursing homes who have no relatives to visit them. Another wrote about two nuns studying at the university. One student reported on local Mexican and black soul food restaurants while another profiled local Hispanic and African-American newspaper publishers. The students were required to make at least three visits to the people they wrote about.

According to Bramlett-Solomon, cultural sensitivity training can help move journalists past stereotypes. She wrote that sensitivity training can help people learn "not to rely on long-held impressions about particular social groups. Instead, they learn the value of double-checking the validity of earlier impressions, both through their own eyes and through the eyes of participants."

Felix Gutierrez

Felix Gutierrez, a senior vice president of The Freedom Forum, is also an author and a former journalism professor. Gutierrez said that coverage of cultures is "better than it used to be but just as clearly not as good as it should be," and that newspapers are still playing a game of catch-up as they try to keep pace with the rapidly changing racial demographics in many communities.

Gutierrez noted that in the 1970s and 1980s, many newspapers started to target more affluent suburban readers for coverage. "That meant the newspapers didn't pay sufficient attention to the growing racial diversity in their central cities and now, in many cases, in the suburbs," he said. "Basically, you can't be the *Los Angeles Times* or *The New York Times* if you don't cover the inner city effectively. If your readers are outside of your core [of coverage] you don't represent the readers of the city that is on your masthead."

Gutierrez also stressed that striving to provide better coverage of minority affairs cannot be approached simply within a black-white context. "All groups of our society must be covered," he said. "Minority issues don't affect just blacks and whites; they cut across all groups."

Actually, because the United States is a nation of increasing diversity, the term *minority* is simply not accurate in a number of cities. "In many of our larger cities, minorities are the majorities," Gutierrez said. "We are becoming a society where almost everyone can claim to be in the minority. If you are looking to the future of the media, I think you would have to conclude that they will thrive only if they report accurately and completely on a multiracial society."

Gutierrez said that, because of the Kerner Commission report, too much attention has been placed only on hiring practices—the sheer numbers—and not enough has been devoted to improvements in coverage. "Too often both the industry and the advocacy organizations have relied on the employment numbers as the only measure of success," he said. "That might be appropriate in some industries—but, for the media, what is most important is the content—the message—and how it is being received."

Caesar Andrews

Caesar Andrews, the editor of Gannett News Service, said that the quest to improve coverage of minority affairs is "a movement that meanders." He elaborated: "It is one of those classic cases where the concept makes sense and the rhetoric sounds good. But the execution has not been solid. It seems that the only things that really move us are the crises—the Los Angeles outrage being a prominent case. I guess I feel that part of what it will take to fix what is wrong is for newspapers to be more forceful in pursuing coverage of people who have been previously ignored, misconstrued or simply not treated the right way. Because of the past pattern of not covering people of color and certain other groups there is almost a need to exaggerate the efforts now—to go well beyond the call of duty."

Andrews envisions a two-prong mission. First, people within the newsroom must be convinced that reporting on cultures consistently and accurately is the right thing to do. "Many journalists have a traditional mindset," he said. "Traditionally, people of color have not been part of journalism's coverage pattern. They haven't been part of what we define as news. They have had their incidents and stereotypes covered, but not their broader humanity. A lot of the efforts to turn the media mindset around have met with resistance to change, with some journalists being unwilling to alter those traditional patterns, to restructure their definition of news. So, we end up perpetuating what is wrong with coverage."

Second, Andrews said, the media must convince people in groups historically excluded from news coverage that they will be included in the future. "I've seen cases where newspaper editors have worked hard to cover all parts of the community—even doing some outstanding journalism in the process—and it goes almost totally unappreciated in certain circles," he said. "We have to better educate people inside the newsroom and we have to make the case with those people on the outside that we do care and that we want to cover them in a more complete way."

Andrews said coverage of minority affairs is better now than ever before, but it is still lacking. "More papers are talking about it now," he said. "I think editors are seeing the wisdom of a business strategy that includes covering all of these varied groups. At the same time, it is not enough yet. It is going to take more energy, more creativity, more hiring and more promoting of people of color throughout the whole range of jobs in newsrooms."

Mary Lou Fulton

Mary Lou Fulton was the founding editor of *City Times*—a once-a-week section in the *Los Angeles Times* launched in partial response to the 1992 riots in that city to focus on central-city issues. She noted that "newspapers have neglected urban areas." She said: "The inner city should be covered as completely as we cover every other area of the county. There are 'good' community stories and there are 'tragedy' community stories. But newspapers often end up with a distorted picture of what happens in the city because we tend to respond only in times of crisis. Then we cover issues only on the surface and we don't look at the underlying causes of why the cities have evolved as they have. As a result, we don't have credibility with people in the city."

Fulton said that consistent coverage is the key to giving a newspaper credibility. "Minority communities should be covered as a beat," she said. "That is not to say that stories about minority issues would come exclusively from that beat. But if you are to understand a community and its history, you need a beat reporter in that area."

Fulton emphasized that each ethnic group has its own history, its own customs and traditions, its own ways of dealing with issues. "Minority communities should not be lumped together," she said. "Minorities are not all alike. In fact, there often are many divisions within each community that should be recognized along with the things they have in common.

"Very simply, we need to pay regular attention to issues that face minority groups in order to have a true understanding of what each group is all about. Newspapers need to reflect, in their stories, both the pain and the glory of all groups."

Fulton noted that most issues affect all residents of a community, "but some issues affect minorities disproportionately." For example, education is of interest to nearly all readers but, because the dropout rates of minorities are often higher, that issue is of particular relevance.

Dorothy Gilliam

Dorothy Gilliam, a *Washington Post* columnist and former associate editor of *Jet* and *Ebony* magazines, said that she worries when she hears editors say they are "tired of the sensitivity issue and are getting 'diversity burnout.' " She pointed out: "The fact of the matter is that they haven't started to truly understand some of the basic issues involved. Part of the challenge of the future is to get past the old ways and to look for new ways to approach the issue."

Gilliam said that it is imperative for newspapers to employ "a critical mass of minorities in numbers that are sufficiently reflective of the community a newspaper serves to really give an authentic voice to the various minorities in the community."

She said that one of the problems facing the United States is that diversity has not truly been recognized as an asset. "We still consider diversity to be a liability, especially in terms of race relations. The newspaper industry has to commit itself to helping this nation do a basic shift in the whole paradigm of diversity—moving from diversity as a liability to diversity as an asset."

Gilliam said that, by and large, the newspaper industry, in its attempts to diversify, has merely made cosmetic changes. She said that the industry needs to put forth the same effort to diversify as it expended when it made the transition from typewriters to computer technology. "No mere Band-Aid approach would have gotten us to where we are now—in the high-tech era of satellites and pagination. Similarly, if we are going to truly meet the challenge of diversity, media will have to be leaders in this transformation. Most Americans get their information about people of color from the media, and when those images are not just negative but often false and misleading, the media are contributing to a very serious social problem."

Diversity in Cultural Reporting: A Commitment to Change

Clearly, reporters face the challenge of reporting with depth, consistency, accuracy and feeling in a nation that is culturally and ethnically diverse. This challenge must be met through diversification of media staffs as well as of coverage itself.

Diversification of Media Staffs

Despite industry efforts, the 2001 census conducted by the American Society of Newspaper Editors found that, for the first time in 23 years, the percentage of minority journalists in newsrooms declined, from 11.85 percent to 11.64 percent.

Newspapers in 2000 actually hired more minorities—nearly 600—than in any single year since 1991. But, 698 minority journalists left newspapers that year—pointing to a retention challenge.

ASNE's leadership, according to the organization's Internet site, quickly "launched a multiyear initiative to study newsroom management and practices as they relate to retention."

Charlotte Hall, managing editor at *Newsday* and chair of the ASNE Diversity Committee, was quoted: "Now we must direct our energies to making newsrooms places where journalists of color can flourish, where they feel welcome, where they can build rewarding careers."

Other major findings of the 2001 survey, according to the Internet site:

- The total number of minority journalists (Asian-Americans, African-Americans, Hispanics and Native Americans) fell from 6,665 to 6,563 of the country's 56,393 total newsroom staffers.
- The 2,951 African-Americans in newsrooms outnumber Hispanics (2,064), Asian-Americans (1,299) and Native Americans (249).
- Most minority journalists (nearly 67 percent) work at newspapers that circulate more than 100,000.
- Women account for 37.35 percent of all daily newspaper journalists, with 14.28 percent of them being minorities.

Diversification of Coverage

Many newspapers are making an increasing commitment to strengthen their coverage of minority affairs and to meet the information needs of their demographically changing readers. As America moved into the 1990s, David Shaw, the media critic for the *Los Angeles Times,* put together an impressive four-part series that examined multiculturalism in American newsrooms.

The lead paragraph of one installment was an attention-grabber:

> Overt racism in the press is rare now, and some newspapers—most notably *USA Today,* others in the Gannett and Knight-Ridder chains and *The Seattle Times*—have even tried as a matter of formal policy to include people of color in the mainstream of their daily coverage. But minority journalists (and many of their white colleagues and supervisors) say the overwhelming majority of press coverage still emphasizes the pathology of minority behavior—drugs, gangs, crime, violence, poverty, illiteracy—almost to the exclusion of normal, everyday life.

Shaw wrote that "the same criticism can be made of press coverage of whites," but still the media generally cover "a much broader range of white life than of minority life."

Shaw's thoroughness in preparing the series is noteworthy. He interviewed more than 175 reporters, editors and publishers from more than two dozen newspapers across the country. Shaw cited the most common criticisms:

The press too often engages in harmful stereotyping of African-Americans, Latinos, Asian-Americans and Native Americans.

Journalists are generally ignorant of cultural differences.

The press too often uses racially biased or insensitive language.

The media often make unfair comparisons between different ethnic groups.

The media often use unrepresentative minority "spokespersons," often "automatically lumping together all Latinos, or, in particular, all Asian-Americans as a single community, without recognizing the substantial differences in culture and language among the varied elements of those communities."

Shaw concluded that "even the most caustic critics of the press acknowledge that most white journalists mean well; it's not the intent but the results that trigger widespread criticism—and those results stem largely from ignorance, insensitivity, the absence of minority journalists from most newsrooms and, more important, the absence of minorities from most editors' offices."

Approaches to Multicultural Coverage

Guidelines for Media and Reporters

No magic formula exists that would ensure superb coverage of minority affairs and cultural issues. However, some guidelines follow.

1: Provide consistent, daily coverage. During recent years, many newspapers have increased their coverage of minority affairs. But that coverage, for the most part, is predictable. Often, it focuses on calendar events such as Black History

Month, the Chinese New Year and so forth. Many of these stories are good, but they do not put the cultures into context. "Newspapers often cover once-a-year or infrequent happenings," said Felix Gutierrez, who has written extensively on coverage of minority affairs. "Readers are given a view of the culture, but it is not a full vision. Once-a-year festivals do not provide readers with the full context of the community. The coverage should be done on a daily basis."

Mary Lou Fulton also believes that consistent coverage is the key to good cultural reporting. "Too often, newspapers assign reporters to the generic city beat," she said. "Each city, though, consists of neighborhoods that should be covered regularly by beat reporters. Most newspapers never would think of assigning just one or two reporters to cover all of suburbia. It follows that they shouldn't assign a single reporter to cover all of the inner city."

2: Get to know the communities you cover. "You soon will realize that there are honest differences of opinion and that no one person can expect to speak for an entire race or neighborhood," Gutierrez said. "Just because you have one black source for a story doesn't mean that you have the black viewpoint. You have to go beyond tokenism when you write about communities."

Dorothy Gilliam, the *Washington Post* columnist, said that it is also important to bring people from the community to the newspapers and "really listen to them." Gilliam said that it is imperative for newspapers to have regular exchanges with the people they cover.

3: Develop multicultural links and friendships. "It is important for students, reporters and editors to take some cross-cultural journeys," Gilliam said. "If newspapers are to cover all aspects of their communities effectively, reporters are going to have to go to places where they might initially feel uncomfortable." For example, whites might visit a black church; Hispanics might go to a function at an African-American college. "The biggest challenge will be for white Americans," Gilliam said. "They have had the luxury throughout the history of this country of telling everybody that they would have to conform to the standards that had been set. As a result, whites have become very insular."

Gutierrez pointed out that everyone has something in common with people of other cultures. "Look for ways to establish links," he said. "You might find those links in where you enjoy eating or the type of music you like."

4: Expand coverage beyond the "problem people" perspective. "Too often minorities are depicted only as 'problem people,' people beset by problems or people causing problems for the larger society," Gutierrez said. Such stereotypes become entrenched: stories often focus only on the poor, on unwed mothers, on the unemployed. Frequently, reporters use an "up-from-the-ghetto" angle in success stories. "Minorities too often are framed within problems that they have overcome or are trying to overcome," Gutierrez said.

5: Mainstream sources for all stories. The news pages should reflect the fullness of society's cultures. Reporters should find minority sources for stories—pieces about the economy, the weather, the first day of school—and **mainstream** those sources: blend them together with all the others that make up the community.

Caesar Andrews, the editor of Gannett News Service, said that journalists at *USA Today,* in particular, also understand that visual presentation makes a difference for how people perceive the newspaper. "*USA Today* works to get minorities represented in the images—the photos and graphics—as well as in the stories," he said. "But the paper takes that philosophy one step further: it not only includes people of color in the mix of stories and visuals, but it also makes sure that the stories and visuals end up in prominent places—on Page 1 and other section fronts."

In mainstreaming, the burden is on reporters and editors to obtain opinions and quotations on various topics from a mix of people. "Journalists have a tendency to call people they have quoted previously, and the sources tend to be people like them," Andrews said. "All of that is a natural process. I wouldn't criticize that. But there is a great need to go beyond those natural processes, and that is what mainstreaming is all about—getting sources beyond one's natural set."

"The Gannett method of mainstreaming sources could serve as a model," Gilliam said. "All stories should contain multiple sources that reflect the *ethnic and gender mixes* of communities."

Andrews noted that, on a certain level, mainstreaming could look like a gimmick—when one gets into counting sources and faces. "With the focus in the industry on numbers, I think that plays into the perception of some that it merely is a fad," he said. "We need to look past all of that and cut to the chase—to look at the role of newspapers, the role of journalism. We need to cover all of the community. That is really what diversity and mainstreaming are about. Diversity and mainstreaming are not just about techniques. They really go to the heart of how you should cover the community."

Dawn Garcia, city editor of the *San Jose Mercury News* in California, strongly recommends that newspapers develop a master **minority source list** that can be shared by all reporters, not just those covering minority affairs. "To do this," she said, "any reporter who comes across a good source in the minority community—and not just sources who speak for minority interest groups—can type that source's name and number into an alphabetically organized computer file easily accessible to all reporters and editors. This helps reporters avoid the trouble of always using the same person as the 'spokesman for the black community,' for instance, when we all know that the black community is not monolithic.

"This also provides all reporters with a good reference for articulate minorities in many professions—professors, lawyers, union leaders, business owners, doctors, sociologists—the 'experts' that reporters so often rely on when doing daily stories. Too often, reports rely on the same white men as their 'experts,' overlooking many qualified minorities who should be portrayed in stories other than minority-issue stories."

6: Periodically assess the representativeness of sources. During performance reviews, some editors evaluate how well reporters have diversified sources in their stories over a period of time. Reporters must be constantly reminded that diverse sources are important in diverse communities in order to paint an accurate picture of topics.

7: Don't "overcredential" sources. If you call a source a "Latino leader," for example, make sure that the person, on the basis of his or her credentials, really is a leader. Lazy journalists who do not bother to consult multiple sources often resort to the term *leader* whether or not it is accurate.

8: Recognize that there is diversity within cultures. Reporters should not put people under the same umbrella just because they look the same or have names that sound the same. "There are a lot of similarities among different groups in our society," Gutierrez said. "But there also are some distinctive differences among people within the same culture." Just as foreign correspondents need to be aware of the various cultures they must cover, city beat reporters should approach diversity in multicultural societies with the same level of understanding and sophistication.

9: Bring your own perspective to the newsroom. Andrews emphasized that journalists should not be afraid to let their special perspectives show through. "Often when people start in newsrooms there is an expectation of conformity," he said. "You are judged on how you conform to the people already in place. There is, indeed, a need to have a newsroom culture, but it should not be at the expense of killing the special qualities and perspectives of individuals. The individual has to struggle to make sure that his or her special perspective [on story ideas, for example] is not crowded out by the overriding culture of the newsroom. This advice really applies to all journalists, but it is especially important to minority journalists. Too often they are expected to think just the same as everybody else. Sometimes, then, you end up without a net gain in perspective in the newsroom."

Andrews also emphasized that once newspapers are committed to inclusivity and their reporters have a high degree of sensitivity, those newspapers must still be willing to practice hard-hitting journalism. "That means that you can't back off of things that need to be covered," he said. "Good coverage doesn't mean doing all positive stories and eliminating the so-called negative stories. I think you should cover all of the above. Some people can become a little hypersensitive about covering certain realities. That shouldn't be the case either. Covering things that aren't so good is not bad—that is part of the job. The bad part is not covering the other stuff: the achievements, accomplishments and success stories of day-to-day life."

Where to Turn Online

Reporters can turn to a number of online sites for background on diversity issues or for help in enhancing multicultural coverage.

Good sources include the Poynter Institute for Media Studies' online site (*www.poynter.org*), which provides a comprehensive list of online resources including the Asian American Journalists Association (*www.aaja.org*), Maynard Institute (*www.maynardije.org*), National Association of Black Journalists (*www.nabj.org*), National Association of Hispanic Journalists (*www.nahj.org*), National Lesbian and Gay Journalists Association (*www.nlgja.org*) and Native American Journalists Association (*www.naja.com*).

Sources that could prove helpful to reporters covering issues involving disabilities include: The Center for an Accessible Society (*www.accessiblesociety.org*), Disability Resources on the Internet (*www.disabilityresources.org*) and Disability Data (*www.infouse.com/disabilitydata*).

✔ A Checklist for Improving Coverage

Presenters at a seminar on "riot & reconstruction: covering the continuing story" distributed a checklist for improving news coverage. The tips were adapted from recommendations of *The Seattle Times'* Racial Awareness Pilot Project; Sandy Rivera, KHOU-TV, Houston; Sherrie Mazingo, a journalism professor at the University of Southern California; and Mervin Aubespin of *The Courier-Journal* in Louisville, Ky.

- ❑ Have I covered the story with sensitivity, accuracy, fairness and balance regarding all of the people involved?
- ❑ What are the likely consequences of publication? Who will be hurt and who will be helped?
- ❑ Have I sought a diversity of sources for this story?
- ❑ Am I seeking true diversity or using **tokenism** by allowing one minority person to represent a community or point of view?
- ❑ Have I allowed preconceived ideas to limit my efforts to include diversity?
- ❑ Am I flexible about the possibility that the focus of the story may change when different sources are included?
- ❑ Have I thought about using quotations from minority experts in non-traditional fields? (For example, a black lawyer, a Hispanic accountant or an Asian physician can be consulted for quotations in general stories.) Creating a minority source list is highly advisable.
- ❑ Have I spent time in minority communities and with residents to find out what people are thinking and to learn more about lifestyles, perspectives, customs, etc.?
- ❑ Have I written about achievements on their own merits, rather than as "stereotype breakers"?
- ❑ Have I guarded against allowing place names to become code words for crime?
- ❑ As I seek diversity, am I being true to my other goals as a journalist?
- ❑ Will I be able to explain my decision clearly and honestly to anyone who challenges it—and not to rationalize?

In their article in *Journalism & Mass Communication Educator,* Marie Hardin and Ann Preston emphasized that most tips that help journalists cover cultural issues better apply also to enhanced coverage of people with disabilities and disabilities issues. They wrote: "Without the same type of awareness that journalists have developed in regard to coverage of other minority groups, their own personal misunderstandings and prejudice will continue to bias coverage of the disabled community."

A Multicultural Reporter at Work: Dawn Garcia's Strategies

Dawn Garcia, the *San Jose Mercury News* city editor, wrote scores of minority-issue stories when she was a projects reporter for the *San Francisco Chronicle.* During her five years at the *Chronicle,* she was involved in both short- and long-term projects, about half of which involved **minority-affairs reporting**.

As a projects reporter, she was not immune from covering daily stories. "I once covered a bank robbery simply because I was the first person in the office and the editors needed someone quickly," she said. "Another time I was available to do a breaking story on a toxic spill in the Sacramento River that poisoned some of the most pristine water in California."

Garcia didn't start her career at the *Chronicle* as a projects reporter. She was hired as a general assignment reporter and quickly took on major front-page stories, including the October 1986 earthquake in El Salvador. She was selected as lead reporter to cover San Francisco Mayor Art Agnos' first two years in office before she took a short leave for a journalism fellowship in Mexico. When she returned, she joined a four-person investigative team that produced a number of award-winning projects.

Garcia stressed that the *Chronicle*'s reporting of minority affairs extends beyond stories produced by reporters who specialize in **ethnic coverage**. "Because California has such a large minority population, on a daily basis reporters who have beats completely unrelated to minority affairs still often end up doing minority-related stories," she said.

No particular organizational structure guarantees effective coverage of minority affairs. "I don't know that any newspaper has found the perfect balance yet," she said. "Newspapers still are struggling to find the best way to cover minority affairs with the proper background and perspective. The *Chronicle* setup is serviceable and it works mainly because the reporters take an interest and strive to write good stories.

"A problem you can run into when you designate a minority-beat reporter is that other reporters might hesitate to get involved in the coverage. Minority-affairs reporting can cross all kinds of beats; all reporters should be capable of and interested in doing the stories. There can be a fear that the story will be 'ghettoized' in the paper. Another problem newspapers should avoid is creating what sometimes is called the 'taco beat,' where a Hispanic reporter covers only Hispanic issues. Certainly, though, you need reporters with an understanding of ethnic communities and people who speak the language."

Garcia noted that the Asian community is particularly difficult to cover in California because it includes so many cultures. "You've got many, many languages and cultures, and no one person can handle them all. Papers have to find their way little by little as they develop effective minority-affairs coverage. I think, though, that all reporters, regardless of their beats, should have a piece of covering minority affairs. Minority-affairs reporting is as much an ongoing awareness of potential stories as it is a beat."

Garcia's minority-issue reporting has been varied and has included investigative, enterprise and daily stories. In an impressive two-part investigative series, she reported on fraud and abuse in a federal minority-business program that cheated minority businesses and made contractors rich. In an enterprise story on how Cinco de Mayo had become so popular, she eschewed the trite approach of "featurizing" the holiday in favor of examining its historical roots and the "multimillion-dollar extravaganza" marketing professionals have made it. Her daily stories on deadline covered topics such as the increasing number of undocumented, single women immigrants in the Bay Area.

Many of Garcia's stories have centered on trends and changing patterns. Even when the focus of a story is on minority affairs, the impact of the issues explored generally goes far beyond the ethnic community being examined. Changing demographics and the concomitant evolution of minority issues and concerns often have a profound impact on entire communities. Logically, then, minority-affairs stories both deserve and command attention in newspapers.

Example: A Story on a Changing Neighborhood

In a story published in the *San Francisco Chronicle,* Garcia and Lisa Chung homed in on the fear of San Francisco Hispanics that the city's Mission District was losing its Latin flavor. Their story illustrates the impact changing demographics can have on an area. Their four-paragraph lead block culminated with the story's nut graph:

> Young Latino civic leaders in San Francisco's Mission District, for nearly 30 years the heart and soul of the Bay Area's Hispanic community, are on a crusade to preserve it as a hub of Latino culture.
>
> As Hong Kong investors, Asian grocers and bohemian artists discover the neighborhood—attracted by its sunny weather, relatively affordable housing and busy shopping districts—longtime residents are voicing fears that the district's strong Latino flavor is being diluted.
>
> Reflecting its growing diversity, the Mission District now includes San Francisco's first distinctly lesbian neighborhood along Valencia Street. With its women-oriented businesses, the area has become a cultural and social center for lesbians from throughout the city.
>
> The demographic changes in the Mission have been noted by a group of young, energetic, college-educated Latino merchants and neighborhood organizers. They say they appreciate the Mission's growing diversity, but they are organizing an effort to preserve the core of the neighborhood as a cultural mecca for Latinos.

Garcia and Chung went on to do several other things. They included several direct quotations from residents. One quotation was particularly vivid:

> "We're just trying to hold onto our turf," said Roberto Hernandez, 34, president of Mission Economic and Cultural Association and leader in the move to revitalize the Latino center of the Mission. "Our parents built the neighborhood and we, the young Chicanos, have a responsibility to preserve it."

They also explained the plans organizers had to preserve the district's culture (by developing everything from Latin-style "mercados" to Mexican art galleries), and they described how the neighborhood organizers were working with the San Francisco Convention and Visitors Bureau.

Through description, they contrasted the district today with what it had been only a few years ago. This section of the story was introduced effectively by a transition:

> Standing at 16th and Mission Streets, Hernandez can see a neighborhood vastly different from the place where he sold tamales on the church steps for youth group fundraisers years ago.

They discussed how the changing demographics of the district "have required some adaptation by businesses trying to overcome cultural barriers," such as Asian business owners learning Spanish.

The story concluded with the following direct quotation from a third-generation resident:

> "It'll take a long time before you stop hearing Spanish in the Mission," he said. "We have to roll with the changes, accept them, adapt to them and make it positive for the overall well-being of San Francisco."

Garcia decided that she wanted to write the Mission District story when, after she had been reporting on the area for several years, she started to notice an increasing number of Asian businesses. "I realized that something was evolving there," she said. "At the same time, I was interviewing and talking with a number of people in the district because I had heard there was going to be a formal push to retain at least a corridor that was largely Latino in character and nature."

Garcia didn't know the Asian community as well as Chung, who was working with her. "We soon discovered that there was some animosity among both the Asian and Latino merchants," Garcia said.

When Garcia pitched the story idea to her editor, he wondered whether life was getting violent in the district. "He almost seemed disappointed when I said it was not," Garcia recalled. "This story was much more subtle. Newspapers need to get away from covering minority issues strictly from the standpoint of crime and people fighting. Different kinds of struggles need to be covered." Chung and Garcia did not want to blow the story out of proportion. Violence had not erupted, but an important shift was evolving. That development was newsworthy.

The reporters soon discovered that some merchants were starting to work together in the neighborhood—people were cooperating and "breaking away from the stereotype of conflict," Garcia said. "Some of the Asian merchants who were coming into the neighborhood realized that they had to learn at least a little Spanish to talk to their customers. Some of the Latino merchants also were trying to reach out to the Asian merchants to bring them into their organizations."

Reactions to Garcia's story on the Mission District were both positive and negative. "Whenever you do stories on minority affairs you will find they often are sensitive and difficult," Garcia said. "And as sensitive as you try to be, sometimes you write things that people might interpret differently from what you meant."

Garcia said there was a lot of good reaction. People in the Mission District often complain that they don't get written about as much as those in the middle-class and white areas of the city. Many people appreciated the fact that the story was written at all.

However, one Mission District resident, Roberto Hernandez, complained about the use of his statement concerning the need for Latinos to protect their "turf." "He said it but he didn't like it when I used that quote," Garcia said. "He said it conjured up gang images. He took a lot of heat in his community for saying that. It is a loaded word. When I wrote it I frankly didn't think someone would connect that word to gangs because the story was not about gangs. I certainly didn't think about that angle. All reporters can do, though, is reflect accurately what sources say and try to be fair."

To further complicate matters, a photo accompanied the story that showed Hernandez and some other fairly young neighborhood people who were behind the push for revitalization. They were standing together in an intersection of the district. "It was a nice photo but those in it thought it made them look too mean," Garcia said. "Some weren't smiling. That, coupled with the quote about protecting turf, conveyed to some of them that we were trying to stereotype them as young toughs trying to take over the neighborhood."

Garcia said that reporters should always be conscious of loaded words like *turf*. "It was such an appealing, strong, clear word to convey what he meant that it was a great quote," Garcia said. "But I did not think about the connection between turfs and gangs until after he pointed it out. I wrote the story because I have an interest in that area and not because I was trying to make people look like thugs. It is sometimes painful when things like that happen, but you just have to try to explain to your sources that it was not your intent."

Garcia emphasized how important it is to humanize stories. "You need people in your stories," she said. "Too often we talk about minorities and immigrants as numbers. We need to talk about them as people and what their lives are like: their hopes, their problems, their dreams."

Clearly, the changing demographics of the United States have caused astute editors and reporters to expand their definition of news and to report aggressively and with feeling on minority issues. Stories by Dawn Garcia and other talented reporters around the country show that most of the emerging minority issues will have or are already having a profound impact on virtually all readers, regardless of race or gender.

Terminology for Multicultural Coverage

The Associated Press Stylebook and Briefing on Media Law lists several terms and entries relevant for multicultural reporting—ranging from *black* to *nationalities and races*. Check the stylebook if you have any questions about the meanings of terms or about which terms are appropriate. In addition, some newspapers have developed supplemental style sheets for multicultural terms, and some minority organizations have issued glossaries to guide reporters and editors. These additional sources could serve as valuable aids.

CHAPTER NINETEEN

CITY GOVERNMENT

Most newspapers, radio stations and television stations take pride in their coverage of city government. Audiences are interested in issues that affect the roads they drive on, the parks they play in, the water they drink, the police protection they depend on and the taxes they pay.

Many reporters launch their careers by covering government at the grass-roots levels. Coverage of city government is often one of the first assignments young reporters receive—particularly if they go to work for small- or medium-sized newspapers, where

(*Tony Gutierrez / Reuters / TimePix*)

extensive coverage of local government is a primary goal. A typical example is *The East Valley Tribune*, a morning daily in suburban Phoenix.

The Tribune circulates in Tempe, a university community of 160,000 that is in a metropolitan area of more than three million. Tens of thousands of Tempe residents also subscribe to the morning *Arizona Republic* (circulation 435,000 weekdays), the state's dominant newspaper that is published in Phoenix. *The Republic* provides detailed coverage of state government and devotes some space to Tempe's local affairs, but like any community newspaper, *The Tribune* is able to provide a more comprehensive package of local government news than metropolitan newspapers that serve a large area.

Adrianne Flynn covers city government for *The Tribune.* Flynn's primary responsibility is coverage of local government. She does her share of city council stories, planning board stories and budget stories, but she has earned good play with enterprise pieces such as these:

> The city, as seen through the eyes of garbage collectors. "I spent the day in a garbage truck, bouncing through alleys," Flynn said. "It was fun to see the backside of the city—the side no one ever wants to see."

> Cemetery space—or the lack of it—in the city. Flynn found that Tempe did not have enough cemetery space to last beyond a calendar year.

Flynn pursued these stories—and dozens like them—after picking up on off-the-cuff remarks made by various city officials as she made her daily rounds and as she sat through various meetings.

Good city beat reporters obviously do not limit their coverage of the community to daily government developments, although contact with elected and appointed officials does provide the foundation—the building blocks—for effective reporting.

Understanding Municipal Government Systems

Forms of Municipal Governments

When she took over the city beat, Flynn realized that she had to learn about the structure of government and about the officials who had power and influence. Forms of government vary from city to city. Nicholas L. Henry wrote in "Governing at the Grassroots" that municipalities use two primary types of government: the "weak executive" model and the "strong executive" model. Forms of municipal governments within these categories are mayor-council, council-manager and commission.

In **mayor-council** systems, the mayor can be categorized as "weak" or "strong," depending on the powers assigned to the position. In a "strong" mayor-council system, the mayor has the power to form budgets and to make and administer policy. This system, according to Henry, exists in six of the nation's 10 largest cities as well as in other communities. Under this system the mayor is a primary source of news, for he or she is attuned to all city government activity. In a "weak" mayor-council system the mayor is, in essence, the chairperson of the city council; most managerial functions are divided among other elected officials and the council.

In **council-manager** systems, the city manager, according to Henry, "controls the administrative apparatus of the city." The manager possesses significant power, but the council retains the authority to hire and fire the manager. Henry noted that the council-manager plan is used by more than one-third of all cities with more than 2,500 people and by more than one-half of all cities with a population of more than 25,000. As more cities moved to a council-manager form of government in the 1960s, 1970s and 1980s, the mayor became more of a figurehead. The main source of city government expertise became the city manager, a trained professional adept at administering a community's affairs.

In **commission** systems, which are used by about 5 percent of the nation's municipalities, a committee of city leaders assumes both executive and legislative functions.

Labels can be placed on various systems, but it is important to remember that there are variations within the systems. Tempe, for example, has a council-manager form of government. The city has a mayor, but the mayor's vote counts the same as that of others on the council. The mayor is elected every two years; the council, every four years in staggered terms. Elections are non-partisan. The mayor chairs the council and conducts the meetings. The mayor also has authority to appoint short-term boards and commissions. The council approves all action in the city and sets policy to be carried out by the city manager. The illustration on page 276 diagrams the government structure of Tempe.

A Day on the City Beat

Flynn said that there is no typical day in covering city government. "The smaller the paper, the more your beat crosses over into others, because there just aren't enough reporters to go around," she said. "I cover some police issues, do a smattering of features, cover awards ceremonies, plus all the boards and commissions. I also cover Tempe's state legislators and Tempe's U.S. congressman. I also occasionally cover a fire, a traffic accident or a hazardous waste spill."

Flynn's hours vary, depending on the meetings she has to cover. But she's usually in the office by 9 a.m. "The first thing I do is read our paper," she said. "I get all my gripes about how my stories were treated out of the way, read the editorials in case someone asks me about them and find out what's going on in other people's beats in case I have to cover for them.

"Next, I read the competition. If I have been beaten on anything, I hustle to catch up. Fortunately, because all we cover is Tempe, we rarely get beaten on the day-to-day stuff. On some of the bigger stories, we get shelled because we don't have the resources in Washington, D.C., or Costa Rica or even the state capital."

Flynn then checks her **story budget**—a list of articles she is to work on—and her date book. "I probably do 70 percent of my work by telephone. I get on the horn and call the sources for my stories and ask them all kinds of stupid questions until I understand what they're talking about."

She likes to deal with her primary City Hall sources face to face. "It is harder for people to lie to you when you're sitting across from them," she said. "I always get better and more information in a face-to-face interview than I do on the phone."

Flynn checks in at City Hall at least twice each day—even if she has absolutely nothing to talk about. "This is a terrific way to get story ideas," she said. "It also keeps you informed of ongoing issues and lets the people know you are around."

While at City Hall, Flynn reads the agendas for posted meetings to see which ones she might sit in on and possibly write about. By midafternoon she is usually back in the office, where she writes her stories for the following day's paper. "*The Tribune* likes us to keep our stories short, and so my stories average about 12 to 15 inches," Flynn said. "Unless it is a really big issue, I never write more than 20 inches."

After she writes her stories, Flynn checks her date book for the next day's schedule and assigns art to accompany stories she is working on, particularly features. She then writes her next day's budget. Occasionally, she is home by 6 p.m. Usually, however, she is still in the office, reworking a story, rewriting or localizing wire copy and eating dinner while waiting to go to a meeting.

The Tempe City Council meets every Thursday night. The planning and zoning commission meets Tuesdays, design review meets Wednesdays and other boards compete for attention on the remaining nights. Most of the meetings do not end until 9:30 or 10 o'clock. By the time Flynn gets back to the office and writes her story for the next morning's newspaper, it is usually 11 o'clock.

"I love it, though," Flynn said. "The variety of stories is stimulating. Working for a small newspaper keeps you busy constantly, and even dull meetings seem interesting when you know what goes on behind the scenes."

City Council Meetings

An important aspect of covering city government is reporting on city council meetings. For example, one of Flynn's primary assignments is coverage of the Tempe City Council. Let's look at her handling of this assignment.

Before the Meeting

The Agenda

Reporters who cover city council meetings should always pick up, *before* the meeting, a copy of the **agenda**—an outline of matters to be considered. The agenda for the Thursday night meetings of the Tempe City Council is available to Flynn after 5 p.m. on Tuesdays.

Here is an agenda for a Tempe City Council meeting that Flynn covered:

7:00—1. STUDIES AND SURVEYS—Mobile Home Parks—Committee Report

7:20—2. PLANNED DEVELOPMENT—Warner Ranch Village—Plan Modification UDC, SE & SWC Warner Rd/Warner Ranch Rd

7:40—3. STUDIES AND SURVEYS—Aircraft Noise, Michael Brandman Report

8:00—4. PARKS—Tempe Soccer Club—Request for use of Diablo Stadium for Thanksgiving Tournament (Please bring booklets delivered to you)

8:15—5. ADMINISTRATION AND POLICY MANAGEMENT—Real Estate Signs, Police Enforcement

Government Structure of Tempe, Ariz.

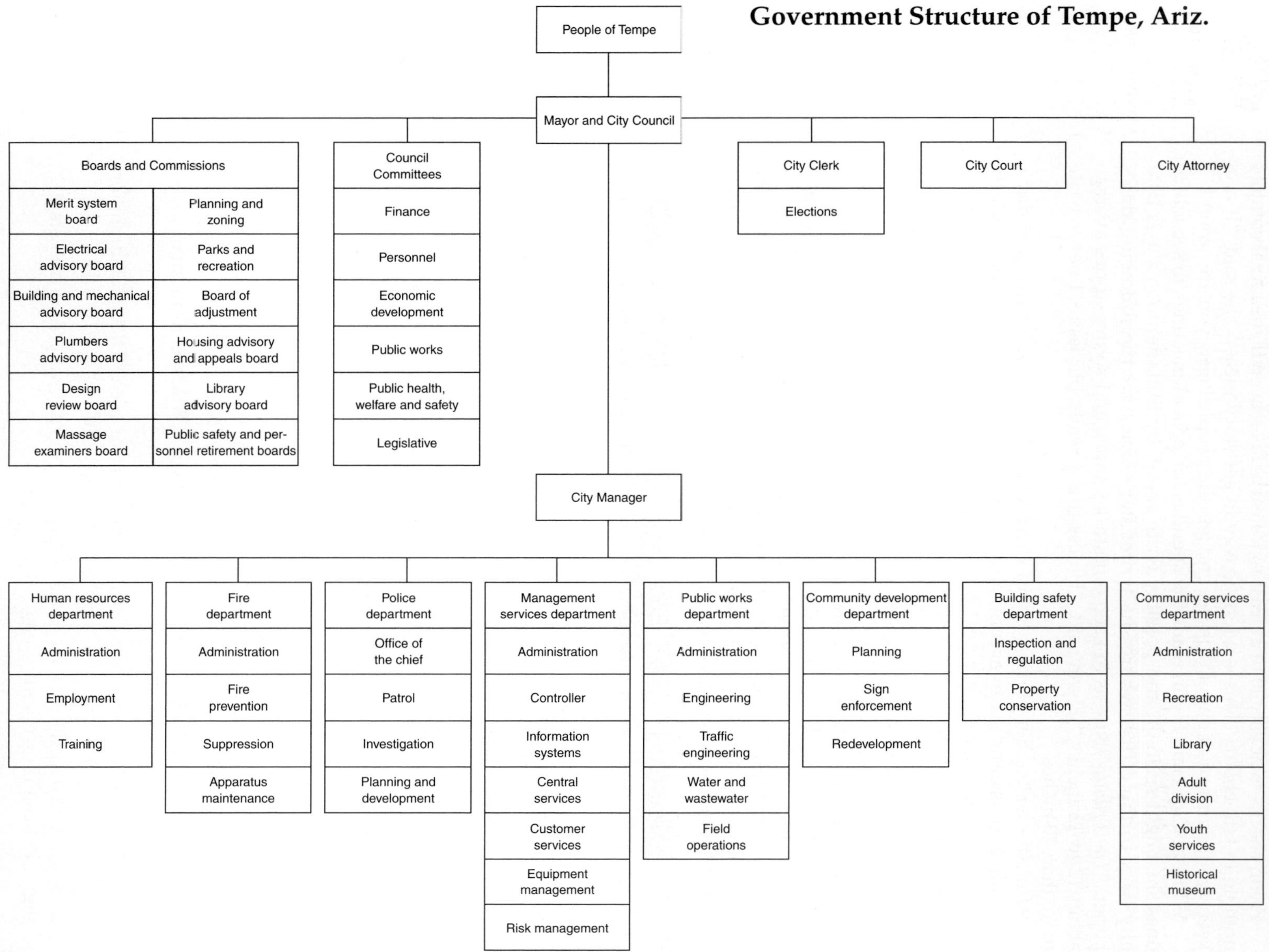

8:30—6. COMMUNITY SERVICES FACILITIES/ACTIVITIES—Latchkey Program, Mary Lou Burem

8:45—7. PARKS—Rolling Hills

9:00—8. ZONING AMENDMENT—Mixed-Use Parking Formula

9:20—9. REAL PROPERTY MANAGEMENT—Use of Parking Garage

9:30—10. ENVIRONMENT—Noise Ordinance Proposed Modification

9:40—11. PUBLIC SAFETY—Fire Truck Bid

9:45—12. STREETS—Street Name Change

9:55—Adjourn

The Advance Story

Flynn usually reads the agenda on Tuesday night and writes an advance (premeeting) story on Wednesday. Because she covers the council regularly, she seldom finds an agenda item that surprises or confuses her. When this occurs, however, she calls appropriate city officials for background. Her advance stories are published in Thursday's edition.

Flynn's advance stories normally focus on what she predicts will be the most important item on the agenda. After discussing this issue in the first few paragraphs of her story, Flynn uses bullets (•) to precede a synopsis of other agenda items. Her advance story this time led with the fact that a consultant would report the results of a study concerning airplane noise over Tempe.

The noise issue had been a long-running news story. Articles had been written when the consulting firm was commissioned to study the problem. Thus, it was logical that the report would be of interest to readers.

The Reporter's Preparation

Preparation is essential before covering a city council meeting. To prepare for a meeting, reporters should review the agenda and should talk to council members and other city officials about any "hidden" issues that may surface.

Flynn always does this. "Most of the issues have already been discussed at study sessions (the Tempe council meets for one hour before regular meetings)," she said. "Because reporters can attend the study sessions, most of us have ample background on the issues before they are considered formally at the regular meetings."

Reporters are not, however, allowed to attend **executive sessions** of the council (meetings at which no official action can be taken and from which members of the press and public are excluded). State laws specify the types of items that can be considered in executive sessions. When a council goes into executive session, it is often to discuss personnel matters or financial matters such as the purchase of property.

Reporters can frequently find sources who will tell them what occurred at executive sessions on the condition that it cannot be printed or that it can be printed but not attributed. "I have a couple of good sources who trust me," Flynn said. "I can usually get them to tell me what happened during the session. If it is not of earth-shattering importance, I hold off until it comes up at a regular meeting. But by finding out about it ahead of time, I can be better prepared to deal with the issue when it does come before the public."

Writing the Meeting Story: An Inverted-Pyramid Story

Occasionally, items will surface at council meetings that turn out to be more important than the projected primary topic. That was not the case this time, however.

Flynn wrote her meeting story as an inverted pyramid, with a summary lead that focused on the report on noise:

> Tempe is getting most of the noise pollution and too little of the benefits from Phoenix Sky Harbor International Airport, a consultant told the City Council Thursday.
>
> "It seems to me you deserve to have the noise levels reduced," said Sam Lane, a consultant with Michael Brandman Associates. "They are dumping their noise garbage all over you, and you're having to clean up the garbage and you're not getting paid for it."

After Flynn presented readers with the thrust of the report and a vivid direct quotation in the first two paragraphs, she provided background:

> Lane's company was hired by Tempe to study the airport noise problem and to recommend technical solutions. A second consultant, Stewart Udall, is considering political solutions and will submit his report to the city within a month.

After this background paragraph, Flynn continued with more new facts from the report:

> Lane said Tempe derives about 10 percent of the economic benefits from Sky Harbor while receiving about 75 percent of its noise. He said the situation will not improve without city action.
>
> Lane said predictions made 10 years ago are far short. Sky Harbor's daily departures are now almost twice those estimates.
>
> He said city and citizen action will "break the monopoly" that the airport and the Federal Aviation Administration have on information. He also said Sky Harbor has insulated itself and is "beholden to the airline industry, not to the general public, even though federal money has been used by them in the past."
>
> "The cost and the benefits are not equitable," Lane said. He recommended Tempe focus on what he considered immediate solutions.
>
> Among these solutions are to send more flights to the west over Phoenix, to require aircraft to follow the river bottom longer before turning and to reduce low-altitude approaches over Tempe.
>
> The council will study the proposals while waiting for Udall's report. It also will wait for analysis by Tempe's Airport Noise Abatement Committee, which will consider Lane's report April 9. ANACOM will meet at 7:30 p.m. in Pyle Adult Recreation Center, 655 E. Southern.

Flynn devoted nearly half of her main meeting story to the issue of airport noise. This is common when one topic is of overriding importance. Because none of the remaining items considered by the council merited expanded treatment, Flynn employed a writing device that many reporters use when covering meetings where multiple issues are discussed. Flynn wrote:

> In other action, the council:

Those transitional words opened the door for a brief discussion of other council issues. Flynn used a bullet to precede each separate item, thus providing a concise, capsulized overview of how the council treated them. Here is part of the remainder of Flynn's story to illustrate this common, punchy style:

- Reviewed the final report of the Ad Hoc Commission on Mobile Home Parks. The group was formed to give mobile home park tenants more rights through recommended changes in state and local law. It asked for more time to read the report and will make recommendations at a future meeting.
- Gave informal approval to a proposal by Universal Development Corporation to change plans for Warner Ranch Village condominiums. The company wants to make the units smaller and wants to bypass Planning and Zoning Commission approval for the change.
- Gave informal approval to a request by the community development department that confiscated illegal signs be considered non-returnable abandoned property. The signs now are locked in a city maintenance yard.
- Reviewed a proposal by the Community Services Department to run a program for latchkey children—kids that are left alone after school until their parents return from work. The report was for the council's information only.

Note that Flynn was careful to write grammatical bulleted items. Because she included the subject *(council)* in her introductory phrase *(In other action, the council:)*, she started each bulleted entry with a verb.

After the Meeting

Writing a complete, understandable story on a city council meeting requires not only diligent preparation before the meeting but also industrious, painstaking checking of facts after the meeting.

City council meetings are often a study in chaos and confusion. To write a good story, reporters must follow up with lots of questions; and double-checking of facts is essential. For example, sometimes a vote count is in doubt and must be checked with the meeting recorder.

✔ A Checklist for Covering Public Meetings

As is the case at community newspapers across the country, the 20,000-circulation *Daily Hampshire Gazette*, Northampton, Mass., prides itself on coverage of public meetings.

Jim Foudy, editor, and Joan Livingston, a community editor at the *Gazette* who worked previously as a town correspondent and staff reporter, recently rewrote a handout of techniques for covering public meetings. The original handout had long been in use at the newspaper.

Here are the techniques:

- ❑ Get it all down in your notebook. What may appear to be an inconsequential conversation early on can lead to an important issue. Clearly mark in your notes which are direct quotes and who said them.

- ❑ Note ideas that might later be turned into stories.
- ❑ Make notations of dates of hearings, when the board will take a final vote on an issue, etc.
- ❑ Look for humor and human interest that could be written separately as a sidebar or for one of the *Gazette*'s people columns.
- ❑ Arrive early to chat with officials. Informal talk can lead to story ideas. Introduce yourself to town, school officials, the highway superintendent, etc. Many town officials are volunteers who are rarely in Town Hall. Collect phone numbers and ask them when are good times to reach them. Some will even allow reporters to call them at work. Likewise let them know how they can easily get in touch with you.
- ❑ Check the clips. Does the issue before the board have a history? Has anything like it come up before?
- ❑ Keep the readers' perspective in mind. What do they need to know to understand the issue and how it affects them?
- ❑ Check and recheck spellings.
- ❑ Question officials when they choose to go into executive session.
- ❑ When there are handouts, ask for a copy.
- ❑ If you don't understand what's happening, ask questions. When you ask depends on the town and the meeting. Some boards don't mind fielding a reporter's questions in the midst of discussion. Others prefer you wait until the end of the meeting. Ask the board ahead of time which they prefer.
- ❑ On occasion, a town official or resident will make a comment and then declare it is off the record. Under the Massachusetts Open Meeting Law there is nothing off the record. The reporter must decide whether the comment is relevant to the story.
- ❑ When votes are taken the story should tally up who voted and what position (Yea or Nay) they took on the issue.
- ❑ Is this more than a meeting story? If the meeting produces a story of significance that you think deserves play on a section front or even the front page, alert your editor before you start writing.
- ❑ If for some reason you can't stay until the end of the meeting for the results of an important vote, arrange ahead of time to link up by telephone with one of the town officials.

The City Budget Process

One of the most important tasks undertaken by a city government each year is developing and implementing a financial budget—and one of the most important aspects of covering city government is reporting on the budget process.

We'll now consider the budget process in Tempe, and Flynn's coverage of it.

Covering the Steps in the Budget Process

In Tempe, the fiscal year runs from July 1 to June 30, but the budget process for the next fiscal year begins in late November or in early December and is spread over nearly seven months.

Here are the steps in Tempe's budget process, which are similar to those in the budget processes of other cities:

1. Individual departments compile budgets with requested increases and justification.
2. Departments submit budgets to the management services director. The management services director compiles the total requests and matches them with financial resource projections to identify the preliminary total budget targets. This preliminary budget is the basis for the city manager's recommendations, which are submitted to the City Council.
3. The council sees the preliminary budget in a study session, usually an all-day affair, where major policy items are considered.
4. Management services takes the direction given by the council during the study session and incorporates it into a more formal budget proposal. Any questions at this point go back to the council in a study session for more direction.
5. After the questions or concerns are resolved, a tentative budget gets a formal hearing at a regular council session. If no objections are raised, the tentative budget is approved.
6. Once the tentative budget is approved, a second public hearing is scheduled. The tentative budget, once adopted, cannot be increased through any subsequent changes.
7. The final budget is formally approved by the City Council.
8. The amount of property tax revenue to be raised is submitted to the county assessor, who sets the tax rate on the basis of the assessed valuation of property within the city limits.
9. After the tax rate is set, another public hearing is held at a council meeting. If no more questions are raised, the budget passes.

All these steps, which vary slightly among communities, are potentially newsworthy.

Developing Sources of Information

When covering the budget process for the first time, it is wise to seek the counsel of various city officials and editors or reporters who are experts. Flynn had been introduced to budgets in college, but when she was thrown head first into the budget reporting process, she went to her best sources in city government. She talked, for example, to the mayor, the city clerk, the city attorney and the management services director.

"I said, 'Look, I'm a novice, and I've had little experience in covering the budget process,' " Flynn said. "I asked officials to explain it to me. I tried to sit down an hour or so with them. Once you understand the process, it is relatively easy to plug in the numbers."

Flynn found Tempe's management services director, Jerry Geiger, to be her best source. "He's more than a number cruncher," she added. "He's an expert on the bureaucracy. He was the key guy in showing me how the process would take place."

Geiger's role as the chief financial officer of Tempe is to prepare a budget the city manager can recommend to the council. Someone like Geiger fills this role in every community. The title for this individual varies. In larger cities, the designation is often *finance director* or *management services director;* in smaller communities, the city clerk often assumes primary responsibility for preparation of the budget.

Reporters need to identify these people and to tap them for budget information—taking full advantage of their expertise. In addition, department heads who submit their individual budget proposals to the finance directors are good sources.

"The average citizen is easily overwhelmed by the budget," Geiger said. "Most people are not totally aware of the organization of local government and of how money is gathered and spent. A budget is a series of numbers—and numbers are sometimes difficult to comprehend and write about. Numbers bore most people.

"I always try to humanize the information when I talk to reporters and other citizens. The best way to do this is to de-emphasize the numbers themselves and to concentrate instead on the level of service that the budget will provide. People want to know how the budget will affect them.

"They might want to know, for example, how many police officers will be on the streets as a result of a budget cutback or increase; they might want to know whether they will have more recreational facilities; and they might want to know if the streets they drive on will be improved. I think readers are more interested in these things than in a mass of line-item figures from a budget."

Indeed, if reporters can present budgetary information in human terms—focusing on the services citizens will receive as a result of expenditures—then the dollar figures are more easily comprehended.

Geiger warns reporters not to get totally embroiled in the figures. Numbers standing alone mean little. Naturally, reporters must have a working knowledge of budgets and of the procedures in forming them, but that is only the first step. The next and most important step is to *explain* the numbers—to tell readers *how* the dollars will affect not only their pocketbooks but their lifestyles. Good sources, like Jerry Geiger, can help them do this.

Examining Budgets

Reporters need to know the intent of the budget—that is, the services the city intends to provide—in order to put the dollars into perspective for their readers. Budgeting is a planning process. A budget is a device through which the government entity goes on record with regard to how it will provide services to the community.

"In the old days, there was more distrust of local officials, and the focus of the media was often on line items, such as expenditures for office supplies and the like," Geiger said. "Today, however, the reporting emphasis is more on relating the dollars budgeted and spent to the services provided."

City budget managers develop a total financial program. This total financial program includes two primary types of budgets: capital budgets and operating budgets.

Capital budgets are made up of projects that often are large-scale, are long-range and have a physical presence. Capital budgets earmark dollars for such things as storm drains, streets, water and sewer lines and parks. The capital budget is often referred to as the "hard" budget.

Operating budgets, as the term connotes, provide details on the dollars required to finance government entities on a day-to-day basis. Operating budgets, which are known as "soft" budgets, include funds to pay the salaries of employees as well as money for the paper clips that the employees use.

The two budgets must relate. For example, money to build new parks comes from the capital budget, but money to care for the parks once they are built comes from the operating budget. For the most part, legal constraints will not permit money to be moved from capital budgets to operating budgets, or the other way around.

Tempe's total financial program for a recent fiscal year was nearly $127 million. The operating budget totaled about $95 million; and the capital budget, about $32 million.

Sources that would generate the nearly $127 million for the total financial program are shown in the illustration on page 285. A breakdown of expenditures is shown in the illustration on page 286. These two pie charts illustrate where the money comes from and where it goes. Readers can relate better to a budget that is divided into major parts than to a staggering total of multiple millions.

It is best for reporters to grasp the broad budget picture before ferreting out and presenting more specific information. The illustrations certainly provide a vivid view, in a general sense, of where Tempe's money comes from and where it goes.

Reporters must decide, on a case-by-case basis, which figures are relevant to readers. Don't strangle readers with numbers. Use judgment to determine which numbers are most relevant. Generally, it would be sufficient, for example, to tell readers that $18.7 million (nearly 15 percent) of the $126.8 million to be generated in Tempe will come from local excise taxes. Most of that, about $17.7 million, will come from the city sales tax. Under most circumstances, there would be little point in breaking down the total further to indicate, for example, that $125,000 of the $18.7 million will come from the cable television franchise tax. If, however, the city had been wrangling with cable television companies over the excise tax, that amount might be pertinent to a budget story.

The reporter who has been diligently following the budget process and who has kept in close touch with sources in City Hall should have a good feel for the numbers that are most relevant and important to readers.

Writing the Budget Story

Essential Ingredients of Budget Stories

As the budget process evolves, stories will naturally emphasize different elements. Here, however, is the basic information that should be included in some or all of the stories:

- Bottom line—the total budget (for example, $126.77 million)
- Total of last year's budget (for example, $106 million)
- Percentage increase or decrease (in the above examples, the writer would report an increase of 19.6 percent)

- Breakdown of budget expenditures (which should include details on where the money will be spent—how much will go to the police department, to the city clerk's office and so forth)
- Reasons for the budget increase or decrease (for example, because of a rising crime rate, more money is needed to add 21 officers to the police department)
- Breakdown of budget revenues (report some of the primary sources of revenue: property taxes, $6.9 million; federal programs, $2.9 million; etc.)
- Details on the impact of tax increases or decreases on residents

If property taxes are being raised, for example, the reporter should not merely note that the new budget calls for a property tax rate of $1.15 per $100 of assessed valuation compared with $1.05 for the current year. Those numbers would not mean much to most readers. Instead, the reporter should put the figures into perspective. This can be done by explaining that a tax rate of $1.15 per $100 of assessed valuation equals a rate of $11.50 per $1,000. Therefore, property taxes on a house assessed at $100,000 would be $1,150, an additional $100 a year; and taxes on a house assessed at $200,000 would be $2,300, an increase of $200. The reporter could also note, for example, that a tax increase will mean that swimming pools will be open longer hours, that new tennis courts will be built and that downtown roads will be resurfaced. Or, if appropriate, the reporter could note that, because of inflation, higher taxes are needed merely to maintain the status quo.

Property taxes are only one source of revenue for municipalities. The illustration on page 285, for example, shows that Tempe needs to raise $6.9 million from property taxes, about 5.4 percent of its $126.8 million total. In some cities, property taxes account for a much larger portion of the revenues generated. School districts also rely heavily on property taxes for revenue.

The taxes that owners must pay are based on the assessed valuations of their property. Normally, assessment is only a proportion of market value. For example, if the government assesses property at 30 percent of its value, a $100,000 house would be assessed at $30,000. Levies are imposed on property values by the municipality or by the school district in order to raise the necessary money. A standard way of computing the amount is by using the mill as a unit of measure. A mill is ⅒ of a cent. Thus, if a district must raise $1 million from property taxes, a formula is used to establish the mill levy. The only purpose in using the mill is to have a unit of measure smaller than one penny. In many parts of the country, the mill is no longer used as a unit of measure.

If the mill is used as a measure, the money to be raised is divided by the total assessed property value of the district. For example, if the district must raise $1 million and the total assessed property valuation of the district is $50 million, the mill levy would be determined by dividing $1 million by $50 million. This computes to 0.02—or two cents on the dollar. Because a mill is ⅒ of a cent, the levy would be 20 mills. Thus, a taxpayer would have to pay $2 on every $100 in assessed value, or $20 for every $1,000 in assessed value. A home with an assessed value of $50,000, for example, would be assessed $1,000 in taxes.

A reporter may also include details on political maneuvering in a budget story. Sources in individual departments can be invaluable in ferreting out this information. For example, if the police chief is particularly upset at the finance

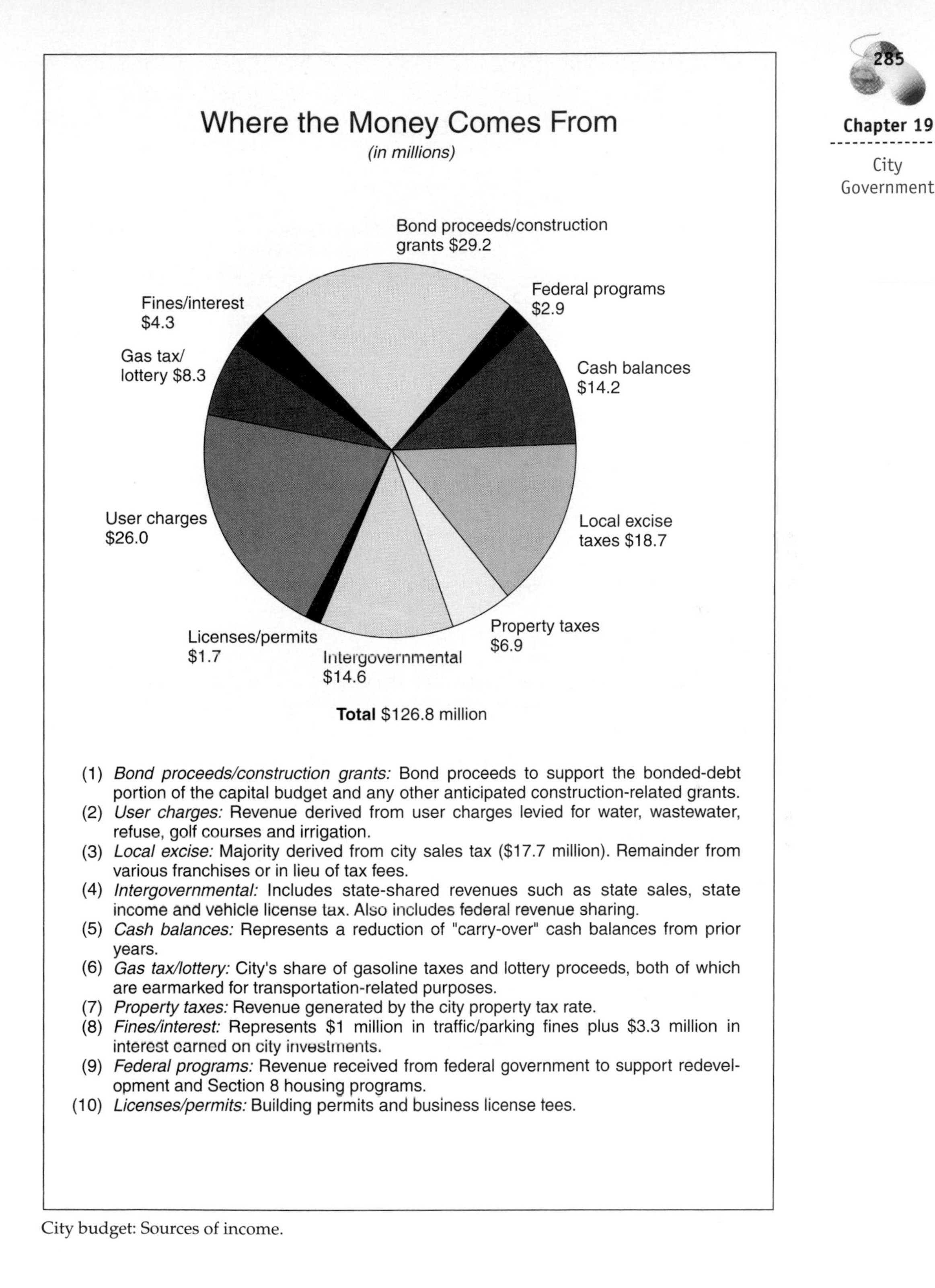

(1) *Bond proceeds/construction grants:* Bond proceeds to support the bonded-debt portion of the capital budget and any other anticipated construction-related grants.
(2) *User charges:* Revenue derived from user charges levied for water, wastewater, refuse, golf courses and irrigation.
(3) *Local excise:* Majority derived from city sales tax ($17.7 million). Remainder from various franchises or in lieu of tax fees.
(4) *Intergovernmental:* Includes state-shared revenues such as state sales, state income and vehicle license tax. Also includes federal revenue sharing.
(5) *Cash balances:* Represents a reduction of "carry-over" cash balances from prior years.
(6) *Gas tax/lottery:* City's share of gasoline taxes and lottery proceeds, both of which are earmarked for transportation-related purposes.
(7) *Property taxes:* Revenue generated by the city property tax rate.
(8) *Fines/interest:* Represents $1 million in traffic/parking fines plus $3.3 million in interest earned on city investments.
(9) *Federal programs:* Revenue received from federal government to support redevelopment and Section 8 housing programs.
(10) *Licenses/permits:* Building permits and business license fees.

City budget: Sources of income.

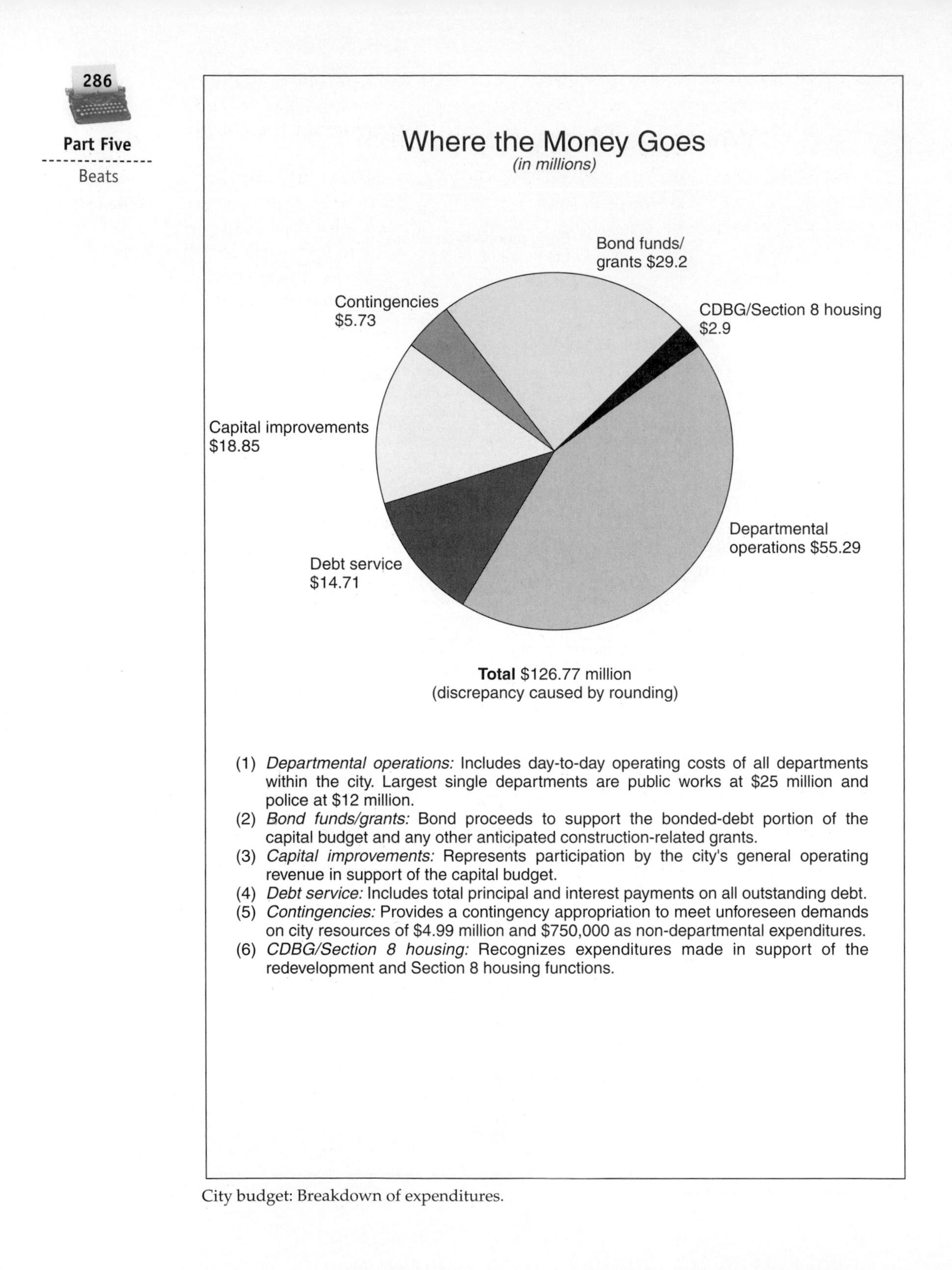

City budget: Breakdown of expenditures.

director's unwillingness to upgrade a section of the police department's budget, this can make for an interesting angle. Interview the police chief, interview the finance director and interview the mayor. Explore and write about the controversy, if that is warranted.

Details on the input of private special-interest groups seeking city appropriations might also be appropriate. Some organizations, although they are not part of city government, can receive funds from the municipality. For example, directors of a fine arts center, a food bank or a shelter for the homeless might seek city council appropriations. During the budgeting process, these special-interest groups often become vocal because they are vying for a limited amount of money.

Details on citizens' groups that are for or against budget increases in specific areas often belong in the budget story. For example, if a group does not think that the city is doing a good job maintaining streets, it might appear before the council during the budgeting process to push for increased expenditures in this area. Reporters should analyze the motives and the effect of such a group.

In writing about city budgets and finances, reporters should also be aware of any limitations imposed by the state legislature on revenues and expenditures. "Caps" on revenue and spending can restrict the flexibility of the city council. Sometimes, though, these limitations can be overcome by a vote of the city's residents in a referendum.

Structuring a Budget Story

After Adrianne Flynn reached the point where she understood the intent of the Tempe budget and the numbers in it, she structured a story in such a way that readers would be drawn into it. She presented figures, but she was careful not to scare the readers away with an avalanche of statistics.

Tempe was in the middle of a heat wave; the temperature had exceeded 112 degrees for three consecutive days. Flynn's lead was a natural:

> It's sweltering. A dip in the pool sounds great, but every Tempe swimming hole is packed. The city's proposed $126.77 million budget hopes to change that.

Flynn's lead paragraph quickly let readers know that the city budget would affect more than their pocketbooks; it would affect their lifestyles. The story continued:

> The spending plan for the upcoming fiscal year sets aside money for a Kiwanis Park pool. And it doesn't stop there.
>
> It would establish a fourth paramedic unit and add nine holes to Rolling Hills Golf Course.
>
> On top of that, there would be no tax increase.

In the fifth paragraph, Flynn gave the total budget figures again; then, in subsequent paragraphs, she began to break them down:

> The Tempe City Council is expected to approve the $126.77 million budget Thursday, after a public hearing that day.
>
> The proposed budget is $20 million more than this year's spending plan for a city that by all estimates has grown from 136,000 to more than 160,000.
>
> Taxes should remain stable because of population and building increases and rising property values. The rate this year was $1.21 per $100 of assessed valuation, according to Management Services Director Jerry Geiger.

After presenting the essential numbers and after emphasizing how residents would be affected, Flynn explained the budget further:

> Tempe's budget has two main parts: The capital portion, which includes city construction and renovation projects and equipment purchases; and the operations budget, for everything from salaries to telephone service.
>
> A large chunk of the capital budget next year is for the first phase of a five-year improvements package. Storm drains will be upgraded or added, parks beefed up and streets reconstructed under the program.

After devoting the next eight paragraphs to projects that were part of the capital budget, Flynn turned to a breakdown of the operations budget. She wrote that city employees would get a 6 percent cost-of-living increase, that the police department would get 21 additional workers, that the fire department would get six new employees and that building maintenance and sanitation would each get three new workers.

Her story contained significant statistics, but the figures were presented in understandable language. When writing budget stories, a reporter should ask:

- What impact will the numbers have on readers?
- Will the budget mean that residents will receive more or fewer services?
- Will residents have to dig deeper into their pockets?
- If so, how much deeper?

Good budget stories must address people-oriented issues such as these.

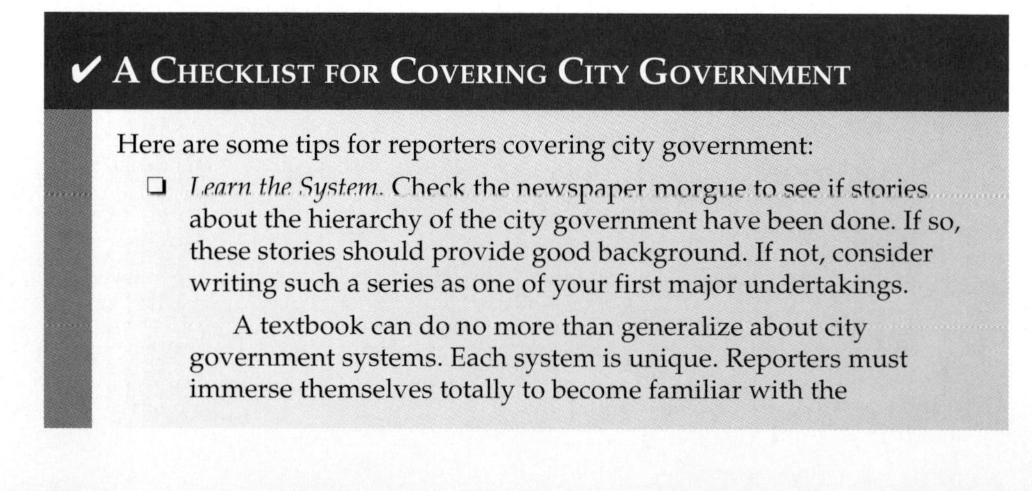

✔ A Checklist for Covering City Government

Here are some tips for reporters covering city government:

❑ *Learn the System.* Check the newspaper morgue to see if stories about the hierarchy of the city government have been done. If so, these stories should provide good background. If not, consider writing such a series as one of your first major undertakings.

A textbook can do no more than generalize about city government systems. Each system is unique. Reporters must immerse themselves totally to become familiar with the governmental structure of the city in which they work. This requires diligence, patience and concentration. Such familiarization must be accomplished quickly; reporters cannot report on city government adequately unless they thoroughly understand its structure.

- *Get to Know the Personalities.* It is one thing to master a city government's organizational chart; it is quite another thing to identify the people listed on the chart who are truly significant. Once this determination has been made, reporters should get to know these people as well as possible. If the city attorney is a Boston Celtics fan, the reporter should learn about the Boston Celtics and should mention the team to the official. It might someday help the reporter get a city government story.
- *Develop Reliable Sources.* Many city government stories are obtained directly from people in elected or appointed positions. Reporters should obviously build a network of sources from within these ranks. It is just as important, however, for reporters to develop a subnetwork of sources. Administrative assistants, secretaries and other staff members can be important sources. Reporters should choose sources wisely, cultivate them and build a bond. But they should never take advantage of their sources.

  "Be honest with your sources," Adrianne Flynn advised. "Let your sources know that you will print all the facts on both sides of an issue, no matter what, but you're not out to do a scandal sheet on every issue. Find two or three really well-informed folks on your beat whom you can find out almost anything from, and cultivate them as sources. Don't butter them up; just be forthright and get to know them as people. Be interested in their personal as well as their professional lives."
- *Be Persistent.* "You catch more flies with honey than with vinegar, but if one method does not work, use the other with gusto," Flynn said. "If you want a story, you must be persistent. Call every day, every hour, if need be. Make your sources so sick of you that they'll have to talk to you just to get you off their backs. I got a great story once by waiting in a developer's office for three hours when he wouldn't return my phone calls. But I finally got to talk to him."
- *Never Let Friendship Interfere with the Job.* Reporters who cover specific beats sometimes spend as much time with officials—their sources—as they do with their circle of personal friends. It is not surprising, then, that reporters and news sources sometimes become friends. Reporters must handle this situation with care—always striving to be fair in their news stories.
- *Always Be Prepared.* To succeed, city government reporters must know more about city government than their competition does. They must have more sources, do more homework on the issues

and work longer hours. Good reporters never skim an agenda casually and write a meeting off as unimportant. Instead, they work harder to find something of value in an otherwise routine meeting.

"It is important to know about the issues in advance," Flynn said. "Ask smart, informed questions. Know how the place operates and who can provide you with facts and figures on any given assignment."

- *Make Note of Story Possibilities.* Many good city government stories do not evolve from coverage of meetings. Rather, they evolve from in-depth follow-ups of news tidbits tossed out at meetings or in informal conversations with city government sources. Even if reporters are working on another story and do not have time to develop the new angle, the idea should be noted and carefully filed away for future reference.
- *Read Other Newspapers, and Listen to Radio and Television News.* Reporters should not operate in a vacuum, smugly assuming that their sources will keep them informed of all possible stories. Other media should be surveyed constantly. Some of the best story ideas arise from less-than-satisfactory handling of stories by other reporters.
- *Write to Inform, Not to Impress, Readers.* Develop city government stories from the standpoint of what an issue means to readers. For example, if a city intends to raise an additional $14 million in property taxes during the next fiscal year, reporters should explain what this increase means to readers as homeowners. What will the increase do to taxes on a house assessed at $50,000, at $75,000 or at $100,000? That is what is relevant to readers.
- *Use Your Brain.* "If you think you're so smart you can conquer the world, you're wrong," Flynn said. "Some of the littlest facts can hang you up. When they do, think your way out of it.

  "I tried once to find out when a local congressman [John McCain, who had been a prisoner of war in Vietnam and who, a decade later, had visited that country] was returning from a trip to Vietnam. I hoped to scoop the competition by meeting him at the airport. It turned out that he arrived too late for our deadline, but I found out, despite the fact that his staff was sworn to secrecy.

  "I tried the airlines and narrowed down the flights to about five possible ones that he could be on. I called the congressman's aide, but he would not tell me which flight it was. I called his wife and said, 'He's going to be on this plane at this time,' but she would not confirm it.

"Then I called his travel agency and almost had it because a new girl in the office was going to give it to me when she suddenly had a guilt attack and checked with her supervisor.

"Finally, I called The Associated Press in New York. They relayed me to the AP bureau in Bangkok, and someone there called McCain and asked him when he was returning. He told the AP correspondent, and the correspondent told me. Because we belong to the AP, we can get all kinds of help from them. Don't be afraid to use the wire service, even when working on a local issue."

- *Do Not Be Afraid to Ask Questions.* If you want to know something, ask. This is better than seeing your mistakes in print or seeing the competition get the jump on you.

CHAPTER TWENTY

POLICE AND FIRE

Scenes from old movies perpetuate the stereotype: police and fire reporters are booze-guzzling, cigar-chomping hacks who have difficulty stringing together complete sentences. They are devious, unscrupulous (but usually likable) fellows who gather facts, frantically call their newsrooms, always ask for rewrite and feverishly tell their sordid stories of crime. Only when they hang up the telephone and look in a mirror at their press hats and baggy pants do they return to reality: they are not really cops.

For the most part, this outdated image is disappearing. Today's police and fire reporters

(*Erlend Aas / Scanpix*)

are likely to be well-educated men and women who do not wear baggy pants and who do know how to write. Roger Aeschliman, a law enforcement reporter for the *Topeka Capital-Journal* in Kansas, is one of this new breed.

Aeschliman, a graduate of Kansas State University, majored in journalism and political science. He took a variety of mass communication classes, including radio and television, and worked on the campus newspaper, the *Kansas State Collegian.* He served as a staff writer, as arts and entertainment editor and eventually as managing editor.

He was a midterm graduate, and so he spent the fall semester pestering Rick Dalton, managing editor of the *Capital-Journal.* "I think he decided to hire me just to get me off his back," Aeschliman said.

Aeschliman was offered a job as a staff writer two days before graduation. It was a great gift. After six months, he started filling in on the weekend police beat. He was named one of the two *Capital-Journal* law enforcement reporters as he started his second year on the job.

Staffing Police and Fire Beats

The size of a newspaper, television station or radio station usually determines how its reporters cover police and fire news. At newspapers with circulations of less than 20,000 and at small-market radio and television stations, one person might juggle coverage of police and fire news while reporting on all other city and county institutions (such as the mayor's office, the engineer's office, the civil defense office, the assessor's office and the clerk's office). At newspapers with larger circulations, a reporter might be responsible only for coverage of law enforcement agencies and the fire department. Large-circulation newspapers generally have more than one reporter covering the police and fire departments.

At *The Oregonian* in Portland, for example, an eight-person Crime Team provides readers with comprehensive coverage that extends well beyond the tendency of some newspapers to play up primarily the sensational.

Breaking crime news, of course, still garners Page 1 play in *The Oregonian,* when warranted, but the 335,000-weekday circulation newspaper has committed itself to systematic, broad-based, topical coverage.

The Crime Team includes six beat reporters (two of whom cover night cops and law enforcement/violence and four of whom cover topical beats such as juvenile justice, white-collar crime and neighborhood crime) and two legal affairs reporters who focus on trends as well as day-to-day cases.

Susan Gage, Crime Team leader, was quoted in an article in "Civic Catalyst," published by The Pew Center for Civic Journalism: "I like the stories we're able to do. They're more thoughtful, more intelligent, more interesting, and they get not only a better response from readers but a better response from the newsroom. For a long time, we felt inferior in the newsroom. . . . But right now we have a team of very experienced reporters—the best in the room—and they're able to sink their teeth into stories."

Regardless of the newspaper's circulation or the community's population, police and fire reporters cover similar stories. Routine crime news is often played down at the major metros and by television and radio, but small-circulation dailies and weeklies generally report on all minor crime stories and accidents. Sometimes these stories are given play on the front page.

At the *Capital-Journal,* a morning newspaper with a weekday circulation of about 60,000, there are two law enforcement reporters: Steve Fry, who works from 6 a.m. until 2:30 p.m.; and Aeschliman, who works from 2:30 p.m. until 11 p.m. Both reporters work out of the *Capital-Journal's* newsroom. At some metropolitan papers, police reporters work out of pressrooms at the stations and are connected to their newsrooms by telephones and computers. The *Capital-Journal* publishes two editions: the 3 a.m. press run is distributed statewide; the 5 a.m. press run is distributed to Topeka residents and to residents of the immediate surrounding counties.

"I enjoy my job," Aeschliman said. "It is very exciting. Every day is different. Some days, though, can be depressing: all you see happening are bad things. That's the only drawback as I see it."

Aeschliman's days pass quickly; he spends much of his time away from the office reviewing records and talking to sources. During the late afternoon and evening hours, he routinely types into his computer terminal 50 one- or two-line items that come from police, fire or court records. These are published in the newspaper's daily record section. He also writes four or five short stories (three to 12 paragraphs) on events that merit elaboration and a longer story on a significant breaking news event or feature.

Covering Police and Fire Departments

Aeschliman's primary responsibilities are coverage of the Topeka Police Department; the Shawnee County Sheriff's Department; the Kansas Highway Patrol (northeast Kansas); the Kansas Turnpike Authority (which has highway patrol-type duties for northeast Kansas); the Topeka Fire Department; four Shawnee County township fire departments; and Medevac MidAmerica (the Shawnee County area ambulance).

His secondary responsibilities are the police, sheriffs' and fire departments and the ambulances of seven surrounding counties. Tertiary responsibilities include police and fire developments for the state of Kansas on weekends and evenings, if the state desk or The Associated Press does not get the story.

Mastering Organizational Structures

Before police or fire reporters can effectively cover their departments and agencies, they must master the various **organizational structures.** These structures vary among cities and states, and so textbooks can only generalize. Many structures, however, are similar to the departments that Aeschliman covers:

- *Topeka Police Department.* The chief of police is appointed by the mayor with the approval of the city council. Under the chief is a lieutenant colonel, who is second in command and in charge of personnel. Next are six majors who are division commanders of Patrol, Traffic, Detectives, Services, Administration and Topeka Emergency Communication (dispatch). Captains, lieutenants, sergeants, patrol officers and traffic officers complete the structure. There are also civilians in records, dispatch, housekeeping and so forth.

- *Shawnee County Sheriff's Department.* This department's sheriff is elected countywide, including Topeka. Three county commissioners are elected countywide, including Topeka. The sheriff is not directly responsible to the commissioners, but they control the budget.

  An undersheriff is appointed by the sheriff with the approval of the commission. The only person in the sheriff's department who holds the rank of major leads the uniformed officers. In addition, the chain of command lists captains, lieutenants, sergeants and corporals. There are eight territories. Officers do not work inside the Topeka city limits. Unlike the Topeka police, who have from 20 to 40 officers on the street at any one time, the sheriff has from three to seven officers out on patrol.
- *Topeka Fire Department.* The fire department is headed by a chief who is appointed by the mayor with the approval of the council. There are 20 assistant chiefs. Three assistant chiefs supervise each shift and live in the stations during their shifts. The firefighters work a 24-hour shift every three days. The other 11 assistant chiefs work on inspections, training and education. In the stations, captains are the leaders (there are 10 stations in Topeka), and there is a lieutenant in charge of each company. There are 17 companies active all the time and two in reserve. Topeka averages three fire calls a day. The department also responds to helicopter landings at three major hospitals about once a day and performs medical first response about six times a day.

Developing Sources

After reporters have a working understanding of the organizational structures of the agencies and departments they cover, sources must be developed and cultivated. Some of Aeschliman's primary sources within the Topeka Police Department, for example, are detectives, patrol and traffic officers, record keepers and high-ranking captains and majors.

In Topeka, detectives work two rotating shifts: they work mornings for two weeks and evenings for two weeks. Aeschliman figures that two or three detectives on each shift are his best sources. He does not try to gain the trust of these detectives overnight. "I start slowly in cultivating them," he said. "I use their names in feature articles or in routine stories to put them in a favorable light. After this, they often are more willing to help me with stories that are not routine."

Aeschliman always tries to determine whether sources like to see their names in print. "If I perceive that they like to see their names used, I will use them," he said. "Some sources like to provide information, but do not like to see their names in print. If that is the case, I do not overuse their names. It all depends on the person and the circumstances."

Aeschliman relies extensively on patrol and traffic officers. "They know exactly what is happening because they are close to the action," Aeschliman said. He estimated that of the 75 officers on the shift he covers, about 20 "would tell me almost anything," another 20 "would be friendly and generally helpful" and the remainder would not be as cooperative (they are the "I'm-kind-of-busy types, so please don't bother me"). "Since more than one officer usually works a case, I am not bothered much by those who don't want to be helpful. If I am at the scene of a crime or accident and one officer tells me to stay back and not bother him, I'll go to another officer who might be helpful."

Some of Aeschliman's best sources are the keepers of records at the department. "These sources are the hardest to get, though, because they operate under strict legal requirements," Aeschliman said. "Occasionally, I try to buy them a cup of coffee or a soft drink. If you work at it long enough, you can earn their trust. After several months, I was on a first-name basis with many of them. Now, I get some good tips from them. It is always off the record, and I respect their wishes."

Aeschliman relies on upper-echelon officers—majors and captains—for information for some stories. "I find that these officers are always looking to be placed in the best possible light," he said. "I never go out of my way to write fluff pieces about them, but it is good to use their names as favorably as possible in routine stories. That way, when you are writing an unfavorable story about the department, they might be more willing to talk to you about it. If they remember you only for the bad stories, they will provide little information to you."

Aeschliman does not have the time to cultivate sources within other departments on his beat, particularly the fire department, to the extent he does at police headquarters.

"Not as many stories come out of the fire department," he said. "But I try to write a couple of nice fire prevention stories now and then. I quote the fire officials. Then, they are more willing to talk when I am covering breaking news stories."

Aeschliman realizes that coverage of hard news is his main responsibility. But he added that "writing soft features about the departments, their activities and their officers plays a big part in cultivating sources for the hard news stories."

Naturally, many of the stories police reporters write are not favorable to the department. Sometimes, the timing of a story may conflict with a police investigation. At other times, the reporter must criticize law enforcement officials for abuse of power or for other questionable activities. These stories obviously do nothing to solidify relations between the department and the reporter. Reporters, though, must overcome these obstacles. The best way is to be as fair, professional and diplomatically aggressive as possible. Officers will often respect you for handling stories fairly, even if it puts them in a bad light.

"I never try to snow my sources," Aeschliman said. "If I make a mistake, I admit it and I try to recover my credibility as best I can."

Using Departmental Records

Reporters write many of their stories about fires, crimes, accidents, arrests and bookings after examining reports that are on file at various departments. Many times, reporters will follow up information from these reports by interviewing officials. The types of reports and the level of legal access to them vary. It is imperative that reporters fully understand reports and records that are available to them in the states and cities in which they work.

Accident Forms and Coverage of Accidents

Unrestricted access to forms. Reporters often have **unrestricted access** to some official accident forms. Aeschliman, for example, has complete unrestricted access to the Topeka Police Department's accident forms; he also has access to the accident report forms of the Kansas Department of Motor Vehicles.

However, some of the supplemental accident reports filled out by police officers are restricted—although officers will sometimes voluntarily tell reporters about information on these supplemental forms.

Information on accident forms. Accident reports vary, but the information found on the Kansas Department of Revenue Motor Vehicle Accident Report forms is representative:

- Location of accident
- Name of investigating officer
- Owner of vehicle
- Driver of vehicle
- Age and occupation of driver
- Names of passengers and witnesses
- Severity of injuries
- License number of vehicle
- Owner's liability insurance company
- Year, make, model and type of vehicle
- Damage (to fixed objects, such as utility poles, as well as injuries to animals, pedestrians and so on)
- Damage to vehicle (windshield, trunk, hood and so on)
- Severity of damage to vehicle (disabling, functional and so on)
- Time authorities were notified
- Time authorities arrived at scene
- Time emergency medical service was notified
- Time emergency medical service arrived at scene
- Hospital to which injured parties were removed and by whom
- Narrative that contains the drivers' and investigating officers' opinions of what occurred
- Principal contributing circumstances (condition of the driver, condition of the vehicle, human behavior and so on)
- Drivers' and pedestrians' condition before accident (ill, fatigued, apparently asleep, apparently normal, taking prescription drugs, taking illegal drugs, consuming alcohol and so on)
- Results of chemical tests
- Road surface (dry, wet, slippery and so on)
- Weather
- Light conditions
- Vehicle defects (turn lights, tires and so on)

- Visibility (vision not obscured, rain, snow, fog and so on)
- Diagram of what happened (drawing of the scene as observed; vehicles, drivers and pedestrians are normally referred to by numbers assigned in the report). The diagram includes an outline of the street and access point paths of units before and after impact, skid marks and point of impact; location of signs, traffic controls and reference points; location of other property hit or damaged; special features at the location (bridge, overpass, culvert and such); location of temporary highway conditions; and all measurements to locate the accident relative to a specific, fixed, uniquely identifiable and locatable point.

Determining newsworthiness of accidents. Most small-circulation dailies and weeklies publish stories about all accidents reported to the police—no matter how minor. The *Capital-Journal,* a larger-circulation daily, does not publish stories about insignificant fender benders, but it does publish daily agate listings of all accidents involving injuries. Each short item contains information about the location of the accident, names of people injured and condition reports from hospitals.

"Any injury reported by the police in their forms is listed as an injury in the paper," Aeschliman said. "We contact the hospital to see if the injured were seen, admitted or treated and released. In the event the police say a person was injured but no hospital has a record of the person, we write 'Police reported John Smith was possibly injured but no record of hospital treatment was found.' "

For a story to graduate from the agate listings in the *Capital-Journal* to a regular article, someone must have been severely injured or killed, or the accident must have an interesting feature, such as a 10-car pileup in a fog or a truck jackknifing across a highway.

Aeschliman said that stories about people who are seriously injured usually rate 5 to 6 inches near the classified ad pages. Stories about life-threatening injuries are often played on the second page. "Fatalities or some spectacular accident merits Page 1 treatment," he said. "Topeka, for example, sees only five to 10 fatal wrecks a year. When they occur in a city of 110,000, many readers know the victims or someone who knew the victims, and so it's news. We're also big on follow-ups. We report the victims' condition until they are out of the hospital. Occasionally, we do a feature story a year later, of the 'how life has been since' type."

Aeschliman glances through dozens of accident reports each day. Because stories will not be written about all of them, here are some key items he looks for to determine which reports are newsworthy:

- *Time and Location of Accident.* "The location helps to give me an idea of how many people might have seen the accident," Aeschliman said. "A minor injury accident at 8 a.m. on the freeway may be more newsworthy than a more severe injury accident at 2 a.m. on a rural gravel road."
- *Names of Those Involved.* "The names are necessary to obtain information about victims' condition from hospitals," Aeschliman said. "It is also important not to overlook the names of passengers, who may have been more seriously injured than the drivers. I always check the names of the vehicle owners as well. You might find that the son or daughter of a respected citizen was out joyriding. The owner's name also gives you another person to contact for more information."

- *Severity of Injuries.* The Kansas form that Aeschliman works with is coded: 0 means no injury; 1 means a death; 2 means an ambulance injury; 3 means obvious but not ambulance-worthy injuries; and 4 means possible injuries. "Of all the items in a report, this one throws up the red flag for a reporter," Aeschliman said. "If the number indicates an injury, the form deserves further attention. If no injury is listed, I usually only glance at the report to see if the mayor was in an accident while driving drunk, or something like that."
- *Results of Chemical Tests.* Any number that appears in this box on the Kansas form shows alcohol consumption. In Kansas, any number more than 0.1 indicates that the person was legally drunk. "If the number indicates consumption, I check into it," Aeschliman said.
- *Ambulance Service.* The Kansas form indicates which ambulance service arrived at the scene. "Finding out which ambulance was involved saves me time trying to find out where the injured were taken," Aeschliman said.
- *Diagram Section.* "This is an important section because it gives you a quick once-over of the wreck and how it occurred," Aeschliman said. "The diagram allows you to understand the wreck and to then ask intelligent questions of the officers or the people involved."
- *Statements Made by Drivers.* "I often quote people involved in an accident," Aeschliman said. "But I am always careful to note that the statement was attributed to the people by the police in their report."
- *"Nuts and Bolts" Section That Provides Information on Road Conditions, Light Conditions, Visibility, Use of Seat Belts and So On.* "If properly read, this section allows you to write a story as if you were there when the crash occurred," Aeschliman said. "For example, you might write: 'The car's tires were bald and the road was slick with spilled oil, the police report said.' Also, at the *Capital-Journal,* at the risk of sounding preachy, we often use information about seat belts, such as, 'Police said that Jones might not have been injured if he had been wearing a seat belt.' "

Example: An accident story. Accident stories normally lead with deaths, then injuries and then damage to vehicles or property. Aeschliman worked much essential information from the police report into the first three paragraphs of an accident story published in the *Capital-Journal.* He also called a hospital for a condition report. Here are his first three paragraphs:

> A Grantville man was thrown from his car and died instantly in a three-car collision Friday, and the driver of another car was seriously injured.
>
> Police said the man, Richard Bigham, 55, was westbound in the 800 block of US-24 when he lost control of his car and slid across the median broadside and into the eastbound lanes where his car was struck by two other vehicles.
>
> Marcella Conklin, 19, Shawnee, the driver of one of the eastbound cars, was admitted to St. Francis Hospital and Medical Center for treatment of broken ribs, a broken kneecap and cuts and bruises, a hospital spokesman said. She was in serious but stable condition late Friday in the intensive care unit, the spokesman said.

The story then provided condition reports on a passenger in one of the cars and on two firefighters who had been sprayed in the eyes with hydraulic fluid while pulling people from the vehicles. Then, attributing information to a police accident investigator, Aeschliman provided additional details on the collision:

> The traffic accident happened at 3:28 p.m. at 851 E. US-24, said police accident investigator Lyndon Weddle. Bigham was westbound in the left lane when another vehicle turned west onto US-24 from Goldwater Road in front of Bigham, Weddle said.
>
> Apparently, Bigham swerved to avoid that car, and in doing so dropped his two left side tires off the road onto the shoulder, Weddle said. When Bigham tried to steer his car back onto the road, it went out of control on the snowy shoulder and spun broadside into the median ditch, she said.
>
> Bigham's car slid on into the eastbound lanes of US-24, facing south, directly in front of Conklin, eastbound in the interior lane, and a third car in the exterior lane, driven by John Stein, 54, Valley Falls, Weddle said.

The story continued with additional details about the accident, a preliminary autopsy report and information about how rush-hour traffic was routed around the accident.

Aeschliman's story shows that reports can provide an abundance of details which, if gathered carefully, can be woven into a complete, understandable story.

Offense Reports and Coverage of Crimes

Limited access to forms. Reporters typically have **limited access** to police departments' forms recording crimes—that is, to standard offense reports.

For example, while Aeschliman has complete access to most accident forms, he has only *limited access* to the Topeka police department's standard offense reports. Access to these is legally limited to the top half of the form's front page. (See the form on page 301; the names and the incident are not real.) Here, such information as the date and time when the alleged offense took place, where it took place, the name of the victim and a brief synopsis is presented. The bottom half of the form provides information on property that might have been stolen or recovered and details about other evidence found at the scene. Also, estimates of the value of stolen property can be provided. Aeschliman does not have a legal right to the information at the bottom of the page, but quite often friendly sources within the department will grant him access.

Often, according to Aeschliman, detectives ask him to withhold some information. For example, the police might ask Aeschliman to withhold information about the theft of the coin bank described in the limited-access portion of the standard offense report. Detectives might reason that including this information in the story could tip off the suspect that the police are aware that it is missing, and this could hinder their investigation. In such instances, Aeschliman might decide to abide by their wishes.

Example: A rape story. The *Capital-Journal* seldom publishes particularly long rape stories unless the victim has severe injuries in addition to the rape itself, or the circumstances are unusual. Like many other newspapers that respect the privacy of rape victims and their families, the *Capital-Journal* never uses the person's name or address; thus, Aeschliman would observe this policy when writing a story based on the information in the form shown on page 301.

Standard Offense Report

LIMITED ACCESS

NAME OF AGENCY	ORI KS
TOPEKA POLICE DEPT. 204 W. 5th Topeka, Kansas 66603	KS 0890100
	1. CASE NO. 0021-02

2. OFFENSE–List Most Serious First	3. OFFENSE CODE	4. DATE OF OFFENSE (MMDDYY)	5. TIME OCC.	6. DATE & TIME RPTD.
RAPE AGG. ASSAULT THEFT		1/15/02	3:25	1/15/02 10:45

7. REPORT AREA

8. TYPES OF PREMISES; CHECK IF VACANT, NOT NORMALLY IN USE ☐

__ STREET X RESIDENCE __ RESTAURANT
__ COMMERCIAL __ BANK __ VEHICLE
__ GAS STATION __ PHARMACY __ OTHER
__ CONVENIENCE STORE __ DRS. OFFICE ______

9. LOCATION OF OFFENSE: 1111 Main Street

10. VICTIM'S NAME–Last, First, Middle (Firm if Business)	11. RESIDENCE ADDRESS–PHONE
Elizabeth B. Baker (not real name)	1111 Main Street

12. RACE	13. SEX	14. AGE	15. DOB (MMDDYY)	16. HT.	17. WT.	18. HAIR	19. EYES	20. OCCUPATION	21. BUSINESS ADDRESS–PHONE
W	F	17	2/15/84	5'1	105	Br	Br	student	N/A (not applicable)

CODES: V-Victim W-Witness P-Parent DC-Discovered Crime RP-Reporting Party Check if More Names in Supplement ____

22. NAME–Last, First, Middle	23. CODE	24. RESIDENCE ADDRESS–PHONE
Mary J. Baker (not real name)	RP	1111 Main Street

25. RACE	26. SEX	27. AGE	28. DOB (MMDDYY)	29. HT.	30. WT.	31. HAIR	32. EYES	33. OCCUPATION	34. BUSINESS ADDRESS–PHONE
W	F	42	NA	NA	NA	NA	NA	housewife	N/A

35. NAME–Last, First, Middle	36. CODE	37. RESIDENCE ADDRESS–PHONE

38. RACE	39. SEX	40. AGE	41. DOB (MMDDYY)	42. HT.	43. WT.	44. HAIR	45. EYES	46. OCCUPATION	47. BUSINESS ADDRESS–PHONE

48. DESCRIBE BRIEFLY HOW OFFENSE WAS COMMITTED.

Mother brought daughter to station after mother found daughter beaten in bed. Victim Baker (not real name) reports a man entered her window and threatened her with a knife and raped her, then left. See Supplement 0022-02.

PROPERTY STATUS: S-Stolen RA-Recovered for your agency RO-Recovered for other agency F-Found RV-Recovered by Victim E-Evidence

49. STATUS	50. QTY	51. DESCRPITION OF PROPERTY	52. CODE	53. MODEL-SERIAL-OWNER APPLIED NO.	54. VALUE	55. COLOR
	1	coin bank		unknown quantity change	$15-25	

56. PROPERTY DAMAGE INCURRED DURING OFFENSE	57. PROPERTY DAMAGE INCURRED DURING ARSON	65. TOTAL VALUE
X UNDER $100 ______ OVER $100	$ NONE	PROPERTY STOLEN $15-25

59. REPORTING OFFICER	60. DATE	61. TYPED BY	62. DATE	63. REVIEWED BY	64. DATE	65. COPIES TO:
						__ DET __ JUVENILE __ KBI __ OTHER

Standard offense report form of a police department.

Aeschliman could lead the story this way:

> A 17-year-old east Topeka girl was raped in her bed early Tuesday by a man armed with a knife.

All this information is available from the standard offense report. But Aeschliman would not rely exclusively on information from the report to structure the remainder of his story. He would also:

- Talk to the officers who investigated and filed the report.
- Check to see if other rapes had been reported in the area during recent weeks.
- Telephone the hospital for a report on the victim's condition.

The remainder of the story might read like this:

> Police reported that the girl said she was beaten by the man and was threatened with a long hunting-type knife. The girl was in satisfactory condition at a local hospital Wednesday night suffering a broken nose. She was admitted for observation, a hospital spokeswoman said.
>
> According to police, this is what the girl said happened: The rape occurred at 3:25 a.m. when a man cut a window screen and then raised the window to get into her room. She woke up when the man crawled into bed with her and clamped a hand over her mouth.
>
> A detective investigating the case reported that the girl said the man held a knife to her throat and then hit her in the face and stomach several times when she tried to cry out. She said that the man raped her, threatened to kill her if she called the police and then left through the same window.
>
> Police said that the victim apparently passed out and was discovered by her mother in the morning. The woman was sleeping in an upstairs room during the attack, the detective said.
>
> The suspect was described as a white man, about 25, 5-feet-8-inches, 180 pounds. He was wearing blue jeans and a plaid shirt.

Note the attribution. Attribution is particularly important in crime stories. Readers need to know the source of the information, and it is the obligation of reporters to provide it. In the story above, for example, the reporter relied primarily on the police, who had been supplied with most of the information by the victim and the victim's mother.

A Day on the Police and Fire Beat

This section provides an overview of a typical day on the job with Roger Aeschliman. A composite day is presented to illustrate Aeschliman's thought processes and writing strategies on a variety of stories common to the police and fire beats. It is realistic in the sense that one major story dominates the day while several smaller ones need to be written and routine work still needs to be accomplished.

Assignments: The Day Begins

At about noon, the telephone rings at Aeschliman's house. Steve Fry, the *Capital-Journal*'s police reporter for the morning shift, says: "It's going to be a big day, Rog. Can you come in an hour early? I'm all tied up with the sheriff's contract negotiations, and there's been a fatal fire."

Aeschliman reports to the office at 1:30 p.m., instead of his usual 2:30. The notes and requests to return calls piled on his desk indicate that he will probably not be going home at 11 p.m. as he normally does.

Fry has wrapped up coverage of the contract negotiations for the day; and he fills Aeschliman in on the session. The deputies approved the contract; but the county did not.

Fry then tells Aeschliman that two children were killed and their father was injured in a fire in a mobile home this morning. "That's big news anywhere," Aeschliman said.

Fry would normally have been at the scene, but he was locked up in the contract meeting, and no one on the skeleton morning staff heard the call go out on the police scanner.

Aeschliman goes to the city desk to talk to his boss, the city editor. Today, Don Marker says only one thing to him: "Do a good job on the fire story."

"On another day, he might have a news tip or a feature story idea for me," Aeschliman said. "In any case, a check-in at the city desk is vital. All the reporters clear through the city editor, and if there is something happening, he's probably going to know about it.

"Back at my desk I start calling around. I make routine checks to find out what's happening. Included are calls to the highway patrol, police traffic, patrol and detectives, the ambulance service, our sheriff, the sheriffs from the surrounding counties and the fire department."

On-the-Scene Coverage: A Major Fire

On this day the big news comes from the fire department. The preliminary report from the inspector is fragmentary: "A mobile home fire at 245 E. 29th was reported at 10:11 a.m. The fire destroyed the structure, doing an estimated $10,000 damage. Two girls, ages 3 and 1, were killed. A man was severely burned."

"That's all I am going to get from them for the rest of the day," Aeschliman said. "It's up to me. This is the kind of story that can't wait until later. Firefighters and police change shifts soon, and witnesses have a way of disappearing. I'm going to the scene; the boss agrees."

The area is still cordoned off, and the fire chief is shuffling through the debris. He comes out to make a statement for the television crews. Again, he uses no names. The cause and origin of the fire are unknown. But he does give some details of the fire and some good quotations.

"I can use the quotes," Aeschliman said. "A door-to-door canvass is next on my list. Do you know who lived there, sir? Do you know the names of the children? Where was the mother?

"A half hour of that and I've got the names of the injured man and his wife, and I've found out that they had moved here recently from a small town north of

Topeka. I've also got the name and address of a man who restrained the father from going back into the blaze to try to rescue the girls. My next stop is the witness.

"He is a shy man with children of his own. He just happened to be shopping across the street when the fire broke out. He didn't know any of the victims, but he saw what happened and he tells about it vividly. I can sure use him.

"It feels as though the day is half gone, but it's only 3:30 p.m. I check back in at the office. Nothing is new. It's time to follow up on some leads. I call the victims' hometown sheriff and ask if he's heard of the deaths. 'Sure, sure, it's the talk of the town,' he says. I tell him the names of the mother and father, and he confirms them."

The sheriff also provides the names of the girls: Shena and Kimberly.

"Now I've got the story no one else has: the victims' names and an eyewitness account of the disaster. I tell the boss, and he sends a photographer out to work up some kind of photo from the scene."

Making the Rounds

After Aeschliman has gathered most of the information for the fire story, he must make his regular stops on the beat. There is still a lot of day left; and he will write the major fire story later.

The *Capital-Journal* publishes a **police log** (a daily report of activity involving the department), **fire reports** and court dockets in small print. That job, tedious as it is, falls to the police reporters. Fry gets the night shift reports, and Aeschliman picks up the morning shift reports when he makes afternoon rounds. That means checking in at the sheriff's office for traffic and offense reports. Then he goes to the police department for the same type of information. Aeschliman summarizes each report in one or two lines.

A typical item from the police blotter might read: "Fleet Service and Equipment, 1534 N. Tyler, burglary of business and theft of tools." A typical item from the fire department log might read: "7:53 p.m. Wednesday—3700 W. 29th, fire started in water heater caused by short in wiring, burned wiring and water heater, $50 loss."

"Even if the paper did not run the small print, I'd still be looking through the reports," he said. "There are important stories hidden in the pile, and you've got to find them."

On this day, he finds one that he regards as worthy of more than a mention in small print: the arrest of a person accused of purse snatching.

Aeschliman returns to his office and calls the fire department again. This time, he asks for the entire list of fire reports. He enters them quickly on his computer terminal and sends them, along with the rest of the short items for the small print, to the city desk.

It is 6:35—five minutes past deadline. "Because of the time I spent on the fire story, no one yells at me for missing the deadline," Aeschliman said.

The reporter has nearly an hour for a dinner break. But instead of eating dinner, he spends the time lifting weights at the YMCA. Now, back in the office, he is ready to write.

Writing the Stories

Planning for Deadlines

Gathering information is only half the job. A beat reporter must organize his or her time to meet deadlines. Aeschliman's next deadline is 10:15 p.m. All copy should be in, but some minor local stories do not have to be rushed. It is 7:30 p.m.

Aeschliman figures that two hours and 45 minutes should be enough time to get everything written—that is, if nothing else happens.

"In addition to writing for the next deadline, I've got to monitor the scanners to keep on top of any breaking news," he said. "If everything breaks loose, some of my stories could be reassigned to another reporter or dumped entirely if something more important happens."

Writing the Fire Story

Aeschliman always sets priorities when writing on deadline. He turns initially to his major story; on this day, it is the mobile home fire.

Developing the lead: Deaths go first. Aeschliman's first task is to develop a strong, concise, accurate lead. That takes thought.

"The deaths go first," Aeschliman said. "Everything is secondary to that. It would be good to identify the girls in the first paragraph because I know who they are and no one else does. I play around with that idea a bit, but every lead comes out extremely long. The boss suggests a simple lead: 'Two young girls were killed when a fire destroyed their mobile home Saturday.'

"That is a nice starting place, but I know I can do better," Aeschliman said. "I look through my notes and decide to go with a little extra about the injured father trying to get back in." Aeschliman writes:

> Two Topeka girls, 3 and 1 years old, died Friday in a mobile home fire, and their critically burned father had to be restrained from re-entering the inferno to try to rescue them.

"That tells the story," Aeschliman said. "The lead may be a tad long, but I like it."

Constructing the story: Ingredients. Stories about fires should answer several basic questions. First, was anyone killed? Beyond that, fire stories should obviously provide additional information. Aeschliman tries to work in most of the following details:

- Identification of the dead
- Cause of death (for example, smoke inhalation, burns and so forth)
- Results of or status of autopsies
- Location of the fire
- Cause and origin of the fire
- If arson is suspected, details on leads or arrests
- Identification of the injured
- Description of the scene
- Details of treatment to the injured at the scene
- Details of where the injured were taken
- Current condition of the injured (generally obtained from hospitals)
- Time of the fire
- When the fire was reported and by whom

- Response time of the firefighters
- Length of time to get the fire under control
- Length of time the firefighters spent on the scene
- Heroics by the firefighters
- Extent of property damage (including damage to adjacent buildings)
- Estimated damage in dollars
- Insurance details
- Quotations from police and fire officials, witnesses, neighbors and so forth

"I like to use good quotes high in the story; they attract attention and keep the reader interested," Aeschliman said. "In this case, using quotes from the witness in the first paragraph would be confusing. I have to tell the readers generally about the fire, so that the quotes can be read in context. But I don't have to overdo it, and the quotes can be used about halfway through the body. The witness has a story to tell, and so I just let him. I've done rearranging to make more sense of it, and I've paraphrased when he wasn't very clear, but I try to use as much of what he said exactly the way he said it."

Aeschliman's story continues:

The girls, Shena and Kimberly Bryan, were killed in the fire at their mobile home, 245 E. 29th, lot 1, at the Crest Mobile Home Park, a fire department spokesman said.

Kenneth Bryan, father of the girls, was burned over most of his body and was taken to St. Francis Hospital and Medical Center before being transferred to the burn center of the Kansas University Medical Center in Kansas City.

He was in critical condition late Friday, but hospital officials would not release further information.

His wife was not at home when the fire broke out, fire department officials said.

Providing attribution. Note that Aeschliman is careful to attribute factual information to reliable sources. Reporters should always tell readers the source of information.

Aeschliman obtained information for the first paragraph by:

Ingenuity (scouring the neighborhood for witnesses and for background information on the family)

A telephone call to the sheriff who served the nearby small community where the family used to live (to verify the parents' names and to get the names of the girls)

Routine reporting work (talking to fire department officials at the scene and, back at the office, calling the hospital for a report on the father's condition)

Describing the scene. Aeschliman's next paragraphs provide additional details from the scene of the fire—details that he would not have been able to relay to readers if he had not gone to the site:

The mobile home was destroyed, with only the skeleton of charred 2-by-2 timbers still standing after the fire. The aluminum siding was mostly melted away, the strips remaining dangling and pockmarked from the heat.

The body of one girl was found in a rear bedroom, the area that had the least fire damage. Officials at the scene said she was not severely burned and probably died from smoke inhalation. The other girl was found in the front living area and was burned beyond recognition, a spokesman said.

"You had to move debris before you saw the body, and even then it was hard to tell what it was," he said.

Autopsies are pending.

Both the cause and origin of the fire are under investigation. No details as to how or where the fire began were available late Friday.

The fire was reported at 10:11 a.m. by neighbors, but Jerry Fitzgerald, 25, 2834 Topeka Ave., the first person to arrive on the scene, said the fire was burning about 15 minutes before anyone called for help.

Aeschliman strengthened his story—and earned an advantage over his competition from other newspapers and from the electronic media—by locating and interviewing Fitzgerald. His description of the scene was indeed vivid. Aeschliman's story continues:

He [Fitzgerald] said he was shopping across the street when he saw a single cloud of smoke billow skyward. Fitzgerald said he drove over right away, and when he arrived he saw Bryan run out of the front door and saw the interior of the residence explode into flames behind Bryan.

Fitzgerald tried to help Bryan, who was covered with burns. But Bryan broke away and ran around to the rear of the trailer where he wrenched open a second door in an attempt to get inside. But flames roared out at him, and Fitzgerald restrained him.

Aeschliman then incorporates some vivid direct quotations into the story:

"He tried to get back inside, so I grabbed him and another man grabbed him and pulled him back and sat him down," Fitzgerald said.

"He just kept saying that his girl was in there and for somebody to go in and get her out. I just said no way, the heat was ungodly."

The smoke pouring out was so thick "it was like you could reach out and hold it in your hand," he said.

Aeschliman then quotes Fitzgerald on how the police and the firefighters were summoned and when the ambulance arrived.

Using vivid details: A question of taste. Aeschliman's city editor objects to a vivid, gruesome quotation that the reporter uses near the end of his story. It reads:

"You could tell he [Bryan] was realizing what had happened to him. He was looking at his hands and they were bleeding, and he had shoes on and there was blood coming from the shoes. His skin was peeling off like wallpaper. And he still wanted to go into the house," he said.

"The quote graphically details the man's injuries and his feelings at the time," Aeschliman said. "I believe it has value in demonstrating the horror of a fire. It is not just sensationalism; it may scare people, but we might save a life because of the morbid paragraph."

The reporter persuades the city editor to let the quotation run. A lot of newspaper editors and reporters, however, would undoubtedly have deleted the quotation as being too gruesome. They would have reasoned that the survivors had already suffered enough and that the vivid description was not necessary to tell the story. Matters of taste often crop up. It is the reporter's job to consider his or her position carefully with regard to material that could be offensive to some readers, and to discuss the matter with an editor.

As Aeschliman closes his story with more details from fire department officials, a couple of fire alarms go out, but they both turn into false calls. "We don't run out on every alarm," Aeschliman said. "Fire trucks are almost always at the scene in three minutes or less, and they immediately report the extent of the fire upon arrival. We can wait three minutes to decide."

Writing the Purse-Snatching Story

After completing the major fire story, Aeschliman is ready to write a short story about the arrest in the purse snatching. He always tries to work most of the following ingredients into his arrest stories:

- Name of the suspect arrested
- Identification (for example, address and occupation)
- Site and time of the arrest
- Name and identification of the victim of the alleged crime
- Time of the alleged crime
- Details of the alleged crime
- Details of the capture and arrest of the suspect
- Details of the booking and charges
- Details of bail
- Quotations from police officials, the victim and the suspect

One officer used the words *cornered* and *flushed out* when he was interviewed by Aeschliman. The reporter's lead reads:

> A man who police think took a purse from a woman Friday was cornered in a nearby alley and arrested when a police dog flushed him out.

Aeschliman uses direct quotations in the second and third paragraphs:

> Police in the area closed in on the alleged purse snatcher and cordoned off the area of 7th and Jewell, while the police helicopter circled overhead. He was in custody "before he knew what hit him," an officer at the scene said.
>
> The arrest was "one of those things when everybody was at the right place at the right time," one officer said. "It was very satisfying."

"The story can be told without repeated reference by name to the suspect. In this way I can identify the arrested person early in the copy block and then later in the story refer to him merely as a man," Aeschliman said. "Officers and I never say, for example, that 'John Smyth took the purse and then hid' or anything close to that. I have to be especially careful when writing my stories to avoid convicting the suspect in print. Libel is always on my mind." (See Chapter 21 on covering the courts and Chapter 25 on law for further details.)

Aeschliman's story continues:

> The suspect, John C. Smyth [not his real name], 19, of Wichita, was arrested in an alley behind 704 Lindenwood and booked into Shawnee County Jail in connection with burglary and theft, officer Mike Casey said.

Note that Aeschliman says that Smyth was booked *in connection with* burglary and theft. Aeschliman is careful not to write that Smyth was booked *for* burglary and theft. Use of the word *for* would imply guilt and could be libelous.

Aeschliman goes on to provide additional details on the booking of the suspect and uses direct quotations from the officers:

> Smyth remained in jail late Friday in lieu of $5,000 bond with surety.
>
> Casey said the theft happened at 2:48 p.m. An 81-year-old woman had just gotten out of her car near 6th and Franklin when a man leaped past her, into the car, grabbed her handbag and ran away.
>
> The woman and a witness tried to chase the suspect but stopped and phoned police. The victim was not injured.
>
> Officer J. W. Harper was patrolling a few blocks away and on a hunch circled to 7th Street where he saw a man walking down the middle of the street. Harper said he drove to within 100 feet of the suspect before the man looked up and sprinted away down an alley.
>
> "He pulled a vanishing act," Harper said. "I was only seconds behind him and couldn't see him, so I figured he was holed up in a garage or something."

Aeschliman then went on to describe the arrival of a police helicopter, additional officers and a police dog. He quoted Harper again: "We put so much coverage in there so fast that he [the suspect] just froze up." Aeschliman also quoted Detective Greg Halford who said that the suspect had been interrogated and that the woman's purse and money had been recovered.

Again, it is clear that reporters can add considerable spice and detail to their coverage of relatively routine events by interviewing the officers involved. Also, one sentence in this story could have alerted reporters to a follow-up article: it is not every day that an 81-year-old woman chases a 19-year-old burglary suspect.

Aeschliman emphasized that he likes to have officers tell of their participation in an event. "Detective Halford has always been good to me," he said. "He really didn't do much in the arrest, but it never hurts to stroke a few egos by putting a name in print."

Final Deadline: The Day Ends

Aeschliman still has unanswered questions about several stories. "As the stories are being processed, I double-check the spelling of the name of the purse-snatch suspect. It's OK. I try to run down the condition of the burned man. Nothing is new there. I try to find out how old the man is, and which child was 3 and which was 1 in the major fire story. No one who knows is available. All the family are at the hospital; officials are unsure themselves, but they do confirm (off the record) that I have the right names."

It is 10:50 p.m. The newspaper's final deadline is midnight, "but for all practical purposes, it's 11 p.m. when the boss and everyone else goes home," Aeschliman said. "I make a series of late calls to ferret out any last-minute news. Usually there's none. Tonight a detective says that narcotics officials have just finished a drug raid. It's not spectacular, and so I bounce it off the boss. He says to write it—short. Out goes the innovation, and in comes the formula":

> Three women were arrested Friday night and another arrest is expected in a cocaine ring drug bust.

Aeschliman provides additional details in the second paragraph and lists the names of persons booked in the third paragraph. A telephone call to the jail reveals that they have been released on bond. He closes his story—and his day—with that.

✔ A Checklist for Beat Reporters

There is no foolproof formula for competent reporting on the police and fire beats, but here are some suggestions:

- ❑ *Develop and Cultivate Sources.* Get to know sources as people—not merely as officials. Hang out at the departments as much as possible. "I don't stay in the newspaper office any longer than I have to," said Aeschliman. "You can't cultivate sources sitting in the newsroom."
- ❑ *Learn How to Handle Hostile Sources.* Reporters on the scene of investigations run the risk of being perceived as interfering with official business. Some front-line police officers and firefighters dislike talking to reporters under these circumstances. If reporters persist, they run the risk of being arrested. Officers do not have to cooperate with reporters. In these cases, begging or shouting does not usually do much good. It is best to go to fire or police supervisors, who should provide information or instruct those under them to provide it. (See Chapter 10 for additional details on how to deal with hostile sources.)
- ❑ *Know the Job Responsibilities of Sources.* Titles can be deceiving. Know what their jobs entail.
- ❑ *Don't Deceive Sources.* If reporters make an error, they should admit it.
- ❑ *If a Big Story Comes Along—One That Places the Department in a Bad Light—Go After It Aggressively.* Work hard on the story, even if it costs you some sources. Make sure, though, that the story is important enough to justify the loss of several major sources. If it is a piddling story, think twice about whether it is worth losing valuable sources.

- ❑ *Know the Territory.* Spend time driving around; get to know the streets and alleys in the community. Know where the major crime areas are. That will make it easier to write stories when the *where* element is important.
- ❑ *Learn the Terminology.* The police might say that they are *interrogating an individual* who is in custody. A journalist should report, however, that the police are *questioning a suspect.* Learn the terminology and jargon, but always write in clear, understandable language for readers.
- ❑ *Be Aware of the Special Vocabulary of an Agency.* In turn, explain terms to readers. For example, the terms *one-alarm, two-alarm, three-alarm* and *four-alarm fires* can have different meanings, depending on the community. In general, more firefighters and equipment are dispatched to two-alarm fires than to one-alarm fires. More still are sent to three-alarm and four-alarm fires. The number of firefighters and the amount of equipment sent, however, will depend on the size of the community and the size of the fire department. Don't assume that readers understand these terms.
- ❑ *Double-Check Spellings of Names and Streets Mentioned on Law Enforcement Department Reports.* Police officers are not trained journalists. Always verify information.
- ❑ *After Reading a Police Report in Which Injuries Are Mentioned, Always Check with the Hospital or the Morgue to Update or Verify the Information.* If the new information conflicts, another story angle might materialize.
- ❑ *Be Particularly Careful When Reporting Arrests.* Remember always to write, for example, that John Jones was arrested *in connection with* (or *in the investigation of*) a burglary at 1122 E. Norwood. Don't write that Jones was arrested *for* a burglary at 1122 E. Norwood. This implies guilt.
- ❑ *Don't Confuse an Arrest with the Filing of a Charge.* A lot of suspects who are arrested are subsequently released and are never charged with a crime. Also, if someone is arrested and you report it, write a follow-up story when the person is charged or released.
- ❑ *Be Leery of Libel.* Journalists have the privilege of reporting most of the information on public records, but they must do so fairly and accurately. And during interviews, the fact that a police officer utters a potentially libelous statement about a suspect does not give reporters the right or the legal privilege to reiterate that statement to readers.
- ❑ *Be Sure to Know an Organization's Policy on the Use of Minors' Names.* Some newspapers have a policy against using the names of juveniles who are involved in misdemeanors. Also, be familiar with the state laws that govern coverage of juvenile proceedings.

CHAPTER TWENTY-ONE

COURTS

Month after month, millions sat mesmerized as the media reported, often in excruciatingly vivid detail, the significant and the seemingly trivial aspects of the O. J. Simpson murder trial.

It was only natural that The Associated Press would assign a special correspondent, Linda Deutsch, to cover the trial. This senior reporter has covered some of the most celebrated cases of the last three decades, including the trials of Patty Hearst, Sirhan Sirhan, Charles Manson, William Kennedy Smith and the officers accused of beating Rodney King.

(*Lester Sloan / Getty Images*)

"The Simpson trial, to me, was a TV trial," Deutsch said. "Everything about it seemed choreographed for television."

Each day, though, her stories for newspaper readers would summarize the most significant developments—often with a twist—in clear, understandable language.

After the preliminary hearing, Deutsch wrote from Los Angeles:

> O.J. Simpson spends his 47th birthday in jail today, facing a double murder trial after a judge found there was enough evidence to link him to the brutal knifings of his ex-wife and her friend.

The story went on to provide background of the case and quotations from attorneys for the prosecution and defense as well as from witnesses who testified. She ended her story with a vivid description:

> Simpson struggled for composure, sighing heavily, looking away, rubbing his face and wiping away tears. . . .

Throughout the trial, the AP stories, in straightforward style, captured the drama of the setting. Focusing on Simpson's appearance and bearing, another story led with these paragraphs:

> No longer a morose, distracted man barely able to utter his own name, O. J. Simpson declared himself "absolutely, 100 percent not guilty" Friday in the slayings of his ex-wife and a friend of hers.
>
> Standing tall and speaking firmly, the 47-year-old former football star entered his plea in a nationally televised arraignment, the latest step in what promises to be one of the most closely watched murder trials in U.S. history.
>
> When he left the courtroom for a nearby holding cell, Simpson—who once said he couldn't bear to return to a similar lockup—gave a thumbs-up to friends. They smiled back.

As jury selection was launched, Deutsch again managed to find a unique angle:

> O. J. Simpson quietly sang, "A new day has begun . . ." before facing some of his potential jurors Monday as the most-watched murder trial in U.S. history got under way.
>
> Jury candidates were identified only by numbers, and the first to be questioned was No. 0032. Simpson wore No. 32 as a college and professional football star, and that didn't go unnoticed.
>
> "I don't know if this is an omen," Superior Court Judge Lance Ito said.
>
> Simpson nodded his head as if to say, "Yes."

Then, after nine months of testimony, the trial ended. Deutsch's AP colleague Michael Fleeman led his story with these three paragraphs:

> O. J. Simpson was acquitted today of murdering his ex-wife and her friend, a suspense-filled climax to the courtroom saga that obsessed the nation.
>
> With two words—"not guilty"—the jury freed the fallen sports legend to try to rebuild a life thrown into disgrace.
>
> Simpson looked toward the jury and mouthed, "Thank you," after the panel was dismissed. He turned to his family and punched a fist into the air. Then he hugged his lead defense attorney, Johnnie Cochran Jr., and his friend and attorney Robert Kardashian.

"I tried to cover the story straight," Deutsch said, adding that she was "astonished and horrified" that some reporters had been quoted giving their opinions of Simpson's guilt or innocence.

Noting that the trial will probably be remembered for the impact of the tabloids, Deutsch contrasted their sensationalized coverage with her philosophy: "My idea is to give the public both sides."

No sentence could provide more succinct advice to reporters who cover the courts.

Indeed, Deutsch has carved a reputation for attention to detail and for providing complete, accurate coverage of court proceedings. Precise language is the staple of her coverage. Through her words, she conveys to readers the relevant facts. But beyond that, she routinely provides context, observation and background—all of which are readily apparent in the first nine paragraphs of her story about another high-profile case.

SANTA MONICA, Calif.—A young man with a history of gang affiliations was found guilty Tuesday in the slaying of Bill Cosby's only son, Ennis, as he changed a flat tire on a dark and lonely road last year.

Mikail Markhasev, a 19-year-old Ukranian immigrant, also was convicted of attempting to rob Ennis Cosby and using a firearm in the commission of attempted robbery.

The six-man, six-woman jury's finding on all counts automatically mandates a life prison term with no possibility of parole.

"The Cosby family is satisfied with the judicial process that has led to this conviction," Cosby spokesman David Brokaw said. "They have no comment on the sentencing."

In the courtroom, members of the Cosby family began to weep and hug each other as the verdicts were announced. Although Bill Cosby and his wife, Camille, were not present, two of their daughters—Erika and Erinn—sat with several other relatives in the front row.

Also in the family group was Phil Caputo, the man who played basketball with Ennis Cosby hours before he was killed. Caputo had tears in his eyes as he heard the word "guilty."

The family of Markhasev never made it to the courtroom in time to hear the verdicts. Markhasev and his lawyer stood stonefaced, staring at the jury as the verdicts were read.

Cosby, 27, a vacationing graduate student from Columbia University, was fatally shot Jan. 16, 1997, while changing a flat tire on a dark road near Bel Air. Markhasev was arrested nearly two months later.

The jury, which heard testimony over two weeks, spent less than six hours talking over the case before accepting the prosecution's argument that Markhasev had been convicted by his own words.

A Demanding Assignment

Coverage of the courts is clearly one of the most demanding assignments a reporter can receive. During one day of testimony in a criminal trial, enough words can be spoken to fill 200 manuscript pages. From the testimony, the reporter must extract the significant points and construct a readable, concise newspaper account of perhaps fewer than 500 words.

"The biggest challenge in court reporting is getting a grasp of the system," said Robert Rawitch, a suburban editor of the *Los Angeles Times* who covered the federal courts in Los Angeles for more than four years. "It is difficult to develop an understanding of legal procedures and jargon. You must strive diligently not to exaggerate or to underplay the importance of any happening."

Metropolitan dailies generally assign more than one reporter to the courts. For example, one reporter might be assigned to the federal courts, one to the state criminal courts and another to the state civil courts. In addition, some metropolitan dailies have legal affairs reporters who are not responsible for daily developments in the various court systems but who write on broader issues, such as the workings of grand juries, civil rights prosecutions of police officers, sentencing patterns of judges, unaccredited law schools and the trend toward national law firms. The largest-circulation dailies also assign a reporter to cover the Supreme Court full time in Washington, D.C.

At most dailies with circulations of less than 100,000, one person has primary responsibility for coverage of local and state courts. These newspapers rely primarily on the wire services for coverage of federal courts.

The Judicial System

Reporters need to have a basic understanding of the judicial system, at both the federal level and the state level—an understanding a veteran reporter such as Deutsch has honed through the years. To help develop that understanding, aspiring court reporters should take appropriate college courses such as law and society, public law, American national government and constitutional law. The following overview serves as a starting point.

The Federal Judicial System

The Supreme Court is the nation's highest court. Its term begins the first Monday in October and usually lasts until late June or early July. It is divided between sittings and recesses. During sittings, cases are heard and opinions announced. During recesses, the nine justices consider the business before the court and write opinions. Sittings and recesses alternate at approximately two-week intervals.

The wire services, the largest newspapers and the networks assign reporters to cover the Supreme Court regularly. Reporters who cover it must have a solid understanding of the law and legal procedures in addition to being capable journalists. Complex legal language filling scores of pages must be deciphered when the written opinions are distributed. The facts of the case and the significance of the holding must be grasped. Reporters often select pertinent direct quotations from the majority, concurring or dissenting opinions. For background, law school professors or practicing attorneys are sometimes consulted for an interpretation of the significance of the case or for direct quotations.

Below the Supreme Court, at the intermediate level in the **federal judicial system,** are various circuits of the U.S. Court of Appeals. At the next level are U.S. District Courts, where trials in the federal system are generally held. There are nearly 100 such courts. Each state has at least one; the more heavily populated states have more than one.

State Judicial Systems

There are about as many types of state court systems as there are states. Usually, a **state judicial system** has three layers:

- Trial courts, where proceedings are initiated
- Intermediate courts, where appeals are first heard
- Supreme courts, which are state panels of final resort

The names assigned to the courts at each of these levels vary, but generally the highest is called the *state supreme court.* The intermediate level (used by about half the states) is called an *appellate court.* Trial-level bodies, often called *superior courts,* are the highest trial courts with general jurisdiction in most states. Sometimes they are given other names; for instance, in New York the trial-level body is the Supreme Court.

Several other courts complete the various state systems. These include probate courts (which handle wills, administration of estates and guardianship of minors and incompetents); county courts (which have limited jurisdiction in civil and criminal cases); municipal courts (where cases involving less serious crimes, generally called **misdemeanors,** are heard by municipal justices or municipal magistrates); and, in some jurisdictions, justice of the peace and police magistrate courts (which have very limited jurisdiction and are the lowest courts in the judicial hierarchy). Justice courts in Arizona, for example, hear matters that involve less than $500.

Types of Court Cases

Court cases can be lumped in two divisions: criminal and civil. **Criminal cases** involve the enforcement of criminal statutes. Suits are brought by the state or by the federal government against a person charged with committing a crime such as murder or armed robbery.

Civil cases involve arriving at specific solutions to legal strife between individuals, businesses, state or local governments or agencies of government. Civil cases commonly include suits for damages arising from automobile accidents, for breach of contract and for libel.

In the next two sections, we'll look at coverage of criminal cases and civil cases.

Criminal Cases

As noted, criminal cases involve the enforcement of criminal statutes. In his book "The Reporter and the Law," Lyle Denniston, a veteran Supreme Court reporter, wrote: "Crime is the main staple of legal reporting. Of course, crime alone does not make all the news on the court beat. But it does dominate the beat."

Denniston continued: "Criminal law is simply more 'newsworthy' than civil law. More often, a criminal case will have in it the ingredients of human interest, public policy and clear-cut controversy that make news. At a more fundamental level, criminal law provides the most vivid test of a community's sense of justice and morality."

The Basic Criminal Process

Criminal charges may be brought against a person through an indictment or through the filing of an information. According to Black's Law Dictionary, an **indictment** is "an accusation in writing found and presented by a grand jury . . . charging that a person has done some act or been guilty of some omission which by law is a public offense." An **information,** according to the dictionary, differs from an indictment in that it is "presented by a competent public officer [such as a prosecuting attorney] on his oath of office, instead of a grand jury on their oath."

According to "Law and the Courts," published by the American Bar Association, the steps that occur after an indictment has been returned or an information has been filed are basically as follows. (Naturally, these steps and the names assigned to them can vary slightly among jurisdictions; reporters need to understand the process in jurisdictions in which they work.)

- The clerk of the court issues a **warrant** for the arrest of the person charged (if the person has not been arrested already). According to Black's Law Dictionary, a warrant is "a written order issued and signed by [an appropriate official], directed to a peace officer or some other person specially named, and commanding him to arrest the body of a person named in it, who is accused of an offense."
- An **arraignment,** where the charge is read to the accused, is held. The arraignment is often held in a lower court. Typically, a plea is entered. In some states, this step is referred to as an **initial appearance.**
- **Plea bargaining,** when the prosecutor negotiates with the defense lawyers over the kind of plea the suspect might enter on a specific charge, can take place at any juncture. It often takes place after the arraignment but before the preliminary hearing. At this time, the prosecutor might propose that, in exchange for a plea of guilty, the state will bring a lesser charge against the suspect. The prosecutor might propose, for example, that the state bring a charge of assault instead of a charge of aggravated assault, a more serious crime that carries a more stringent penalty. In return, the defendant would plead guilty as charged, and the state would be spared the time and the expense of further proceedings. Plea bargaining, which helps unclog the courts, is a common practice. According to Denniston's "The Reporter and the Law," the "terms of a plea bargain ordinarily will have to be disclosed in open court, and usually will be subject to some inquiry by the judge as to the advisability of the bargain." Denniston wrote that the purpose of plea bargaining "is to determine whether a trial might be avoided, and a just result reached, by encouraging a person whose guilt is not in serious doubt to plead guilty or 'no contest.' " Criminal cases often conclude through plea bargaining.
- A **preliminary hearing** is held at which the state must present evidence to convince the presiding judge that there is probable cause to believe that the defendant committed the crime he or she is being charged with. If the judge agrees that there is probable cause, he or she will order the defendant bound over for trial.

- In some states, in lieu of a preliminary hearing, a **grand jury** is convened to determine if there is probable cause that a crime has been committed and if there is probable cause that the person charged with the crime committed it. A finding of probable cause is not, however, the same as a finding of guilty. That is determined at a trial. A grand jury is so labeled because it has more members than a trial jury. The number of people who serve on a grand jury varies among jurisdictions. In Arizona, for example, 16 people are impaneled. Nine are needed for a quorum.
- A date for another arraignment is set. The second arraignment is held in a court that has jurisdiction over the case.
- The **defendant** appears at the arraignment, where the judge reads the charge and explains the defendant's rights.
- The defendant then pleads guilty or not guilty. If the defendant pleads not guilty, a trial date is set. If the defendant pleads guilty, the judge sets a date for sentencing.
- For defendants who plead not guilty, a jury is selected.
- Once the trial is under way, opening statements are made by the prosecuting attorney and by the defense attorney.
- The prosecuting attorney presents evidence (the state's evidence is always presented first).
- The defense attorney then presents evidence.
- Final motions and closing arguments are heard.
- The judge then reads instructions to the jury.
- The jury deliberates and returns with a verdict.
- The judge enters a judgment on the verdict.
- If the defendant is found guilty, the judge sets a date for sentencing.
- After a presentence hearing, the judge will pronounce sentence.
- The defendant, if unhappy with the verdict, may appeal to a higher court. In most states, the death penalty is appealed automatically.

All these steps are potentially newsworthy. Reporters must of course be extremely careful to attribute statements to legal documents or to the person who makes the statements in court. Accurate reporting based on legal documents or statements made in court is virtually libel-proof. (See Chapter 25 for a discussion of libel defenses, including the privilege of reporting.) The source of information should be clear to the reader. It is always sound practice to attribute information, but it is particularly important when covering litigation.

For a complete discussion of the steps in a criminal case and the role of the journalist in the process, Denniston's book "The Reporter and the Law" is an excellent source.

Reporting Criminal Cases

As stated earlier, steps in criminal proceedings can vary. To illustrate general reporting procedures, however, this section will trace the coverage of a criminal case by *The East Valley Tribune* in suburban Phoenix.

The Incident

Coverage of this case started in May with a story about a missing 13-year-old girl. More than 13 months and 100 stories later, a man was convicted of murdering and raping the teen-ager.

Tonia Twichell, a police beat reporter, wrote the first story about the girl's disappearance. It began:

> Officers combed alleys, flew over canals and poked through garbage Thursday in search of clues to the disappearance of 13-year-old Christy Fornoff who vanished Wednesday while collecting for her Tempe newspaper route.
>
> Police, dogs, Tempe's mounted patrol, a Phoenix police helicopter, the Tempe police ultra-light aircraft and officers in squad cars and on foot blanketed central Tempe neighborhoods and fields.
>
> After peering under every desert bush for a mile, Tempe officers closed their command post Thursday afternoon at Bekin's Van Lines, 1888 E. Broadway Road.
>
> Christy, a Connolly Junior High School seventh-grader, who turned 13 on May 3, last was seen by her mother at the Rock Point Apartments complex at 2045 S. McClintock Drive.

The story went on to say that Christy's parents were confident that she would be found. The story quoted investigating officers; it noted that Tempe police were questioning felons living in the area who had been convicted of assaults and sexually related crimes; it described the girl; and it noted that *The Arizona Republic/The Phoenix Gazette* had offered a $5,000 reward for information concerning the girl's whereabouts.

A story published the following day, also written by Twichell, contained the bad news. The summary lead told the story:

> A maintenance man discovered the body of 13-year-old Christy Fornoff—dead of asphyxia—at 5:50 a.m. Friday, wrapped in a white bedsheet behind a dumpster in the same apartment complex where she was last seen.

The second paragraph included background on the girl's disappearance and the necessary attribution for the cause of death:

> Christy, who disappeared Wednesday evening while collecting on her paper route, died of asphyxia, according to the Maricopa County Medical Examiner's Office. She was wearing the same clothing she was last seen in: blue shorts, a white pullover, white tennis shoes and a black bathing suit underneath.

The story concluded with additional background but noted that further details about the girl's death were not available because the police had ordered a blackout of all information about the slaying. In the sixth paragraph, the story mentioned the name of the maintenance man who had found the body: Don Beaty.

The Tribune's police reporters and general assignment reporters continued to keep pace with developments in the slaying. One follow-up story noted that the police were making progress in the investigation, but that they declined to say whether they had any suspects or if they expected an arrest soon. Another story focused on the fact that Beaty had lost his job as maintenance man at the apartment complex. The reporter John D'Anna's story opened with a summary lead and contained background. It began:

> The maintenance man who found the body of 13-year-old Christy Fornoff, the Tempe newspaper carrier raped and smothered to death eight days ago, says he has lost his job because of the furor over the investigation. He also said he plans to sue.
>
> Don Beaty, 29, has worked at the Rock Point Apartments, 2045 S. McClintock Road, for eight weeks. Beaty found the girl's body behind a dumpster in the complex two days after she disappeared while collecting for her *Phoenix Gazette* route.
>
> Since then, Beaty said he has been continually harassed by Tempe police, who initially told him he was a prime suspect. Beaty said since then police have told him he is not a suspect.
>
> On Friday, the management company that owns Rock Point told Beaty he could resign or be fired because he lied about having a criminal record on his employment application. He was given until 5 p.m. Monday to move out of his apartment.

The story included several extensive direct quotations from Beaty. Beaty's name was not well-known when the story appeared, but that was soon to change.

Arrest

When an arrest was made, the police reporter, Twichell, carefully crafted a summary lead. The first part of her story naturally focused on:

- The fact that an arrest had been made
- Details on charges that were being requested
- Subsequent steps in the judicial process

The story began:

> The 29-year-old maintenance man who found the body of 13-year-old newspaper carrier Christy Fornoff on May 11 was arrested Monday in connection with her death.
>
> After 10 days of undercover police surveillance, Don Edward Beaty was taken to the Tempe City Jail, where he is awaiting an initial appearance today in Tempe Justice Court.
>
> First-degree murder, robbery and sexual abuse charges are being requested by the Maricopa County Attorney's Office and Tempe police.
>
> Beaty, who refused to talk to police and asked for a lawyer, could be released on his own recognizance after the court appearance, but probably will be ordered held on bail in the Maricopa County Jail in Phoenix.
>
> Beaty was arrested at 4:15 p.m. in the manager's office of Rock Point Apartments, 2045 S. McClintock Drive, where he worked until Friday.
>
> Police Chief Arthur Fairbanks refused to say what led to the Monday arrest, but other police officers said the department had been awaiting test results from the Department of Public Safety crime laboratory.

Twichell was careful to write that Beaty had been arrested *in connection with* the death of the teen-ager (some newspapers prefer to use *in suspicion of* or *in the investigation of*). Twichell did not write that Beaty was arrested *for* the death; doing so would imply guilt and could lead to a libel suit. Also note that the story said the arrest was made in connection with the *death*—not the *murder*. The AP Stylebook emphasizes that reporters should not write that a victim was murdered until someone is convicted of murder. The stylebook advises that reporters should use the words *killed* or *slain*.

Lower-Court Arraignment

The Tribune followed with a story about the lower-court arraignment, which is called an *initial appearance* in Arizona. In most states, an arraignment in a lower court (designations of these courts vary, but they include *police courts, municipal courts, magistrate courts* and *justice courts*) generally takes place within a specified short period after the arrest. At the arraignment, the charge is read to the accused, who then enters a plea. The plea normally becomes the story's lead. For the first time, *The Tribune* used in the lead paragraph the name of the accused, who by now was well-known to readers.

> Donald Edward Beaty pleaded innocent to charges of first-degree murder and child molesting in the death of 13-year-old Christy Fornoff Tuesday in a heavily guarded courtroom.
>
> After receiving phone calls threatening the 29-year-old Beaty's life, police switched courtrooms for the hearing, beefed up security and searched everyone who came to his initial appearance.
>
> Beaty, looking disheveled after a night in Tempe City Jail, was ordered held under $685,000 bail in Maricopa County Jail in Phoenix.
>
> Tempe Justice of the Peace Fred Ackel read Beaty the charges—which included robbery—and ordered him to appear May 31 for a preliminary hearing.
>
> Beaty is accused of killing Fornoff after she disappeared May 9 while collecting for her *Phoenix Gazette* paper route at Rock Point Apartments, 2045 S. McClintock Drive. Beaty, who worked as a maintenance man at the apartments until Friday, found Christy's body May 11 in the complex behind a trash dumpster.

The story went on to provide attributed, documented details on Beaty's prior criminal record.

Note that the story said Beaty pleaded *innocent.* Actually, a defendant would plead *not guilty.* But newspapers long ago adopted the style of using the word *innocent* instead of the words *not guilty* to avoid the possibility that the word *not* would be inadvertently dropped from the story and thus render it inaccurate.

Preliminary Hearing or Grand Jury Proceeding

At a preliminary hearing, the judge must decide if the state's case is adequate to bring the accused to trial. The state, often without revealing all the information it has, must nevertheless present sufficient evidence to convince the judge that there is probable cause to believe that the defendant committed the crime. The state's case at the preliminary hearing often includes specifics on the testimony of law enforcement officers or other officials. Their testimony will probably be pivotal in deciding whether there is sufficient reason for the accused to stand trial.

As noted earlier, the procedure in some states is to bypass a preliminary hearing by referring the case to a grand jury, which will determine if there is probable cause that the person charged with the crime committed it. If the grand jury determines that there is sufficient evidence, it will return an indictment known as a

true bill. If the grand jury decides that sufficient probability does not exist that the accused committed the crime, it will return a **no bill.**

In Arizona, both procedures are used: a preliminary hearing will sometimes be held; at other times a case is referred to a grand jury. The prosecutor can exercise either option. The Beaty case was referred to a grand jury.

The Tribune's police and general assignment reporters had been covering the Beaty story to this point. Once the case went to the grand jury, however, a court reporter, Mike Padgett, took over. Grand jury proceedings are held behind closed doors. Details are given to the press if a true bill is returned. Padgett's first paragraphs were punchy and to the point:

> A Maricopa County grand jury has indicted Donald Edward Beaty on charges of sexual assault and first-degree murder in the death of 13-year-old Christy Ann Fornoff of Tempe.
>
> And a county official said Thursday tighter security will surround Beaty's arraignment next week.
>
> Beaty, 29, was indicted by the grand jury late Wednesday. News of the indictment was not released to reporters until Thursday after Beaty received his copy, said Jane Bradley, spokeswoman for the county attorney's office.
>
> Beaty's bond remains at $685,000. His scheduled arraignment is at 8:45 a.m. Wednesday before Maricopa County Superior Court Judge John H. Seidel.
>
> Bradley said Seidel's courtroom is the smallest in Superior Court and easier to guard.

Higher-Court Arraignment

If the judge at the preliminary hearing decides that the evidence is sufficient, or if a grand jury returns a true bill, the accused is arraigned in a court that has jurisdiction. In Arizona, felony cases are heard in Superior Court. A **felony,** according to the American Bar Association's booklet "Law and the Courts," is "a crime of a graver nature than a misdemeanor [and generally is] an offense punishable by death or imprisonment in a penitentiary." The same source defines a **misdemeanor** generally as an offense "punishable by fine or imprisonment otherwise than in penitentiaries."

Padgett always makes an effort to sit in on arraignments, even though most last only a few minutes. "You never know when someone—usually one of the attorneys—will come up with something newsworthy," he said. Generally, however, most arraignment stories lead with how the accused pleads to the charge. *The Tribune* story began:

> Donald Edward Beaty pleaded innocent Wednesday to charges of first-degree murder and sexual assault in the slaying of Tempe newspaper carrier Christy Ann Fornoff.
>
> At Beaty's arraignment, Superior Court Judge John Seidel scheduled a July 5 pretrial conference and a July 25 trial before Judge Rufus C. Coulter.
>
> Both court dates are expected to be postponed by defense and prosecution motions.
>
> Beaty, 29, remained in the Maricopa County Jail Wednesday in lieu of posting $685,000 bail.
>
> Seidel accepted Beaty's pleas of innocent from a public defender, Mary Wisdom, who was appointed to defend Beaty.

Note that Padgett's story contains background on the circumstances that led to the arraignment. Reporters should always provide background. Background information can be developed by reviewing clippings of previous stories written about the case and by interviewing attorneys and others close to the case. Even when reports of judicial proceedings are in the news for an extended time, journalists must assume that most readers do not know the background of the case.

The Trial

Pretrial developments. Before a trial, newspapers will generally publish stories that summarize past developments and inform readers of new information. The Beaty trial, for example, was delayed eight times. Naturally, *The Tribune* followed the developments closely. One of Padgett's pretrial stories focused on the pervasive publicity that the Beaty proceedings were generating.

A story by Tonia Twichell focused on Beaty's hunger strike in the county jail to protest what he alleged to be poor conditions and threatening behavior by guards.

One of Padgett's main pretrial stories discussed the issuance of a gag order. A **gag order,** which is sometimes called a **protective order,** is a judicial mandate ordering the press to refrain from disseminating specific information or ordering those associated with the trial or the investigation not to discuss the case with the press. (See Chapter 25 for a discussion of legal ramifications of the fair trial–free press issue.) Padgett's story began:

> A Maricopa County Superior Court judge Friday issued a gag order and banned camera coverage of all pretrial proceedings in the Christy Ann Fornoff murder case.
>
> On two other motions, Judge Rufus C. Coulter Jr. said he would decide later whether to ban cameras during the trial of Donald Edward Beaty, and whether it should be moved because of publicity.
>
> The trial is scheduled to start next Wednesday, but it is expected to be reset. If it appears an unbiased jury cannot be chosen in Maricopa County, Coulter said he then would rule on defense attorney Michael A. Miller's motion to move the trial.
>
> "But it's consistently been my policy to wait until at least an attempt has been made to select a jury," the judge said.

After providing background on the case, Padgett elaborated on the gag order. He wrote:

> Since his arrest, Beaty and his attorney have granted interviews with reporters. But now the court's gag order means Beaty, Miller, police, witnesses, court staff, county prosecutors, Department of Public Safety laboratory staff and anyone else associated with the investigation cannot discuss the case with reporters.
>
> "In the future, all information about this case will flow through (Superior Court information officer) Rob Raker," the judge said Friday.
>
> When attorney David J. Bodney, representing the First Amendment Coalition, attempted to argue the judge's gag order and asked whether the judge would accept a written objection, the judge said he won't change his mind.

Jury selection. More than six months after Beaty was arrested and arraigned, the case was ready to go to trial. A jury was selected. This generally merits a news story. Padgett wrote:

> From a crowd of 150 prospective jurors, nine men and seven women were selected Tuesday to hear the first-degree murder trial of Donald Edward Beaty, the man charged in the slaying of 13-year-old Christy Ann Fornoff of Tempe.
>
> After jury selection, defense attorney Michael A. Miller objected to public questioning of the jurors, saying they should have been interviewed individually. Maricopa County Superior Court Judge Rufus Coulter said there was no need for that.
>
> "I'm satisfied we have a fair and impartial jury," the judge told Miller.
>
> Beaty's trial, which is expected to last a month, is set to begin Thursday, even though attorneys still are waiting for the return of some evidence and a final scientific report.

Testimony. Reporters provide gavel-to-gavel coverage of only the most important trials. Certainly the Beaty trial fell into that category for *The Tribune* and Padgett.

"I try never to miss the opening day of a trial," Padgett said. "On that day, most prosecuting attorneys are going to say, 'That guy did it and we have the evidence to back up the charge.' Once they are finished, the defense attorneys will say something like, 'The evidence is not there. My client did not do it.' They will try to shoot holes in the opening statement of the prosecutor. You want to get the opening statements down for the readers. I often use a tape recorder because I want to get as much color as possible. I also take notes. I have found, however, that tape recorders allow me to be more productive and more accurate."

Relatively minor cases might go to the jury within a day or so. Major trials, however, run much longer. Beaty's first trial lasted seven weeks (and then, after it ended in a mistrial, a second trial lasted six weeks more).

Reporters must diligently follow the testimony in long-running major trials. "You have to spend several hours each day in the courtroom," Padgett said. "It does not do much good to drop in for an hour or so, because you have no way of predicting what will happen. One hour is not enough. You simply must sit and listen. Sometimes it gets really tedious. There were days at the Beaty trial when it would be 4 p.m. and I still did not have a strong lead for the day. On several days, key testimony during the last 30 minutes of the session gave me my lead. If you are not there for the duration, you risk missing the most significant angle."

Also, reporters must often keep track of developments in less significant trials. Padgett, for example, was following other cases while he was devoting most of his time to the Beaty trial. "You often have to call the judge's secretary to keep up with other trials," Padgett said. "It is important to get to know the judge's staff—the secretary, the bailiff, the court reporter. Get to know them on a first-name basis. It helps when you have to telephone them for updates because you are tied up with a major case like Beaty's. Secretaries are very helpful. They keep the judges' schedules, and so they always know what is happening."

Reporters occasionally trade information. Padgett, however, does not like to do this because he can never be sure how accurate the information is. "I don't want to risk getting duped," he said. "If other reporters ask me for basic (nonexclusive) information, I provide it, but I always refer them to an attorney or to someone involved for verification."

There is no substitute for being in court, always looking for the most interesting, most significant developments. Without warning, for example, shouting matches can erupt. Because these spur-of-the-moment developments are often important to a story, reporters have to be alert for them. They will be difficult to reconstruct if you have to rely on secondhand information.

Attribution is also imperative when reporting key testimony. It is absolutely essential that quotations be accurate and that readers be made aware of who is making statements or articulating opinions. (See Chapter 8 for guidelines on methods and placement of attribution.) Here are the first four paragraphs from one of Padgett's stories on the trial (note how careful he was to attribute all information):

Christy Ann Fornoff, the 13-year-old girl found killed last May in an apartment parking lot, died of asphyxiation after a brief struggle, a medical expert testified Tuesday.

Dr. Heinz Karnitschnig, chief Maricopa County medical examiner, also said a lack of decomposition indicated the girl's body was kept in a cool place for nearly two days before she was found May 11 in the parking lot of the Rock Point Apartments, 2045 S. McClintock Drive. Karnitschnig said he performed the autopsy within hours after the body was found. A few bruises were found on her, but nothing to indicate there was a violent struggle before she died.

"There may have been (a struggle), but only a minimal amount of struggle," he said. "Her airway was occluded in some kind of way; either a hand was held over her or she was pushed into some permeable materials (such as a pillow)."

Karnitschnig was the fourth person to testify Tuesday in the trial of Donald Edward Beaty, charged with first-degree murder and sexual assault in the Fornoff girl's death.

Padgett also provided quotations from other testimony and closed his story with the fact that the names of 147 persons were on a list of potential witnesses.

On another day, Padgett focused on testimony from a forensic expert. Note how Padgett did not identify the expert by name—only by occupation—in the lead paragraph. That way, the lead was more streamlined and the authoritative attribution was sufficient. Here are the first three paragraphs:

Human hairs found throughout Donald Edward Beaty's Tempe apartment exhibit "similar characteristics" to hair taken from Christy Ann Fornoff, the 13-year-old girl he is accused of slaying, a forensic expert testified Tuesday.

In addition, a pubic hair taken from the girl's body is similar to Beaty's pubic hair, according to testimony of Edward Trujillo, a state Department of Public Safety laboratory technician.

Trujillo said human head hair found in Beaty's apartment doorway, on the bathroom floor, on and under his living room couch, from a bed sheet found in his spare bedroom closet and from vacuumed particles from the closet are similar to the victim's head hair.

Mistrials. Padgett followed the case day by day for seven weeks. The case was sent to the jury, but the jury was unable to break a 10–2 deadlock. A mistrial was declared, and a second trial was scheduled.

About a month after the mistrial was declared, the second trial began. A new jury was in place. The second trial might be a new experience for members of the jury, but some of the testimony and evidence will be familiar to other participants in the trial and to reporters. Reporters nevertheless must stay alert for new developments. During the fifth week of the second trial, for example, Padgett's story led with a significant development. His story began:

Saying "I didn't mean to kill her . . . I'm not the terrible man they say I am," Donald Edward Beaty confessed last December to slaying 13-year-old Christy Ann Fornoff, a jail psychiatrist testified Monday.

Dr. George S. O'Connor, under a judge's orders to tell Beaty's private conversation with him, testified: "He (Beaty told me he) didn't mean to kill her. She had been making a lot of loud sounds and her mother was outside."

O'Connor's testimony came in the fifth week of Beaty's second trial, and it was by far the most incriminating evidence to date in a case that has been built on circumstantial evidence.

The first trial—less the psychiatrist's testimony—ended earlier this year in a hung jury.

Beaty, 30, is charged with first-degree murder and sexual assault in the Fornoff girl's death. She vanished May 9 while on her newspaper route at the Rock Point Apartments, 2045 S. McClintock Drive in Tempe.

The vivid direct quotation was the natural lead. Sometimes it is best to paraphrase testimony to streamline the first paragraph. But when the quotation is extremely powerful, it is best to use it verbatim. Note also how Padgett was careful to weave background information into his story relatively high. The story continued with a discussion of the appropriateness of the psychiatrist's testimony.

Closing arguments. Padgett was in court for the closing arguments. "Just as I never want to miss opening statements, I never want to miss the closing arguments," he said.

After the closing arguments, the case goes to the jury. If the closing occurs late in the afternoon, the judge will generally instruct the jury members to return the next morning to begin deliberations.

"I always try to stay in the courtroom when the jury is locked in its room deliberating," Padgett said. "I want to be there when the jury comes out."

Verdict. The climax of a criminal trial is the verdict. There is no sacrosanct formula for writing verdict stories, but they should contain these essential ingredients:

- Outcome (was the accused found guilty or not guilty?)
- Precise charge (for example, murder)
- Length of jury deliberations
- Date of sentencing
- Range of penalties established by law
- Reactions of the defendant, the defendant's family and the defense attorneys
- Reactions of the victim or the victim's family
- Reaction of attorneys for the prosecution
- Background of the case
- Review of key testimony throughout the trial
- Possibility of appeal

Here are the first six paragraphs of Padgett's story on the verdict (note how he worked many of the key ingredients into the first part of his story):

A Maricopa County Superior Court jury deliberated less than 10 minutes Thursday before finding Donald Edward Beaty guilty of murdering and raping 13-year-old Christy Ann Fornoff of Tempe.

Beaty, 30, is scheduled to be sentenced July 22. He could face the death sentence for first-degree murder.

Defense attorney Michael Miller said he probably would appeal.

> Reaction to the verdict ranged from relief by the girl's family to anger from a woman who sat behind Beaty in court and who had taken charge of having his clothes cleaned and pressed.
>
> The victim's parents, Roger and Carol Fornoff, were not in court Thursday morning because they hadn't expected a decision so quickly. After the verdict was announced, they met with reporters in the county attorney's office.
>
> "It's a relief for us, knowing this man has been convicted," Carol Fornoff said. "We know he won't be on the streets. He won't be doing it again."

Note that the word *murdering* is used after the conviction.

Often, the lead practically writes itself in a verdict story, but the reporter must work hard to assemble the remainder of the account. Padgett, for example, always concentrates on the reaction of the defendant. "I keep my eyes on the defendant," Padgett said. "I want the defendant's reaction—or lack of reaction. Some do not react; some almost crumble; and some will sit down and put their heads on the table."

Padgett also likes to interview spectators, lawyers and jurors. "The primary job is to get quotes from the jurors," he said. "While the trial is going, they can't talk to anyone. But once they render a verdict, they can talk to the press if they want to. I like to talk to them. I want to know what convinced them one way or the other. It also is important to talk to the attorneys. It is very hectic. You try to be in several places at the same time, but it doesn't work very well. I always try to get to the jurors first. They sometimes disappear in a hurry. I can usually get back to the lawyers."

The Tribune reporter always tries to interview the defendant. "It is almost impossible to get to a defendant—right away—who has been found guilty," Padgett said. "Sometimes, you might be able to get in a couple of questions walking down the hallway, but that's about it."

Padgett routinely tries to get word to the defendant—through the defense attorney or through the bailiff—that he would like to interview him or her. "If the defendant agrees to talk, you've got an exclusive," Padgett said. "The worst that can happen is that the defendant will say no."

Padgett was surprised after the Beaty trial; the defendant got word to the reporter that he would like to be interviewed. "I can't take much credit for getting the interview," Padgett said. "Beaty had not liked the coverage by some of the other newspapers, and so he called me." *The Tribune* ran the interview story on the front page with the verdict story. It began:

> "I don't care what the jury said—I know I am not guilty," Donald Edward Beaty declared shortly after a jury convicted him of first-degree murder and sexual assault in the death of 13-year-old Christy Ann Fornoff.
>
> In a jail-house interview after the verdict was returned, Beaty contended that key witnesses lied under oath, that his attorney gave up toward the end of the trial and that he had wanted to testify in his own defense.
>
> "I'm innocent, and I intend to fight it," Beaty said. "I didn't even see her that night. That's the whole deal."

The story continued with more vivid quotations.

Coverage of criminal proceedings generally does not end with the verdict. There will be a presentence hearing, a sentencing and often an appeal. Let's look at these.

Presentence hearing. Padgett was in court for Beaty's presentence hearing. The lead summarized the testimony of Beaty's former wife. The story began:

The ex-wife of convicted child-murderer Donald Beaty testified Thursday that he molested several children, including his newborn daughter, and sold their son for $1,000 and a pickup.

Mary Gray said the day she returned from the hospital with their daughter, Beaty fondled the baby and "would laugh about it."

More than 50 spectators sat silently and listened intently during a presentence hearing as Gray and six others graphically described Beaty's past sexual conduct.

Their frank testimony became the only evidence presented to Superior Court Judge Rufus Coulter, who will pronounce either a life or a death sentence Monday.

The damaging testimony never came to light during Beaty's first or second trial. The first ended in a hung jury.

Defense Attorney Michael A. Miller called Thursday's presentence hearing "a mud-slinging contest" by people "who don't like Don Beaty." He said he asked Beaty if he wanted to testify and Beaty said no.

In fact, no one testified for Beaty. His brother and sister in Tennessee, whose transportation to Phoenix had been paid, failed to appear. Another brother in Phoenix, Fred Beaty, who was in court, didn't testify and declined to talk to a reporter after the hearing.

Sentencing. Padgett was well-prepared to write the story of the sentencing. He had been covering the Beaty trial for months; he had background information at his fingertips; and he understood the nuances of the case. His lead was straightforward:

Donald Edward Beaty, convicted last month of the first-degree murder of 13-year-old Christy Ann Fornoff, Monday was sentenced to die in the gas chamber.

Maricopa County Superior Court Judge Rufus Coulter Jr. told Beaty he had "committed the offense in an especially heinous, cruel and depraved manner."

The death penalty will be appealed automatically.

Coulter also sentenced Beaty, 30, to the maximum term of 28 years in prison for sexually assaulting the girl.

Beaty, who has maintained his innocence, stood before the judge handcuffed and dressed in blue jail fatigues and soiled red tennis shoes. Almost imperceptibly, he began trembling after he was sentenced to death.

Appeal. Four years after Beaty was sentenced to die, the case was still in the judicial system. *The Tribune* continued to follow developments. Richard Polito's lead was to the point:

The U.S. Supreme Court on Monday rejected the appeal of Donald Edward Beaty, an apartment complex maintenance man who is on death row for the sex-slaying of 13-year-old Christy Ann Fornoff, a newspaper carrier.

The girl vanished while collecting at a Tempe apartment complex where Beaty worked.

The justices let stand rulings that Beaty received a fair trial and properly was sentenced to death.

The story went on to quote the victim's mother, who said that she was disheartened to hear that further appeals were likely. Background on the slaying followed.

The story ended with this paragraph: "There has not been an execution in Arizona since 1963, and Beaty still has avenues of appeal through the federal courts."

The Aftermath

Three years after Beaty's appeal was rejected, the story continued to develop when the Fornoffs entered into a settlement in a wrongful-death suit they had brought. Lynn DeBruin's story in *The Tribune* began with these paragraphs:

> Roger Fornoff says he'll never get over the murder of his youngest daughter, Christy Ann.
>
> He and his wife, Carol Ann, still celebrate her birthday. On May 3 this year, she would have been 21.
>
> "We stopped crying for the time being. But a song can set you off, or meeting a friend," Roger Fornoff said.
>
> What has helped most has been talking it out in bereavement groups.
>
> "There's a lot of need for it. People hurt," the Tempe resident said.
>
> With that in mind, he said he and his wife hope to use part of their $1.5 million settlement from the wrongful-death suit for such programs.
>
> The Fornoffs reached the settlement this week in their suit against the operator of the apartment complex where their 13-year-old daughter was killed . . . by maintenance man Donald Edward Beaty.
>
> "I have to believe that (if they had done more background checks), Christy would still be alive," Fornoff said.
>
> The Fornoffs filed suit . . . accusing Continental American Management Corp. of negligence in hiring Beaty to work at Rock Point Apartments.

The second half of DeBruin's story provided background on a case that had been in the news for nearly eight years. It also gave additional details on how the Fornoffs had devoted considerable time in recent years to calling attention to the need for schools and businesses to run sufficient checks on potential employees.

Analysis and Feature Articles on Criminal Cases

Coverage of the Beaty case by *The Tribune* illustrates that there are several newsworthy points as a case makes its way through the judicial system. The coverage often extends beyond courthouse drama. Analysis pieces and feature articles can accompany coverage of litigation. Alert reporters often pick up on items of interest to readers by keeping their eyes and ears open.

Padgett wrote several features and analysis pieces during the months of the Beaty litigation. Here are the first four paragraphs of one of Padgett's analysis pieces:

> On the periphery of the testimony and drama of Donald Edward Beaty's murder trial, a quiet circus of sorts is taking place.
>
> There is the judge's secretary who, in addition to her regular duties of supervising the judge's hectic daily calendar, is answering phone calls from prospective onlookers who ask directions to Maricopa County Superior Court in Phoenix. They ask whether parking is available, is it expensive, how is the food in the cafeteria, is the courtroom packed and show times.
>
> They pack the courtroom and those who don't get in wait until a seat becomes available. They know the cameras are rolling, too, some even hopeful they'll get on TV. And curiously, one juror appears to take catnaps during this trial, one of the Valley's most publicized in recent years.
>
> They come to see Beaty, the Tempe maintenance man indicted on charges of first-degree murder and sexual assault in the May 9 death of 13-year-old Christy Ann Fornoff.

Again, Padgett was careful to put background information on the case relatively high in the story. After inserting the background, Padgett provided direct quotations from sources and more observation.

Dealing with Sources

Whether they are covering murder cases or misdemeanors, reporters must develop a reliable network of sources. In addition to gaining the respect of judges and lawyers, reporters should strive to be on a first-name basis with sources such as:

- Secretaries
- Bailiffs
- Court public information officers
- Clerks
- Record-keeping personnel

These sources can help alert reporters to new cases and to developments in ongoing cases. Sources should be cultivated and never taken for granted.

Experience can help reporters deal with sources. Some attorneys and law enforcement officers, for example, crave publicity. Sometimes the information they provide is helpful. At other times they are clearly supplying less-than-essential information for their own political gain.

Experience helps reporters recognize the motives sources might have for parting with information. "Clerks are good sources because they do not have a vested interest in most cases," Robert Rawitch of the *Los Angeles Times* said. "Prosecuting attorneys and defense lawyers, although they can be helpful, do have such a vested interest. As a reporter, you must be wary of that."

Sources, particularly lawyers and judges, sometimes try to evade questions by giving rambling answers packed with legalese. Persist. Continue to repeat the question until the answer is clear and understandable.

Padgett's coverage of the Beaty proceedings illustrates the diligence and the attention to detail that are necessary when reporting on litigation. Naturally, not all the criminal cases reporters cover gain the attention that the Beaty proceedings generated. Padgett's comments on gathering information, writing stories and dealing with sources and fellow reporters apply equally, however, to less spectacular cases such as burglaries and assaults.

Civil Cases

Often, dozens of **briefs** (written reports in which lawyers set forth facts that support their positions) are filed in civil suits. Reporters must periodically check court **dockets** that record progress in specific cases. All complaints filed, motions made and other developments in a case are recorded chronologically on a docket.

In Superior Court for Los Angeles, to take one example, the average civil suit is in the system—from time of **filing** until trial or settlement—approximately four years. It is not unusual for cases to extend six or seven years. Metropolitan court systems are often short on personnel for civil cases, and legal requirements force them to give priority to criminal cases. The normal criminal cases in Superior Court for Los Angeles will generally conclude from two to four months after the arrest.

Understanding record-keeping systems is a critical element in good court coverage. Reporters in small cities do not face the crunch of cases that metropolitan reporters do, but regardless of the case load, reporters must watch dockets and calendars closely. In Superior Court for Los Angeles, the civil courts reporter for the *Los Angeles Times* is usually following the progress of more than 500 pending suits. "It is a bookkeeping nightmare," Rawitch said.

The filing system in Los Angeles' civil division of Superior Court is efficient and detailed, but Rawitch said that reporters must spend more than an hour each day checking case numbers listed on the court calendar.

The Basic Civil Process

Steps taken in a civil suit vary. Procedural maneuverings can be complex and time-consuming. According to "Law and the Courts," here is the basic process:

- The **plaintiff** (the party bringing the suit) selects the proper jurisdiction (federal or state system, and the appropriate court thereof).
- The plaintiff files a **complaint** (sometimes called a **petition**) against a party (called the *defendant*). The complaint usually contains a precise set of arguments that include the damages sought. **Damages** are the estimated monetary value for the injury allegedly sustained. Of course, the filing of a complaint does not ensure that the plaintiff has a cause of action.
- The defendant is served with a **summons,** a writ informing him or her that he or she must answer the complaint.
- After a specified period, the defendant is required to file his or her **pleading,** or answer, to the plaintiff's charges.
- **Depositions** (out-of-court statements made by witnesses under oath) are taken.
- After all the pleadings have been filed, attorneys for both parties appear before a judge at a pretrial conference to agree on the undisputed facts of the case. (Often a **settlement** is reached at this point without trial.)
- If no settlement is reached, the case is scheduled for trial.
- Testimony as to the dispute is presented, and arguments are heard at the trial.
- After the arguments, the judge instructs the jury (unless the defendant has waived his or her right to a jury proceeding) on legal considerations.
- The jury goes to its room for deliberations.
- The jury returns with a verdict.
- The verdict is announced, and the judge enters a judgment on the verdict.
- If either party is unhappy, an appeal can be made.

Reporting Civil Cases

Scores of civil suits are filed each day in metropolitan jurisdictions. Certainly not all of them are newsworthy. Reporters must decide which suits are important and then must constantly check court dockets for developments. The following suit—the

William Westmoreland suit—involved a well-known Army general and the Columbia Broadcasting System, and thus would clearly be considered newsworthy.

Examining a Complaint in a Civil Suit

In the Westmoreland suit, the complaint, filed in the U.S. District Court for the District of South Carolina, Greenville Division, was assigned Civil Action No. 82-2228-3.

The beginning of the complaint looked like this:

GENERAL WILLIAM C. WESTMORELAND,
United States Army (retired)
P.O. Box 1059
Charleston, South Carolina 29402
(803) 577-3156

Plaintiff

v.

COLUMBIA BROADCASTING SYSTEM, INC.,
51 West 52nd Street
New York, New York 10019
(212) 975-4321
and
VAN GORDON SAUTER, President
of CBS News
524 West 57th Street
New York, New York 10019
(212) 975-4153
and
GEORGE CRILE,
555 West 57th Street
New York, New York 10019
(212) 975-2915
and
MICHAEL WALLACE,
555 West 57th Street
New York, New York 10019
(212) 975-2997
and
SAMUEL A. ADAMS
Route 3, Box 442
Leesburg, Virginia 22075
(703) 882-3351

Defendants

Complaint

(Libel, False Light)

(1) Jurisdiction herein is founded on 28 U.S.C. Sec. 1332 (a). Plaintiff and defendants are residents of different states and the amount in controversy exceeds $10,000, exclusive of interest and costs.

(2) Venue is proper in this Court under 28 U.S.C. Sec. 1391 (a).

(3) Plaintiff, General William Childs Westmoreland, United States Army, Retired, is a resident of Charleston, South Carolina. General Westmoreland was the Commander in Chief of the United States Military Assistance Command in Vietnam ("MACV") from June 1964 until June 1968. General Westmoreland was also the chief U.S. advisor to the Vietnamese military forces during the same four year period.

(4) Defendant, Columbia Broadcasting System, Inc. ("CBS"), is a corporation organized under the laws of the State of New York, whose principal place of business is located at 51 West 52nd Street, New York, New York, 10019. CBS News is a division of CBS and its principal place of business is located at 524 West 57th Street, New York, New York, 10019.
(5) Defendant Van Gordon Sauter is President of CBS News, and has been since March 1, 1982. Upon information and belief, he is a resident of the State of New York.
(6) Defendant George Crile is an employee of CBS. Defendant Crile was the producer of the CBS broadcast "The Uncounted Enemy: A Vietnam Deception" (hereinafter "the Broadcast"). Crile also participated in the Broadcast as an on and off camera interviewer. Upon information and belief, he is a resident of the State of New York.
(7) Defendant Michael Wallace is an investigative reporter employed by CBS. Wallace served as narrator and interviewer for the Broadcast. Upon information and belief, he is a resident of the State of New York.
(8) Defendant Samuel A. Adams served as a paid consultant to CBS for purposes of the Broadcast, receiving $25,000 therefor, and appeared as an interviewee in the Broadcast. Upon information and belief, he is a resident of the Commonwealth of Virginia.
(9) On January 23, 1982, CBS aired the Broadcast at issue, a "CBS Report" entitled, "The Uncounted Enemy: A Vietnam Deception." The Broadcast was aired on stations WLTX-TV in Columbia, South Carolina, WBTW-TV in Florence, South Carolina, and numerous other CBS affiliates in all 50 states. The number of viewers of the Broadcast was estimated by the Nielsen Company to have been 20,041,920.
(10) The Broadcast dealt with the U.S. military's handling of intelligence regarding enemy troop strength estimates in the year prior to the 1968 Tet Offensive of the Vietnam War. The Tet Offensive began on or about January 30, 1968.

Count One

(Libel)
(11) Plaintiff adopts herein by reference paragraphs 1 through 10.
(12) On Friday, January 22, 1982, CBS placed identical full page advertisements in The Washington Post, The New York Times and upon information and belief in other newspapers across the country (hereinafter the "Advertisements"). A copy of the Advertisement which appeared in The New York Times is attached hereto as Exhibit A. The Advertisements announced a CBS Report, to be aired on January 23, 1982 and entitled, "The Uncounted Enemy: A Vietnam Deception." The Advertisements were composed of a drawing of men in uniform, seated around a conference table, with the word "Conspiracy" superimposed in large letters. The text of the Advertisement read in part:

> CBS Reports reveals the shocking decisions made at the highest level of military intelligence to suppress and alter critical information on the number and placement of enemy troops in Vietnam. A deliberate plot to fool the American public, the Congress and perhaps even the White House . . .

The complaint continued with six more paragraphs under Count One. It went on to list four additional **counts** [parts of a civil complaint claiming specific wrong done] of allegedly libelous information broadcast about Westmoreland by CBS. The complaint concluded with the following:

WHEREFORE, plaintiff, General William Childs Westmoreland respectfully prays that the Court award him the following relief:

(A) Judgment in his favor and against each defendant, and all of them, jointly and severally, in the amount of $40,000,000 compensatory damages.
(B) Judgment in his favor and against each defendant, and all of them, jointly and severally, in the amount of $80,000,000 punitive damages.

(C) Judgment in his favor for the costs of this action, including attorneys' fees.
(D) Interest on all amounts awarded.
(E) Such other relief as to the Court may deem just and proper.

Jury Demand

Plaintiff hereby demands trial by a jury of 12 on all issues.

Essential Ingredients of Stories on Civil Suits

A story about the Westmoreland civil suit—like all court-related articles—should contain certain essential ingredients:

- It should tell who is bringing the suit (the plaintiff).
- It should tell who is being sued (the defendant).
- It should tell when the suit was filed.
- It should identify the parties as fully as possible.
- It should provide background on the circumstances that brought about the suit.
- It should give specifics on the damages sought.
- It should give the defendant's response to the complaint.
- It should fully attribute all information. When appropriate, it should make absolutely clear to the readers that the information came from court records.

As mentioned earlier in this chapter, reporters and their newspapers can defend themselves against libel charges by quoting accurately from official court documents.

If they are on deadline, reporters will sometimes report the filing of a complaint on the basis of information supplied by the attorneys in the case or by the clerk of the court; but the safest, soundest journalistic procedure is to write the story from a copy of the complaint. Comments from attorneys can be used to further explain the filing.

Most of the essential ingredients of civil-suit stories can be found in the first two paragraphs of an article by Sally Bedell published in *The New York Times:*

> Gen. William C. Westmoreland, former commander of United States military forces in Vietnam, filed a libel suit yesterday against CBS Inc. for its portrayal of him in January in a documentary, "The Uncounted Enemy: A Vietnam Deception." The documentary said he was the head of "a conspiracy at the highest levels of American military intelligence, to suppress and alter critical intelligence on the enemy" during the Vietnam War.
>
> The suit asks for $120 million in compensatory and punitive damages. General Westmoreland said that if he were to win, he would donate the money to charity.

The 19-paragraph story went on to provide details on where the suit was filed; it named the other defendants in addition to CBS; it quoted an attorney who specializes in First Amendment cases; it quoted one of the defendants in the suit; it quoted the lawyer for Westmoreland; and it gave a synopsis of the current state of American libel law.

The first five paragraphs of an Associated Press story also provided essential information:

> Gen. William Westmoreland filed a $120 million suit against CBS Monday, charging the network libeled him in January in a documentary saying the U.S. military falsified reports on enemy troop strength in Vietnam.
>
> The suit was filed in federal court in Greenville, S.C., according to Dan Burt, Westmoreland's attorney. The retired general, who headed the Army in Vietnam for four years, lives in South Carolina.
>
> Westmoreland asked for $40 million in general damages and $80 million in punitive damages. If he wins, the money will be donated to charity, he said.
>
> Westmoreland called the show "vicious, false and contemptible."
>
> "When CBS first asked me to participate in the making of this documentary," Westmoreland told a news conference, "I had no idea that they had prejudged my participation in that war, nor that they would attempt to prove that I or anyone else was in any way capable of any illegal or improper acts."

The AP article went on to quote a CBS official, to provide background on an internal investigation of the documentary that CBS had conducted, to refer to an article in *TV Guide* magazine about the documentary and to quote Westmoreland's attorney further.

Because of a deadline, the AP story was apparently written without the reporter's having reviewed the actual complaint that had been filed. Attribution, however, was made to Westmoreland's attorney. As mentioned earlier, it is always sound practice for the reporter to have a copy of the complaint so that there can be no doubt that the information used is indeed accurate and fully attributable to the document.

The approaches used in the *Times* and AP articles were similar in that each provided complete, essential, accurate information in easy-to-understand language. Some civil suits can be extremely complicated and technical; reporters must always translate the "legalese" into understandable language.

Considerations in Covering a Civil Suit

Most civil suits do not involve high-ranking officials or major networks; and more than 90 percent never make it to trial. According to Tom Spratt, a courthouse reporter for *The Phoenix Gazette,* many civil suits merely "fade away" after an initial filing.

Still, if a story has been written about the filing, a reporter must be diligent in following the case to its conclusion. It is important to report dismissals, settlements or judgments. Many civil suits make headlines when they are filed, but as they become tangled in the shuffle of paperwork and forgotten in the passage of time, they are not followed up by reporters. This, of course, is unfair to the parties involved. If a newspaper reports that a malpractice suit seeking $15 million in damages was filed against Dr. John Jones, the newspaper owes it to its readers and to the parties in the suit to report how the case is ultimately decided.

No magic formula determines if a civil suit is newsworthy. Spratt, however, tries to examine all civil complaints systematically. He glances at the general headings listed at the tops of the complaints: contract; tort motor vehicles (a **tort,** according to "Law and the Courts," is "an injury or wrong committed, either with or without force, to the person or property of another"); tort non-motor vehicles (this category includes personal wrongs and is often newsworthy); and non-classified (which includes an assortment of cases that do not fit under common headings).

Spratt also looks at the damages sought. But the fact that a plaintiff is seeking more than $1 million does not necessarily make the complaint newsworthy. "After the reporter is on the courthouse beat for a while, he or she will begin to recognize which lawyers consistently file suits seeking huge damages that never get very far in the judicial process," Spratt said.

After Spratt isolates cases of potential interest by reading the headings and determining the damages sought, he reads the complaints in their entirety to see if they seem to be particularly important, interesting or significant.

Once a civil suit has been filed and Spratt decides that it deserves coverage, he often calls the attorney who filed it for a further explanation. "I make an effort to talk to attorneys for both parties, whenever possible," Spratt said. "This is particularly important in civil cases where filings and rulings are very complicated." Sometimes, to get additional background, he also calls attorneys who are not involved in the suit but who are experts in the area being litigated.

Newspapers do not cover most civil suits at every step in the judicial process. Often, a short story is written when a suit is filed, and another story is written when the suit is dismissed or settled or when there is a judgment. Some civil cases, however, because of the huge damages sought or because of the parties or issues involved, merit expanded coverage.

Example: A Suit for Damages

An example of a civil suit that did receive expanded coverage is a case filed by a Phoenix family after a natural-gas explosion in their apartment. This suit had a number of newsworthy elements: astronomical damages were sought, the defendants included public utilities and it had been a spectacular explosion.

The filing. The story of the filing, which was published in *The Arizona Republic,* contained the essential items of importance. The lead paragraph focused on the damages sought:

> Members of a Phoenix family critically injured April 20 by a natural-gas explosion in their apartment have filed a $92 million suit in Maricopa County Superior Court.

The next two paragraphs provided background on the plaintiffs. The story concluded by listing the defendants, by providing details outlined in the complaint and by quoting the parties.

Developments during the suit. Procedural maneuverings are extensive in complicated civil suits, but generally they are not newsworthy. As noted earlier, civil suits can drag on for years. Occasionally, however, between the filing and the conclusion of litigation, developments arise that are newsworthy and deserving of coverage. This was the case in our example.

Jeff South's story in *The Phoenix Gazette* revealed a new development:

Because of their desperate plight, burn victims Gloria Crawley and her children will get their day in court sooner than expected.

Judge James Moeller of Maricopa County Superior Court has approved a motion giving priority to the Crawleys' lawsuit in connection with an April 20 explosion that ripped through their apartment at 6565 N. 17th Ave.

At the request of the Crawleys' attorney, Moeller set the case for trial next April.

The story went on to list the defendants, to provide background on the $90-million-plus suit, to explain the reasoning advanced by the Crawleys' lawyer concerning the need for the accelerated process and to explain that Mrs. Crawley's husband had died from burns 30 days after the explosion. The story also quoted from documents filed by the Crawleys' attorney, Charles Brewer:

The Crawleys' "desperate physical, financial and mental situation may become irreversible and irrecoverable" unless the case goes to trial soon, Brewer said in court documents.

The settlement. As is often the case in civil actions, the suit in our example was settled out of court. Naturally, this settlement merited a major story. Brent Whiting of *The Arizona Republic* used a straightforward lead:

An out-of-court settlement of $8.1 million was reached Thursday in a suit filed by members of a Phoenix family critically injured last year when a natural-gas explosion ripped through their apartment.

Background on the suit was given in the next two paragraphs. Then, in the fourth and fifth paragraphs, Whiting provided details of the settlement. Note how he was careful to attribute the information.

Charles M. Brewer, Mrs. Crawley's attorney, said the settlement will be paid by Arizona Public Service Co. and by Palo Verde Apartments Inc., owner of the 16-unit complex.

Brewer said that under the terms of the settlement, APS and its liability-insurance carrier will pay $7.1 million, and the remaining $1 million will be paid by the carrier for the apartment owner.

A logical question naturally surfaced: had there been other civil suits in the state that involved such a large settlement? If the answer could be documented, it would probably belong in the lead. Here, it was merely an opinion that was placed lower in the story and was fully attributed:

"This is probably the biggest settlement in Arizona history," Brewer said. "I would have liked to have tried the case, but when you have this kind of settlement offer, you have to accept it."

The story went on to provide other pertinent particulars: an update on Mrs. Crawley and her children and background on the filing.

✔ A Checklist for Covering the Courts

Robert Rawitch of the *Los Angeles Times* estimated that it takes a reporter six months to a year to become attuned to covering courts in a metropolitan setting. Naturally, it does not take as long to gain a grasp of the judicial system in a non-metropolitan setting. But the job of court reporters for big-city dailies and for community dailies or weeklies is the same: they must inform their readers accurately, in understandable language.

"The role of the court reporter is to break through the legal jargon—to translate the special role of the court to the everyday role of the reader," Rawitch said. "But just like the specialist on any beat, the court reporter must be careful—once he or she begins to feel comfortable with the system—not to lose sight of what is important to the reader."

Covering the courts involves more than reporting on procedural filings in civil suits or on spectacular criminal trials. Many good court-related stories are the result of a reporter's persistence in searching for information that can lead to in-depth stories on the workings of the judicial system or on the interaction among those involved in the system.

Following are some specific steps to follow.

- ❏ *Learn the Judicial System.* Reporters need to master the intricacies of the court systems in their jurisdictions. State systems vary. Do not be afraid to ask questions. It is imperative to grasp the workings of the system.
- ❏ *Learn the Record-Keeping System.* Once the procedural and structural aspects of a court system are mastered, reporters need to know how to ferret out information. Knowledge of the record-keeping system is essential.
- ❏ *Provide Sufficient Background for the Reader.* For example, even though the Beaty case was in the news for more than a year, reporter Mike Padgett never failed to provide a background paragraph in each story that explained how the case had started.
- ❏ *Double-Check Facts.* Names, ages, addresses and the specific charges should always be verified. The stakes are high. Reporters never want to make errors, but there is a monumental difference between saying that John Jones was the leading scorer for his basketball team (when he was really only the second-leading scorer) and saying that John Jones was charged with driving while intoxicated (when he was really charged with running a stop sign).
- ❏ *Use Complete Names and Addresses or Occupations.* To avoid confusion—and to head off potential lawsuits—list full names with middle initials, ages, addresses and occupations of persons charged with crimes.

CHAPTER TWENTY-TWO

SPORTS

During a seminar on "Sports: A Cultural Obsession," which focused on the role and responsibilities of the media, William L. Winter, president and executive director of the American Press Institute, said: "The enterprise of sports permeates our society. . . . Newspaper sports sections are rife with stories of colleges that cheat to get athletes in their doors and to keep them there, even when they break the law. The same sections carry frequent reports of professional athletes who have been arrested for illegal use of drugs, or spousal abuse, or for nightclub brawls, drunken driving or other violations of the law or of commonly accepted standards of behavior."

(*Steve Manuel*)

Clearly, the impact of sports on our society has become greater, just as the games themselves have changed.

Athletes are bigger, stronger and faster. They also often behave differently from those who went before them.

"Imagine, if you will, the great Jim Brown pulling himself up off the end zone turf of Cleveland Stadium, slamming the football into the ground, ripping off his helmet and engaging in a vulgar dance designed for nothing other than calling attention to the wonders of Jim Brown," Winter said. "It was Jim Brown's coach, Paul Brown, who, you may recall, reacted to an end zone dance by one of his players by saying, 'Son, act like you've been there before.' "

The content of America's sports pages has changed dramatically in recent years, but one thing has not: On each Sunday morning from late summer through autumn, millions of college football fans turn quickly to the sports sections of their daily newspapers.

The panorama of America comes to life through the datelines of Associated Press stories:

SOUTH BEND, Ind.—So what if Notre Dame started its celebration a few seconds early? After a summer of discontent, can anyone blame the Fighting Irish?

As the final seconds ticked down on No. 22 Notre Dame's 36-20 upset of No. 5 Michigan on Saturday, Irish fans rushed the field, players lifted Coach Bob Davie on their shoulders and there was a good old-fashioned pep rally going on.

But a timeout had been called. The field was cleared and the final two plays were run. Then the celebration began all over again.

MORGANTOWN, W. Va.—It was a display so impressive that West Virginia Coach Don Nehlen shuddered.

"I hope that team is Number 1," he said while shaking his head moments after top-ranked Ohio State slammed the door on Nehlen's 11th-ranked Mountaineers, 34-17.

SYRACUSE, N.Y.—Tee Martin, understudy the past two years to Peyton Manning, threw for two touchdowns and ran for one Saturday as No. 10 Tennessee eked out a 34-33 victory over mistake-prone Syracuse in the season-opener for both teams.

Jeff Hall won it with a 27-yard field goal as time expired, but it was Martin who wouldn't let Tennessee lose.

EUGENE, Ore.—The Oregon offense picked up where it left off last season. Now it looks as if the Ducks might actually have a defense to make all those points stand up.

Akili Smith threw four first-half touchdown passes and Reuben Droughns rushed for 202 yards and scored three touchdowns as Oregon flattened No. 23 Michigan State 48-14.

But there are few datelines any bigger during the college football season than Lincoln, Neb., where from 1962 through 1972, Coach Bob Devaney's teams captured two national championships, and from 1973 through 1997, Coach Tom Osborne's squads claimed three national titles and won at least nine games each year while compiling a record of 255-49-3.

Nebraskans who didn't know the outcome of the post-Osborne era season-opener likely were few and far between. Still, readers turned to the *Omaha World-Herald* for details the morning after the game.

LINCOLN—Louisiana Tech's record-setting passing show Saturday failed to spoil the coming-out party Nebraska threw for Frank Solich.

The Huskers relied on offensive efficiency to make up for some defensive deficiencies in registering a 56-27 victory over the Bulldogs in the Eddie Robinson Football Classic at Memorial Stadium. The win, before the 221st consecutive sellout crowd of 76,021, provided Solich with a successful debut as Tom Osborne's replacement.

The *World-Herald's* Lee Barfknecht, who covered the Cornhuskers for the last 15 years of the Osborne era, could probably handle almost any journalistic assignment. A Phi Beta Kappa, he was graduated from the University of Nebraska with high distinction. He majored in journalism and minored in English, history and economics.

"I'm happy as a sportswriter," Barfknecht said. "I think our pages are as well-read as most other sections of the newspaper, and people often read them critically because many readers consider themselves to be sports experts."

When he first joined the *World-Herald,* Barfknecht was primarily responsible for high school sports coverage in the Omaha-Council Bluffs, Iowa, metropolitan area. On autumn Saturdays, though, he helped cover the Nebraska Cornhuskers. After a few years, he moved to the University of Nebraska beat exclusively. His responsibilities included coverage of all 21 varsity sports at NU.

While covering the NU beat, Barfknecht has made hundreds of round trips from Omaha to Lincoln (approximately 50 miles each way) to cover events on campus. He averages about five trips a week during the fall sports season, four trips a week during the winter and three trips a week in the spring.

The main focus of his coverage is obviously sports such as football, men's basketball, baseball and track. But in recent years, 17 of Nebraska's 21 sports programs have been ranked in the top 20 nationally. So Barfknecht's assignments and enterprise ideas have been broad-based. He has won several Associated Press state sports writing awards and, on multiple occasions, he has been Nebraska sportswriter of the year.

Trends in Sports Coverage

Sports Writing Styles

One of the best-known American sportswriters, Grantland Rice—a Phi Beta Kappa graduate of Vanderbilt who majored in Greek and Latin—was fond of using verse. More than half a century after Rice penned his first sports stories for the *Nashville* (Tenn.) *Daily News,* he wondered in his book "The Tumult and the Shouting" why he had never gotten around to giving the score in a piece he wrote in 1901. It began:

Baker Was an Easy Mark
Pounded Hard Over Park
Selma's Infield Is a Peach
But Nashville Now Is Out of Reach
All of the Boys Go Out to Dine
And Some of Them Get Full of Wine

After their long, successful trip the locals opened up against Selma yesterday afternoon at Athletic Park, and when the shades of night had settled on the land the difference that separated the two teams had increased by some dozen points.

Throughout the whole morning a dark, lead-colored sky overhung the city, and a steady rain dripped and drizzled, only stopping in time to play the game, but leaving the field soft and slow. . . .

During the first part of this century, flowery prose like this adorned the sports pages. Today, however, sports writing styles have changed.

It is true that some writers still use such **sports writing clichés** as "flashy freshmen," "sophomore sensations," "brilliant field generals," "lanky leapers" and "diminutive, sparkplug point guards," but in general today's sports pages are filled with better, more balanced writing than ever before.

That change has been a while coming. Stanley Woodward, the sports editor of the old *New York Herald Tribune,* may have been a bit optimistic when he wrote in his book "Sports Page" (published in 1949) that the better sportswriters had started to abandon hyperbole, profuse praise and strained similes. He wrote: "The horrendous clashes of fearsome Tigers and snarling Wolverines, which usually were concluded in purple sunsets, now are taboo in the better sports departments. The sports editor doesn't mind picturesque writing if the reporter can handle it, but he no longer wishes to see his vehicle smeared with wild and indiscriminate pigments."

Woodward wrote that sportswriters should strive for the middle ground; they should avoid the **"gee whiz" school** (where athletes perform nothing but heroic feats) just as they should avoid the **"aw nuts" school** (where gifted athletes and great games are treated with near disdain).

Many of today's sportswriters are providing readers with the high-quality coverage and writing that Woodward sought in 1949. Woodward has theorized that World War II helped to put sports into better perspective. Writers no longer routinely extended hero status to mere athletes. A more spartan, streamlined sports writing style evolved after World War II, with an emphasis on the five W's and H—and on a horde of statistics. And that style in turn started to give way, in the 1970s and 1980s, to a more balanced approach. Some of today's best sports writing certainly includes valuable statistical information and essential ingredients (who won, what the score was, who starred), but it is more literary than the bare-boned scores-and-statistics approach that held sway at many newspapers after World War II.

An examination of today's sports pages shows that clichés and hyperbole are not extinct, but they are found less frequently, and praise is not as lavish or gushing as it once was. Soft news approaches are used more frequently on stories that would once have been topped only with summary leads. Even morning newspapers are providing more analytical writing than ever before.

High School Sports Coverage

Nearly all the country's daily and weekly newspapers provide readers with extensive coverage of high school sports. The prep sports beat can be viewed as the best and the worst of assignments. The *Omaha World-Herald* reporter Terry Henion, a former prep sports editor of the *Colorado Springs Gazette Telegraph* and a former sports editor of *The Hastings* (Neb.) *Tribune,* described it:

> It is a genuine pain in the neck sometimes to have to keep statistics and never get to see the game. It's a pain to listen to a wild-eyed mother question your roots because you misspelled her daughter's name in a summary. It's a pain—and somewhat frightening—to have a father scream wildly at you because you are not giving his son enough ink. It's a pain to cover six or seven games a week and rarely see your family.

But it's a pleasure to watch an awkward and timid sophomore develop into a poised and polished senior. It's a pleasure to see kids play games for the fun of it without the pressure and hard sell of college and pro sports. It's a pleasure to see the smiles on their faces and in a way a pleasure to see their tears when they lose because the emotions are honest.

In the long run, Henion said, "The pleasures of covering high school sports greatly outweigh the pains, and that's why I enjoy it so much. High school sports are what sports were always meant to be: kids playing kids' games."

At high schools there are no sports information directors cranking out play-by-play charts, keeping statistics and providing quotations from players after the game. The work must be done by the sports reporters, who usually find themselves walking the sideline at a football game or crammed into tight quarters at a basketball game. *Covering* a prep game is almost a misnomer, according to Henion. He thinks that *documenting* might be a better term. Henion said that the prep writer cannot always concentrate on doing what a good writer should do—answer the human interest questions that fans would ask if they had access to the locker room. Instead, reporters must keep the statistics (or rely on a 14-year-old student manager who tends to inflate his or her team's numbers), interview the coaches and players and then formulate a readable account of the game. Often the work is done under deadline pressure.

One of the best ways for a college student to gain professional journalism experience is to work as a stringer covering high school sports. A **stringer** is a part-time newspaper or broadcast correspondent who covers a specific geographical area or team for a news medium that is often located elsewhere. Sports editors of area dailies generally hire stringers during busy football and basketball seasons. Even the smallest dailies often cover at least a handful of local prep teams. By serving as stringers, young journalists get an opportunity to cover sports, write sports and occasionally see their bylines. A stint as stringer often leads to a spot on the staff.

Lee Barfknecht said that preparation for a high school game is more difficult than preparation for a college game. Before college games, constantly updated Web sites and mounds of releases from sports information offices provide easy access to statistics and other background. The reporter who covers a high school game, however, must generally dig up statistics and background by reviewing clippings and by talking to coaches, players or athletic directors.

Also, there is sometimes a logistical problem when covering high school sports. Barfknecht pointed out that most Omaha high schools play their games in a handful of major stadiums in the city.

"A lot of times, the coach puts the players on the bus almost immediately after the game," Barfknecht said. "You almost have to tackle them to get an interview. My strategy is to hit the losing coaches first—they tend to be the ones who want to get out of the stadium quickly. Also, by getting to them immediately after the game, you often get a very honest reaction from them."

After Barfknecht talks with the losing coach, he heads to the winning coach. "I always congratulate the coach and ask if a couple of star players can stick around for a minute to be interviewed," Barfknecht said.

The *World-Herald* sports department has no guidelines on who should be interviewed after a high school contest. Barfknecht, though, likes to gather quotations from both winning and losing coaches along with what he calls "kid quotes." "Some people think high school athletes don't have much to say," Barfknecht noted. "But sometimes they make for better interviews than college athletes."

Some high school coaches, however, prefer that reporters not talk to players after games. The wise reporter will respect those wishes. A quotation taken out of context can harm a player, a coach or an entire program. An important thing to remember when interviewing high school athletes is that these are youngsters—they are not the presumably poised athletes in college or professional programs.

As Henion said: "You're dealing with kids who usually never have felt the sting of a razor, let alone the cutting edge of a perhaps cynical and bored writer. Temperance is the word when quoting high school athletes."

College Sports Coverage

Coverage of major college football is a choice assignment; it is also a demanding one. Barfknecht is one of four reporters who cover Nebraska Cornhusker football games for the *World-Herald*. "We arrive at the stadium about an hour and a half before the game," Barfknecht said. "We have lunch and discuss things going on in college football that day, and as game time approaches, we get our notebooks out to outline basically what we will be doing once the game starts. We don't preplan coverage too much because we don't want to limit our flexibility. We all know our basic assignments."

The four reporters watch the game from the press box. One writes the primary account of the game; one does sidebar material and the Nebraska postgame account; and one writes sidebars and covers the opposing team's locker room. The fourth reporter, the sports editor, writes an analytical column. In addition, a team of photographers in the press box shoots sequential black-and-white photos of every play. Photographers are also stationed around the field, two shooting color photos and the rest shooting black-and-white.

Even on days when Barfknecht is writing sidebars and covering the opponent's locker room, he keeps a play-by-play chronology of the game action. The sports information office provides complete play-by-play accounts at the half and after the game, but Barfknecht said that he has a better grasp of turning points and trends if he charts the games himself.

The *World-Herald* writers talk as the game progresses. "We pretty much know the writing approaches each of us will use," Barfknecht said. That way, when the four writers are scrambling to file stories after the game, there will be a minimum of duplication.

Most of the Cornhusker fans who file out of the stadium after a game probably relax and savor a victory over dinner. But the real work begins for the *World-Herald* reporters once the final gun sounds.

The first *World-Herald* sports deadline for some outstate editions (those that are delivered to counties in the western part of Nebraska) is 6:15 p.m. Games that begin at 1:30 are usually over by 4:30. Thus, the reporters have less than two hours to conduct interviews and file their stories. When starting times are moved to 2:30 or 3 o'clock to accommodate television, the deadline pressure is even more intense.

The reporter responsible for the main game story will write about 10 inches of narration on first-half highlights during the halftime. That way, after the game is over, the reporter can immediately structure a top to the story, write a transition and move directly to the second-half narration.

When the game ends, the reporters go to different areas of the stadium. "We all use tape recorders," Barfknecht said. "It is an individual decision, but we all rely strongly on them. The NU locker room is sometimes so crowded that you can't get your pen and pad out to write freely, and so we record."

The "cooling off" period for players and coaches is generally 10 minutes in the Nebraska locker room. Then the interviews begin. The writer responsible for the game story interviews the head coach; the sidebar writer interviews the Husker players. In the opponent's locker room, another *World-Herald* reporter interviews both the head coach and the players.

Within a half hour—at about 5:15—the *World-Herald* reporters are back in the press box. They strive to assemble a 25-inch game story, two sidebars and a column for the first outstate editions.

After the 6:15 p.m. deadline has been met, the reporters have 2½ hours before their next deadline.

"The writer doing the game story usually starts completely over," said Barfknecht. "All of us go back and transcribe our tapes fully. Then we try to analyze what we have. We decide how many stories we have and who and what we are going to write about."

After these decisions are made, the reporters call the Omaha newsroom, where three editors—who are assigned to the "Husker Desk"—are in a corner focusing exclusively on coordinating coverage of the Nebraska game.

"We try to let them know who and what we are going to write about so they can start gathering art and photos to supplement our stories," Barfknecht said. "Also, if any of us have ideas for the photo page (a full page of pictures that runs after every game), we pass them on to the desk. For example, if there is a great run that might be good in photographic sequence, we will suggest that. We try to keep the line open to Omaha from the NU press box as the evening wears on."

After the writers transcribe their notes, they then "sit down and sweat a lot," Barfknecht said.

Barfknecht, who normally covers the opponent's locker room, is sometimes hard-pressed to write lively sidebars. "I've seen a lot of long faces and quiet players in opponents' locker rooms," Barfknecht said. Nebraska's opponents have had little to cheer about. Since 1962, the Cornhuskers have won about 80 percent of their games.

The day is still not over for the reporters after they meet their 9 o'clock deadline. Deadline is 10 o'clock for editions that will be distributed in the Omaha metropolitan area. The reporters take the extra 60 minutes to determine if they have overlooked anything and to compile information for the fixture items: "What Others Said" (the lead paragraphs written by writers from other newspapers who covered the game) and the "Answer Box" (where some interesting tidbits about the game appear in question-answer format).

"We usually struggle out of the press box at about 10 o'clock," Barfknecht said.

The crew then heads back to Omaha. Barfknecht does not get much rest, however. On Sunday, he prepares his agenda for the coming week.

Reporting Sports

Working with Statistics

A City Hall reporter must know how to read a budget; a court reporter must know how to interpret a legal brief; a sports reporter must be able to work with statistics. Every sport has its own statistical language. Reporters do not necessarily have to be experts on each phase of every sport (although that certainly helps), but they must have a working knowledge of scoring procedures and significant statistics of the sports that they cover.

Deciphering Statistics

A portion of a **box score** for a basketball game follows:

ASU	Mn	FG	FT	Rb	At	PF	St	Tr	Pt
Deines f	22	2–7	0–1	7	0	5	0	0	4
Everett f	20	2–3	1–1	9	0	5	0	0	5
Taylor c	26	1–4	1–1	4	1	2	0	5	3
Thomson g	34	6–17	4–4	1	7	1	5	0	16
Beck g	35	4–10	5–6	7	3	4	1	2	13

The numerals listed above tell us a lot about what five players did in a basketball game. We know, for example, that they play for Arizona State University. We also know how many minutes each of them played in the regulation 40-minute game, how many field goals they made (and attempted), how many free throws they made (and attempted), how many rebounds they grabbed, how many assists they had, how many personal fouls they accumulated, how many steals they made, how many turnovers they committed and how many points they scored.

At a glance, we can tell that guards Bobby Thomson and Steve Beck were the leading scorers with 16 and 13 points, respectively. We can also tell that Thomson and Beck played most of the game; that center Jon Taylor had a rough night (he had more turnovers than he had points); that forward Warren Everett led the team in rebounds; and that Everett and forward Jim Deines both fouled out.

Team statistics are computed by adding numerals from individuals. For example, after adding the **individual statistics** of the Arizona State substitutes to the statistics listed above, we find that in an 81-72 loss to the University of Oregon in a Pacific 10 Conference basketball game, ASU made 28 of 70 shots from the field (a frigid .400); made 16 of 20 free throws (a respectable .800); snared 44 rebounds (10 more than Oregon); had 14 assists (compared with 19 for Oregon); made 29 personal fouls (compared with 18 for Oregon); had 8 steals (compared with Oregon's 4); and committed 15 turnovers (the same as Oregon). These are significant statistics.

Sports reporters, of course, could delve deeper. They could, for example, determine how many points both teams scored within 5 feet of the basket (this might reveal which team was able to get the ball consistently deep inside the lane); they could determine which team had the most blocked shots; or they could determine how many times the lead changed hands.

Depending on available space, on readers' interest in the game or on the importance of the contest, the reporter would decide which statistics are worth mentioning in the story.

The key is this: Reporters covering basketball or any other sport must know which statistics are relevant and important. For instance, what are the magic numbers in football? For starters, there are scores by quarters, first downs, rushing yards, passing yards, return yards, passes attempted and completed, number of punts and average distances, number of fumbles and fumbles lost, number of penalties and yards penalized, and time of possession. Many of these statistics are also relevant for individuals. In gymnastics, it is important to know that judges score a routine or exercise by totaling points from four areas for a maximum of 10.0. Those four areas are execution; combination; difficulty; and risk, originality and virtuosity (known as ROV).

It is not the purpose of this chapter to provide a comprehensive summary of applicable statistics for all sports. It is imperative, however, for aspiring sports reporters to realize that they must understand the statistical undercurrents of the sports they cover. If they do not, they cannot report or write intelligently.

Using Statistics Effectively

Following are suggestions for using statistics in sports writing.

- *Provide Readers with Statistical Information That Is Useful for Understanding the Contest or Its Trends.*
- *Avoid Being a "Statistics Junkie."* There is a difference between providing readers with information necessary to understand what happened at the contest and inundating them with irrelevant strings of numerals that interrupt the flow of the story.
- *Review Team and Individual Statistics before a Contest.* Preparation is a key ingredient in solid coverage of any sport. If you review team and individual statistics before a basketball game, when you write your story after the game you can note, for example, that a 22-points-per-game scorer was held to 11 points; that a team normally making 53 percent of its field goal attempts shot a cold 37 percent; or that a team averaging 11 turnovers a game made 23. These statistical differences help put a victory or a loss into perspective.
- *Review Statistics after a Game for Trends and Turning Points.* It is standard to focus on individual and team totals, but running **play-by-play charts** can help the reporter piece together important sequences in the contest. Play-by-play charts provide a chronology of a basketball game. The chart notes who scored, on what kind of shot, who fouled, who turned the ball over and what the score was at the time of the play. For example, the play-by-play chart could tell a reporter whether one team went 6 minutes and 23 seconds without scoring a field goal (while the other team was making 10 field goals) or whether one team made six consecutive field goals midway in the half without a miss. These factors will probably be worth mentioning in the game story.

Going beyond Statistics

Reporters could put together accurate, readable game accounts merely by reviewing statistics. That, however, would not make for complete coverage of a contest.

Non-statistical information—insight and information not known even by readers who might have watched the game themselves—lifts a story beyond the ordinary.

Here are some ways for sports reporters to go beyond statistics.

- *When Walking the Sidelines or Sitting in the Press Area, Do Not Focus Exclusively on the Field or Court.* If you stalk the sidelines during a football game, you can often pick up on strategy discussed by players and coaches. If you sit in the stands or in the press box, you might notice the nervous parents of a star player.
- *Find Out Policies for Post-Game Interviews.* Gaining access to players immediately after a game can sometimes be difficult, but it is often essential to complete coverage. Many coaches demand a **"cool down" time** of 10 to 15 minutes before the press is allowed into the locker room after a game. Many teams have developed policies in response to female sportswriters who have sought equal access to male locker rooms. Some teams have made locker rooms off limits to all reporters; these teams often provide an interview room where athletes go after they have showered and dressed. This, of course, creates delays and could cause some reporters to miss their deadlines. Most teams try to accommodate writers of both sexes. It is important, however, to know the policies of the teams being covered.
- *Talk to Coaches.* Touch base with them before the event if possible. That way, you will not be a stranger in the post-contest interview. Strive to ask intelligent questions. If a team loses an opportunity to win a basketball game because of a controversial traveling call with 8 seconds remaining, don't ask the coach what the turning point of the game was.
- *Talk to Players.* Do not select only the stars for interviews. Others might have some interesting insights into the game. How did the unsung offensive tackle in a football game, for example, feel after butting heads the entire game against an all-conference defensive lineman?
- *Talk to Trainers.* In addition to providing you with information about specific individual injuries, trainers might pass along other useful tidbits such as the general condition of the team and whether any special conditioning drills will be conducted during the next week's practice sessions.

Writing a Sports Story

Writing for Morning Newspapers

For the most part, morning and afternoon newspapers cover the same athletic events played the night before, but the writing angles should be different. Reporters at morning (A.M.) newspapers face tight deadlines because their newspapers are printed late at night, often right after the athletic event. Traditionally, morning newspapers give a straightforward account of the preceding night's game; although as noted earlier, even these newspapers are increasingly opting for softer analytical leads. Readers who open their morning newspapers might not know the score of the game they are interested in; thus, even when using a soft lead, writers for A.M. newspapers generally try to get the scores of games high in the stories. The reporter who covers the contest is generally rushed to meet a deadline; the story must be complete, but quite often there is not sufficient time to conduct extensive interviews or to develop an extended feature lead.

When Nebraska played a second-round National Invitation Tournament game at Ohio State, morning newspapers and the wire services could have led with a terse, to-the-point summary paragraph such as this:

> COLUMBUS, Ohio—Seven-foot center Grady Mateen scored 20 points to lead Ohio State past Nebraska 85-74 Monday night in a second-round National Invitation Tournament game.

This summary lead provides key information—*who, what, when, where, why* and *how.*

Lee Barfknecht covered the game for the *Omaha World-Herald.* He was under deadline pressure, but his newspaper had allotted space for his story. Barfknecht saved the score for the second paragraph, but being aware that many of his morning readers would be eager for details of the game, he jammed mounds of essential information into the first five paragraphs of his story:

> COLUMBUS, Ohio—Even without its steering wheel, Ohio State's basketball machine stayed on the right path long enough to run over Nebraska.
>
> "This just shows that Ohio State is a good team with or without Jay Burson," NU forward Dapreis Owens said after the Buckeyes beat the Huskers 85-74 in the second round of the National Invitation Tournament before a sellout crowd of 13,276 at St. John Arena.
>
> Owens, a freshman from Mansfield, Ohio, scored a career-high 18 points and senior guard Eric Johnson added 23. But it wasn't enough to avoid a loss that ended NU's season at 17-16.
>
> Ohio State, 19-14, played without Burson, the All Big-Ten guard who fractured a neck vertebra a month ago.
>
> But the Buckeyes made up for his 22-point average and stayed on course for a third NIT final four trip in the past four years by driving the ball inside.

Writing for Afternoon Newspapers

Sports reporters working for afternoon (P.M.) newspapers have time to write comprehensive stories that encompass not only the essential ingredients (victor, score, team records, key statistics and so on) but also a unique angle or feature lead. They therefore cannot use the standard excuse for a poorly written story—they cannot say they were under extreme deadline pressure. These sports reporters should analyze the games they cover—probing into the *why* and the *how*—because most of their readers know the score before they open their newspapers. The reporters should combine a synopsis of the game, a statistical summary and an angle not covered in the morning newspapers or by the electronic media. The afternoon account should not be primarily a play-by-play rehash.

Barfknecht, when writing his story for the afternoon editions of the *World-Herald,* relied more extensively on direct quotations and analysis. He had more time to write his story. He conducted several post-game interviews to put the trends and the statistical accounts of the contest into better perspective. Because it was the last game of the season for the Cornhuskers, Barfknecht, in his P.M. version, chose to look ahead to the next campaign. Barfknecht once again placed the score in the second paragraph, but the first part of his story was laden with quotations.

COLUMBUS, Ohio—Danny Nee didn't sugar-coat it.

Nebraska's basketball coach told his team after Monday's season-ending 85-74 loss at Ohio State in the second round of the NIT that the Huskers' 17-16 record wasn't anything to brag about.

"Basically, I felt this team never really reached its potential," Nee said. "We could have done better."

Were there nods of agreement in the locker room to that statement?

"I don't care what they say," Nee said. "I want them to show me."

Showtime for NU's returning players apparently starts immediately.

"Coach Nee said next year starts tomorrow," forward Dapreis Owens said, "and that we can't quit working or take vacation.

"We have to work hard to get better for the years to come."

Owens, a freshman from Mansfield, Ohio, showed his stuff with a career-high 18 points plus seven rebounds, while senior guard Eric Johnson poured in 23 points. But it wasn't enough to upset the 19-14 Buckeyes before a sellout crowd of 13,276 at St. John Arena.

Providing Extensive Coverage: A College Football Game

Most sports events can be covered effectively simply by writing a single game story. This was the case for the basketball game discussed in the previous section. Some sports events, such as the Olympic Games, the Super Bowl, the World Series and major college football games, however, are of such interest and importance to readers that more than one story will be written about them. The *Omaha World-Herald*'s coverage of Nebraska football games falls into this category.

For a Nebraska-Iowa State football game, Barfknecht wrote the main story for the *World-Herald.* His 78-paragraph game story was supplemented with the following:

Column by the sports editor

Four sidebars

Scoring summary in agate type

Color photo

Four black-and-white photos scattered throughout the Sunday section

Full picture page with an additional 11 black-and-white photos

Barfknecht's game story contained all the essential ingredients:

- Teams and score
- Reference to whether it was a conference or a non-conference game
- Site of the game
- When the game was played
- Key plays (who made them, which coach was responsible for calling them, etc.)
- Scoring summary
- References to star players
- Key offensive statistics (rushing and passing)
- Key defensive statistics (tackles, interceptions, fumble recoveries)
- Direct quotations by players
- Direct quotations by coaches

- Weather and its effect on the game
- Injuries and condition updates
- Results of previous games between the teams (the series record or outcomes of most recent games, whichever is most relevant)
- Overall records
- Conference records
- Reference to national rankings, if relevant
- Next games for both teams
- Historical significance, if any, of the game

Every sports fan in Nebraska probably knew the final game score before opening the Sunday *World-Herald.* Most fans had probably also listened to at least part of the game on the radio. With this in mind, Barfknecht waited until the 18th paragraph before providing narration of significant plays and scoring drives. In his lead paragraphs, he concentrated on presenting information that most readers may not have been aware of: the Husker defense held center stage in the Iowa State game. Barfknecht provided details early in his story:

> AMES, Iowa—The Nebraska defense felt it owed Iowa State something for what happened a year ago in Lincoln.
>
> Stamp that debt "PAID IN FULL," because Nebraska held Iowa State to 53 total yards in 54 offensive plays and never let the Cyclones inside the NU 37-yard line Saturday during a 44-0 victory at Cyclone Stadium.
>
> "We were embarrassed by the way we performed last year," safety Bret Clark said.
>
> "They just ran up and down the field on us," defensive coordinator Charlie McBride recalled.
>
> Though Nebraska won that game 72-29, the Cyclones gained 502 total yards, the most the Blackshirts allowed all season.
>
> But on Saturday, Iowa State did not run up the field. Or down the field. Or across the field—at least without somebody in a white jersey and red pants running next to them. The defensive effort, in allowing Iowa State 53 total yards, is Nebraska's best of the season.

If Barfknecht had been writing a single story about the game—with no accompanying sidebars focusing on star players and comments by coaches—he probably would not have placed so much emphasis on significant statistics so early in his story. But because his story was supported with thousands of additional words, he was able to focus on the staggering statistical documentation. And he did so without ruining the rhythm of his writing. It is also apparent that Barfknecht had done his homework. He was writing the story on deadline, but he was able to weave statistics, direct quotations and background efficiently into his early paragraphs.

Beyond the Game—Contracts, Courtrooms and Boardrooms

When readers turned to the sports pages two decades ago, they read primarily about heroes: high-scoring basketball players; swift, elusive running backs; and fence-rattling baseball sluggers. Those stories, of course, remain the staple of sports coverage. But on any given day, readers can also find several stories about off-the-field happenings.

Stories about strikes by players and umpires, probes by the National Collegiate Athletic Association, drug investigations, antitrust actions, franchise moves, trials and contract negotiations have not taken over the sports pages, but on some days it might seem that way.

"We're definitely seeing more coverage in these areas," said Dennis Brown, the former sports news editor of *The Phoenix Gazette.* "I remember an instance when, as we approached deadline, we were looking for a story to put in an 8-inch hole. Somebody suggested that we put in the story about the Pirates being purchased and staying in Pittsburgh. Somebody else said that we could put in the story about drug allegations in the NFL. A third staffer, with a trace of a smile, suggested that we put in a 'real' sports story. We started looking through the copy, but all we could find was stuff on contracts, drugs and franchises. It's getting harder to tell if you are a sportswriter or a lawyer."

Brown said that he is not sure how extensively readers want to be informed about lawsuits, contract squabbles and drug trials. He suspects, however, that many of them prefer to read about the competitive on-the-field aspects of sports.

Still, sports pages need to provide coverage of off-the-field developments. Brown said, however, that the pendulum might have swung too far; he said that newspaper sports pages sometimes devote too much space to legal and business issues.

"We should cover these developments," he said. "But I think more of these stories should be handled in briefs columns unless they are really extraordinary. (*USA Today,* for example, often carries short items under the standing headline "Jurisprudence.") I'm not sure readers need to have a lengthy blow-by-blow account of where parties stand on contract negotiations. They need to know about such matters, certainly, but sports editors need to decide how many inches should be devoted to them."

✔ A Checklist for Sportswriters

Obviously, there is no magic formula for writing sports stories, and the approach will always depend on the circumstances. Here, though, are some general tips:

- ❑ *Go with a Summary Lead If It Is Warranted, but You Are Not Wedded to It.* The wire services will generally provide summary leads, and so many sportswriters take other approaches.

- ❑ *Avoid Chronological Approaches.* Always lead with the most significant aspect of the contest. For example, "Chuck Johnson hit a 15-foot jump shot with three seconds left to give Grand Junction a 61-60 basketball victory over Wymore Friday night." The game story would not begin like this: "Chuck Johnson controlled the opening tip for Grand Junction, and his team went on to beat Wymore 61-60 in basketball Friday night."

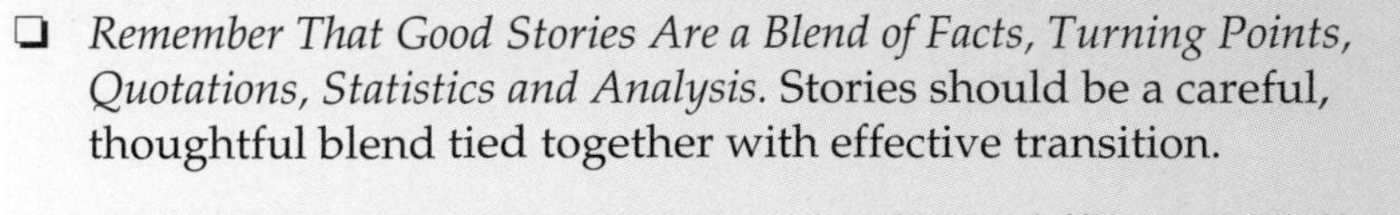

- ❑ *Remember That Good Stories Are a Blend of Facts, Turning Points, Quotations, Statistics and Analysis.* Stories should be a careful, thoughtful blend tied together with effective transition.

- ❑ *Avoid Clichés.* One-point victories are indeed "cliffhangers"; effective offensive line blocking often opens holes "big enough to drive the student body through"; and dominant teams often "take it to" the losers. Good writers, though, find more original descriptions.

- ❑ *Avoid "Ridiculous" Direct Quotations.* "We whipped 'em good," has a down-home ring to it, but it doesn't add much to the story.

- ❑ *Use Vivid Description When Appropriate.* You could write, "John Jones caught the winning touchdown pass with 14 seconds left." But it might be better to write, "John Jones swerved between two defenders, stretched high in the air, cradled the ball in his left hand and pulled it to his chest for the game-winning touchdown with 14 seconds left."

- ❑ *Double-Check Spellings.* Particularly at high school contests, spellings listed in the official score book and on the program can be different. Find out which one is correct.

- ❑ *Do Your Homework.* The more background information you take with you to a contest, the easier and the faster it will be for you to write the story once the contest is over.

Where to Turn Online

The National Collegiate Athletic Association maintains a comprehensive site (*www.ncaa.org*). It includes timely news and features; sports and championships, including comprehensive links to colleges, conferences and affiliated members; education/outreach, ranging from diversity programs to gambling/sports wagering to student-athlete advisory committees to the Youth Education through Sports (YES) program; administration and governance, which includes information ranging from committees to insurance to the NCAA Foundation; rules and eligibility, which includes information ranging from agents and amateurism to regional rules compliance seminars; enforcement and reinstatement, which includes information ranging from bylaw manual searches to a secondary infractions database; and marketing and awards, which includes information ranging from corporate sponsors to television schedules.

Professional sports leagues also maintain far-reaching sites that include up-to-the-minute information on standings, schedules, statistics, drafts, tickets and more. The National Basketball Association (*www.nba.com*), the National Football League (*www.nfl.com*) and Major League Baseball (*www.mlb.com*) are among the best. ESPN's site (*www.espn.go.com*) also is an informative destination for sportswriters.

In addition, the high-school activities or athletic associations in most states maintain sites that are invaluable to reporters covering prep sports.

IN-DEPTH AND INVESTIGATIVE REPORTING

Some of her neighbors watched as Ana Romero was beaten, but they won't have to answer to the law.

This subhead told readers that before them was a story about a woman who was savagely beaten, and about the lack of laws to protect her. It was a major in-depth article, the result of extensive research and writing.

The article, written by Monique Brouzes, a student at Arizona State University, was published in a campus newspaper called *The Bulldog*. It won a scholarship award in an in-depth

(*The Seattle Times*/Jake Batsell)

writing competition sponsored by the William Randolph Hearst Foundation Journalism Awards Program for college journalists.

The article began:

> Ana Romero is a 5-foot, 100-pound, 23-year-old student nurse with nerve damage to her face.
>
> Six metal anchors are embedded in her gums.
>
> She has lost 30 pounds. She rarely goes out, and she now carries a gun.
>
> Romero sat on the edge of her overstuffed couch with her two young daughters by her side as she began recalling the terror of Aug. 29 outside her east Phoenix apartment.
>
> "A bunch of people saw what happened but nobody helped me," Romero said in a quiet and slightly slurred voice. Her large brown eyes filled with tears.
>
> "He was like a lion or something. I was not a girl to him."
>
> At least five people from the apartment complex where she lives saw her attacker beat her and break her jaw.
>
> Someone did call the police, but no one rushed to her side.
>
> Two of the witnesses, one man who owned a gun, the other a single mother of one child, were less than six feet from the attack.
>
> Only four states have "duty to aid" laws that compel the public to physically intervene in helping those in jeopardy. That means 46 states, including Arizona, have no such laws.
>
> Only six states have "duty to report" laws that require people to report a crime. Arizona is not one of them.

What Is an In-Depth?

Writers no longer cover only routine stories that can be summarized in a few inches. They often spend weeks, perhaps months, researching a compelling topic and then writing about it in depth.

An **in-depth** article—through extensive research and interviews—provides an account that goes far beyond a basic news story.

In-depths report the news, and they also provide detailed information that allows people to lead more enjoyable, safer, more profitable or better-informed lives. Such stories cover a broad range of topics:

- A lengthy news feature looks at a new state program to help reduce child abuse. Another story tells about an American family that adopted a boy and girl from China and is doing all that it can so the children will retain much of their culture as they grow up.
- An in-depth personality profile presents a psychiatrist in a state mental institution.
- A first-person article discusses the writer's painful experience of going through cancer treatments.
- A hard-hitting investigative story proves that toxic chemicals from two construction sites have polluted a water supply, and the article leads to changes in the law.

Investigative stories that reveal wrongdoing by an agency or person are excellent examples of in-depth articles that allow a reporter to step back from everyday deadlines and spend extensive time researching and writing.

Journalists have always been civic watchdogs, and this means that they have always been involved in investigations and in-depth work. The idea that this type of reporting is a result of the Watergate era of the 1970s is a misconception. So is the notion that an in-depth or investigative reporter is different from any reporter gathering facts. In a way, all stories are investigative stories because they require research, digging, interviewing and writing. Also, all reporters are investigators who are trained to ask questions, uncover information and write the most complete stories possible.

Some reporters, however, concentrate solely on investigations of wrongdoing. They deal with reporter-adversary relationships that are usually not found in beat reporting or other in-depth coverage. These reporters are trying to ferret out well-guarded information from often hostile sources.

Most American newspapers and online sites devote space to in-depth or investigative reports. Even local broadcast outlets are devoting an increasing amount of air time to stories that require in-depth or investigative work. The networks also devote time to in-depth reports, either on their newscasts or through news magazine shows.

This increased emphasis on longer, more comprehensive stories that require extensive research and interviews gives reporters an opportunity to be more than technicians following a rigid set of guidelines. It gives them a chance to be creative, to become part of their readers' emotional lives and, sometimes, to uncover an injustice and correct it.

A Reporter as Investigator

"Any beat reporter or feature writer can, and should, also do investigative reporting," said Duff Wilson, who has worked as an investigative reporter for *The Seattle Times* since 1989 and, before that, for *The Seattle Post-Intelligencer.* "It just takes some extra work, but it's worth it. Investigative reporters strive to go beyond the press release, news conference or meeting. We dig beneath the surface. We try to uncover secrets, presumably ones of some public significance. I like to call it public service reporting. I also don't mind the tag 'muckraker,' though in today's climate, that sounds pretty pejorative."

Wilson worked for The Associated Press and *Everett* (Wash.) *Herald* and covered City Hall, state government and police beats before he became an investigative reporter. He has won more than 30 journalism awards. His 1997 series of articles "Fear in the Fields—How Hazardous Wastes Become Fertilizer" won numerous awards and was a finalist for the Pulitzer Prize for public service.

He has never been sued for libel. His articles have sparked numerous changes in law. A King County, Wash., Superior Court judge committed suicide on the eve of Wilson's 1988 story detailing his pedophilia as a teacher and judge. This series of articles led to a state constitutional amendment passed by the voters to open up the process of disciplining judges.

In his work, Wilson said he constantly uses public records. "We actively cultivate sources who will give us information and leak us documents," he added. "I used to be shy about asking people to leak stuff and tip me off to things. No more. I find that many people actually like to play Deep Throat, even though he stayed in the shadows in the movie ['All the President's Men']. Hey, they think it's fun. And it is."

He said that while beat reporters and feature writers often write about trends, investigative reporters "look for patterns and stories where others may not think to look. We try to buck trends and be counterintuitive. We have two criteria for stories: (1) Is it interesting? The same criteria as for a feature. And (2) is it really important?"

Still, every beat or feature story should have elements of investigative reporting in it, Wilson said. "A beat reporter can sow the seeds of investigative reporting by filing a public-records request for inside information or files after the reporter writes a daily story. It only takes a minute."

He added that investigative, public service reporting carries the best traditions of historical American journalism. "We challenge authority," Wilson said. "That's one reason beat reporters may have a hard time with such an adversarial process as investigative reporting. Imagine a sports writer challenging the managers' explanation for what happened in a game. This writer relies on the manager for access to information. Investigative reporters burn a lot more bridges."

Wilson said there are other differences between beat and investigative reporting. "At its root, investigative reporting demands accountability," he said. "My favorite technique is to find a law or a promise and then to compare it with the actual performance. Every investigative story needs this feature. Sometimes, identifying the standard is the hardest part of the reporting. This applies to investigative reporting on private businesses as well as public officials.

"Also I think it is important to use our power for social issues reporting, 'comfort the afflicted.' Finally, investigative reporting demands excellent writing, and with all the material you will have gathered, that can be a challenge. I am a big believer in third, fourth and fifth drafts."

Reporter's Accountability

Whenever investigative reporters reveal wrongdoing, they often are criticized for their work, particularly by the people or agencies that are accused of the wrongdoing. Wilson knows that firsthand.

He has done considerable research and writing about Seattle's Fred Hutchinson Cancer Research Center. In a five-part investigative series in 2001 Wilson and another *Times* reporter, David Heath, described how patients had died prematurely in two clinical trials at the center, which is known in Seattle as "The Hutch."

Once the series was published, officials at the center raised questions about the fairness and accuracy of the series. The newspaper responded to letters and e-mails by asking the reporters and *Times* editors about the series and publishing the answers on its Web site (*www.seattletimes.com*). Staffers were asked why they didn't talk about all of the good work that has gone on over the years at The Hutch. They responded in part:

> The Hutch's groundbreaking work in cancer research was noted repeatedly throughout the series. On the first day, a separate story recounted the history and accomplishments of the center. Further, the good works of The Hutch have been covered thoroughly by *The Times* in the center's quarter-century of existence.

Some critics wondered if the newspaper published the series during "sweeps week," the week newspapers count their circulation numbers. The answer:

> Newspapers have no such "sweeps week." This was not about selling newspapers any more than any of the journalism we do here—from coverage of the Legislature to

> international news to movie reviews to Mariner game stories—is about selling newspapers. It was about our commitment to serving the community through quality journalism.

In an important question, the reporters were asked how they, who are not medical professionals, could understand the technical aspects of the clinical trials. They were asked, "What did you do to ensure accuracy?" Their answer:

> It's true the reporters who wrote these stories are not doctors. But we interviewed dozens of them, both at The Hutch and elsewhere, in the course of doing these stories. And when we were ready to publish, we had the stories reviewed for technical accuracy by a nationally regarded bone-marrow specialist from a major research institution.

Gathering Information for an In-Depth

In-depths are choice assignments because they allow reporters to explore a topic thoroughly, learn things that most people do not have a chance to learn and tell a story without the fear of its being cut to 6 inches for a small hole on Page 4. The final story may be written as hard news or as soft news. It may be one long piece that starts on the front page and jumps to one or more inside pages, or it may be a series that runs several days. It usually is proactive rather than reactive, as are most other stories that fill newspapers.

A newspaper often will anchor Page 1 of its Sunday edition with an in-depth article. Readers tend to spend more time with their Sunday paper, which means the longer stories that require more reading time and concentration are well suited for that day.

In-depths are usually grueling assignments because they require the reporter to spend days, weeks or even years investigating a topic in front of a computer and in the field, asking questions over the phone, in person and in writing. For example, reporter Fred Schulte, an investigative team leader at the *Sun-Sentinel* in Fort Lauderdale, Fla., spent four years looking at Veterans Administration (VA) hospitals in general and at the one in Miami in particular. He and his newspaper also had to fight a court battle to win the right to examine medical "quality-assurance" records. His series of articles revealed excessive deaths during 11 years in the cardiac unit at the Miami hospital, underused facilities, botched surgical techniques, chronic staff shortages and substandard care.

An in-depth story "gives you a chance to work on something you believe is worthwhile rather than working eight hours and covering routine meetings," Schulte said. "You evolve into looking for a bigger challenge than covering routine stories. Investigative reporting gives you a chance to do that. On the other hand, it's a long time between bylines. Some reporters have a short attention span, and it's difficult to stay on track for months at a time. A newspaper shouldn't try to make everyone work on in-depths. It needs to have good feature writers. It also has to have people who can cover and write a good story in three hours. Good investigative reporters can do this, too, but they do it after an investigation is announced, after their stories have run."

Of course, many reporters do not have the luxury of investigating a single topic for an extended time. Often, they must work on in-depths while they continue their regular beats.

An in-depth is a combination of research, interviews, observation, writing and rewriting. All these areas require careful attention.

Before Monique Brouzes at Arizona State University wrote her article on "duty to aid" and "duty to report" laws, she had to spend weeks researching the topic. She found out that only four states have laws compelling the public to physically help people in jeopardy. Only six states have laws that even require people to report a crime.

Brouzes also had to win the confidence of a young mother who had been brutally beaten in front of her neighbors and would have to recount the attack. She even needed to ask the woman if a photographer could take pictures of her.

The reporter spent hours with her source. She spent even more time on the phone, calling law professors who have researched the laws and attorneys who have had to deal with them in court.

When it was finally time to write—and, of course, rewrite—Brouzes was able to tell the story of a courageous woman who continues to battle her way back to health. The story began with a description of Romero. Her ordeal was woven throughout.

Brouzes' writing clearly showed that she had researched her topic in depth. She cited several studies and sources on state "duty" laws. She also interviewed Romero's neighbors—the ones who saw her beaten but did not come to her aid. Here is an example of the writing:

In the beating of Romero, one witness, David Pruitt, a 21-year-old grounds-keeper, said he did not come out to help, even though he owns a gun. He said he lives with his grandmother and feared for her safety.

"I got woken up by this lady (Romero) just screaming her head off," Pruitt said.

"I heard some guy, he was roaring like a bear. I looked out the window and saw her (Romero) running and screaming around the pillar and he (her attacker) caught her right there by my apartment."

Pruitt gestured toward a cement pillar about 5 feet from his front door.

He said he did not actually see the man's face because the pillar was blocking his view.

Pruitt said he started to get dressed, but the animal-like grunts of the man stopped him.

"I knew he was crazy," Pruitt said. "I didn't want to come out because I have an 87-year-old grandma in there."

By the end of her article, Brouzes brought her readers back full circle, to Romero sitting on her couch, this time talking about the future:

Romero said she still can't open her mouth and has to exercise it with a tongue depressor by gently forcing her jaw open.

"The doctor said my jaw will be fine, but the upper right side of my face is going to be paralyzed permanently," she said.

Romero said she is looking forward to going back to school in the spring at Glendale Community College.

She has also taken a part-time position as a medical assistant for a private doctor.

"It's just a matter of fact now," she said. "Reality starts to hit you when the bills start coming in. It's like, OK, this happened to me. You're OK, go on now.

"I have changed. I can't stand to have anybody walk behind me. When I walk alone, I have this insecurity like somebody's going to come up from behind.

"But not everybody is bad. This man was mentally ill."

Romero said she still carries her gun and will never be without one again.

She has given notice where she lives and hopes to be out of her apartment by Jan. 1.

"I'll be fine," she said. "I just need to move."

Smelling a Story

When a man stumbled into the *Sun-Sentinel* newsroom, complaining that the Miami VA hospital had scrapped its heart surgery unit two weeks before he was supposed to have an operation, Fred Schulte did what many reporters do when they receive such a tip. He played a hunch, and in this case, it paid off.

Schulte smelled a story. He could just as easily have shrugged the man off, saying to himself, "Why should I listen to this guy or believe him?" But he had a hunch, he followed it and he ultimately wrote a hard-hitting series.

Ideally, reporters write their stories on the basis of facts that they have gathered at news events and have then synthesized. The story is there, and they go out and cover it. In reality, reporters often smell a story and chase it. They let their emotions, intuition, past experiences and gut reactions guide them in the stories they research and write. These feelings arouse reporters to begin working on a story. These feelings influence the gathering of facts, and they become the basis for what is written.

Of course, some hunches turn up nothing. Reporters do not get lucky all the time. More often than not, however, hunches do lead to stories. Experienced reporters, particularly investigative reporters, continually follow hunches. Their stories may reveal a major problem or may point out that the rumors were false.

"We all play hunches," said Jack Anderson, a longtime investigative reporter who wrote the syndicated "Washington Merry-Go-Round" and won a Pulitzer Prize for his reporting on the secret relations between the United States and Pakistan in its war with India. "With experience you develop a certain sense of things. You learn after a while how the crooks operate. When you see a senator get up and pontificate a certain way, it raises an antenna. Many times I've said to my reporters, 'Keep your eye on this or go check this out.' "

Anderson also warned against drawing conclusions about a hunch before the reporting process is complete. "Don't make your mind up until you have the facts," he said.

Conducting Research

Importance of Research

As in any story, the first step in writing an in-depth is to study the topic and the sources. Doing careful research is vital because research:

- *Introduces a Reporter to the Language of a Complex Topic.* That prepares the reporter to talk to specialists and helps eliminate the problem of having to ask continually, "What does this mean?" or "Can you explain that procedure to me?"
- *Introduces a Reporter to People Who Have Been Sources for Similar Stories in the Past.* Usually, if they spoke to a reporter before, they will do it again.
- *Helps a Reporter Formulate a List of Questions.* Reporters should know what subjects they want covered and what questions they want answered. It is best to know the answers or partial answers to the questions before the interviewing even begins.

- *Provides Other Articles Written on the Same Topic.* There are few major topics that have not been covered by the media at some time. There may not be any articles on the individuals involved in a story, but there is usually something about the topic.
- *Uncovers Some of the Good Things and Bad Things to Look for during Interviews.* Careful study of records and documents can turn up much information.

Sources of Information

The most common places to look for background information—clippings and reference—are the Internet, newspaper library, electronic databases and the public library. The in-depth reporter often has to dig deeper than traditional sources, however. Obscure public records often become the key to a major story.

"I almost always go to the courthouse first," Schulte said. "That is a simple way to get a ton of information. All you have to know are the names of the plaintiffs and defendants, and you can look them up in an index. You also have to know all the names of the people involved in the story. If you are doing a story on a big hospital, for instance, you should know all the key staff people. You always should know the name of the administrator. Then you can see if a suit naming the administrator has been filed."

Interviewing

An in-depth is not written after merely interviewing a source or two. Like the research and writing, the interviewing process for an in-depth requires extensive work.

For example, the story on Ana Romero and state "duty" laws could never have been written if Brouzes had interviewed only two or three sources. She had to call a law professor in San Diego who had written a 58-page report on helping strangers in need. She needed to talk to the county prosecutor who was handling the case against the suspect in the attack, to Romero's neighbors, to a special assistant to the county attorney and to dozens of other people.

Of course she did not include in her story everyone she interviewed. Reporters often interview more people than they need, if only because they want to make certain before they write that they are getting the same information from more than one source.

Here are some tips on interviewing for an in-depth article:

- *Talk to Everyone You Can.* Sometimes the best sources for stories are people who have clues that will lead to something big.
- *Interview as Long as You Can.* You don't get bonus points for finishing the interviewing process and turning in a completed story days before deadline. Keep talking as long as you can to as many people as possible.
- *Ask Sources for Names of Additional Sources.* Sources can provide names of people you never even thought about. If you interview six people and ask each of them for a name, you then have a dozen sources.
- *Know the Answers to Incriminating Questions Before You Ask Them.* Be ready for sources who deny the truth. Save the toughest sources for last, after you have gathered most of your information.

- *Use a Tape Recorder for In-Depth or Particularly Sensitive Interviews.* You should still take some notes, but if you are spending hours with a source, you don't want to be writing the entire time.

Interviews from the Outside In

Investigative reporters often use **interviews from the outside in**, much like an ever-tightening circle, from the least important to the most important players.

Instead of going to the major source first, at the bull's-eye of the circle, most investigative reporters begin at the outer rings, where people are more likely to give them information about the people in the center. For instance, in a story about a sleazy ambulance firm, most reporters would begin their interviews with former drivers for the firm, the most likely people to have an ax to grind. Then they would talk to current drivers and other officials. The last interview would be with the owner of the firm, who would be much less likely to deny wrongdoing after being presented with well-documented evidence.

"My strategy is to know everything about the person before I go in there," Schulte said. "Once you have everything, interviewing is a breeze because it is clear to the interviewee that you have done your homework. I always begin by asking questions that I know the answers to."

Smoking-Gun Interviews

John Stossel, a correspondent for ABC News' "20/20," told an Investigative Reporters and Editors seminar on the special problems of interviewing for broadcast investigations that he knows the interviewee is guilty even before he conducts an interview. Instead of going into an interview to ask general questions, the reporter goes in with videotape or other evidence of wrongdoing by the interviewee and asks direct questions about a specific incident. The interviewee denies it, and the reporter then shows the incriminating evidence, hoping that the person will confirm, on camera, that he or she really is one of the bad guys.

Such an interview is called a **smoking-gun** or **shotgun interview**. "It's the best type of interview," Stossel said. "I've done all the research, and I go into the interview mad. I know the bad guy is guilty. I knew it before the interview. A hidden camera gets the bad guy doing something. Then we interview the person, and he denies everything. Then we show him the tape."

Stossel added that, to get decent television, he is also obnoxious during an interview with someone who he knows is guilty. "I ask questions such as, 'Do you sleep well at night?' or 'Are you ashamed?'" he said. "They have pat answers. They say 'no comment.' They smile. They try to manipulate. They go into gobbledygook. I try to jar them out of that language. It seems the only way I get anything from stiffs on camera is to be a little wild."

Many reporters scorn smoking gun interviews, for the simple reason that they believe all interviewees should be given a chance to tell their side of the story. Many editors and news directors remind their reporters that there is always a chance, no matter how small, that the interviewee may not be as guilty as all the evidence indicates; therefore, that person should have a chance to express his or her opinions on camera or in print.

"Confrontation interviews may look good on television, but they don't make it in print," Fred Schulte said. "You don't want to do things in that sort of fashion, coming in swaggering about how bad you are. You don't want to go in there like a prosecutor.

"I prefer an informed discussion with the person, where it is clear that both of you have studied the issue sensibly. A lot of people are glad to talk to someone who shares their interest. You usually find that people are very responsive. Then as they get deeper and deeper, you can start with a little of the shotgun. You let them dig their own grave."

Double-Checks and Triple-Checks

Reporters who work on in-depth and investigative stories do not have the same deadline pressures as reporters covering breaking or quickly developing news. They should have time to double-check and triple-check everything their sources tell them.

It is not unusual for a beat reporter or a general assignment reporter under a tight deadline to go with a single source. However, reporters working on in-depths generally have the time to develop their stories carefully, and they seldom rely on a single source. When working on in-depth articles, reporters should confirm everything three, four or more times. The general rule they follow is that *two sources are usually enough, but it is better to have more.*

Confidential Sources

Most reporters avoid unnamed sources if they can. But there are some important stories that simply would never be reported if the daily media did not rely on confidential sources. Remember Watergate and Deep Throat, the anonymous source who was never identified but who helped bring down the presidency of Richard Nixon? (See Chapter 8 for more more on confidential sources.)

There are other examples:

> *The Dallas Morning News* reported that "a Federal Aviation Administration official who asked to remain anonymous" said he had been told that a stalled jet engine led to the crash of a Delta Air Lines jet at the Dallas-Fort Worth International Airport.

> The *San Francisco Examiner* reported that "law enforcement sources" indicated that a New York crime family was seeking a foothold in San Francisco, a city considered relatively free of traditional organized-crime activity.

> An in-depth series in *The Arizona Republic* on sex for sale used first names but no last names for many of its sources. In one article a woman named Paula said that giving good phone sex is legal, and it's safe if a person remembers to scrub the receiver with disinfectant to ward off colds and ear infections from colleagues.

Most reporters follow the same general guidelines when using confidential sources:

- During an interview, they try to talk a reluctant source into going on the record by telling him or her how important the information is to the story.
- If the source is still unwilling to talk on the record, they listen anyway because he or she can provide important information.

- They ask if the source knows of anyone who is willing to provide the same information on the record.
- If possible, they find another source who can be named.

Going Undercover

Sometimes, while reporters are working on an in-depth article, they go **undercover** and do not tell sources for the story that they are reporters.

For example, a reporter in Chicago applied for and got a job as a guard at the state prison but never told the officials who hired him that he was a reporter. Afterwards, he wrote a first-person article. When a reporter in Albuquerque, N.M., enrolled in a local high school and then wrote a series on what goes on there, she never told school officials that she was a reporter. The *Chicago Sun-Times* once purchased a tavern in the city, renamed it the Mirage and operated it for four months with the Better Government Association, which provides investigators to work with newspaper and broadcast reporters to uncover corruption and mismanagement in government. Reporters and investigators worked as bartenders, never telling patrons who they really were.

When the *Sun-Times* ran its Mirage series, the stories detailed payoffs to city inspectors to ignore health and safety hazards, shakedowns by state liquor inspectors who demanded cash for silence about liquor violations, illegal kickbacks from jukebox and pinball machine operators and misconduct by public employees who loafed on the job.

The series was nominated for a Pulitzer Prize for best investigative series and was a finalist, but it was turned down because some members of the Pulitzer board thought that reporters going underground and operating a bar as a front for a sting operation raised serious questions about journalistic ethics. Many editors continue to argue that going undercover is a deceptive practice that is not in the best interest of a news organization's credibility. They do not want their reporters to misrepresent themselves, and they will not allow this type of investigative journalism—ever.

Of course, it can also be argued that many good stories would be impossible to get if a reporter walked into a situation and quickly announced that he or she was a reporter and that everything everyone said might turn up in print. Doing this would probably have meant that the reporter in Albuquerque would not have been able to purchase drugs in a girls' restroom at the high school. The reporter in Chicago would not have been treated like all the other guards in the state prison if the officials and inmates knew he was a reporter. Certainly, the reporters who worked as bartenders at the Mirage would not have experienced extortion and payoffs.

Undercover journalism is practiced at some newspapers. Generally, however, it is a last resort, used only after editors and reporters have concluded that a story is extremely significant and that there would be no other means of obtaining it. In situations where criminal activity is being investigated, some editors contend that the end justifies the means.

William Recktenwald, a former *Chicago Tribune* reporter who once worked as a prison guard to get a story and who has been involved in numerous undercover investigations, agreed that reporters should avoid going undercover unless it is absolutely necessary. Recktenwald, who now teaches journalism at Southern Illinois University, gives the following advice about undercover work:

- Remember that the first duty of a reporter assuming another role is to do the job right and not jeopardize anyone's life. If a reporter is going to work in a nursing home, the duties of the job come before those of a journalist.
- If something is not there, do not make it up. Do not embellish. Never encourage people to break the law to help make the story.
- A reporter using a phony background should make it as close to the truth as possible. A reporter using a false name will usually use his or her real first name. That way, there is no hesitation when someone calls out the reporter's name. When filling out applications, use a real birthday and hometown and actual schools and work experience, except jobs as a reporter. It is always easy to list two years' experience when there may have been only six months. Most of the time, backgrounds are not checked. Do not lie on forms, such as a driver's license, that require an oath.
- Never break the law. The news-gathering process is not protected by the First Amendment. The Ninth Circuit Court Judge Shirley Hufstedler made it clear in a 1971 court decision (*Dietemann* v. *Time Inc.*) that the "First Amendment has never been construed to accord newsmen immunity from torts or crimes committed during the course of news gathering."
- Avoid **leak journalism**. Stories based on "leaks" rely too heavily on unnamed sources. Instead, rely on **enterprise journalism**. Just stay enthusiastic and work at it. Dig through those boring records. The key to success is perseverance and digging.

Writing an In-Depth Story

Finding the Right Lead

Summaries are the most common leads on investigative stories that reveal wrongdoing or break news for the first time. On other in-depths, reporters often use narrative, contrast, direct-address or other types of leads. (See Chapter 5 for a discussion of special leads.)

Summary Lead

Fred Schulte's investigation of VA hospitals took four years and involved two lawsuits before his four-day series began. Each day, the *Sun-Sentinel* ran a mainbar story detailing a major revelation. It also ran sidebar stories that described programs in other cities or specific cases in Miami.

Schulte's first mainbar story started with a hard summary lead, as do most in-depth investigative stories that reveal something:

> Excessive patient deaths, inept disciplining of doctors and dangerously unrestrained growth have plagued heart-surgery programs for America's veterans for more than a decade, a *Sun-Sentinel* investigation has found.
>
> The findings are based on Veterans Administration documents federal attorneys fought three years to suppress. The investigation is the first independent review of the $27 million-a-year heart-surgery network, run by a coterie of VA doctors who conduct their affairs in secret.

Lead Block and Nut Graph

Because an in-depth is longer than a news account and may not be delivering news firsthand, the reporter may want to paint a picture and draw readers into the story before giving them the news peg. To do that, the reporter writes a lead block. Then several paragraphs later, one or more nut graphs are used to give an audience the "so what" of the story.

Monique Brouzes used a lead block of descriptions, narrative and quotations in her article on state "duty" laws. Her nut graphs told readers that Ana Romero lives in one of the 46 states where there are no laws compelling people to physically intervene when someone is in trouble, and that Arizona is one of 44 states with no laws requiring people to report a crime.

Using Bulleted Paragraphs to Summarize Findings

In his first story on the VA hospitals, Schulte did what many writers do in the first part of an in-depth series. He used several bulleted paragraphs that summarized the major findings of the investigation:

> The *Sun-Sentinel* found:
>
> • Cardiac-surgery death rates are five times higher in some veterans hospitals than others—differences VA doctors cannot justify or explain.
>
> • Death rates jumped to excessive levels 59 times at 37 VA hospitals between April 1978 and March 1982.
>
> • VA cardiac units in four cities—including Miami—were closed after too many patients died.
>
> • Low-use VA programs report the highest death rates. VA officials have disregarded numerous safety warnings to shut down the small units.
>
> • Cardiac surgery is safest for veterans sent to university hospitals. VA officials are phasing out these transfers to save money.

In his series of stories, Schulte delved extensively into each of these items and much more.

Using Anecdotes and Observations

An anecdote—a short, entertaining account of a personal happening—is a valuable tool in writing an in-depth story or series. The simplest formula to follow when writing an anecdote is to have one of the characters in the story do something that will evoke some emotion from the readers. Remember, though, to stay away from cliché-filled "atmospheric" phrases, such as these:

> It was a dark and stormy night when John started the car.

Or:

> As the sun slowly crept over the mountain, John started his car.

It is better to use observations in which a source is reacting to something such as the weather:

> John started his red convertible, looking at the bank, waiting for her to walk out into the sunlight.

Or:

> John puffed on a cigarette as he started his red convertible. He stared at the bank, waiting for her to walk out into the sunlight.

Finding the Thread

The key to a successful in-depth article is a strong thread throughout to keep readers interested. The thread may be a real-life situation, strange twists or suspense leading to a surprise ending, but it is used to keep readers interested in the entire story.

In her article on "duty" laws, Brouzes used Romero as the thread. The story began with the woman sitting on her couch, talking about the night she was attacked. After the nut graphs, the story moved to a legal expert, who talked about "duty" laws.

Next, Brouzes moved to one of the neighbors, who said that the beating occurred right outside his window and that he called the police but was afraid to help.

Then the county prosecutor was featured. She said that the suspect had broken out of the county hospital and stolen a car before he got to Romero.

Brouzes then used transition to bring readers back to Romero, the story's thread. Romero's compelling and sad story of her night of terror was a theme throughout the article. It held the story together and kept readers emotionally attached.

> She recounted the events that led to her attack.
>
> She and her husband, Juan, came home about 2 a.m. on Aug. 29 with their daughters, her brother-in-law and a cousin.
>
> Romero said they had been drinking. Her brother-in-law left as soon as they got home. Her cousin stayed.
>
> Gifts had been left in the truck and Romero decided to go get them.
>
> "Something told me 'Don't go,' but I was stubborn and I went," she said.
>
> While she was at the truck, she said she noticed someone swinging furiously on the playground swings and then moving to the merry-go-round.
>
> "(Then) he jumped over the fence (6 feet) like nothing," she said.
>
> "At first I thought he knew me or lived here."
>
> Romero said the man somehow made it seem as if he would walk past her, but as soon as he got a few feet behind her, he started after her.
>
> "I could hear his feet running in the grass," she said. "I dropped everything and started running and screaming. I just remember the terror. It was like a nightmare of being chased and knowing I would get caught."

Brouzes moved next to another witness and then several more sources before coming back to Romero. That was the pattern of the story. As is typical of many in-depth articles, this one:

- Began with a key player, the thread of the story.
- Used transition to introduce and develop other key sources.

- Came back to the thread.
- Used transition to move to other sources.
- Came back to the thread.
- Developed other sources.
- Came back full circle to the thread.

Writing a First-Person Article

News stories are seldom written in the first person because reporters are taught to stay out of their writing, to present both sides of a story. In the name of objectivity, reporters are trained to be intermediaries, to witness an event and then recall it in words so that readers, viewers or listeners who were not there can feel as if they were.

Unlike a hard news story written as an inverted pyramid, an in-depth meant to involve its readers in an emotional story can be effective in the first person. In these stories, the writer invites an audience into a personal experience. First-person articles can make a highly intense and personal subject much more real. Examples include, "I was an inmate at the county jail" and "I worked as a guard at the state prison."

Here is the beginning of a first-person in-depth written by a journalism student whose husband was dying of cancer. The story worked better in the first person because it allowed the writer to tell her highly personal and emotional story directly to readers. The article was purchased by *The Arizona Republic.*

> I was standing at the kitchen sink washing fresh vegetables for dinner. Dennis walked in from work and said he had just heard a song on the radio that described how he felt.
>
> "Better be good to yourself cause you're no good for anyone else," he said while he kissed me and reached around for a glass. (Dennis is in a low mood, and I had better just drift with him for a while, I thought.)
>
> My husband Dennis is 24 years old. We've been married 2 1/2 years, but are never sure how much longer we have together. Dennis has cancer of the soft tissue. His doctors have told us his cancer is a rare form and they can do no more than experiment with various drugs in their search for a cure. The doctors have said that the longer he goes without another growth, the greater his chances of survival.
>
> We think the will to live is the most important factor. Somehow, this will carry us through even the lowest moods.

First-person stories are powerful because, in them, a writer must relive for a mass audience a personal and sometimes painful experience. In the cancer story, the writer had to talk about her insecurities, her finances and the rest of her family. None of that was easy to do.

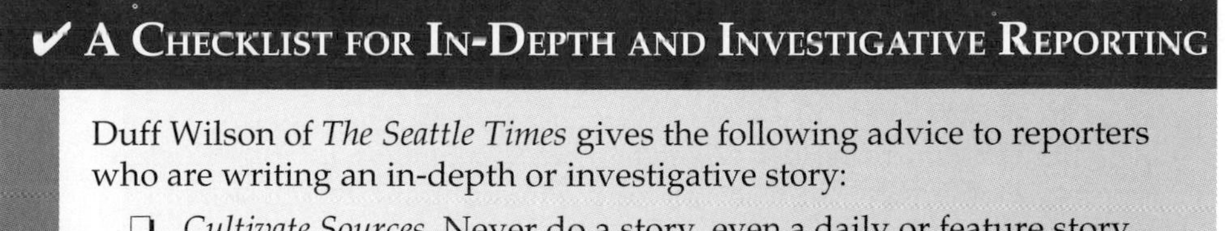

✔ A Checklist for In-Depth and Investigative Reporting

Duff Wilson of *The Seattle Times* gives the following advice to reporters who are writing an in-depth or investigative story:

- ❑ *Cultivate Sources.* Never do a story, even a daily or feature story, with fewer than three named sources. To do less would be to embarrass yourself. It just takes a few extra minutes to get a couple of extra voices in your story.

- *Use the Public Records Law to Dig.* You can say you're "just doing your job," and the people you cover will respect you for it.
- *Be Careful.* Check every word.
- *Strive to Be Fair.* "After every story, I phone the main targets or sources and ask them if they think the story was completely fair, accurate and complete. I encourage their feedback either on the record or off the record. I ask them if there were any unfair nuances. I initiate this contact. I really want their candid feedback. That is much better than waiting for the phone to ring. This technique has probably been the single most important thing I do in the reporting process. It helps to assure that my stories are fair, accurate and complete. The contact also generates some good follow-up stories. Most of all, it builds trust, respect and care in our craft."
- *Read about the Great Investigative Reporters.* Join Investigative Reporters and Editors.

Here are some additional guidelines to follow when writing an in-depth or investigative story:

- *Always Know before an Interview Which Questions Are to Be Answered or Which Major Topics Are to Be Covered.* Be flexible enough to follow the flow of the interview when it moves away from predetermined questions, because the interview can be steered back to them later.
- *Talk to Off-the-Record Sources.* Even people who refuse to allow you to use their names can provide valuable information. Tell them how important their information is, and try to talk them into going on the record. If they still refuse, ask them if they know of a source who will go on the record.
- *Conduct Investigative Interviews in an Ever-Tightening Circle.* Work from the least important to the most important players. That will make interviewing the person in the middle of the circle much easier.
- *Use the Right Lead.* A hard news summary lead belongs on an investigative article that reveals wrongdoing or other news firsthand. A narrative, contrast, direct-address or another special lead can be used on an in-depth that is not delivering news firsthand. On stories that are illuminating a previously reported news event, it is better to invite and draw readers inside before giving them the news peg.
- *Use Bullets Early in a Lengthy Article to Summarize It for Readers.* Don't make them search for the major points of the story.
- *Use Anecdotes and Observations.* They help readers become emotionally attached to a story.

- *Use a Strong Thread throughout the Story.* Many in-depth writers begin their stories with one person or event. Then they refer to the person or event in the body and at the end of the story.
- *Consider Writing a Series of Articles.* Instead of writing a single extremely long story, it may be better to write a mainbar and several sidebars. A series can make a subject more palatable to an audience. Most newspapers also use informational graphics and photographs with in-depth articles.
- *Consider First-Person Articles.* Sometimes the most effective in-depth is written in the first person, especially if the story involves a highly personal topic. Be prepared to tell an editor all the reasons that a first-person article may be the best.

CHAPTER TWENTY-FOUR

BUSINESS NEWS AND OTHER SPECIALTIES

STRASBOURG, France—The European Union blocked General Electric Co.'s $41 billion purchase of Honeywell International Inc. on Tuesday, the first time a proposed merger between two U.S. companies has been blocked solely by European regulators. The veto of one of the world's largest industrial mergers by the EU's 20-member executive commission was widely expected after the American companies failed to allay European fears the deal would create an unfairly dominant position in markets for jetliner engines and avionics. (Associated Press)

(*Rick Wiley*)

The National Association of Theater Owners has promised to "tighten up enforcement" of movie ratings, proposing 12 initiatives Monday to improve the system.

The group promises to ban coming-attractions trailers for films rated R from being shown before any G- or PG-rated film. And it will prohibit trailers for R-rated films before PG-13 films—unless the "tone and content are consistent with the feature film, and nothing in the trailer itself is likely to offend the audience."

The announcement is in response to the year-long Federal Trade Commission study that found that Hollywood studios and other entertainment companies market violent material to children. (*USA Today*)

In an unusually assaultive movie season, even for the summer, "The Score" is a refreshingly quiet and methodical heist picture. So I kept wondering why I didn't like it more.

After all, it lays the groundwork for its enormous, sizzling set piece—a break-in at a high-security cage in Montreal's Customs House—with enough specificity for us to appreciate the thieves' expertise and enough mystery for us to be surprised at how completely they work out their plan.

The Montreal settings are superb in their European-American texture and filigree; how wonderful it is to see a Hollywood movie made in Canada that doesn't just show us Toronto masquerading as New York. (Michael Sragow, *USA Today*)

One of the most arresting and telling images in "California Crazy & Beyond: Roadside Vernacular Architecture" by Jim Heimann (Chronicle Books, $18.95, 180 pages) appears on the title page of the book. A grinning carpenter stands in front of a half-finished restaurant under construction on Whittier Boulevard on a sunny day in 1932, and behind him we can see the 2-by-4s and tar paper and chicken wire that will give the structure its fanciful shape—the restaurant is called the Chili Bowl, and that's exactly what it will look like. (*Los Angeles Times*)

Sultry. Alluring. Passionate and mysteriously edgy—it's the nearly forgotten music of nearly forgotten men brought together by chance to revisit the dreams of their youth.

Nights at Havana's Buena Vista Social Club came alive again through film and music. Ibrahim Ferrer and Ruben Gonzalez, two members of that traditional Cuban jazz group, give Detroit a taste of island life at the Meadow Brook Music Festival at 8 p.m. Wednesday. (*The Detroit News*)

Each day, people look for news about the global economy and environment, interest rates, mutual funds, movies, books, concerts and so on. The media have responded.

Indeed, much of today's news has become specialized. What was once tucked into the back of newspapers, or not mentioned at all, is often now big news. The media have hired experts to cover business and consumer news, the arts, architecture, technology, medicine, legal affairs, the environment, religion and other specialties.

Unlike a beat reporter, who obtains stories by making regular stops at or telephone calls to the courthouse, the police station or the county attorney's office, a specialty reporter obtains stories by cultivating and contacting a variety of experts and news sources. The beat reporter is generally concerned only with news that is occurring now; the specialty reporter is often interested in long-range stories, the roots of problems and the reasons behind the news. A specialty reporter must be sufficiently informed about a complicated field to report and write on it exclusively and intelligently.

It would be impossible to report on all the established and emerging specialty reporting areas. The specialty areas discussed in this chapter, however, are representative.

Business

The success of *The Wall Street Journal, USA Today,* other financial publications, syndicated columns on personal finances and financial reports on radio, television and the Internet has shown that people are keenly interested in news about business and the world economy. Today, business writers not only report the traditional financial news from bankers and brokers but also explain to average readers what it means and how it affects them. Business stories are regularly front-page news.

On a typical day a financial page may include news stories on Federal Reserve decisions about interest rates, European regulators blocking a proposed merger between two U.S. companies, an airline deciding to expand its terminal space at the local airport or a trade agreement between a local company and the People's Republic of China. There also may be feature stories on people in the business world. Newspapers and broadcast outlets still use handouts, annual reports and government reports for stories, but they are also sending reporters into the field to uncover stories. This increased coverage requires reporters who are specialists in the complex field of business and who can develop contacts with many news sources.

The Business Reporter

As in any specialty, business writing is more than covering events that occurred in the last 24 hours and then reporting back to an audience. Business writers do cover breaking news such as store openings, speeches by business leaders, corporate meetings and changes. But, like all specialists, they also sit back and analyze what something means, why it occurred and what effects it will have on an audience.

For example, if a department store in town announces that it is laying off 75 employees because of financial difficulties, business writers will report the announcement to their audiences immediately. They will also dissect the announcement to try to find the reasons behind it and what effects it will have in the future. If the company is publicly owned, the reporters will study annual reports to find out how the firm has used its revenues. They will conduct extensive interviews with company executives. Audiences—and reporters—want to know if the announcement is a harbinger of worse things to come or merely a temporary setback. Here is where specialty reporters earn their salaries, for they are hired specifically to examine events with the eyes of an expert and then write about them in easily understandable language.

The increased coverage of financial news has made business reporting more attractive to journalism students. To prepare themselves, students are studying economics and business along with journalism. They are finding out that editors are impressed by reporters who understand how the government, stock markets, money system and business world operate.

Mary Beth Sammons is a reporter who covers business and finance in Chicago and its northwestern suburbs for the *Chicago Tribune, Crain's Chicago Business* and other publications. She also has been a beat reporter and a business writer and columnist for *The Daily Herald* in Arlington Heights, Ill.

"I took a lot of business courses in college," Sammons said. "As a beat reporter I covered Schaumburg, the town with the most business development in our area, and much of my job was covering businesses. When there was an opening for a business writer at *The Daily Herald,* I applied for it."

During her career, Sammons has written all types of local business stories. She also has localized national and international business stories. For example, in response to the release of the monthly unemployment figures by the U.S. Labor Department, Sammons has reported reactions from state employment experts, local business leaders and sometimes the unemployed workers themselves.

"When I was covering municipal government (as a beat reporter), I was always trying to find the *great* story," she said. "I was always checking the people in power and looking for corruption. I had a cast of characters that I could call every day. Now the cast of people I use as sources is too big. I have to look at so many things now, such as the banking industry and the real estate industry, that I can't keep as much of a check on people. In order not to feel like an imbecile, I have to read so that I will know something about different industries."

Sammons said that the best part of writing about business is that she has an opportunity to learn about the world of finance from the people at the top. She said her work has taken her "into the offices of chief executive officers and other leading personalities that most people, including the employees in their own companies, rarely meet."

The Business Story

Types of Business Stories

Business stories range from hard news to soft features, handouts to personal finance columns, people items to business openings. Hard news reports generally have summary leads; features have softer leads.

Here are three examples of summary leads that topped inverted-pyramid business stories. They are typical of what readers will find on the front pages of business sections.

WILMINGTON, Del.—DuPont Co., the second largest chemical maker, said second-quarter profit fell 55 percent and the third quarter will be "substantially more challenging" because of low demand for the company's chemicals, paints and fibers. (Bloomberg.com)

Colorado has led the nation in personal income growth for much of the last year with a 10.1 percent increase, but the state's days at the top of the heap could be numbered.

"I'd be surprised if it stays at that level going forward," said economist Rich Wobbekind, director of the University of Colorado's Business Research Division. "I'm hearing anecdotally that people are being more cautious about giving significant wage increases, when everyone is scrutinizing their bottom line." (*Rocky Mountain News*)

LONDON (AP)—Share prices on the London Stock Exchange were lower at midday Wednesday.

The Financial Times-Stock Exchange 100-share index was down 31.9 points at 5,288.3.

Daily business pages also include feature stories, which generally begin with softer, non-summary leads. For example, Max Jarman, a writer for *The Arizona Republic,* began his business feature on "friends" in the workplace by teasing his readers.

There's Lady, Maxwell, Happy and Sweeper. Odd names for co-workers, even by today's standards. But they are regulars at Phoenix-area businesses where they help to boost employee loyalty and build customer satisfaction.

Lady is a shelty. Maxwell and Happy are cockers and Sweeper is a long-haired dog of unspecified pedigree.

Pets such as these are increasingly finding their way into businesses and offices where they can relax and motivate stressed workers and help promote better relations with customers.

Annual Reports

A **publicly held company** is owned by investors who purchase its stock on an exchange. The value of the stock is determined by demand—what investors are willing to pay for it. A **privately,** or **closely, held company** is controlled by a family or a small group. The value of its stock, which is not traded on an exchange, is set by the owners.

Each year, a publicly held company must issue an **annual report,** which stockholders receive and may read to determine their company's financial health and find out what is in store for the future. Although the annual reports are public relations statements to stockholders, business reporters read them, too, because their audiences include stockholders, future investors and employees of publicly held companies.

Business reporters must wade through the jargon in annual reports and synthesize it into understandable language. That is not always easy, but reporters follow certain steps. They must read between the lines to get an accurate picture of a firm's health. The personal-finance columnist and commentator Jane Bryant Quinn, in an article entitled "How to Read an Annual Report," which she wrote for the International Paper Co., suggested that the best place to begin reading a report is in the back. Many reporters follow her advice. They read the numbers after they have read and interpreted three other important sections.

Let's look at some important aspects of annual reports.

Auditor's report. The auditor's report, by independent certified public accountants, is in the back of the book, but it should be read first. It informs reporters whether the annual report conforms to generally accepted accounting principles.

Business reporters can spot potential trouble within a company by looking for the words *subject to* in the auditor's report. According to Quinn, those words mean that the financial report is "subject to" the "company's word about a particular piece of business." The words could be a signal that the reporter needs to do some more digging.

Notes to financial statements. Footnotes in the back of the annual report can also help reporters spot trouble. They should be read after the auditor's report because they explain things such as major accounting principles, deductions made on receivables, unusual charges, the effect of interest income on investments, the selling off of plants or divisions and expenses of retirement plans. All these could signal bigger stories.

Letter from the chairperson. Now reporters move to the front of the report, where the chairperson discusses the company's well-being and its goals for the next year. Quinn noted that reporters should also look for buzz words here, which could indicate trouble in the company. *To reach these goals . . . , Despite the . . .* and *Except for . . .* need to be checked carefully.

The actual numbers. Now reporters can look at the numbers contained in the annual report's financial statements and can have a better understanding of them.

One set of numbers, the *balance sheet,* gives the company's **assets**—what it owns. *Current assets* are things that can be turned into cash quickly. The balance sheet also gives **liabilities**—what the company owes. And it notes **shareholders' equity**—the difference between total assets and all liabilities. *Current liabilities* are debts due in one year, which are paid out of current assets.

Another important source of numbers is the *statement of income,* or earnings. It shows how much money a company made or lost in the last year. The statement of income will show a company's *sales,* its cost of doing business and its **net income**—its profit or loss after taxes. Business reporters also look at **net income per share.** An increase in income per share is an indication that a company is healthy. But reporters also check the notes in the back of the report to see why the earnings per share increased. It could have happened because of budget cutbacks or the selling off of a plant, rather than because of an increase in business.

Quarterly Reports

Public companies also issue reports at the end of each quarter of their fiscal year. Like annual reports, these are read carefully by business reporters. They should be read in the same way as annual reports.

Stories are also written from the quarterly reports, which provide sales and earnings information for the quarter.

Example: A Business Story from Idea to "30"

Mary Beth Sammons covers many events at Chicago's O'Hare International Airport. She said that she often noticed air express planes at the airport and decided that a story on overnight air delivery would be worthwhile. The steps she followed, from her idea to the final story, illustrate how a typical business writer operates.

The research. Like any reporter, Sammons had to devote plenty of time to the research phase of her story. Here are some of the things she did:

- *Check Internet Sources.* Sammons said that she looked up the names of local companies and realized that there were more overnight air delivery firms than she had thought.
- *Check the Electronic and Paper Clips.* Sammons went to her newspaper's library and the public library to find out if anything had been written on the industry. There had been stories written on individual companies but nothing on the industry itself.
- *Contact Professional Associations.* During her research, Sammons found that there were two associations dealing with the air express industry, both based in Washington, D.C.: Airfreight Association of America and Air Transportation Association. She called both of them to find out which companies are the largest and to gather financial data on the firms and phone numbers and addresses.

- *Telephone or Visit Local Companies.* Sammons said that she discovered quickly that most of the companies were not based in her area. She was told by nearly every firm that she had to call or write the public relations departments at their headquarters to get permission to interview local people.
- *Set Up Interviews.* Once she got permission from the companies ("Not all of them gave it") to conduct local interviews, Sammons called to set up appointments. She was able to get some data over the phone for her story, but most of the material she needed would have to come from people at the airport. As she was gathering information, Sammons also contacted local businesses that use overnight air delivery most. She asked about advantages and disadvantages of shipping by air express. She talked to security people about what measures are taken to protect precious cargo, and she talked to customs agents about how international cargoes are handled.

The writing. "A photographer and I spent five straight days at the airport," she said. "The first day we realized that all the activity happens from midnight to 6 a.m., and so that's when we had to go there. In fact, what impressed me most while I was at the airport was all the activity at night. A businessperson can leave the office at 5 p.m., but here is all this activity late at night getting the business done. I wanted my lead to reflect that."

She said that she went with the first lead she wrote. In most cases, a reporter will change the lead several times to improve it, but Sammons said that she did not have to this time. She wrote a narrative lead block that set the stage for her readers by putting them in the middle of the nighttime activity.

Here are the story's first five paragraphs:

When most businesses are closing up shop for the night, a group of several service firms are just beginning to gear up for their busiest hours.

Hundreds of trucks, vans, station wagons and jet aircraft converge on O'Hare Airport to meet up with hundreds of workers who will labor until the pre-dawn at breakneck speed, loading, unloading, sorting and stacking. The situation is repeated at airports across the country.

The competition is hot among the companies whose employees work in close proximity to each other at O'Hare. But all have one goal in mind: to get a package or envelope to another point overnight and in a way that is economical, convenient and—most important to customers—on time.

Mention overnight air delivery and Federal Express immediately comes to mind. The Memphis-based company's funny television commercials and crisp advertising slogan, "When it absolutely, positively has to be there overnight," have brought overnight express service to the attention of even those people who never use it.

But while Federal Express may be the industry leader—growing from a tiny operation that handled a dozen packages on its first day in 1973 to one that now delivers more than 42 million packages each year—it is only one company in a very crowded field. Hundreds of firms are vying for a piece of the billion dollar industry, with more constantly entering the competition.

Sammons based her article on a combination of interviewing and observations; this is typical for business writers working on in-depths. "If I hadn't been outside, I couldn't have seen what was going on," she said. "I couldn't have interviewed the pilots, mechanics and other workers. I even got to go inside one of the planes. They're all gutted inside."

Her story included scores of quotations and paraphrases, many facts and figures and a list of who's who in the business. It ended with a look into the future by Paul Hyman, director of cargo services for Airfreight Association of America and one of the sources she introduced earlier:

> The forecast for the overnight air cargo is bright. Industry experts predict that the economic recovery will bolster the business climate and result in a fantastically high growth rate that Hyman puts at about 30 percent a year.
>
> "There is no question that the air cargo industry will continue to grow, because the demand is there for rapid transport of business materials," Hyman said. "In fact, many companies are already starting same-day service. As long as corporations and businesses can afford to pay for air delivery, it will be a thriving industry."

Sammons wrote a lengthy story, but she still had to make cuts. Like every reporter, she writes for limited space, and she cannot get in everything she would like to.

"I had to concentrate on a description of the services rather than much of the color at the airport," she said. "I interviewed pilots who fly from New York City to Japan and back to New York City in two days, but I couldn't get that in."

✔ A Checklist for Business Reporting

Mary Beth Sammons gives the following advice to aspiring reporters who would like to specialize in business writing:

- ❑ *Major in Journalism and Minor in Business.* "I would encourage people to study journalism," she said. "I could go into other fields, and my writing skills could be used in any of them. People can talk for an hour, and in one minute I can pick out the key thing they say. This ability would help me in many fields."
- ❑ *Build a Clip File.* "The fact that you have a degree does not mean that you have a job," Sammons said. While she was in college, Sammons served as a reporter and then as city editor for her campus daily. At various times during college, she had internships at United Press International and at a community daily. She also founded a student magazine and was its editor.
- ❑ *Don't Stop Learning about Business.* To succeed as a specialty reporter "you have to stay with it and keep studying," Sammons said. "For business writing an M.B.A. (master's degree in business administration) could be an extra bonus. Most of all, experience counts, and you have to be able to hustle constantly."

Consumers

Trends in Consumer Journalism

Consumer reporting has come a long way since its emergence during the 1960s and early 1970s—a period that became the era of advocacy journalism. Ralph Nader can be credited with introducing consumer reporting to the nation in 1965 with the publication of "Unsafe at Any Speed: The Designed-In Dangers of the American Automobile," in which he took on General Motors. For a long time after "Unsafe at Any Speed" appeared, consumer reporting consisted mainly of stories that compared various products or uncovered fraud in the marketplace. Reporters turned to **advocacy journalism** as consumerism and a mistrust of big business grew.

Today, consumer reporting consists of more than comparing grades of meat or prices of automobile repairs. Issues such as Interstate Commerce Commission regulations, state and local consumer protection laws and consumer rights are being covered in depth by consumer reporters at newspapers and broadcast outlets. Stories range from how and when to mail Christmas packages to an investigation that reveals the long-term dangers of using common materials in the home. Consumer reporters are now specialists who are reporting consumer news, reasons behind the issues and long-range effects.

Another outgrowth of the consumer journalism movement of the 1960s and 1970s is the **action-line column.** When a news outlet offers an action-line column, people are encouraged to write or telephone to describe their problems. Then, the outlet's own reporters try to solve these problems.

Consumer reporters usually work in several specialty or general areas while researching a single story. For example, a story on how to prepare for traffic court would require some police beat work, courthouse work and research into types of traffic violations, fines and sentencing. A story on the U.S. Food and Drug Administration's campaign against ineffective prescription drugs would require interviews with government officials, doctors, pharmacists and consumer advocates.

Television is well-suited for hard-hitting consumer stories because reporters can actually show children playing with dangerous toys, crop dusters spraying hazardous pesticides too close to homes or the results of a tragic rollover caused by faulty tires. This type of reporting has become a specialty of cable and network television magazine shows. Many local television stations also have consumer reporters.

Because their own staffs are not large enough to cover consumer news extensively, many small newspapers and small broadcast outlets rely on consumer stories that are supplied by the wire services. The Associated Press and other news services supply consumer stories to thousands of newspapers and broadcast outlets throughout the United States. Consumer news is also available on the Internet.

To gather information for their stories, consumer reporters rely on local, state and national governmental agencies; various public action and consumer groups; corporate officials and public relations departments; economists; university professors; and stock analysts. By keeping an extensive file of sources, a consumer reporter knows whom to call as a source for a breaking news story or whom to call for background information on an important issue. Extensive sources are also important because reporters depend on them for tips.

Consumer News Stories

There is incredible consumer information available in newspapers, on TV and on the Internet. Stories can range from late-breaking news to feature stories. When the 34,000 members of the Communications Workers of America went on strike against US West in 13 states, consumers felt it. In a story about families and businesses facing delays and frustrations, Joe Heim of *The Seattle Times* reported:

> Don't call us, we'll call you.
>
> That's the message frustrated US West customers say the company is sending in response to requests for new telephone service and repairs in the midst of a 10-day-old strike.

When Jake Batsell of *The Seattle Times* reported on rising prices in the area, here's how he began his story:

> If you're a transplant to the Seattle area, with monthly rent payments, a lengthy grocery list and a hankering for the occasional microbrew, chances are you've been spending more money lately.
>
> But if you're a landlord or longtime homeowner with a marathon commute, you probably haven't felt the pinch.
>
> Prices Puget Sound-area consumers pay for everything from housing to groceries have risen an average 2.9 percent over the past 12 months, a rate roughly twice the current national pace of 1.5 percent.

"The fact that inflation in Seattle was running roughly twice the national average caught the interest of the paper's news editors, who were interested in a follow-up story from a feature-type perspective explaining the reasons behind the figures," said Batsell, a business reporter who also writes consumer stories.

He added that consumer news is a paradoxical brand of "specialized reporting" because it examines a broad topic anyone can relate to: spending money. "The best consumer-oriented articles come across as personable and accessible, taking information that's often complex and turning it into something that's useful and practical for readers," Batsell said. "I tried to take that approach in the inflation story by using the categories with the most visible price jump (rent, groceries and beer) to create a profile of the type of person most affected by inflation in Seattle. Those kinds of mental pictures give readers an image they can identify with."

Batsell said that in consumer reporting, curiosity and a common sense approach are much more important than any sort of specialized expertise. "Just as a metro reporter starts from scratch in going out to cover a shooting or a fire, consumer reporting requires asking lots of questions and peeling away the layers," he added. "But specialized beats such as labor, trade and high-tech often require industry contacts and a sense of history and context that you won't have if you're always parachuting into stories."

Where to Turn Online

There are hundreds of Internet sites that offer business and consumer news and public relations items. They include standard news sites and scores of specialized sites.

Here is a sampling of sites that deals with consumer news:

- *www.safetyforum.com*, which provides information about products and practices that cause harm.
- *www.consumer.gov*, a resource for consumer information from the federal government.
- *www.natlconsumersleague.org*, which has as its mission "to identify, represent and advance the economic and social interests of consumers and workers."
- *www.consumerreports.org*, a site that provides evaluations of thousands of products.
- *www.fda.gov*, which offers press releases and much more from the U.S. Food and Drug Administration.
- *www.olen.com*, a site that contains Food Finder in which consumers can search for information on fast-food items sold at various restaurants.
- *www.cnsweb.com*, an information and news media company that provides data to newspapers, radio and television.

✔ A Checklist for Reporters Specializing in Consumer Journalism

Here are some tips for aspiring consumer reporters:

- ❏ Try to get a well-rounded liberal arts education.
- ❏ Read as much about consumer affairs as possible.
- ❏ Learn the language of consumer reporting.
- ❏ Try to get an internship in consumer reporting.
- ❏ After college, take more advanced training courses.

Technology

Expanding Coverage in New Technologies

Technology is moving faster than we are, and the nation's media are trying to keep up by devoting more and more space to covering it. Reporters are becoming specialists in technology and then are trying to explain it simply to their audiences.

Technology reporting is an outgrowth of or an extension of science writing. It requires reporters who are journalists as well as specialists. For instance, when the

St. Louis Post-Dispatch advertised for a science journalist, it sought someone to "lead a team of six to eight reporters covering science, health (including medicine) and technology." The newspaper's ad also noted, "A background in science is a plus."

When the *Star Tribune* in Minneapolis was hunting for two technology reporters, it sought one who could cover technology companies and one who could cover the Internet and electronic commerce.

"The reporter who covers the tech companies must be a good basic business journalist, familiar with financial statements and savvy about finding stories in numbers," said *Star Tribune* recruiter Brenda Rotherham. "The reporter covering the Internet should know the technology and be comfortable with it, but not be so much involved with it that he or she cannot see the stories most people would want to read about. We want an idea person, a strong writer, someone who can spot trends and see the so-what, who-cares about this new part of the world."

Dan Gillmor, technology columnist for the *San Jose* (Calif.) *Mercury News,* said, "You need to have some knowledge and, more important, journalism skills."

Gillmor was at the *Detroit Free Press* before going to the *Mercury News.* He also has worked at the *Kansas City Times* and several newspapers in Vermont. He has free-lanced for numerous publications.

He is in the heart of the Silicon Valley, where he writes extensively on subjects ranging from the ups and downs of technology stocks to computer language and programmers to business practices at Microsoft Corp.

"I cover anything to do with technology, tech issues and policy that touches on technology," Gillmor said. Still, he considers himself a reporter who also is a columnist, "which is different by definition. I inject opinion into what I write."

Kim Komando, who writes a syndicated column about technology and is the host of a national talk show, said: "In technology reporting, you have to remember who your audience is. You have to understand technology but also write so that if someone just got on a computer they would understand what you write."

Stories about Technology

Newspapers throughout the country are not only running technology stories as they break but also devoting a page or section each week to the specialized field.

For example, one column by Kim Komando began:

> If you still haven't bought that new back-to-school computer system, the wait may have paid off.
>
> This is the season for back-to-school rebates, and computer manufacturers and software publishers alike have jumped right in.

Dan Gillmor wrote about personal data being sold to companies.

> The business community loves knowing all about you, and it particularly loves trading what it knows about you with other companies.
>
> Your personal data represents big money, because it lets companies target you more efficiently—to make you a customer, or keep you as one.
>
> As public worries grow amid a spate of privacy abuses, companies have increasingly—if reluctantly—begun to offer consumers a way out: a loophole-ridden system in which you can "opt out" of any future solicitations. The real scandal is their refusal to give you a far preferable choice: opt in.

When *The East Valley Tribune* in suburban Phoenix ran a story on a local man who builds large-format cameras by hand, it put the piece on its weekly "Silicon Desert" section. The story by Booyeon Lee began:

> Nineteen years ago Keith Graham started building large-format cameras for himself because, on a public teacher's salary, he could not afford to buy one. Now, his $2,150 large-format cameras are selling by the hundreds across the country and Europe.
>
> Graham, who taught math, physics and photography at Mountain View High School for 15 years, started selling his cameras when other photographers saw them and wanted to buy them. Now he devotes all his time to K.B. Graham Inc.

These stories are representative of technology reporting as well as specialty reporting in general. They run the gamut from breaking news to features to opinion columns. They require someone who knows how to report and write, and who also has specialized knowledge about a complicated field.

Becoming a Technology Writer: Tips for Reporters

Dan Gillmor of the *San Jose Mercury News* said students interested in technology reporting should "learn how to think with a liberal-arts degree, but learn as much as you can about technology in the process. It's not necessary to live and breathe tech to cover it. Having a life is just as important as having a great beat."

Syndicated columnist and author Kim Komando said that as in any specialty reporting field, knowing how to report and write is essential. "It's hard to find people who can write who also understand how technology works, how it affects people and what new technologies are coming down the pike," she added.

Komando said students interested in specialty reporting need to "immerse themselves, whether it's sports, health or gardening. For instance, I could not write a political column. I'm totally immersed in this. As a student you need to find someone who is doing what you want to do and latch on to them. Offer to be a grunt, to work for them for hardly anything. It's worth it for what you'll learn."

She also sees continuing growth in technology reporting. "Before we had one general computing column," Komando added. "Now we have a Macintosh column, an Internet column and editorials about general technology. With the Internet we have interactive television, telecommunications and more."

Environment

Coverage of the Environment

Specialty reporters at major metropolitan newspapers and the television networks have been writing about the environment for decades. What the reporters cover has changed significantly, however. In the late 1960s and into the 1970s, environmental writing focused on what people could see, touch and smell, such as air and water pollution. Today, much environmental reporting focuses on what people cannot see, such as holes in the ozone, climate changes, toxic chemicals and nuclear waste.

Although this specialty is not new, most newspapers and broadcast outlets still get their environmental stories from the wire services or from reporters covering issues part time along with their regular beats.

As in any specialized field, environmental reporting requires expertise in complicated and highly technical areas. It also requires a reporter who can communicate with sources in areas ranging from all levels of government to the sciences.

Two Reporters and Their Jobs

John G. Mitchell of *National Geographic* magazine and Casey Bukro of the *Chicago Tribune* have covered the environment since the 1960s.

"The first thing I did was a series on air pollution in the old *New York Journal-American* in about 1961," said Mitchell, a senior assistant editor, writer, text editor and senior assistant editor for environment at *National Geographic*. "They put it opposite the comics page because they thought, 'What the hell is this?' No one was doing much back then. Now, there often are Page One stories in *The Washington Post* dealing with the environment. It has become more politically charged than before."

Bukro began covering the field in 1967. He started at the *Tribune* as a general assignment reporter and then became an assistant day city editor. "Among my jobs was to go through the mountains of mail and make sure we got the right mail to the right people," he said. "We started getting material on water pollution, and I started keeping it because there was no one to handle it. I started doing water pollution stories on a part-time basis."

He said that in the early days of reporting about the environment, his stories, like Mitchell's, dealt mainly with pollution. "You could see the stuff," he added. "You could hear, taste and touch pollution in those days. That's why the public responded so strongly to it."

Mitchell worked several jobs and wrote about the environment before he joined *National Geographic.* He was a writer and science editor at *Newsweek,* editor-in-chief for Sierra Club Books and a writer and editor for *Audubon* magazine. He authored seven books and also wrote pieces for *American Heritage, Smithsonian, Field & Stream* and *Sports Afield.*

"I think there are two kinds of writing about the environment," he said. "There's the highly technical writing that you'd find in journals and there's the type that I do, which is done by a generalist. The first type never appealed to me personally. I prefer to write narrative stories about some issue that include a good amount of information. The main thrust is telling a story rather than just telling the facts."

Bukro said environment reporting is a specialty. "I try to look for the root causes of things no matter where I have to go," he said. "I've been to the state house, I've been to City Hall, I've been to the White House to cover the environment. Some people just sit back and look at the long-range stuff. I do some of that. But I treat it as a newsy beat where things are happening almost every day."

Becoming an Environmental Writer: Tips for Reporters

"No kid steps out of school and goes into a beat like this," Bukro said. "You have to be a solid reporter and solid writer, and you have to know how journalism works before you get involved in a specialty. You have to know how to be a good reporter and get details. You have to be a good writer to present the details. I am dealing with scientists who use highly specialized terms. It takes years to pick up the lingo and ask intelligent questions.

"Then you have to make it into compelling reading. You don't just say what they said. You can't use their fancy terms. That's the quickest way to lose a reader. You have to take this mountain of material from highly technical people and make it into a story that a reader wants to read and can't put down."

Bukro said there will be plenty of opportunities for future reporters who want to cover the ever-changing environment. He added: "One of the things that sometimes scares me is I'm not sure we have been covering the issues that really need to be covered. If you look at journalism historically, we tend to cover conventional wisdom. How long did it take for us to see auto pollution as a real hazard? Who saw some of the problems we're having with toxic chemicals? It wasn't until this stuff slapped us in the face that we started to write about it.

"There are so many issues. The comet heading our way. Garbage. Food. Radioactive waste. These may turn out to be more of a problem than they are supposed to be. There's a lot of stuff lying around, toxic waste that already has soaked into the ground. It's a real problem. We've really messed up a lot of water. I sometimes think we don't really know yet what all these things mean together."

Mitchell said: "You need to be interested in the subject. That's dangerous ground to start with because most people still have this idea that a good reporter has to be objective. I think a good reporter needs to be fair and balanced.

"You have to care about clean landscape or clean air or clean water. You have to have a concern and secondly you have to be able to mute that concern to the extent that you will be fair. Of course there also are places on some publications for advocacy journalism."

He suggested that aspiring journalists who want to write about the environment for a good publication "do have to have that journalism pedigree, but I think you also need the broadest kind of education. Get an education in as many subjects as possible."

LAW

More than three decades ago, when the U.S. Supreme Court considered cases that involved the mass media, reporters and editors predictably climbed onto their soapboxes and pointed majestically to the First Amendment, smugly assured that the Constitution provided them with ironclad protection to gather and print news as they wished.

Most journalists today are less confident and certainly more realistic. Lyle Denniston, a veteran Supreme Court reporter, vividly summarized what a lot of journalists think. He

Congress shall make no law
respecting an establishment of religion,
or prohibiting the free exercise thereof;
or abridging the freedom of speech, or of the press,
or the right of the people peaceably to assemble,
and to petition the Government for a
redress of grievances.

(*Courtesy of The Freedom Forum*)

wrote in *The Baltimore Sun:* "Reporters, editors, publishers and broadcasters can be less sure than ever before about their constitutional freedom. The law has discovered the press in a big and threatening way, and as a result the 'free press' clause is not as strongly protective as the press has thought."

Henry Kaufman, general counsel for the Libel Defense Resource Center in New York, called the American climate "tumultuous" with regard to freedom of the press. He said: "There is a lot of attention being paid to journalism, the power of the press and the influence of controversial stories in a wide variety of contexts. Everything goes in cycles. We seem to be in a cycle where the public questions media methods and is less willing to question what the media are exposing."

The depth of freedom of the press indeed runs in cycles. The late Zechariah Chafee Jr., a Harvard law professor, summarized freedom of the press in the first half of the 20th century. He called World War I a "period of struggle and criminal prosecutions"; the 1920s a "period of growth"; 1930 to 1945 a "period of achievement"; and the Cold War a "period of renewed struggle and subtle suppressions." Freedom of the press blossomed under the liberal Earl Warren Court in the 1960s; but if there has been no erosion, there has been scant expansion during the decades that have followed.

The First Amendment and the Press

Very simply, the First Amendment does not mean literally what it says: "Congress shall make no law . . . abridging the freedom of speech, or of the press." There are exceptions to its seemingly ironclad language. Only seven years after ratification of the First Amendment, Congress passed the Alien and Sedition Laws of 1798, designed to stifle criticism of the government. Those laws expired when Thomas Jefferson became president in 1801, but more than a century later, in 1918, Congress approved another Sedition Act for basically the same reason.

In 1919 Justice Oliver Wendell Holmes Jr. wrote that "the First Amendment, while prohibiting legislation against free speech as such, cannot have been, and obviously was not, intended to give immunity for every possible use of language."

In 1942 Justice Frank Murphy wrote: "It is well understood that the right of free speech is not absolute at all times, and under all circumstances. There are certain well-defined and narrowly limited classes of speech, the prevention and punishment of which have never been thought to raise any constitutional problem."

The courts have repeatedly held that the First Amendment is not an absolute. Thus, they are constantly called on to decide whether actions taken by the press are legally permissible. As the courts consider issues on a case-by-case basis, journalists are obligated to stay abreast of significant decisions.

A national survey reported in *Journalism Quarterly* showed that editors are increasingly cognizant of the need to keep pace with developments in communication law. Student journalists—as well as professionals—certainly need to be aware of the effects of court decisions on reporters and editors. Applicable court decisions should not be looked on as esoteric ramblings by scholarly justices; working journalists should view the decisions as fragments of wisdom that help them to function effectively—day by day.

Areas of particular concern to reporters are libel, protection of sources and the fair trial–free press controversy. We'll examine these in turn.

Libel

Libel Law and Libel Suits

Libel—holding someone up to public hatred, ridicule or scorn—is the communication of false information that damages an individual in his or her profession, business or calling. This tort has become "politicized," according to Henry Kaufman. "Libel litigation was intended to bring about the vindication of an individual at an individual level," he said. "But it has moved into the political arena where people are vying for more power. This is a troubling development. The press, being a powerful institution itself, inherently always has been subject to this tugging and pulling within the political process. But putting libel into the political process is coercive and threatening."

Five requirements must be met before a libel action can be successfully brought against a media outlet: (1) publication (communication to a third party); (2) identification (though this is not limited to calling an individual by name); (3) harm to reputation; (4) proof of falsity; and (5) proof of fault.

William Prosser, the late dean of the University of California Hastings College of the Law, wrote: "There is a great deal of the law of defamation which makes no sense. It contains anomalies and absurdities for which no legal writer ever has a kind word." Indeed, libel law is complex. Large-circulation newspapers have the luxury of retaining attorneys with special expertise in this area; most smaller-circulation papers retain lawyers, but they probably do not specialize in communication law. Knowing that virtually every story is potentially libelous is enough to make any reporter timid. It is imperative, therefore, that reporters have at least a basic understanding of libel law; then, at least, they need not call an attorney—particularly one who does not specialize in communication law—every time they write a controversial story.

Lyle Denniston thinks that reporters are too dependent on attorneys. He wrote in *Quill* magazine that lawyers in the newsroom are "as much of a threat to the press as judges sitting on the bench deciding what we can print. I think you have to go to hell for election with your stories and then take the consequences and I do mean prepare to go to the slammer." Translation: Newspaper attorneys are retained to keep their newspapers out of court; the easiest way to do so is to avoid printing controversial stories.

What Leads to Libel?

Most libel suits do not grow from hard-hitting, aggressive reporting of matters of monumental importance. The majority of suits evolve from—to use the newsroom vernacular—stupid, idiotic mistakes, such as failure to copy information correctly from public records. For example, John Jones is found *not guilty* of aggravated assault, but the reporter hurriedly skims the court records and writes that Jones was found *guilty* of aggravated assault.

Bruce Sanford, a reporter-turned-attorney who represents the Society of Professional Journalists and Scripps-Howard, said at the First Amendment Survival

Seminar held in Washington, D.C., that the "chief cause of libel suits is plain old unromantic carelessness." Sanford estimated that 80 percent of all libel suits flow from "the simple, routine story that nobody would have missed if it hadn't appeared in the newspaper or been broadcast." Sanford cautioned that reporters must be very careful with rewrites, condensations and summaries.

Four potential paths to libel are certain explosive words, certain categories of words, defamation by implication, and quotations. Let's consider these.

"Red Flag" Words

Sanford listed the following "red flag" words in "Libel and Privacy." Reporters and editors should handle these words carefully; potentially they are legally explosive and could lead to libel litigation because harm to reputation is apparent.

adulteration of products
adultery
AIDS
alcoholic
altered records
ambulance chaser
atheist
bad moral character
bankrupt
bigamist
blacklisted
blackmail
blockhead
booze-hound
bribery
brothel
buys votes
cheats
child abuse
collusion
con artist
confidence man
corruption
coward
crook
deadbeat
deadhead
defaulter
divorced
double-crosser
drug abuser
drunkard
ex-convict
fawning sycophant
fraud
gambling den
gangster
gay
graft
groveling office seeker
herpes
hit-man
hypocrite
illegitimate
illicit relation
incompetent
infidelity
informer
insider trading
intimate
intolerance
Jekyll-Hyde personality
kept woman
Ku Klux Klan
liar
Mafia
manipulate
mental illness
mobster
moral delinquency
mouthpiece
Neo-Nazi
paramour
peeping Tom
perjurer
plagiarist
pockets public funds
price cutter
profiteering
prostitute
rape/rapist
scam
scandalmonger
scoundrel
seducer
sharp dealing
shyster
slacker
smooth and tricky
smuggler
sneaky
sold influence
sold out
spy
stool pigeon
stuffed the ballot box
suicide
swindle
taken
thief
unethical
unmarried mother
unprofessional
unsound mind
unworthy of credit
vice den
villain

Reporters can steer clear of many libel suits by scrutinizing the meaning of the words and the sentences they write. A warning bell should sound any time a reporter writes a story that contains any of the "red flag" words. In certain contexts, these words could damage a person's reputation.

Classes of Libelous Words

When writing sensitive stories, always be alert for potentially libelous statements. Libel in the state of Illinois, for example, includes these classes of words: (1) words imputing the commission of a criminal offense; (2) words that impute infection with a loathsome communicable disease of any kind which would tend to exclude one from society; (3) words that impute inability to perform, or want of integrity in the discharge of, duties of office or employment; and (4) words that prejudice a particular person in his or her profession or trade. Classes of libelous words can, of course, vary slightly among the states, but this list is representative. Following are examples of each category.

1: Words imputing the commission of a criminal offense. Avoid statements such as this:

> John Crandall was taken into custody Wednesday for murdering Sally Smith Tuesday night.

Think again. Is that really what happened? Remember to choose your words carefully. Crandall is not guilty of murder until a court says that he is. It would be better to write:

> John Crandall was taken into custody Wednesday in connection with (or in the investigation of) the Tuesday night slaying of Sally Smith.

2: Words that impute infection with a loathsome communicable disease of any kind that would tend to exclude one from society. Don't write:

> John Crandall, who was elected Wednesday to be president of the local chapter of the Fellowship of Christian Athletes, was treated last summer for a venereal disease, the *Daily Bugle* has learned.

Such an accusation is hardly a major scoop. There is no reason to publish it. It is an example of going out on a legal limb for the type of story that Sanford mentioned earlier: one that "nobody would have missed if it hadn't appeared in the newspaper or been broadcast." The lesson is clear: the danger of libel constantly lurks; if you are going to tempt fate, do so with a story that is worth the risk.

3: Words that impute inability to perform, or want of integrity in the discharge of, duties of office or employment. Don't write:

> Public school groundskeeper John Crandall is unfit by temperament and intelligence to adequately perform his duties, sources who wish to remain anonymous said Wednesday.

This lead paragraph is another example of using a verbal sledgehammer to bludgeon an ant. Why risk a suit for such a revelation? Again remember: Be aggressive when you report, but make sure that the story justifies the potential harm to your subject and to your employer's pocketbook.

4: Words that prejudice a particular person in his or her profession or trade. Don't write:

> Attorney John Crandall, who will represent the widow in the embezzlement case, is the most incompetent lawyer in town, according to courthouse observers.

Obviously, Crandall is not going to take kindly to the accusation. Can the reporter document the charge, and is there sufficient justification for making it? The reporter who wrote the paragraph had better hope so.

The examples and suggestions above illustrate one principle: Handle with care any story that could injure a person's reputation. This does not mean that you should back away from a story that should be told. But it does mean that you should choose your words carefully. Ask yourself: Am I being fair? Am I being accurate? Is this story worth the legal risk?

Defamation by Implication

In addition to the laundry list of specific words identified by Bruce Sanford and the four categories of words described above that create potential libel liability, journalists also must be aware of something called *defamation by implication.* In this situation, it is not the use of any particular words that creates liability, but rather the *implication created by the reporter's organization of facts.* For instance, a brief story reads:

> John Jones was seen entering the Shady Oaks motel yesterday with a woman. The motel is located in a known prostitution area.

The reasonable implication to be drawn from these two sentences is clear—that Jones engaged in illegal conduct by soliciting a prostitute. Although the reporter never directly said this, he or she could nonetheless be held accountable if this implication turns out to be false. Be aware, then, that libel suits can arise from not only what you write, but how you write it. A defamatory implication may be just as dangerous as a defamatory statement.

Quotations

Remember: The reporter and the news medium are responsible for statements aired or printed—even if someone is being quoted directly or indirectly. Assume, for example, that a reporter interviews the neighbor of a man who has just been charged with murder. The neighbor says that the man is a "no-good drunken bum who beats his kids regularly and belongs to the Communist Party." The fact that the neighbor made the observation does not reduce the newspaper's level of liability; *the news medium must assume responsibility for the statement if it is used.*

As the attorney Neil Rosini has pointed out, misquotations can defame not only third parties whom a speaker mentions but also the quoted speaker. The U.S. Supreme Court ruled in 1991 that deliberate misquotations may injure reputation by attributing harmful assertions to the speaker if the misquotations result in a "material change" in the meaning intended by the speaker.

Reporters must always keep the following points in mind when using quotations.

1: The fact that information was provided by a source does not necessarily mean that it is correct. Assume, for example, that a nurse tells a reporter that

Dr. John Jones is the only physician practicing at Memorial Hospital who has been sued successfully for malpractice during the preceding year. The reporter could sit at a computer terminal and type:

> Dr. John Jones is the only physician who practices at Memorial Hospital to be sued successfully for malpractice during the past year, according to a nurse.

The lead sounds like the start of a great story. The problem is that the reporter did not verify the information. Jones had been sued, but he won his case. The nurse had him confused with another doctor. The lesson is clear: do not rely on secondhand information when printing accusations of such gravity. Check and double-check. And then go to the person who has been accused for his or her side of the story. By failing to do so, the reporter invites a libel action.

2: Beware of off-the-record tips passed along by sources, even high-ranking officials or law enforcement officers. Always confirm potentially libelous accusations. Prefacing an accusation with the word *alleged* will not help when you get to court. Do not, for example, write:

> Police said that the alleged crook is in custody.

Instead, write:

> Police said that the man charged with the crime is in custody.

Defenses against Libel

No matter how careful a reporter is, libel suits can materialize. In this section, we'll examine defenses against libel.

If a libel suit is filed, a defendant can use a number of defenses. Some defenses are conditional: they are viable if certain conditions or qualifications are met. Others are absolute: if proven, there are no conditions or qualifications. A defense may be based on common or statutory law or on the Constitution.

Common Law and Statutory Defenses

Conditional defenses. In their book "Libel: Rights, Risks, Responsibilities," Robert H. Phelps and E. Douglas Hamilton, two authorities on libel law, discuss conditional defenses that have evolved through the common law (judge-made law based on prior court decisions) and statutory law. These defenses include the following.

Privilege of reporting The defense known as *privilege of reporting* flows from fair and accurate reporting of official proceedings—city council meetings, state legislative sessions, congressional hearings and so forth—and the fair and accurate reporting of information contained in official documents and court records. Obviously, this defense is often cited by reporters. As emphasized, however, the defense is limited to fair and accurate reporting. Extraneous libelous matter cannot be intertwined. If, for example, during a city council meeting the mayor accuses the council president of embezzling city funds, the reporter is free to report that the charges were made—so long as the story accurately conveys what the mayor said. Any elaboration or interpretation of the mayor's remarks by the reporter would not necessarily be protected.

Many jurisdictions have extended this qualified privilege to include reporting on matters in the public interest that flow from *unofficial but open* meetings such as those taking place when citizens gather to consider construction of a nuclear waste facility or when political parties assemble to discuss pressing community issues. Check to see if this protection applies in your jurisdiction.

Fair comment and criticism As a defense against libel, *fair comment and criticism* applies only to opinions about matters of public concern. The defense does not protect erroneous factual reporting. It must be clear that the allegedly libelous statement—whether it appears in an editorial, a book review or a personal viewpoint column—is a statement of opinion, not an expression of fact. This defense is not available to the reporter who covers an event and then writes a factual news account. However, if a reporter were to comment on the news event and offer an analysis of it in a personal column, this defense possibly could be used.

Neutral reportage In 1977 the 2nd U.S. Circuit Court accepted neutral reportage as a conditional defense; that is, it is defensible to report charges made by one responsible person or organization about another when both parties are involved in a public controversy. This defense has not been widely accepted, however, and at least one circuit has specifically rejected it. Where it applies, though, it makes additional protection available to the defendant in a libel suit. Check to see if it applies in your state.

The defense was cited in *Edwards* v. *National Audubon Society*. In this case, a *New York Times* reporter wrote a story concerning accusations by officials of an Audubon Society periodical, *American Birds,* that scientists who contended that the insecticide DDT did not have a negative impact on bird life were being paid to lie. The *Times* story included a short denial by some of the named scientists who had sent to the reporter extensive research material to refute the charges. The 2nd U.S. Circuit Court said that even when a newspaper seriously doubts the truth of the charges, the publication is protected under the defense of neutral reportage—objective and dispassionate reporting of the charges.

Absolute defenses. The following are absolute defenses against libel.

Statute of limitations Statute of limitations is the most ironclad of the defenses. If a suit is brought after a specified period—in most states the statute of limitations on libel is one, two or three years—the plaintiff has no standing to sue.

Truth Truth is an absolute defense in most states. But its practical value as a defense against libel has been considerably diminished because the burden now rests with the plaintiff to prove falsity, especially when the challenged statement relates to a matter of public interest; the burden is no longer on the defendant to prove truth.

Professor Rodney A. Smolla of the University of Richmond noted in his book, "Law of Defamation," that the courts have shifted the burden from the defendant, who previously had to prove the passage in question was truthful, to the plaintiff, who must now provide proof of falsity as part of his case. Smolla wrote: "Although the 'truth' issue is now properly classified as part of the plaintiff's principal case, lawyers continue to refer colloquially to the 'truth defense,' . . . though it would be more technically correct to drop the word 'defense.' "

Privilege of participant The defense called *privilege of participant* applies to participants in official proceedings: a city council member's remarks during a meeting, the testimony of a witness during a trial, a senator speaking on the protected floor of the Senate. This, then, is not a defense reporters would generally be able to use. Reporters normally report the news—not make it.

Consent or authorization If a reporter writes a libelous passage, calls the person in question and gets his or her permission to publish it, this defense can be used. Obviously, this situation is not likely to happen.

Self-defense or right of reply If publicly criticized, the recipient of the criticism has a right to respond. He or she must be careful, however, to keep the response within the framework of the original accusation. For example, suppose that a newspaper's drama critic treats the opening of a play harshly. The star of the play could respond, but the privilege of response covers only a response to the original criticism. In other words, the star could not launch a salvo critical of the reviewer's home life.

Journalists would not often have occasion to use this defense.

Partial defenses. If conditional or absolute defenses (including the conditional *New York Times* "actual malice" defense, which will be discussed in the next section) cannot be used successfully, the defendant will probably be assessed damages. He or she can, however, cite partial defenses to mitigate the damages. Partial defenses represent good faith on the part of the defendant, and a judge can take them into consideration when levying damages. Partial defenses include publication of a retraction (a clear admission of erroneous reporting) or of facts showing that, though the newspaper erred, there was no gross negligence or ill will or that the reporter relied on a usually reliable source.

A Constitutional Defense: The Actual Malice Standard

***The New York Times* rule.** Clearly, the reporter is not without common law and statutory defenses. However, most of these defenses are limited compared with the federal rule, commonly called the *actual malice* defense. This is a constitutional defense first articulated by the U.S. Supreme Court in 1964. In the landmark case of *New York Times Co.* v. *Sullivan,* the court nationalized the law of libel in part to provide a constitutional defense when *public officials* are plaintiffs. Suit was brought against *The Times* for publication of an advertisement in 1960 that, in essence, said that the civil rights movement in the South was being met with a wave of aggression by certain Southern officials. L. B. Sullivan, a Montgomery, Ala., commissioner, filed the suit. Portions of the advertisement were false, and under existing statutory and common law, a defendant had to prove the literal truth of the statements. The Alabama courts awarded Sullivan $500,000 in damages.

The Supreme Court, however, reversed this ruling. It held that, to collect damages, a public official—which Sullivan clearly was—would have to prove that the defendant acted with "actual malice." Justice William Brennan said that this would constitute disseminating information "with knowledge that it was false or with reckless disregard of whether it was false or not." Brennan wrote that the advertisement, "as an expression of grievance and protest on one of the major public issues of our time, would seem clearly to qualify for the constitutional protection." The media would be protected against suits brought by public officials, even when the statements were false—so long as the statements were not made with actual malice. Essentially, the case put to death the concept of seditious libel in the United States.

The conditional actual malice defense provides reporters with a primary defense to add to their arsenal of common law and statutory defenses. The condition on which the *Times* rule was based, of course, is that the publication must concern a public official. From 1964 on, the status of the plaintiff—whether public or private—has been the first consideration a defendant makes when formulating possible defenses against a libel action. In 1967 the Supreme Court said that **public figures**—in addition to public officials—also have to show actual malice to recover libel damages. The message is clear: As a reporter, you don't want to get tied up in a libel action, but if you do, there is more protection if the plaintiff is a public person.

The *Times* rule was extended again in 1971. A plurality of the court said in *Rosenbloom* v. *Metromedia* that private persons involved in events of general or public interest also have to show actual malice to recover libel damages. The press was elevated to its most protected position ever regarding libel defenses.

***Gertz* v. *Robert Welch*.** In 1974, however, the press was dealt a setback. In *Gertz* v. *Robert Welch Inc.,* the court said that it had gone too far in *Rosenbloom* and that unless a plaintiff in a libel suit were to be awarded presumed or punitive damages, private persons involved in events of general or public interest need only prove a lower fault standard—presumably **negligence**—to receive damages. Negligence would certainly be easier to prove than actual malice, the standard still required with public officials and public figures.

In addition to stripping the press of some of the protection it had come to enjoy as a result of *Rosenbloom, Gertz* also restructured the definition of a public figure. The court said that to be categorized as a public figure, an individual must "voluntarily thrust" himself or herself into the vortex of the particular controversy that gave rise to the litigation with the intention of influencing its outcome (for example, leading a movement to recall a city council member) or must assume a role "of especial prominence" to the extent that, for all purposes, he or she is to be considered a public figure (for example, celebrities such as David Letterman or athletes such as Tiger Woods).

The court also said that each state would define the appropriate level of liability—presumably negligence—when suits were brought by non-public persons involved in events of general or public interest. Some 34 states have since defined negligence, but few definitions are uniform. Some states define it as "gross negligence," and others as "failure to act as a reasonable person."

Professor W. Wat Hopkins of Virginia Polytechnic Institute and State University wrote in *Journalism Monographs:* "Negligence is a nebulous word. And other nebulous words—reasonable, prudent, ordinary, careful, proper—are being used to define it."

The article focused on the various standards of negligence that had been established. Hopkins concluded: "While courts may not have always agreed on the legal definition of negligence, most courts, thus far anyway, have recognized sloppy reporting. And the best protection from the finding of negligence is the elimination of sloppy reporting."

It is important that reporters check to see what definition applies in the states where they work. Some state supreme courts agreed to review cases for the sole purpose of defining the standard of liability for libel of private persons involved in public events. In reviewing such a case, for example, the Arizona Supreme Court said that negligence is "conduct which creates an unreasonable risk of harm. It is the failure to use that amount of care which a reasonably prudent person would use under like circumstances."

As emphasized earlier, with the status of the plaintiff an all-important consideration when defending against libel actions, *Gertz* took away some of the certainty editors and reporters had when deciding who might be categorized as a public figure. In *Gertz,* for example, the plaintiff was a well-known Chicago attorney who had been reasonably active in civic affairs. But the court reasoned that his reputation as a lawyer was not pervasive enough to stamp him as a public figure for all purposes; and in this particular case, he had not thrust himself to the forefront of the controversy.

As we have seen, the press has the most protection when sued by either public officials or public figures; if the plaintiffs are so categorized, to recover damages they must prove that the defendant acted with actual malice. When plaintiffs are private persons involved in events of public concern, they must prove that the defendant acted with negligence—a less stringent standard. Reporters naturally do not want to become embroiled in libel suits. If they are, however, as we stated above, the chance of a successful defense is greater if the plaintiff is a public official or a public figure. This was apparent in a libel action in the mid-1980s that attracted considerable attention: *Sharon* v. *Time, Inc.*

The Sharon case. Ariel Sharon, former minister of defense for the state of Israel, brought a $50 million libel action against Time Inc., on the basis of a single paragraph in an article entitled, "The Verdict Is Guilty: An Israeli Commission Apportions the Blame for the Beirut Massacre."

While Sharon was minister of defense, Israel invaded Lebanon, hoping to eliminate Palestine Liberation Organization strongholds from which the PLO had been attacking Israel. Members of the Christian Phalangist militia—by arrangement with the Israel Defense Forces—entered Palestinian refugee camps at Sabra and Shatilla. While there, the Phalangists slaughtered hundreds of Palestinian civilians, including women and children. Israel then established a commission to determine who was responsible for the slaughter.

Time's article included a discussion of the commission's findings. *Time* said that the report was a "stinging indictment" of Sharon. Sharon based his libel claim not on the thrust of the story, but on this paragraph:

> One section of the report, known as Appendix B, was not published at all, mainly for security reasons. That section contains the names of several intelligence agents referred to elsewhere in the report. Time has learned that it also contains further details

> about Sharon's visit to the Gemayel family on the day after Bashir Gemayel's assassination. [Gemayel was Lebanon's president elect.] Sharon reportedly told the Gemayels that the Israeli army would be moving into West Beirut and that he expected the Christian forces to go into the Palestinian refugee camps. Sharon also reportedly discussed with the Gemayels the need for the Phalangists to take revenge for the assassination of Bashir, but the details of the conversation are not known.

The federal District Court for the Southern District of New York noted:

> Sharon claims that this paragraph is false, both because he never discussed the need for revenge with the Gemayels and because the Commission Report contains no details of such discussion. He claims that this paragraph is defamatory both because it suggests that he instigated, encouraged, or condoned the massacres at Sabra and Shatilla, and because it suggests that the Commission had secret evidence or found secretly that he had lied when he testified that he had not known in advance that a massacre would occur.

Sharon, who was forced to resign his defense post after the commission's findings were released, said that he had visited Phalangist leaders one day before the slaughter, but he denied that he had ever discussed gaining revenge against the PLO.

Time labeled Sharon's libel action "an unprecedented case of a major foreign official suing for libel in a U.S. court over a story about his official actions." *Time*'s defense was complicated by the fact that Israel refused to turn over requested documents, for reasons of national security. This evened the odds somewhat because Sharon, as a public figure, faced the burden of showing that *Time* had acted with actual malice.

The trial attracted pervasive media attention. Federal Judge Abraham Sofaer was praised for his instructions that the jury announce its findings in stages before reaching a verdict:

First, the jury announced that the paragraph in question was defamatory. (Sharon's reputation had been tarnished.)

Next, it announced that the paragraph was false. (Appendix B made no mention of Sharon's speaking of a need for revenge.)

But, after considering the third and most important point—whether *Time* had acted in reckless disregard for the truth—the jurors found for the magazine.

The Associated Press quoted Sharon's attorney, Milton Gould, who said: "The only thing we don't get is money, and the reason we don't get any money is that we're dealing with a peculiar law of actual malice which makes it almost impossible for a public figure to prove."

The AP also reported that the jury issued a statement saying that certain *Time* employees, even though they had not published the story in reckless disregard for the truth, had acted "negligently and carelessly in reporting and verifying the information which ultimately found its way" into the paragraph.

Both sides claimed victory, but one fact emerges: *Time* did not have to pay damages. The case illustrates that the protection flowing from the actual malice standard is considerable. Clearly, it is not enough for a public figure to show that a media defendant carelessly published a defamatory or false report—even when the report caused significant damage to the plaintiff's reputation. The public person must also show that the defendant published the report with a high degree of awareness of probable falsity—and that is a stringent standard to overcome.

Libel in Cyberspace: A New Frontier

The U.S. Supreme Court did not hand down a decision on a First Amendment case until 1918—127 years after ratification of the free-speech clause. It is not surprising, then, that the courts—and legislatures—are groping their way in establishing parameters for "cyberlibel."

In the mid-1990s, discussion concerning liability for the dissemination of defamatory or obscene statements centered primarily on whether an online service was a *distributor* or a *publisher.*

In essence, a distributor, while choosing the material it provides over a bulletin board, still does not actually control the content of the information. It functions much like a library or bookstore, merely as a passive conduit—not like a publisher, which exercises editorial control over its product.

Then, in 1996, Congress passed the Communications Decency Act (CDA), which protects online service providers from liability for publication of defamatory material. The federal statute makes no distinction between publishers and distributors in providing immunity from liability. The law states: "No provider or user of an interactive computer service shall be treated as the publisher or speaker of any information provided by another information provider."

In 1997, the U.S. Court of Appeals for the 4th Circuit, in interpreting the CDA, held that the law prohibits libel suits that "seek to hold a service provider liable for its exercise of a publisher's traditional editorial functions—such as deciding whether to publish, withdraw, postpone or alter content."

More recently, a federal district court in the District of Columbia granted America Online Inc.'s motion for summary judgment in a libel action involving the Drudge Report, an Internet gossip column. The Drudge Report, which claimed that a presidential aide had "a spousal abuse past," was carried on AOL. The district court held AOL immune from the lawsuit because the CDA effectively immunized online service providers from liability for libelous information disseminated by them but created by others.

✔ A Checklist for Dealing with Libel

Guidelines for Reporters

Following is some advice for reporters with regard to libel.

❑ *Be Aggressive—But Don't Take Foolish Risks.* Fear of losing a libel suit probably chills the reporting process. Lyle Denniston advised reporters not to take "foolish risks" but also not to be overly cautious. "Reporters should not compromise," he said. "Journalists must take chances when reporting stories. They have to be aggressive.

"Reporters should not consider legal ramifications as they gather information and as they write a story. They should go after the story and worry about the law later. It is a risk, but when reporters and editors operate on legal premise, they inhibit the reportorial processes.

"If reporters follow ethical restraints, they should be within legal bounds. Reporters shouldn't try to gauge in advance what will fly legally. They aren't equipped to think legally—they inhibit themselves too much."

- ❑ *Be Fair—Keep an Open Mind.* The First Amendment scholar Marc A. Franklin of the Stanford Law School noted that reporting "involves substantial responsibility on the part of the journalist." He advised: "No reporter acts without a hypothesis. But that hypothesis must be open to change and modification continually. The reporter should not seek facts that support a strongly held hypothesis. Instead, reporters should seek as much information as will shed light on the situation. This requires an open mind, but not necessarily one that is unable to draw conclusions. If the reporter honestly concludes, after careful research and investigation, that the facts support a conclusion that is negative about someone—perhaps even defamatory—the reporter should lean over backwards to make sure that he or she has been reasonably careful in acquiring the facts and reasonably fair in considering them.

  "Reporters should recognize that the fairness with which a story is published may go a long way in avoiding the filing of a lawsuit. Working to be fair does not compromise the reporter's integrity in any way whatsoever. The point is that many subjects of defamation, though obviously unhappy, will respond to fair treatment in an article.

  "This kind of press behavior is in no way inconsistent with the notion of a strong, aggressive and inquiring media."

- ❑ *Seek Advice If You Are Unsure of Your Turf.* Henry Kaufman pointed out that legal rules are complex. "Reporters should take advantage of advice from legal counsel and from editors, and they should draw on what they learned in school," he said. "No matter how well-advised you are or how much you know, though, you can't completely guarantee that you are going to avoid litigation. A claim always can be filed, even if it is not meritorious. In fact, it would probably be a negative thing if the focus of reporters was on trying to guarantee a 100 percent libel-proof story. The only way to guarantee that would be to make a story completely inoffensive to public people. I don't think that would be good for journalism or in the public interest. The best thing reporters can do is to be good journalists. That means be careful and hope that you have a good lawyer if it comes down to defending the story."

Here are additional tips provided by The Reporters Committee for Freedom of the Press in its First Amendment Handbook:

- ❑ Check sources thoroughly. Get independent corroboration whenever possible. A source could have a vendetta against the subject and willfully or unintentionally misrepresent the facts for his or her own purposes. Confidential sources, such as government employees, may disappear or recant in the face of a lawsuit. Don't rely on someone else to be accurate.
- ❑ Do not let your opinion about whether someone is a public figure or official color your decision to verify the accuracy of a story. Juries do not respond favorably to reporters who fail to confront their subjects with defamatory information and to provide them with an opportunity to comment.
- ❑ If you cover the police or courthouse beat, make certain you understand criminal and civil procedure and terminology. Be especially careful to restate accurately any information obtained about arrests, investigations and judicial proceedings.
- ❑ Be cautious when editing. Make sure the story does not convey the wrong information because of a hasty rewrite.
- ❑ Watch for headlines and cutlines that might be defamatory even though the text explains the story.
- ❑ Make sure news promos or teasers used to stir audience interest are not misleading or defamatory.
- ❑ Do not use generic film footage or file photos when reporting on an activity that might be considered questionable.
- ❑ Just because someone else said it does not mean that a news organization cannot be sued for republishing it. This includes letters to the editor. Check out any factual allegations contained in them as carefully as you would statements in a news story.
- ❑ Be sensitive about using words that connote dishonest behavior, immorality or other undesirable traits, whether in your published story or in marginal comments in your notes. Remember that a judge may order a news organization to produce reporters' notes, drafts and internal memoranda at a libel trial.

Guidelines for Potential Defendants

Concern over libel actions is real enough that the New York State Newspapers Foundation, in its "Survival Kit for Reporters, Editors and Broadcasters," provided this advice for the potential defendant:

- ❑ *Be Courteous and Polite.* Nothing is gained by antagonizing a person who claims to have been libeled.
- ❑ *Do Not Admit an Error When a Person Initially Claims That He or She Has Been Libeled.* Take advantage of the complexity of the law.

Even though it is conceivable that you have libeled the person, the wrong may not be sufficient to sustain a libel suit.

- *Agree to Look into the Matter.* If nothing else, this will get the caller to leave you alone, at least temporarily.
- *If an Attorney Calls You about the Potential Libel, Refer the Call to Your Attorney.* Libel law is full of traps for the unwary; do not assume that you can discuss a case on an attorney's turf. The attorney probably knows the territory; you do not.
- *Notify Your Editor or Attorney at the First Mention of Libel.* Reporters should not attempt to resolve the problem without proper advice or counsel.

Reporters and Their Sources

Background

Historically, reporters have guarded the identity of anonymous sources. It is theorized that once a reporter betrays a confidential source, the reporter's other anonymous contacts will soon vanish. Why, after all, would sources who want to remain unnamed give information to reporters if the sources think that they might be betrayed?

Attorneys and police, however, have turned to reporters for information with increasing frequency. The problem is real. To date, the U.S. Supreme Court has considered only one case that focuses on **journalists' privilege**. In 1972 the court held in a fractured opinion that the First Amendment does not provide an absolute testimonial privilege to reporters who have witnessed a crime if they are called on to testify before a grand jury *(Branzburg* v. *Hayes).*

The Branzburg Case

Paul Branzburg, a reporter for the *Courier-Journal* in Louisville, Ky., had witnessed illegal drug use and had written articles about it. He was subpoenaed and asked to testify before a grand jury. He refused, claiming a First Amendment privilege. Justice Byron White, who wrote the majority decision when the case was reviewed by the Supreme Court, said that to contend that it is better to write about a crime than to do something about it is absurd. White's opinion, though not well-received by the press, did provide some hope. He emphasized that official harassment of the press in an effort to disrupt the reporter's relationship with his or her sources would not be tolerated. White also said that states were free to implement statutory laws—**shield laws**—to protect reporters.

Justice Lewis F. Powell Jr., in a concurring opinion, attempted to put *Branzburg* into perspective. He said that the ruling was "limited"; courts would still be available to reporters who think that their First Amendment rights have been violated. Furthermore, he said that the press could not be annexed as an "investigative right arm" of the government or the judiciary, and if the requested testimony was "remote," news reporters could move to quash the subpoena. The information sought had to be relevant and had to go to the heart of the issue; it could not be a fishing expedition by the authorities.

Justice Potter Stewart dissented. He proposed a three-part test to be considered whenever a reporter was asked by the government to reveal confidential information. Stewart wrote:

> [I] would hold that the government must (1) show that there is probable cause to believe that the newsman has information which is clearly relevant to a specific probable violation of law; (2) demonstrate that the information sought cannot be obtained by alternative means less destructive of First Amendment rights; and (3) demonstrate a compelling and overriding interest in the information.

The legal scholar Todd F. Simon of Kansas State's School of Journalism and Mass Communications noted that "the trio of tests . . . have become the basis for decisions in many of the cases that followed *Branzburg*." Simon said that "virtually every jurisdiction now has some form of the privilege, and most use Stewart's test." Simon noted, in fact, that the privilege is nearly absolute in civil suits in which the reporter is not a party.

Because of Justice Powell's carefully worded concurring opinion and Justice Stewart's dissent, a number of state and lower federal courts have often upheld the right of news reporters to protect their sources under certain conditions. In some circumstances, however, several lower courts have not upheld the reporter's rights. Courts consider questions of testimonial privilege on a case-by-case basis.

What if news reporters "burn" their confidential sources by revealing names? Indeed, in recent years some journalists have shown an increasing tendency to disregard promises of confidentiality when they believe that the public interest demands names of sources. The U.S. Supreme Court, though, held in *Cohen* v. *Cowles Media Co.* (1991) that the First Amendment does not immunize the press from a lawsuit if it breaks a promise of confidentiality to its sources. Be aware, then, that if you make a promise of confidentiality to a source, you should do your best to keep it.

Shield Laws

Although the Supreme Court made it plain that the First Amendment would not provide absolute protection for journalists called to testify, it did leave the door open for states to pass laws and for state courts to fashion rules that would shield reporters from testifying. More than 40 of the states have done so. Some states have relatively stringent shield laws that provide a great deal of protection, whereas others have qualified shield laws. It is important to remember, however, that even the most stringent laws probably have some loopholes.

Nebraska has one of the country's more stringent laws. The Nebraska law is designed to ensure the free flow of news and other information to the public and to protect the reporter against direct or indirect governmental restraint or sanction. The statute states that "compelling such persons to disclose a source of information or to disclose unpublished information is contrary to the public interest and inhibits the free flow of information to the public." The law protects reporters from testifying before any federal or state judicial, legislative, executive or administrative body.

No matter how ironclad shield laws appear, however, they are subject to interpretation by the judiciary. The constitutionality of most shield laws has never been contested, and even if their constitutionality was upheld, hostile judicial interpretation could strip protection from the reporter. In essence, reporters should never assume that the law will keep them out of jail.

The Arizona shield law, for example, did not provide sufficient protection for the *Arizona Republic*'s investigative reporter Jerry Seper. Seper had written articles saying that a wealthy Arizona liquor distributor was under investigation by the Internal Revenue Service. Presumably, Seper had obtained this confidential information from an IRS employee. Later, the IRS officially declared the liquor distributor innocent of any wrongdoing in connection with his tax returns. Lawyers for the distributor then filed suit in federal district court in Arizona against an IRS agent who they claimed had provided Seper with the confidential information. The agent named in the suit denied that he had given information to Seper; the reporter's testimony supported the denial. Attorneys for the liquor distributor then substituted an unnamed "John Doe" as the defendant.

Seper was asked to give the name of his source; he refused, citing Arizona's shield law (which was nearly half a century old) and the First Amendment. The district judge ruled that, under *Branzburg,* Seper did not have First Amendment protection. Clearly, the information sought went to the heart of the matter and was available from no other sources. The judge also ruled that, since suit was filed in federal district court, Arizona's state shield law was not applicable. Still, Seper steadfastly refused to reveal his source.

Ultimately, the liquor distributor's lawyers requested that Seper be held in contempt of court for failure to identify sources necessary to their case. At this point, Seper invoked his Fifth Amendment right against self-incrimination. (Federal law prohibits unauthorized publication of confidential tax information.) The judge, on the basis of Seper's Fifth Amendment claim, denied the request that the reporter be held in contempt of court.

Seper was fortunate, but it was not the First Amendment or the state shield law that kept him out of jail. The case clearly illustrates that reporters cannot always depend on state laws for protection.

In addition to worrying about revealing names of confidential sources during investigations of criminal wrongdoing, reporters must also face the possibility that plaintiffs, while bringing suit for libel, will seek to identify persons who supplied the information on which a story was based. In fact, shield laws in some states specifically say that protection is not extended to journalists under these circumstances. Though shield laws might not help reporters involved in libel actions, the journalists are not without protection.

In December 1970, for example, Jack Anderson's syndicated newspaper column, "Washington Merry-Go-Round," reported that the president of the United Mine Workers (UMW), Tony Boyle, and its general counsel, Ed Carey, had been removing boxfuls of documents from Boyle's office. Later, Carey made an official complaint to Washington police that burglars had stolen a boxful of "miscellaneous items." Because the United Mine Workers union was under investigation by the Justice Department, Carey contended that the column had, essentially, falsely accused him of obstruction of justice.

Carey brought a libel suit against Anderson and the reporter Brit Hume. To prove that Anderson and Hume had acted in "reckless disregard for the truth"—a necessary condition to collect damages—Carey had to show that Anderson and Hume had obtained their information from an unreliable source. The U.S. Court of Appeals for the District of Columbia reasoned that this was a heavy burden to meet and that the identity of the source was therefore critical to Carey's claim. Hume was prepared to go to jail for contempt, fully intending not to reveal his source. However, the source, a former UMW employee, voluntarily stepped forward to testify at the jury trial. This probably saved Hume from going to jail.

Circumstances were similar in another libel suit brought against Anderson and his "Merry-Go-Round" column (*Shelton* v. *Anderson*). Turner B. Shelton, a former ambassador to Nicaragua, sought damages for a column critical of his performance as a public official. Shelton claimed that several of the allegations made against him were false. Like Carey, Shelton attempted to compel Anderson to reveal confidential sources who had supplied information. Anderson supplied the names of several non-confidential sources, but he refused to supply the names of sources who had been promised anonymity. The U.S. District Court for the District of Columbia reasoned that because Shelton had made no effort to question any non-confidential sources, it could hardly be concluded that the identities of unnamed sources were essential to his case. Thus Anderson was not forced to reveal the names.

It becomes apparent, then, that the flexibility of *Branzburg* can be used to protect journalists who are asked to reveal their confidential sources, particularly when the information sought is not directly relevant to the issue or if other equally valuable sources have not been tapped.

Fair Trial versus Free Press

Background: An Ongoing Conflict

Cases involving the inherent conflict between the First Amendment rights of the press to report and the Sixth Amendment rights of the accused to a speedy and public trial by an impartial jury have surfaced with regularity during the past several decades. Such cases represent an ever-present dilemma. As early as 1807, Chief Justice John Marshall was confronted with the responsibility of seeing that Aaron Burr was not deprived of his constitutional rights during a treason trial that gained widespread public attention.

Journalists have long contended that the press is entitled to cover litigation. Reporters recognize the Sixth Amendment rights of defendants but argue that these rights can be maintained without trampling on the freedom to report. **Procedural safeguards** such as change of venue (changing the location of a trial), change of venire (transporting jurors in from another jurisdiction), sequestering jurors (keeping them away from news reports) and effective voir dire (questioning potential jurors to determine if they have prejudicial feelings about one of the parties) are available to judges who wish to ensure that defendants are not deprived of the judicial serenity and fairness to which they are constitutionally entitled.

Though procedural safeguards are available, they are sometimes not used. In fairness to the judiciary, however, publicity for some particularly notorious trials has been so prejudicial and so pervasive that the safeguards might not have provided sufficient protection. This was evident in some cases during the early 1960s. In *Irvin* v. *Dowd* (1961), the U.S. Supreme Court, for the first time in history, reversed and remanded a state criminal conviction because of intense prejudicial publicity. The barrage of publicity leveled at Leslie Irvin in Evansville, Ind., was so intense that of 430 potential jurors examined under voir dire, about 85 percent said that they believed Irvin was guilty. Even before Irvin had been found guilty a radio station conducted man-on-the-street interviews to determine what kind of punishment he should receive.

Two years later, the court considered a case in which a station in Lake Charles, La., had televised, complete with sound, a sheriff securing a confession from a man accused of murder (*Rideau* v. *Louisiana*). The height of press irresponsibility, however, probably came in the trial of Dr. Sam Sheppard, who had been accused of murdering his wife (*Sheppard* v. *Maxwell,* 1966). His trial was later described by the Supreme Court as a "carnival" that rendered virtually impossible any private communication between the defendant and his attorney. Reporters jammed the 26- by 48-foot Ohio courtroom. Only 14 seats were reserved for family members. Seven of the 12 jurors had one or more Cleveland newspapers delivered to their homes; local papers cried for "justice" in front-page editorials. Not surprisingly, the high court reversed and remanded the case, contending that "bedlam reigned at the courthouse."

Balancing Conflicting Rights: Guidelines for the Bar and the Press

Cases such as these that focused on media irresponsibility at its crudest brought the issue to the forefront. Shortly after *Sheppard,* the American Bar Association's Advisory Committee on Fair Trial and Free Press released its findings. The committee sought to provide guidelines that would balance the conflicting constitutional rights. Though the report was aimed primarily at lawyers, law enforcement officers and judges, it had an indirect effect on the press. Also, the committee recommended that judges use the contempt power against reporters who communicate information that could be damaging to the accused.

Several states, including Nebraska, used the ABA report as a model as lawyers, judges and journalists put their heads together in an attempt to develop guidelines for the coverage of litigation.

The Nebraska guidelines, which are drawn from the ABA report, are representative of other states. The guidelines are included in a booklet published by the Nebraska Press Association and the Nebraska Broadcasters Association.

Portions of the Nebraska Bar–Press guidelines follow:

> These voluntary guidelines reflect standards which bar and news media representatives believe are a reasonable means of accommodating, on a voluntary basis, the correlative constitutional rights of free speech and free press with the right of an accused to a fair trial. They are not intended to prevent the news media from inquiring

into and reporting on the integrity, fairness, efficiency and effectiveness of law enforcement, the administration of justice, or political or governmental questions whenever involved in the judicial process.

As a voluntary code, these guidelines do not necessarily reflect in all respects what the members of the bar or the news media believe would be permitted or required by law.

Information Generally Appropriate for Disclosure, Reporting

Generally, it is appropriate to disclose and report the following information:

(1) The arrested person's name, age, residence, employment, marital status and similar biographical information.

(2) The charge, its text, any amendments thereto, and, if applicable, the identity of the complainant.

(3) The amount or conditions of bail.

(4) The identity of and biographical information concerning the complaining party and victim, and if a death is involved, the apparent cause of death unless it appears that the cause of death may be a contested issue.

(5) The identity of the investigating and arresting agencies and the length of the investigation.

(6) The circumstances of arrest, including time, place, resistance, pursuit, possession of and all weapons used, and a description of the items seized at the time of arrest. It is appropriate to disclose and report at the time of seizure the description of physical evidence subsequently seized other than a confession, admission or statement. It is appropriate to disclose and report the subsequent finding of weapons, bodies, contraband, stolen property and similar physical items if, in view of the time and other circumstances, such disclosure and reporting are not likely to interfere with a fair trial.

(7) Information disclosed by the public records, including all testimony and other evidence adduced at the trial.

Information Generally Not Appropriate for Disclosure, Reporting

Generally, it is not appropriate to disclose or report the following information because of the risk of prejudice to the right of an accused to a fair trial:

(1) The existence or contents of any confession, admission or statement given by the accused, except it may be stated that the accused denies the charges made against him. This paragraph is not intended to apply to statements made by the accused to representatives of the news media or to the public.

(2) Opinions concerning the guilt, the innocence or the character of the accused.

(3) Statements predicting or influencing the outcome of the trial.

(4) Results of any examination or tests or the accused's refusal or failure to submit to an examination or test.

(5) Statements or opinions concerning the credibility or anticipated testimony of prospective witnesses.

(6) Statements made in the judicial proceedings outside the presence of the jury relating to confessions or other matters which, if reported, would likely interfere with a fair trial.

Prior Criminal Records

Lawyers and law enforcement personnel should not volunteer the prior criminal record of an accused except to aid in his apprehension or to warn the public of any dangers he presents. The news media can obtain prior criminal records from the public records of the courts, police agencies and other governmental agencies and from their own files. The news media acknowledge, however, that publication or broadcast of an individual's criminal record can be prejudicial, and its publication or broadcast should be considered very carefully, particularly after the filing of formal charges and as the time of the trial approaches, and such publication or broadcast should generally be avoided because readers, viewers and listeners are potential jurors and an accused is presumed innocent until proven guilty.

Press Coverage of Trials

Supreme Court Decisions

Another major case involving the issue of fair trial versus free press reached the U.S. Supreme Court in 1975. Jack Murphy—who was sometimes referred to as "Murph the Surf"—was convicted in Dade County, Fla., of breaking and entering. He had a criminal background. The Florida press gave substantial coverage to his arrest and trial. Murphy sought a reversal on the basis of prejudicial publicity. The Supreme Court refused, emphasizing that prejudicial publicity is not necessarily synonymous with pervasive publicity. The majority distinguished *Murphy* from *Irvin, Rideau* and *Sheppard.* In *Murphy,* though the media coverage had been extensive, it had been responsible. Voir dire did not reveal pervasive hostility.

A grave threat to press coverage of criminal trials came in the autumn of 1975 when a Nebraska judge issued a *gag order*—a protective order—prohibiting the press from publishing some information from a public murder trial (*Nebraska Press* v. *Stuart*). The Reporters Committee for Freedom of the Press estimated that there had been 174 cases involving gag orders between 1967 and 1975, with 62 of the instances occurring in 1975.

Obviously, the controversy was ripe for adjudication. Among other things, a Nebraska district county judge, Hugh Stuart, prohibited the press from reporting contents of a confession that had been mentioned in open court, statements made by the accused to others, medical testimony that had been introduced at the preliminary hearing and the identity of victims of sexual assault. (Six members of the Henry Kellie family of Sutherland, Neb., had been killed; some were assaulted sexually.) In addition, Stuart gagged the press from reporting the contents of the gag.

The U.S. Supreme Court in 1976 reversed the ruling, holding that though the First Amendment is not absolute, barriers to a constitutional prior restraint on the press are high. A "heavy burden" would have to be met to justify a prior restraint on the press, and in this instance, that burden had not been met. Chief Justice Warren Burger, in his majority opinion, criticized the trial judge for not exploring available procedural safeguards before resorting to a gag order. The majority conceded, however, that under the most extreme circumstances, some gag orders could conceivably be upheld as constitutional. In a concurring opinion, Justice William Brennan said that prior restraint could never be placed on the press in covering litigation.

Because *Nebraska Press* did not slam the door on the possibility that the press might sometimes be excluded from coverage of litigation, it was only logical that future cases would develop. In 1979 the U.S. Supreme Court held that the Sixth Amendment is for the benefit of the defendant—not the media—in a case (*Gannett* v. *DePasquale*) that was such a debacle that the court was forced to correct itself only 12 months later. The majority said the Constitution does not give the press an "affirmative right" of access to criminal trials. In a concurring opinion, Chief Justice Burger noted that the ruling applied only to pretrial hearings. Justice William Rehnquist, however, disagreed; in his concurring opinion, he said it applied to all stages of a public trial. Confusion prevailed. During public speeches after the decision, several justices took contrasting stances about what it meant. Critics of the decision contended that lower court judges would take advantage of the uncertainty of the ruling and close trials, as well as preliminary hearings, without substantial reason to believe that the press would deprive the defendant of the right to a fair trial.

Fortunately for the press, a case that could clarify the *DePasquale* ruling was already making its way up through the judicial system. Reporters had been denied access to a murder trial in Virginia on the request of the defense attorney. As in *DePasquale,* the reporters present did not object to the closure. A few hours later, however, attorneys for the newspaper asked that the order be vacated. The court refused. Though the case was technically moot, the U.S. Supreme Court agreed to hear it (*Richmond Newspapers Inc.* v. *Virginia*). One year to the day after *DePasquale,* the court held that the Virginia closure was not proper. The majority said that the First Amendment guarantees the right to attend public trials, absent "overriding considerations." The 7-1 decision helped clarify the murky waters left by *DePasquale.* Though it had long been assumed, *Richmond Newspapers* was the first formal articulation by the court that the press had a right of access under the First Amendment to gather news at public trials.

In 1984, in *Press-Enterprise Co.* v. *Riverside County Superior Court,* the Supreme Court recognized the right of the public and the media to attend the examination of potential jurors (voir dire). Two years later, in a case bearing the same name, the court said that, absent overriding considerations, the public and the press enjoy a First Amendment right to attend pretrial hearings. When considered in tandem, these cases certainly bring into question the continued applicability of *Gannett.* For all practical purposes, barring a "substantial probability that the defendant's right to a fair trial will be prejudiced by publicity," the public and the press enjoy an affirmative right of access to attend pretrial proceedings as well as trials.

Though the court made it clear in *Richmond Newspapers* and in both *Press-Enterprise* cases that reporters could be banned from covering public litigation only in the most extreme circumstances and that a heavy burden would be placed on the person requesting a closure to show that the defendant would otherwise be deprived of fair proceedings, reporters undoubtedly will continue to be confronted with similar situations. The rulings, however, should make judges hesitant to close public proceedings.

Closed Trials: A Statement of Objection for Reporters

If a proceeding is ordered closed, several media organizations and newspapers have prepared cards for their reporters to carry. Printed on each card is a brief statement of objection that the reporter is urged to read for the court record. The Gannett card reads:

> Your honor, I am ________, a reporter for ________, and I would like to object on behalf of my employer and the public to this proposed closing. Our attorney is prepared to make a number of arguments against closings such as this one and we respectfully ask the Court for a hearing on these issues. I believe our attorney can be here relatively quickly for the Court's convenience and he will be able to demonstrate that closure in this case will violate the First Amendment, and possibly state statutory and constitutional provisions as well. I cannot make the arguments myself, but our attorney can point out several issues for your consideration. If it pleases the Court, we request the opportunity to be heard through Counsel.

Time is clearly important to any reporter involved in closed proceedings. Editors and attorneys should be notified promptly. It is also important that reporters attempt to state on the record that they object to the closure. Of course, reporters do not have a right of access to all judicial proceedings. Grand jury proceedings and juvenile hearings are examples of judicial situations from which the press is normally barred.

Electronic Coverage in Courtrooms

As is emphasized in Chapter 17, television news teams constantly strive to coordinate video with words. In 1981 the Supreme Court handed down a decision that pleased broadcast journalists who had long ago advocated the televising of state court proceedings. The question that faced the court was whether, consistent with constitutional guarantees, a state could provide for radio, television and still photographic coverage of a criminal trial for public broadcast—even when the accused objected.

This was not an overnight issue. In 1937 the American Bar Association had passed Canon 35—a "suggestive code"—that banned cameras from state courtrooms. In 1952 an amendment was approved that included television cameras in the ban. Most states adopted the rationale of Canon 35. In 1972 the Code of Judicial Conduct replaced the Canons of Judicial Ethics, and Canon 35 was replaced by Section 3A(7). Rule 53 of the Federal Rules of Criminal Procedure—enacted in 1946—effectively banned cameras from federal courtrooms.

By the mid-1970s, however, some states had launched movements to allow camera coverage of state court proceedings. In 1978 a *Washington Post* survey showed that 56 percent of lawyers, state supreme court justices and law professors favored electronic coverage of trials. About 31 percent disapproved; 13 percent were uncertain.

The only previous time the U.S. Supreme Court had considered the camera issue was in 1965 (*Estes* v. *Texas*). In that case, it held that Billy Sol Estes, who had been charged with theft, swindling and embezzlement involving the federal government, had been deprived of a fair trial because of cumbersome camera coverage of portions of it. The decision, of course, was based on the state of the technology at that time. Justice Tom Clark, who wrote the majority opinion, said that the cameras had an impact on the jurors, the quality of the testimony and the defendants. He also said that the cameras placed additional responsibilities on the judge to control the courtroom. In a concurring opinion, however, Justice John Marshall Harlan said that the door should be left open for future camera coverage as the technology became sufficiently sophisticated.

When the Supreme Court considered the question of the constitutionality of cameras in state courtrooms in January 1981, more than 20 states were experimenting or had already experimented with them.

In July 1977 two Miami Beach policemen, Noel Chandler and Robert Granger, were charged in Florida with conspiracy to commit burglary, grand larceny and possession of burglary tools. The case was widely publicized.

Chandler and Granger's counsel sought to ban electronic coverage of the trial. The judge refused. A small portion of the proceedings was broadcast. The jury returned a guilty verdict on all counts. Chandler and Granger appealed, claiming that because of the television coverage, they had been denied a fair and impartial trial. The lower courts said that they had not.

The Supreme Court voted 8-0 to affirm the lower courts. Chief Justice Warren Burger said that *Estes* did not announce a constitutional rule that all photo, radio and television coverage of criminal trials was inherently a denial of due process. Burger said, "It does not stand as an absolute ban on state experimentation with an evolving technology, which in terms of modes of mass communication, was in its relative infancy in 1964, and is, even now, in a state of continuing change."

Burger said that any criminal case "that generates a great deal of publicity presents some risks that the publicity may compromise the right of the defendant to a fair trial." Trial courts would have to be "especially vigilant to guard against any impairment of the defendant's right." Still, an "absolute ban" on camera coverage could not be justified "simply because there is a danger that, in some cases, prejudicial broadcast accounts . . . may impair the ability of jurors to decide the issue of guilt or innocence uninfluenced by extraneous matter."

Burger also talked about the Florida program. The chief justice seemed pleased with the safeguards built into it, which were similar to those of other states. The Florida guidelines provided the following: Only one television camera and one technician were allowed in the courtroom; coverage had to be pooled; there could be no artificial lighting; equipment had to be placed in fixed positions; videotaping equipment had to be remote from the courtroom; film could not be changed when the court was in session; the jury could not be filmed; the judge had sole discretion to exclude coverage of certain witnesses; and the judge had discretionary power to forbid coverage whenever satisfied that it could have a "deleterious effect on the paramount right of the defendant to a fair trial."

Electronic media journalists generally regarded the *Chandler* decision as a much-deserved victory. The American Bar Association's House of Delegates in August 1982 also reacted in a positive way and repealed Section 3A(7), passed in 1972.

In 1991, several federal courts decided to permit electronic coverage of proceedings as part of a three-year experiment authorized by the U.S. Judicial Conference. At the end of 1994, however, the Judicial Conference voted down a proposal to make the experiment permanent.

Then, in 1996, the Judicial Conference, which is the policy-making body for the federal court system, voted 14-12 to allow each of the 13 federal appeals courts to determine independently whether to allow camera coverage in appellate proceedings.

USA Today quoted Gilbert Merritt, a Nashville, Tenn., federal appeals judge who chaired the Conference's executive committee: "There is general opposition to cameras among federal judges. This (the vote that opened the door to coverage in federal appellate courts) was as much as the judges wanted to do."

Electronic coverage of the U.S. Supreme Court and federal criminal trials is forbidden.

A Warning about Aggressive News Techniques

Journalists may be sued for two basic activities—how they *report* the news and how they *gather* the news. Libel, discussed earlier in the chapter, focuses on how journalists report the news. It creates liability for journalists when they report false facts that harm a person's reputation. The actual malice standard, along with the other defenses and privileges, creates a very tough burden for public officials and public figures seeking to recover for libel.

Because of these high hurdles in libel law, individuals suing the media today increasingly are focusing their efforts on the news *gathering* tactics of journalists, rather than on news reporting. The primary reason is that the First Amendment defenses that apply to news reporting are not as prevalent in the area of news gathering. While a complete discussion of legal theories that affect news gathering is beyond the scope of this chapter, one general principle is important to remember: *Journalists have no special First Amendment protection or immunity when it comes to violating laws that apply to all members of the public.*

For instance, journalists cannot claim a First Amendment defense to engage in trespass (the unauthorized entry onto private property possessed by another) simply because newsworthy information is on the property. As the U.S. Supreme Court observed in *Cohen* v. *Cowles Media Co.*, "generally applicable laws do not offend the First Amendment simply because their enforcement against the press has incidental effects on its ability to gather and report the news." The court added that "the press may not with impunity break and enter an office or dwelling to gather news." Likewise, the First Amendment does not allow journalists to enter disaster scenes that are otherwise off limits to the public (although a few states have statutes that give the press greater access to such areas). State statutes that govern stalking, harassment and even false imprisonment also may apply to journalists when they are overly aggressive in pursuing subjects for photographs or videotape.

Campus Rights and Restrictions

As this chapter makes clear, student journalists—when carrying out the workday functions of the press—must follow the legal prescriptions of their professional counterparts. The catch is that they do not *always* enjoy the same legal protections or benefits of the professional media. Much of the law that has developed over time regarding student expression grew up around the rights of students enrolled in the public school system, and although these rulings typically do not spill over to college campuses, the ripple effect certainly has been spotted there in recent years.

More than three decades ago, the U.S. Supreme Court observed that students enrolled in a public school do not "shed their constitutional rights to freedom of speech or expression at the schoolhouse gate" (*Tinker* v. *Des Moines Independent Community School District*, 1969). Despite the liberalizing nature of this aphorism, courts throughout the ensuing decades have chipped away at student expression, including the rights of the student press. In fact, a Supreme Court case from the late 1980s made clear that student journalists can be treated differently from mainstream practitioners without violating First Amendment principles. This ruling stemmed from a controversy at Hazelwood East High School in St. Louis County, Mo.

Hazelwood East students published their high school newspaper as part of a journalism class. Three days before the final issue of the school year was slated to go to press, the newspaper's adviser delivered proofs—as was customary—to Hazelwood East's principal. After reviewing the pages, the principal objected to two stories—one involving teen-age pregnancy and the other dealing with the impact of divorce on teens—and ordered their removal from the paper. The newspaper's editor sued the school district, claiming a violation of the First Amendment.

After two contrasting lower court decisions, the U.S. Supreme Court ruled that the student newspaper was not a public forum or a conduit for student views. The court further rationalized its decision by suggesting that a "school must be able to set standards for the student speech that is disseminated under its auspices—standards that may be higher than those demanded by some publishers or theatrical producers in the 'real' world—and may refuse to disseminate student speech that does not meet those standards" (*Hazelwood School District* v. *Kuhlmeier*, 1988).

The court noted that the ruling applied only to the high school press, but hinted that questions as to the level of deference afforded to college and university officials in similar circumstances could come at a later time. While the Supreme Court has not revisited this question, a handful of lower courts have squarely faced the issue of extending the *Hazelwood* ruling to the college press. So far, the news has been good for student journalists. For instance, the U.S. Court of Appeals for the 6th Circuit, sitting as a full court in early 2001, found that a college yearbook was a "limited public forum" and indeed deserved constitutional protection (*Kincaid* v. *Gibson*). The ruling was important for college journalists because it reversed two earlier decisions in the case that had held to the contrary. The court relied on the fact that the speech in question did not take place at a high school, suggesting that "the university context mitigates in favor of finding that the yearbook is a limited public forum."

The mere fact that the speech in question involves a college-age audience will not always be enough to cloak it in constitutional protection. That point was driven home sharply by the U.S. Court of Appeals for the 3rd Circuit in a case involving the University of Pittsburgh's *Pitt News*—but with wider ramifications for college media. When Pennsylvania amended its liquor code in 1996, lawmakers provided for criminal penalties against businesses that advertised alcoholic beverages in media "published by, for or in behalf of any educational institution." The amendment, known as Act 199, not only cut into a revenue stream for college newspapers but also drew a dividing line between the college and professional press—the latter obviously not subject to the tightened controls.

The *Pitt News* sued, seeking an injunction against enforcement of Act 199, claiming its First Amendment rights had been violated. The newspaper argued

that the decline in its advertising revenue would directly reduce the amount of space that could be devoted to news and information and thereby impinge upon its press freedom. The Court of Appeals disagreed. The court characterized the loss of revenue as an "incidental economic effect" of the regulation and found no First Amendment violation because the act did not "directly restrict the content of the newspaper." (*The Pitt News* v. *Fisher,* 2000). The U.S. Supreme Court has declined to hear the case. The decision clearly has an impact on the collegiate press. It demonstrates that college media, indeed, are viewed differently.

Liquor advertisements are not the only source of controversy in the college press. More than two dozen papers ran an advertisement during the 2000–2001 academic year that set off a nationwide debate over whether college newspapers should be more selective when selling space to those with offensive viewpoints. The Center for the Study of Popular Culture and author David Horowitz prepared an advertisement entitled "Ten Reasons Why Reparations for Slavery Is a Bad Idea—And Racist Too." For weeks the ad led to protests and commentaries across the country about the appropriate role of a campus newspaper in fueling controversy through its acceptance of political and editorial advertisements.

While the Horowitz advertisement does not raise any specific *legal* questions, it should remind campus journalists that the newspaper is ultimately responsible for the content of it pages—including advertisements. Should an advertisement be libelous or an invasion of privacy or violate one of the principles articulated earlier in this chapter, the newspaper may have to answer in a court of law just as many papers have answered in the court of public opinion for the Horowitz ad.

Where to Turn Online

Reporters can turn to a number of online Web sites for background on law-related issues or for help in locating various types of legal information. Some Web sites provide primary source material directly; others provide hypertext links to a variety of other Web sites. Caution: unfortunately, Web sites often change address or cease to exist altogether.

Among the best online sources are the Cornell Law School's Law Information Institute online site (*www.law.cornell.edu*), which is especially useful for U.S. Supreme Court cases and for court rulings; Emory University School of Law's federal courts finder (*www.law.emory.edu/FEDCTS*), which is arguably the best site for locating decisions of various federal circuit courts; and FindLaw (*www.findlaw.com*), which is the best starting point for online legal research and includes U.S. Supreme Court cases, state law resources and law reviews. The U.S. Supreme Court's own Web site (*www.supremecourtus.gov*) recently was placed online and features a wealth of information about the court, from its history to current cases.

The most comprehensive Web site for virtually anything law-related and especially for finding state law materials is Villanova Law School's Center for Information Law and Policy (*vls.law.vill.edu*). The National Center for State Courts' site (*www.ncsconline.org*) is a valuable source for finding information on court statistics and caseloads.

For access to the Code of Federal Regulations, Federal Register, U.S. Code, bills in the U.S. House and Senate and so forth, the home page of the Government Printing Office is an excellent source (*www.access.gpo.gov*). Thomas (*thomas.loc.gov*), which is the legislative server of the Library of Congress, provides legislative information on the Internet for access to bills, legislative histories and the *Congressional Record.*

CourtTV (*www.courttv.com*) is an excellent source for background information about high-profile cases. Martindale-Hubbell Lawyer Locator (*www.martindale.com*) is an online version of the Martindale-Hubbell Law Directory, which includes lawyers' e-mail addresses and firm Web sites.

The Reporters Committee for Freedom of the Press (*www.rcfp.org*) offers an excellent site that features both brief news updates on current cases and controversies affecting the news media and an extensive First Amendment Handbook online that covers the nuts and bolts of topics such as libel, privacy, confidential sources, gag orders and access to courts and documents.

ETHICS AND FAIRNESS: RESPONSIBILITY TO SOCIETY

As the 20th century drew to a close, George Langford, public editor of the *Chicago Tribune,* wrote: "There is a consensus in the news business that the journalism profession has had better days."

He pointed to a rash of incidents in which journalists had been "accused . . . of lying, stealing, racing into print with inadequately sourced stories and abusing the anonymous-sources crutch."

Interestingly, in many respects the mainstream media never have been fairer and more professional. They employ the best-educated journalists in history. Never have they been

(*Dirck Halstead / Getty Images*)

more dedicated to holding often lengthy, introspective, in-house conversations about how stories should be handled and played.

However, as technology has advanced at warp speed—with the electronic and online media bringing stories into millions of homes instantaneously and with virtually all media rushing as never before to communicate news developments before the context might be known—journalists increasingly have found themselves on the hot seat of public opinion.

"There is inflation in news coverage today, with too many reporters chasing too little information," Walter Mears of The Associated Press said. "And there is no [journalistic] immunity for other people's excesses."

Sandra Mims Rowe, editor of *The Oregonian* in Portland and former president of the American Society of Newspaper Editors (ASNE), told the Organization of News Ombudsmen: "It is true that in many newsrooms, standards are unclear or, given recent evidence, wildly inconsistent. Editors routinely talk about the gap between the journalistic values they hold most dear and those they think guide the reporters they work beside."

She cited early coverage of the President Bill Clinton-Monica Lewinsky story as a primary example. That story broke with a rush, spurring special prosecutor Kenneth Starr to investigate whether Clinton had had an affair with the White House intern, lied about it under oath and attempted to cover it up.

"The salient standard [during much of the Clinton-Lewinsky coverage] appears to have been that someone said it, therefore we wrote it; the wire service sent it, therefore we printed it.

"Further diminishing our credibility were the rush to judgment obvious in the early reporting, the incessant blathering of the talking heads on TV and some isolated instances of sloppy editing by respected publications. No good editor harbors delusions of adequacy. Yet, never in my memory has a single story reinforced that so much for so many."

Michael Schudson, a professor at the University of California, San Diego, wrote in the *Media Studies Journal:* "Today's journalistic fairness in the United States is a blend of high hopes, historic traditions, contemporary political culture and the expediencies journalists face in keeping audiences, owners and sources at bay. It is a shifting set of principles and practices that will be tested and reformulated by a changing information environment whose shape will not hold still."

In that same issue of the *Media Studies Journal*—which was devoted to the theme "what's fair?"—the editors wrote:

> The demarcation of public and private life that once ruled certain kinds of stories out of bounds has eroded, leaving reporters with the unenviable challenge of having to cover events whose seaminess inevitably taints all who touch them. Old certainties that gave credibility to journalists, such as trust in government sources, have broken down—weakening the authority of journalists as well. Commercial pressures, and a tidal wave of information and entertainment media, have engulfed the news business—leaving the definitions of journalism and journalistic standards vague and uncertain. And the technology of news reporting is speeding up news cycles in ways that leave little time for sober and measured judgments.

The Fairness Movement

The movement to extricate journalists from the swamp of public opinion they increasingly find themselves in has taken on a sense of urgency. The American Society of Newspaper Editors launched a five-year effort in the late 1990s to, very simply, improve the credibility of newspapers.

Sandra Mims Rowe told the nation's newspaper ombudsmen that the erosion of press credibility "is serious business, and we are serious about confronting it. The nation's editors have placed the credibility issue at the top of the agenda."

So have other organizations such as The Freedom Forum, a nonpartisan, international foundation dedicated to free press, free speech and free spirit for all people, which embarked on a multimillion-dollar project to study and make recommendations for improving fairness in journalism.

The Freedom Forum's Free Press/Fair Press project began with this premise: *Public standards for the news media are higher than ever. Some journalists may not understand that. Conversely, the mainstream press has improved greatly. The public may not be aware of that.*

The goal of the project was to help both the public and the press understand better the role and responsibilities of a free and fair press.

In Freedom Forum roundtable discussions with the public and with journalists in communities around the country, two major themes emerged:

- The public expressed serious concerns about press performance, particularly about the procedures and practices of journalism, that is, how journalists do their jobs. Reporters and editors can faithfully follow the accepted rules and procedures of journalism and still produce a story that the public sees as unfair.
- Journalists expressed a deep yearning for help. They welcomed the chance to talk about fairness and issues of fairness in their newsrooms. They want guidance. They want to do better.

Robert H. Giles, longtime metropolitan daily newspaper editor and publisher, directed the Free Press/Fair Press project for The Freedom Forum. He said: "The lessons that emerged from the discussions are central to the practice of journalism. Five major concerns raised by the public go to the heart of the journalistic process and should be reflected in the teaching of journalism on the nation's campuses."

Giles outlined the five concerns.

- *News Coverage Does Not Adequately Reflect All of Reality.* The public observed that by seeking polar opposites to bring conflict into stories, journalists tend to normalize radical behavior and radical thinking while giving little attention to the large middle ground where public decisions typically are made. Others contended that negative news dominates the coverage and squeezes out good news.
- *Lack of News Staff Diversity Leads to Missing Stories, Failing to Provide Important Context or Using Language in Stories That Reflects Unconscious Prejudices and Stereotypes.* The point was made repeatedly by the public that a diverse staff contributes a sensitivity to issues that otherwise would be

ignored. Especially important is having racial minorities involved in assigning stories and determining the play of stories. A serious consequence for the lack of diversity is the perception that *I don't see myself in news coverage.* This concern was expressed by Hispanics and gays who maintained that local newspapers and television news ignore the issues that most interest them.

- *Reporters Come to Stories with Preconceived Notions of the Story Line and the Roles Different Sources Are to Play.* Minorities noted that they normally are contacted by reporters only when the story subject is race. Public officials complained that they are typecast, that reporters seek them out only when they want a quotation that fits the reporter's need for a certain response, such as a comment from a liberal to balance that of a conservative.
- *Reporters Lack Expertise in the Subjects They Are Covering.* The public offered two significant consequences:
  1. Stories are oversimplified and often misleading because reporters are not grounded in a fundamental understanding of the issues. Stories about economics, science, education and race were most often cited as examples.
  2. Turnover on beats makes it difficult for news sources to establish long-term relationships with reporters and help them build an authoritative grasp of the subject. Many public officials see this as a key to ensuring fairness in coverage.
- *Trying to Get Corrections Published or Broadcast Is an Exercise in Futility.* It was widely noted by the public, and acknowledged by television journalists, that corrections rarely appear on a television newscast. One television news executive dismissed the idea that corrections are important because the nature of coverage is such that errors made early in a story are fixed in later broadcasts, thus negating the need for on-air corrections. The public also found it a difficult and frustrating process to get the local newspaper to publish corrections. Many who had experience in trying concluded that it was better to "simply let it go."

During the early stages of The Freedom Forum initiative, Charles L. Overby, chairman and chief executive officer, said he heard a recurring refrain from people across the country who were concerned about fairness in the media.

"From these discussions, I have broken down the components of fairness into five basic categories that provide an easy-to-remember formula: a + b + c + d + e = f (fairness)," he wrote.

Here is how Overby broke down the categories:

- *Accuracy.* This is the basic component of fairness, but it generated lots of discussion, especially in the area of corrections. Most newspapers still are doing a superficial job of correcting their errors. Procedures often are not reader-friendly. The better newspapers run more corrections, not fewer, every day than average newspapers. Forget corrections with television.
- *Balance.* Many in the public think stories reflect definite points of view. Often, the other side is given scant, secondary attention, far down in the news report.

- *Completeness.* This was the biggest complaint that we heard. Our respondents said reporters fail to tell the whole story because of inexperience, ineptitude, laziness or lack of space or time. The lack of completeness affects context.
- *Detachment.* The frequent complaint lodged by people who deal with the media was that reporters and editors construct their stories in advance and only want news sources to confirm their preconceived notions. Once the news "hook" is established, there is not much fair and open reporting that follows.
- *Ethics.* This involves the way reporters and editors pursue stories, the feeling that editorial viewpoints drive news content, placement and headlines. This category also focuses on methodology of reporting, ranging from paparazzi photography to insensitivity to victims.

Overby said that editors and news directors should be able to find ways to improve performances in each area.

"If the public could see improvements and regular explanations about these basic elements, they probably would develop more trust in the mainstream media," he wrote.

The task of putting shine back on journalism's tarnished image, however, will not be easy. When the public thinks about press irresponsibility, it tends to lump all media into the same batch. Most people don't make distinctions between conscientiously edited daily newspapers and hurry-to-press tabloids. Further complicating matters is a racier approach to news selection that has infiltrated many mainstream dailies.

Ann Compton, a White House correspondent for ABC News, wrote in the *Media Studies Journal:* "Fairness is not in any user's manual handed to us with a White House press pass. Fairness is a principle, a way of working that we learn to apply to every story, every script, the choice of every sound bite and every stand-up close despite the rush to report in this era of competition."

Sandra Mims Rowe acknowledged the challenge of maintaining and reinforcing "the standards that both outward and inward credibility require." She wrote: "How do we do this? One reporter, one editor, one day at a time, making decisions worthy of claiming as their own."

Some "Best Practices"

As part of its Free Press/Fair Press Project, The Freedom Forum asked Robert Haiman, president emeritus and distinguished editor in residence at the Poynter Institute in St. Petersburg, Fla., to write a handbook of best practices.

Haiman, who worked at the *St. Petersburg Times* for a quarter century, including 10 years as managing editor and seven years as executive editor, noted that Best Practices for Newspaper Journalists "is intended to help those who would restore public trust by raising the standards for fairness in their newspapers."

Haiman's readable practical handbook—which features nine examples of unfairness in newspapers—is available through The Freedom Forum and serves as a superb source for journalists and journalism students.

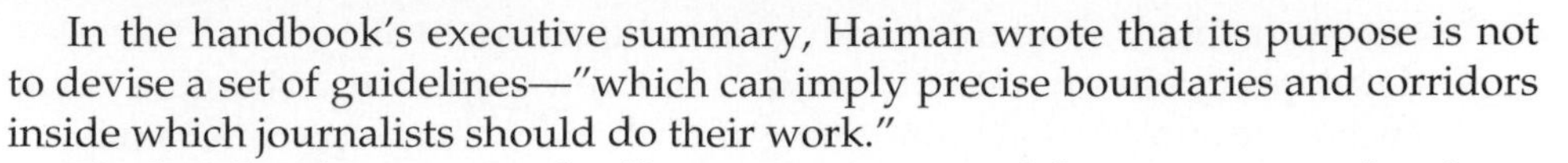

In the handbook's executive summary, Haiman wrote that its purpose is not to devise a set of guidelines—"which can imply precise boundaries and corridors inside which journalists should do their work."

The handbook, very simply, "is an examination of the concerns readers have expressed about newspapers and a list of best practices used in many of the nation's newspapers."

Best Practices for Newspaper Journalists should be read in its entirety, but an outline of the concerns discussed at length follows in skeleton form.

- *Newspapers are unfair when: They get the facts wrong.* Haiman wrote that "although many journalists may think that spelling and grammar errors, wrong names, wrong titles, wrong addresses, wrong dates and other similar mistakes have relatively little to do with the press's credibility, the public sees it otherwise."

  Among the "best practices to address the problem": The *Chicago Tribune's* formal tracking system, which even makes use of an outside proofreading agency to detect errors, calls for a form to be completed for each mistake that traces the problem to its root and seeks input on ways it could have been avoided.

- *Newspapers are unfair when: They refuse to admit errors.* Haiman wrote that "there is a broad feeling in the public that newspapers not only make too many mistakes, but that they also are unwilling to correct them fully and promptly. Television gets even more criticism for this, but newspaper people should take no comfort from that."

  Among the "best practices to address the problem": Publishing prompt corrections not only of factual errors but also "clarifications when all facts published may have been correct but the overall impression was misleading, or important details were omitted, or significant nuances were missed."

- *Newspapers are unfair when: They won't name names.* Haiman wrote that, during Freedom Forum roundtables in cities across the country, "representatives of the general public seemed unfamiliar with the complicated lexicon journalists use in defining a range of practices on sourcing, such as off the record, not for attribution, background, deep background, the two-source rule. [See Chapter 8 for a fuller discussion of the use of anonymous sources.] But they stated clearly their belief that allegations of wrongdoing from unnamed persons were unfair."

  Among the "best practices to address the problem": The Associated Press's rules (see the AP Stylebook), "which are among the most direct and rigorous of any publication or news agency," and the guidelines provided in the Gannett Newspaper Division Principles of Ethical Conduct for Newsrooms (see the Principles in Appendix A).

- *Newspapers are unfair when: They have ignorant or incompetent reporters.* Haiman wrote that "business, community and civic leaders say they and their organizations often are covered by reporters who simply do not know enough about the subjects they are trying to report on," particularly in technical areas.

  Among the "best practices to address the problem": Newspapers should look favorably on candidates for reporting positions who took a concentration or second major in a subject that would allow them to develop a reporting specialty in that area. Newspapers also should encourage and facilitate continuing education for their reporters, ranging from freeing them for special fellowship programs to short courses to taking full advantage of various Internet sources.

- *Newspapers are unfair when: They prey on the weak.* Haiman wrote that "the public believes the press too often takes unfair advantage of people who are suddenly and unexpectedly thrust into the news and who are not prepared to deal with questioning by reporters . . . . That powerful images of sorrow or tragedy are newsworthy and are captured openly, utilizing traditional photojournalism practices, does not persuade those who believe people in such circumstances are entitled to a zone of privacy from the press."

  Among the "best practices to address the problem": Editors should regularly lead case-study discussions with reporters who might find themselves suddenly covering stories that involve people unaccustomed to dealing with the press in general, let alone in particularly trying circumstances; private citizens who find themselves involuntarily thrust into tragic events should be accorded more respect while children, in particular, deserve special treatment.

- *Newspapers are unfair when: They concentrate on bad news.* Haiman wrote that "the concern that the press focuses too much on what is wrong, violent and bizarre and that it never prints 'good news' may be the longest-running complaint of the public." He noted that many of the roundtable participants spoke of "their frustration in getting fair coverage of legitimate positive accomplishments, both in the public and private sectors, and the problems of dealing with reporters who seemed interested only in aberrations and sensational exceptions to the norm."

  Among the "best practices to address the problem": Designation of a new beat at the Washington Bureau of Newhouse Newspapers called "Doing Good"; attempts by *The Oregonian* in Portland to add context to crime coverage by naming a Crime Team of experienced reporters who would spend less time reacting to and reporting on acts of violence and crime and more time developing trend stories (see Chapter 20 for a discussion of coverage of police and fire); the efforts by some newspapers, such as *The Arizona Republic,* to do a more conscientious job explaining, usually in columns by editors, *why* they cover news the way they do.

- *Newspapers are unfair when: They lack diversity.* Haiman wrote that "in all of our roundtables, both community leaders and ordinary citizens expressed strong feelings about gaps in coverage of race, gender, age, ethnicity, economic and social class, and sexual orientation. Members of racial minority groups took the lead in many of these conversations. . . . But many white participants also gave voice to the belief that the local newspaper was not always a model of diversity, sensitivity and fairness to members of minority groups."

  Among the "best practices to address the problem": *Hiring* more minority staff members, *retaining* them, *promoting* them and *encouraging* them to put forward their points of view and ideas for coverage; expanding, through diversification, sources on all subjects and topics; and conducting systematic content audits to ensure coverage reflects the diversity of the community.

- *Newspapers are unfair when: They allow editorial bias in news stories.* Haiman wrote that "the most powerful concern about bias we encountered in our roundtables was the perception that news organizations had a 'negative' bias . . . [that] reporters too often seemed to seek out the most extreme views and ignored the broad middle, where most opinion resides and where decisions typically are made." Readers also noted what they perceived to be "political bias," although in smaller numbers than those concerned about "negative bias."

  Among the "best practices to address the problem": Editors should let their reporters know—in no uncertain terms—that they expect news coverage to reflect the positive as well as the negative. And editors should back up their directions by ensuring that "negative" stories do not receive disproportionate top play on Page 1.
- *Newspapers are unfair when: They can't admit that sometimes there's no story.* Haiman wrote that roundtable participants "often felt that reporters had their minds fully made up by the time they approached key figures to get their versions of events." He noted also: "Even the emergence of new facts or different dimensions or a broader context fails to enable them to open their minds to the possibility that the story has changed or that there may be no story at all."

  Among the "best practices to address the problem": Editors need to consistently emphasize "fairness" in staff meetings, making clear to reporters that stories always need to be framed in ways that are fair to all parties—common sense advice that most reporters say is seldom part of everyday newsroom conversations. There is constant questioning about whether stories are "right," to be sure, but far less about whether they are "fair."

A Theory of Press Systems

Reporters must recognize that today's society expects them to behave more responsibly. This expectation fits in with the "social responsibility" theory outlined by Theodore Peterson in "Four Theories of the Press," a book he wrote more than four decades ago with Wilbur Schramm and Fred S. Siebert. Peterson wrote that "freedom carries concomitant obligations; and the press, which enjoys a privileged position under our government, is obliged to be responsible to society for carrying out certain essential functions of mass communications."

Siebert, Peterson and Schramm grouped the press systems of the world under four headings: authoritarian, Soviet Communist (which, because of its inapplicability to the American system, will not be discussed here), libertarian and social responsibility.

Authoritarian System

In an **authoritarian system,** which is the oldest of the four, criticism of the government is not tolerated. Although most newspapers are privately owned, their content is controlled by the state through licensing or the issuance of patents. If newspapers want to be unceremoniously shut down, they criticize the government. If newspapers want to stay in business, they print what the state wants them to print. Some colonial American newspaper editors went along with the system; they were content to publish innocuous newspapers that did not offend the government or check on it. Other, more courageous colonial American journalists sought to escape suppression under the authoritarian system.

Libertarian System

As authoritarian controls on the press were resisted, the **libertarian system** developed. Under this philosophy, humans are rational thinking beings capable of separating truth from falsehood, good from evil. Thus, newspapers must provide information on a variety of topics—particularly government—so that citizens are in a position to make enlightened decisions. This romantic concept flourished during the early 1800s and continued into the 20th century.

As might have been expected, the libertarian philosophy opened the door for unscrupulous reporters to be blatantly irresponsible. Some 19th-century American newspapers were particularly vicious. They were, however, regarded as the primary instrument for checking on the government and its officials.

Social Responsibility Theory

In reaction to perceived shortcomings of the press under the libertarian system, the Commission on Freedom of the Press was formed shortly after World War II. Made up of scholars and philosophers, it was particularly concerned about the shrinking newspaper marketplace (the number of daily newspapers had been declining since shortly after the turn of the century) and the accompanying loss of potential philosophies. The commission said that the press should exercise more responsibility; it should make a concerted effort to discuss divergent views, even if the views were not compatible with those of management. The commission said that it was the responsibility of the press not only to present diverse viewpoints but also to interpret them responsibly.

What has been called the **social responsibility theory** of the press emerged from the commission's report. According to this philosophy, everyone who wants to express views should be given access to the press, which is bound by professional ethics. Community opinion helps to keep the press in check. And if the press fails to live up to its obligations of social responsibility, the government can step in to ensure public service.

In exploring the evolution of the social responsibility theory, Peterson wrote:

> A rather considerable fraction of articulate Americans began to demand certain standards of performance from the press. . . . Chiefly of their own volition, publishers began to link responsibility with freedom. They formulated codes of ethical behavior, and they operated their media with some concern for the public good—the public good as they regarded it, at least.

Today's reporters, then, find themselves working in a libertarian system that is making increasingly strong demands for journalistic responsibility. The challenge is formidable.

The courts, however, have not been willing to impose a standard of responsibility on the press. In 1974 Chief Justice Warren Burger wrote in a court opinion: "A responsible press is an undoubtedly desirable goal, but press responsibility is not mandated by the Constitution and like so many virtues it cannot be legislated. . . . A newspaper is more than a passive receptacle or conduit for news, comment and advertising. The choice of material to go into a newspaper . . . constitutes the exercise of editorial control and judgment."

The Media and the Public

Criticism of the Press

Americans have grown increasingly outspoken in their criticism of perceived irresponsibility on the part of the news media. A national opinion poll conducted by the Public Agenda Foundation showed that the majority of Americans surveyed support laws requiring fairness in newspaper coverage of controversial stories or political races.

The message to the media is clear: society is demanding responsibility. In an article published in *Editor & Publisher,* the pollster George Gallup wrote: "The press in America is operating in an environment of public opinion that is increasingly indifferent—and to some extent hostile—to the cause of a free press in America."

Many Americans feel that journalists should exercise greater restraint in choosing stories to publish or to air. A Gallup poll showed that Americans think the media "exaggerate the news in the interest of making headlines and selling newspapers," and that the media "rush to print without first making sure all facts are correct."

The Press Responds

Many newspapers have looked inward to determine, address and find solutions to the shortcomings for which they have been criticized. Some have appointed ombudsmen to see that readers' complaints are acted upon. A few metropolitan newspapers, such as the *Los Angeles Times,* have hired **media critics**—reporters who write stories about the strengths, the weaknesses and the trends of daily media coverage.

Media Critics

David Shaw, a national press reporter, has been the media critic for the *Los Angeles Times* since 1974. Shaw, who was a general assignment reporter, was asked by then-editor William H. Thomas to write in "exhaustive fashion" about the American press and the *Times.* Shaw was somewhat unsure of his turf.

But Thomas quickly cleared the air. In his book, "Journalism Today," Shaw wrote that Thomas told him that "the one thing the press covers more poorly today than anything else is the press." Shaw paraphrased Thomas: "We don't tell our readers what we do or how we do it. We don't admit our mistakes unless we're virtually forced to under threat of court action or public embarrassment. We make no attempt to explain our problems, our decisions, our fallibilities, our procedures." Thomas wanted the media critic to confront these issues directly.

Shaw wrote that his job was unique—he was to function neither as beat reporter nor as ombudsman. Thomas wanted him "to provide long, thoughtful overviews on broad issues confronting the press today, to analyze, criticize and make value judgments, to treat my own newspaper as I would any other."

Shaw's pieces are not always greeted with enthusiasm by fellow journalists who come under scrutiny, but the *Times* has been a pacesetter in media introspection.

Ombudsmen

The Washington Post has been a leader in the use of ombudsmen. Most newspapers that have ombudsmen instruct reporters and editors to respond to, not ignore, complaints or suggestions forwarded by the ombudsman. These responses take several forms—argument, agreement, disagreement, rebuttal, frustration or even anger—but the reporters and the editors must respond to the independent positions of the ombudsman. To establish rapport with these reporters and editors and to gain their respect, each ombudsman must be scrupulously fair and unbiased. It is not an easy job.

Indeed, *Editor & Publisher* noted that staffers at the *Hartford* (Conn.) *Courant* once used a photo of the newspaper's ombudsman as a dart board. The magazine quoted the ombudsman, Henry McNulty: "I think they meant it as a joke—at least I hope they did."

The Post created the position of ombudsman in 1970—one year after *The Courier-Journal* in Louisville, Ky., did. Robert J. McCloskey, a retired ambassador who for 10 years was the State Department's press spokesman, is a former ombudsman at *The Post.* According to McCloskey, an ombudsman can funnel complaints primarily in three ways: (1) go directly to the editor or reporter involved, say that an issue has been raised that should be considered and pose a possible solution; (2) write memos, which are distributed to senior editors and the publisher, outlining complaints and possible solutions; or (3) write a column outlining shortcomings and posing solutions. The column is published.

The Ethics of Journalism

Professors John Merrill of Louisiana State University and Ralph D. Barney of Brigham Young University, noting that journalistic ethics had received scant attention in the literature between the 1930s and the early 1970s, decided to edit a book of readings. The book, which they titled "Ethics and the Press," was published in 1975 and featured a variety of ethical topics.

Merrill said that the resurging interest in journalistic ethics at that time was a result of increasing criticism of press excesses such as leak journalism—where anonymous sources provide presumably confidential information to reporters. "A better informed, more critical, more skeptical population began to question many of the things the press does," Merrill said. "Before this time, the general public was more or less naive and trusting of the press."

Merrill put the issue of journalistic ethics into perspective in another of his books, "The Imperative of Freedom." He wrote:

> Ethics is that branch of philosophy that helps journalists determine what is right to do in their journalism; it is very much a normative science of conduct. Ethics has to do with "self-legislation" and "self-enforcement"; although it is, of course, related to

> law, it is of a different nature. Although law quite often stems from the ethical values of a society at a certain time (i.e., law is often reflective of ethics), law is something that is socially determined and socially enforced. Ethics, on the other hand, is personally determined and personally enforced—or should be. Ethics should provide the journalist certain basic principles or standards by which he can judge actions to be right or wrong, good or bad, responsible or irresponsible.
>
> It has always been difficult to discuss ethics; law is much easier, for what is legal is a matter of law. What is ethical transcends law, for many actions are legal, but not ethical. And there are no "ethical codebooks" to consult in order to settle ethical disputes. Ethics is primarily personal; law is primarily social. Even though the area of journalistic ethics is swampy and firm footing is difficult . . . , there are solid spots which the person may use in his trek across the difficult landscape of life.
>
> First of all, it is well to establish that ethics deals with voluntary actions. If a journalist has no control over his decisions or actions, then there is no need to talk of ethics. What are voluntary actions? Those which a journalist could have done differently had he wished. Sometimes journalists, like others, try to excuse their wrong actions by saying that these actions were not personally chosen but assigned to them—or otherwise forced on them—by editors or other superiors. Such coercion may indeed occur in some situations (such as a dictatorial press system) where the consequences to the journalist going against an order may be dire. But for an American journalist not to be able to "will" his journalistic actions—at least at the present time—is unthinkable; if he says that he is not able and that he "has to" do this or that, he is only exhibiting his ethical weaknesses and inauthenticity.
>
> The journalist who is concerned with ethics—with the quality of his actions—is, of course, one who wishes to be virtuous.

Merrill once said that there is often no general agreement on what is right or what is wrong. "It always boils down to an individual journalistic concept," he said. "In life, a journalist who believes that anything goes to get a story—that the ends justify the means—will apply that concept in journalism. Some people, for example, believe that it is ethical to surreptitiously tape an interview; this is a personal belief. There are others, however, who believe that it is dishonest because it is not being frank or forthright with the source. Ultimately, it boils down to personal ethics—personal values applied to the work of journalism."

Codes of Ethics

As the growing concern about media ethics and responsibility gathered steam in the 1970s, The Associated Press Managing Editors Association, the American Society of Newspaper Editors, the Society of Professional Journalists, the National Conference of Editorial Writers and The Associated Press Sports Editors were among the groups that revised existing codes. The American Society of Newspaper Editors Statement of Principles, for example, was adopted in 1975. It replaced a code of ethics that was about a half-century old.

The **codes of ethics** developed by national groups that sincerely wished to strengthen the profession were broad statements of principle. However, Merrill wrote in "Existential Journalism": "Acting journalistically is the main thing; having a theory about journalism is another, and of much lesser import. A code of ethics hanging on the wall is meaningless; a code of ethics internalized within the journalist and guiding his actions is what is meaningful."

Merrill said that he did not know how helpful a code of ethics drawn up by a committee could be. "The codes do indicate a desire on the part of organizations to be ethical—whatever that means to them," Merrill said. "But ethics always boils right back to the individual. Ethical values are acquired all through life from a number of sources, such as church, family and friends. Reporters can't separate the ethics of journalism from the values they hold as individuals."

Although individual journalists need to assume personal responsibility for the ethical decisions that they make, it is important to examine codes of ethics that have been structured by various media organizations.

The formulation and updating of codes show an awareness by individual newspapers that ethical matters are a growing concern. However, a former managing editor of the no-longer-published *Washington Star,* Charles B. Seib, contended that most codes "share a weakness—they are toothless."

No matter how broad some codes are, they do represent legitimate attempts by the industry to police its own ranks. The codes are often helpful—particularly to the working reporter—but journalists are regularly confronted with ethical and moral issues that must be reacted to on a case-by-case basis.

✔ A Checklist for Doing Ethics: Ask Good Questions to Make Good Ethical Decisions*

- ❑ What do I know? What do I need to know?
- ❑ What is my journalistic purpose?
- ❑ What are my ethical concerns?
- ❑ What organizational policies and professional guidelines should I consider?
- ❑ How can I include other people, with different perspectives and diverse ideas, in the decision-making process?
- ❑ Who are the stakeholders—those affected by my decision? What are their motivations? Which are legitimate?
- ❑ What if the roles were reversed? How would I feel if I were in the shoes of one of the stakeholders?
- ❑ What are the possible consequences of my actions? Short-term? Long-term?
- ❑ What are my alternatives for maximizing my truthtelling responsibility and minimizing harm?
- ❑ Can I clearly and fully justify my thinking and my decision? To my colleagues? To the stakeholders? To the public?

*By Bob Steele, director, Ethics Program, Poynter Institute for Media Studies, St. Petersburg, Fla.

Ethical Issues

Few would argue with the assertion that journalists are more concerned than ever about the ethical ramifications of their work. Scores of articles and books that focused on media ethics have been published in the past quarter century; conversations in newsrooms and at seminars about the ethics of journalism have become increasingly common. Edmund B. Lambeth, a professor at the University of Missouri, wrote in his book, "Committed Journalism":

> Accumulated distrust of the news media, skepticism of journalists' ethics and a resentment of media power are very nearly permanent features of the contemporary American scene. While the media themselves are not alone responsible for this state of affairs, it is past time for journalists and owners of newspapers and radio and television stations to articulate principles of performance that are publicly visible, ethically defensible and rooted clearly in a philosophic tradition that continues to justify a free press.

It has been pointed out, however, that in their well-intentioned zeal to be increasingly ethical, some journalists may avoid stories that should be brought to the attention of the public. At a Poynter Institute conference, Roy Peter Clark said that a "few, well-publicized ethical scandals . . . (had) prompted journalists to be overly cautious, keeping important information out of newspapers and newscasts." The institute's newsletter, "The Poynter Report," also quoted Robert M. Steele, who directs its ethics program, as saying that "journalists must still be principled" when they make decisions but they should not be less aggressive. He also noted that the "restraint mentality has been exacerbated by the legal climate in which many newspapers failed to cover significant public policy stories out of fear of libel suits."

Do reporters adhere to the same stringent ethical standards for which they hold public officials accountable? Journalists are trained to report the first hint of governmental impropriety. Government officials, after all, have a responsibility to their constituents. Reporters should remember, however, that they too have a responsibility to their readers. Should reporters:

Jump at the chance for free movie tickets?

Stock personal libraries with review books sent out by publishers?

Look forward to gulping down free liquor from friendly sources?

Expect—and accept—small favors in return for complimentary stories?

Though the acceptance of "freebies" is often the first thing that comes to mind when discussing media ethics, the issues faced by journalists are sometimes considerably more complicated.

More than 150 editors of daily newspapers across the United States responded to two surveys that explored their opinions about and their handling of ethical issues. The first survey was conducted in the mid-1980s, the second in the early 1990s. Among other things, the editors were asked to discuss what they considered the most pressing ethical issues facing journalists. A synthesis of their responses results in the following list, which we'll examine item by item. We'll then take up an additional issue: journalistic arrogance.

- Fairness and objectivity
- Misrepresentation by reporters
- Economic pressure
- Privacy versus the public's right to know
- Conflicts of interest
- Anonymous sources
- Gifts
- Compassion versus policy

Fairness and Objectivity

Approximately one-fourth of the editors listed fairness and objectivity as the most pressing ethical issue facing journalists today. This concern far outdistanced the others.

Gilbert M. Savery, the former managing editor of the *Lincoln* (Neb.) *Journal,* explored the issue in some detail. He wrote:

> To answer the question of what I would consider to be the most pressing ethical issues facing reporters and editors today, I have to ask: "What is unethical and why should it be avoided?"
>
> Presumably when reporters or editors accept favors of magnitude, they are beholden to the donor. The question then arises as to whether that donor or his personal or corporate interests will be given more favorable treatment than other persons, businesses or institutions.
>
> Ethics, under this interpretation, translates into fairness. Therefore, the major ethical issues facing journalists today are those dealing with fair and balanced treatments of all viewpoints expressed on such issues as abortion, nuclear arms, nuclear power, a host of national issues including fiscal policy, education, religion and economics.
>
> Journalistically, the challenge is to deliver to readers, listeners and viewers a fair and balanced representation of viewpoints held by persons who differ markedly in their perceptions of what public policy should be.

Mark Baker, the managing editor of the *Shawano Evening Leader* in Wisconsin, said that it is imperative for reporters to write a balanced story. "Making sure a reporter provides access to all sides of a dispute—whether or not he or she agrees with the point of view rather than closing the door to those whose views or opinions are thought to be stupid, biased or just plain wrong—is important," Baker said. "Reporters, to some extent, must be like glass windows—allowing sunlight to come through with as little distortion as possible. Readers then get a true picture of the world."

Professor Merrill, who has written extensively about journalistic ethics, wrote in *Journalism Quarterly* that acceptance of the assumption that "objective reporting is ethical reporting" raises interesting questions. He said that such acceptance would "mean that a journalist who was objective—or tried diligently to be objective—could forget about additional ethical decisions per se; for the journalist would have already entered the ethical field simply by applying technique. In short, the journalist accepting objective-reporting-as-ethics as a valid concept would have to concentrate on the technique of being objective, thereby satisfying any journalistic ethical demands which might be placed upon him."

Merrill pointed out, however, that the terms *objectivity* and *ethics* "are filled with semantic noise, and when they are brought together in tandem in this objectivity-as-ethics sense, the abstractness is greatly increased." Merrill wrote that we are "immediately aware of the intriguing question as to the possibility of ever reaching 'objective' news coverage" because of the many variables that go into the selection, writing and presentation of stories.

Misrepresentation by Reporters

Should reporters misrepresent themselves when working on stories? Yes? No? Sometimes? According to editors who responded to the surveys, this is a major ethical issue facing journalists today.

Tim Harmon, the managing editor of *The Journal-Gazette,* Fort Wayne, Ind., said that he saw ethical problems in misrepresentation "and any of the various other ways journalists foster the stereotype of the callous, get-the-story-at-any-price reporter or editor." Harmon said that journalists "don't put enough thought into how we get the information for our stories or whether we should use all of it."

Tim Wood, the managing editor of *The Weatherford* (Texas) *Democrat,* emphasized that reporters must take care to be open with sources. "Reporters must clearly identify themselves as reporters when they contact a source and make it clear that anything the source says may end up in the newspaper," he wrote. "Anyone being interviewed for publication must be aware of the purpose of the interview. Even asking vague questions without revealing the context in which the answers will be put is a practice that borders on being unethical. Sources should not be surprised when the story appears in print."

David Shaw, after conducting a non-random survey of reporters across the country, wrote in the *Los Angeles Times:* "Most journalists argue that it is unethical for a reporter to pretend he is not a reporter—or to fail to identify himself as a reporter—when interviewing someone."

The fact remains, however, that at some metropolitan newspapers undercover journalism is occasionally practiced. Generally, it is resorted to only after editors and reporters have concluded that a story is extremely significant and that there would be no other means of obtaining it. Many journalists criticize undercover journalism, but others view it as a necessary means of gathering information, particularly when criminal activity is being investigated. In those situations, some newspaper editors and reporters contend that the ends justify the means.

Brian Walker, the managing editor–news of *The Muncie* (Ind.) *Evening Press,* said that the issue of misrepresentation or "masquerading" by reporters is often discussed at his newspaper. "Some reporters have wanted to try it while others have been particularly sensitive about using even information given freely by sources who simply were not aware that their listeners were reporters. I oppose masquerading, but differentiate between reporters deliberately misidentifying themselves to sources and reporters accepting information or quotes from sources who didn't know their identity but simply didn't ask. The reporter's intent is important here. If the source was not intentionally misled about the reporter's identity, then the information is probably usable. If a source is willing to talk freely to someone without knowing who that someone is, then it is fair to assume that the source is speaking for public consumption."

Certainly, most editors and most reporters realize that purposeful misrepresentation to gain information should be considered only as a last resort, if ever.

Economic Pressure

Interestingly, several of the editors tied ethical concerns to a weak economy. The majority of these comments came from editors of smaller dailies. One editor, for example, said that "the line between advertising and news becomes less clear every day; news people must keep the news untainted."

An editor of a midsized daily wrote: "Advertorial approaches by executives outside the newsroom are my top ethical concern. More and more, papers are tying in 'stories' and photos based on advertising. We could easily mislead readers into believing that news articles can be bought. I understand a slumping newspaper economy is causing publishers to take a hard look at increasing ad revenue. We are treading on very dangerous ground."

An editor of a small-circulation daily who wrote the following comments was articulating a common theme: "With newspapers both large and small facing declining advertising revenues, I believe one area that is particularly troublesome is the relationship between editorial and advertising departments. Facing constant pressure from advertising, news departments often must decide whether to pursue a story that may put a major advertiser in a bad light. On the other hand, a story suggested by advertising, while possibly newsworthy, is—at least in my mind—immediately suspect because one wonders about the motivation behind the idea."

Historically, of course, there has been some sensitivity to the intrusion of advertising salespeople into newsrooms. But a common strain of forcefully articulated fears emerged from this survey, indicating that a sour economy could exacerbate an old problem. Many of today's editors are worrying about the ethical ramifications that ensue from the impact of revenue concerns on editorial decisions.

Critics have asserted that television, in particular, has allowed economics to influence its news programming. During recent years, the networks have aired more and more programs in which the line that separates news from entertainment has grown increasingly fuzzy.

Privacy versus the Public's Right to Know

We have all watched the scenes on television or read the stories in the newspaper: a man has just died in a traffic accident caused by a drunken driver. The victim's widow, barely able to compose herself, is confronted by reporters who want to know how she feels and whether there should be stiffer sentences for people found guilty of driving while intoxicated.

To what extent should reporters invade privacy in an effort to get a story? Wickliffe R. Powell, the managing editor of *The Daily Independent* in Ashland, Ky., said that he thinks this issue becomes most sensitive when interviews are sought with "people who are thrust into the public eye because of circumstances beyond their own control."

In April 1992, one of the world's best-known athletes, the tennis player Arthur Ashe, was talking to a reporter for *USA Today*, Doug Smith, who had been a friend in high school. Smith's primary purpose, though, was not to talk about old times. Rather, he was at Ashe's house to ask him to respond to the rumor that he had AIDS.

Ashe, who asked also to speak to the newspaper's executive editor for sports, did not confirm the rumor. Because Ashe didn't confirm the rumor and because of its policy not to use unnamed sources, *USA Today* did not publish the story.

But the conversations spurred Ashe to hastily call a press conference for the following day to make public what a small circle of friends already knew: the former tennis star did indeed have AIDS. Ashe thought he had contracted the disease through tainted blood during an operating-room transfusion nearly a decade earlier; he died of it in February 1993.

Just before the press conference, when *USA Today* journalists were able to confirm what Ashe intended to announce, they immediately prepared a story for the newspaper's international edition and for the Gannett News Service.

As one would expect, reaction to the story and its handling was strong and emotional. *USA Today* created a special telephone line to receive calls. Hundreds of readers made their feelings known; most of them were critical.

Debra Gersh, writing in *Editor & Publisher* magazine, assembled reactions that had been published in the media and solicited opinions from a sample of journalists. The lead on her story was compelling: "The media found out last week that the boundaries of good journalism are not as clear as the service line on a tennis court."

Included in her story were some excerpts from a column Ashe had written for *The Washington Post:*

> I know there are tradeoffs in life. I understand that the press has a watchdog role in the maintenance of our freedoms and to expose corruption. But the process whereby news organizations make distinctions seems more art than science.
>
> I wasn't then, and I am not now, comfortable with being sacrificed for the sake of the "public's right to know."

Gersh went on to quote some journalists who were outraged at what they perceived to be an invasion of Ashe's privacy. Other journalists, though most of them admitted to feeling uneasy about the situation, said that the media had no choice but to write the story once the rumor was circulating and had been confirmed.

USA Today sportswriter Smith said he later talked with Ashe about the story.

"A few days after the story was published he called because he knew I was catching some flak," Smith said. "He told me that he wanted me to know that he didn't hold me personally responsible. Arthur and I remained friends. Despite the discomfort that the disclosure caused him, he called frequently and insisted that I update and edit his book, 'A Hard Road to Glory.' "

"I think the thing that helped me most was what he did with his life afterwards. Within two months of his coming out, he formed a foundation to combat AIDS, which raised several million dollars for indigent AIDS patients. And his speeches helped a lot of people change their attitudes toward those who had AIDS. He became an advocate and I think that he helped change a great number of people—both those who had AIDS and those who had to deal with the people who had AIDS."

Smith, a Hampton University graduate who served in the Army in the 1960s, was among the early wave of blacks to enjoy distinguished newspaper careers.

"I never considered being a reporter during my undergraduate years at Hampton (where he was a math major) primarily because journalism was among numerous professions that didn't really exist for blacks during that time. Actor Sidney Poitier was the most powerful black achiever and role model for my generation. I yearned to see blacks excel in other fields, besides entertainment and athletics."

Smith possesses more than a quarter-century of journalism experience. Before he joined *USA Today* in 1986, he worked for *Newsday*, the *New York Post* and for Howard University, where he edited publications.

"The Ashe story was, by far, the most difficult thing I ever had to deal with as a reporter," said Smith, who now covers tennis for *USA Today*. "But, as a journalist, you must make decisions that you can live with. When I was an Army captain, I had to make decisions that were difficult personally, but they were decisions that had to be made. The most important thing to be able to say is 'This is what I think should be done,' and then go with it."

Conflicts of Interest

Mike Foley of the *St. Petersburg* (Fla.) *Times* sees conflicts of interest as a major ethical issue facing journalists. Foley said that these conflicts—real or perceived—can involve such things as club memberships, friendships and even a spouse's political involvements.

Reporters and editors cannot be expected to live like hermits or to develop no friendships. But friendships can pose potential problems. Arthur C. Gorlick, the assistant managing editor of the *Seattle Post-Intelligencer*, called these problems "cronyism." He said: "It seems manifested in many ways at various levels of news organizations. Reporters, editors and publishers establish friendships with many of the people involved with things news organizations are expected to report about fairly. It is difficult for reporters or editors to maintain the impression of being impartial in a news report about a legislator if they have been socializing the previous evening or have a weekend golf date. It is difficult for journalists to function easily in reporting about a business leader knowing the publisher has invited the business leader to join the board of a civic fund-raising effort, however good the cause."

Reporters can also feel an ethical squeeze when they are asked to write newsletters for organizations to which they belong. Media policies vary with regard to the level of outside involvement their reporters and editors can have. New reporters should familiarize themselves with the codes of ethics of organizations for which they work.

Anonymous Sources

"The anonymous source—its use or misuse—is an issue of growing concern for us and other newspapers, particularly as it relates to the issue of newspaper credibility and public confidence in the media," said William T. Newill, the editor of the *Burlington* (N.J.) *County Times*. "There are times when it is absolutely necessary to guarantee anonymity in exchange for vital information. But the process has been abused by politicians and reporters up and down the system to the point where readers must certainly believe that the anonymous sources quoted in so many stories are none other than the reporters themselves. And who can blame our readers for thinking that way?"

In a speech at a journalism education conference in Chicago, then *Washington Post* ombudsman Geneva Overholser noted the complexities inherent in the use of anonymous sources.

"When we use anonymous sources, we allow our news sources to be depicted in ways they would not be [otherwise]," she said. "We all know that the quality of conversation is different when we're saying something off the record rather than on. Some would argue that's when the real truth comes out, and sometimes it does. But too often, it's not the truth that comes out but somebody's ax or venom, and it's certainly unfair to the people we cover."

David Shaw, media critic for the *Los Angeles Times,* noted in an article in the *Media Studies Journal* that "the accelerated news cycle and the absence of standards and gatekeepers in cyberspace have both expanded the use of unnamed sources and exacerbated its consequence."

Shaw elaborated: "Who has the time to think—let alone try to talk someone into going on the record, or, failing that, to find, cultivate and persuade a second or third or fourth source to go on the record—when Matt Drudge (or someone of his ilk) is already online with the latest unconfirmed, unreliable rumor from the most clever (or most available) unnamed source?"

Later in his article, Shaw was critical of the journalistic convention that often is observed at newspapers and magazines—that, under certain circumstances, anonymous sources can be used, but only if confirmed by a second source: "Some journalists seem to feel that if they have *two* unnamed sources, it automatically validates a story. I've heard many reporters speak of the 'two-source' rule as if it were either a clause in an insurance policy or one of the Ten Commandments. But I don't think readers necessarily accept this. The overuse of unnamed sources is probably the single biggest complaint I hear about the media from people outside the profession—bigger even than bias, sensationalism and inaccuracy."

Gifts

Presumably all editors and reporters agree that it is unethical to accept any gift of value from a news source. Some editors contend that it is unethical to accept any gifts—period. There are, however, some gray areas.

Tim Wood of *The Weatherford Democrat* said: "Accepting gifts usually is a judgment call. For example, several organizations bring food to our office during the holiday season. Is it unethical to accept this food? The food has little monetary value. Turning it down could be interpreted as an insult. The people who give us the food don't expect anything in return. However, if an organization wanted to treat the staff to a nice dinner at a local restaurant, that would be a different matter."

Many of the national and individual newspaper codes deal with the matter of gifts. The code of the Society of Professional Journalists says "journalists should refuse gifts, favors, fees, free travel and special treatment." The Associated Press Sports Editors' code says: "Gifts of insignificant value—a calendar, pencil, key chain or such—may be accepted if it would be awkward to refuse or return them. All other gifts should be declined. A gift that exceeds token value should be returned immediately with an explanation that it is against policy. If it is impractical to return it, the gift should be donated to a charity by your company." *The Washington Post*'s code says: "We accept no gifts from news sources. Exceptions are minimal (tickets to cultural events to be reviewed) or obvious (invitations to meals). Occasionally, other exceptions might qualify. If in doubt, consult the executive editor or the managing editor or his deputy."

Codes also often address the matter of free travel. The code of the *Chicago Sun-Times* says: "As a general principle, we will continue to pay for all travel. If an exception is required, a decision will be made on the merits of each case, with the understanding that conditions of any free travel are to be fully explained in connection with the subsequent news coverage."

Mitch Kehetian of *The Macomb Daily* in Michigan said that he thinks too much attention is given to accepting a lunch or dinner because he has "too much faith in the journalists of today to insinuate that they could be bought off with a Big Boy burger."

The biggest problem for reporters at smaller newspapers, according to Kehetian, is dealing with "informational trips." Reporters and editors are often offered trips by groups such as the National Guard, which might provide transportation to training exercises at a summer camp. "The downtown dailies have unlimited sources, and can preach ethics at accepting such offers—but small daily staffers, and more so at weekly levels, find that the free offer is the only way of getting the story," Kehetian said. "That's sometimes the price for good ethics. In most cases, however, questionable examples are resolved by maintaining an open discussion line in the newsroom and always stressing that it is in the best interest of the reporter's professional integrity and, in the general run, that of the newspaper."

Compassion versus Policy

Reporters and editors of smaller dailies and weeklies are most likely to encounter those ticklish, awkward day-to-day situations when a subscriber, acquaintance or friend walks in the front door of the newsroom and asks, for example, that his or her name be kept out of the court news.

Most journalists have been threatened with, "Do you want to be responsible for the consequences if you print this story?" Such threats occur with frequency, but even veteran reporters never grow completely calloused to them.

It is not uncommon for court reporters—particularly those who work for smaller newspapers—to be confronted by people charged with criminal offenses. It is surprising how many of them have relatives with heart trouble or other medical problems—conditions that would quickly worsen if a story were published. Most reporters have received telephone calls from ministers or other community leaders urging that a drunken-driving story not be printed because of the disastrous effects such a story would have on the family of the accused. Sometimes, policies are in place to handle such matters. At other times, reporters or editors must make individual decisions.

"The real ethical issues are the hard choices faced in reporting day-to-day news," said Bill Williams, the editor of *The Paris* (Tenn.) *Post-Intelligencer*. "Do I publish the name of the rape victim? Do I wait until the defendant appears in court before publishing news of the arrest? Do I allow the mayor to provide information off the record? Does my birth column list illegitimate children?"

Williams told of an incident that occurred at his newspaper. It illustrates that, particularly in small-town journalism, editors are sometimes darned if they do and darned if they don't.

"The child of divorced parents won an honor," he said. "The mother reported the information, and we identified the child with her mother's name. The father called to object, said he was proud of the kid, too, even though the mother had custody, and he wanted to be identified as the father. So we ran a correction. The mother stormed in [subscribers don't have to get by security guards at small dailies and weeklies], said the father was a louse who had forfeited any claim. The child had subsequently been adopted by the stepfather, she said, and he should be identified as the father. I agreed with her that the guy was a louse, but I said he was still the biological father and we didn't see that we had any choice. She slapped me in the face and stalked out. That's how I 'solved' the issue."

T. J. Hemlinger, the editor of the *Hartford City* (Ind.) *News-Times,* said that, at his small-town (population 7,600) newspaper, staffers don't face some of the ethical problems encountered by larger newspapers. " 'Free travel' [for us] means riding a bus to the state capital with the Farm Bureau members to attend the state convention. Our ethics questions are: Should we run a picture of a suicide victim covered by a sheet, or a picture of someone injured in a traffic accident? Should we run a picture of a woman who probably is mentally ill as she goes into court to face charges of murdering her 9-month-old infant? My answers are all 'yes,' by the way."

Thad Poulson, the editor of the *Daily Sitka Sentinel* in Alaska, said: "We are regularly asked, by acquaintances and strangers alike, to 'keep my name out of the paper' in connection with the police news we publish. We often would prefer to comply, but we never do. Everyone on the staff, editorial and in other departments, knows that exceptions cannot be made even for employees of the newspaper."

Policies often provide ironclad rules for journalists, but it is clear that sometimes difficult decisions must be made on the spot. As Professor Merrill pointed out, ethics involves personal values. Journalists must decide what, under the circumstances, is the correct course of action.

Journalistic Arrogance

Editors who were surveyed spoke at length on some of the ethical issues discussed above. In their continuous effort to be responsible to their readers, their sources and themselves, however, reporters and editors also need to consider the issue of journalistic arrogance.

David Shaw of the *Los Angeles Times* touched on the issue of journalistic arrogance in an article he wrote for the magazine of the Society of Professional Journalists' national convention.

Shaw described one of the characters in Irving Wallace's novel "The Almighty": "The protagonist . . . is a power-mad, megalomaniacal, second-generation newspaper publisher who makes such observations as, 'There's not enough hard news around, exclusive news. Usually, my competitors have the same thing to sell that I have. But we here want our news alone. Since it's not around, we might have to invent some of it.' "

Shaw noted that this hyperbolic view is held by a lot of people who read novels and watch movies about newspapers. Still, Shaw said that the press likes to point majestically to the First Amendment, claiming that it "separates us from other institutions in our society." He wrote: "Like lawyers—and doctors and politicians and athletes and movie stars and everyone else I know—we don't like to be criticized."

The *Los Angeles Times* reporter said that "the arrogance of the press may be one of the greatest problems we, as an institution, face today." Shaw said that he was convinced "that the press must be held morally accountable to itself and to the society it serves." He said that it was important for the press to tell the public what it does and why—and, when necessary, to admit its mistakes.

In Conclusion: The Journalist's Responsibility

Clearly, there are no absolute or certain answers to many of the ethical questions that regularly confront journalists. As Professor Merrill noted, "Ethics has to do with 'self-legislation' and 'self-enforcement.' " Merrill vividly summarized the issue of ethics and journalism in his book "The Imperative of Freedom": "When we enter the area of journalistic ethics, we pass into a swampland of philosophical speculation where eerie mists of judgment hang low over a boggy terrain. In spite of the unsure footing and poor visibility, there is no reason not to make the journey. In fact, it is a journey well worth taking for it brings the matter of morality to the individual person; it forces the journalist, among others, to consider his basic principles, his values, his obligations to himself and to others. It forces him to decide for himself how he will live, how he will conduct his journalistic affairs, how he will think of himself and of others, how he will think, act and react to the people and issues surrounding him.

"Ethics has to do with duty—duty to self and/or duty to others. It is primarily individual or personal even when it relates to obligations and duties to others."

During a lecture at Penn State University, Pulitzer Prize-winning journalist Michael Gartner brought home the importance of writers exercising responsibility: "You can be a good writer and write terribly unfair stories, but you can't be a good newspaper writer and do that. Not, at least, for a mainstream newspaper. Fairness is vital for every story and every newspaper, for the unfair story hurts the credibility of the reporter and the editor and the newspaper. What this means is that the good writer avoids cheap shots. And I know that is hard to do. Cheap shots are just so much fun. Sometimes, they just roll out of the computer like Fords off an assembly line. They are sharp and snappy and pretty and appealing. But they're also deadly—for the writer."

Clearly, journalists bear an awesome responsibility to themselves and to their audience; this they should never forget.

Indeed, *Oregonian* editor Sandra Mims Rowe told the nation's ombudsmen:

> Credibility is not theoretical, philosophical or remote from our work. It is at the heart of our professional lives.
>
> Credibility is not about selling more newspapers. It is about building the quality and integrity of our news.
>
> It is not about finding some new journalistic fad or silver bullet to solve our problems. It is about thoroughly understanding, clearly articulating and relentlessly applying the highest professional and ethical standards.
>
> It is not even about what we have the right to do; obviously, we have the right to print just about anything we want. It is about doing the right thing.

Appendix A Gannett Newspaper Division

I. Principles of Ethical Conduct for Newsrooms

We Are Committed to:

Seeking and Reporting the Truth in a Truthful Way

- We will dedicate ourselves to reporting the news accurately, thoroughly and in context.
- We will be honest in the way we gather, report and present news.
- We will be persistent in the pursuit of the whole story.
- We will keep our word.
- We will hold factual information in opinion columns and editorials to the same standards of accuracy as news stories.
- We will seek to gain sufficient understanding of the communities, individuals and stories we cover to provide an informed account of activities.

Serving the Public Interest

- We will uphold First Amendment principles to serve the democratic process.
- We will be vigilant watchdogs of government and institutions that affect the public.
- We will provide the news and information that people need to function as effective citizens.
- We will seek solutions as well as expose problems and wrongdoing.
- We will provide a public forum for diverse people and views.
- We will reflect and encourage understanding of the diverse segments of our community.
- We will provide editorial and community leadership.
- We will seek to promote understanding of complex issues.

Exercising Fair Play

- We will treat people with dignity, respect and compassion.
- We will correct errors promptly.
- We will strive to include all sides relevant to a story and not take sides in news coverage.
- We will explain to readers our journalistic processes.
- We will give particular attention to fairness in relations with people unaccustomed to dealing with the press.

- ❑ We will use unnamed sources as the sole basis for published information only as a last resort and under specific procedures that best serve the public's right to know.
- ❑ We will be accessible to readers.

Maintaining Independence

- ❑ We will remain free of outside interests, investments or business relationships that may compromise the credibility of our news report.
- ❑ We will maintain an impartial, arm's length relationship with anyone seeking to influence the news.
- ❑ We will avoid potential conflicts of interest and eliminate inappropriate influence on content.
- ❑ We will be free of improper obligations to news sources, newsmakers and advertisers.
- ❑ We will differentiate advertising from news.

Acting with Integrity

- ❑ We will act honorably and ethically in dealing with news sources, the public and our colleagues.
- ❑ We will obey the law.
- ❑ We will observe common standards of decency.
- ❑ We will take responsibility for our decisions and consider the possible consequences of our actions.
- ❑ We will be conscientious in observing these Principles.
- ❑ We will always try to do the right thing.

Appendix

B The Associated Press Stylebook and Briefing on Media Law Rules

Here is a summary of the major rules from The Associated Press Stylebook and Libel Manual. These rules are only a sampling of what can be found in the stylebook, which you should also have.

Abbreviations and acronyms The notation *abbrev.* is used in this book to identify the abbreviated form that may be used for a word in some contexts.

A few universally recognized abbreviations are required in some circumstances. Some others are acceptable depending on the context. But in general, avoid alphabet soup. Do not use abbreviations or acronyms which the reader would not quickly recognize.

Guidance on how to use a particular abbreviation or acronym is provided in entries alphabetized according to the sequence of letters in the word or phrase.

Some general principles:

BEFORE A NAME: Abbreviate the following titles when used before a full name outside direct quotations: *Dr., Gov., Lt. Gov., Mr., Mrs., Rep., the Rev., Sen.* and certain military designations listed in the military titles entry. Spell out all except *Dr., Mr., Mrs.* and *Ms.* when they are used before a name in direct quotations.

AFTER A NAME: Abbreviate *junior* or *senior* after an individual's name. Abbreviate *company, corporation, incorporated* and *limited* when used after the name of a corporate entity.

WITH DATES OR NUMERALS: Use the abbreviations *A.D., B.C., a.m., p.m., No.* and abbreviate certain months when used with the day of the month.

Right: *In 450 B.C.; at 9:30 a.m.; in room No. 6; on Sept. 16.*

Wrong: *Early this a.m. he asked for the No. of your room.* The abbreviations are correct only with figures.

Right: *Early this morning he asked for the number of your room.*

IN NUMBERED ADDRESSES: Abbreviate *avenue, boulevard* and *street* in numbered addresses: *He lives on Pennsylvania Avenue. He lives at 1600 Pennsylvania Ave.*

Addresses Use the abbreviations *Ave., Blvd.* and *St.* only with a numbered address: *1600 Pennsylvania Ave.* Spell them out and capitalize when part of a formal street name without a number: *Pennsylvania Avenue.* Lowercase and spell out when used alone or with more than one street name: *Massachusetts and Pennsylvania avenues.*

All similar words (*alley, drive, road, terrace,* etc.) always are spelled out. Capitalize them when part of a formal name without a number; lowercase when used alone or with two or more names.

Always use figures for an address number: *9 Morningside Circle.*

Spell out and capitalize *First* through *Ninth* when used as street names; use figures with two letters for *10th* and above: *7 Fifth Ave., 100 21st St.*

Abbreviate compass points used to indicate directional ends of a street or quadrants of a city in a numbered address; *222 E. 42nd St., 562 W. 43rd St., 600 K St. N.W.* Do not abbreviate if the number is omitted: *East 42nd Street, West 43rd Street, K Street Northwest.*

Capitalization In general, avoid unnecessary capitals. Use a capital letter only if you can justify it by one of the principles listed here.

Capitalization—(*cont.*) Many words and phrases, including special cases, are listed separately in this book. Entries that are capitalized without further comment should be capitalized in all uses.

If there is no relevant listing in this book for a particular word or phrase, consult Webster's New World Dictionary. Use lowercase if the dictionary lists it as an acceptable form for the sense in which the word is being used.

As used in this book, *capitalize* means to use uppercase for the first letter of a word. If additional capital letters are needed, they are called for by an example or a phrase such as *use all caps.*

Some basic principles:

PROPER NOUNS: Capitalize nouns that constitute the unique identification for a specific person, place or thing: *John, Mary, America, Boston, England.*

Some words, such as the examples just given, are always proper nouns. Some common nouns receive proper noun status when they are used as the name of a particular entity: *General Electric, Gulf Oil.*

PROPER NAMES: Capitalize common nouns such as *party, river, street* and *west* when they are an integral part of the full name for a person, place or thing: *Democratic Party, Mississippi River, Fleet Street, West Virginia.*

Lowercase these common nouns when they stand alone in subsequent references: *the party, the river, the street.*

Lowercase the common noun elements of names in all plural uses: *the Democratic and Republican parties, Main and State streets, lakes Erie and Ontario.*

POPULAR NAMES: Some places and events lack officially designated proper names but have popular names that are the effective equivalent: *the Combat Zone* (a section of downtown Boston), *the Main Line* (a group of Philadelphia suburbs), *the South Side* (of Chicago), *the Badlands* (of North Dakota), *the Street* (the financial community in the Wall Street area of New York).

The principle applies also to shortened versions of the proper names for one-of-a-kind events: *the Series* (for the World Series), *the Derby* (for the Kentucky Derby). This practice should not, however, be interpreted as a license to ignore the general practice of lowercasing the common noun elements of a name when they stand alone.

DERIVATIVES: Capitalize words that are derived from a proper noun and still depend on it for their meaning: *American, Christian, Christianity, English, French, Marxism, Shakespearean.*

Lowercase words that are derived from a proper noun but no longer depend on it for their meaning: *french fries, herculean, manhattan cocktail, malapropism, pasteurize, quixotic, venetian blind.*

SENTENCES: Capitalize the first word in a statement that stands as a sentence.

In poetry, capital letters are used for the first words of some phrases that would not be capitalized in prose.

COMPOSITIONS: Capitalize the principal words in the names of books, movies, plays, poems, operas, songs, radio and television programs, works of art, etc.

TITLES: Capitalize formal titles when used immediately before a name. Lowercase formal titles when used alone or in constructions that set them off from a name by commas.

Use lowercase at all times for terms that are job descriptions rather than formal titles.

Comma The following guidelines treat some of the most frequent questions about the use of commas.

For detailed guidance, consult the punctuation section in the back of Webster's New World Dictionary.

IN A SERIES: Use commas to separate elements in a series, but do not put a comma before the conjunction in a simple series: *The flag is red, white and blue. He would nominate Tom, Dick or Harry.*

Put a comma before the concluding conjunction in a series, however, if an integral element of the series requires a conjunction: *I had orange juice, toast, and ham and eggs for breakfast.*

Comma—(*cont.*) Use a comma also before the concluding conjunction in a complex series of phrases: *The main points to consider are whether the athletes are skillful enough to compete, whether they have the stamina to endure the training, and whether they have the proper mental attitude.*

WITH EQUAL ADJECTIVES: Use commas to separate a series of adjectives equal in rank. If the commas could be replaced by the word *and* without changing the sense, the adjectives are equal: *a thoughtful, precise manner; a dark, dangerous street.*

Use no comma when the last adjective before a noun outranks its predecessors because it is an integral element of a noun phrase, which is the equivalent of a single noun: *a cheap fur coat* (the noun phrase is *fur coat*); *the old oaken bucket; a new, blue spring bonnet.*

WITH INTRODUCTORY CLAUSES AND PHRASES: A comma is used to separate an introductory clause or phrase from the main clause: *When he had tired of the mad pace of New York, he moved to Dubuque.*

The comma may be omitted after short introductory phrases if no ambiguity would result: *During the night he heard many noises.*

But use the comma if its omission would slow comprehension: *On the street below, the curious gathered.*

WITH CONJUNCTIONS: When a conjunction such as *and, but* or *for* links two clauses that could stand alone as separate sentences, use a comma before the conjunction in most cases: *She was glad she had looked, for a man was approaching the house.*

As a rule of thumb, use a comma if the subject of each clause is expressly stated: *We are visiting Washington, and we also plan a side trip to Williamsburg. We visited Washington, and our senator greeted us personally.* But no comma when the subject of the two clauses is the same and is not repeated in the second: *We are visiting Washington and plan to see the White House.*

The comma may be dropped if two clauses with expressly stated subjects are short. In general, however, favor use of a comma unless a particular literary effect is desired or it would distort the sense of a sentence.

INTRODUCING DIRECT QUOTES: Use a comma to introduce a complete, one-sentence quotation within a paragraph: *Wallace said, "She spent six months in Argentina and came back speaking English with a Spanish accent."* But use a colon to introduce quotations of more than one sentence.

Do not use a comma at the start of an indirect or partial quotation: *He said his victory put him "firmly on the road to a first-ballot nomination."*

BEFORE ATTRIBUTION: Use a comma instead of a period at the end of a quote that is followed by attribution: *"Rub my shoulders," Miss Cawley suggested.*

Do not use a comma, however, if the quoted statement ends with a question mark or exclamation point: *"Why should I?" he asked.*

WITH HOMETOWNS AND AGES: Use a comma to set off an individual's hometown when it is placed in apposition to a name: *Mary Richards, Minneapolis, and Maude Findlay, Tuckahoe, N.Y., were there.*

If an individual's age is used, set it off by commas: *Maude Findlay, 48, Tuckahoe, N.Y., was present.*

NAMES OF STATES AND NATIONS USED WITH CITY NAMES: *His journey will take him from Dublin, Ireland, to Fargo, N.D., and back. The Selma, Ala., group saw the governor.*

Use parentheses, however, if a state name is inserted within a proper name: *The Huntsville (Ala.) Times.*

WITH YES AND NO: *Yes, I will be there.*

IN DIRECT ADDRESS: *Mother, I will be home late. No, sir, I did not do it.*

SEPARATING SIMILAR WORDS: Use a comma to separate duplicated words that otherwise would be confusing: *What the problem is, is not clear.*

IN LARGE FIGURES: Use a comma for most figures higher than 999. The major exceptions are: street addresses *(1234 Main St.),* broadcast frequencies *(1460 kilohertz),* room numbers, serial numbers, telephone numbers and years *(1876).*

PLACEMENT WITH QUOTES: Commas always go inside quotation marks.

Courtesy titles Refer to both men and women by first and last name: *Susan Smith* or *Robert Smith.* Do not use the courtesy titles *Mr., Miss, Ms.* or *Mrs.* except in direct quotations, or where needed to distinguish among people of the same last name (as in married couples or brothers and sisters), or where a woman specifically requests that a title be used (for example, where a woman prefers to be known as *Mrs. Susan Smith* or *Mrs. Robert Smith*).

In cases where a person's gender is not clear from the first name or from the story's context, indicate the gender by using *he* or *she* in a subsequent reference.

Dates Always use Arabic figures, without *st, nd, rd* or *th.*

Directions and regions In general, lowercase *north, south, northeast, northern,* etc., when they indicate compass direction; capitalize these words when they designate regions.

Some examples:

COMPASS DIRECTION: *He drove west. The cold front is moving east.*

REGIONS: *A storm system that developed in the Midwest is spreading eastward. It will bring showers to the East Coast by morning and to the entire Northeast by late in the day. High temperatures will prevail throughout the Western states.*

The North was victorious. The South will rise again. Settlers from the East went West in search of new lives. The customs of the East are different from those of the West. The Northeast depends on the Midwest for its food supply.

She has a Southern accent. He is a Northerner. Nations of the Orient are opening doors to Western businessmen. The candidate developed a Southern strategy. She is a Northern liberal.

The storm developed in the South Pacific. European leaders met to talk about supplies of oil from Southeast Asia.

WITH NAMES OF NATIONS: Lowercase unless they are part of a proper name or are used to designate a politically divided nation: *northern France, eastern Canada, the western United States.*

But: *Northern Ireland, South Korea.*

WITH STATES AND CITIES: The preferred form is to lowercase compass points when they describe a section of a state or city: *western Texas, southern Atlanta.*

But capitalize compass points:

—When part of a proper name: *North Dakota, West Virginia.*
—When used in denoting widely known sections: *Southern California, the South Side of Chicago, the Lower East Side of New York.* If in doubt, use lowercase.

IN FORMING PROPER NAMES: When combining with another common noun to form the name for a region or location: *the North Woods, the South Pole, the Far East, the Middle East, the West Coast* (the entire region, not the coastline itself), *the Eastern Shore, the Western Hemisphere.*

Doctor Use *Dr.* in first reference as a formal title before the name of an individual who holds a doctor of dental surgery, doctor of medicine, doctor of osteopathy, or doctor of podiatric medicine degree: *Dr. Jonas Salk.*

The form *Dr.,* or *Drs.* in the plural construction, applies to all first-reference uses before a name, including direct quotations.

If appropriate in the context, *Dr.* also may be used on first reference before the names of individuals who hold other types of doctoral degrees. However, because the public frequently identifies *Dr.* only with physicians, care should be taken to assure that the individual's specialty is stated in first or second reference. The only exception would be a story in which the context left no doubt that the person was a dentist, psychologist, chemist, historian, etc.

In some instances it also is necessary to specify that an individual identified as *Dr.* is a physician. One frequent case is a story reporting on joint research by physicians, biologists, etc.

Do not use *Dr.* before the names of individuals who hold honorary doctorates.

Do not continue the use of *Dr.* in subsequent references.

House of representatives Capitalize when referring to a specific governmental body: *The U.S. House of Representatives, the Massachusetts House of Representatives.*

Capitalize shortened references that delete the words *of Representatives: the U.S. House, the Massachusetts House.*

Retain capitalization if *U.S.* or the name of a state is dropped but the reference is to a specific body:

BOSTON (AP)—The House has adjourned for the year.

Lowercase plural uses: *the Massachusetts and Rhode Island houses.*

Apply the same principles to similar legislative bodies such as *the Virginia House of Delegates.*

Hyphen Hyphens are joiners. Use them to avoid ambiguity or to form a single idea from two or more words.

Some guidelines:

AVOID AMBIGUITY: Use a hyphen whenever ambiguity would result if it were omitted: *The president will speak to small-business men.* (*Businessmen* normally is one word. But *the president will speak to small businessmen* is unclear.)

Others: *He recovered his health. He re-covered the leaky roof.*

COMPOUND MODIFIERS: When a compound modifier—two or more words that express a single concept—precedes a noun, use hyphens to link all the words in the compound except the adverb *very* and all adverbs that end in *ly: a first-quarter touchdown, a bluish-green dress, a full-time job, a well-known man, a better qualified woman, a know-it-all attitude, a very good time, an easily remembered rule.*

Many combinations that are hyphenated before a noun are not hyphenated when they occur after a noun: *The team scored in the first quarter. The dress, a bluish green, was attractive on her. She works full time. His attitude suggested that he knew it all.*

But when a modifier that would be hyphenated before a noun occurs instead after a form of the verb *to be,* the hyphen usually must be retained to avoid confusion: *The man is well-known. The woman is quick-witted. The children are soft-spoken. The play is second-rate.*

The principle of using a hyphen to avoid confusion explains why no hyphen is required with *very* and *ly* words. Readers can expect them to modify the word that follows. But if a combination such as *little-known man* were not hyphenated, the reader could logically be expecting *little* to be followed by a noun, as in *little man.* Instead, the reader encountering *little known* would have to back up mentally and make the compound connection on his own.

TWO-THOUGHT COMPOUNDS: *serio-comic, socio-economic.*

COMPOUND PROPER NOUNS AND ADJECTIVES: Use a hyphen to designate dual heritage: *Italian-American, Mexican-American.*

No hyphen, however, for *French Canadian* or *Latin American.*

AVOID DUPLICATED VOWELS, TRIPLED CONSONANTS: Examples: *anti-intellectual, pre-empt, shell-like.*

WITH NUMERALS: Use a hyphen to separate figures in odds, ratios, scores, some fractions and some vote tabulations.

When large numbers must be spelled out, use a hyphen to connect a word ending in *y* to another word: *twenty-one, fifty-five,* etc.

SUSPENSIVE HYPHENATION: The form: *He received a 10- to 20-year sentence in prison.*

Legislative titles

FIRST REFERENCE FORM: Use *Rep., Reps., Sen.* and *Sens.* as formal titles before one or more names in regular text. Spell out and capitalize these titles before one or more names in a direct quotation. Spell out and lowercase *representative* and *senator* in other uses.

Spell out other legislative titles in all uses. Capitalize formal titles such as *assemblyman, assemblywoman, city councilor, delegate,* etc., when they are used before a name. Lowercase in other uses.

Legislative titles—*(cont.)* Add *U.S.* or *state* before a title only if necessary to avoid confusion: *U.S. Sen. Nancy Kassebaum spoke with state Sen. Hugh Carter.*

FIRST REFERENCE PRACTICE: The use of a title such as *Rep.* or *Sen.* in first reference is normal in most stories. It is not mandatory, however, provided an individual's title is given later in the story.

SECOND REFERENCE: Do not use legislative titles before a name on second reference unless they are part of a direct quotation.

CONGRESSMAN, CONGRESSWOMAN: *Rep.* and *U.S. Rep.* are the preferred first-reference forms when a formal title is used before the name of a U.S. House member. The words *congressman* or *congresswoman*, in lowercase, may be used in subsequent references that do not use an individual's name, just as *senator* is used in references to members of the Senate.

Congressman and *congresswoman* should appear as capitalized formal titles before a name only in direct quotation.

Legislature Capitalize when preceded by the name of a state: the Kansas Legislature.

Retain capitalization when the state name is dropped but the reference is specifically to that state's legislature:

TOPEKA, Kan. (AP)—Both houses of the Legislature adjourned today.

Capitalize *legislature* in subsequent specific references and in such constructions as: *the 100th Legislature, the state Legislature.*

Although the word *legislature* is not part of the formal, proper name for the lawmaking bodies in many states, it commonly is used that way and should be treated as such in any story that does not use the formal name.

If a given context or local practice calls for the use of a formal name such as *Missouri General Assembly*, retain the capital letters if the name of the state can be dropped, but lowercase the word *assembly* if it stands alone. Lowercase *legislature* if a story uses it in a subsequent reference to a body identified as a general assembly.

Lowercase *legislature* when used generically: *No legislature has approved the amendment.*

Use *legislature* in lowercase for all plural references: *The Arkansas and Colorado legislatures are considering the amendment.*

In 49 states the separate bodies are a *senate* and a *house* or *assembly*. The *Nebraska Legislature* is a unicameral body.

Military titles Capitalize a military rank when used as a formal title before an individual's name.

See the lists that follow to determine whether the title should be spelled out or abbreviated in regular text. Spell out any title used before a name in a direct quotation.

On first reference, use the appropriate title before the full name of a member of the military.

In subsequent references, do not continue using the title before a name. Use only the last name.

Spell out and lowercase a title when it is substituted for a name: *Gen. John J. Pershing arrived today. An aide said the general would review the troops.*

In some cases, it may be necessary to explain the significance of a title: *Army Sgt. Maj. John Jones described the attack. Jones, who holds the Army's highest rank for enlisted men, said it was unprovoked.*

In addition to the ranks listed, each service has ratings such as *machinist, radarman, torpedoman*, etc., that are job descriptions. Do not use any of these designations as a title on first reference. If one is used before a name in a subsequent reference, do not capitalize or abbreviate it.

Military titles—(*cont.*)

ABBREVIATIONS: The abbreviations, with the highest ranks listed first:

MILITARY TITLES

Rank	*Usage before a Name*

ARMY

Commissioned Officers

Rank	Usage before a Name
general	Gen.
lieutenant general	Lt. Gen.
major general	Maj. Gen.
brigadier general	Brig. Gen.
colonel	Col.
lieutenant colonel	Lt. Col.
major	Maj.
captain	Capt.
first lieutenant	1st Lt.
second lieutenant	2nd Lt.

Warrant Officers

Rank	Usage before a Name
chief warrant officer	Chief Warrant Officer
warrant officer	Warrant Officer

Enlisted Personnel

Rank	Usage before a Name
sergeant major of the Army	Sgt. Maj. of the Army
command sergeant major	Command Sgt. Maj.
sergeant major	Sgt. Maj.
first sergeant	1st Sgt.
master sergeant	Master Sgt.
sergeant first class	Sgt. 1st Class
staff sergeant	Staff Sgt.
sergeant	Sgt.
corporal	Cpl.
specialist	Spc.
private first class	Pfc.
private	Pvt.

NAVY, COAST GUARD

Commissioned Officers

Rank	Usage before a Name
admiral	Adm.
vice admiral	Vice Adm.
rear admiral upper half	Rear Adm.
rear admiral lower half	Rear Adm.
captain	Capt.
commander	Cmdr.
lieutenant commander	Lt. Cmdr.
lieutenant	Lt.
lieutenant junior grade	Lt. j.g.
ensign	Ensign

Warrant Officers

Rank	Usage before a Name
chief warrant officer	Chief Warrant Officer
warrant officer	Warrant Officer

Enlisted Personnel

Rank	Usage before a Name
master chief petty officer of the Navy	Master Chief Petty Officer of the Navy
senior chief petty officer	Senior Chief Petty Officer
chief petty officer	Chief Petty Officer
petty officer first class	Petty Officer 1st Class
petty officer second class	Petty Officer 2nd Class
petty officer third class	Petty Officer 3rd Class
seaman	Seaman
seaman apprentice	Seaman Apprentice
seaman recruit	Seaman Recruit

MARINE CORPS

Ranks and abbreviations for commissioned officers are the same as those in the Army. Warrant officer ratings follow the same system used in the Navy. There are no specialist ratings.

Others

Rank	Usage before a Name
sergeant major of the Marine Corps	Sgt. Maj. of the Marine Corps
master gunnery sergeant	Master Gunnery Sgt.
master sergeant	Master Sgt.

Military titles—(*cont.*)

first sergeant	1st Sgt.
gunnery sergeant	Gunnery Sgt.
staff sergeant	Staff Sgt.
sergeant	Sgt.
corporal	Cpl.
lance corporal	Lance Cpl.
private first class	Pfc.
private	Pvt.

AIR FORCE

Ranks and abbreviations for commissioned officers are the same as those in the Army.

Enlisted Designations

chief master sergeant of the Air Force	Chief Master Sgt. of the Air Force
chief master sergeant	Chief Master Sgt.
senior master sergeant	Senior Master Sgt.
technical sergeant	Tech. Sgt.
staff sergeant	Staff Sgt.
senior airman	Senior Airman
airman first class	Airman 1st Class
airman	Airman
airman basic	Airman

PLURALS: Add *s* to the principal element in the title: *Majs. John Jones and Robert Smith; Maj. Gens. John Jones and Robert Smith; Spcs. John Jones and Robert Smith.*

RETIRED OFFICERS: A military rank may be used in the first reference before the name of an officer who has retired if it is relevant to a story. Do not, however, use the military abbreviation *Ret.*

Instead, use *retired* just as *former* would be used before the title of a civilian: *They invited retired Army Gen. John Smith.*

FIREFIGHTERS, POLICE OFFICERS: Use the abbreviations listed here when a military-style title is used before the name of a firefighter or police officer outside a direct quotation. Add *police* or *fire* before the title if needed for clarity: *police Sgt. William Smith, fire Capt. David Jones.*

Spell out titles such as *detective* that are not used in the armed forces.

Months Capitalize the names of months in all uses. When a month is used with a specific date, abbreviate only *Jan., Feb., Aug., Sept., Oct., Nov.* and *Dec.* Spell out when using alone, or with a year alone.

When a phrase lists only a month and a year, do not separate the year with commas. When a phrase refers to a month, day and year, set off the year with commas.

EXAMPLES: *January 1972 was a cold month. Jan. 2 was the coldest day of the month. His birthday is May 8. Feb. 14, 1987, was the target date.*

Numerals A number is a figure, letter, word or group of words expressing a number.

Roman numerals use letters *I, V, X, L, C, D* and *M.* Use Roman numerals for wars and to show personal sequence for animals and people: *World War II, Native Dancer II, King George VI, Pope John XXIII.*

Arabic numerals use the figures *1, 2, 3, 4, 5, 6, 7, 8, 9* and *0.* Use Arabic forms unless Roman numerals are specifically required.

The figures *1, 2, 10, 101,* etc. and the corresponding words—*one, two, ten, one hundred one,* etc.—are called cardinal numbers. The term ordinal number applies to *1st, 2nd, 10th, 101st, first, second, tenth, one hundred first,* etc.

Follow these guidelines in using numerals:

LARGE NUMBERS: When large numbers must be spelled out, use a hyphen to connect a word ending in *y* to another word; do not use commas between other separate words that are part of one number: *twenty; thirty; twenty-one; thirty-one; one hundred forty-three; one thousand one hundred fifty-five; one million two hundred seventy-six thousand five hundred eighty-seven.*

SENTENCE START: Spell out a numeral at the beginning of a sentence. If necessary, recast the sentence. There is one exception—a numeral that identifies a calendar year.

Wrong: *993 freshmen entered the college last year.*

Numerals—(*cont.*)

Right: *Last year 993 freshmen entered the college.*

Right: *1976 was a very good year.*

CASUAL USES: Spell out casual expressions: *A thousand times no! Thanks a million. He walked a quarter of a mile.*

PROPER NAMES: Use words or numerals according to an organization's practice: *3M, Twentieth Century Fund, Big Ten.*

FIGURES OR WORDS?

For ordinals:

—Spell out *first* through *ninth* when they indicate sequence in time and location—*first base, the First Amendment, he was first in line.* Starting with *10th,* use figures.

—Use *1st, 2nd, 3rd, 4th,* etc. when the sequence has been assigned in forming names. The principal examples are geographic, military and political designations such as *1st Ward, 7th Fleet* and *1st Sgt.*

SOME PUNCTUATION AND USAGE EXAMPLES:

—*Act 1, Scene 2*

—*a 5-year-old girl*

—*DC 10* but *747B*

—*a 5-4 court decision*

—*2nd District Court*

—*the 1980s, the '80s*

—*The House voted 230-205.* (Fewer than 1,000 votes.)

—*5 cents, $1.05, $650,000, $2.45 million*

—*No. 3 choice,* but *Public School 3*

—*0.6 percent, 1 percent, 6.5 percent*

—*a pay increase of 12 percent to 15 percent*

Or: *a pay increase of between 12 percent and 15 percent*

Also: *from $12 million to $14 million*

—*a ratio of 2-to-1, a 2-1 ratio*

—*a 4-3 score*

—*(350) 262-4600*

—*minus 10, zero, 60 degrees*

OTHER USES: For uses not covered by these listings: Spell out whole numbers below 10, use figures for 10 and above. Typical examples: *They had three sons and two daughters. They had a fleet of 10 station wagons and two buses.*

IN A SERIES: Apply the appropriate guidelines: *They had 10 dogs, six cats and 97 hamsters. They had four four-room houses, 10 three-room houses and 12 10-room houses.*

Party affiliation Let relevance be the guide in determining whether to include a political figure's party affiliation in a story.

Party affiliation is pointless in some stories, such as an account of a governor accepting a button from a poster child.

It will occur naturally in many political stories.

For stories between these extremes, include party affiliation if readers need it for understanding or are likely to be curious about what it is.

FORM FOR U.S. HOUSE MEMBERS: The normal practice for U.S. House members is to identify them by party and state. In contexts where state affiliation is clear and home city is relevant, such as a state election roundup, identify representatives by party and city: *U.S. Reps. Thomas P. O'Neill Jr., D-Cambridge, and Margaret Heckler, R-Wellesley.* If this option is used, be consistent throughout the story.

FORM FOR STATE LEGISLATORS: Short-form listings showing party and home city are appropriate in state wire stories. For trunk wire stories, the normal practice is to say that the individual is a *Republican* or *Democrat.* Use a short-form listing only if the legislator's home city is relevant.

Periods Follow these guidelines:

END OF DECLARATIVE SENTENCE: *The stylebook is finished.*

END OF A MILDLY IMPERATIVE SENTENCE: *Shut the door.*

Use an exclamation point if greater emphasis is desired: *Be careful!*

END OF SOME RHETORICAL QUESTIONS: A period is preferable if a statement is more a suggestion than a question: *Why don't we go.*

END OF AN INDIRECT QUESTION: *He asked what the score was.*

INITIALS: *John F. Kennedy, T.S. Eliot.* (No space between *T.* and *S.*, to prevent them from being placed on two lines in typesetting.)

Periods—(*cont.*)

Abbreviations using only the initials of a name do not take periods: *JFK, LBJ*.

ENUMERATIONS: After numbers of letters in enumerating elements of a summary: *1. Wash the car. 2. Clean the basement.* Or: *A. Punctuate properly. B. Write simply.*

PLACEMENT WITH QUOTATION MARKS: Periods always go inside quotation marks.

Plurals Follow these guidelines in forming and using plural words:

MOST WORDS: Add *s: boys, girls, ships, villages.*

WORDS ENDING IN CH, S, SH, SS, X AND Z: Add *es: churches, lenses, parishes, glasses, boxes, buzzes.* (*Monarchs* is an exception.)

WORDS ENDING IN IS: Change *is* to *es: oases, parentheses, theses.*

WORDS ENDING IN Y: If *y* is preceded by a consonant or *qu*, change *y* to *i* and add *es: armies, cities, navies, soliloquies.* (See PROPER NAMES below for an exception.)

Otherwise add *s: donkeys, monkeys.*

WORDS ENDING IN O: If *o* is preceded by a consonant, most plurals require *es: buffaloes, dominoes, echoes, heroes, potatoes.* But there are exceptions: *pianos.*

WORDS ENDING IN F: In general, change *f* to *v* and add *es: leaves, selves.* (*Roof, roofs* is an exception.)

LATIN ENDINGS: Latin-root words ending in *us* change *us* to *i: alumnus, alumni.*

Most ending in *a* change to *ae: alumna, alumnae* (*formula, formulas* is an exception).

Most ending in *um* add *s: memorandums, referendums, stadiums.* Among those that still use the Latin ending: *addenda, curricula, media.*

Use the plural that Webster's New World lists as most common for a particular sense of a word.

FORM CHANGE: *man, men; child, children; foot, feet; mouse, mice; etc.*

Caution: When *s* is used with any of these words it indicates possession and must be preceded by an apostrophe: *men's, children's*, etc.

WORDS THE SAME IN SINGULAR AND PLURAL: *corps, chassis, deer, moose, sheep*, etc.

The sense in a particular sentence is conveyed by the use of a singular or plural verb.

WORDS PLURAL IN FORM, SINGULAR IN MEANING: Some take singular verbs: *measles, mumps, news.* Others take plural verbs: *grits, scissors.*

COMPOUND WORDS: Those written solid add *s* at the end: *cupfuls, handfuls, tablespoonfuls.*

For those that involve separate words or words linked by a hyphen, make the most significant word plural:

—Significant word first: *adjutants general, aides-de-camp, attorneys general, courts-martial, daughters-in-law, passers-by, postmasters general, presidents-elect, secretaries general, sergeants major.*

—Significant word in the middle: *assistant attorneys general, deputy chiefs of staff.*

—Significant word last: *assistant attorneys, assistant corporation counsels, deputy sheriffs, lieutenant colonels, major generals.*

WORDS AS WORDS: Do not use *'s:* His speech had too many *ifs, ands* and *buts.* (Exception to Webster's New World.)

PROPER NAMES: Most ending in *es* or *z* add *es: Charleses, Joneses, Gonzalezes.*

Most ending in *y* add *s* even if preceded by a consonant: *the Duffys, the Kennedys, the two Kansas Citys.* Exceptions include *Alleghenies* and *Rockies.*

For others, add *s: the Carters, the McCoys, the Mondales.*

FIGURES: Add *s: The custom began in the 1920s. The airline has two 727s. Temperatures will be in the low 20s. There were five size 7s.* (No apostrophes, an exception to Webster's New World guideline under "apostrophe.")

SINGLE LETTERS: Use *'s: Mind your p's and q's. He learned the three R's and brought home a report card with four A's and two B's. The Oakland A's won the pennant.*

MULTIPLE LETTERS: Add *s: She knows her ABCs. I gave him five IOUs. Four VIPs were there.*

Possessives Follow these guidelines:

PLURAL NOUNS NOT ENDING IN S: Add *'s: the alumni's contributions, women's rights.*

PLURAL NOUNS ENDING IN S: Add only an apostrophe: *the churches' needs, the girls' toys, the horses' food, the ships' wake, states' rights, the VIPs' entrance.*

NOUNS PLURAL IN FORM, SINGULAR IN MEANING: Add only an apostrophe: *mathematics' rules, measles' effects.* (But see INANIMATE OBJECTS below.)

Apply the same principle when a plural word occurs in the formal name of a singular entity: *General Motors' profits, the United States' wealth.*

NOUNS THE SAME IN SINGULAR AND PLURAL: Treat them the same as plurals, even if the meaning is singular: *one corps' location, the two deer's tracks, the lone moose's antlers.*

SINGULAR NOUNS NOT ENDING IN S: Add *'s: the church's needs, the girl's toys, the horse's food, the ship's route, the VIP's seat.*

Some style guides say that singular nouns ending in *s* sound such as *ce, x* and *z* may take either the apostrophe alone or *'s*. See SPECIAL EXPRESSIONS below, but otherwise, for consistency and ease in remembering a rule, always use *'s* if the word does not end in the letter *s: Butz's policies, the fox's den, the justice's verdict, Marx's theories, the prince's life, Xerox's profits.*

SINGULAR COMMON NOUNS ENDING IN S: Add *'s* unless the next word begins with *s: the hostess's invitation, the hostess' seat; the witness's answer, the witness' story.*

SINGULAR PROPER NAMES ENDING IN S: Use only an apostrophe: *Achilles' heel, Agnes' book, Ceres' rites, Descartes' theories, Dickens' novels, Euripides' dramas, Hercules' labors, Jesus' life, Jules' seat, Kansas' schools, Moses' law, Socrates' life, Tennessee Williams' plays, Xerxes' armies.*

SPECIAL EXPRESSIONS: The following exceptions to the general rule for words not ending in *s* apply to words that end in an *s* sound and are followed by a word that begins with *s: for appearance' sake, for conscience' sake, for goodness' sake.* Use *'s* otherwise: *the appearance's cost, my conscience's voice.*

PRONOUNS: Personal, interrogative and relative pronouns have separate forms for the possessive. None involve an apostrophe: *mine, ours, your, yours, his, hers, its, theirs, whose.*

Caution: If you are using an apostrophe with a pronoun, always double-check to be sure that the meaning calls for a contraction: *you're, it's, there's, who's.*

Follow the rules listed above in forming the possessives of other pronouns: *another's idea, others' plans, someone's guess.*

COMPOUND WORDS: Applying the rules above, add an apostrophe or *'s* to the word closest to the object possessed: *the major general's decision, the major generals' decisions, the attorneys general's request.*

Also: *anyone else's attitude, John Adams Jr.'s father, Benjamin Franklin of Pennsylvania's motion.* Whenever practical, however, recast the phrase to avoid ambiguity: *the motion by Benjamin Franklin of Pennsylvania.*

JOINT POSSESSION, INDIVIDUAL POSSESSION: Use a possessive form after only the last word if ownership is joint: *Fred and Sylvia's apartment, Fred and Sylvia's stocks.*

Use a possessive form after both words if the objects are individually owned: *Fred's and Sylvia's books.*

DESCRIPTIVE PHRASES: Do not add an apostrophe to a word ending in *s* when it is used primarily in a descriptive sense: *citizens band radio, a Cincinnati Reds infielder, a teachers college, a Teamsters request, a writers guide.*

Memory Aid: The apostrophe usually is not used if *for* or *by* rather than *of* would be appropriate in the longer form: *a radio band for citizens, a college for teachers, a guide for writers, a request by the Teamsters.*

An *'s* is required, however, when a term involves a plural word that does not end in *s: a children's hospital, a people's republic, the Young Men's Christian Association.*

Possessives—*(cont.)*

DESCRIPTIVE NAMES: Some governmental, corporate and institutional organizations with a descriptive word in their names use an apostrophe; some do not. Follow the user's practice: *Actors' Equity, Diners Club, the Ladies' Home Journal, the National Governors' Association.*

QUASI POSSESSIVES: Follow the rules above in composing the possessive form of words that occur in such phrases as *a day's pay, two weeks' vacation, three days' work, your money's worth.*

Frequently, however, a hyphenated form is clearer: *a two-week vacation, a three-day job.*

DOUBLE POSSESSIVE: Two conditions must apply for a double possessive—a phrase such as *a friend of John's*—to occur: 1. The word after *of* must refer to an animate object, and 2. The word before *of* must involve only a portion of the animate object's possessions.

Otherwise, do not use the possessive form on the word after *of: The friends of John Adams mourned his death.* (All the friends were involved.) *He is a friend of the college.* (Not *college's,* because college is inanimate).

Memory Aid: This construction occurs most often, and quite naturally, with the possessive forms of personal pronouns: *He is a friend of mine.*

INANIMATE OBJECTS: There is no blanket rule against creating a possessive form for an inanimate object, particularly if the object is treated in a personified sense. See some of the earlier examples, and note these: *death's call, the wind's murmur.*

In general, however, avoid excessive personalization of inanimate objects, and give preference to an *of* construction when it fits the makeup of the sentence. For example, the earlier mentioned references to *mathematics' rules* and *measles' effects* would better be phrased: *the rules of mathematics, the effects of measles.*

Quotation marks The basic guidelines for open-quote marks (") and close-quote marks ("):

FOR DIRECT QUOTATIONS: To surround the exact words of a speaker or writer when reported in a story:

"I have no intention of staying," he replied.

"I do not object," he said, "to the tenor of the report."

Franklin said, "A penny saved is a penny earned."

A speculator said the practice is "too conservative for inflationary times."

RUNNING QUOTATIONS: If a full paragraph of quoted material is followed by a paragraph that continues the quotation, do not put close-quote marks at the end of the first paragraph. Do, however, put open-quote marks at the start of the second paragraph. Continue in this fashion for any succeeding paragraphs, using close-quote marks only at the end of the quoted material.

If a paragraph does not start with quotation marks but ends with a quotation that is continued in the next paragraph, do not use close-quote marks at the end of the introductory paragraph if the quoted material constitutes a full sentence. Use close-quote marks, however, if the quoted material does not constitute a full sentence. For example:

He said, *"I am shocked and horrified by the incident.*

"I am so horrified, in fact, that I will ask for the death penalty."

But: *He said he was "shocked and horrified by the incident."*

"I am so horrified, in fact, that I will ask for the death penalty," he said.

DIALOGUE OR CONVERSATION: Each person's words, no matter how brief, are placed in a separate paragraph, with quotation marks at the beginning and the end of each person's speech:

"Will you go?"

"Yes."

"When?"

"Thursday."

NOT IN Q-AND-A: Quotation marks are not required in formats that identify questions and answers by *Q* and *A.*

Quotation marks—*(cont.)*

NOT IN TEXTS: Quotation marks are not required in full texts, condensed texts or textual excerpts.

IRONY: Put quotation marks around a word or words used in an ironical sense: *The "debate" turned into a free-for-all.*

UNFAMILIAR TERMS: A word or words being introduced to readers may be placed in quotation marks on first reference:

Broadcast frequencies are measured in "kilohertz."

Do not put subsequent references to *kilohertz* in quotation marks.

AVOID UNNECESSARY FRAGMENTS: Do not use quotation marks to report a few ordinary words that a speaker or writer has used:

Wrong: *The senator said he would "go home to Michigan" if he lost the election.*

Right: *The senator said he would go home to Michigan if he lost the election.*

PARTIAL QUOTES: When a partial quote is used, do not put quotation marks around words that the speaker could not have used.

Suppose the individual said, *"I am horrified at your slovenly manners."*

Wrong: *She said she "was horrified at their slovenly manners."*

Right: *She said she was horrified at their "slovenly manners."*

Better when practical: Use the full quote.

QUOTES WITHIN QUOTES: Alternate between double quotation marks ("or") and single marks ('or'):

She said, "I quote from his letter, 'I agree with Kipling that "the female of the species is more deadly than the male," but the phenomenon is not an unchangeable law of nature,' a remark he did not explain."

Use three marks together if two quoted elements end at the same time: *She said, "He told me, 'I love you.'"*

PLACEMENT WITH OTHER PUNCTUATION: Follow these long-established printers' rules:

—The period and the comma always go within the quotation marks.

—The dash, the semicolon, the question mark and the exclamation point go within the quotation marks when they apply to the quoted matter only. They go outside when they apply to the whole sentence.

Semicolon In general, use the semicolon to indicate a greater separation of thought and information than a comma can convey but less than the separation that a period implies.

The basic guidelines:

TO CLARIFY A SERIES: Use semicolons to separate elements of a series when individual segments contain material that also must be set off by commas:

He leaves a son, John Smith of Chicago; three daughters, Jane Smith of Wichita, Kan., Mary Smith of Denver, and Susan, wife of William Kingsbury of Boston; and a sister, Martha, wife of Robert Warren of Omaha, Neb.

Note that the semicolon is used before the final *and* in such a series.

TO LINK INDEPENDENT CLAUSES: Use a semicolon when a coordinating conjunction such as *and, but* or *for* is not present: *The package was due last week; it arrived today.*

If a coordinating conjunction is present, use a semicolon before it only if extensive punctuation also is required in one or more of the individual clauses: *They pulled their boats from the water, sandbagged the retaining walls and boarded up the windows; but even with these precautions, the island was hard-hit by the hurricane.*

Unless a particular literary effect is desired, however, the better approach in these circumstances is to break the independent clauses into separate sentences.

PLACEMENT WITH QUOTES: Place semicolons outside quotation marks.

Senate Capitalize all specific references to governmental legislative bodies, regardless of whether the name of the nation or state is used: *the U.S. Senate, the Senate, the Virginia Senate, the state Senate, the Senate.*

Senate—(*cont.*) Lowercase plural uses: *the Virginia and North Carolina senates.*

The same principles apply to foreign bodies.

Lowercase references to non-governmental bodies: *The student senate at Yale.*

State names Follow these guidelines:

STANDING ALONE: Spell out the names of the 50 U.S. states when they stand alone in textual material. Any state name may be condensed, however, to fit typographical requirements for tabular material.

EIGHT NOT ABBREVIATED: The names of eight states are never abbreviated in datelines or text: *Alaska, Hawaii, Idaho, Iowa, Maine, Ohio, Texas* and *Utah.*

Memory Aid: Spell out the names of the two states that are not part of the continental United States and of the continental states that are five letters or fewer.

ABBREVIATIONS REQUIRED: Use the state abbreviations listed at the end of this section:

—In conjunction with the name of a city, town, village or military base in most datelines.

—In conjunction with the name of a city, county, town, village or military base in text. See examples in PUNCTUATION section below.

—In short-form listings of party affiliation: *D-Ala., R-Mont.* See **party affiliation** entry for details.

The abbreviations, which also appear in the entries for each state (ZIP code abbreviations in parentheses):

Ala. (AL)	Ind. (IN)	Mont. (MT)
Ariz. (AZ)	Kan. (KS)	Neb. (NE)
Ark. (AR)	Ky. (KY)	Nev. (NV)
Calif. (CA)	La. (LA)	N.H. (NH)
Colo. (CO)	Md. (MD)	N.J. (NJ)
Conn. (CT)	Mass. (MA)	N.M. (NM)
Del. (DE)	Mich. (MI)	N.Y. (NY)
Fla. (FL)	Minn. (MN)	N.C. (NC)
Ga. (GA)	Miss. (MS)	N.D. (ND)
Ill. (IL)	Mo. (MO)	Okla. (OK)
Ore. (OR)	S.D. (SD)	Wash. (WA)
Pa. (PA)	Tenn. (TN)	W.Va. (WV)
R.I. (RI)	Vt. (VT)	Wis. (WI)
S.C. (SC)	Va. (VA)	Wyo. (WY)

Following are the ZIP code abbreviations for the eight states that are not abbreviated in datelines or text:

AK (Alaska), HI (Hawaii), ID (Idaho), IA (Iowa), ME (Maine), OH (Ohio), TX (Texas), UT (Utah).

Use the two-letter Postal Service abbreviations only with full addresses, including ZIP Code.

PUNCTUATION: Place one comma between the city and the state name, and another comma after the state name, unless ending a sentence or indicating a dateline: *He was traveling from Nashville, Tenn., to Austin, Texas, en route to his home in Albuquerque, N.M. She said Cook County, Ill., was Mayor Daley's stronghold.*

MISCELLANEOUS: Use *New York state* when necessary to distinguish the state from New York City.

Use *state of Washington* or *Washington state* when necessary to distinguish the state from the District of Columbia. (*Washington State* is the name of a university in the state of Washington.)

Time element Use *today, this morning, this afternoon, tonight,* etc., as appropriate in stories for afternoon editions. Use the day of the week elsewhere.

Use *Monday, Tuesday,* etc., for days of the week within seven days before or after the current date.

Use the month and figure for dates beyond this range.

Avoid such redundancies as *last Tuesday* or *next Tuesday.* The past, present or future tense used for the verb usually provides adequate indication of which *Tuesday* is meant: *He said he finished the job Tuesday. She will return on Tuesday.*

Time element—(*cont.*) Avoid awkward placements of the time element, particularly those that suggest the day of the week is the object of a transitive verb: *The police jailed Tuesday.* Potential remedies include the use of the word *on*, rephrasing the sentence or placing the time element in a different sentence.

Titles In general, confine capitalization to formal titles used directly before an individual's name.

The basic guidelines:

LOWERCASE: Lowercase and spell out titles when they are not used with an individual's name: *The president issued a statement. The pope gave his blessing.*

Lowercase and spell out titles in constructions that set them off from a name by commas: *The vice president, Nelson Rockefeller, declined to run again. Paul VI, the current pope, does not plan to retire.*

COURTESY TITLES: See the courtesy titles entry for guidelines on when to use *Miss, Mr., Mrs.* and *Ms.*

The forms *Mr., Mrs., Miss* and *Ms.* apply both in regular text and in quotations.

FORMAL TITLES: Capitalize formal titles when they are used immediately before one or more names: *Pope Paul, President Washington, Vice Presidents John Jones and William Smith.*

A formal title generally is one that denotes a scope of authority, professional activity or academic accomplishment so specific that the designation becomes almost as much an integral part of an individual's identity as a proper name itself *President Clinton, Sen. Dianne Feinstein, Dr. Marcus Welby, Pvt. Gomer Pyle.*

Other titles serve primarily as occupational descriptions: *astronaut John Glenn, movie star John Wayne, peanut farmer Jimmy Carter.*

A final determination on whether a title is formal or occupational depends on the practice of the governmental or private organization that confers it. If there is doubt about the status of a title and the practice of the organization cannot be determined, use a construction that sets the name or the title off with commas.

ABBREVIATED TITLES: The following formal titles are capitalized and abbreviated as shown when used before a name outside quotations: *Dr., Gov., Lt. Gov., Rep., Sen.* and certain military ranks listed in the military titles entry. Spell out all except *Dr.* when they are used in quotations.

All other formal titles are spelled out in all uses.

ROYAL TITLES: Capitalize *king, queen,* etc., when used directly before a name.

TITLES OF NOBILITY: Capitalize a full title when it serves as the alternate name for an individual.

PAST AND FUTURE TITLES: A formal title that an individual formerly held, is about to hold or holds temporarily is capitalized if used before the person's name. But do not capitalize the qualifying word: *former President Ford, deposed King Constantine, Attorney General-designate Griffin B. Bell, acting Mayor Peter Barry.*

LONG TITLES: Separate a long title from a name by a construction that requires a comma: *Charles Robinson, undersecretary for economic affairs, spoke.* Or: *The undersecretary for economic affairs, Charles Robinson, spoke.*

UNIQUE TITLES: If a title applies only to one person in an organization, insert the word *the* in a construction that uses commas: *John Jones, the deputy vice president, spoke.*

Women Women should receive the same treatment as men in all areas of coverage. Physical descriptions, sexist references, demeaning stereotypes and condescending phrases should not be used.

To cite some examples, this means that:

—Copy should not assume maleness when both sexes are involved, as in *Jackson told newsmen* or in *the taxpayer . . . he* when it easily can be said *Jackson told reporters* or *taxpayers . . . they.*

Women—(*cont.*)

—Copy should not express surprise that an attractive woman can be professionally accomplished, as in: *Mary Smith doesn't look the part, but she's an authority on . . .*

—Copy should not gratuitously mention family relationships where there is no relevance to the subject, as in: *Golda Meir, a doughty grandmother, told the Egyptians today . . .*

—Use the same standards for men and women in deciding whether to include specific mention of personal appearance or marital and family situation.

In other words, treatment of the sexes should be even-handed and free of assumptions and stereotypes. This does not mean that valid and acceptable words such as *mankind* or *humanity* cannot be used. They are proper.

Appendix

C Glossary

A wire Main news wire of The Associated Press that transmits the most significant national and international stories of the day. The wire is sometimes written as **AAA** or **Aye.**

Absolute defenses In libel suits, defenses that, if proven, are viable with no conditions or qualifications. For example, under the statute of limitations, suit must be brought within a specified period or the plaintiff has no standing to sue.

Abstracts Brief summaries of articles or books that are contained in some computer reference searches.

Accident forms Reports available in police stations that outline the circumstances surrounding accidents investigated by the department. Larger-circulation newspapers generally cover only spectacular accidents. Smaller-circulation dailies and weeklies routinely report all accidents, no matter how minor.

Action-line column Consumer-oriented column that helps people solve their problems. People write or call to describe their problems, and a reporter tries to solve them.

Active voice Term describing the verb form used when the subject of a sentence acts upon an object. For example: *The mayor denied the charge.* Active voice is generally preferred in journalistic writing because it is more vigorous than passive voice (see page 467).

Actual malice Fault standard in libel law, first articulated by the Supreme Court in 1964, that must be met by plaintiffs who are public officials or public figures. Such plaintiffs must prove that the information was communicated "with knowledge that it was false or with reckless disregard of whether it was false or not."

Actuality Audiotape excerpt, sometimes called a **soundbite,** that is inserted in a broadcast news story.

Add Each subsequent page of a story written on hard copy. For example, the second page of a story is the first add, the third page is the second add and so forth. When wire copy is electronically transmitted, an add is additional information to a story that is filed under the same key word as the original story.

Advance Story announcing a coming event.

Advance text A copy of the speech a source is expected to deliver. Reporters use advance texts to help them prepare for covering speeches. They do not write stories from advance texts, however, because speakers often wander from their prepared remarks.

Advocacy journalism News writing in which a reporter defends or maintains a proposal or a cause.

Agate Type size smaller than regular text type; agate is generally 6 points or 7 points. (A **point** is 1/72nd of an inch.) Sports statistics and public-record items are commonly set in agate.

Agenda Outline of matters to be considered by a government body.

A.M. Morning newspaper.

A.M. cycle Morning newspapers usually report news that breaks on the A.M. cycle, generally the time from noon to midnight.

Analysis piece Feature story, also called a **backgrounder,** that adds meaning to current issues in the news by explaining them further.

Anchor On-camera person who reads the script for a broadcast news show. Some anchors write their own scripts; some read only what reporters and other off-camera newspeople have written.

Annual report Report issued by a public company and sent to its stockholders, informing them of the company's financial health and what is in store for the future.

Anonymous sources People who are willing to provide information on the condition that their names not be used in the story.

AP members Newspapers and broadcast stations that receive news from The Associated Press (see page 458), a not-for-profit cooperative.

Appropriation Type of invasion of privacy that involves using someone's name or likeness for commercial gain.

Area editor See **state editor.**

Arraignment Step in the judicial process involving the reading of the charge to the accused. The arraignment is often held in a lower court, where a plea is typically entered.

Assets What a company owns. A company's assets are listed in its report to stockholders.

Assignment editor Editor who coordinates all assignments in a broadcast newsroom. He or she makes assignments, keeps track of crews in the field, makes follow-up calls for reporters and takes incoming calls.

Associated Press Generally referred to as the **AP,** the world's oldest cooperative news-gathering service.

Attribution Telling readers the source of information.

Authoritarian (press) system System in which criticism of the government is forbidden. Most newspapers in countries that operate under this philosophy are privately owned, but their content is controlled by the state through licensing or the issuance of patents.

"Aw nuts" school Premise subscribed to by some sports reporters that even great games and gifted athletes should be treated with near disdain.

B wire News wire of The Associated Press that transmits national and international news of secondary importance.

Background Sentences in a news story that explain important elements. Background can explain something technical or provide details that were reported in earlier stories.

Backgrounder See **analysis piece.**

Banner Headline that stretches across a newspaper page.

Baud Measure of speed of data transmission.

Beat reporter Reporter who covers a specific geographic or subject area each day. Beats include police and fire; county and federal courts; and city, county and state governments.

Blind lead-in A smooth transition into a soundbite that makes sense standing alone, and is not dependent on the soundbite to finish the idea or thought.

Body Portion of a news story or a feature between the lead and the conclusion. The body should keep readers interested in the story and hold them until the conclusion.

Boldface Dark type that is thicker and blacker than ordinary text type. Also: **boldface caps,** which are capital letters set in type blacker than ordinary type. Boldface or boldface caps are often used for bylines.

Box score Statistical summary for various sports.

Breaking news News that is available for publication and that reporters try to cover as quickly as possible.

Brief Written report in which a lawyer sets forth facts that support his or her position.

Brightener Short, often humorous story that emphasizes quirks in the news. Brighteners are used to give an audience a break from hard news. They allow people to sit back and smile.

Broadcast producer Person who puts a broadcast news show together. He or she chooses which stories will be broadcast, in what order they will appear, how long they will be and in what production style they will be (how much videotape of a scene, how many interviews, etc.).

Broadcast wire News wire of The Associated Press that transmits stories written in a shorter, more conversational style than those transmitted for print media.

Browser A program that allows a computer user to find and access documents from anywhere on the Internet.

Bulldog Newspaper's first edition of the day.

Bulletin Priority designation used by wire services. A bulletin contains at least one publishable paragraph but not more than two; it alerts newsrooms that a major story is developing.

Bullets Bold dots that introduce and highlight items in a news story or a feature.

Bureau Geographically removed extension of a news medium's headquarters. The Associated Press, for example, has its headquarters in New York, but it has bureaus in every state and in scores of foreign countries.

Buried lead Term for a news story's most important point when it is not in the opening paragraph, where it belongs.

Byline Line, usually at the top of a story, that names the author.

Capital budget Sometimes called a "hard" budget, the capital budget provides the dollars for government projects that are often large and long-range and have a physical presence, such as storm drains, streets and parks.

Caps Media shorthand reference to capital letters.

Change of venue Moving a trial to another location to reduce the possibility that prejudicial opinions, emotions and publicity will deprive the accused of a fair, impartial hearing.

Citation Information found on a database that tells the searcher where an article, news story, report or document can be found. A citation usually contains name of author, title of article, title of publication in which it appeared, volume number, date and page number. It may also include a summary of the article's contents.

Citation database Electronic storage facility accessible by computers connected to it with telephone lines. It contains citations, or information that indicates where an article or document can be found.

City editor Editor who runs the city (or metropolitan) desk and is in charge of city-side general assignment, beat and specialty reporters. The city editor makes certain that news in the city (or metropolitan area) is covered and that as many local stories as possible get into each edition.

Civic journalism Stories resulting from journalists' connections with residents in their communities.

Civil case Case that involves arriving at specific solutions to legal strife between individuals, businesses, state or local governments or agencies of government. Civil cases include suits for breach of contract and for libel.

Closed-ended question Question that is structured to elicit a short, precise answer. Reporters often ask closed-ended questions that require only "yes" or "no" responses. Sometimes, such questions have answers built into them. For example: *John Johnson and Bill Blodgett are candidates for mayor. Which of these candidates will you vote for?*

Clutter lead Awkward and difficult-to-understand lead that contains too many elements.

Codes of ethics Guidelines for journalists developed by national groups and by some individual news media. Codes often cover matters such as responsibilities of journalists, use of unnamed sources, accuracy, objectivity, misrepresentation by reporter, acceptance of gifts and favors from sources, political activities that journalists should or should not take part in and business dealings that could present conflicts of interest.

Color Observations, narrative or anecdotes in a story that give an audience a clearer picture of a person or an event.

Column inch Measure of space in a newspaper; a column inch is one column wide and one inch deep. Stories are often measured in column inches.

Commission government Municipal government system in which a committee of city leaders assumes both executive and legislative functions.

Complaint In law, a document that is filed by a plaintiff against a defendant in a civil suit. The complaint usually contains a precise set of arguments against the defendant.

Complete direct quotation Source's exact words, set off by quotation marks.

Complex sentence Sentence that has only one independent clause and at least one dependent clause. For example, *Johnson is the coach who will be elected to the hall of fame. Johnson is the coach* is an independent clause because it would make complete sense when left standing alone; *who will be elected to the hall of fame* is a dependent, or subordinate, clause (it does not make sense standing alone).

Composing room Production area of a newspaper where each edition's pages are put together according to an editor's instructions on layout sheets.

Computer reference services Services provided by many libraries to search for information via computer. The search is similar to a volume-by-volume search of a printed index, except that the requested information is returned electronically.

Conditional defense Defense against libel suits that involves certain conditions or qualifications. For example, privilege of reporting may be used as a defense when reporting information from official proceedings, public documents and court proceedings. This defense is limited, however, to *fair* and *accurate* reporting that does not intertwine extraneous, libelous matter.

Contrast lead Lead that compares or contrasts one person or thing with one or more other people or things.

Convergence Reaching audiences by combining the strengths of newspapers, TV and the Internet in collecting and delivering information.

Conversational style Less formal, less stilted style of writing for broadcast than is normally found in print media.

"Cool down" period Relatively short time, generally 10 or 15 minutes, set aside by coaches after a game during which the locker room is off limits to reporters who seek interviews with players.

Cop shop Old-time journalism term for *police station* that is still used today by many reporters.

Copy Written material produced by journalists.

Copy desk Desk inside a newsroom where copy editors process copy written by journalists and then write headlines.

Copy editor Editor who checks stories to make certain that they follow proper style, usage, spelling and grammar rules. The copy editor also makes certain that a story is well-organized and not libelous. After editing the story, the copy editor writes a headline for it.

Correction Material that corrects something in a previously disseminated story.

Correspondent Journalist who contributes news stories to a medium that is located elsewhere. Metropolitan newspapers, for example, normally have correspondents stationed in the nation's capital as well as in countries around the world.

Council-manager government Municipal government system in which the city manager controls the administrative apparatus of the city. The main source of government expertise is the city manager, a trained professional adept at administering a community's affairs.

Counts In law, parts of a complaint or indictment claiming a specific wrong done.

Courtesy titles Titles such as Mr., Mrs. or Miss that precede names. Most newspapers limit courtesy titles to second references in obituaries.

Criminal case Case that involves the enforcement of a criminal statute. Actions are brought by the state or federal government against an individual charged with committing a crime, such as murder or armed robbery.

Criss-cross directory Directory that lists a city's residents by names and addresses. By looking up an address in the directory, a reporter can find the identity and phone number of the person at the address.

Crop Mark on a photograph or other piece of art indicating that it will not be used full frame. Art is cropped to eliminate unneeded material or to make it fit into a predetermined hole.

Cultural sensitivity Awareness of and sensitivity to the manifestations and structures of diverse cultures and their people.

Culturally inclusive Term describing newsrooms where reporters, editors and photographers with various racial, linguistic or religious ties work together to cover diverse communities.

Current assets Those things owned by a company that can be turned into cash quickly.

Current liabilities Debts of a company that are due in one year. Current liabilities are paid out of current assets.

Cursor Flashing light on a computer screen that indicates where the next character would appear.

Cut Another term for a printed photograph or some other piece of art. Stories are also *cut, trimmed* or *sliced.*

Cutline Copy accompanying a photograph or other piece of art that explains what is occurring or being shown.

Damages In law, the monetary value of an injury allegedly sustained through the unlawful act or negligence of another.

Dangling modifiers Grammatical errors that occur when a phrase used to begin a sentence is not followed by a subject, or when the subject is not correctly connected to the phrase or modifier. For example: *By working diligently, the job was accomplished.*

Dateline Opening line of an out-of-town story that gives the place of origin.

Death notice Story or listing of information about someone who has died. Many newspapers consider death notices and **obituaries** synonymous.

Defendant Party against whom a lawsuit is brought.

Demographics Distribution, density, size and composition of a population.

Dependent clause Clause that would not make complete sense if left standing alone. For example: *John studies hard before he takes a test.* The clause *before he takes a test* is dependent upon *John studies hard* in order to make sense. It cannot be left standing alone.

Deposition Out-of-court statement made by a witness under oath.

Direct-address lead Lead that communicates directly with an audience by including the word *you.*

Docket Court record that documents progress in a specific case. All complaints filed, motions made and other developments in a case are recorded chronologically.

Double truck Story or advertisement that covers two facing pages of a newspaper or magazine, including the **gutter** (the space down the center of the two pages).

Dummy Mock-up of a newspaper or magazine page that has advertisements with specific sizes keyed in. News stories, features and photographs are laid out around the ads.

Dupe Abbreviation for *duplicate* and a designation for a copy of a story.

Editor Person in charge of the editorial function of a newspaper. The role of the editor changes depending on the size of the newspaper.

Editorial news hole Space on a newspaper page that does not contain an advertisement and is reserved for stories or art. The ads are laid out on the page first; the editorial news hole consists of the remaining column inches.

Electronic camera Computerized camera that uses no film. Instead, pictures are recorded on a video floppy disk that resembles a computer floppy disk.

Electronic carbons Designation by The Associated Press for the transmission of stories directly from newspapers' computers to regional AP bureaus.

Electronic mail Facility for exchanging messages using central computer storage. A writer can type a message on a computer and then store it in a central electronic file accessible only by the addressee. The remote computers and central file are connected by telephone lines.

Electronic morgue Electronic storage facility that holds clippings of published stories for instant retrieval.

Element of immediacy Asset of the broadcast media that allows them to give up-to-the-minute reports and to write copy in a way that makes it sound fresh and lively.

Enterprise journalism Stories that require reporters to go beyond their daily routine. For example, a police reporter routinely writes stories from accident logs. An enterprise story would examine why a particular intersection has more accidents than any other in the city and would require multiple sources, statistical information and extensive quotations.

Ethnic coverage Reporting on the trends, events and issues of particular ethnic groups, people who have ties of ancestry, culture, nationality or language that distinguish them from the majority in society.

Executive producer Person who runs a television newsroom. He or she is responsible for story content, reading and editing reporters' scripts, long-range planning and scheduling, and countless other decisions. At smaller stations, the executive producer may also make assignments and decide the layout of each news show.

Executive session Meeting at which no official actions can be taken by government officials and from which members of the press and public are excluded.

False light Type of invasion of privacy that involves painting a false, though not necessarily defamatory, picture of a person or event.

Feature story Story that analyzes the news; entertains; or describes people, places or things in or out of the news.

Federal judicial system Branch of the federal government that is responsible for interpreting the law. The Supreme Court is the nation's highest court.

Feeds Program content sent to a television station via satellite, microwave or land lines from a network's headquarters or from another station.

Felony Serious crime for which punishment is normally imprisonment in a penitentiary.

Field producer Person who directs broadcast reporters and photographers in the field. At many stations the reporter is also the field producer. In some operations, however, a separate field producer directs the news gathering.

Filing In law, the formal lodging of a complaint in a civil action.

Filler Short story of less importance that is used to fill a small open space on a newspaper page.

Financial editor Editor in charge of handling business news. Most newspapers have a business page or section each day, and many have a staff of financial reporters who cover local businesses.

Financial wire News wire of The Associated Press that transmits business news stories, some stock tables and other market data.

Fire reports Daily reports of activity involving the fire department.

Five W's and H Six primary elements of a news story: *who, what, where, when, why* and *how.*

Flash Top-priority designation used by wire services. It usually contains only a few words and may not be a complete sentence. A classic flash: *DALLAS (AP)—Kennedy shot.*

Floppy disk Portable storage device that is inserted into a computer's disk drive.

Fluff Superfluous, overwritten and untimely information from a press release.

Focal point Thrust of a summary lead. A reporter determines the lead's focal point by choosing which of the five W's and H to emphasize.

Focal question Primary question in a survey directly addressing the main issue. Other survey questions flow from this umbrella query.

Follow Sometimes referred to as a **second-day story,** a second or later story written about a newsworthy event. A follow provides the latest news in the lead or early in the story, but it also repeats the major news that was reported earlier.

Follow-up question Rearticulated or new question that a reporter asks to elicit a new or more specific response.

Foreign editor Editor who supervises reporters who cover news events outside the United States.

For immediate release Line at the top of a press release informing the media that the information it contains can be used immediately.

Fragmentary quotations Extremely small parcels of the precise words of a source that are spread throughout a sentence or paragraph. Fragmentary quotations look confusing when set in type and generally should not be used.

Free ad Information in a press release that is clearly of no news value and tries to seek free publicity for a person, business or organization.

Freedom of Information Act Generally referred to as the **FOI Act,** the law that provides for access to federal materials that are not statutorily exempt.

Free-lance To produce news stories for several publications, none of which is a full-time employer.

Frequency distribution In surveys, the percentage of responses to each question.

Full-text database Electronic storage facility accessible by computers connected to it with telephone lines. It contains the entire text of an article or document.

Funnel interview Most common type of interview, in which the reporter begins with nonthreatening background and open-ended questions. The toughest questions, those that may put the source on the spot, are saved for near the end of the interview.

Gag order Judicial mandate, sometimes called a **protective order,** that requires the press to refrain from disseminating specific information or that restricts those associated with the trial or investigation from discussing the case with the press.

Gang interview Press conference in which every reporter is given the same information and the source refuses to meet with reporters individually.

Gatekeepers People who make news decisions. Editors and reporters, on a story-by-story basis, decide what items to include and what angles to emphasize.

"Gee whiz" school Premise of some sports stories that athletes perform nothing but heroic feats.

General assignment reporter Reporter who covers a breaking news story or a feature that has been assigned by an editor. A general assignment reporter does not cover a specific beat.

Grand jury Jury of citizens convened to determine if there is probable cause that a crime has been committed and that the person charged with the crime committed it. A grand jury is so labeled because it has more members than a trial jury.

Graph Media shorthand for *paragraph.* Also spelled **graf.**

Graphics editor Editor who serves as a liaison between reporters, editors, photographers, artists and designers to coordinate the production of maps, charts, diagrams, illustrations and other informational graphics that accompany stories.

Guild Union of journalists formed to bargain collectively over such things as wages and benefits. For example, many newspaper journalists belong to the Newspaper Guild.

Handout Another term for **news release** or **press release.** Corporations, businesses, universities, organizations and political parties send handouts to alert the media to something they are doing.

Hard copy Product of a story composed on a typewriter or printed out from a computer.

Hard news Events that are timely and are covered almost automatically by print and electronic media. A speech by a ranking public official is an example.

Hardware Physical components of a computer such as terminal, cables, disk drives and so forth.

Head sheet Paper on which a headline is written or typed. Computerized newsrooms no longer use head sheets.

Hoax Deceptive or fraudulent story. An example is a call or letter that dupes a newspaper or broadcast station into disseminating an obituary for someone who has not died or does not exist.

Hostile source Uncooperative, close-lipped source who does not want to talk to reporters.

Hourglass style Style of writing in which the major news of a story is reported in the first few paragraphs and then a transitional paragraph introduces a chronology of the events of the story.

House ad Advertisement that promotes a publication.

HTML Hypertext Markup Language The language used to write pages for the World Wide Web.

Human angle Approach to a story that readers can relate to. The human angle is common on weather-related stories that reporters write to emphasize how the weather will affect people.

Human interest story Feature story that shows a subject's oddity or emotional or entertainment value.

Hyperbolic adjectives Overused references (most common in sports writing) that stretch beyond controlled, accurate description. Phrases such as *phenomenal freshman, sensational sophomore* and *game of the century* are examples.

Immediate news value Term descriptive of a breaking story, such as a fire, an accident or an election, that reporters try to cover as quickly as possible.

In-camera inspection Judge's examination of materials in a private room or with all spectators excluded from the courtroom.

Independent clause Clause that makes complete sense when left standing alone. For example: *John studies hard before he takes a test.* The clause *John studies hard* could stand alone; it expresses a complete thought.

In-depth story Story that, through extensive research and interviews, provides a detailed account well beyond a basic news story. An in-depth story can be a lengthy news feature that examines one topic extensively; an investigative story that reveals wrongdoing by a person, an agency or an institution; or a first-person article in which the writer relives a happy or painful experience.

Indictment Written accusation by a grand jury charging that a person has committed a public offense.

Indirect quotation Paraphrase of a source's statement that retains its meaning. Attribution must be provided.

Individual statistics Data compiled for each player in an athletic contest. For example, field goals made, free throws made, fouls, rebounds and total points are important individual statistics for basketball players.

Information In law, a written accusation, presented by a public officer such as a prosecuting attorney instead of a grand jury, that charges a person with committing a public offense.

Initial appearance Step in the judicial process at which the charge is read to the accused. In most states, this is referred to as an **arraignment.**

Insert Copy that is placed, or inserted, into a story to make the story more complete or to clarify what has been written already.

Internet Worldwide networks that connect thousands of supercomputers, mainframes, workstations and personal computers so that they can exchange information.

Interview from the outside in (See **outside-in interview**).

Intrusion Type of invasion of privacy in which the defendant intrudes upon an individual's solitude, either physically or by electronic eavesdropping.

Invasion of privacy Legal wrong against what evolved in the 20th century as the right "to be let alone." There are four types of invasion: intrusion, appropriation, public disclosure of embarrassing private facts and false light.

Inverted-funnel interview Type of interview in which the key questions, often the toughest, are asked immediately. This style of interview is used when sources are experienced in fielding closed-ended or adversarial questions or when there is little time to ask questions.

Inverted pyramid Traditional news writing form in which the key points of a story are put in the opening paragraph and the news is stacked in the following paragraphs in order of descending importance.

Issues reporting Reporting that examines complex matters of interest rather than simply providing the *who, what, where, when, why* and *how* of a newsworthy event.

Italics Type that slants to the right *like this.*

Java A computer language invented by Sun Microsystems that runs on any modern computer and delivers application programs over the Internet.

"Jell-O journalism" News reporting that overemphasizes soft writing, which is decried by some editors.

Journalists' privilege Assertion that journalists have a privilege, under certain conditions, not to reveal information sought by a court or grand jury. No such absolute privilege exists.

Jump To continue a story from one newspaper page to another.

Kerner Commission National commission appointed by President Lyndon B. Johnson and headed by Otto Kerner (then governor of Illinois) to study the effect of the mass media on riots. The official name of the group was the National Advisory Commission on Civil Disorders.

Keyword approach Method of selecting data from the holdings in a database. It involves writing a computer command citing concepts and terms central to the research topic.

Kid quotes In sports writing, quotations gathered from junior-high and high-school athletes.

Lay out To position stories and art elements on a newspaper page. A **layout,** or **dummy,** is an editor's plan of how the page will look when it is printed.

Lead Opening paragraph of a story. Also spelled **lede.**

Lead-in In broadcast writing, a sentence or phrase that sets listeners up so that they are mentally prepared for what follows. For example, *Reporting from the scene of the fire, Tom Johnson describes. . . .*

Lead block Multiparagraph lead that builds up to the major point of the story.

Leak journalism Reliance on "leaks" from unnamed sources to construct a story. Most editors and news directors discourage this practice.

Level of confidence In a random-sample survey, the probable error because of chance variations. The most common interval is the 95 percent level of confidence. This means that the probability is only 5 in 100 that the true answer is not within the range found.

Liabilities What a company owes. A company lists its liabilities in its reports to stockholders.

Libel Legal offense of publishing or broadcasting a false story that damages a person's reputation by holding him or her up to public ridicule, hatred or scorn.

Libertarian (press) system Developed in the United States beginning early in the 19th century. A system in which the media flood the marketplace with information so that citizens can make enlightened decisions. The press is regarded as a primary instrument for checking on the government and its officials.

Lifestyle editor Person, also called the **features editor,** who leads what is usually a newspaper's main features section. The section may include articles by lifestyle writers, a food editor, an entertainment writer, a drama critic, a television writer and other reviewers and critics.

Limited access Designation for police reports that cannot be examined in their entirety, under all circumstances, by members of the public or journalists.

Listserv Named after the software that maintains the list, a virtual community of people who are linked together by some common interest.

Localizing Putting a local emphasis on a story with broader ramifications. For example, if a wire-service report datelined Washington mentions a local or state official in the body of the story, the local newspaper may rework the story to move the local reference to the top of the story.

Local news value Characteristic of a story of particular interest to local readers, viewers or listeners.

Local weather forecasts Stories that discuss and predict weather for a local area.

Lowercase Small letters of type, in contrast to capital letters.

Mainbar Main story in a group of articles about the same topic in a single edition of a newspaper.

Mainframe Powerful central computer to which other computers are connected. The mainframe usually holds a system's software.

Mainstreaming Practice at newspapers of citing and quoting in stories a variety of sources that represent and reflect the ethnic and gender mixes of communities.

Makeup editor Person who dummies (lays out) pages of a newspaper.

Managing editor Top editor in most newspaper newsrooms. This editor makes certain that the paper is out on time each day and that costs are kept within a budget. The managing editor is responsible for hiring and firing newsroom personnel and is usually involved in selecting stories, photos and graphics.

Masthead Box that appears inside a newspaper, often on the editorial page, identifying its top executives.

Mayor-council government Municipal government system in which the mayor can be categorized as "weak" or "strong," depending on the powers assigned to the position. In a "strong" mayor system, the mayor has the power to draw up budgets and to make and administer policy. In a "weak" mayor system, the mayor is, in essence, the chairperson of the city council, with most managerial functions divided among other elected officials and the council.

Media critic Reporter who writes stories about the strengths and weaknesses of and trends in daily media coverage. David Shaw of the *Los Angeles Times* is among the best known. Also called a **press critic.**

Media event News occurrence, such as a presidential press conference, in which both the interviewee and the reporters are in the limelight.

Memorials Gifts in honor of a person who has died. In obituaries, most newspapers note when families suggest memorials to a specific cause or organization.

Menu approach Method of selecting data from the holdings in a database. The searcher gets computer access to a generic list of topics from which one is chosen. That action brings a second list of subtopics to the computer screen from which, again, one is chosen. This process continues until the precise information is uncovered.

Meteorologist Person trained in the science of weather and climate. Metropolitan-area television and radio stations often employ meteorologists to provide weather forecasts and news.

Mill levy Tax imposed on property values by a municipality or school district in order to raise necessary money. The **mill** is the unit of measure (1/10 of a cent) used by municipalities and school districts in computing property taxes.

Minor sports Non-revenue-producing sports such as gymnastics, volleyball, cross country and swimming.

Minority-affairs reporting Reporting on the trends, events and issues of people who are not part of the larger, more dominant group in a given society.

Minority source list List of names of minority people in a variety of professions and capacities, developed at media outlets to help reporters find sources for stories that reflect the ethnic mixes of communities.

Misdemeanor Crime considered less serious than a felony. Punishment is normally a fine or imprisonment in a facility other than a penitentiary.

Modem Short for *modulator-demodulator.* Device that translates computer-generated signals into signals that telephone lines can transmit.

More Word written at the end of a page to indicate that another page follows.

Morgue Traditional name for a newspaper library where clippings files and reference books are kept. Reporters do much of their research in the morgue. Stories (clips) are generally filed under subject and reporters' bylines.

Mugshot Head-only photograph of a source. One-column mugshots of primary sources often accompany news stories. They are used to show readers what the sources look like, as well as to break up long stretches of gray type.

Multiple-element lead Lead, also called a **double-barreled lead,** that gives two or more of the primary elements of a news story equal rating and that informs an audience immediately that more than one major event is occurring.

Nameplate Name of a newspaper on the front page; also called the **flag.**

Narrative lead Lead, also called an **anecdotal lead,** that uses narrative to draw people into a story by putting them in the middle of the action. A narrative lead is the most popular on features and non-breaking news stories.

National editor Editor who supervises reporters covering news events in cities other than the city in which the newspaper is published.

Negligence Fault standard in libel law articulated by the Supreme Court in 1974 that can vary from state to state. In some states, the level of liability is "gross negligence"; in others, it is "failure to act as a reasonable person" when gathering information for and writing a story.

Net income Company's profit or loss after taxes.

Net income per share How much each share of a public company earned in a quarter or for the year.

New lead Updated information that replaces the original lead. The wire services, during a 12-hour cycle, are constantly transmitting new leads to developing stories.

News director Top person in a television newsroom. He or she reports to a station manager or a general manager or both and does many of the jobs that a managing editor of a newspaper does. The news director is responsible for what goes on the air, the newsroom budget and the hiring and firing of most reporters and other personnel.

News editor Editor who decides which news appears in the newspaper and where. This editor is in charge of the copy desk, where copy editors work.

Newsgroups Also known as Usenet, a popular way to read or take part in discussions on the Internet.

News hole Number of column inches available for news.

News meeting Daily meeting of a newspaper's editors, also called a **news huddle, doping session,** a **news conference,** an **editors' meeting** or an **editorial conference.** In this meeting the editors discuss and then decide which of the top foreign, national, state and local stories, and photographs and graphics will make it into the paper.

News mix Combination of hard news stories and feature pieces. The news mix can also include a blend of longer and shorter local, regional, national and international stories.

News peg Sentence or paragraph linking a story to a news occurrence.

News release See **handout.**

News story Write-up or broadcast piece that chronicles the *who, what, where, when, why* and *how* of timely occurrences.

Newsworthy element Peg of a story that should often be reported in the lead paragraph. In stories based on survey research, for example, the most significant statistical finding would be the newsworthy element that belongs in the lead.

No bill Finding returned by a grand jury if it determines that a sufficient probability does not exist that the accused committed the crime with which he or she is being charged.

Nose for news Reporter's instinct, which is used to gather information and to make news decisions as quickly as possible.

Nut graph Explanatory paragraph, also called a **"so-what" paragraph,** that follows the introductory lead block and explains the significance of a story.

Obit Common journalism term for **obituary,** a story about someone who has died.

Objective verbs of attribution Verbs of attribution such as *said* or *added* that reporters can use when quoting sources, to avoid interjecting personal feelings or perceptions about the way the source sounded.

Observation What a reporter sees, hears, smells, tastes or touches while working on a story. Observations add color to news stories and features.

Off the record Agreement reached by a reporter and a source before an interview that disallows use of the material revealed. Often, reporters refuse to accept information off the record, choosing instead to try to obtain it from another source.

Ombudsman "Middle person," or theoretically objective employee of a newspaper, who listens to complaints from readers and, when they are justified, passes them on to appropriate reporters or editors. About 30 newspapers employ ombudsmen.

On background Agreement reached by a reporter and a source before an interview that the material can be used, but attribution by name cannot be provided.

On deep background Agreement reached by a reporter and a source before an interview that the material can be used, but not in direct quotations and not accompanied by attribution.

Online Connected. Information held in computer memory that is available to searchers using computers remote from the memory unit is said to be "online."

Online journalism A computer reporting medium that utilizes multimedia to tell stories.

On the record Agreement reached by a reporter and a source before an interview that the material can be used, complete with the name of the source and identification.

Op-ed page Page that runs next to an editorial page, giving readers a mix of opinion columns and illustrations.

Open-ended question Question that is structured to allow a source time to develop an answer. Open-ended questions are a good way to break the ice between a reporter and a source because they give the source time to expand at length. For example: *What do you think about the quality of sports coverage in your local daily?*

Open-meeting laws Statutes in all 50 states that provide for public access to meetings of government bodies. The laws are not uniform, and all list exceptions to access.

Open-records laws Statutes that provide for access to state-level information. Most of these statutes, which also list specific exceptions to access to public records, specify that the laws should be construed liberally in favor of people seeking the records.

Open sentences Clearly constructed sentences that present no confusing ambiguities to the reader. Open sentences normally contain a straight subject-verb sequence and are seldom introduced with distracting dependent clauses and phrases.

Operating budget Sometimes called the **"soft" budget,** the operating budget provides dollars required to finance government entities on a day-to-day basis. One of the largest components of operating budgets is salaries.

Organizational structures Chains of command that outline the titles and duties of executives and employees. Beat reporters, for example, must master the organizational structures of the agencies they cover.

Outcue (OC) The last few words of a broadcast soundbite that tell the newscaster when to open the microphone and continue the story.

Outside-in interview Technique, used by investigative reporters, of interviewing acquaintances, associates and friends of a source first, before going to the source. By the time the reporter is ready to interview the source, he or she is well-armed with information and already knows many of the answers to critical questions.

Pagination Layout process in which stories, photographs, graphics, cutlines and headlines are assembled electronically on a computer screen.

Paper of record Newspaper that offers comprehensive, straightforward news accounts of what happened in the world, nation, state and community since the last edition. A paper of record is also a source for future historical reference.

Paraphrase Sentence or sentences providing the essence of what a source said, but not in the source's precise words.

Partial defense Defense, sometimes called a **mitigating factor,** that can be employed against libel suits if conditional or absolute defenses cannot be used successfully. Partial defenses, such as publication of a retraction, represent good faith on the part of the defendant and can be taken into consideration when damages are assessed.

Partial quotation Specific portions of a lengthier complete direct quotation that are reported and set off by quotation marks.

Passive voice Term describing the verb form used when the subject of a sentence is acted upon by the object. For example: *The child was hit by the car.* Passive voice should be used in news writing only when the person or thing receiving the action is more important than the person or thing doing the acting.

Personal computer Stand-alone computer that can be used for a variety of functions, including the input of stories. Material produced on a personal computer (PC) can be stored in the computer's built-in storage device, which is called its *hard disk,* or on a portable storage device called a *floppy disk.*

Personality profile Feature story that brings an audience closer to a person in or out of the news. Interviews, observations and creative writing are used to paint a vivid picture of the person.

Petition In law, a document that asks a court to take a particular action.

Photo editor Editor who supervises a newspaper's photographers. This editor may also write the captions that run with photographs.

Plaintiff Party who is bringing a lawsuit.

Planning editor Also called a **metropolitan editor,** the person who is in charge of long-term planning in a broadcast newsroom. The planning editor coordinates coverage of future events, such as trials or elections.

Play-by-play charts Tables produced at sports events such as football and basketball games to help reporters piece together important sequences in the contests. In basketball, for example, the chart would note who scored, on what kind of shot and what the score was at the time of the play.

Plea bargaining Negotiation between the prosecutor and defense lawyers over the kind of plea a suspect might enter on a specific charge. Prosecutors often propose that, in exchange for a plea of guilty, the state would bring a lesser charge against the suspect.

Pleadings In law, a written statement by all the parties setting forth assertions, denials and contentions.

P.M. Evening newspaper.

P.M. cycle Evening newspapers usually report news that breaks on the P.M. cycle, generally the time from midnight to noon.

Police log Daily report of activity involving the police department.

Population In surveys, the total number of subjects in the group to be studied. For example, in a survey conducted to find out where local high school seniors will attend college, the population would be all seniors in all local high schools.

Precision journalism Use of social science research methods—such as methodologically sound sampling procedures and computer analysis—to gather facts, leading to more precise, accurate news stories.

Preliminary hearing Step in the judicial process at which the state must present evidence to convince the presiding judge that there is probable cause to believe that the defendant committed the crime with which he or she is being charged.

Press critic See **media critic.**

Privately held company Also called a **closely held company,** a privately held company is a firm controlled by a family or small group. The value of the company's stock, which is not traded on an exchange, is set by the owners.

Procedural safeguards Steps, such as a change of venue, available to judges who want to ensure that defendants are not deprived of the judicial serenity and fairness to which they are constitutionally entitled.

Proof Copy of a typeset story.

Proofreader Person who reads a proof of a story to ensure that it is set the way the editors wanted and that it is free of typographical errors.

Public disclosure of embarrassing private facts Type of invasion of privacy that involves communicating information not of public concern in violation of standards of "common decency" perceived by persons of "ordinary sensibilities."

Public figure In libel cases, a person who has "voluntarily thrust" himself or herself into the vortex of a particular controversy to resolve that controversy, or a person who has assumed a role "of especial prominence" to the extent that, for all purposes, he or she is to be considered a public figure.

Public official In libel cases, a government employee who has substantial responsibility for or control over the conduct of governmental affairs.

Public relations people People who work for public relations (PR) firms and whose job it is to gain media attention for the businesses, organizations, people or institutions that they represent.

Public relations wire Wire over which news releases and other public relations transmissions are sent to wire-service bureaus and to other news outlets that subscribe to it.

Publicly held company Company owned by investors who purchase its stock on an exchange.

Queue File in a newsroom computer system. Stories and other information are stored in and pulled out of queues.

Question lead Lead that asks a question. The key to writing a question lead is to answer the question as quickly as possible.

Quote lead Lead that allows a central character to begin a news story or a feature by talking directly to the audience. The quotation may be the most powerful one in the story, or it may set the tone for what is to follow.

Rambling quotations Long, drawn-out direct quotations that journalists should avoid when possible by paraphrasing or by using indirect quotations.

Random selection Process by which each entity in a group has an equal chance of being selected.

Release date Date at the beginning of a press release or a wire story that informs the media of the earliest time that they can use the information. Many press releases are stamped *for immediate release,* which means that the information can be used as soon as it is received.

Religious News Service Supplemental news service established in 1933 to supply religion stories to news outlets.

Same-day obits Obituaries, written on the day of a person's death, in which the lead paragraph reports that the person has died.

Sample Portion of a population being studied. For example, in a survey conducted to find out where local high school seniors will attend college, a news medium might question one out of every 10 students.

Sampling error Margin of error that should be reported in all stories based on random-sample surveys. A mathematical formula is used to compute the percentage. An error margin of 5 percent, for example, means that the result could vary 5 percentage points either way because of chance variations in the sample.

Scanner Multichannel radio that monitors police and fire dispatches.

Search warrant Court document issued in the name of the state that directs a law enforcement officer to search specified premises.

Second-day obits Obituaries, written one or more days after a person dies, in which the lead paragraph features the time of services.

Second-day story Follow-up story written after the breaking news has been reported.

Settlement In law, an agreement reached by the parties, often before the case goes to trial.

Shareholders' equity Difference between a company's total assets and its liabilities.

Shield laws Statutes (existing in about half the states) that allow journalists and other specified people who are questioned by grand juries or under other circumstances to protect their sources under certain conditions.

Shotgun interview See **smoking-gun interview.**

Sidebar Story that runs with a mainbar. A sidebar isolates a person, place or thing usually mentioned in a mainbar and further explains, examines or illustrates it.

Simple sentence Sentence that has only one independent clause. For example: *The high jumper won.*

Skip interval In random selections from a list, every *n*th entry. E.g., if 10 names are to be chosen from a list of 100, the skip interval is 10. If the fourth name on the list is the first chosen, every 10th name thereafter would be chosen.

Slot editor Person who supervises copy editors. The slot editor distributes stories to copy editors and then checks their editing and headlines.

Slug One- or two-word label on a story. The slug identifies a story and keeps it separate from other stories.

Smelling a story In reporting a story, letting emotions, intuition, past experiences and gut reactions be a guide in gathering information.

Smoking-gun interview Question-and-answer session (also called a **shotgun interview**) in which a reporter, armed with videotape or other evidence of wrongdoing, asks direct questions about specific incidents. When the source denies any wrongdoing, the reporter shows the incriminating evidence in the hope that the source will admit guilt.

Social responsibility theory Philosophy, which emerged as a theory in the United States in the post-World War II years, that all views should be disseminated through the media, which are bound by professional ethics. The theory holds that if the press fails to live up to its obligations to present diverse views and to interpret them responsibly, the government can step in to ensure public service.

Soft news Events that are usually not considered immediately important or timely to a wide audience. Many of these events still merit coverage. A math fair at an elementary school or a faculty member's prize-winning rose garden might be covered as soft news, for example.

Software Program that tells the computer how to carry out specific functions such as word processing.

Soundbite See **actuality.**

Source Written material or a person that a reporter uses for information.

Source file File a reporter keeps of names, phone numbers, addresses and the expertise of useful sources.

Specialty reporter Reporter who covers breaking news stories or features in a highly specialized area, such as transportation, energy, education, religion, aviation, the arts and legal affairs. Like the sources they cover, specialty reporters must be experts in a particular field.

Spending caps Limitations imposed by government bodies on revenue or expenditures. Such caps can sometimes be overcome by a referendum.

Splitscript Television writing format in which the video descriptions are placed on the left side of the page and the audio, or reporter's narrative, is on the right.

Sports editor Editor in charge of sportswriters and the desk people who process their copy. The sports editor often writes a column.

Sports writing clichés Phrases, such as *brilliant field generals* and *sparkplug guards,* often overused by reporters.

Spot news News event covered by reporters as it is occurring.

Staccato lead Lead made up of a short burst of phrases that carry readers into a story by dangling some of its key elements in front of them. It is meant to tease readers and to set the mood for the story.

Standard offense forms Forms available at police and sheriff's departments, providing information such as when the alleged offense took place, where it occurred, the names of any victims and a brief synopsis of what reportedly happened.

State editions Issues of a metropolitan daily newspaper that have earlier deadlines than other editions and are delivered to counties and towns outside the metropolitan area.

State editor Person who supervises reporters covering communities and areas outside the city in which the newspaper is published; alternatively called the **area** or **suburban editor.**

State judicial systems Third branch of government for each of the 50 states. State judicial systems usually have three layers: trial courts, intermediate courts and supreme courts.

State news only (SNO) wire News wire that carries virtually all of the state news and sports produced by The Associated Press for a particular state.

State weather forecasts Stories that discuss and predict weather for a state.

Steady advance Term used to describe writing that flows smoothly and logically. Sentences are constructed in such a way that readers glide efficiently from the first word to the last.

Story budget List of stories that have been written or are to be written. Individual reporters sometimes keep their own budgets. The wire services move international, national and state budgets that contain overviews of the most important stories on each day's cycles.

Stringer Part-time newspaper or broadcast correspondent who covers a specific subject or geographical area for a news medium often located elsewhere.

Sub Substitute. Reporters are often asked to write subs, which may provide later information or which may be better written than the original material.

Subpoena Court order for an individual to give testimony or to supply documents.

Suburban editor See **state editor.**

Summary lead Terse opening paragraph that provides the gist of a story and lets readers decide right away if they are interested enough in the story to continue.

Summons In law, a writ informing a person that an action has been filed against him or her in court and that he or she must answer the complaint.

Supplemental news services Services more limited in scope and resources than The Associated Press. Supplemental services, for a fee, provide news media with materials ranging from cartoons to in-depth political analysis. An example is the Newspaper Enterprise Association.

Survivors Persons who live after the death of someone closely related to them. In obituaries, most newspapers list names of surviving spouses, children, sisters, brothers and parents.

Team statistics Data computed by totaling individual statistics for sports contests. For example, if a team used eight basketball players in a game and each accumulated three fouls, the team total would be 24.

Text type Type in which newspaper stories are set. Text type is generally 8-, 9-, or 10-point. (One point equals 1/72 inch.)

-30- Symbol used to indicate that a story has ended.

Thread Common element, usually a narrative about a person or event, that is intertwined throughout a story to connect the beginning, body and conclusion.

Throw line In broadcast writing, an introduction to the reporter. For example: *KFAB's John Johnson reports from the scene . . .*

Tight pages Pages on which there are so many advertisements that comparatively little space is available for news stories and features.

Time element The *when* of a news story. Generally, the time element is included in the lead paragraph.

Tokenism Practice, which should be avoided, of quoting or citing in stories a single minority person who ostensibly represents the point of view of an entire community or group.

Tort In civil law, a wrongful act committed against a person or against his or her property.

Transition Word, phrase, sentence or paragraph that ushers an audience from one area of a story to another. Transition alerts an audience that a shift or change is coming.

Transitional paragraph Paragraph that shifts readers smoothly from one area of a story to another.

Trend story Type of feature story that examines people, things or organizations having an impact on society.

True bill Indictment returned by a grand jury if it determines that there is probable cause that a person charged with a crime committed it and should stand trial for it.

Truncation Means of using root words plus extra symbols to broaden a computer keyword search of a database. For example, **report???** in a command would elicit articles with keywords such as *reporter, reportage* and *reporting.*

Turn Transitional paragraph to introduce a chronology of the events of the story.

Turn word Transitional word that moves readers from one area to another. Some of the most common turn words are *now, today, but* and *meanwhile.*

Typo Typographical error.

Undercover journalism Type of reporting in which the journalist does not reveal to a source that he or she is working on a story.

United Press International Privately held corporation formed in 1958 when United Press and International News Service merged; generally referred to as **UPI.**

Unrestricted access Term for unlimited availability of police reports to members of the public or to journalists. The types of reports permitted unrestricted access vary among cities and states, but accident reports are often unrestricted.

URL (Uniform Resource Locator) The specific name of a file on the Internet. Typing in the URL allows a computer user to access the file on the World Wide Web.

Video display terminal Computer terminal at which a reporter "inputs" (types) a story. A video display terminal, or **VDT,** is normally connected to a publication's mainframe computer.

Verdict Decision of a trial jury after it has considered the directions given to it by the judge and after it has weighed the evidence presented.

Visitation Hours established for viewing a decedent at a funeral home. Most newspapers provide details about visitation in obituaries.

Visuals Non-word elements of a printed page, including photographs, illustrations and graphics.

Voice "Signature" or personal style of every writer. Using voice in a story allows writers to put an individual stamp on their work. Voice reveals a reporter's personality and subtly tells readers that this story is not by any writer, but by *this* writer.

Voice track Words of a television reporter that accompany an anchor's words and the videotape.

Warrant Writ issued by a magistrate or by another appropriate official to a law enforcement officer, directing that officer to arrest a person and to bring him or her before a court to answer a charge.

Weather forecasting services Sources of information for journalists working on weather-related stories. The National Weather Service is a primary source, although some larger newspapers and television stations also contract with private weather forecasting services.

Wide-open pages Pages on which there are few or no advertisements.

Wind-up line In broadcast writing, the final sentence or "punch line" of a story. The last sentence can be a summary line, a future angle or merely a repetition of the main point of the story.

"Words in your mouth" technique Method used occasionally by journalists when interviewing inarticulate or tight-lipped sources. For instance, the reporter asks: *Did you feel ecstatic when you won the race?* and the source says, *Yes.* The journalist reports: *Jones said that he felt ecstatic when he won the race.*

World Wide Web (WWW) An Internet information server that allows users to view text, photographs, art, videos, sound and animation at the same time. It was developed at the European Laboratory for Particle Physics (CERN) in Geneva, Switzerland, and is viewed through a browser.

Wrap Also called a **donut.** In preparing a broadcast story, to place a reporter's words around one or more actualities.

Writethru Designation used by wire services to tell newsrooms that a story replaces all earlier stories on the same news event.

Year-end weather summaries Stories routinely published by newspapers on Jan. 1 that recap the weather for the previous year and present the most relevant statistics, such as rainfall amounts.

PERMISSIONS AND CREDITS

Chapter 1 Pages 2–3: Jerry Schwartz. 2–3: The Associated Press; used by permission of The Associated Press.

Chapter 3 Page 29–32: Reprinted with permission from the *Washington Journalism Review.* 32–40: Adapted from Robert Gunning, "The Technique of Clear Writing," rev. ed. (New York: McGraw-Hill, 1968); used with permission of the Gunning-Mueller Clear Writing Institute, Inc. 33: Reprinted with permission of *The Arizona Republic.* 33–34: Greta Tilley, *Greensboro* (N.C.) *News and Record.* 40: *The Orlando Sentinel.*

Chapter 6 Pages 74, 77: Jerry Schwartz. 74–77, 78–79: The Associated Press; used by permission of The Associated Press. 82–83: Roy Peter Clark. 83–84: Reprinted from the *Philadelphia Inquirer,* Jan. 9, 1985, by permission. 86–87: Reprinted with permission of Mohave County Miner, Inc.

Chapter 7 Pages 91–96: Judi Villa.

Chapter 8 Page 105–106: Edward Sylvester. 107, 116–117: The Associated Press; used by permission of The Associated Press. 110: *The Tribune.*

Chapter 9 Pages 123, 128, 132, 134–135: *State Press,* Arizona State University. 123–124, 131, 133–136: Mary D. Gillespie. 124, 128–129, 135: Carol B. Lutyk. 124–125, 135: John G. Mitchell.

Chapter 10 Pages 144–145, 151: Maren S. Bingham. 144–145: Marie C. Dillon. 146: Jerry Guibor.

Chapter 11 Page 172, 179: Reprinted with permission from the *Washington Journalism Review.* 180–183: James Simon.

Chapter 12 Page 185: *Berkshire Eagle.* 188, 190–191, 193, 195–196: *New Haven* (Conn.) *Register.* 189, 194–195: Tom Tuley. 189–190, 196–197: *News-Journal,* Daytona Beach, Fla. 190, 195: *Trentonian,* Trenton, N.J. 190: *Fargo* (N.D.) *Forum.* 191: Kent Ward. 192–193: *Findlay* (Ohio) *Courier.* 193, 196: *Jamestown* (N.Y.) *Post-Journal.* 197: Reprinted with permission of *The Birmingham* (Ala.) *News.*

Chapter 15 Page 215: Kenneth Reich.

Chapter 16 Page 224: Jack Williams. 225–226: *Fairbanks* (Alaska) *Daily News-Miner.* 236: Karen McCowan.

Chapter 17 Page 239–243: Donald E. Brown. 243, 249–250: Ben Silver. 244–245: Reprinted with permission of KFAB. 246–247: Dan Fellner. 247–248: KPNX-TV, Phoenix, Ariz. 249–251: Wendy Black.

Chapter 18 Page 259–260, 264, 266: Felix Gutierrez. 260–261, 265–266: Caesar Andrews. 261, 264: Mary Lou Fulton. 261–262, 264: Dorothy Gilliam. 265, 268–271: Dawn Garcia. 269–270: © *San Francisco Chronicle.*

Chapter 19 Page 273–275, 277–279, 281, 289–291: Adrianne Flynn. 278–279, 287–288: Reprinted with permission of *The Tribune.* 279–280: Reprinted with permission of the *Daily Hampshire Gazette.* 282: Jerry Geiger, management services director, Tempe, Ariz.

Chapter 20 Page 293–300, 303–311: Roger Aeschliman. 299–300, 305–310: Reprinted with permission of the *Topeka* (Kan.) *Capital-Journal.*

Chapter 21 Page 313–314, 335: The Associated Press; used by permission of The Associated Press. 316: Description of state court systems from a chart in "Mass Communication Law," by Donald M. Gillmor, Jerome H. Barron, Todd F. Simon and Herbert H. Terry, West Publishing Co., 1990. 319–323, 325–329: *The Tribune.* 322–324, 326–327: Michael Padgett. 336: Reprinted with permission of *The Arizona Republic.* 337: Reprinted with permission of *The Phoenix Gazette.*

Chapter 22 Page 341, 343–345: Lee Barfknecht. 341: From "The Tumult and the Shouting," by Grantland Rice; published by A. S. Barnes; copyright, 1954. 342–344: Terry Henion. 349–351: Reprinted with permission of the *Omaha* (Neb.) *World-Herald.* 352: Dennis Brown.

Chapter 23 Pages 355–356, 360, 368: *The Bulldog,* Arizona State University. 357–358, 369–371: Duff Wilson. 359, 361, 363: Fred Schulte. 365–366: William Recktenwald.

Chapter 24 Pages 374–375, 378–379: Mary Beth Sammons. 381: Jake Batsell. 383: Brenda Rotherham. 383–384: Dan Gillmor. 383–384: Kim Komando. 385–386: John G. Mitchell. 385–386: Casey Bukro.

Chapter 25 Page 387–388, 399–400: Lyle Denniston. 388–389, 400: Henry R. Kaufman. 390: From "Synopsis of the Law of Libel and the Right of Privacy," by Bruce W. Sanford; used with permission of Scripps-Howard Newspapers. 400: Reprinted with permission of Reporters Committee for Freedom of the Press. 400: Marc A. Franklin. 401–402: New York State Newspapers Foundation.

Chapter 26 Page 417, 420, 435: Media Studies Center and The Freedom Forum. 418–419: Robert H. Giles. 419–420: Charles L. Overby. 420–423: The Freedom Forum. 426–428, 430–431, 438: John C. Merrill. 428: Bob Steele, Poynter Institute for Media Studies. 433–434: Doug Smith. 429–437: *Newspaper Research Journal,* Winter/Spring, 1992.

Appendix A Reprinted with permission of Gannett Co., Inc.

Appendix B Portions of The Associated Press Stylebook are used by permission of The Associated Press.

INDEX

B

D

G

H

I

J

K

L

M

N

O

P

Q

R

S

T

U

Y

Z